HISTORY OF
AMERICAN JOURNALISM

.

A Da Capo Press Reprint Series

THE AMERICAN SCENE
Comments and Commentators

GENERAL EDITOR: WALLACE D. FARNHAM
University of Illinois

MAIN CURRENTS
IN THE HISTORY OF
AMERICAN
JOURNALISM

By Willard G. Bleyer

DA CAPO PRESS · NEW YORK · 1973

Library of Congress Cataloging in Publication Data

Bleyer, Willard Grosvenor, 1873-1935.
  Main currents in the history of American
journalism.

    (The American scene: comments and commentators)
    Bibliography: p.
    1. Journalism — United States.   2. Press — United
States.   I. Title.
PN4855.B6   1973   071'.3   70-77720
ISBN 0-306-71358-6

This Da Capo Press edition of
*Main Currents in the History of American
Journalism* is an unabridged republication
of the first edition published by Houghton
Mifflin Company in 1927. It is reprinted
by arrangement with the estate of the author.

Published by Da Capo Press, Inc.
A Subsidiary of Plenum Publishing Corporation
227 West 17th Street, New York, New York 10011

HISTORY OF
AMERICAN JOURNALISM

HORACE GREELEY
1811–1872

MAIN CURRENTS
IN THE HISTORY OF
AMERICAN JOURNALISM

205588

BY

WILLARD GROSVENOR BLEYER, PH.D.

*Director of the Course in Journalism and Professor of Journalism
in the University of Wisconsin; Author of "Newspaper Writing
and Editing," "Types of News Writing," "How to Write
Special Feature Articles," and "The Profession
of Journalism."*

HOUGHTON MIFFLIN COMPANY

BOSTON NEW YORK CHICAGO SAN FRANCISCO

The Riverside Press Cambridge

The Riverside Press
CAMBRIDGE · MASSACHUSETTS
PRINTED IN THE U.S.A.

PREFACE

In order to understand the present-day American newspaper and its problems, it is necessary to know something of the influences that have shaped the course of the press since its inception. This book undertakes to furnish an historical background sufficient for an intelligent understanding of the American newspaper of to-day. Since it is manifestly impossible to present in a single volume a complete history of the press in the United States, the scope of this book has been limited to a consideration of outstanding newspapers and editors that have exerted a strong influence on the evolution of the press. Other editors and other newspapers have made contributions of significance, but their inclusion would have extended the book beyond the limits that seemed desirable for a handbook intended for students of journalism and for the general reader.

Because of the importance of English journalism as an influence on American journalism previous to 1800, the first chapter has been devoted to sketching the development of the English press, particularly in those phases that were imitated by American newspapers. Later journalistic practices in England that influenced newspapers in the United States have been discussed in connection with various American papers.

Newspaper files in this country and in England have furnished the basis for most of the facts and conclusions presented, and a large number of excerpts from newspapers have been included. In a few instances where files were not available, secondary sources have been used for these quotations. Biographies of editors supplied data concerning their lives, as well as material from their letters. The original spelling, capitalization, punctuation, and peculiarities of typographical style have been reproduced in all quotations as far as it seemed feasible to do so.

For readers who desire to make further study of the subject, a list of readings has been appended, arranged according to the chapter divisions, and a supplementary list of readings on nineteenth and twentieth century English journalism has been in-

cluded. These readings are not intended to be a complete bibliography. Other sources of material are given in the footnotes.

While working in the British Museum during the summer of
1923 on the beginnings of English journalism, the author discovered in the Burney Collection of early English newspapers a
practically complete file for the first two years of James and Benjamin Franklin's *New-England Courant.* The file contains all but
one of the first sixteen numbers, none of which was known to
have survived. On almost all of the first forty-three issues some
one has written in ink the names of the contributors. From a
comparison of the hand-writing of Benjamin Franklin with that
in which these names were entered, the conclusion was reached
that he had written them. The new light thus thrown on the beginnings of the *Courant* has been discussed briefly in Chapter II.
At about the same time, Mr. Worthington C. Ford of the Massachusetts Historical Society also found that the British Museum
possessed a file of the *Courant,* and later, after examining photo-
stat copies of it, arrived at the same conclusion as to Benjamin
Franklin's handwriting. The results of his study of these photo-
stat copies are given by Mr. Ford in the *Proceedings of the Massachusetts Historical Society* for April, 1924.[1]

Valuable suggestions were obtained from the researches in the
history of early English journalism made by Mr. J. G. Muddiman, who has usually published his results under the name of
J. B. Williams; and from Miss Elizabeth C. Cook's monograph,
Literary Influences in Colonial Newspapers, 1704-1750.

The author is indebted to Mr. Richard Hooker of the *Springfield Republican* for a photograph of Samuel Bowles; to Mr.
Arthur H. Yunker of the same paper for a zinc etching of the
first page of the first issue of that paper; to Mr. Irwin Kirkwood
of the *Kansas City Star* for a photograph of William Rockhill
Nelson; to Mr. John O'Hara Cosgrave of the New York *World*
for a portrait of Joseph Pulitzer; to Professor James Melvin Lee
of New York University for reproductions of two early corantos;
to Mrs. Hiram F. Hunt of Kingston, Rhode Island, for a rare
Sunday "extra" of the *New York Transcript* containing an account of the Robinson-Jewett murder case; to Mr. Roy W.
Howard for data concerning the Scripps-McRae and the Scripps-

---

[1] *Massachusetts Historical Society Proceedings, 1923-24,* vol. 57, pp. 336-53.

Howard newspapers; and to the State Historical Society of Wisconsin for permission to photograph material in its newspaper files.

To the critical judgment and untiring assistance of his wife, Alice Haskell Bleyer, the author acknowledges his deepest gratitude.

UNIVERSITY OF WISCONSIN
    MADISON

CONTENTS

ILLUSTRATIONS

MAIN CURRENTS
IN THE HISTORY OF
AMERICAN JOURNALISM

..

CHAPTER I

EARLY ENGLISH JOURNALISM

1. THE RISE OF THE PRESS

THE period of English colonization in what is now the United States coincides almost exactly with the period during which journalism in England came into existence and developed into a vital force in the social and political life of the nation. Despite the barriers that separated the New World from the Old, the ties that bound the colonists to the mother country were so close that the rise of news periodicals in England could not fail to have a profound influence on the beginnings and the development of American colonial journalism. The printing presses and type used by American printers were imported from England. The names, form, and make-up of colonial newspapers were copied from English papers. American newspaper publishers depended upon English papers, not only for most of their English and European news, but for much of their editorial matter in the form of essays and letters addressed to the publishers. Such original material as the colonial papers contained was generally written in a form and style closely imitating similar contributions in the English press. In short, the newspapers of the colonies were modeled on those of the mother country.

A brief review, therefore, of the significant steps in the evolution of the English news periodicals in the seventeenth and eighteenth centuries makes possible a better understanding of the American papers of the same period.

That a century and a half should have been allowed to pass between the time when Caxton set up the first printing press in

England, in 1476, and the publication in 1621 of the first coranto, the earliest English prototype of the modern newspaper, seems incomprehensible today. So necessary has the newspaper become in modern life that we should naturally assume that one of the first uses to which the printing press would be put would be to print the news. The long delay, however, is easily accounted for by the political, religious, and social conditions during this period.

In times of political and religious unrest like the sixteenth and seventeenth centuries, the dangers of unrestricted printing as a possible means of spreading sedition and heresy could not be overlooked. Restrictions on freedom of discussion, made by both the Church and the State, and extremely limited means of communication, imposed great handicaps on the publication of news. The lack of postal facilities made well-nigh impossible the collection of news and its dissemination in printed form.

Printing was early recognized as one of the prerogatives of the Crown, to be carried on under royal supervision. Caxton and his fellow craftsmen, enjoying royal encouragement and privileges, were not inclined to risk disfavor by printing anything that might give offense. Later, royal patents were issued to a limited number of printers. By thus restricting the business of publishing, the Government could the more easily supervise the products of the presses. The licensing of all books before they could be printed was provided for in a proclamation issued by Henry VIII in 1534. The King's efforts to reform the Church led Parliament in 1542–43 to pass an "Act for the Advancement of true Religion and for the Abolishment of the Contrary," which confirmed the absolute power of the Crown to regulate printing and all other forms of discussion. The licensing system for all publications, enforced in the reigns of Edward VI and Mary, was promptly upheld by Queen Elizabeth in a proclamation issued soon after she came to the throne. The Stationers' Company, incorporated in 1556 by master printers, was a recognized organization which could regulate printing and coöperate with the authorities in supervising publications. Star Chamber ordinances of 1566 and 1586, reënforcing the royal decrees, established severe penalties for unauthorized printing. No relief from these drastic restrictions on freedom of printing and discussion was granted by James I. Under such circumstances unlicensed publication of current news and comment would have been fraught with great danger.

News, however, was disseminated through means other than periodical publications. An interesting forerunner of the news-paper, for example, is to be found in the broadsheet ballad de-scribing some recent crime, catastrophe, scandal, battle, or death of a notable personage. The journalistic character of these bal-lads was indicated by the Elizabethan dramatist, Thomas Middle-ton, when in 1620 he wrote that a ballad monger never lacked a subject to write of; "one hangs himself today, another drowns himself tomorrow, a sergeant stabbed next day; here a pettifogger a' the pillory, a bawd in the cart's nose, a pander in the tail; *hic mulier, hæc vir*, fashions, fictions, felonies, fooleries; — a hun-dred havens has the balladmonger to traffic at, and new ones still daily discovered."[1] These ballads were often sung by hawkers who offered them for sale on the street, quite as newsboys today shout the most important news in their papers.

Contemporary criticism shows that some of these ballads were regarded as quite as sensational, and quite as often concerned with trivial events, as were some newspapers of a later date. Chettle in his *Kind-Harts Dreame* (1592) describes the ballad-mongers of the period thus:[2]

> A company of idle youthes, loathing honest labour and dispising lawful trades, betake themselves to a vagabond and vicious life, in every corner of Cities and market Townes of the Realme, singing and selling ballads and pamphlets full of ribaudrie, and all scur-rilous vanity, to the prophanation of God's name, and withdraw-ing people from Christian exercises, especially at faires, markets, and such public meetings.

Equally critical of these forerunners of the newspaper is the author of a pamphlet entitled *Martine Mar-Sixtus*, who in 1591 wrote:[3]

> ... scarce a cat can look out of a gutter, but out starts a half-peny Chronicler, and presently *A propper ballet* [ballad] *of a strange sight* is endited.

[1] Middleton, Thomas. *The World Tost at Tennis*, A. H. Bullen, ed., vol. vii, p. 154.

[2] *Percy Society*, vol. 5, p. 13.

[3] *Martine Mar-Sixtus — A second replie against the defensory and Apology of Sixtus the fift late Pope of Rome*, p. 2 of *The Epistle Dedicatorie*.

As the ballad-maker was the journalist for the masses, so the educated intelligencer in Elizabethan and Jacobean England served as news-gatherer and news-letter writer for the statesman, or man of affairs, who desired to be informed regarding the news of London. When public men went abroad, they arranged with their secretaries or with these intelligencers to keep them in touch with events at home by means of written letters of news.

Some foreign news was also available in England during the sixteenth and seventeenth centuries in the form of printed pamphlets called "relations," generally translated from Continental originals. These "relations," however, were not periodical publications.

It was in Holland, not in England, that the first sheets of foreign news were printed in English. Considerable printing in English was done in Holland, particularly of books and pamphlets that could not be published in England with impunity.[1] The first extant news-sheet appeared in Amsterdam, without title or headline, dated December 2, 1620. It contained an account of the battle of Weissenberg, near Prague, on November 8, which had resulted in the defeat of Frederick, Elector of the Palatinate and head of the Protestant Union, whom the Bohemians, revolting against the Hapsburgs, had chosen as their king. England was interested in the fate of Frederick, because he had married Elizabeth, daughter of James I. His defeat at Weissenberg, which marked the beginning of the Thirty Years' War, resulted in his losing, not only the throne of Bohemia, but the title of Elector of the Palatinate.

Besides this first sheet of news, others printed in Holland have survived, dated at irregular intervals from December 23, 1620, to September 18, 1621, and bearing such headlines as *Corrant out of Italy, Germany, &c; Courant Newes out of Italy, Germany, Bohemia, Poland, &c;* and *Corante, or, Newes from Italy, Germanie, Hungarie, Spaine and France.* These two-page news-sheets, dealing entirely with foreign news, doubtless were sent from Holland to England to meet the English demand for news of the struggle

---

[1] Two of the Pilgrim Fathers, William Brewster and Edward Winslow, were engaged in printing English pamphlets in Leyden, Holland, before they came to America in 1620.

CORANTE, OR, NEVVES FROM
Italy, Germanie, Hungarie, Spaine and France. 1621.

From Lyons the 6 of Iune 1621.

OVr King in person lies before S Iohn Dangely, wherein the Duke of Roans brother is gouernour; whereof the Towne issued out 2. mile towards their enemie : First Beaumont regiment, and after them a company of light horsemen, after that a trate for 8.dayes was made therein to intreate for peace : In the meane time preparation is made to besiege Rochell, and the Duke de Guise is gon to Marsellis, there to prepare an armie by Sea, to besiege Rochell by water, Monsieur Ladignier is not permitted to goe from the Court, it may be, because they feare, that he being a Souldier of great experience might seeke to aide those of the religion; it is sayd that there shalbe a new gouernour chosen in his place of gouernment in Daulphinois.

In Paris in regard of certaine marshall matters, the spiritualtie assembled together, and as the Bishop of Bollonia desired to haue obedience before the Parliament, as he beginne to frame his Oration, his speach beganne to faile him, and when he would haue giuen it in writing, he could not doe it, but within three houres after he died speachlesse.

From Venice the 21 of Iune 1621.

From Millane it is written, that although there hath 2.commissions already bin sent out of Spaine to restore Valtelnia againe : the gouernour to the contrarie sends more men thether, the like doth the Arch Duke Leopoldus, and see that 14. companies of Switzers entred into Leopoldus gouernement; and therein burnt an Abby the restitution is stayed, yet the Spaniards were forced to giue backe, who won-er much, that the Duke of Sauoy masters many Souldiers, and they know ther his own ent.

From Constantinople it is written that the great Turke with his principall officers, is gon to Adrianopolie, with a great number of Ianizeries and Spaggyans his armie, besides the Tartarians being 300 thousand strong, that haue taken 4. millions and a halfe of Suldanes out of the treasurie with them to pay their Souldiers, and he hath deliuered 4.hundred thousand Suldanes to his generall of the Seas, who with 70. shippes or gallies is gon into the blacke Sea, to keepe the Coslackers backe, that with their gallies, used to goe almost to Constantinople, and other letters certifie, that the great Turke, will goe into Polonia with 150.thousand men, and will send 100. thousand into Moldauia, and as many into Hungaria, to withstand the Emperor of Germanie if he attempteth any thing.

From Lenisch in Hungarie the 4.of Iune, 1621.

Here is great trouble, there are 400 Dutch souldiers in the Towne, and there shall 1200.more come, which will trouble vs much.

The 6 of Iune at Eperies there shall an assemblie be holden without doubt, because Bethlem Gabor is desirous to know of the Nobilitie there small resolution, whether they will hold with him or not : it is thought, that the 15 of Iune he will march forward with all his forces, and that the Marquis of Iagemedors will ioyne with him strange thing, will shortly be heard of, whosoeuer liues to see them; seeing hee can doe nothing in the treatie of peace, because they sought to betray him : it is sayd that 30 thousand Turkes, and 20 thousand Tartarians are marching forward, that are to fall vpon Krain and Kaeneten God be mercifull vnto vs, if it comes to that, that the Turkes and Tartarians should destroy this goodly Countrie, God turne it all to the best.

From Lenisch the 10 of Iune 1621.

To morrow the generall assembly of the States is to begun at Eperies, and this day there are certaine letters come, one from the Emperor wherein he writes very friendly vnto the States, another from the Lords Palatine, and the third from Setfeld Georgen, with all to a manner are sent vnto Bethlem Gabor as there King. What answere shall be giuen them,

and this assemblie will effect, we shall heereafter know

From Neus the 13 of Iune 1621.

On Whitsunday his grace let Balthasar Hoffman Van Goritz that was agent for the Emperor heere, vntill this present, goe out of prison, who was forced to deliuer the key of his Maste. and it was opened to see what was therein.

Lieutenant Lohane hath a good number of men by him againe, yesterday caused 10.barrels of beere, and some wine to be sent into his quarter, a great number of men come to him with his grace, entertain es, and the money giuen them in hand is payd in Bethlemish luckets, and Rhens gold Nobles; he giues a horse man 15. Florins in hand; it is thought that they will shortly gne to Otmachaw a mile and a halfe from hence, which for that it is a strong Fort, therefore they intend to fortifie themselues therein : Leischwitz. was yesterday more then halfe burnt by fire that fell in a Malt house.

It is said 6.or 700 of these stubee Souldiers horsemen shall come hether, yesterday about 2. of the clocke at night there came 2.Posts hether to what end we know not, but all the Captaines that were here in the Towne, were sent for to the Marquis, and presently posts were sent into the quarter, and the people willed to come. The Towne-gates were kept shut till nine of the clocke in the morning, and at last none but the gate vnder the toll sowre was set open, and all the company that lay in the new Towne, stood still in armes about 10.of the clocke, the same company came in hether and were set before the Ianet Captaines house, with commandement to charge there peeces, after that they were sent into the Castle, and therein also are some of the Burgers with them that lay therein before, while this company went into the Castle, the Lorrehouse company, stood still behind the Castle, which procured no small feare.

Yesterday it was reported, that Beuten belonging to the Marquis was burnt by the Polanders, and Iagerendorp taken by the Emperors forces, whether it be so or not, by the next we shall know : Since the gilders are daily caried by the Captaines and Commaunders into the quarter to pay the Silesian Souldiers.

From Vianna the 25.of Iune 1621.

Although Stenzel Tuerso is in treatie with Bucquoy, the Hungarians in Newheusel will not grant to yeild, but will rather cut Tuerso in peeces, then graunt to yeild : Therefore great store of great Ordinance, bullets and powder are this weeke sent thether to batter the Towne; there is likewise 600 thousand Florins in money, and 200.thousand Florins in iewels sent, to giue euery one of our Souldiers 3 moneths pay : in the meane time the Hungarians daily skirmish with our men, and it is sayd that B-thlem at Caschew prepares a great strength to releiue Newheusel, and that Setsehy George seekes to stop his passage.

On this side the Earle of Colaldo hath gotten the Budianers goods out of the inuincible Castle called Gissingen, where he himselfe is, whereof there is a deale of corne and wine come, which is sent backe to Papa and the comisselhen borders.

In Morauia, there are more principall Lords and Purgers committed to prison, whose expectation, as also in Prague of the prisoners shall this weeke be done, and Erasmus & George Van Landaw shall be brought prisoners hether.

The Emperors iourney to Prague shall begin the fift of Iulie, and the Rickes day at Regenspurg shall begin the 1. of Septpember.

From Prague the 26.of Iune 1621.

The seuenth of this moneth, as 8.daies since it was written, old Srnewin, one of the imprisoned directors, in the night time threw himselfe headlong out of the white Tower into the ditches and there died, his body was yesterday cut in 4. quarters.

The First Page of a Single-Sheet Coranto, Printed at Amsterdam in July, 1621.

Size of page, 6⅜ in. by 11¾ in.

between Protestant and Catholic forces at the outset of the Thirty Years' War.

The first of these sheets of foreign news, or "corantos," to be printed in England probably appeared in July, 1621. The earliest ones were doubtless reprints of corantos published in Amsterdam, for, on August 4, 1621, an intelligencer in London wrote to his patron, the English ambassador to Holland, that there were printed "every week, at least, corrantos, with all manner of news, and as strange stuff as any we have from Amsterdam." [1] Thomas Archer was evidently the publisher of these first English newssheets printed in London, for, according to another letter, dated September, 1621, he was punished "for making, or adding to, his corrantos." [2] None of them, however, has come down to us.

The earliest extant prototype of the newspaper printed in England is a coranto, issued by Nicholas Bourne, under the date of September 24, 1621. Like those printed in Holland, it bore only a headline and not a title. This headline read, *Corante, or, newes from Italy, Germany, Hungarie, Spaine and France, 1621.*[3] At the end this legend appeared: *London   Printed for N. B.   September the 24. 1621.   Out of the Hie Dutch Coppy printed at Franckford.* Five similar corantos, also published by Bourne, bearing the dates September 30, October 2, 6, 11, and 22, 1621, with variants in type and spelling of the headline, *Corant or Weekly Newes, from Italy, Germany, Hungaria, Polonia, Bohemia, France, and the Low-Countries,* have survived as further evidence that the publication of foreign news at more or less regular intervals began at this time. The legend at the end of the issue of October 11, *Out of the Low Dutch Coppy,* like that at the end of the issues of September 24 and October 2, *Out of the Hie Dutch Coppy,* indicates the sources of these early corantos — Dutch or German news-sheets. All of these corantos were single sheets printed on both sides.

In 1622 the single-sheet form was superseded by the news-book coranto, a pamphlet consisting of from eight to forty pages. From this time until the establishment of the *Oxford Gazette* in

---

[1] Quoted in Thomas Birch's *The Court and Times of James the First*, vol. II, p. 272.

[2] *Ibid.*, p. 276.

[3] This headline is practically identical with one used in the English corantos printed in Amsterdam by Broer Jonson, between July 9, 1621, and August 2, 1621, and by Adrian Clarke at the Hague in August, 1621.

The 23. of May.

VVEEKELY
Nevves from Italy,

GERMANIE, HVNGARIA,
BOHEMIA, the PALATINATE,
France, and the Low Countries.

Tranſlated out of the Low Dutch Copie.

LONDON,
Printed by *I. D.* for *Nicholas Bourne* and *Thomas
Archer*, and are to be ſold at their ſhops at the
Exchange, and in *Popes-head Pallace*.
1622

The First Page of the Earliest News-Book Coranto, London, 1622
Size of page, 4 in. by 6¾ in.

1665, all English news periodicals were in pamphlet form. The earliest extant issue of these news-book corantos, dated May 23, 1622, was published by Thomas Archer and Nicholas Bourne, and bore the headline, *Weekely Newes from Italy, Germanie, Hungaria, Bohemia, the Palatinate, France, and the Low Countries*. Another weekly news-book, begun on August 2, 1622, by Nathaniel Butter, and continued by him in conjunction with Bourne, Archer, and others for over two years, was numbered consecutively beginning with the issue of October 15, 1622. Like the other corantos, Butter's had a headline of contents that was different in each issue, rather than a title, and hence was not, as has been erroneously stated, entitled *The Weekly Newes*. That Butter, however, appreciated the value of continuity in the issue of news-books, is shown by the explanation of his purpose in the third number, dated August 23, 1622: [1]

> If any gentleman or other accustomed to buy the weekly rela-
> tion of Newes, be desirous to continue the same, let them know
> that the writer, or transcriber rather, of this Newes, hath published
> two former newes, the one dated the 2d and the other the 13th of
> August, all of which do carry a like title . . . and have dependence
> upon one another; which manner of writing and printing he doth
> propose to continue weekly by God's assistance, from the best and
> most certain intelligence.

At the close of the year 1624, Butter and Bourne headed their news-book *The Continuation of our Weekly Newes*, a title taken over at the beginning of 1625 by a publisher styling himself *Mercurius Britannicus*, possibly Thomas Archer. As this designation was continued for at least twenty-three successive weekly issues, it may be regarded as the first instance of the use of a title for a coranto news-book.

Butter and Bourne were the principal publishers of the corantos until 1632, when all of them were suppressed at the request of the Spanish ambassador, because some of their foreign news reflected on the house of Austria. They were not revived until 1638, when, by royal letters patent, Butter and Bourne were given the exclusive right to print foreign news.

These corantos, first as single sheets, then as news-books, con-

[1] Quoted in *Tercentenary Handlist of English and Welsh Newspapers, Magazines and Reviews*, p. 18.

taining only foreign news gleaned largely if not entirely from Continental news periodicals, constitute the first stage in the evolution of English journalism.

The forerunners of periodicals of domestic news, as distinct from the corantos of foreign news, are apparently to be found in the written news-letters recording the proceedings of Parliament that were sent out from London by scriveners, or clerks, as early as 1628. Out of these written parliamentary news-letters developed the first printed periodicals of domestic news, the so-called "diurnals." [1] These printed diurnals, or news-books, devoted primarily to parliamentary proceedings, were the first periodicals of domestic news, and hence mark the second stage in the development of journalism in England.

The diurnals grew out of the struggle between Charles I and Parliament culminating in the Civil War, which, like most wars since that time, in both England and America, had a tremendously stimulating effect on journalism. After the abolition of the Star Chamber on August 1, 1641, Parliament, ignoring the long-recognized royal prerogative to control all printing, permitted the publication of the journals of its proceedings, the diurnals, in order to lay before the people its side of the controversy. Immediately various forms of news-book diurnals were published, as many as fifteen often appearing on a Monday in time for the mail which left London on Tuesday. The earliest of these diurnals, published by John Thomas on November 29, 1641, bore the title, *The Heads of Several Proceedings in this Present Parliament*, and the inside heading, *Diurnall Occurrences*. With the third issue, *Diurnall Occurrences, or, The Heads of several proceedings in both Houses of Parliament* became the outside heading. As this title continued to be used through seven issues, it may be regarded as the first instance of a title on a periodical of domestic news. One of these news-books was *A Perfect Diurnall*, edited by Samuel Pecke, a scrivener of Westminster Hall. Because it dealt with events involving the struggle between the two parties both in and out of Parliament, and continued with interruptions from 1643 to 1655, it may be considered the first important periodical of domestic news. Many of the diurnals contained, not only

[1] Cf. Notestein, Wallace, and Reif, Frances H. *Commons Debates for 1629, University of Minnesota Studies in the Social Sciences*, No. 10, pp. xlii–lv.

reports of parliamentary proceedings, but also news of political and military affairs.

The first news-book established to uphold the King's side was published at Oxford from 1643 to 1645, with the title, *Mercurius Aulicus*, or "mercury of the court." It was followed between 1647 and 1649 by some forty royalist news-books. The use of *Mercurius* in the title of the *Mercurius Aulicus* and in that of other royalist news-books, as well as in the parliamentary party's *Mercurius Britanicus* (1643–46), gave currency to the term "mercury" to designate any news periodical.[1] The figure of Mercury, the winged messenger of the gods, came to be used as an emblem in the title of news periodicals.[2]

Between 1641 and 1649 the outpouring of parliamentary and royalist news-books was very great, in sharp contrast with the meager publication of corantos before this time. Over two hundred periodicals appeared, although only a few of them survived for more than a year. This recognition by both parties of the value of the news-book as an effective means of carrying on political controversy, marks an important step in the development of the press as a medium for influencing public opinion.

After the execution of the King and the establishment of the Commonwealth in 1649, a drastically repressive act was passed inflicting heavy penalties upon writers, printers, and publishers of unauthorized printed matter, exacting a bond from all printers, and forbidding the hawking of news-books on the streets. This act, renewed in 1653 and made still more stringent in 1655, resulted in a great decline in all writing for publication. The licensed news-books were suppressed. In their place Cromwell authorized an official news-book, *Mercurius Politicus*, with Marchamount Needham as editor. To this publication was added in 1655 the *Publick Intelligencer* (1655-1660), the two together constituting a semi-weekly periodical.

When with the Restoration a system of licensing was renewed, Henry Muddiman was given the exclusive right of publishing news-books, a privilege that he held from 1660 to 1663. By an

---

[1] The term "mercurius" was originally used to designate the author of a news periodical, as in the case of the semi-annual chronicle in Latin, *Mercurius Gallobelgicus* (1594), and the coranto published by *Mercurius Britannicus* (1625).

[2] It appears in the title of the third newspaper published in the colonies, the *American Weekly Mercury*, which was begun in Philadelphia in 1719.

A Perfect Diurnall

OF SOME
PASSAGES
IN
PARLIAMENT,

And the daily proceedings of the Army under his Excelleney
Sir *Thomas Fairfax.*

From Munday the 10 of *Ianuary* till Munday the 17 of *January.* 1647

Collected by S.P.G. for the satisfaction of such as desire to be truly informed.

Printed by E.G. and F.L. for *Francis Coles* and *Laurence Blaiklock* : And are to
be so d at their Shops in the *Old-baily,* and at *Temple-bar.*

Beginning Munday, Ianuary 10.

He house of Commons this day had reported to them ;
from the Committee formerly appointed to view all
letters and papers taken in the late war, certaine papers of warrants of moment, some of His Majesties
own hand writing, As a warrant for diverting the
ships pretended for the reliefe of Rochel, An other
about the Ordnance and Ammunition designed for
York at the first beginning of the war with others ;
And it was Ordered that this Committee should appoint secretaries to translate and copie cut letters and
papers of concernment. And this Committee are to
publish in print such of them as they shall think fit for the clearing of all objections ;
and undeceaving the people by answering such papers as they shall think fit in vin-
dication of aspersions cast upon the Parliament.

The Commons this day voted severall Sheriffes for the Counties of Carmer-
then, Radnor and Cardigan.

They Ordered a Judge to go down into Hamptshire for the tryall of the late mu-
tiners in the Isle of Wight by Commission of *Oyer* and *Terminer.*

The house was moved in behalfe of Bridgenorth, for the losse they sustained by
fire, amounting to 70000 l. and upwards : whereupon a briefe was granted for collections, some other places were moved for, that have bin burnt these late wars, and

11 D   they

A Typical First Page of *A Perfect Diurnall,* a News-Book Published
from 1643 to 1649

Size of page, 5 in. by 7⅝ in.

act of 1662 regulating printing, Roger L'Estrange became licenser of the press. The following year he succeeded Muddiman as publisher of the two official news-books, the *Intelligencer* and the *Newes*, which together, in accordance with previous practice, formed a semi-weekly publication.

L'Estrange, doubtless like many others of his time, had little confidence in the value of news periodicals for the masses of the people. He wrote in the first issue of the *Intelligencer*, published on August 31, 1663:

> First, as to the point of Printed Intelligence, I do declare myself . . . that supposing the Press in Order; the People in their right Wits, and Newes, or No Newes, to be the Question; a Publick Mercury should never have My Vote; because I think it makes the Multitude too Familiar with the Actions, and Counsels of their Superiors; too Pragmaticall and Censorious, and gives them, not only an Itch, but a kind of Colourable Right and License, to be Meddling with Government. . . .

Nevertheless, L'Estrange appreciated the possibilities of influencing public opinion, particularly the views of the common people, through the "prudent Menage [management] of a Gazett," for he wrote in the same issue:

> . . . 'tis none of the worst wayes of Address to the Genius, and Humour of the Common People; whose Affections are much more capable of being tuned and wrought upon, by convenient Hints, and Touches, in the Shape and Ayre of a Pamphlet, then by the strongest Reasons, and best Notions imaginable, under any other, and more sober Form whatsoever.

During the period of repression, written news-letters were the common means of disseminating both foreign and domestic news, especially among the upper classes in the country districts. In the cities these written news-letters were available to the patrons of the coffee-houses, the social clubs of that day. Their circulation, however, was considerably restricted by the comparatively high subscription price. The news, after being gathered and written, was copied by a staff of clerks, and enough copies of each news-letter were made to supply all the subscribers. Although the method of writing these letters by hand was slow and expensive, it made possible the dissemination of news that could not with impunity be printed. Since their circulation was practically limited to the upper classes, the Government was inclined to be less concerned about their contents than it was about matter published in printed form. Henry Muddiman, publisher of the two official news-books after the Restoration, and editor of the first newspaper, the *Oxford Gazette*, enjoyed the privilege of sending his written news-letters post free, and was thus able to do a thriving business in news-letter writing until his retirement in 1689, long after the printed newspaper had become established.[1]

The period of the news-book may be said to end, and that of the newspaper to begin, with the publication in 1665 of the single-sheet, semi-weekly *Oxford Gazette*, the first English newspaper. Renamed the *London Gazette*, it has continued from that day to this as the official paper of the Court. Begun on November 16, 1665, with Henry Muddiman as editor, while the Court was sojourning at Oxford because of the black plague, it followed the Court to London, and, with No. 24 on February 5, 1665/6, became the *London Gazette*. Printed on both sides of a half-sheet folio with two columns on each page, it was designated as a "paper" or "slip" of news to distinguish it from a news-book. The term, "newspaper," was not coined until 1670. Henry Muddiman, the writer of the first twenty-three issues of the *Oxford Gazette* and of the first two issues of the *London Gazette* may be said to be the father of the English newspaper.[2]

The refusal of Parliament in 1679 to renew the act of 1662 regulating printing, resulted in the appearance, during the following three years, of some twenty newspapers of importance. This revival in journalism took place despite a royal proclamation of 1680 embodying an opinion given the King by the judges to the effect "That His Majesty may by Law Prohibit the Printing and Publishing of all News-Books and Pamphlets of News whatsoever, not Licensed by His Majesties Authority, as manifestly tending to the breach of Peace, and disturbance of the Kingdom."[3]

[1] In the colonies, John Campbell, postmaster of Boston, sent out written news-letters to the governors of some of the other colonies for a year at least before he began the first regular newspaper published in America (1704), to which he gave the name, significant in this connection, of the *Boston News-Letter*.

[2] The application of the term, "gazette," to this official newspaper led to its adoption for the titles of the official and semi-official newspapers in most of the colonies, as, for example, the *Boston Gazette*, the *Pennsylvania Gazette*, the *New-York Gazette*, and the *South-Carolina Gazette*.

[3] *London Gazette*, May 3–6, 1680.

The London Gazette.

Published by Authority.

From **Monday** June 14. to **Thursday** June 17. 1680.

Moscow, April 27.

THE Person which this Court had sent privately to *Constantinople*, to learn the Sentiments of the Grand Signior and the Divan, concerning a Peace, is returned with an account, That according to the best Information he could get, the Grand Signior was resolved not to depart from his demand of having all the *Ukraine*, from the *Black Sea* to the *Borisihenes*, yeilded to him; and that besides, he pretended satisfaction for the Charges of the War: Whereupon the Czar, after having consulted with his Principal Ministers and Officers, has resolved to send a second Embassy to *Poland*, to strengthen the Negotiation of the Ministers he has already at that Court, as likewise to send an Ambassador to *France*, to demand the Assistance of that King against the Turks, and in consideration thereof to offer his Subjects several advantageous Priviledges in their Commerce.

Warsaw, May 28. This Week arrived here an Express sent by the Resident of this Crown at *Constantinople*, to acquaint his Majesty, That he had good grounds to believe that the Ottoman Forces would Advance this Summer to the Frontiers of this Kingdom, That their Army would be much more considerable then was now believed, That Orders had been sent to *Mahomet Bassa*, who lyes encamped with an Army on the *Danube*, to Detach 20000 men to joyn with the *Tartars*, That the Turks had Built two Bridges over the River *Niester* for the Passage of their Army; And that the Hospedar of *Wallachia* did make great Provision of Victuals, which he sent to *Caminiec* to be kept in the Magazines there, for the use of the Turkish Army.

Dantzick, June 1. From *Warsaw* they write that the King had appointed a great Council to be held there the 10th Instant, to consider what resolutions to take in the present State of Affairs, with relation to the Moscovites, especially considering that the late Advices from *Constantinople* led them see that the Designs of the Port are not only against the Moscovites, but likewise against *Poland*; After which the King will go to *Jaworow* on the Frontiers, more narrowly to observe the Motions of the *Ottomans*.

Hamburg, June 14. The French Envoy, Monsieur d'*Arcy*, is gone from *Zell* to *Hanover*, and Sir *Gabriel Silvius* is now at *Cassel*. We may in a short time expect to know the Resolutions of those Princes upon the Overtures made to them by the said Ministers. The Duke of *Zell*, having received the last Payment of the Moneys stipulated by the Treaty of Peace, or at least those Moneys being ready here, it is not doubted but *Boeckshoede* will be evacuated in few days, and restored to the

Suedes. It is said that the Elector of *Brandenburg* is going to raise eight new Regiments, which if true, will probably give other Princes occasion to do the like. Yesterday Count *Anthony* of *Oldenburg* came hither from *Copenhagen.* The King of *Denmark*, they say, will be, before the end of the Month, in these parts. The new Fortifications here are carrying on with all the dilligence possible.

Genoua, May 26. We are expecting here the French Galleys, Commanded by the Duke *de Vivonne*, of which the French Resident has it's said given the Senate Notice, and that the Duke *de Vivonne* has positive Orders to oblige the Spanish Galleys, wherever he meets them, to salute the Kings Flag. From *Rome* they write, that Prince *Radzevill*, Ambassador from *Poland*, was at last arrived there.

Milan, May 29. Our Governor, the Count *de Melgar*, having received advice of the Arrival of several Spanish Troops at *Final*, has sent Orders for the disposing of them into several Quarters. It is still said that there is an intention of making a considerable Levy in *Swisserland* for the Service of this Country.

Strasburg, June 12. The Baron *de Monclar*, the French King's Lieutenant in *Alsace*, continues encamped at *Landaw*, the number of his Forces encreasing daily. The French do now pretend to the Sovereignty of all the Baillages of the Palatinate on this side the *Rhine*, as well as those belonging to this City. Our Magistrates have desired time to declare themselves, and are busy to find out such antient Papers and Records as may make it appear that the said Baillages, belonging to them, do not in the least depend on the great Baillage of *Haguenaw*, which the French make the Foundation of their Pretention. Some days since arrived here two Boats laden with several Field Pieces and Ammunition, for the Service of the French Camp. The Governor of the Castle of *Falkenburg* cannot yet be prevailed with to Surrender it, which the French have made use both of Threats and Promises to persuade him to do.

Cologne, June 14. There are several French Officers here and in our Neighbourhood who List men, which being known, the people here are much dissatisfied at it. It is reported that several French Troops will come and live in this Diocess, and in the Country of *Juliers*, for their Money, as they did in 1641. before the breaking out of the War

Brussels, June 18. The Prince of *Nassaw* is returned from *Flanders*, where he has been to settle the new Magistrates in the several Cities of that province: and about the end of this Week his Excellency goes for *Antwerp*, where he will expect the return of the Marquis *de Bourgomanero* from *Holland*, and give him his Dispatches in order to his beginning his Journey to the Emperors Court. The Prince of *Vaudemont*, as Admiral of these Provinces, has received 20000 Crowns, to

---

A Typical First Page of the *London Gazette*, the First English Newspaper

Size of page, 5½ in. by 9½ in.

First and chief among these twenty newspapers was Benjamin Harris's *Domestick Intelligence, or News both from City and Country. Published to prevent false reports*, which began on July 9, 1679, and continued with interruptions until 1681. As Harris in 1690 made the first attempt to print a newspaper in America, his career in England is of peculiar interest. In 1679 he was convicted of publishing a pamphlet offensive to the Government, and was sentenced to pay a fine of £500, to stand in the pillory, and to give surety for his good behavior for three years. Failure to pay the fine resulted in his imprisonment for two years, but during this time he resumed the publication of his paper, then called *The Protestant (Domestick) Intelligence*, which had been suspended for eight months. In 1686 a quantity of pamphlets that he had printed were seized, and warrants were issued for his arrest, but, before he could be apprehended, he fled to America and settled in Boston.[1]

After the House of Commons refused in 1695 to reënact the licensing system in force since 1685, even though the House of Lords had voted its renewal, the press in England was free from licensing in advance of publication. William III did not insist on the royal prerogative in the matter of printing, and from that time on, newspapers were subject only to the laws of seditious libel. Although this new freedom did not immediately result in the establishment of many papers, it eventually led in the eighteenth century to the development of journalism as a vital force in the social and political life of England. Papers of the period, such as the *Postman*, the *Flying Post*, and the *Post Boy*, were single sheets printed on both sides, like the *London Gazette*. Like the *Gazette*, also, they were published semi-weekly, on Tuesday and Saturday, the two days of the week when mail went out from London.

A popular innovation in journalism was introduced in March, 1689/90, by John Dunton, a London bookseller, when he began the *Athenian Mercury*, a weekly publication devoted to questions asked by readers and answered by the editors. Whole numbers were given up to questions and answers on love and marriage,

---

[1] These facts concerning his career are set forth by Harris in a petition to the House of Commons, a facsimile of which is given by Worthington C. Ford in his *Boston Book Market*, p. 88.

quite in the manner of present-day "advice to the lovelorn." The popularity of this paper led, not only to the establishment of others like it, but to the introduction of question and answer departments into regular newspapers. The first periodical for women, the *Ladies Mercury* (1693), consisted entirely of questions and answers concerning love, courtship, and marriage. The *Spectator* in several essays satirized these questions and answers on affairs of the heart.[1] The popularity of this feature of journalism no doubt led readers to write letters to newspapers on matters of everyday life, in an easy, familiar style.[2]

The first daily paper, the *Daily Courant*, appeared on March 11, 1702. It was a single small sheet, printed on only one side, so that, as the publisher, Elizabeth Mallet, announced in the first issue, the news might be "confin'd to half the Compass, to save the Publick at least half the Impertinences, of ordinary News-Papers." Two interesting details of its policy were announced by the editor in the initial number: first, "at the beginning of each Article he will quote the Foreign Paper from whence 'tis taken, that the Publick, seeing from what Country a piece of News comes with the Allowance of that Government, may be better able to Judge of the Credibility and Fairness of the Relation"; and second, "Nor will he take upon him to give any Comments or Conjectures of his own, but will relate only Matter of Fact; supposing other People to have Sense enough to make Reflections for themselves."[3] Elizabeth Mallet, the first publisher, seems to have abandoned the undertaking within the first two weeks, but publication was resumed by Samuel Buckley a month later. In reprinting her original announcement of policy, he expanded the points quoted above, thus:[4]

[1] Cf. *Spectator*, Nos. 591, 607, 614, and 625 (September 8, October 15, November 1, and November 26, 1714).

[2] Benjamin Franklin's first journalistic effort at the age of sixteen, the "Silence Dogood" letters, contributed to his brother's paper, the *New-England Courant*, in 1722, was of this type. In this connection it is interesting to note that the *Athenian Oracle*, a reprint in three volumes of questions and answers taken from the *Athenian Mercury*, was among the books in the library of the *New-England Courant*, according to a statement in that newspaper on June 25–July 2, 1722.

[3] The first American newspaper, the *Boston News-Letter*, begun in 1704, two years after the establishment of the *Daily Courant*, followed the practice of giving the name of the paper from which its foreign news was taken, and had little or no comment on the news.

[4] *Daily Courant*, April 25, 1702.

The Daily Courant.

Wednefday, March 11. 1702.

From the Harlem Courant, Dated March 18. N. S.

Naples, Feb. 22.

ON Wednefday laft, our New Viceroy, the Duke of Efcalona, arriv'd here with a Squadron of the Galleys of Sicily. He made his Entrance dreft in a French habit ; and to give us the greater Hopes of the King's coming hither, went to Lodge in one of the little Palaces, leaving the Royal one for his Majefty. The Marquis of Grignl is alfo arriv'd here with a Regiment of French.

Rome, Feb. 25. In a Military Congregation of State that was held here, it was Refolv'd to draw a Line from Afcoli to the Borders of the Ecclefiaftical State, thereby to hinder the Incurfions of the Tranfalpine Troops. Orders are fent to Civita Vecchia to fit out the Galleys, and to ftrengthen the Garrifon of that Place. Signior Cafali is made Governor of Perugia. The Marquis del Vafto, and the Prince de Caferta continue ftill in the Imperial Embaffador's Palace; where his Excellency has a Guard of 50 Men every Night in Arms. The King of Portugal has defir'd the Arch-Bifhoprick of Lisbon, vacant by the Death of Cardinal Soufa, for the Infante his fecond Son, who is about 11 Years old.

Vienna, Mar. 4. Orders are fent to the 4 Regiments of Foot, the 2 of Cuiraffiers, and to that of Dragoons, which are broke up from Hungary, and are on their way to Italy, and which confift of about 14 or 15000 Men, to haften their March thither with all Expedition. The 6 new Regiments of Huffars that are now raifing, are in fo great a forwardnefs, that they will be compleat, and in a Condition to march by the middle of May. Prince Lewis of Baden has written to Court, to excufe himfelf from coming thither, his Prefence being fo very neceffary, and fo much defir'd on the Upper-Rhine.

Francfort, Mar. 12. The Marquifs d' Uxelles is come to Strasburg, and is to draw together a Body of fome Regiments of Horfe and Foot from the Garifons of Alface ; but will not leffen thofe of Strasburg and Landau, which are already very weak. On the other hand, the Troops of His Imperial Majefty, and his Allies, are going to furm a Body near Germefhein in the Palatinate, of which Place, as well as of the Lines at Spires, Prince Lewis of Baden is expected to take a View, in three or four days. The Englifh and Dutch Minifters, the Count of Frife, and the Baron Vander Meer ; and likewife the Imperial Envoy Count Lowenftein, are gone to Nordlingen, and it is hop'd that in a fhort time we fhall hear from thence of fome favourable Refolutions for the Security of the Empire.

Liege, Mar. 14. The French have taken the Cannon de Longie, who was Secretary to the Dean de Mean, out of our Caftle, where he has been for fome time a Prifoner, and have deliver'd him to the Provoft of Maubeuge, who has carry'd him from hence, but we do not know whither.

Paris, Mar. 13. Our Letters from Italy fay, That moft of our Reinforcements were Landed there ; that the Imperial and Ecclefiaftical Troops feem to live very peaceably with one another in the Country of Parma, and that the Duke of Vendome, as he was vifiting feveral Pofts, was within 100 Paces of falling into the Hands of the Germans. The Duke of Chartres, the Prince of Conti, and feveral other Princes of the Blood, are to make the Campaign in

Flanders under the Duke of Burgundy ; and tho Duke of Maine is to Command upon the Rhine.

From the Amfterdam Courant, Dated Mar. 18.

Rome, Feb. 25. We are taking here all poffible Precautions for the Security of the Ecclefiaftical State in this prefent Conjuncture, and have defir'd to raife 3000 Men in the Cantons of Switzerland. The Pope has appointed the Duke of Berwick to be his Lieutenant-General, and he is to Command 6000 Men on the Frontiers of Naples : He has alfo fettled upon him a Penfion of 6000 Crowns a year during Life.

From the Paris Gazette, Dated Mar. 18. 1702.

Naples, Febr. 17. 600 French Soldiers are arrived here, and are expected to be follow'd by 3400 more. A Courier that came hither on the 14th. has brought Letters by which we are affur'd that the King of Spain defigns to be here towards the end of March ; and accordingly Orders are given to make the neceffary Preparations againft his Arrival. The two Troops of Horfe that were Commanded to the Abruzzo are pofted at Pefcara with a Body of Spanifh Foot, and others in the Fort of Montorio.

Paris, March. 18. We have Advice from Toulon of the 5th inftant, that the Wind having long ftood favourable, 22000 Men were already fail'd for Italy, that 2500 more were Embarking, and that by the 15th it was hoped they might all get thither. The Count d' Eftrees arriv'd there on the Third inftant, and fet all hands at work to fit out the Squadron of 9 Men of War and fome Fregats, that are appointed to carry the King of Spain to Naples. His Catholick Majefty will go on board the Thunderer, of 110 Guns.

We have Advice by an Exprefs from Rome of the 18th of February, That notwithftanding the preffing Inftances of the Imperial Embaffador, the Pope had Condemn'd the Marquis del Vafto to lofe his Head and his Eftate to be confifcated, for not appearing to Anfwer the Charge againft him of Publickly Scandalizing Cardinal Janfon.

ADVERTISEMENT.

IT will be found from the Foreign Prints, which from time to time, as Occafion offers, will be mention'd in this Paper, that the Author has taken Care to be duly furnifh'd with all that comes from Abroad in any Language. And for an Affurance that he will not, under Pretence of having Private Intelligence, impofe any Additions of feign'd Circumftances to an Action, but give his Extracts fairly and Impartially ; at the beginning of each Article he will quote the Foreign Paper from whence 'tis taken, that the Publick, feeing from what Country a piece of News comes with the Allowance of that Government, may be better able to Judge of the Credibility and Fairnefs of the Relation : Nor will he take upon him to give any Comments or Conjectures of his own, but will relate only Matter of Fact ; fuppofing other People to have Senfe enough to make Reflections for themfelves.

This Courant (as the Title fhews) will be Publifh'd Daily : being defign'd to give all the Material News as foon as every Poft arrives : and is confin'd to half the Compafs, to fave the Publick at leaft half the Impertinences, of ordinary News-Papers.

LONDON. Sold by E. Mallet, next Door to the King's-Arms Tavern at Fleet-Bridge.

The Whole of the First Number of the *Daily Courant*, the First Daily Paper in England, London, 1702

Size of page, 6¼ in. by 11½ in.

By following this Method [of giving the name of the foreign paper from which each piece of news was taken], he hopes he shall be thought to perform what he takes to be the proper and only Business of a News-Writer; first, giving the freshest Advices from all Quarters, which he will certainly be able to do (let the Post arrive when it will) by coming out Daily: And next, delivering Facts as they come related, and without inclining either to one Side or the other: And this he will be found to do, by representing the same Actions, according to the different Accounts which both Sides give of them: For which the Papers that he cites will be his Vouchers. And thus having fairly related, What is done, When, Where, by which Side reported, and by what Hands transmitted hither; He thinks himself obliged not to launch out of his Province, to amuse People with any Comments and Reflections of his own; but leave every Reader to make such remarks for himself as he is capable of.

The first half of the eighteenth century, during which American colonial newspapers originated and developed, was a brilliant period in English journalism. Men of letters like Defoe, Swift, Addison, Steele, Fielding, and Samuel Johnson, as writers and editors, raised journalistic style to a higher level than it had previously attained. These Augustans of the "age of prose and reason," with their devotion to classical clearness, to so-called "wit," common sense, and critical taste, developed in the periodical essay a type of journalistic writing closely akin to the present-day editorial. Although their best work dealt with social, moral, and literary topics, they did not eschew political discussion. The development of the two-party system in English politics led both Whigs and Tories to seek the aid of literary men as well as of political hack writers. The rise of the middle class, and the popularity of the coffee-houses among all classes, also stimulated journalism. The coffee-houses, like the clubs and public drinking houses of a later day, were convenient places in which to read papers and discuss their contents. As early as 1680, one newspaper editor satirically described the eagerness of frequenters of coffee-houses for both foreign and domestic news, however trivial, and noted the enterprise of publishers in satisfying this curiosity. He wrote:[1]

The lower Sort, they sit at Coffee-Houses, and judge of the

[1] *Mercurius Infernus*, No. 1, n. d. [1680].

Actions of great Persons: so that you shall hear as much Confusion
of Languages over Coffee and Tea, as ever there could be imagined
at *Babel* . . . And how to satisfie all these several sorts of Curiosi-
ties what a Dicker have we of *Forreigns* and *Domesticks;* from
Harris, from *Thomson*, from *Harford*, from *Smith*, from *How*,
from *Paris*, from *Brussels*, from *Cologne*, from *Haerlem*, so exact
to the Visits and *How d'ye's* of Grandee-folk, so that the Dauphin-
ess cannot scratch her Ears, or pare her Nails, but we hear of it.
The Countess of *Soissons* cannot hire a House, but you know who
is her Landlord. Nay, the Duke of Luxemburgh cannot make a
Contract with the Devil, but all *Europe* must ring with it. And
for home Intelligence, we have it Daily, and Hourly, and Minutely,
and half Minutely. So that there is that ample provision made
for divulging and publishing the Affairs of this World that greater
diligence cannot possibly be used.

The part played by the coffee-house fifty years later is briefly
sketched in the *Daily Gazetteer* of July 4, 1737:

. . . there's scarce an Alley in City or Suburbs but has a Coffee-
house in it, which may be called the School of publick Spirit,
where every Man over Daily and Weekly Journals, a Mug, or a
Dram, . . . learns the most hearty Contempt of his own Personal
Sordid Interest to which he owes his Bread only, and devotes himself to that glorious one, his Country. . . .

In short, the spirit of the age, as it found expression in literature,
politics, and social life, tended to develop a marked degree of interest in all forms of journalistic writing.

The greatest single influence on the journalistic style of the
eighteenth century was that of Addison and Steele. Their *Tatler*
(1709–11) and *Spectator* (1711–12, 1714), the first of the so-called
"essay papers," enjoyed great popularity and were freely imitated. These periodical essays may be regarded as the earliest
prototypes of the editorial. Steele began the *Tatler* on April 12,
1709, as a tri-weekly penny paper consisting of one sheet printed
on both sides. Of its contents he wrote in the first issue: [1]

. . . we shall not, upon a dearth of news, present you with
musty foreign edicts, or dull proclamations, but shall divide our
relation of the passages which occur in action or discourse throughout this town, as well as elsewhere, under such dates of places as

---

[1] *Tatler*, April 12, 1709.

may prepare you for the matter you are to expect, in the following manner.

All accounts of gallantry, pleasure, and entertainment, shall be under the article of White's Chocolate-house; poetry, under that of Will's Coffee-house; learning, under the title of Grecian; foreign and domestic news, you will have from Saint James's Coffee-house; and what else I have to offer on any subject shall be dated from my own apartment.

The only news published in the *Tatler* dealt with foreign affairs and constituted a small and unimportant part of the contents. Familiar essays on a variety of subjects, including the fads and foibles of the day, with letters from correspondents, real and fictitious, occupied the greater part of the paper. At first several short essays were printed in each issue; later one longer essay, with advertisements, constituted the whole contents. Addison contributed essays to the *Tatler*, and, when that paper was discontinued in 1711, joined with Steele in bringing out its successor, the *Spectator*. The *Spectator*, which was published daily, consisted of a single sheet printed on both sides, and contained only an essay and advertisements. Its purpose was set forth in these words: [1]

...I shall endeavour to enliven Morality with Wit, and to temper Wit with Morality, that my Readers may, if possible, both Ways find their account in the Speculations of the Day. And to the End that their Virtue and Discretion may not be short transient intermitting Starts of Thought, I have resolved to refresh their Memories from Day to Day, till I have recovered them out of that desperate State of Vice and Folly, into which the Age has fallen. . . . It was said of *Socrates*, that he brought Philosophy down from Heaven, to inhabit among men; and I shall be ambitious to have it said of me, that I have brought Philosophy out of Closets and Libraries, Schools and Colleges, to dwell in Clubs and Assemblies, at Tea-tables, and in Coffee-houses.

In less than two weeks the *Spectator* attained a circulation of 3000 copies, which meant, according to Addison, that it reached 60,000 persons daily. [2] In the last issue of the year Addison expressed gratification that his paper had succeeded without including news, discussions of party politics, or objectionable reading matter such as were found in other papers. He wrote: [3]

[1] *Spectator*, No. 10, March 12, 1711.   [2] *Ibid*.
[3] *Ibid*., No. 262, December 31, 1711.

I think my self highly obliged to the Publick for their kind Acceptance of a Paper which visits them every Morning, and has in
it none of those *Seasonings* that recommend so many of the Writings which are now in vogue among us.

As, on the one Side, my Paper has not in it a single Word of
News, a Reflection in Politicks, nor a Stroke of Party; so, on the
other, there are no fashionable Touches of Infidelity; no obscene
Ideas, no Satyrs [satires] upon Priesthood, Marriage, and the like
popular Topicks of Ridicule; no private Scandal, nor anything
that may tend to the Defamation of Particular Persons, Families,
or Societies.

There is not one of these abovementioned Subjects that would
not sell a very indifferent Paper, could I think of gratifying the
Publick by such mean and base Methods: But notwithstanding I
have rejected everything that savours of Party, everything that is
loose and immoral, and every thing that might create Uneasiness
in the Minds of Particular Persons, I find that the Demand for
my Papers has encreased every Month since their first Appearance
in the World. This does not perhaps reflect so much Honour upon
my self, as on my Readers, who give a much greater Attention to
Discourses on Virtue and Morality, than ever I expected, or indeed could hope.

When I broke loose from that great Body of Writers who have
employed their Wits and Parts in propagating Vice and Irreligion,
I did not question but I should be treated as an odd kind of Fellow
that had a mind to appear singular in my Way of Writing: But
the general Reception I have found, convinces me that the world
is not so currupt as we are apt to imagine; and that if those Men of
Parts who have been employed in viciating the Age had endeav-
oured to rectify and amend it, they needed not to have sacrificed
their good Sense and Virtue to their Fame and Reputation. No
Man is so sunk in Vice and Ignorance, but there are still some
hidden Seeds of Goodness and Knowledge in him; which give him
Relish of such Reflections and Speculations as have an Aptness in
them to improve the Mind and make the Heart better.

So popular was the *Spectator* that innumerable essay papers
sprang up in avowed imitation of it. The *Female Tatler*, the
Whisperer, the *Hermit*, the *Free Thinker*, the *Lay Monk*, the
Growler, were some of the names they bore. Newspapers published essays like those of the *Spectator*, often as the leading feature on the front page. The Addisonian style became a model.
"Whoever wishes to attain an English style," declared Dr.

Johnson, "familiar, but not coarse, and elegant, but not ostenta-
tious, must give his days and nights to the volumes of Addison"; [1]
and many an English and American writer for a century after the
appearance of the *Spectator* followed this advice. Reprinted in
book form, not only the *Tatler* and the *Spectator*, but a number of
the other periodical essays, enjoyed an even larger circulation in
England and in the colonies than they had had in their original
form. [2]

Another prototype of the editorial was the so-called "letter introductory," developed by Daniel Defoe in *Mist's Journal*, which
he edited during most of the three years from 1717 to 1720.
Addressed to the printer of the *Journal* and signed with various
pen names, these letters dealt with a variety of topics, in a direct,
persuasive style well calculated to appeal to the average reader.
Although now popularly known only as the author of *Robinson
Crusoe*, Defoe deserves recognition as the master journalist of the
eighteenth century. It was from the *Mercure Scandale*, later called,
Advice from the Scandalous Club, which constituted one part of
Defoe's *Review*, that Steele got the idea for the *Tatler*. Defoe's power of realistic description and detailed circumstantial
narrative made him the best of news writers, whether portraying
the destruction of the island of St. Vincent or recounting the exploits of the daring highwayman, Jack Sheppard. Because he
possessed a constructive imagination that enabled him to describe
vividly scenes that he himself had not witnessed, his critics have
found evidence in his work of "the little art he is truly master of,
of forging a story and imposing it on the world for truth," [3] in
other words, of the art of "faking," but he always professed to
hold high ideals as to the importance of accuracy in news writing.
He wrote in *Applebee's Original Weekly Journal:* [4]

> ... I would argue, not the Justice, the Necessity, the Reason-
> ableness of our News-Papers giving out no false Accounts of
> Things, no false Reports upon Persons and Nations, but the Ad-
> vantage which it would be to themselves.

[1] Boswell, James. *Life of Samuel Johnson;* George B. Hill, ed., vol. I, p. 261.
[2] In the colonies almost every newspaper, beginning with the Franklins' *New-
England Courant* (1721–26), reprinted essays from the *Spectator* and published
essays and letters that showed plainly the influence of Addison and Steele.
[3] Quoted by William Minto in his *Daniel Defoe*, p. 123.
[4] *Applebee's Original Weekly Journal*, March 16, 1723.

... the only way to establish a Paper, is always to write Truth,
... by a constant adhering to Truth, of Fact, and correcting any
Mistake that may inadvertantly happen, an Author cannot fail
to Establish the Character of his Writings.

His was a long career in journalism, beginning with his *Review* in
1704 and continuing almost until his death in 1731. At times he
edited several papers simultaneously. *Robinson Crusoe* was the
first popular story published serially in an English newspaper. It
was printed in the *London Post*, beginning in October, 1719, six
months after it appeared in book form.[1]

In the political controversies between the Tories and the Whigs
during the eighteenth century, newspapers gradually displaced
pamphlets as a medium of discussion. On the Tory side were the
powerful controversialists, Dean Swift, who edited the *Examiner*
(1710) and wrote political pamphlets, and Nicholas Amhurst,
editor of the *Craftsman* (1726-36), who for more than ten years
vigorously assailed the Walpole ministry. Viscount Bolingbroke,
under the signature, "Humphrey Oldcastle," contributed to the
Craftsman a series of letters, afterwards reprinted as *A Disserta-
tion on Parties*, which attracted wide attention. Another series of
political letters, written by John Trenchard and Thomas Gordon
and signed "Cato," appeared weekly from 1720 to 1723, first in
the *London Journal* and then in the *British Journal*, and enjoyed
great popularity both in England and in America. The theories
of liberty and of representative government set forth in *Cato's
Letters*, as they were called when issued in four volumes in 1724,
met with so hearty an approval in the colonies that some of the
letters were reprinted and quoted in almost every colonial newspaper, beginning in 1721 with Franklin's *New-England Courant*.
They helped to crystallize the political ideas that finally found expression in the Declaration of Independence. The famous letters
by "Junius," published in the London *Public Advertiser* from 1769
to 1772, critical years in American colonial affairs, were also
effective in bringing, both to the colonists and to the citizens of
England, a clearer understanding of their constitutional rights
and a stronger determination to retain them. This method of
carrying on political discussion in series of letters contributed to

[1] Defoe's *Religious Courtship* was the first serial in an American newspaper;
Samuel Keimer began its publication in his *Pennsylvania Gazette* in 1729.

newspapers by political leaders, usually writing under the names of famous Romans, was very popular both in England and in America.

In 1712 the Tory Government, by placing a tax of "one half-penny sterling" on each printed half-sheet, and one of "twelve pence sterling" on every advertisement, sought both to raise revenue and indirectly to curb the press. Papers like the *Spectator* were compelled to double their price, with a consequent loss of subscribers. The number of advertisements in papers was also greatly reduced by reason of the shilling tax. Many papers ceased publication entirely. These "taxes on knowledge," as they came to be called, were not abolished until the middle of the nineteenth century.

During the greater part of the eighteenth century, the amount of news in English newspapers was comparatively small. Their two or four pages, each of which was often scarcely larger than a sheet of letter paper, afforded little room for news, particularly when essays and advertisements occupied considerable space. Without organized methods of news gathering at home or abroad, publishers depended largely on Continental newspapers, private letters furnished them by merchants, reports from travelers and from ship captains, coffee-house gossip, criminal records, and similar sources. News, brought in the mails by sailing vessels and by relays of horses traveling over poor roads, was often weeks and even months old when published. Both foreign and domestic news was, as a rule, very briefly presented. Since political news might be held by the Government to be seditious, it was usually omitted to avoid prosecution for seditious libel.

Domestic news consisted largely of reports of crimes, trials, executions, accidents, disasters, deaths, and marriages. As Defoe wrote:[1]

> This Article call'd Home News is a new Common Hunt, tho' upon a cold scent after Casualties; the Miseries of Mankind are the chief Materials, such as Death and Marriage in the first Class; the Disasters of Families, such as Robberies and Bankrupts, that's the second Class; the Jail Deliveries, either to or from the Gallows, that's the third Class.
>
> If indeed a flaming Rogue comes upon the Stage, such as a

[1] *Applebee's Original Weekly Journal*, August 21, 1725.

Sheppard, a Gow, a Jonathan Wild, or a Blueskin, they are great Helps to us, and we work them, and work them till we make Skeletons of the very Story, and the Names grow rusty as the Chains they are hang'd in.

Eustace Budgell, a cousin of Addison, in his paper, the *Bee*, pointed out the fact that news of crime and accidents was what many readers wanted. He wrote:[1]

We have been so teized and tormented, by our middling Sort of Readers, to be more particular in our Domestick Occurrences, that in order to gratify them, we have taken on Mr. Hum-Drum, an honest stupid Fellow, into our Society: We are pretty well assured, that this Gentleman's Taste is the same with their own: Mr. Hum-Drum reads the first News-Paper that falls in his way, without Distinction; but never minds or remembers what is doing in Foreign Parts; the Articles that chiefly affect him, are Robberies, bloody Murders, Accounts of Draymen's Carts that have run over People, with the Adventures of Post-Boys, Tide-Waiters, and Messengers &c. The Promotions, Deaths, and Marriages of the Nobility, Gentry and Clergy, and of the Days when some of the Royal Family go to the Play-House, or take the Air, are the most abstruse Points in Politicks, about which he ever troubles his Head.

In the first issue of the *Bee* he also promised to furnish his readers some accounts of exploits of criminals taken from *Applebee's Original Weekly Journal*. That paper, as he wrote, owed not a little of its popularity to the fact that it published the confessions of criminals about to be executed. He wrote:[2]

Mr. Applebee takes Care to purchase from all our dying Criminals the private Memoirs of their Lives and Conversations; and tho' many of these Pieces have been wrote or dictated under great Perturbation of Mind, and consequently have not been very Coherent, they still incite the Curious and Inquisitive to peruse Mr. Applebee's Journal. Whenever the Case or Behaviour of a condemned Criminal has something in it extraordinary, we shall consult this ingenious Biographer for the most exact and authentick Account of it.

Foreign news, usually translated from Continental news periodicals, almost invariably took precedence over domestic news. The *Grub-Street Journal* in 1733 pointed out that it was "a great im-

[1] *The Bee*, vol. i, p. 242 (1733). [2] *Ibid.*, p. 29 (1733).

propriety to begin with Foreign news, and end with Domestic; and that it was like travelling into foreign countries before we have taken a survey of our own"; but, although for three years this paper had set an example by putting home news first, the editors called attention to the fact that their example had been "followed by none of our Daily, and but by one of our Weekly historians," "a remarkable instance," they declared, "of that tenacious adherence to old ways and customs, good and bad, for which the English are famous."[1]

The most important political news, the doings of Parliament and of its committees, could not be printed with impunity.   In 1722 the House of Commons passed the following resolution:

> Resolved, That no News Writers do presume in their Letters, or other Papers, that they disperse as Minutes, or under any other Denomination, to intermeddle with the Debates, or any other Proceedings, of this House or any Committee thereof.
>
> Resolved, That no Printer, or Publisher, of any printed News Papers, do presume to insert in any such Papers any Debates, or any other Proceedings, of this House, or any Committee thereof.[2]

Monthly periodicals, such as Boyer's *The Political State of Great Britain*, Cave's *Gentleman's Magazine*, and the *London Magazine*, braved Parliamentary disfavor and published accounts of the doings of Parliament, but they disguised them under such designations as "Proceedings of a Political Club"[3] and "Debates in the Senate of Magna Lilliputia."[4] Without attending any sessions of Parliament, Dr. Samuel Johnson wrote fictitious speeches in the reports of Parliament printed in the *Gentleman's Magazine*, which were long considered authentic.[5]

The final struggle of the press for freedom, not only to report parliamentary proceedings, but to criticise the King and the ministry, coincides with the struggle of the American colonies against the oppression of the mother country.   In fact, it was the illiberal policies of George III and his ministers, in both English and colonial affairs, that caused popular discontent on both sides of

---

[1] *Grub-Street Journal*, July 5, 1733.
[2] *Journals of the House of Commons*, vol. 20, p. 99.
[3] *London Magazine*, vol. VII, p. 209 (May, 1738).
[4] *Gentleman's Magazine*, vol. VIII. p. 283 (June, 1738).
[5] Boswell, James. *Life of Samuel Johnson;* George B. Hill, ed., vol. I, p. 174-75.

the Atlantic, and that led to bold assertions of the rights of the people. One of the leading figures in the fight for the liberty of the press was John Wilkes, who in his weekly paper, the *North Britain* (1762–63), attacked the ministry, and finally, in the famous "Number 45," the King himself. This offense led to his being deprived of his seat in the House of Commons and later to his conviction and imprisonment for seditious libel. Although a profligate and a demagogue, he was hailed by the London populace as a champion of the rights of the people, and "Wilkes and Liberty" became the rallying cry of those opposed to the Government. In America the "Sons of Liberty" of Boston thanked him for his brave fight; the South Carolina Assembly voted £1500 toward a fund being raised by his English friends to pay his debts; [1] and his release from prison was celebrated by a flag raising at the Liberty Tree in Boston and by drinking his health in a toast to "That illustrious Martyr to Liberty." [2] In 1771, as a London alderman, he took a leading part in the fight made by the London newspapers to prevent Parliament from punishing them for publishing its proceedings, a fight that ended in victory for the newspapers and in recognition of their right to report the doings of Parliament as fully as they pleased.

Another milestone in the struggle for freedom of the press was the trial and acquittal of Henry Sampson Woodfall, publisher of the *Public Advertiser*, in connection with the printing in that paper of the famous *Letters of Junius*. In one of these letters Junius, whose identity has never been definitely established, addressed to the King himself a protest against the policies of the Government, [3] with the result that Woodfall, as publisher, was arrested and tried for seditious libel. Despite the judge's charge to the jury to the effect that it could only decide whether or not the alleged libelous statements were published by the defendant and could not decide the question as to their libelous character, the jury virtually acquitted the publisher by finding him "guilty of printing and publishing *only*." In this case the judge's charge to the jury and its verdict involved the same moot question of the law of seditious libel that was at issue in 1735 in the American case of John Peter Zenger and his *New-York Journal;* that is, whether the jury had

---

[1] *Annual Register* for 1770, p. 71.   [2] *Boston Gazette*, April 23, 1770.
[3] *Public Advertiser*, December 19, 1769, Letter No. xxxv.

the right to judge both the fact and the law, or only the fact, leaving to the judge the decision whether or not the statements published were libelous.   Finally, in 1792, twenty-one years later, Parliament settled the matter by passing the Fox Libel Act, which assured freedom of the press by leaving it to the jury to decide what constitutes seditious libel.

Thus were two great victories won.   The undisputed publication by the newspapers after 1771 of the proceedings of Parliament had greater results than fortifying the freedom of the press, for, by removing the secrecy that had surrounded parliamentary proceedings, it led to recognition of the responsibility of Parliament to the people.   The Libel Act of 1792, by leaving to the jury the decision as to what constitutes seditious libel, assured to the press the right to criticise the Government to any extent that would appeal to the average citizen as reasonable.

2. Criticism of the Press

It is interesting to note that from the very dawn of English journalism newspaper writers and publishers were criticised and satirized for the character of their work.   In 1620, the year that the first corantos appeared in England, Ben Jonson in his masque, *News from the New World Discovered in the Moon*, assigns to a printer the words:

> I am a printer, and a printer of news; and I do hearken after 'em whatever they be at any rates; I'll give anything for a good Copy now, be it true or false, so 't be news.

Of the writers of news Shirley in his play, *Love Tricks* (1622), wrote:

> . . . a peace concluded is a great plague upon them, and if the wars hold out we shall have a store of them . . . these, I say, will write you a battle in any part of Europe at an hour's warning, and yet never set foot out of a tavern; describe you towns, fortifications, leaders, the strength of the enemy, what confederates, every day's march — not a soldier shall lose a hair, or have a bullet fly between his arms, but he shall have a page to wait on him in quarto; — Nothing destroys them but want of a good memory, for if they escape contradition they may be chronicled.

Both Ben Jonson, in his *Staple of News* (1625), and Fletcher, in the *Fair Maid of the Inn* (1625), took occasion to pun on the name of Nathaniel Butter, one of the first of the coranteers. Fletcher implied that falsehood was the stock in trade of that stationer, for one of his characters says:[1]

> It shall be the ghost of some lying Stationer,
> A Spirit shall look as if *butter* would not melt in his mouth. A
> new *Mercurius Gallo-belgicus*.

Abraham Holland, in *A Continued Inquisition against Paper-Persecutors* (1624), thus referred to Butter in describing the "shameful lies" of news writers:

> To see such Batter everie weeke besmeare
> Each publicke post, and Church dore, and to heare
> These shameful lies, would make a man in spight
> Of Nature, turne Satyrist and write
> Revenging lines, against these shamelesse men
> Who thus torment both Paper, Presse, and Pen
> Th' Impostors that these Trumperies doe utter
> Are, A, B, C, D, E, F, G, and (......)

Holland, in referring to the writers of the corantos published by Butter could not refrain from a pun on his name:

> ... But to behold the wals
> Butter'd with weekly Newes compos'd in Pauls
> By some Decaied Captaine, or those Rooks
> Whose hungry braines compile prodigious Books.

Whether or not they were justified in their charges that the news of the day was often "faked," these authors, particularly the three dramatists, evidently counted on meeting popular approval by their implied charges against news writers and publishers, and especially against Butter, the best known among them.

The bitterness of partisan journalism, beginning with the struggle between Charles I and Parliament, and extending to the first years of the eighteenth century, was so great that charges of falsifying news were constantly made. George Wither, the Puritan poet, in undertaking the publication of *Mercurius Rusticus* in 1643, frankly declared his policy thus:[2]

> I hope you will not be so severe to expect Truth in every circum-

---

[1] *The Works of Francis Beaumont and John Fletcher;* A. R. Waller, ed., vol. IX, p. 195.
[2] *Mercurius Rusticus; or A Country Messenger*, No. 1, October 26, 1643.

stance; for all Mercuries having the Planet *Mercurie* predominant in their Nativities, cannot but retaine a twang of Lying; Yet this I will assure you, that (though it not be all exact literall truth which I present) here are no such down-right Lies as my other *Cousin-Mercuries* make no bones of; but onely Rhetoricall, Metaphoricall, Parabolicall, or Poeticall Lies, insinuating that which may prevent deceit, without purpose of deceiving any to their dammage.

Of the contemporary periodical publications he wrote in the same issue: [1]

> . . . the *Diurnals*, *Informations* and *Relations* which come weekly and daily abroad (except some few published by Authority) are for the most part either Lies, Mistakes, Vanities, or Impertinences multiplyed & patched out of each other.

That charges of misrepresentation and deliberate lying should have been frequently made against news-books in this period was no doubt due, partly to the heat of controversy, and partly to the fact that many of the writers before the Restoration were men of little education and no character or reputation.   War-time journalists were less zealous to present the truth than to uphold their side.   Mercenary motives led some of these hack writers to change their allegiance from one side to the other.   That some of the leaders recognized the advantages to be derived from employing writers for the diurnals to magnify their achievements is indicated by Mrs. Lucy Hutchinson in her life of her husband, Colonel John Hutchinson of the Parliamentary party, in which she wrote: [2]

> This man [Sir John Gell] kept the diurnal-makers in pension, so that whatever was done in the neighbouring counties, against the enemy, was attributed to him; and thus he hath indirectly purchased himself a name in story, which he never merited.

In the eighteenth century, writers of repute like Addison, Steele, Fielding, and Johnson took occasion to criticise and satirize news writers for their falsehoods, contradictions, and "faking" of news. Addison in an early number of the *Tatler* thus described the methods of news writers in times both of war and of peace: [3]

---

[1] *Mercurius Rusticus; or A Country Messenger*, No. 1, October 26, 1643.

[2] *Memoirs of the Life of Col. Hutchinson, By his Widow Lucy*, C. H. Frith, ed., vol. 1, pp. 11 and 355.

[3] *Tatler*, No. 18, May 21, 1709.

The Case of these Gentlemen is, I think, more hard than that of the Soldiers, considering that they have taken more Towns, and fought more Battles. They have been upon Parties and Skirmishes, when our Armies have lain still; and given the General Assault to many a Place, when the Besiegers were quiet in their Trenches. They have made us Masters of several strong Towns many Weeks before our Generals could do it; and compleated Victories, when our greatest Captains have been glad to come off with a drawn Battle. . . . It is impossible for this ingenious Sort of Men to subsist after a Peace: Every one remembers the Shifts they were driven to in the Reign of King Charles the Second, when they could not furnish out a single Paper of News, without lighting up a Comet in Germany, or a Fire in Moscow. There scarce appear'd a Letter without a Paragraph on an Earthquake. Prodigies were grown so familiar, that they had lost their Name, as a great Poet of that Age has it. I remember Mr. Dyer, . . . was particularly famous for dealing in Whales; insomuch that in Five Months Time (for I had the Curiosity to examine his Letters on that Occasion) he brought Three into the Mouth of the River Thames, besides Two Porpoises and a Sturgeon. The judicious and wary Mr. I. Dawks hath all along been the Rival of this great Writer, and got himself a reputation from Plagues and Famines, by which, in those Days, he destroy'd as great Multitudes, as he has lately done by the Sword. In every Dearth of News, Grand Cairo was sure to be unpeopled.

How news writers, lacking accurate information, were given to padding out news reports with conjectures, often self-contradictory, was thus shown by Steele in a later issue of the *Tatler:* [1]

This Way of going on in Words, and making no Progress in the Sense, is more particularly the Excellency of my most ingenious and renowned Fellow-Labourer, the *Post-Man* . . . The being kept up with one Line contradicting another, and the whole, after many Sentences of Conjecture, vanishing in a Doubt whether there is any Thing at all in what the Person has been reading of, puts an ordinary Head into a Vertigo which his natural dulness would have secured him from . . . The Tautology, the Contradictions, the Doubts, and Wants of Confirmations, are what keep up imaginary Entertainments in empty Heads. . . .

When the *Daily Post* in 1719 entered the London field as the only rival of the *Courant*, Defoe, in the introductory address, ex-

[1] *Tatler*, No. 178, May 30, 1710.

plained that "the Multitude of Papers already publish'd is no Discouragement to us at all," because,[1]

> 'Tis the Misfortune of the Town to have much News but little Intelligence; Truth ill-told, — Lies ill-cover'd, Parties ill-serv'd, — and, in a Word, the Readers vilely impos'd upon on all Sides . . . almost every Transaction is set in a false Light . . . Misrepresentation is, as it were, the Business of every Writer, and whether they speak of private Persons or of publick, the character of no Man seems safe, but Scandal and Slander make Havock of Men's Reputation without Mercy.

Again, six years later, Defoe, writing for *Applebee's Original Weekly Journal*, repeated some of these charges against the newspapers and added others to them, as follows:[2]

> . . . one foreign Paragraph serves a whole *Post Boy*, two supplies a Journal, all the rest we owe to Invention, and how barren! or to Domestick Witt, and that how dull! or to Quack Doctors, and they how fulsome! or to Home News, and that how fabulous, how monstrous, and, in itself too, how mean! . . .
>
> Nay, to tell the Truth, we marry Couples that never was, bury those that never die, bankrupt those that never break, and rob those that never met with a Thief, but this goes but a little way: I have thought now of a new Method to restore Plenty to our hungry Palates, and supply the World with News, and that is, to raise a War in the World, that we may have those dear Things called Battle and Blood to talk of again, and that we may not be all undone by Peace and Quietness.

That news of crime and scandal should have been reported in a manner that would not be tolerated today, is not surprising in an age when plain-speaking was common. Nevertheless, this objectionable practice did not escape censure if we are to judge from an essay on modesty in the *Universal Spectator* in which the author writes:[3]

> The proceedings of our *Courts*, in the Tryal of *Rapes, Criminal Conversations*, and *something* still more abominable, at which Trials, whenever they came on, the late Lord Chief Justice *Holt* would often give Notice to his Female Auditors are now printed in Words at length, or with such *Marks* and *Breaks* as are easily

[1] *Daily Post*, October 6, 1719.
[2] *Applebee's Original Weekly Journal*, August 21, 1725.
[3] *Universal Spectator, and Weekly Journal*, September 23, 1732

intelligible. The Proceedings in *Doctors Commons* upon Cases of *Divorce*, have been carefully translated from the *Latin*, in which, according to the Rules of the Court, they are decently conceal'd.

The *True Briton*, soon after it began publication in 1723, claimed credit for having led other papers to devote more space to domestic news, the truth of which could be determined, than to foreign news, which it was easy to falsify. The editor wrote:[1]

> The *True Briton* has already done some Service to the Publick, since he has provok'd the Mercenary and Hackney Scribblers of an abandon'd Faction to entertain the Town with *Domestic Abuses*, and to shorten the *Foreign Intelligence*, which generally used to fill their Papers. What they now seem to attempt, Every-Body can disprove, but their former Method of Entertaining us with Lyes from Abroad, could not so easily be confuted.

The *Craftsman* likewise pointed out that "Brother News-writers, in a Dearth of common Intelligence, frequently entertain their Readers with surprizing Accounts of Monsters, Earthquakes, and floating Islands."[2]

The *Grub-Street Journal* (1730–37) essayed the interesting task of reprinting each week the different reports of the same events as they appeared in the several London newspapers, and of commenting humorously on the discrepancies among them. The editors of this satirical journal also discussed in a series of essays the way in which newspapers handled the various kinds of news, and, among other abuses, called attention to the common practice of exaggerating the importance of persons who figured in what is now called "society news":[3]

> The new-married couple, tho' scarce heard of before, are placed in the brightest light, and raised by the description given of them nearer upon a level with persons of much higher life. . . . By such relations as these the obscure are rendered eminent; batchelors in middling or low circumstances are made rich and wealthy; and maids who are old and hard-favored become young and beautiful.

In 1729, when the proprietors of the coffee-houses in London attempted to boycott the existing newspapers and to set up newspapers of their own, we have an interesting, although naturally

---

[1] *True Briton*, July 19, 1723.   [2] *Craftsman*, December 20, 1729.
[3] *Grub-Street Journal*, September 13, 1733.

not unbiased, criticism of methods of news gathering, published in a pamphlet entitled: *The Case of the Coffee-men of London and Westminster, or, an Account of the Impositions and Abuses, put upon Them and the Whole Town, by the present Set of News-Writers. With the Scheme of the Coffee-Men for setting up News-Papers of their own; And some Account of their Proceedings thereupon.   By a Coffee-Man.*[1]

The Methods made use of by the present Set of News-Writers, to get Intelligence, and fill up their Papers, expose both them and their Productions to the utmost Contempt.

First: Persons are employed (One or Two for each Paper) at so much a Week, to haunt Coffee-Houses, and thrust themselves into Companies where they are not known; or plant themselves at a convenient Distance, to overhear what is said, in order to pick up Matter for the Papers.   By this Means Gentlemen are often betrayed and embarrass'd in the Management of their private Interests and Concerns.   And by this Means too, the greatest Falsehoods and the idlest Fictions are often publish'd as Matters of Fact.   For these Sons of *Mercury* are often distinguish'd by Persons of Discernment; and when they do so, some rouzing Falsehood is Utter'd in their Hearing for Truth; which the next Day comes out, upon *Credible Information*, to the great Wonder and Edification of the whole Town.

The Market-Cross of *Sherborn* in *Oxfordshire* has fallen down twice after this Manner, in my Memory: And the *Conde de las Torres*, at the Siege of Gibraltar, lost his Boot-Heel by a Cannon-Shot the same Way.   The Ministers have been indispos'd, and dead of Apoplexies, at the Time they were in perfect Health: And Grants have been made, and Honours conferr'd, which were never intended or fought for.   Coblers and Bed-rid Old Women have inherited great Estates; and Earthquakes and Inundations done incredible Damage in Places where they never happen'd.

The same Persons are employed to scrape Acquaintance with Footmen and other Servants of the Nobility and Gentry; and to learn from those knowing and ingenious Persons the Motions and Designs of their Lords and Masters, with such Occurrences as come to the Knowledge of those curious and inquisitive Gentlemen.   By this Means Family-Secrets are often betrayed, and Matters sacred to Privacy and the Fire-side, made the Talk of the World.

The same Persons hang and loiter about the Publick Offices, like

[1] Pages 5–13.

House-breakers waiting for an Interview with some little Clerk, or a Conference with a Door-keeper, in order to come at a little News, or an Account of Transactions; for which the Fee is a Shilling, or a Pint of Wine. By this Means Gentlemen in Employment are frequently betrayed in Matters of Secrecy and Importance, the Publick Service hinder'd, and excellent Designs o'erthrown, or thwarted, by getting Air too soon; or suffer in the Sense of the People by Misrepresentation; not to mention the Lies and Absurdities, which Clerks and Door-keepers often report for the sake of the pitiful Reward. The Lords of the Admiralty are well aware of this; and seem to have searched the Matter to the Bottom; since I am inform'd, there are Orders at the Admiralty-Office, that the *Fellow with the Black Wig* be never allow'd to come within the House; and that the Clerks and Door-keepers beware of him; and never speak of any thing transacting in that Office for the Publick Service, for fear of that Mortal, and his Fellows.

The same Persons call in at Ale-houses where they are acquainted; and there from Carmen, Porters and Common Fellows, pick up Matter for the Publick Attention. There is, indeed, no Harm in this, with respect to Method; but here, likewise, they are often *taken in:* For all Men have the same Spirit and Inclination to divert themselves with these Fellows, when they find them out. Accordingly, a famous Dealer in Politicks and old Shoes, near Bartlet's Buildings, often puts in for a Word to the Publick; and makes his Brags over his Beer, that He has the Honour to entertain the Best Lords of the Land with his Notions. "Why," says he "there is Jo——s now, the Trunk-maker that was. He says, the Hammer Craz'd his Brain. He is one of your Collectors of News. The Fellow now and then comes to me for a Story. I tell him what I think fit: And the next Day 'tis all in Print, as plain as the Nose on your Face, and carried all over among Lords and Gentlemen."

But when it happens, that these wretched Scouts, after running a whole Day about Town, or neglecting Business to play *Cribbage* at an Ale-House, are not provided with Intelligence sufficient to recommend their Zeal and Diligence to their Masters, they fall to work with Invention, and *Give, Grant* and *Confer* of their own Heads; raise Armies in Persia, and Hurricanes in the West-Indies; make Treaties and dissolve Alliances; concert Marriages, and inflict Distempers; *hang* for Love, and *drown* for Despair; tell of Deaths, Robberies and Revolutions, and turn the World up-side down; and thus getting rid of the Business of the Day, go to Sleep with great Satisfaction, till the rising Sun calls them again to the same shining Employments.

Another Method practis'd by the present Set of News-Writers, to make up Deficiencies, and impose on the Publick, is to draw up imaginary Accounts and Articles from abroad; Letters from the *Hague* and Advices from *Paris;* with strange Wonders from *Germany* and the *Black Sea*, and new Discoveries of Antiquities in *Italy*. This is always the game when the Wind holds long in the West: And happy is he who has the most fruitful Invention.

A third Method taken by these dexterous Sons of Mercury, to supply themselves with Matter, is to steal from One another. They copy every Tale that is publish'd to their Hands, good and bad, without Distinction; and the most bare-fac'd Lie, as well as the most pitiful Trifle, once published, has the Sanction of them all. But every Body knows this so well, that 'tis needless to dwell on it.

Another Artifice, often practiced by the present Set of News-Writers, especially in a Dearth of News, or in very rainy Weather, is to rummage old Chronicles, Histories of Antiquity, and other Pieces recording Accidents and remarkable Occurrences of Times long since gone, for old forgotten Stories; which they publish as Relations of Matters just happen'd, only changing the Scenes. . . .

. . . These *Death-Hunters* are met by the Collectors of News in certain Parts of the Town; and for a Treat and a little Money tell them what they hear: And by this Means the Publick is informed of the Progress of Death and Distemper among People of Condition. But how often is the Publick imposed on in this Article! And the Reason is a very good One: For there is Something so shocking in Fellows running about Town, like *Jack-alls*, to find out who is Meat for the *Undertakers*, as justly raises everyones Indignation; and stirs up all that know 'em to cramp and discourage the Practice by all the Inventions and idle Stories they can throw in their Way.

Such are the Arts and Methods practised by the present Set of News-Writers, to get Intelligence and fill up their Papers: And such are the Impositions, and Abuses they put upon the Publick: Always excepting the Publishers by *Authority*. By this Means the wise and excellent Designs of honest and able Ministers, are frequently betrayed and misrepresented; and idle and groundless Jealousies spread and fomented among the People. By this Means the Trade and Credit of the Kingdom are often at a Stand. By this Means the Secrets of Families, and the private Interests and Concerns of particular Persons, are often betray'd and blown about the World. By them the Publick is mislead and distracted, and People sent from One End of the Town to the other, and sometimes to the farthest Parts of the Kingdom, upon Fools Errands.

By them the Channels of *History* are corrupted and poison'd with numberless Lies and Absurdities; and all the laudable Ends and Designs of Publick Intelligence defeated.

Dr. Johnson, in two of the *Idler* essays in *Payne's Universal Chronicle*, pointed out the low ethical standards of news writers and their willingness, particularly in time of war, to give the public what it wants. In the first essay he wrote:[1]

> The compilation of News-papers is often committed to narrow and mercenary minds, not qualified for the task of delighting or instructing; who are content to fill their paper, with whatever matter, without industry to gather, or discernment to select.
> Thus Journals are daily multiplied without increase of knowledge. The tale of the Morning Paper is told again in the Evening, and the narratives of the Evening are brought again in the Morning. These repetitions, indeed, waste time, but they do not shorten it. The most eager peruser of news is tired before he has completed his labour, and many a man who entered the Coffeehouse in his night-gown and slippers, is called away to his shop, or his dinner, before he has well considered the state of Europe.

In the second essay he took up the subject again at greater length:[2]

> To write news in its perfection requires such a combination of qualities, that a man completely fitted for the task is not always to be found. In Sir Henry Wotton's jocular definition, *An Ambassador* is said to be *a man of virtue sent abroad to tell lies for the advantage of his country;* a News-writer is *a man without virtue, who writes lies at home for his own profit.* To these compositions is required neither genius nor knowledge, neither industry nor spriteliness, but contempt of shame and indifference to truth are absolutely necessary. He who by a long familiarity with infamy has obtained these qualities may confidently tell to-day what he intends to contradict to-morrow; he may affirm fearlessly what he knows that he shall be obliged to recant, and may write letters from Amsterdam or Dresden to himself.
> In time of war the nation is always of one mind, eager to hear something good of themselves and ill of the enemy. At this time the task of News-writers is easy, they have nothing to do but to tell that a battle is expected, and afterwards that a battle has been

---

[1] *Payne's Universal Chronicle*, May 27, 1758.
[2] *Ibid.*, November 11, 1758.

fought, in which we and our friends, whether conquering or van-
quished, did all, and our enemies did nothing.

Scarce any thing awakens attention like a tale of cruelty. The
Writer of news never fails in the intermission of action to tell how
the enemies murdered children and ravished virgins; and if the
scene of action be somewhat distant, scalps half the inhabitants of
a province.

Among the calamities of War may be justly numbered the
diminution of the love of truth, by falsehoods which interest dictates and credulity encourages.   A Peace will equally leave the
Warrior and Relater of Wars destitute of employment; and I know
not whether more is to be dreaded from streets filled with Soldiers
accustomed to plunder, or from garrets filled with Scribblers accustomed to lie.

Criticism of advertisements in news-books appeared almost as
soon as advertising began to be common.   The first advertisement
— that of a book — was published as early as 1626, in Mercurius
Britannicus' *The Continuation of our Weekly Newes*,[1] but the
innovation apparently did not meet with favor, for no other advertisement appeared until some twenty-one years later.   During
the two years following the publication of this second advertisement, also of a book, in Walker's *Perfect Occurrences*,[2] advertising
in news-books became general.   In 1649 a paper called *The Man
in the Moon* referred to Walker's news-book as "bumbasted out"
with a six-penny advertisement "of a man that lost a wall ey'd
Mare at Islington."[3]   In the next year the same periodical mentioned Samuel Pecke's *Perfect Diurnall*, "the last page which most
commonly he lets out to the Stationers for sixpence a piece to
place therein the titles of their books."   The first criticism of the
character of advertisements in news-books was made in 1652 by
Samuel Sheppard in the first number of his *Mercurius Mastix*.
He wrote: [4]

> . . . they have now found out another quaint device in their
> trading.   There is never a Mountebank who either by professing
> Chymistry, or any other Art, drains money from the people of the
> Nation, but these Arch-cheats have a share in the booty; and be-
> sides filling up his paper (which he knew not how to do otherwise)

---

[1] *The Continuation of our Weekly Newes*, February 1, 1625/26.
[2] *Perfect Occurrences*, April 2, 1647.
[3] *The Man in the Moon*, October 10, 1649.   [4] *Mercurius Mastix*, August 27, 1652.

he must have a feeling to authorise the Charletan, forsooth, by putting him in the News-book. There he gives you a Bill of his Cures; and because the fellow cannot lye sufficiently himself, he gets one of these to do't for him, and then be sure it passes currant; just like those who being about to sell a diseased or stoln horse in Smithfield, are fain to get a Voucher who will say or swear any thing they please for six pence. But why should we be angry with them for this? for it is commonly truer then the rest of their news.

Nay, they have taken Cryers trade from them: for all stoln goods must be inserted in these Pamphlets; the fittest place for them, all theirs being stoln, they do so filch from one another: I dare be bold to say they confer notes: And then judge you whether this be not fine cozenage, when we have that in ten or twelve Pamphlets, which would hardly fill up a page in one.

From the beginning of advertising, quack doctors and the makers of nostrums recognized the value of the news-books as a medium of publicity. They made the most extravagant claims for themselves and for their wares. In an age when knowledge of medicine and surgery was comparatively limited, it is not surprising that charlatanism and quackery should have flourished. "Great Abuses," it was pointed out in How's *Catholick Intelligence: or Infallible News both Domestick and Forreign*, "have been put upon good People by the Cheats, and Pretences of Quacks and Mountebanks." [1] Even to coffee, newly introduced into England, were attributed remarkable qualities, as appears from the advertisement of one of the first coffee-houses published in the *Publick Adviser*.[2]

In Bartholomew Lane on the back side of the Old Exchange, the drink called coffee, which is a very wholesom and Physical drink, having many excellent vertues, closes the Orifice of the Stomach, fortifies the heat within, helpeth the Digestion, quickneth the Spirits, maketh the heart lightsom, is good against Eyesores, Coughs, or Colds, Rhumes, Consumptions, head-ach, Dropsie, Gout, Scurvy, Kings Evil, and many others, is to be sold both in the morning, and at three of the clock in the afternoon.

In the first quarter of the eighteenth century, Addison, Steele,

---

[1] *Catholick Intelligence: or Infallible News both Domestick and Forreign*, March 8, 1679/80.
[2] *Publick Adviser*, May 19-26, 1657.

and Defoe denounced quackery with great vigor. Steele in the *Spectator* declared that "the ordinary Quack Doctors . . . are to a Man Impostors and Murderers; yet such is the Credulity of the Vulgar, and the Impudence of these Professors, that the Affair still goes on, and new Promises of what was never done before are made every Day." [1]   Addison, likewise, published in the *Spectator*, "for the Good of the Publick," as he said, an "Essay against Quacks" contributed by Dr. Zachary Pearce, Bishop of Rochester.[2]   Nevertheless, Addison and Steele permitted the publisher of the *Spectator* to insert a large number of highly objectionable advertisements of quacks and nostrums.   Typical of the absurd claims made for some of these remedies is the following advertisement: [3]

> Angelick Snuff: The most noble Composition in the World, removing all manner of Disorders of the Head and Brain, easing the most excruciating Pain in a Moment; taking away all Swimming and Giddiness proceeding from Vapours, &c, also Drowsiness, Sleepiness and other lethargick Effects, perfectly curing Deafness to Admiration, and all Humours or Soreness in the Eyes, &c strengthening them when weak, certainly cures Catarrhs, or Defluxions of Rheum, and remedies the Tooth-ach instantly; is excellently beneficial in Apoplectick Fits and Falling Sickness, and assuredly prevents those Distempers; corroborates the Brain, comforts the Nerves, and revives the Spirits. Its admirable Efficacy in all the above-mentioned Diseases has been experienc'd above a Thousand times, and very justly causes it to be esteem'd the most beneficial Snuff in the World, being good for all sorts of Persons. Price 1s. a paper with directions.

So, too, despite its high moral tone, the *Spectator* not infrequently contained questionable "personals" and advertisements of swindles, as well as "puffs" of books, plays, and business enterprises that were advertised in its pages.[4]   Thus early in the history of English journalism appears an inconsistency between editorial professions and business policy with reference to undesirable advertisements that may still be observed today.

To Defoe belongs the credit of first pointing out the inconsistency of inveighing in the editorial columns against political

---

[1] *Spectator*, No. 444, July 30, 1712.   [2] *Ibid.*, No. 572, July 26, 1714.
[3] *Ibid.*. No. 88, June 15, 1711.
[4] Cf. Lewis, Lawrence. *Advertisements of The Spectator*, p. 118.

charlatanism while printing in the advertising section of the same issue deceptive advertisements of quacks and nostrums. In a "letter introductory" written by Defoe for *Mist's Journal*, of which he was editor, he not only took Mist to task for printing such advertising but proposed that the publisher should start a crusade against quacks:[1]

> Believe me, I know not how to reconcile one Part of your Paper with another; nor do I see how all that Zeal against the Botchers in Politicks, which you discover in the Beginning of your Journal, is consistent with that Connivance which you shew to those Pretenders toward the Conclusion. You generally begin your Journal with disabusing the Publick, pointing out the Lies, and rectifying the Errors of your Brother Newsmongers; and yet, e'er you leave your Reader, you never fail to send him to ten or a dozen Places, where he is sure of being abused and imposed on in the grossest Manner. The last Page of your Paper never misses of having as many Lies in it as all the rest have Truths; and I am perswaded you cannot do so much Good by the one as you do Harm by the other.
>
> The World has got an Opinion of your Probity, and whatever appears within the Limits of your Paper, passes among the Populace for authentick. This our Quacks are sensible of; and for this Reason it is that they crowd your Paper with their Advertisements more than any other. The Want of Vertue in the Medicine, and of Merit in the Preparer, they think will be abundantly supplied, by Mr. Mist's Publishing the Praises of them both. Thus your Paper, which was designed for a Receptacle of Truth, is become a Refuge of Lies; and the Reputation you have acquired by your Honesty, now serves to recommend the grossest Impostures. . . .
>
> At present, these People disperse their Lies under your Protection to every Part of the Nation, and spread Death and Desolation, by your Assistance through every Corner of the Island. . . . Your Journal . . . carries them thro' Town and Country, gains Admittance for them at Coffee-houses and Tea-Tables, and gives them Opportunity of prating to all Qualities, Ages, Sexes, Constitutions and Parties. . . .
>
> I have been thinking in what Manner you had best begin your Hostilities; and do not find any that promise better, than to draw the Pictures of some of the Ringleaders of the Tribe, and hanging them up by way of Scare-Crows in your Journal.
>
> The lesser Fry will be terrified with the Sight of such Hobgob-

---

[1] *Mist's Journal*, October 31, 1719.

lins, and even the Grandees themselves will be shocked at the View of their own monstrous Features. . . .

I have got the Outlines of such a Picture ready drawn, by me, and if you publish this, I'll take Care to fill it up, and transmit it to you to be expos'd in your next Journal.

One little periodical, the *Knight Errant*, designed to combat the vices and follies of the day, took a definite stand against objectionable advertising, when in the second issue it announced: [1]

> Whereas I have condescended to annex to this Journal of Knight-Errantry, certain Advertisements, for Publick Information, of advantageous Bargains, Books of Learning, and Entertainment, and such kind of innocent Amusement: This is to certify the Ladies, and all Persons of Delicacy, that 'tis inconsistent with the Laws of Knight-hood, to be any Way concern'd with what is indecent or shocking to the most modest Ear, and, consequently, they may be assur'd, that nothing, of that Nature will ever be allow'd to defile this Paper.

That newspapers contained an excessive amount of advertising, and that their publishers derived large revenues from advertisements, were among the charges made against the papers by the coffee-house men of London in 1729, in connection with their proposal to establish newspapers of their own. In the pamphlet already referred to, it was said: [2]

> Another Complaint the Coffee-Men have against the Managers of the present News-Papers, is that they are made Tools and Properties of in the Business of Advertising. They stipulate for *News;* not for Advertisements: Yet the Papers are ordinarily more than half full of them. The *Daily Post*, for Example, is often equipped with Thirty; which yield Three Pounds Fifteen Shillings that Day to the Proprietors, for the least: And sometimes that Paper has more . . . Well may they divide Twelve Hundred Pounds a Year and upwards. . . .

A brief survey of current criticism of English newspapers in the seventeenth and eighteenth centuries shows that such faults as inaccuracy, "faking," coloring of news, triviality, venality, and inconsistency between editorial professions and advertising policies are not of modern origin but are as old as journalism itself.

---

[1] *Knight Errant*, March 5, 1728/9.
[2] *The Case of the Coffee-men of London and Westminster*, p. 16.

CHAPTER II

EARLY COLONIAL NEWSPAPERS, 1690–1750

THE first American colonists were too much engrossed with subduing the wilderness and establishing themselves in a new world to undertake printing of any kind. Although two of the Pilgrim leaders, William Brewster and Edward Winslow, had been printers in Leyden, Holland, for some years before coming to America, Brewster having issued from his press at least a dozen books and pamphlets, they did not attempt to bring a printing press with them to the New World or to secure one later for the Plymouth Colony. Governor Bradford in his history "Of Plimmoth Plantation" tells of Brewster's career as a printer at Leyden, and of his abandonment of printing on coming to America: [1]

> He [Brewster] also had means to set up printing, (by ye help of some friends,) and so had imploymente inough, and by reason of many books which would not be allowed to be printed in England, they might have had more then they could doe. But now removeing into this countrie, all these things were laid aside againe, and a new course of living must be framed unto; in which he was no way unwilling to take his parte, and to bear his burthen with ye rest, living many times without bread, or corne, many months together, having many times nothing but fish, and often wanting that also.

The first press in what is now the United States was set up at Cambridge, Massachusetts, in 1638, through the efforts of the Reverend Joseph Glover. He was a wealthy Puritan clergyman, who had died at sea as he was bringing from England not only the press, with the necessary type and paper, but a young man to operate it. This printing press was closely identified with Harvard College, which gained possession of it in 1654 through the marriage of President Dunster to Mr. Glover's widow. The first printing press in Boston was set up in 1674. There was no other press in the colonies until William Bradford established one at Philadelphia in 1685.

[1] Bradford, William. *History of Plymouth Plantation*, vol. II, p. 348.

The first colonial newspaper was issued in Boston on September 25, 1690, for Benjamin Harris, an exiled English newspaper publisher, who had settled in Boston as bookseller and proprietor of the London Coffee-House.[1]   *Publick Occurrences Both Forreign and Domestick*,[2] as this paper was called, was promptly suppressed by the Governor and the Council, because it "contained Reflections of a very high nature" and "sundry doubtful and uncertain Reports."   From Judge Samuel Sewall's diary we learn that the paper gave "much distaste because not Licensed; and because of the passage referring to the French King and the Maquas [Mohawk Indians]."[3]   In the broadside proclaiming their "high Resentment and Disallowance," the Governor and the Council "strickly" forbade any one "for the future to Set forth any thing in Print without License first obtained from those that are or shall be appointed by the Government to grant the same."[4] This right of the Governor to regulate the press was granted to each of the colonial governors sent over between 1686 and 1730 by the following paragraph in their instructions:[5]

> And forasmuch as great inconvenience may arise by liberty of printing within our said territory under your government you are to provide by all necessary orders that no person keep any printing-press for printing, nor that any book pamphlet or other matter whatsoever be printed without your especial leave and license first obtained.

Thus the licensing system was continued in the colonies for a generation after it was abandoned in the mother country.

The only issue of *Publick Occurrences* that appeared consisted of four pages, each about the size of a sheet of business stationery (6 × 10¼ inches).   The first three pages contained news arranged in two columns to a page; the fourth page was left blank.

----

[1] See p. 15 *supra*.

[2] The title *Publick Occurrences* may have been suggested to Harris by that of an English newspaper, *Publick Occurrences truely stated*, published in London during the greater part of the year 1688.

[3] Sewall, Samuel.   *Diary*, vol. 1, p. 332.

[4] Duniway, C. A.   *The Development of Freedom of the Press in Massachusetts*, p. 69. The broadside is reproduced in Samuel A. Green's *Ten Fac-simile Reproductions Relating to Old Boston and Neighborhood*.

[5] Duniway, C. A.   *The Development of Freedom of the Press in Massachusetts*, pp. 64–65.

PUBLICK
OCCURRENCES

Both *FORREIGN* and *DOMESTICK.*

Boſton, Thurſday Sept. 25th. 1690.

IT is deſigned, that the *Countrey ſhall be fur-niſhed once a moneth* (or if any Glut of Oc-currences happen, oftener,) *with an Ac-count of ſuch conſiderable things as have ar-rived unto our Notice.*

In order hereunto, *the Publiſher will take what pains he can to obtain a Faithful Relation of all ſuch things* ; *and will particularly make himſelf beholden to ſuch Perſons in* Boſton *whom he knows to have been for their own uſe the diligent Obſer-vers of ſuch matters.*

That which is verein propoſed, is, Firſt, *That* Memorable Occurrents *of Divine Providence may not be neglected or forgotten, as they too often are.* Secondly, *That people every where may bet-ter underſtand the Circumſtances of Publique Af-airs both abroad and at home* ; *which may not only direct their Thoughts at all times, but at ſome times alſo to aſſiſt their Buſineſſes and Ne-gotiations.*

Thirdly, *That ſome thing may be done towards the Curing, or at leaſt the Charming of that Spi-rit of Lying, which prevails amongſt us, whe e-fore nothing ſhall be entered, but what we have reaſon to believe is true, repairing to the beſt foun-tains for our Information. And when there ap-pears any material miſtake in any thing that is collected, it ſhall be corrected in the next.*

Moreover, *the Publiſher of theſe Occurrences is willing to engage, that whereas, there are ma-ny* Falſe Reports, *maliciouſly made, and ſpread among us, if any well-minded perſon will be at the pains to trace any ſuch falſe Report ſo far as to find out and Convict the Firſt Raiſer of it, he will in this Paper* (*unleſs juſt Advice be given to the contrary*) *expoſe the Name of ſuch perſon, as* A malicious Raiſer of a falſe Report. *It is ſuppos'd that none will diſlike this Propoſal, but ſuch as intend to be guilty of ſo villanous a Crime.*

THE Chriſtianized *Indians* in ſome parts of *Plimouth*, have newly ap-pointed a day of Thankſgiving to God for his Mercy in ſupplying their extream and pinching Neceſſities under their late want of Corn, & for His giving them now a proſ-pect of a very *Comfortable Harveſt.* Their Example may be worth Mentioning.

'Tis obſerved by the Husbandmen, that altho' the With-draw of ſo great a ſtrength from them, as what is in the Forces. lately gone for *Canada*; made them think it almoſt impoſſible for them to get well through the Affairs of their Husbandry at this time of the year, yet the Seaſon has been ſo unuſually favourable that they ſcarce find any want of the many hundreds of hands, that are gone from them ; which is looked upon as a Mer-ciful Providence

While the barbarous *Indians* were lurking about *Chelmsford*, there were miſſing about the beginning of this month a couple of Chil-dren belonging to a man of that Town, one of them aged about eleven the other aged a-bout nine years, both of them ſuppoſed to be fallen into the hands of the *Indians.*

A very *Tragical Accident* happened at *Wa-ter-Town*, the beginning of this Month an *Old man*, that was of ſomewhat a Silent and Moroſe Temper, but one that had long En-joyed the reputation of a Sober and a Pious *Man*, having newly buried his Wife, The Devil took advantage of the Melancholly which he thereupon fell into, his Wives diſ-cretion and induſtry had long been the ſup-port of his Family, and he ſeemed hurried with an impertinent fear that he ſhould now come to want before he dyed, though he had very careful friends to look after him who kept a ſtrict eye upon him, leaſt he ſhould do himſelf any harm. But one evening eſcaping from them into the Cow-houſe, they there quickly followed him. found him changing by a Rope;which they had uſed to tye their *Calves* withal, he was dead with his feet near touch-ing the Ground.

Epidemical *Fevers* and *Agues* grow very common, in ſome parts of the Countrey, whereof, tho' many dye not, yet they are ſorely unfitted for their imployments; but in ſome parts a more *malignant Fever* ſeems to prevail in ſuch ſort that it uſually goes thro' a Family where it comes, and proves *Mortal* unto many.

The *Small-pox* which has been raging in *Boſton*, after a manner very Extraordinary is now very much abated. It is thought that far more have been ſick of it then were viſi-ted with it, when it raged ſo much twelve years ago, neverthleſs it has. not been ſo Mortal, The number of them that have

---

The First Page of the First and Only Number of *Publick Occurrences*, a News-paper which Benjamin Harris Attempted to Publish in Boston in 1690

Size of page, 6 in. by 10¼ in.

There were no advertisements.   The publisher's purposes were set forth in these words: [1]

> It is designed, that the Countrey shall be furnished once a moneth (or if any Glut of Occurrences happen, oftener,) with an Account of such considerable things as have arrived unto our Notice.
>
> In order hereunto, the Publisher will take what pains he can to obtain a Faithful Relation of all such things; and will particularly make himself beholden to such Persons in Boston whom he knows to have been for their own use the diligent Observers of such matters.
>
> That which is herein proposed, is, First, That Memorable Occurrents of Divine Providence may not be neglected or forgotten, as they too often are.   Secondly, That people every where may better understand the Circumstances of Publique Affairs both abroad and at home; which may not only direct their Thoughts at all times, but at some times also to assist their Businesses and Negotiations.
>
> Thirdly, That some thing may be done towards the Curing, or at least the Charming of that Spirit of Lying, which prevails amongst us, wherefore nothing shall be entered, but what we have reason to believe is true, repairing to the best fountains for our Information.   And when there appears any material mistake in any thing that is collected, it shall be corrected in the next.
>
> Moreover, the Publisher of these Occurrences is willing to engage, that whereas, there are many False Reports, maliciously made, and spread among us, if any well-minded person will be at the pains to trace any such false Report so far as to find out and Convict the First Raiser of it, he will in this Paper (unless just Advice be given to the contrary) expose the Name of such person, as A malicious Raiser of a false Report.   It is suppos'd that none will dislike this Proposal, but such as intend to be guilty of so villanous a Crime.

Unlike colonial newspapers of a later date, the one issue of this paper consisted largely of American rather than foreign news. Of some twenty paragraphs of news only two concerned foreign affairs.   Detailed reports of encounters between the English with their Indian allies and the French and Indians of Canada, occupied considerable space.   Local news included that of the kid-

---

[1] A facsimile of *Publick Occurrences*, the only known copy of which was found in the London Public Record Office in 1845, is given in Samuel A. Green's *Ten Facsimile Reproductions Relating to Old Boston and Neighborhood.*

naping of two children by Indians at Chelmsford, the suicide of an old man at Watertown, "Epidemical Fevers and Agues ... very common, in some parts of the Country," the spread of small-pox in Boston, and a fire in Boston that destroyed among other things "the best furnished Printing-Press, of those few that we know of in America ... a loss not presently to be repaired." As a result of his newspaper experience in England, Harris had a better developed sense of news values, and a better style in news writing, than had many of the later colonial publishers, most of whom were printers rather than editors.

No second attempt to publish a newspaper in America was made until fourteen years later, when, on April 24, 1704, John Campbell, postmaster of Boston, issued the first number of the *Boston News-Letter*. Continued for seventy-two years, eighteen of them under Campbell's editorship, it proved to be the first successful American newspaper. By "waiting on His Excellency or Secretary for approbation of what is Collected"[1] in the way of news, Campbell was able to print conspicuously, "Published by Authority," under the heading of his paper, and thus escaped the penalty of suppression inflicted on Harris' unauthorized publication.

The *News-Letter* grew out of the written news letters that Campbell had been sending to the governors of the other New England colonies for at least a year before its appearance.[2] It consisted of a single small sheet ($6\frac{1}{4} \times 10\frac{1}{2}$ inches) printed on both sides, like its English contemporaries. The first issue, without any prospectus or advertisements, contained foreign news from London newspapers of over four months before, and some local news. The news from abroad was credited to the papers from which it was taken and was given precedence over domestic news, in accordance with the common practice of English papers. In fact, the *News-Letter* was plainly modeled on the newspapers of the mother country.

At the close of the first year, Campbell described his difficulties and his editorial methods thus:[3]

[1] *Boston News-Letter*, April 2–9, 1705.
[2] The contents of nine of these written letters are given in the *Proceedings of the Massachusetts Historical Society*, 1867, vol. 9, pp. 485–501.
[3] *Boston News-Letter*, April 2–9, 1705.

This Publick Printed News-Letter was undertaken to be Published for a Publick Good, to give a true Account of all Foreign and Domestick Occurrences, and to prevent a great many false reports of the same, and was propounded to be Printed for one year for a tryal viz. from the 14th of April last, to the 1st of May next, to see if the Income by the Sale thereof at a moderate price would be sufficient encouragement to defray the necessary Charge expended in the procuring and Printing of the same, which Charge is considerable beyond what most people conceive it to be, besides the trouble and fatigue attending it; all which would be too long here to enumerate, yet for some satisfaction, we will venture to set down some of the Charges and trouble that arises thereby & leave other-some to rational persons to conceive of. 1. The Undertaker has several setts of the several Prints from England, & sent him in several Vessels, that being time of War might have one sett if the rest should be taken, which are ordered to come by all Vessels coming to our Continent where the Post is settled almost 500 miles from E. to W. from N. Hampshire to Pensilvania. 2. Correspondents settled in several other Ports & places our Shipping goes to, for sending Intelligence. 3. Waiting on Masters, Merchants and others when Ships & Vessels arrive to have from them what Intelligence they can give. 4. Waiting on His Excellency or Secretary for approbation of what is Collected. 5. Paper & Printing, &c. And when so done as we said before, we set the half Sheet at a more moderate price than it was set at in Exeter in England, where they began to Print much about the same time that we began here, here it was set at 2d. and there it was at 2d. and that sterling money, & when sent out to any house in Town inclosed, they were to have Twenty Shillings per Annum, and it was propounded here to be sent out for Twelve Shillings per Annum, tho' the paper and labour, & other Charges here is 4 times at least dearer then it is at Exeter. And tho' it was proposed at such moderate Rates for both Town & Country, having had 11 months experience of the Income, & trouble & charge in procuring & Printing it; the Undertaker is money out of Pocket, & has not sufficient to defray the necessary Charge; and unless some better encouragement be given for the future, it must drop: & therefore several being desirous it should not drop but be continued, we thought fit to insert this Advertisement, That either the price for the half Sheet a week, and the Quarterly and Yearly Customers must be augmented, or else there must be more of them Sold, and more Quarterly & Yearly Customers than was last year.

Campbell struggled along, making frequent appeals for support,

The Boston News-Letter.

Publiſhed by Authority.

From Monday May 15. to Monday May 22. 1704.

Weſtminſter, Novemb. 12. 1703.
The Addreſs of the Lords Spiritual and Temporal, preſented Her Majeſty.

WEE Your Majeſties moſt dutiful and loyal Subjects, the Lords Spiritual and Temporal in Parliament Aſſembled, do offer up our hearty acknowledgments to Almighty God, for the preſervation of Your Royal Perſon, ſo eſſential to the happineſs of Your People, & the Safety of *Europe.*

We ſee, with the greateſt ſatisfaction, the zeal with which Your Majeſty eſpouſes the Publick Intereſt, which carries You even beyond the obligations of Your Treaties in Defence of the Houſe of *Auſtria*, againſt the Uſurpations of the Houſe of *Bourbon*, & the glorious reſtitution of that Family to the Monarchy of *Spain*, which we have great reaſon to expect from the late Alliance with the King of *Portugal*, will be chiefly owing to Your Majeſties Arms and Aſſiſtance.

Your Majeſty may depend upon Security at home in the love of Your People, our Perſons & Fortunes ſhall ever be ready to defend You upon all occaſions, and Your Majeſty may therefore, with the greater Safety and Glory, ſend Your Fleets and Armies abroad in the Defence of Your Allies.

The happy Declaration of the Duke of *Savoy*, for the common Intereſt, gives Your Majeſty a ſeaſonable opportunity to ſhew Your Compaſſion and concern for thoſe Proteſtants in the South of *France*, who lie under the heavieſt Perſecution and oppreſſion.

We lament for our ſelves and others the unavoidable expences of War, but have reaſon to thank God and Your Majeſty, that we are free from all the other Calamities of it, having almoſt nothing elſe to wiſh for (being ſecured of a Proteſtant Succeſſion) but Your long and happy Reign over us: And we ſhall moſt willingly pay our proportion of Taxes, encouraged by Your Royal Generoſity for the eaſe of Your People, & by the frugal management of what is given ; being ſenſible, there is no better way to ſave the Wealth of the Nation, than by carrying on the War at this time with the utmoſt vigour.

Your Majeſty may expect from us a moſt ready compliance with all Your deſires, ſo juſtly merited by Your care of the general welfare and happineſs of Your People, extended even to the pooreſt and meaneſt of Your Subjects

This appears yet more eminently in that earneſt and preſſing Recommendation to Your Parliament of Union and Peace amongſt themſelves ; And we, in the moſt ſolemn manner, Aſſure Your Majeſty, That we will not only avoid, but oppoſe whatſoever may tend to create any diſquiet or diſunion amongſt Your Subjects.

We ſhall never be wanting in any part of our Duty towards the Supporting Your Majeſties honour & Your Allies, not doubting but Almighty God will proſper Your Majeſties Arms, ſo gloriouſly employed to protect all thoſe whom the ambition of the *French* King would oppreſs.

To which Her Majeſty return'd Her moſt Gracious Anſwer in theſe words.

My Lords,
I Am extreamly ſenſible of the particular concern You expreſs for me in this Addreſs, and of Your great zeal for the common cauſe of *Europe*.

I rely very much upon the Aſſurances You give me of Your Duty and Affection, and ſhall always uſe my beſt endeavours to eſtabliſh the ſafety and happineſs of the Kingdom.

Piſcataqua, May, 13. Letters thence acquaint us of ſome more damage, done by the Sculking Adverſary, on the 11. inſtant *Nicholas Cole* of *Wells*, with *Nicholas Hogden, Thomas Dane* and *Benjamin Gough*, Souldiers, went about a Mile from Capt. *Wheelwright's* Garriſon to Look after his Cattle, and on their return were Attack't by 12. Indians, who kill'd ſaid *Cole* and *Hogden*, took *Dane* Captive, *Gough* eſcaping, adviſed Capt. *Hales* of it, who immediately called his Souldiers together ; but the Enemy were fled.

Her Majeſties Council by His Excy. direction hath appointed Thurſday the 18. inſtant a day of Publick Faſting with Prayer, being the ſame day appointed by His Excy. & Council in the Province of *Maſſ.Bay* and for ſaid ends contain'd in ſaid Proclamation.

Arrived here *John Holicom* from *Antigua. Richard Shortridge* for *Fyall* wind-bound. Outward-bound, Capt. *Alcock* for *Barbadoes* ready to Sail, *John Froſt* for ſaid Port in Ten days, and *Robert Emery* in about 3 weeks, and *Richard Waterhouſe* for St. Chriſtophers in a Week.

Northampton, May 13. A Company of Indians and French, between day break and Sun-riſing, about 60 Set upon a Garriſon-houſe of *Benj. Jones's*, about two Miles from the body of the Town, and ſet fire to it ere they were aware of it ; Kill'd and carryed Captive about 30. Perſons. The Town being Alarmed, purſued them, the Enemy finding it, ſcattered themſelves into parties ; and ſo did the Engliſh into Ten in a Company, purſuing them ; Capt. *Taylor* was kill'd in the purſuit.

Liſbon, March 27. On the advice brought the King of *Portugal*, of the Fleet from *England*, being on the Coaſt in whom was the King of *Spain* ; he ordered a Wharff to be made from his Palace to the Waterſide, & overlaid it with Cloath of Scarlet, and went in his Barge on board to receive him, returned and the King of *Spain* on his right hand ; who was received with all imaginable Demonſtrations of joy, by diſcharing of Guns, ringing of Bells, bon fires, illuminations, Fireworks, &c. and for a Fortnight nothing but Feaſting. Three days ere the K. of *Spain* Arrived the Princeſs (Daughter of the K. of *Portugal*) deſigned to be his Queen, Dyed ; and that loſs like to made up by her Siſter, ſome two years younger. Seven Grandees of *Spain* (beſides thoſe he brought with him) came to him upon his Arrival, who informed him that all places would ſubmit to him aſſoon as he appeared. The Engliſh and Dutch Forces were about 12 thouſand. The King of *Portugal* had 15. thouſand, and daily leavying of New Forces : Upon his Arrival he ſent the Forces to the Fronteers, ; reſerving a few Companies for guard of his own Perſon to the Army, whither he deſigned to March that Week, that Capt. *Elſon* came away & then directly for *Marid.* Upon the Fleets Arrival in *Liſbon*, conſiſting of about 22 Sail of Men of War, and about 300 Tranſport Ships : A Dutch Privateer being chaſed by 5 Sail of Men of War, informed Admiral *Rook* of and twice during 1706 receiving grants from the Government.[1] Finally, in March, 1709, having published the paper continuously for five years, he was compelled to suspend it for eight months "for want of any Tollerable encouragement to support it."[2]   On January 1, 1710, it "was again sett on Foot at the desire of several in this and the Neighbouring Provinces, particularly of the Town of Boston, in hopes of meeting with a far better reception, both from publick and private hands, for its present support, and future continuance, which hitherto it has not met with."[3]   Despite the fact that for the first fifteen years of its existence it was the only paper in the colonies, it never received adequate support. In 1719 Campbell points out, in one of his periodic complaints of lack of patronage, that "he cannot vend 300 at an Impression, tho' some ignorantly concludes he Sells upwards of a Thousand."[4] Obviously, with so small a circulation to show for fifteen years of struggle, he must have carried on the publication more out of a sense of duty to the community than from any hope of profit.

Campbell edited his paper in a painstaking but conservative and uninspired manner.   He was scrupulously accurate, even to the extent of pointing out in one issue that a comma had been misplaced in a preceding number.[5]   On another occasion he explained that, in an account of a fire at Plymouth in the preceding issue, "whereas it is said Flame covering the Barn, it should be said Smoak."[6]   Occasionally he would point the moral of a piece of news.   When, for example, a woman had committed suicide, he expressed the hope that "the Inserting of such an awful Providence here may not be offensive, but rather a Warning to all others to watch against the Wiles of our Grand Adversary."[7] Again, when a man was punished with a severe whipping for selling tar mixed with dirt, he explains that the account "is here only Inserted to be a caveat to others, of doing the like, least a worse thing befal them."[8]   Such brief comments were the only editorial utterances in the *News-Letter*.

[1] Duniway, C. A.   *The Development of Freedom of the Press in Massachusetts*, p. 78, footnote.

[2] *Boston News-Letter*, June 19–26, 1710.   [3] *Ibid.*

[4] *Ibid.*, August 3–10, 1719.   [5] *Ibid.*, July 15–22, 1706.

[6] *Ibid.*, April 26–May 3, 1708.   [7] *Ibid.*, August 6–13, 1705.

[8] *Ibid.*, October 1–8, 1705.

The first illustration in an American newspaper, a wood-cut reproduction of a new flag to be used by the United Kingdom of England and Scotland, appeared in the *Boston News-Letter* of January 19–26, 1707/8.

With meticulous care Campbell undertook, in the limited space of his paper, "to carry on the Threed of Occurrences" abroad by reprinting in chronological order news gleaned from English newspapers. By this method he was at times from nine to thirteen months behind in publishing foreign news.[1] His difficulties, particularly in winter, he explains in his clumsy style thus:[2]

> Having in our Numb. 207. Given you a Summary of the Publick Occurrences of *Europe* for five months time, *viz.* from the middle of *August* to the middle of *December:* And in our five last and in this, a more particular Account of the most Remarkable Occurrences of *Europe* for six months and an halfs time, *viz.* from the middle of *August* to the first of *March*, in our Numb. 208, 209, 210, 211, 212. And in regard we have not Weekly and Monthly Pacquets, as they have in *Europe* and the *West-Indies*, wherby to carry on the Occurrences regularly; We shall now return back where we left off in our Numb. 207. to carry on the Threed of Occurrences as methodically as it will admit of, . . . until Vessels from *Great Britain*, or from the *West-Indies* do arrive in any part of our Continent, when the Undertaker shall give you as he usually did a Summary and Abridgment of the most Remarkable Occurrences of *Europe*, for the succeeding Months.

After being superseded in the Boston postmastership in 1719, Campbell continued the *News-Letter* for three years. Then, in 1722, he retired in favor of Bartholomew Green, who for many years had been the printer of the paper.

When Campbell refused to turn over the *News-Letter* to the new postmaster, William Brooker, the latter started a rival paper, the *Boston Gazette*, with James Franklin as printer. The *Gazette*, the first issue of which appeared on December 21, 1719, was thus the second newspaper in the colonies. It continued as the organ of four successive postmasters after Brooker. The official status of the *Gazette* was indicated, both by its name, obviously suggested by that of the *London Gazette*, the English government organ, and by the legend, "Published by Authority." In its early years, like

---

[1] *Boston News-Letter*, August 3–10, 1719.   [2] *Ibid.*, May 10–17, 1708.

the *News-Letter*, it was a mere chronicle of foreign and some domestic news, dry and uninteresting.

The appearance of the *New-England Courant* in Boston on August 7, 1721, from the press of James Franklin, marks a new stage in the development of American journalism. The *Courant* was the first newspaper established in any colony in avowed opposition to its recognized leaders, as well as the first to publish essays, letters, and verse. It was the third paper published in Boston, and the fourth in the colonies, having been preceded by the *American Weekly Mercury* of Philadelphia. In the first issue Franklin announced that his paper would be "published fortnightly," but in the second number, a week later, he explained that, "at the desire of several Gentlemen in Town, this Paper is to be published weekly." [1]

Having lost the printing of the *Gazette* through a change in postmasters, Franklin apparently was encouraged to start a paper in opposition to the *Gazette* and to the *News-Letter* by a group of men who were out of sympathy with the influential Puritan leaders of Boston. James Franklin, as his brother Benjamin tells us in his *Autobiography*, "had some ingenious men among his friends, who amus'd themselves by writing little pieces for this paper." [2] In the file of the *Courant* preserved in the British Museum in the Burney collection of early English newspapers, the names of practically all of the contributors are written in, in ink, apparently in Benjamin Franklin's handwriting. From this file it appears that John Checkley was the editor, or "author," of the first three numbers. As Checkley was a devout Episcopalian, who had been forbidden by the authorities two years before to publish a religious tract, and as several of the contributors to the early numbers of the *Courant*, including the Reverend Henry Harris of King's Chapel, Boston, were Church of England adherents, the reason for the *Courant's* attitude toward prominent Puritans is evident. That this sectarian element was involved in the establishment of the *Courant*, is borne out by James Franklin's statement in the fifth number of the paper. He said: [3]

Several Gentlemen in Town believing that this Paper (by what

---

[1] *New-England Courant*, August 7–14, 1721.
[2] *Writings of Benjamin Franklin*, Smyth, A. H., ed., vol. I, p. 246.
[3] *New-England Courant*, August 28–September 4, 1721.

was inserted in No.3) was published with a Design to bring the Persons of the Clergy into Contempt, the Publisher thinks himself oblig'd to give Notice, that he has chang'd his Author; and promises, that nothing for the future shall be inserted, any ways reflecting on the Clergy or Government. . . .

The immediate question at issue was the desirability of inoculation for small-pox, a method of combatting the disease that was being advocated by the Reverend Increase Mather and other leading Puritans. "The chief Design" of the paper, according to a statement by Checkley in the third issue, was "to oppose the *doubtful* and *dangerous* Practice of *inoculating* the *Small Pox.*"[1] Practically all the space in the first four numbers of the *Courant* that was not devoted to news, was taken up with articles and letters opposing inoculation. All of the Boston physicians, with but one exception, are said to have opposed inoculation, and three of these opponents wrote letters or articles against it for the *Courant*.

James Franklin's only contributions to the first four issues were some verses entitled "On the Distress of the Town of Boston, occasioned by the Small Pox,"[2] and a reply in verse to an attack made on him by John Campbell in the *News-Letter*. Writing under the name of "Jack Dulman," which had been given him by Campbell, Franklin addressed these lines to the editor of the *News-Letter:*[3]

> He need not tell you where you're *flat* and *dull;*
> Your Works declare, 'tis in your empty Skull.
> *In reading, hearing, writing, and Pains taking,*
> You set your Reader's Heads and Hearts on aking.

The first issue of the *Courant* called forth a rejoinder from the inoculationists in the form of a broadside, also printed by Franklin. Entitled *The Little-Compton Scourge: or, The Anti-Courant,* it took the form of a letter to the "author" of the *Courant*, signed "Zechariah Touchstone," the pen name of the Reverend Thomas Walter of Roxbury, a grandson of the Reverend Increase Mather.[4]

---

[1] *New-England Courant*, August 14–21, 1721.
[2] *Ibid.*, August 21–28, 1721.   [3] *Ibid.*, August 14–21, 1721.
[4] This broadside is bound in the file of the *New-England Courant* in the Burney collection at the British Museum, and its authorship is ascribed to the Reverend Mr. Walter, apparently in the handwriting of Benjamin Franklin.

In the third number of the *Courant* appeared two replies to this broadside, one by Dr. John Gibbins, a prominent Church of England adherent, and another by Checkley, the editor of the paper. These articles, which charged the Reverend Mr. Walter with immorality and drinking to excess, were in bad taste, and Franklin not only dispensed promptly with the services of Checkley but later expressed regret that he had published these articles.[1]   The journalistic battle thus begun between the rival factions continued for months, the venerable Increase Mather and his party using the *Boston Gazette*, and their opponents, the *Courant*.   Both sides also resorted to pamphlets.   Franklin and his associates on the *Courant* were styled by their opponents the "Hell-Fire Club of Boston," a name obviously suggested by the notorious "Hell-Fire Club" in England.

That the writings of James Franklin and of contributors to the *Courant* deeply stirred the Reverend Increase Mather is evident from his "Advice to the Publick," published in the *Boston Gazette*.   Part of this article read:[2]

> I that have known what *New-England* was from the Beginning, cannot but be troubled to see the Degeneracy of this place.   I can well remember when the Civil Government could have taken an effectual Course to suppress such a *Cursed Libel!* which if it be not done I am afraid that some *Awful Judgment* will come upon this Land, and that the *Wrath of GOD will arise, and there will be no Remedy.*
>
> I cannot but pity poor *Franklin*, who tho' but a *Young Man*, it may be *Speedily* he must appear before the Judgment Seat of GOD, and what answer will he give for printing things so vile and abominable?   And I cannot but Advise the Supporters of this *Courant* to consider the consequences of being *Partakers in other Mens Sins*, and no more Countenance such a *Wicked Paper.*

The manner in which the controversy was carried on may be judged from Franklin's reply in the *Courant* to a letter in the *Boston Gazette*[3] written by Mather Byles, a grandson of the Reverend Increase Mather and a freshman in Harvard College:[4]

> ... a young scribbling Collegian, who has just Learning enough to make a Fool of himself, has taken it in his Head to put a Stop to

this Wickedness (as he calls it) by a Letter in the last Week's *Gazette*. Poor Boy! When your letter comes to be seen in other Countries, (under the Umbrage of Authority,) what indeed will they think of New-England! They will certainly conclude, There is bloody Fishing for Nonsense at Cambridge, and sad Work at the Colledge. The young Wretch, when he calls those who write the several Pieces in the Courant, The Hell-Fire Club of Boston, and finds a Godfather for them, (which by the way is a Hellish Mockery of the Ordinance of Baptism, as administered by the Church of England,) and tells us, That all the Supporters of the Paper will be look'd upon as Destroyers of the Religion of the Country, and Enemies to the faithful Ministers of it, little thinks what a cruel Reflection he throws on his Reverend Grandfather, who was then, and for some time before, a Subscriber for the Paper.

Thus James Franklin himself was occasionally drawn into controversial writing, although most of the original contributions in his paper were the work of other hands.

In accordance with the printer's announcement in the second issue of the *Courant* that he "earnestly desires his Friends may favour him from time to time, with some short Piece, Serious, Sarcastick, Ludicrous, or other ways amusing,"[1] the paper, after the first few issues, included not only discussions of inoculation but also essays, letters, and verse on a variety of subjects, after the manner of contemporary English newspapers. Many of these contributions were original; others were reprints from English sources. One of *Cato's Letters*, on libeling, taken from the *London Journal* of a few months before, appeared in the sixth number, and was followed by others. Essays from the *Spectator* were included, as well as original contributions in imitation of Addison and Steele. For example, "Ichabod Henroost's" letter about his gadding wife,[2] by James Franklin, is an echo of a letter in the *Spectator* by "Nathaniel Henroost," a henpecked husband.[3] The short introductory essays on the first page of the *Courant*, with their Latin mottoes, also suggest strongly the English essay papers. That Franklin aimed to pattern his paper after these publications is indicated, not only by the contents, but by the purpose expressed thus at the end of the first half year:[4]

---

[1] *New-England Courant*, August 7–14, 1721.   [2] *Ibid.*, January 8–15, 1722.
[3] *Spectator*, September 21, 1711 (No. 176).
[4] *New-England Courant*, January 22–29, 1722.

> To expose the Vices and Follies of Persons of all Ranks and
> Degrees, under feign'd Names, is what no honest Man will object
> against; and this the Publisher (by the Assistance of his Corre-
> spondents) is resolv'd to pursue, without Fear of, or Affection to
> any Man: And as the Paper will contain Variety of Speculations,
> every Subscriber will often find a Subject to please him, and 'tis
> presum'd, nothing that shall give just Cause of Offence.

Accordingly letters, essays, and verse criticising and ridiculing
various vices and abuses were a regular feature of the paper. By
thus imitating English methods, Franklin introduced new elements into colonial journalism and made his paper much more
sprightly and readable than those of his predecessors.

When, on a March night in 1722, Benjamin Franklin, a sixteen-
year-old apprentice in his brother's print shop, slipped under the
door of the *Courant* office his first contribution, a letter signed
"Silence Dogood," the paper secured a valuable contributor who
was destined to become one of the ablest of colonial editors.
James Franklin was apparently ignorant at first of the authorship
of these contributions, but in the course of the six months during
which the "Silence Dogood" letters appeared regularly every
other week, he discovered the identity of their author.[1]   From a
literary point of view they constituted the most meritorious part
of the *Courant*.   Modeled on the *Spectator*, which, as Benjamin
Franklin related in his *Autobiography*, he had read and imitated
from the age of twelve, they were marked by a genial humor and
urbanity that contrasted strongly with the coarser, more personal ridicule in most of the other contributions.

If we are to take literally a statement addressed to its readers in
an early number, the *New-England Courant* deserves credit for
being the first American newspaper to have women on its staff.
The statement read in part as follows: [2]

> We are not ashamed the World should know our great Design;
> it being to promote Virtue and real Goodness: And having lately
> admitted two of the Fair Sex into our Society, we hope we shall be
> able to prosecute the same with more advantage; reform things
> that have been amiss, and at once both please and profit others.

[1] The fourteen letters are reprinted in *The Writings of Benjamin Franklin*, A. H.
Smyth, ed., vol. II, pp. 2–49.
[2] *New-England Courant*, June 25–July 2, 1722.

THE [N° 58

New-England Courant.

From M O N D A Y September 3. to M O N D A Y September 10. 1 7 2 2.

Quod eſt in corde ſobrii, eſt in ore ebrii.

To the Author of the New-England Courant.

SIR, [No XII.

T is no unprofitable tho'
unpleaſant Purſuit, di-
ligently to inſpect and
conſider the Manners
& Converſation of Men,
who, inſenſible of the
greateſt Enjoyments of
humane Life, abandon
themſelves to Vice from
a falſe Notion of *Plea-
ſure* and *good Fellowſhip.*
A true and natural Re-
preſentation of any E-
normity, is often the beſt Argument againſt it and
Means of removing it, when the moſt ſevere Repre-
henſions alone, are found ineffectual.

I WOULD in this Letter improve the little Obſervation I have made on the Vice of *Drunkenneſs,* the
better to reclaim the *good Fellows* who uſually pay
the Devotions of the Evening to *Bacchus.*

I DOUBT not but *moderate Drinking* has been improv'd for the Diffuſion of Knowledge among the
ingenious Part of Mankind, who want the Talent
of a ready Utterance, in order to diſcover the Conceptions of their Minds in an entertaining and intelligible Manner. 'Tis true, drinking does not *improve* our Faculties, but it enables us to *uſe* them ;
and therefore I conclude, that much Study and Experience, and a little Liquor, are of abſolute Neceſſity
for ſome Tempers, in order to make them accom-
pliſh'd Orators. *Dic. Ponder* diſcovers an excellent
Judgment when he is inſpir'd with a Glaſs or two
of *Claret,* but he paſſes for a Fool among thoſe of
ſmall Obſervation, who never ſaw him the better for
Drink. And here it will not be improper to obſerve,
That the moderate Uſe of Liquor, and a well plac'd
and well regulated Anger, often produce this ſame
Effect ; and ſome who cannot ordinarily talk but in
broken Sentences and falſe Grammar, do in the Heat
of Paſſion expreſs themſelves with as much Eloquence
as Warmth. Hence it is that my own Sex are generally the moſt eloquent, becauſe the moſt paſſio-
nate. " (ſays an ingenious Author,) that they could talk
" whole Hours together upon any thing ; but it
" muſt be owned for the Honour of the other Sex,
" that there are many among them who can talk
" whole Hours together upon Nothing. I have
" known a Woman branch out into a long extempo-
" re Diſſertation on the Edging of a Petticoat, and
" chide her Servant for breaking a China Cup, in all
" the Figures of Rhetorick. "

BUT after all is muſt be conſider'd, that no Pleaſure can give Satisfaction or prove advantageous to
a *reaſonable Mind,* which is not attended with the
Reſtraints of Reaſon. Enjoyment is not to be found
by Exceſs in any ſenſual Gratification ; but on the
contrary, the immoderate Cravings of the Voluptu-
ary, are always ſucceeded with Loathing and a pal-

led Appetite. What Pleaſure can the Drunkard have
in the Reflection, that, while in his Cups, he retain'd
only the Shape of a Man, and acted the Part of a
Beaſt ; or that from reaſonable Diſcourſe a few Minutes before, he deſcended to Impertinence and Non-
ſenſe ?

I CANNOT pretend to account for the different
Effects of Liquor on Perſons of different Diſpoſitions,
who are guilty of Exceſs in the Uſe of it. 'Tis
ſtrange to ſee Men of a regular Converſation become
rakiſh and profane when intoxicated with Drink, and
yet more ſurprizing to obſerve, that ſome who appear to be the moſt profligate Wretches when ſober,
become mighty religious in their Cups, and will then,
and at no other Time addreſs their Maker, but when
they are deſtitute of Reaſon, and actually affronting
him. Some ſhrink in the Wetting, and others ſwell
to ſuch an unuſual Bulk in their Imaginations, that
they can in an Inſtant underſtand all Arts and Sciences, by the liberal Education of a little vivifying
Punch, or a ſufficient Quantity of other exhilerating
Liquor.

AND as the Effects of Liquor are various, ſo are
the Characters given to its Devourers. It argues
ſome Shame in the Drunkards themſelves, in that
they have invented numberleſs Words and Phraſes
to cover their Folly, whoſe proper Sgnifications are
harmleſs, or have no Signification at all. They are
ſeldom known to be *drunk,* tho they are very often
*boozey, cogey, tipſey, fox'd, merry, mellow, fuddl'd,
groatable, Confoundedly cut, See two Moons,* are A-
*mong the Philiſtines, In a very good Humour, See the
Sun,* or, *The Sun has ſhone upon them* ; they *Clip the
King's Engliſh,* are *Almoſt froze, Feavouriſh, In their
Altitudes, Pretty well enter'd,* &c. In ſhort, every
Day produces ſome new Word or Phraſe which
might be added to the Vocabulary of the *Tiplers :*
But I have choſe to mention theſe few, becauſe
if at any Time a Man of Sobriety and Temperance
happens to *cut himſelf confoundedly,* or is *almoſt froze,*
or *feavouriſh,* or accidentally *ſees the Sun,* &c. he may
eſcape the Imputation of being drunk, when his Miſ-
fortune comes to be related.

I am *SIR,*
Your Humble Servant,

SILENCE DOGOOD.

FOREIGN AFFAIRS.

Berlin, May 8. Twelve Pruſſian Batallions are
ſent to Mecklenburg, but for what Reaſon is not
known. 'Tis ſaid, the Emperor, ſuſpecting the De-
ſigns of the Czar, will ſecure all the Domains of
the Duke of Meckleburg. His Pruſſian Majeſty, to
promote the intended Union of the Reformed and
Lutherans in his Dominions, has charged the Mi-
niſters of thoſe two Communions, not to make the
leaſt mention in the Pulpits of the religious Differences about ſome abſtruſer Points, particularly the
Doctrine of Predeſtination, and to forbear all con-
tumelious Expreſſions againſt one another.

Hamburg, May 8. The Imperial Court has order'd the Circles of Lower Saxony, to keep in Rea-
dineſs

A Typical First Page of the *New-England Courant,* Containing One of
Benjamin Franklin's "Silence Dogood" Letters

Size of page, 6⅛ in. by 10¾ in.

It is not improbable, however, that one of the "fair sex" referred to may have been "Silence Dogood," alias Benjamin Franklin.

That James Franklin should finally be called to account for his freedom in dealing with those in authority was to be expected. A suggestion in the *Courant* of June 4–11, 1722, that the Government had not been so aggressive as it should have been in suppressing pirates on the New England coast, brought him to prison for a month. Just before he was released, the Council proposed to the House of Representatives that he should be placed under bonds and should be required to submit each week for the approval of the Secretary all the material that he proposed to print in the *Courant*. The House, however, refused to concur in these proposals. The charges on which the Council based this proposed action were that "many Passages have been published, boldly reflecting on His Majesty's Government and on the Administration of it in this Province, the Ministry, Churches and College [Harvard]: and it very often contains Paragraphs that tend to fill the Readers Minds with vanity, to the Dishonour of God and disservice to Good Men." [1] Franklin continued his criticism and ridicule, until he was again called to account.

In January, 1723, the *Courant* published an essay on hypocrites and other articles that gave offense, with the result that the Council and the House agreed to appoint a committee to consider what should be done to curb the publication. The report of this committee read: [2]

> The Committee appointed to Consider of the Paper called, The New-England Courant, published Monday the fourteenth Currant, are humbly of Opinion that the Tendency of the said Paper is to mock Religion, and bring it into Contempt, that the Holy Scriptures are therein profanely abused, that the Reverend and faithful Ministers of the Gospel are injuriously Reflected on, His Majesty's Government affronted, and the Peace and good Order of his Majesty's Subjects of the Province disturbed, by the said Courant; And for prevention of the like Offence for the Future, the Committee humbly propose, That James Franklin the Printer and Publisher thereof, be strictly forbidden by this Court to Print or Publish the New-England Courant, or any Pamphlet or Paper of the like Nature, except it be first supervised by the Secretary of

[1] *New-England Courant*, July 9–16, 1722.
[2] *Ibid.*, January 14–21, 1723.

this Province; And the Justices of His Majesty's Sessions of the Peace for the County of Suffolk, at their next Adjournment, be directed to take sufficient Bonds of the said Franklin for [his good Behaviour] Twelve Months Time.

The Council ordered Franklin's arrest, and a warrant was issued on January 28. In the issue of the *Courant* of February 4–11, the following announcement was made:

The late Publisher of this Paper, finding so many Inconveniences would arise by his carrying the Manuscripts and publick News to be supervis'd by the Secretary, as to render his carrying it on unprofitable, has intirely dropt the Undertaking. The present Publisher having receiv'd the following Piece, desires the Readers to accept of it as a Preface to what they may hereafter meet with in this Paper.

What had happened was that James Franklin had substituted the name of his brother, Benjamin, for his own, as printer and publisher of the *Courant*.

This seventeen-year-old boy wrote a characteristic editorial preface to the first issue bearing his name, in which he explained his purpose thus:[1]

The main Design of this Weekly Paper will be to entertain the Town with the most comical and diverting Incidents of Humane Life, which in so large a Place as Boston, will not fail of a universal Exemplification: Nor shall we be wanting to fill up these Papers with a grateful Interspersion of more serious Morals, which may be drawn from the most ludicrous and odd Parts of Life.

In the same number the publisher boasted that his paper had "met with so general an Acceptance in Town and Country, as to require a far greater Number of them to be printed, than there is of the other publick Papers," and that it was "besides more generally read by a vast Number of Borrowers, who do not take it in."[2] But the precocious young Benjamin did not get on well with his brother and finally ran away. He went to New York, and then to Philadelphia, where later, as editor and publisher of the *Pennsylvania Gazette*, he did his most active journalistic work. James Franklin continued to publish the *Courant* until some time

[1] *New-England Courant*, February 4–11, 1723. The complete article is reprinted in *The Writings of Benjamin Franklin*, A. H. Smyth, ed., vol. II, pp. 49–50.

[2] *Ibid.*, February 4–11, 1723.

in 1726, when he, too, deserted Boston. He settled at Newport, Rhode Island, where in 1732 he started the first paper in that colony, the *Rhode-Island Gazette*.

The demise of the *New-England Courant* was followed shortly by the establishment, on March 20, 1727, of the *New-England Weekly Journal*. When a change in Boston postmasters deprived Samuel Kneeland of the printing of the *Boston Gazette*, the organ of the postmaster, he, like James Franklin under similar circumstances, started a paper of his own, the *Weekly Journal*. In the first issue he announced that he had arranged "to settle a Correspondence with the most knowing and ingenious Gentlemen in the several noted Towns in this and the Neighbour-Provinces, who may Take particular Care seasonably to Collect and send what may be remarkable in their Town or Towns adjacent, worthy of Publick View"; and that "a Select number of Gentlemen, who have had the happiness of a liberal Education, and some of them considerably improv'd by their Travels into distant Countries; are now concerting some regular Schemes for the Entertainment of the ingenious Reader and the Encouragement of Wit and Politeness; and may in a very short time, open upon the Public in a variety of pleasing and profitable Speculations."[1] From the latter part of this announcement it is evident that James Franklin's innovation in the *Courant* of publishing *Spectator*-like essays and letters from contributors, was recognized as an interesting addition to the mere recording of current events. The "gentlemen of liberal Education" who contributed "a variety of pleasing and profitable Speculations" to the *Weekly Journal* included the Reverend Mather Byles, grandson of the Reverend Increase Mather, the Reverend Thomas Prince, author of the *Chronological History of New England*, Judge Danforth, and probably Governor Burnet. The essays were palpable imitations of the *Spectator*, and the poems, largely by the Reverend Mather Byles, were in the manner of Pope. In publishing essays and verse the *Weekly Journal* followed the example not only of Franklin's *Courant* but of English newspapers.

That the coffee-houses of Boston, like those in London, served as convenient places in which to read both foreign and local news is indicated by advertisements in the Boston newspapers. The

[1] *New-England Weekly Journal*, March 20, 1727.

proprietor of the Crown Coffee-House, for example, advertises in 1726 that he "had been and still is at considerable Pains and Expence in procuring the London and Boston Newspapers for the Entertainment of the Publick," and that, as these papers are "commonly taken away before they have been read," he is offering a reward of twenty shillings "to any person who discovers who does it." [1] In 1731 an advertisement of the opening of a chocolate house in Boston describes it as a place "where they [gentlemen] may Read the News, and have Chocolate, Coffee, or Tea ready made any time of the Day." [2]

The first newspaper published outside of Boston, and the third in the colonies, the *American Weekly Mercury*, appeared in Philadelphia on December 22, 1719, one day after the first number of Brooker's *Boston Gazette*. It was issued by Andrew Bradford, postmaster of Philadelphia, a son of the William Bradford who in 1685 had set up the first printing press in Philadelphia. Local news was given more space, and was rather better written, in the *Mercury* than in the *News-Letter* or in the *Boston Gazette*. Longer accounts were printed of fires, accidents, crimes, executions, and last speeches of criminals. Even a humorous feature story like the following found its way into the Mercury: [3]

Philadelphia, Sept. 28

Several Bears were seen Yesterday near this Place, and one killed at German-Town, and another near Derby. Last Night a very large Bear, being spied by two Amazons, as he was eating his last Supper of Acorns up a tree, they calling some Inhabitants of this Place to their Assistance, he was soon fetch'd down from thence, and entirely dispatched by em. Afterwards finding no more Sport with Bears, they quarrel'd with one another for the Body as madly as the Centaurs upon a like Occasion. The following Lines were writ in Praise of the Notable Heroine, who spied him first and attended him to his Execution.

> Fair P——r, sure 'twas wisely, bravely done,
> To shew thy self a modern Amazon,
> Unus'd to hunt, or draw the strenuous Bow,
> To poize the Lance, or fatal Dart to throw;
> Yet Atalanta's Courage shone in thee,
> That durst approach the monster-bearing Tree:

---

[1] *Boston Gazette*, June 6–13, 1726.   [2] *Ibid.*, September 13–20, 1731.
[3] *American Weekly Mercury*, September 21–28, 1721.

> For R——r's arm you mark'd the destin'd Prey
> Nor fearful turn'd your Virgin Face away,
> And merited with him the Honour of the Day.

The publisher of the *Mercury*, after printing an account of the action of the Massachusetts General Assembly against James Franklin, vigorously championed Franklin's cause in these words:[1]

> My Lord Coke observes, That to punish first and then enquire, the Law abhors; but here Mr. Franklin has a severe Sentence pass'd upon him, even to the taking away Part of his Livelihood, without being call'd to make Answer. An indifferent Person would judge by this vote against Couranto, That the Assembly of the Province of Massachusetts Bay are made up of Oppressors and Bigots, who make Religion the only Engine of Destruction to the People, and the rather, because the first Letter in the Courant of the 14th of January (which the Assembly censures) so naturally represents and exposes the Hypocritical Pretenders to Religion. Indeed, the most famous Politicians in that Government (as the infamous Gov. D——y and his Family) have been remarkable for Hypocrisy: And it is the general Opinion, that some of their Rulers are rais'd up and continued as a Scourge in the Hands of the Almighty for the Sins of the People.
>
> Thus much we could not forbear saying, out of Compassion to the distressed People of the Province, who must now resign all Pretences to Sense and Reason, and submit to the Tyranny of Priestcraft and Hypocrisy.

Bradford doubtless felt the more keenly this action against Franklin because, just a year earlier, he had been called before the Provincial Council of Pennsylvania for printing a harmless little paragraph, and, after apologizing for its publication, had been warned not to offend again.

The second paper published in the middle colonies, and the first in New York, was William Bradford's *New-York Gazette*, begun on November 8, 1725. After having established the first printing press outside of Massachusetts, at Philadelphia in 1685, Bradford had been invited by Governor Fletcher to go to New York, and in 1693 had accepted the appointment of official printer. As "the King's Printer for the Province of New York," Bradford made his *Gazette* little more than a semi-official paper of news, much after

[1] *American Weekly Mercury*, February 19–26, 1722/23.

the manner of Campbell's *Boston News-Letter*. That his paper, like Campbell's, failed to receive adequate support — possibly because it, too, was merely a chronicle of current events taken largely from foreign newspapers — is shown by a statement that he made after the *Gazette* had been in existence for two and a half years: [1]

> ... having calculated the Charge of Printing and Paper for the same, as also how much will arise to defray that Charge (when all those that take this Gazette have paid in what is due to the first of May last) do find that we shall loose Thirty Five Pounds in the two years and a half, by Publishing this Paper, besides the trouble and Charge of Correspondents, collecting the News, making up Pacquets and conveying the same to those in the Country who take them. And therefore if some further Encouragement be not given, by a larger Number of Subscribers for said Gazette, we must let it fall, and cease publishing the same.

Despite this lack of support, Bradford continued the *Gazette*, doubtless with the encouragement of the colonial governors, and probably with the aid of the salary which he is said to have received as official printer. Without opposition for eight years the *Gazette* continued to furnish news, as well as occasional essays, stories, and verses gleaned from English publications.

The rise of a colonial party in New York opposed to Governor Cosby and his adherents, resulted in the establishment on November 5, 1733, of the second paper in that colony, the *New-York Weekly Journal*. The printer and publisher was John Peter Zenger, a German immigrant, who had been an apprentice of Bradford's and later his partner for a short time. The purpose of the leaders of the popular party responsible for the establishment of the paper, was set forth in a private letter by James Alexander, who seems to have been its editor-in-chief: [2]

> Inclosed is the first of a newspaper designed to be continued Weekly and chiefly to expose him [Governor Cosby] and those ridiculous flatteries with which Mr. Harison [the Recorder and a member of the Council] loads our other Newspaper which our Governor claims and has the privilege of suffering nothing to be in but what he and Mr. Harison approve of.

[1] *New-York Gazette*, June 10–17, 1728.
[2] Rutherfurd, Livingston. *John Peter Zenger*, pp. 28–29.

Governor Cosby, in turn, declared that it was "by the Contrivance of some evil Disposed and Disaffected Persons" that the *Weekly Journal* had "been caused to be Printed and Published by" Zenger.[1] To the *New-York Journal*, accordingly, belongs the distinction of being the first newspaper established in America by a political faction as a means of carrying on a political controversy.

In the early numbers of the *Weekly Journal*, the opponents of the Governor discussed liberty of the press, trial by jury, and other fundamental rights of the people. In their fight for popular government, Zenger and his backers quoted freely from *Cato's Letters* and from the essays of Addison and Steele. How much these English writers were admired is shown by the following excerpt from a letter contributed to the paper:[2]

> Addison, Steel, and the English Cato have been Men Almost Divine, we can hardly Err if we agree with them in Political Sentiments; And yet we ought not to give up our Reason to them Absolutely, because they were Men, and as such Lyable to Errors tho I know not of one Error in either of them.

Bradford, as editor of the semi-official *Gazette*, came to the defense of Governor Cosby and the Government, and, not to be outdone in the matter of marshaling well-known English authorities, repeatedly quoted the *Spectator* to confute Zenger and his party. Thus did English journalism furnish colonial writers with models for political debate.

The significance of this newspaper controversy between rival factions in New York, lies in the fact that it started the discussion of theories of government that culminated in the Declaration of Independence. The leaders who wrote for the *Weekly Journal* upheld the right of the people to a voice in government, to freedom to criticise their rulers, to liberty of the press, and to the privilege of jury trial; and they stressed the responsibility of rulers to the people, from whom they derived their right to rule. Bradford's *Gazette*, on the other hand, stood for maintaining the authority of the Crown and of its representatives, the colonial governors and their councils. Thus these opposing conceptions of

---

[1] Rutherfurd, Livingston. *John Peter Zenger*, plate opposite p. 44.
[2] *New-York Weekly Journal*, February 4, 1733/4.

the nature of government were the subject of newspaper discussion in New York a generation before the Stamp Act of 1765 brought them before all the colonists.

The attacks on the Governor and his party published in the *Weekly Journal* inevitably led to efforts to punish the printer for his temerity, even though Zenger himself did not write the articles that gave offense. On November 17, 1734, Zenger was arrested on a warrant charging him with "printing and publishing several Seditious Libels" in his paper, copies of which were described in the warrant as "having in them many Things, tending to raise Factions and Tumults, among the people of this Province, inflaming their minds with Contempt of His Majesty's Government, and greatly disturbing the Peace thereof." [1] At the same time Governor Cosby in a proclamation offered a reward of £50 to any one "who shall discover the Author or Authors of the said *Scandalous, Virulent* and *Seditious Reflections*." [2] Zenger while in prison was not only deprived for several days of pen, ink, and paper but was refused permission to communicate with any person. He was unable, therefore, to publish the *Journal* that week. The following week, however, it again appeared, with an account of his arrest and imprisonment and the explanation that, since he had been given "the Liberty of Speaking through the Hole in the Door" to his wife and servants, he hoped "to entertain" his readers with his "Weekly Journall as formerly." [3] Through the efforts of his wife and his supporters, the *Journal* continued regularly every week during his eight months' imprisonment. After his acquittal and his release on August 5, 1735, he resumed personal management of the paper.

The plea made in behalf of Zenger by Andrew Hamilton, a prominent lawyer of Philadelphia, who had been secured by Zenger's backers to defend him, was the first legal argument in any American court on two points vital to subsequent discussions of liberty of the press in both England and America — the admissibility of evidence as to the truth of the statements alleged to be libelous, and the right of the jury, not only to pass upon the fact of the publication of the alleged libelous matter, but to de-

[1] Rutherfurd, Livingston. *John Peter Zenger*, pp. 45–46.
[2] *New-York Gazette*, November 18–25, 1734.
[3] *New-York Weekly Journal*, November 18–25, 1734.

termine whether or not the statements published were libelous under the laws of seditious libel.[1] Hamilton argued against the principle of the English law of seditious libel, which held that "the greater the truth the greater the libel," and he sought to prove that, to be libelous, a statement "must be false and malicious, and tend to Sedition." [2]   When the court overruled him on this point and held that it could not be "admitted ... to give the Truth of a Libel in Evidence," [3] he contended that the jury "have the Right beyond all Dispute, to determine both the Law and the Fact, and where they do not doubt the Law, they ought to do so." [4]   Although the Chief Justice declared that "the Jury may find that *Zenger* printed and published those Papers, and leave it to the Court to judge whether they are libellous," [5] Hamilton was so successful in his plea to the jury that they brought in a verdict of "Not Guilty."

The trial, involving as it did the question of the right of newspapers to criticise the Government, as well as moot questions of the law of seditious libel, attracted attention both in the other colonies and in the mother country.   Zenger not only printed a brief account of his trial in the *Weekly Journal* of August 18, 1735, but immediately issued a forty-page report of the trial in pamphlet form.   Four editions of this pamphlet were reprinted in London in 1738; others were issued in Boston and in Lancaster, Pennsylvania.   Shortly after the appearance of the London reprint of the trial, it served as text for an essay in the *Craftsman*,[6] and for one in *Common Sense*.[7]   An enthusiastic correspondent writing to the *Pennsylvania Gazette* quoted the following private letter from London dated February, 1737/8, in regard to the interest that the trial had aroused in England: [8]

> We have been lately amused with Zenger's Trial, which has become the *common* Topic of Conversation in all the Coffee Houses, both at the Court-End of the Town and in the City.   During my

---

[1] William Bradford had raised the point of the right of the jury to decide both the fact and the law in defending himself against a charge of seditious libel at Philadelphia in 1692.

[2] Rutherfurd, Livingston. *John Peter Zenger*, p. 84.

[3] *Ibid.*, p. 81.   [4] *Ibid.*, p. 93.   [5] *Ibid.*, p. 93.

[6] This essay, which appeared in the *Craftsman* on January 21, 1737/8, was reprinted in the *Pennsylvania Gazette*, March 30–April 6, 1738.

[7] *Common Sense*, January 7, 1738.

[8] *Pennsylvania Gazette*, May 11–18, 1738.

Observation, there has not been any piece, published here, so greedily read and so highly applauded. — The greatest Men at the Bar have openly declared, that the Subject of Libels was never so well treated in *Westminster-Hall*, as at New-York. — Our political Writers of different Factions, who never agreed in any thing else, have mentioned the Trial in their public Writings with an Air of Rapture and Triumph. — a *Goliath* in Learning and Politics gave his opinion of Mr. *Hamilton's* Argument in these terms, *If it is not Law it is better than Law, it Ought to be Law, and Will Always be Law wherever Justice prevails.* The Tryal has been reprinted four times in three months, and there has been a greater demand for it, by all ranks and degrees of People, than there has been known for any of the most celebrated Performances of our greatest Geniuses. — We look upon *Zenger's* Advocate, as *a glorious Assertor of Public Liberty and of the Rights and Privileges of Britons.*

Although Hamilton's arguments met with popular approval on both sides of the Atlantic, his contention that juries in cases of seditious libel should be judges of the law as well as of the fact was not established in England until Fox's L bel Act was passed by Parliament in 1792, and his other contention regarding the admissibility of evidence of truth as a defense in libel cases was not recognized as valid in American law until a clause covering this point was added to the Alien and Sedition Act in 1798. Despite the fact that it was in New York in 1735 that the latter argument was raised at Zenger's trial, the State of New York did not recognize by law the validity of the defense of truth in criminal libel suits until 1821. Nevertheless, Hamilton's great speech and Zenger's acquittal are milestones on the road of progress toward freedom of the press.

One of the most ambitious newspaper projects in the early colonial period was *The Universal Instructor in all Arts and Sciences; and Pennsylvania Gazette*, brought out in Philadelphia by Samuel Keimer. On October 1, 1728, nearly three months in advance of the appearance of the first issue, Keimer published a prospectus in which he set forth grandiloquently all the details of the proposed publication. It read in part:

Whereas several Gentlemen in this and the Neighboring Provinces, have given Encouragement to the Printer hereof, to publish a Paper of Intelligence; and whereas, the late *Mercury* has been so wretchedly perform'd; that it has been not only a Reproach to the Province, but such a Scandal to the very Name of Printing, that it may for its unparallel'd Blunders and Incorrectness, be truly stiled *Nonsence in Folio*, instead of a Serviceable News-Paper.

This is therefore to give Notice, that there is design'd to be published the Latter End of November next, a most useful Paper of Intelligence, Entitled, *The Pennsylvania Gazette, or the Universal Instructor*, containing the best and most authentick Accounts of the most remarkable Transactions in Europe; to be continued Weekly, in a fair Letter and well corrected.

As the Proposer hereof has dwelt formerly at the Fountain of Intelligence in *Europe*, he has taken effectual Methods to be furnish'd with the most useful, material, pleasant and remarkable Occurrences that shall happen; to please all, and offend none, and that at the reasonable Expence of 10s *per annum*, Proclamation-Money, allowing every Subscriber to put in an Advertisement *Gratis*, any one Time in the first Half Year.

As this News Paper in a few Weeks Time after Publication, will exceed all others that ever were in *America*, and being always a whole Sheet, it will contain at Times, the Theory of all Arts, both Liberal and Mechanical, and the several Sciences both humane and divine; with the Figures, Kinds, Properties, Pro-ductions, Preparations of Things natural and artificial; also the Rise, Progress and State of Things Ecclesiastical, Civil, Military and Commercial, with the several Systems, Sects, Opinions among Philosophers, Divines, Mathematecians, Antiquaries, &c. after an Alphabetical Order, the whole being the most compleat Body of History and Philosophy yet publish'd since the Creation.

To carry out the latter part of this elaborate program, Keimer devoted the first page of each issue to the serial republication of Chambers' *Dictionary of the Arts and Sciences*, beginning with the letter "A."

In the first issue he made this announcement: [1]

We have little News of Consequence at present the *English* P ints being generally stufft with Robberies, Cheats, Fires, Murders, Bankrupcies, Promotions for some, and Hangings of others; nor can we expect much better till Vessels arrive in the Spring, when we hope to inform our readers what has been doing in the Court and Cabinet, in the Parliament-House as well as in the Session-House, so that we wish, in our *American* world, it may be said, as Dr. *Wild* wittily express'd it of the *European*, viz.

[1] *Universal Instructor*, December 24, 1728.

We all are seiz'd with the Athenian itch,
News and New Things do the whole World Bewitch.

In the mean Time we hope our readers will be content for the
present, with what we can give 'em, which if it does 'em no Good,
shall do 'em no Hurt. 'Tis the best we have, and so take it.

Keimer also sought to interest women readers. In the second
issue, "in the Scarcity of Foreign News," he published the story of
"two Vertuous Women," which, he wrote, "we recommend to our
Female Readers, whom we shall not forget to oblige, in our
Weekly Lucubrations"; and in the fourth issue he printed another
selection recommended to his "Female Readers." He likewise
began the serial republication of Defoe's *Religious Courtship*.

In starting the *Universal Instructor*, Keimer tried to forestall
the publication of a new paper that Benjamin Franklin intended
to establish in Philadelphia. Franklin, incensed at the betrayal
of his plans by a friend to whom he had confided them, contributed six of the "Busybody" essays to Bradford's *American
Weekly Mercury*, in order to enliven it and make it a serious competitor of the *Universal Instructor*. When, after nine months'
effort, Keimer had succeeded in holding only ninety of his subscribers, he was willing to sell his paper to Franklin.[1] On taking
over the publication, with Hugh Meredith as partner, Franklin
reduced the long title to the *Pennsylvania Gazette*, discontinued
the serial republication of Chambers' *Dictionary*, which it would
have taken fifty years to complete, and also ceased reprinting
Defoe's *Religious Courtship*. In the third issue under the new
management, he announced that "from this time forward instead
of publishing a whole sheet once a week, as the first Undertaker
engag'd to do in his proposals, we shall publish a Half Sheet twice
a week, which amounts to the same Thing; only we think it will
be more acceptable to our Readers inasmuch as their Entertainment will by this Means become more frequent." [2] But this first
attempt in America to publish a semi-weekly paper did not prove
satisfactory, and weekly publication was resumed shortly afterwards.

The conditions under which newspapers were begun and de-

[1] Franklin, Benjamin. *Autobiography*, in *The Writings of Benjamin Franklin*,
A. H. Smyth, ed., vol. I, p. 3.
[2] *Pennsylvania Gazette*, October 16–23, 1729.

veloped in the other colonies were not essentially different from those already described in Massachusetts, New York, and Pennsylvania.   Usually, after a printer had established himself in business in the most important city of one of the colonies, he would launch a weekly paper modeled after those in the other colonies and in England.   Thus William Parks, an English printer, started the *Maryland Gazette* in 1727, a year after he had set up at Annapolis the first press in Maryland and had been made public printer for that colony.   Discouraged by a six years' struggle, during which the *Gazette* was discontinued and revived, he migrated to Virginia.   In 1736 he established at Williamsburg the first paper in that colony, the *Virginia Gazette*, and became "printer to the colony."   In South Carolina the first paper was the *South-Carolina Weekly Journal*, brought out in 1730 by a New England printer who had settled at Charleston.   But it lived less than a year and was succeeded in 1732 by the *South-Carolina Gazette*, which with interruptions continued down to 1802.   To James Franklin, as we have seen, belongs the credit of printing the first paper in Rhode Island, the *Rhode-Island Gazette*, which was issued at Newport in 1732.   It survived, however, for less than a year. The second Rhode Island paper, the *Newport Mercury*, founded in 1758 by Franklin's son, proved more successful and has continued to the present time.   The first papers in the other colonies were: the *Connecticut Gazette*, New Haven, 1755; the *New-Hampshire Gazette*, Portsmouth, 1756; the *North-Carolina Gazette*, Newbern, 1755; the *Wilmington Chronicle*, Wilmington, Delaware, 1762; and the *Georgia Gazette*, Savannah, 1763.

With small subscription lists and limited advertising patronage, the early colonial printers generally found their papers far from remunerative, especially as both subscribers and advertisers were slow to pay.   Frequent dunning appeals were made, accompanied by warnings that, unless delinquents paid up, the paper would be compelled to suspend.   Small in size, often poorly printed from well-worn type, and edited, as a rule, without much discrimination by their printer-publishers, these papers had little to commend them either to readers or to advertisers.   Yet their publication involved considerable outlay and effort.   Paper and ink were scarce and expensive.   The wooden hand-presses and the type had to be imported from England.   On these small presses only one or two pages could be printed on one side with each impression. The ink was rubbed over the forms with a deerskin pad attached to a stick. Each sheet of paper was placed in position by hand, and after being printed on one side was removed by hand. The maximum speed of printing under these conditions was 250 impressions an hour; this meant that only 125 papers printed on both sides could be run off in an hour.

The difficulties of publishing newspapers in the early colonial period were increased by the limited communication, both between the colonies and the mother country, and among the several colonies themselves. Vessels crossed the Atlantic under favorable conditions in from five to eight weeks, but in winter their number was very small and the passage often slower. Post riders carried the mail from colony to colony once a week during three quarters of the year, and fortnightly from December to March. During these winter months, some of the papers changed their day of publication to correspond to the day on which the mail arrived, and, when the post rider was delayed, postponed publication for two or three days. Even so, at times a paper would have to go to press without waiting for the mail, as did the *Boston Gazette* in 1730, when it announced in a line across the bottom of the second page, "Monday Morning Ten o'Clock, the Southern Post is not yet come in nor is not expected till Saturday next." [1] The causes of the delays are indicated by such announcements as these:

The Western Post is not yet come in, the Rider not being able to get over the Ferry at New London. [2]

The Eastern Post came in late last Saturday Evening, being obliged to travel the greatest Part of the Way with Snow Shoes, the Snow being so drifted as to make the Roads impassable for Horses. [3]

We have these three Days expected the New York Post, and he is not yet arrived. It is supposed that the late strong Winds have hindered his Ferrage at Amboy, &c. for which reason we are obliged to publish this Weeks News without his Advices and Entries of Vessels from that Port. [4]

Because of such obstacles, the news of a fire in Charleston, South Carolina, in the winter of 1741, that destroyed 300 houses

[1] *Boston Gazette*, Monday, February 2–9, 1730.   [2] *Ibid.*, March 8–15, 1731.
[3] *Ibid.*, February 2–9, 1741.   [4] *American Weekly Mercury*, March 1–10, 1722.

and a million dollars' worth of merchandise, as reported in the
South Carolina Gazette, was not published in the *Boston Gazette*
until over two months after it occurred.[1]

Advertisements constituted a regular but inconspicuous feature
of the early colonial newspapers. Usually set in body type, and
occasionally illustrated with small, rather crude wood-cuts, they
occupied the last column of the last page of the paper. The
number of advertisements in one issue was never large, but the
commodities offered covered a wide range. Lost and found articles were advertised, and "want-ads" appeared not infrequently.
As newspaper publishers were usually printers of books and pamphlets, as well as dealers in a variety of articles, they often used
the columns of their paper to advertise their own wares. Thus,
in his *American Weekly Mercury*, Andrew Bradford advertised for
sale at his shop, not only books and almanacks, but "very good
corks," "very good English Pease and Spanish Snuff," "very good
Lamp-Black," and "very good Chocolate."

Negro slaves were offered for sale, and, when they ran away,
their owners advertised for them. One advertisement in the
Boston Gazette read, "Good Red Herring and Fine Negros, to be
sold by Jacob Royall, Merchant in Boston,"[2] and another,
"Negroes Males and Females to be sold cheap, or 12 Months
Credit."[3] Sometimes a small wood-cut depicting a man running
was used in advertisements of runaway negro slaves or white
indentured servants.

Nostrums were much less frequently advertised in colonial
papers than in English papers of the same period. Sometimes,
however, just as extravagant claims were made for them as for
those offered in England. One "cure-all" was advertised in the
Boston Gazette as follows:[4]

> To be sold, an Excellent Medicine, which cures the Cholick, Dry
> Belly-ack, Loss of Limbs, Fevers and Agues, Asthmas, Coughs,
> and all sorts of Obstructions, Rheumatism, Sickness at the Stom-
> ach, Surfeits by Immoderate Eating and Drinking, Weakness,
> Trembling of the Heart, want of Appetite, Gravel, Melancholy,
> and Jaundice, and is Excellent for the Gout; Which is now Pub-

---

[1] *Boston Gazette*, January 19–26, 1741.   [2] *Ibid.*, August 4-11, 1729.
[3] *Ibid.*, September 27–October 4, 1731.
[4] *Ibid.*, December 18–25, 1727.

lish'd at the desire of several Persons of Note (who have been wonderfully reliev'd by it). . . .

The claims of a cosmetic preparation were set forth in these terms in the *New-York Weekly Journal:* [1]

At Mrs. Edwards next Door to Mr. Jamison, opposite the Fort Garden, an admirable Beautifying Wash for Hands, Face and Neck, it makes the Skin soft, smooth and plump, it likewise takes away Redness, Freckles, Sun-Burning, or Pimples, and cures Postules, Itchings, Ring Worms, Tetters, Scurf, Morphew and other like Deformities of the Face and Skin (Intirely free from any Corroding Quality) and brings out an exquisite Beauty, with lip Salve and Tooth Powder, all sold very cheap.

Among the entertainments and amusements advertised in early Boston papers were bear baitings, horse races, and exhibitions of a lion, of a "captured cattamount," and of a new type of gun. The following description of the catamount was well calculated to arouse curiosity: [2]

To be seen at the Grey Hound Tavern in Roxbury, a Wild Creature, which was caught in the Woods about 80 miles to the westward of this Town, called a Cattamount, it has a Tail like a Lyon, its Leggs are like a Bears, its Claws like an Eagle, its Eyes like a Tyger, its Countenance is a mixture of every Thing that is Fierce and Savage, he is exceedingly Ravenous and devours all sorts of Creatures that he can come near; its Agility is surprizing, it will Leap 30 Foot at one jump, notwithstanding it is but three Month old. Whoever inclines to see this Creature may come to the Place aforesaid, paying a Shilling each, shall be welcome for their Money.

An instructor at Harvard College advertised in the *Boston Gazette* that during the summer vacation he would lecture twice a week on astronomy, using "the Orrery, and all such Machines, instruments and Schemes as are used by Astronomers, . . . except only that it wants one of Sir Isaac Newton's Reflecting Telescopes, which New England has not, as yet, been honoured with." In the same advertisement he also announced that, "If the Curiosity and Desire of Knowledge, justly admired in the Fair Sex should excite any of Them; there will be some Expedient found

[1] *New-York Weekly Journal*, March 29, 1736.
[2] *Boston Gazette*, April 20-27, 1741.

out that They may be gratified twice a week in the Afternoon, with their usual Tea and a Familiar Astronomical Dialogue."[1]   In an advertisement in the *American Weekly Mercury* of Philadelphia, a man offered to teach "his poor Brethren the Pale-Negroes to read the Holy Scriptures in a very uncommon, expeditious, and delightful Manner, without any manner of Expence to their respective Masters or Mistresses."[2]

A dressmaker in Boston advertised the latest London fashions as follows:[3]

> Mrs. Elizabeth Hatton from London makes Manteaus, Cloaks, Manteels, and all sorts of Women's Apparel after the newest Mode, she lives at Mr. Roodes's in Water-Street near the Tan-yard.
>
> She also has new Pattern of Sleves by the last Ships, from the Queen's Manteau and Scarf Maker, from whom she'l constantly be supply'd as the Fashion alters.

The news content of these first colonial papers consisted of short items of foreign news taken from English newspapers; bits of domestic news gleaned from other colonial papers, from private letters, or from letters sent by correspondents; and a little local news such as could be obtained from official or semi-official sources or could easily be picked up by the printer-editor.   The general reading matter was made up of essays and verse clipped from English or other colonial papers, as well as "letters to the printer" and original essays and verse contributed by local writers with literary or political tastes.   The only editorial material was an occasional sentence or two of comment appended to a news item by the printer or by a correspondent.   Whatever distinction any of these colonial papers possessed was generally given to it, not by its printer-editor, but by the contributors who furnished him verse, essays on social and moral topics, usually in imitation of those in the *Spectator*, and letters on political and economic subjects in the manner of *Cato's Letters*.   Conventional though most of these contributions were in subject-matter and style, they occasionally revealed some originality in dealing with such local subjects as could be treated with impunity.   As a whole, the

---

[1] *Boston Gazette*, June 17–24, 1734.
[2] *American Weekly Mercury*, February 5–12, 1722/23.
[3] *Boston Gazette*, May 14–21, 1733.

colonial newspapers previous to 1750 were routine productions of printers, no more distinctive in character than the poorest of present-day country weeklies. Although these papers seem characterless, their publishers nevertheless deserve no little credit as pioneers who established and sustained their publications under adverse conditions without adequate financial rewards.

CHAPTER III

THE PRESS DURING THE STRUGGLE BETWEEN THE COLONIES AND ENGLAND, 1750–1783

ALTHOUGH the newspapers in the several colonies were small weeklies that lacked distinctive qualities, they played their part in developing a feeling of solidarity among the colonists in the struggle against the mother country. When, in anticipation of the approaching French and Indian War, a congress of representatives of the English colonies was called to meet at Albany in the summer of 1754, Benjamin Franklin undertook to impress on his readers the need of united action by printing in his *Pennsylvania Gazette* a one-column, two-inch wood-cut of a snake divided into eight segments, each of which bore the initials of one of the colonies, with the caption, "Join, or Die." This cartoon of the divided snake was immediately reproduced in four other newspapers in Boston and New York. It came to be regarded as symbolic of the necessity for united action, and reappeared in the newspapers, in slightly modified form, during the opposition to the Stamp Act in 1765 and again at the outbreak of the Revolutionary War.

Benjamin Franklin's Snake Cartoon, Printed in the First Column of the Second Page of the *Pennsylvania Gazette*, May 9, 1754

Size of cartoon, 2⅞ in. by 2 in.

Franklin took a prominent part in the Albany congress. After the representatives of the colonies had voted that "a union of all colonies is at present absolutely necessary for their security and defence," Franklin, entrusted with the task of drawing up a plan of union, worked out a method of organization not unlike the Articles of Confederation of 1777. Neither the British Government nor the colonial assemblies, however, were willing to adopt the plan, because, as Franklin wrote in his *Autobiography*, "they [the assemblies] all thought there was too much *prerogative* in it, and in England it was judg'd to have too much of the *democratic*." [1]

Despite the failure of the proposed union of the colonies, the seven years of warfare against a common enemy from 1754 to 1760 drew the colonists closer together. They fought side by side; they acted together when occasion demanded; they taxed themselves heavily for the common defense. The presence of British troops tended to strengthen this feeling of solidarity. The colonists disagreed with their English governors and military commanders over such matters as the raising of funds to carry on the war, the quartering of British troops in Boston, and the rating of colonial military officers below the lowest of the English commissioned officers.

To raise funds for carrying on the war, two of the colonies, Massachusetts and New York, imposed a stamp tax of one halfpenny on every copy of the newspapers printed in these colonies. The Massachusetts tax continued for two years, from 1755 to 1757, and the New York tax for three years, from 1757 to 1760.

Following the accession of George III in 1760 and the appointment of the Grenville ministry in 1763, the British Government adopted a colonial policy that finally resulted in the Revolutionary War. The measures regarded as oppressive by the colonists included the enforcement of various Acts of Trade limiting colonial trade to English or colonial ships and to English merchants, the establishment of permanent garrisons of British troops in America, the taxation of the colonies for the partial maintenance of these garrisons, and finally, in 1765, the Stamp Act. Protests against these measures were immediately made by various colonial assemblies, a patriotic society was organized called

[1] *Writings of Benjamin Franklin*, A. H. Smyth, ed., vol. I, p. 388.

Thursday, October 31, 1765. THE NUMB. 1195.

PENNSYLVANIA JOURNAL;

AND

WEEKLY ADVERTISER.

EXPIRING: In Hopes of a Resurrection to LIFE again.

I AM sorry to be obliged to acquaint my Readers, that as The STAMP-ACT,* is fear'd to be obligatory upon us after the *First of November* ensuing, (the *fatal To-morrow*) The Publisher of this Paper unable to bear the Burthen, has thought it expedient to STOP a while, in order to deliberate, whether any Methods can be found to elude the Chains forged for us, and escape the insupportable Slavery; which it is hoped, from the just Representations now made against that Act, may be effected. Mean while, I must earnestly Request every Individual of my Subscribers, many of whom have been long behind Hand, that they would immediately Discharge their respective Arrears, that I may be able, not only to support myself during the Interval, but be better prepared to proceed again with this Paper, whenever an opening for that Purpose appears, which I hope will be soon. WILLIAM BRADFORD.

Remember, O my friends! the Laws, the Rights,
The generous plan of power deliver'd down,
From age to age, by your renown'd forefathers;
O let it never perish in your hands!
But piously transmit it to your children.
Do thou, great Liberty, inspire our souls,
And make our lives in thy possession happy;
Or our deaths glorious in thy defence. ADDISON'S Cato.

LIBERTY is one of the greatest Blessings, which human beings can possibly enjoy: When we are deprived of this earthly happiness, we are fettered with the Chains of inimical servitude. Nations, who are born for the mutual support of each other, should preserve a steady attachment to the welfare and happiness of that nation with whom they are united, that their mutual alliance of friendship might be sincere and permanent. When this union is separated by the illegal encroachments on that Liberty, which is the Soul of Commerce, and the Support of Life, it degenerates into implacable Enmity, which in time grows inveterate, and finally recoils upon those who have been the means of its unhappy dissolution. The *Liberty of the Press* has very justly been esteemed one of the main Pillars of the Liberty of the People. While this is maintained, the first Steps to Oppression are detected, and the Attention of the People seasonably awakened. When this is suppressed, the Suspicion of the People, and their Ruin may admit of so sudden a transition, as renders the Success of the first impracticable, and the Miseries attending the latter unavoidable. So dangerous is this to lawless Power, that the farthest approaches to it are resolutely opposed, or rigorously punished. So essential is this to Freedom, Property, and Happiness, that the most plausible Attempts to curtail it even in the smallest Degree, have always been most strenuously opposed by the virtuous, free, and unbiassed Patriot. It is the Priviledge of Britons to speak Truth with impunity, and even to fear no Danger from speculative Error whether in Religion or Politicks. The want of attending to this has produced needless Enquiries, and unjustifiable Censures of what is true in Fact or no more than false in Speculation.---But how unhappily is it to be debarr'd from this last Relief in a dangerous and sickly State! How melancholly to pine and die while no kind Physician is allowed to explore the Cause, or prescribe the Cure of our manifold Disorders? The love of Ease, and absence of Pain in some Distempers, is a fatal Symptom of the desperate Circumstances of the Patient.

And in all political Disorders the more contented we are under them, so much the worse are they, and so much the worse are we for them. It is a very happy Circumstance attending public Virtue and public Spirit, that the more it is vilified, the more illustrious it always appears. No Falshood formed against it can prosper, for it at once detects and confutes the darkest and most inveterate Calumny. But although public Virtue cannot be affected by the Indulgence of the most unlimited Freedom of speaking or writing, yet Oppression and Tyranny as it derives all its Influence from its Secrecy, may be extremely benefited by the Reverse: For this reason, in Countries subjected to the insatiable Demands of Power and Avarice, the first Attempts to inspire People with a just Sense of their Condition, are commonly nipt in the Bud. It is of the last Importance to the Views of designing Men to shut up the most successful and universal Channel of Information from the People, when they are forming such Schemes as need only to be known in order to be Opposed. Besides the Deprivation of our whole Liberty may be justified on the same Principles as the Deprivation of any individual Part, such as the Liberty of the Press undoubtedly is.

How amiable is the Enjoyment of Liberty! But how detestable are the Bonds of Servitude! 'Tis therefore sincerly to be hoped, that the old *New-England* Spirit so exemplarily free in former Times, will never condescend in Submission to new and unwarrantable Restrictions.

A Day, an Hour of virtuous Liberty,
Is worth a whole Eternity in Bondage.

May we all as loyal Subjects, and free born Britons exert our utmost to preserve the Rights and Liberties of our Country, in a Manner that shall add Honour to our Endeavours; that future Posterity may reap the Benefit, and bless the Hands which were the Instruments of procuring it.---

That Glory then, the brightest Crown of Praise,
Which every Lover of his Country's Wealth,
And every Patron of Mankind deserves;
Will gracefully adorn such Patriot's Deeds,
And leave behind an Honour that will last
With Praise immortal to the End of Time.

Thursday last arrived here the ship Philadelphia Packet, Capt. Budden, from London, by whom we have the following advices.

R O M E, *July* 24.

THE harvest in this country hath not proved so good as we hoped. This event hath engaged the congregation established for inspecting into the supplies of provisions for this capital, to seek all possible means to prevent a fresh scarcity.

St. James's, August 17. The king has been pleased to appoint the most honourable the Marquis of Rockingham to be lord lieutenant of the west-ridings of the county of York, and of the city of York, and county of the same city; and also Custos Rotulorum of the north and west-ridings in the said county of York and of the city of York, and county of the same city; and Ainsty, otherwise Aynstry, of York.

The king has been pleased to appoint the right hon. William Earl of Dartmouth, Soam Jenyns, Edward Elliot, John York, George Rice, John Roberts, Jeremiah Dyson, and William Fitzherbert, Esqrs; to be commissioners of trade, and for inspecting and improving his majesty's plantations in America, and elsewhere.

The king has been pleased to grant unto the right hon. Richard Viscount How, the office of treasurer of his Majesty's navy.

St. James's, August 27. By the last letters from Col. Desmaretz, his majesty's commissary at Dunkirk, we are assured, that orders were given by the French ministry, for immediately setting about the demolition of the Jettees, which are the support of the harbour of Dunkirk.

Warsaw, August 1. The tribunal of Great Poland, held at Posnania, has granted permission to the Lutherans at Lobseutz to open their church, which has been shut near twenty years, to provide a minister, and to perform divine service in public.

Corunna, July 27. The detachment of one hundred men drafted for Louisiana, are on the march for Ferrol, where they are to embark on board the Unicorn frigate with a governor, two capuchin friars, a commissionary at war, and some civil officers.

Cadiz, July 23. Letters brought by the last post from Gibralter say, the report before spread, that the Algerines have killed their Dey, and declared war against all the European powers except England and France, proves not true.

L O N D O N.

August 17. On Thursday at the king's arms tavern in Cornhill, an elegant entertainment was given by the committee of North-American merchants to Richard Gluver, and Charles Garth, Esqrs; when those gentlemen received the thanks of that body, for their endeavours to prevent the soldiery from being billeted upon the private houses of their fellow-subjects in America.

Part of a letter from an officer in the East-India service, dated from the Ariclur camp, January 8, 1765.

"In my last I acquainted you that we did at last reduce Madure. The army has since conquered the Ariltur country for the Nabob, of 100,000l. revenue a year. We are now under orders to attack another chief, or polygor contiguous to this country; both chiefs have mutually maintained an independency of the Nabob till now; merely on account of the impenetrable woods they are possessed of. You certainly have heard before of the memorable battle Major Munro gained at Bengal over Suja Dowla, one of the most formidable powers of India: The consequence of this battle gives the company the command of trade in the greatest part of the Mogul's dominions; and, without exaggeration, the East-India company at present may be brought in comparison with Alexander the Great, whose command, from the river Indus to the river Ganges, was not so much respected as their's."

It is said the new m----y, taking into consideration the present deplorable situation of the Canadians, have determined to take up all the Canada bills at par, with interest to the present time; and afterwards to demand, in the most spirited terms, *immediate* and *full* payment of France, under pain of all the consequences that can result from a refusal.

The new lords of trade and plantations will hold a board on Monday next, for the first time, at the Cockpit Whitehall.

We hear the rent rolls of the several proprietary estates in America, obtained by former grants under the crown are ordered to be made out, as also an estimate of the annual product of their land tax, in order to introduce a more equitable form of levying his majesty's revenues in that part of the world.

They write from Gibralter, that English officers and seamen are engaging both there and at Minorca by foreign agents, to serve on board his Sardinian majesty's ships of war in the Mediterranean.

August 20. The right honourable the Earl Cornwallis, lieutenant colonel to the 33 regiment of foot, is appointed one of his majesty's aids de camp, with the rank of colonel of foot in the army.

We are informed, that a gentleman lately very popular in this country, is soon to reside at Lousanne, in Switzerland, where he intends publishing his friend Mr. Churchill's poems, with explanatory notes; and we are likewise informed, that he has an intention of publishing, at the same place, a history of England wrote by himself.

By a vessel arrived at Guernsey from Belleisle there is advice, that the French are erecting several batteries at Sandy Bay, on the south east of the island, and in the great road where the descent was made in the late war by the seamen and troops under Admiral Keppel and General Hodgson.

Aug. 21 We hear lord Viscount Spencer is shortly to be created an earl.

All thoughts of any farther changes are said to be entirely laid aside.

It is reported, that a person of high rank, on being lately offered a great employment, refused it, saying, "that he could not possibly accept of it, consistently with the love he bore to the British nation, which would ever be the object of his care and attention."

Monday some dispatches said to be of importance, were received here from Holland, but the subject has not yet transpired.

Private letters from Paris mention that the true reason

An Emblem of the Effects of the STAMP.

O! the fatal STAMP.

The "Tombstone" Number of William Bradford's *Pennsylvania Journal*
October 31, 1765, the Day before the Stamp Act Went into Effect

the "Sons of Liberty," and threats were made to boycott English goods. The Stamp Act brought the opposition to a head in the form of a colonial congress held in New York in the fall of 1765. This congress sent petitions to the British Government, adopted a "Declaration of Rights and Grievences of the Colonies of America," and protested against "taxation without representation."

The Stamp Act directly affected all colonial newspapers. Following the principle of the newspaper stamp taxes of 1712 in England, it imposed a tax on newspapers of from a half-penny to a penny according to their size, and a tax of two shillings on every advertisement. It also required that the name of the publisher should appear on every newspaper. All the papers undertook to evade the payment of the tax. A few suspended publication temporarily, others threatened to do so, and still others came out without their titles or without the names of their publishers. In New York a mob seized the stamped paper upon which the newspapers were to have been printed. The most striking protest against the newspaper stamp tax was made by William Bradford, when, on October 31, 1765, the day before the Act was to go into effect, his *Pennsylvania Journal and Weekly Advertiser* appeared with a front-page "make-up" in imitation of a tombstone. The announcement was made in this issue that the paper was "Expiring: In Hopes of a Resurrection to Life again," and was bidding "Adieu, Adieu to the Liberty of the Press." In the lower right-hand corner of the first page was printed a skull and cross-bones, with the legend, "An Emblem of the Effects of the Stamp. O! the fatal-Stamp." The *Boston Gazette* and the *Maryland Gazette* employed the skull and cross-bones in a similar manner. These graphic remonstrances, as well as the various means of evading the tax adopted by other newspapers, helped to stimulate popular opposition to the Stamp Act.

In this and subsequent controversies, American leaders who opposed or supported the British colonial policies made use of the newspapers and of pamphlets to carry on their discussion. The usual means adopted by these contributors to newspapers, who included statesmen, lawyers, scholars, and clergymen, were letters, singly or in series, addressed to the printer, or "author," of the newspaper, and signed with pen names, like *Cato's Letters* and the *Letters of Junius* in English newspapers. Letters that

No *Stamped Paper* to be had.

B O S T O N, *October* 28.

WE hear from Halifax, in the province of Nova-Scotia, that on Sunday, the 13th inst. in the morning, was discovered hanging on the gallows behind the Citadel-Hill, the effigies of a stampman, accompanied with a boot and devil, together with labels suitable to the occasion (which we cannot insert, not being favoured with the same) this we are informed gave great pleasure and satisfaction to all the friends of liberty and their country there, as they hope from this instance of their zeal, the neighbouring colonies will be charitable enough to believe that nothing but their dependent situation, prevents them from heartily and sincerely opposing a tax unconstitutional in its nature, and of so destructive a tendency as must infallibly entail poverty and beggary on us and our posterity, if carried in execution.

On the 23d instant the Great and General Court met here, according to adjournment; and we hear that almost every member of the honourable house of representatives have received instructions from their constituents; and that they are of the same import with those already published.

We hear that the merchants and friends to America in England, were determined to use their utmost endeavours the next session of Parliament, in order to get the stamp act repealed.

N E W - Y O R K, November 4.

The late extraordinary and unprecedented preparations in Fort George, and the securing of the stamped paper in that garrison, having greatly alarmed and displeased the inhabitants of this city, a vast number of them assembled last Friday evening in the commons, from whence they marched down the Fly (preceded by a number of lights) and having stopped a few minutes at the Coffee-house, proceeded to the Fort walls, where they broke open the stable of the L-------t G--------r, took out his coach, and after carrying the same through the principal streets of the city, in triumph marched to the commons, where a gallows was erected; on one end of which was suspended the effigy of the person whose property the coach was; in his right hand he held a stamped bill of lading, and on his breast was affixed a paper with the following inscription, *The rebel drummer in the year* 1715: At his back was fixed a drum, the badge of his profession; at the other end of the gallows hung the figure of the devil, a proper companion for the other, as 'tis supposed it was intirely at his instigation he acted: After they had hung there a considerable time, they carried the effigies, with the gallows intire, being preceded by the coach, in a grand procession to the gate of the Fort, where it remained for some time, from whence it was removed to the Bowling-green, under the muzzles of the Fort guns, where a bon-fire was immediately made, and the drummer, devil, coach, &c. were consumed amidst the acclamations of some thousand spectators, and we make no doubt, but the L-------t G-------r, and his friends, had the mortification of viewing the whole proceeding from the ramparts of the Fort: But the business of the night not being yet concluded, the whole body proceeded with the greatest decency and good order to Vaux-Hall, the House of M----r J----s, who, it was reported, was a friend to the stamp act, and had been over officious in his duty, from whence they took every individual article, to a very considerable amount; and having made another bon-fire, the whole was consumed in the flames, to the great satisfaction of every person present; after which they dispersed, and every man went to his respective habitation. The whole affair was conducted with such decorum, that not the least accident happened. The next evening another very considerable body assembled at the same place, having been informed that the L---t G-----r had qualified himself for the distribution of the stamped paper, were determined to march to the Fort, in order to insist upon his delivering it into their hands, or to declare that he would not undertake to distribute the same; but before this resolution could be executed, the minds of the people were eased by the L---t G---r's sending the following declaration from the Fort, viz.

THE Lieutenant Governor declares he will do nothing in relation to the stamps, but leave it to Sir Henry Moore, to do as he pleases on his arrival.

Council-Chamber, New-York, November 2, 1765.

By Order of his Honour, Gw. BANYAR, D. Cl. Con.

We have certain information from Boston, that the printers there intend to continue their papers, and to risk the penalties--- and that if any of them were to stop on account of the stamp act, their offices would be in danger from the enraged people.

At a general meeting of the Freemen, inhabitants of the county of Essex, in New-Jersey, at the free Borough of Elizabeth, on the 25th day of October, in the year of our Lord 1765, being the anniversary of the happy accession of his present Majesty King George the Third, to the crown of Great-Britain, &c. upon which occasion the said freemen unanimously, and with one voice declared,

FIrst. That they have at all times heretofore, and ever would bear true allegiance to his Majesty King George the Third, and his royal predecessors, and wished to be governed agreeable to the laws of the land, and the British constitution, to which they ever had, and for ever most chearfully would submit.

Secondly. That the stamp act, prepared for the British colonies in America, in their opinion, is unconstitutional; and should the same take place, agreeable to the tenor of it, would be a manifest destruction and overthrow of their long enjoyed, boasted and invaluable liberties and privileges.

Thirdly. That they will, by all lawful ways and means, endeavour to preserve and transmit to posterity, their liberty and property, in as full and ample manner as they received the same from their ancestors.

Fourthly. That they will discountenance and discourage, by all lawful measures, the execution and effect of the stamp act.

Fifthly. That they will detest, abhor, and hold in the utmost contempt, all and every person or persons, who shall meanly accept of any employment or office, relating to the stamp act, or shall take any shelter or advantage from the same; and all and every stamp pimp, informer, favourer and encourager of the execution of the said act; and that they will have no communication with any such person, nor speak to them on any occasion, unless it be to inform them of their vileness.

CITY of NEW-YORK, October 31, 1765.

AT a general Meeting of the Merchants of the City of New-York, trading to Great-Britain, at the House of Mr. George Burns, of the said City, Innholder, to consider what was necessary to be done in the present Situation of Affairs, with respect to the STAMP ACT, and the melancholy State of the North-American Commerce, so greatly restricted by the Impositions and Duties established by the late Acts of Trade: They came to the following Resolutions, viz.

FIRST, That in all Orders they send out to Great-Britain, for Goods or Merchandize, of any Nature, Kind or Quality whatsoever, usually imported from Great-Britain, they will direct their Correspondents not to ship them, unless the STAMP ACT be repealed: It is nevertheless agreed, that all such Merchants as are Owners of, and have Vessels already gone, and now cleared out for Great-Britain, shall be at Liberty to bring back in them, on their own Accounts, Crates and Casks of Earthen Ware, Grindstones, Pipes, and such other bulky Articles, as Owners usually fill up their Vessels with.

SECONDLY, It is further unanimously agreed, that all Orders already sent Home, shall be countermanded by the very first Conveyance; and the Goods and Merchandize thereby ordered, not to be sent, unless upon the Condition mentioned in the foregoing Resolution.

THIRDLY, It is further unanimously agreed, that no Merchant will vend any Goods or Merchandize sent upon Commission from Great-Britain, that shall be shipped from thence after the first Day of January next, unless upon the Condition mentioned in the first Resolution.

FOURTHLY. It is further unanimously agreed, that the foregoing Resolutions shall be binding until the same are abrogated at a general Meeting hereafter to be held for that Purpose.

In Witness whereof we have hereunto respectively subscribed our Names.

[*This was subscribed by upwards of Two Hundred principal Merchants.*]

In Consequence of the foregoing Resolutions, the Retailers of Goods, of the City of New-York, subscribed a Paper, in the Words following, viz.

WE the under-written, Retailers of Goods, do hereby promise and oblige ourselves not to buy any Goods, Wares, or Merchandizes, of any Person or Persons whatsoever, that shall be shipped from Great-Britain, after the first Day of January next; unless the STAMP ACT shall be repealed----As Witness our Hands.

October 31, 1765.

Extract of a Letter from a principal House in England to a Gentleman in New-York.

THE present Situation of the Colonies is really alarming to every Person who has large Sums to come from them.---We feel the Force of the late Act, in a very sensible Manner, being drove to our Wits End to pay our Tradesmen, agreeable to the Time their Payments become due; and if a Method is not taken, diametrically opposite to the former, you and we, and indeed every Person of Property, must unavoidably sink under the present Restrictions. The Colonies, at this present Moment, owe us One Hundred Thousand Pounds and upwards, too large a Sum to be kept out of above two Years, and no Remittances; and though two Vessels are arrived at London from New-York, the whole Remittance was a single Hundred Pounds.---This is what we cannot bear, therefore are determined to stop our Hands in the Export Way, and will not ship off a single Shilling's Worth, but to Persons who can and will pay us: If this cursed Act is not repealed, we shall be great Sufferers, and our Manufacturers thrown on their Parishes, for want of Support, whilst People who employed them, will not be in a much better Situation. The Avenues of Remittances are stopped with you, and Trade, the Basis and Foundation of England's Wealth, is intirely shut up. We dread the Consequence, and know not to what Fatality we are destined.

P H I L A D E L P H I A, November 7.

An Agreement of the same Kind, with that under the New-York Head, relating to the Importation of Dry Goods, &c. from England, is now on Foot here.

On Friday and Saturday last, the DREADFUL FIRST and SECOND Days of November, our Bells were rung muffled, and other Demonstrations of Grief shewn.

From Lisbon we learn, that they had Advice there of Musegong, a Settlement belonging to the Portugueze, on the Coast of Barbary, being besieged by a strong Body of Moors.

Captain Steel, from Leith, on the 11th of September, in Lat. 48 : 30, Long. 27, spoke the Brig Olive Branch, Captain Robinson, from this Place for Rotterdam, out 29 Days, all well. On the 11th of October, in Lat. 26 : 27, Long. 57 : 30, he spoke the Schooner Industry, Captain Davis, from Boston for Dominica, out 21 Days.---- In Lat. 27 : 30, Captain Steel met with a Sloop belonging to Egg-Harbour, that had been blown off the Coast, without a Navigator on board, and brought her safe in with him.

Captain Adams, from Barbados, on the 29th ult. off Sinepuxent, spoke a Schooner from Rhode-Island, bound to Virginia.---Captain Adams left Bridgetown the 11th of October, when the Stamped Paper for that Island was not arrived

Captain Hunter, from Lisbon, on the 24th of last Month, in Lat. 37 : 43, Long. 67, spoke two Sloops; from New-London for Barbados, out three Days; a third Sloop was in Company, but he did not speak with her.

Captain Keith, from Londonderry, on the 12th ult. in Lat 44 : 47, spoke a Brig from Philadelphia for Glasgow. And on the 15th, in Lat. 38 : 51, spoke a Snow from Boston for South-Carolina.

We hear from Georgia, that neither the Stamp Master, nor Stamp Paper, had arrived there the 20th ult.

From Bermuda we have Advice, that Captain Copperthorn, in a Ship from Virginia for London, having lost her Main-mast, ran ashore, the Sixth of September, on the Rocks of that Island, when the Vessel was entirely lost, but the People, and Part of the Cargoe, saved.

Arrived. Captain Hervey at Barbados, and Captain Aldborough at Jamaica, both from this Port. And Captain Thompson, at Jamaica, from New-York.

Hugh Gaine's *New-York Mercury*, Printed Without a Title on November 4, 1765, just after the Stamp Act Went into Effect

appeared in one newspaper were often republished by papers in other colonies. For wider circulation, a series of these newspaper letters was sometimes reprinted in pamphlet form. Some controversialists preferred the pamphlet to the newspaper, because it made possible a more detailed, comprehensive, and coherent presentation of arguments than did a single letter or a number of letters published serially. Thus the colonial newspapers, although containing no editorials, served to influence public opinion through these voluntary contributions made by leaders on both sides of current controversies.

The newspapers, both by protesting in a striking manner against the effects of the Stamp Act upon themselves and by printing arguments against the obnoxious Act, played an important rôle in creating sufficient sentiment among the colonists to lead Parliament to repeal the Act in 1766. This successful outcome of their remonstrances taught the colonists the effectiveness of strong, wide-spread protests, and made their leaders realize the value of the press in shaping public opinion. The lull in the controversy, however, was only temporary, because Parliament in repealing the Stamp Act reaffirmed its right to legislate for the colonies. In the following year Parliament enacted a new measure of colonial taxation, imposing import duties on several articles including glass, paper, and tea. To provide more effective control over the colonies, a colonial department was created in the British Government headed by a secretary of state. From this time on, one coercive measure followed another, until the colonies finally declared their independence.

Boston was the storm center of the controversy. There a group of Patriots, including Samuel Adams, James Otis, Joseph Warren, Josiah Quincy, Samuel Cooper, and John Adams, made the *Boston Gazette* their mouthpiece. The printing office of Edes and Gill, publishers of the *Gazette*, served as the headquarters of Samuel Adams and his little band. How this group of writers was regarded by prominent Loyalists, is shown in a letter written in 1769 by Andrew Oliver, Governor Hutchinson's brother-in-law, and lieutenant-governor after 1771, in which he said, "If there be no way to take off the original incendiaries [by sending them to England, as was proposed, to be tried for treason] they will still continue to instil poison into the minds of the people through the vehicle of the *Boston Gazette.*" [1]   Early in 1769 the authorities instituted proceedings against Edes and Gill as "authors of numberless treasonable and seditious writings," but popular sentiment was with these Patriot printers and with the writers for their *Gazette.*   As Governor Hutchinson declared in 1770, "The misfortune is that seven eights of the people read none but this infamous paper, and so are never undeceived." [2]   So strong was Loyalist hatred against these writers and publishers by 1774 that some Loyalists distributed a letter in the British camp at Boston to incite the troops to put them "to the sword, destroy their houses and plunder their effects," declaring that "it is just that they should be the first victims of the mischiefs they have bro't upon us." [3]   The printers of the *Gazette*, Edes and Gill, were referred to by name in this letter as "trumpeters of sedition."

Samuel Adams was the most prolific and the most effective of the Patriot writers for newspapers.   In signing his letters and articles he used some twenty-five different pen names.   His policy in controversial writing, as he himself expressed it, was "to put and keep the enemy in the wrong." [4]   That his methods proved efficacious was admitted by Governor Hutchinson, a Loyalist, who wrote of Adams: [5]

> ... for nearly twenty years a writer against government in the public newspapers, at first but an indifferent one; long practice caused him to arrive at great perfection, and to acquire a talent of artfully and fallaciously insinuating into the minds of his readers a prejudice against the character of all whom he attacked, beyond any other man I ever knew.

Hutchinson's further characterization of Adams as "the Grand Incendiary of the Province" [6] is an accurate one, for probably no single Patriot did more to bring about the rupture between England and her colonies than did Adams.   As early as 1773, in letters printed in the *Boston Gazette*, Adams advocated, not only that a "congress of American states be assembled as soon as possible," but that the colonies "Form an Independent State — An American Commonwealth." [7]

[1] Wells, W. V. *Life of Samuel Adams*, vol. I, p. 237.   [2] *Ibid.*, vol. I, p. 244.
[3] *Boston Evening-Post*, September 19, 1774.
[4] Letter by Samuel Adams quoted in Wells's *Life of Samuel Adams*, vol. II, p. 281.
[5] Hutchinson, Thomas. *History of the Colony of Massachusetts Bay*, vol. III, p. 295.
[6] Wells, W. V. *Life of Samuel Adams*, vol. I, p. 500.
[7] *Boston Gazette*, September 27 and October 11, 1773.

To counteract the effect of the *Boston Gazette*, the Loyalists printed letters and articles in the other Boston papers, two of which — the *Boston News-Letter* and the *Boston Chronicle* — were avowedly governmental in their sympathies. The old *Boston News-Letter*, taken over from its founder, John Campbell, by Bartholomew Green, and continued by him until his death in 1733, had been carried on, first by his son-in-law, John Draper, and after 1762 by the latter's son, Richard Draper. The elder Draper was for thirty years "Printer to the Governor and Council of the Province." When his son was duly appointed to succeed him, he introduced the Royal Arms into the title head of the *News-Letter*. Later he changed the name of the paper to the *Massachusetts Gazette and Boston News-Letter*, doubtless to indicate its official character. Naturally the Governor and his Loyalist followers used this paper as their organ. This is shown, not only by its contents, but by one of Governor Hutchinson's letters, dated December 3, 1771, in which he wrote: [1]

> I have taken much pains to procure writers to answer the pieces in the newspapers which do so much mischief among the people, and have two or three engaged with Draper, besides a new press, and a young printer who says he will not be frightened, and I hope for some good effect.

One of the writers referred to in this letter was Jonathan Sewall, attorney-general of Massachusetts, who, writing under the name of "Philanthrop," had engaged in a protracted newspaper discussion with Samuel Adams as "Vindex," over the outcome of the trial of the British soldiers engaged in the Boston Massacre. [2] The *News-Letter*, published by Richard Draper until his death in 1774, then by his widow, and finally by John Howe, continued to serve as the mouthpiece of the Tories. Thus it had the distinction of being the only paper printed in Boston during the occupation of that city by the British. On February 22, 1776, a few weeks before the British evacuated Boston, it ceased publication, after an existence of seventy-two years. It was an unkind fate that made the first American newspaper the organ of the opponents of the colonists' cause, but the willingness of its founder, John Campbell,

[1] Wells, W. V. *Life of Samuel Adams*, vol. I, p. 439.
[2] *Ibid.*, p. 442.

from the first, to bow to authority characterized its policy during practically its whole career.

How the *Boston Gazette* and the *Massachusetts Gazette* were employed for the purposes of political discussion is illustrated by a series of letters contributed by two prominent leaders, Daniel Leonard, a Loyalist lawyer of Taunton, Massachusetts, and the Patriot, John Adams, of Boston. In December, 1774, the *Massachusetts Gazette and Post Boy* contained the first of seventeen letters by Leonard, signed "Massachusettensis," attacking the measures adopted by the first Continental Congress. John Adams, after returning from that Congress, undertook to answer these Loyalist attacks with a series of letters, signed "Novanglus," contributed to the *Boston Gazette*. The debate continued, week by week, until cut short by the temporary suspension of the *Boston Gazette*, which ceased publication for two months immediately after the battle of Lexington. These letters attracted much attention, not only when they appeared in these papers, but when they were reprinted in pamphlet form both in the colonies and in England.

The other Boston paper that eventually became an opponent of the Patriots, the *Boston Chronicle*, was established in 1767 by two Scotchmen, John Mein and John Fleeming. It was the best printed and the cheapest paper in the colonies, considering its quarto size and the character of its contents. During its first year the *Chronicle* seemed neutral, for it reprinted such material on the Patriots' side as John Dickinson's *Letters from a Farmer in Pennsylvania* and extracts from the writings of John Wilkes, the English champion of the people's rights. At the beginning of the second year, it became a semi-weekly, the first in New England. Then Mein, who was a successful stationer and printer and had established a circulating library, not only refused to join the other Boston merchants in their agreement not to import English goods, but in the *Chronicle* undertook to prove that John Hancock and the other "well-disposed" merchants who had signed the agreement were violating it for their own profit. A well-educated man and a vigorous writer, he proved a strong controversialist when assailed by his opponents in the *Boston Gazette*. So unpopular did he become that he was hanged in effigy, he and his partner were attacked in the streets, and finally, when he wounded one of his assailants, he was compelled to take refuge on a warship in the harbor. In consequence of its unpopular policy, the *Chronicle*, which had claimed a circulation of 1400, lost so many of its readers that it was discontinued with the issue of June 21–25, 1770. Mein fled to England to escape arrest for wounding one of his attackers, then returned in an attempt to straighten out his tangled affairs, and finally went back to England in 1771 to enter the employ of the British Government. Like others who opposed the Patriots' cause, he was charged with being in the pay of the authorities while editing the *Chronicle*.

The only Boston newspaper that remained neutral throughout the struggle was the *Boston Evening-Post*. For forty years, from 1735 to 1775, it had been the brightest and liveliest paper in the colonies. Succeeding in 1735 to Jeremy Gridley's literary period-ical, the *Weekly Rehearsal* (1731–35), it had enjoyed popularity under the proprietorship of Thomas Fleet until his death in 1758, and after that, under his sons, Thomas and John Fleet. By devoting some issues entirely to domestic news, by making brief satirical or impudent comments in brackets after news items, and by writing clever advertisements for the wares that he sold, the elder Fleet had produced a very readable sheet. In religious and political controversies, he had permitted both sides to use his columns freely, realizing, no doubt, the interest thus created in his paper. His sons, continuing this policy of independence, gave equal space and prominence to the letters of Patriot and Loyalist writers. During 1774–75, however, as the relations between the colonies and England approached a crisis, the Patriots resented its publication of Loyalist arguments and abuse. In self-defense, the Fleets early in 1775 felt it necessary to declare that their paper was not among those that were charged with being "hired, or rather bribed, (from a Fund said to be established for that Use) for the vile Purposes of publishing Pieces . . . tending to favor Despotism and the present arbitrary and tyrannical Proceedings of the Ministry relative to America."[1] At the same time they explained that the *Post* had "always been conducted with the utmost Freedom and Impartiality," and gave notice "that their Paper shall, as usual, be open for the Insertion of all Pieces that shall tend to amuse or instruct, or to the promoting of useful

[1] *Boston Evening-Post*, March 6, 1775.

Knowledge and the general Good of Mankind, as they themselves (who are the sole Directors and Proprietors thereof) shall think prudent, profitable, or entertaining to their numerous Readers." [1] But popular feeling was running too high in those critical days to tolerate such independence and moderation.   Consequently, on April 24, 1775, five days after the battles of Lexington and Concord, the publishers announced "that they shall desist publishing their Papers after this Day, till Matters are in a more settled State." [2]   In the column of local news just preceding this announcement, they informed their readers that "the unhappy Transactions of last Week are so variously related that we shall not at present undertake to give any particular Account thereof." To have dismissed in this summary fashion the occasion when

> . . . . the embattled farmers stood,
> And fired the shot heard round the world,

seems to-day a sad lack of journalistic enterprise, not to say of patriotism, but, since that was the last issue of their paper, perhaps they regarded discretion as the better part of valor.   At any rate, they continued to carry on a successful job-printing business long after they ceased to be newspaper publishers.

Another important Boston paper entered the lists shortly before the Revolution — the *Massachusetts Spy*.   Established in July, 1770, by Zechariah Fowle and his twenty-one-year-old apprentice, Isaiah Thomas, it was distinctive as a small, cheap, tri-weekly, designed "to obtain subscriptions from mechanics, and other classes of people who had not much time to spare from business." [3] When this innovation in journalism proved unsuccessful, Fowle withdrew, in November, 1770, and Thomas published the paper twice a week for three months.   This plan also was abandoned on February 1, 1771, and for a month the *Spy* suspended publication completely.   Then in March, 1771, Thomas revived the paper as a large, four-page weekly, with the motto, "Open to all Parties, but Influenced by None."   Possibly it was Thomas whom Governor Hutchinson described as "a young printer who says he will not be frightened," and whose "new press" the Governor hoped could be used to put the Loyalists' cause before the people. [4]   At

---

[1] *Boston Evening-Post*, March 6, 1775.   [2] *Ibid.*, April 24, 1775.

[3] Thomas, Isaiah. *History of Printing in America*, vol. II, p. 61.

[4] Cf. Wells, W. V. *Life of Samuel Adams*, vol. I, p. 439; also p. 83, *supra*.

first the *Spy* lived up to its motto by printing letters contributed by writers of both factions. But when it became known that Thomas himself was an ardent Patriot, the Loyalists not only withdrew their support and contributions but attacked him vigorously. The *Spy* thereupon became an even bolder advocate of the colonists' cause than was the *Boston Gazette*, and Thomas was denounced, with Edes and Gill, as one of the "trumpeters of sedition" whose lives and property the Loyalists in 1774 urged the British soldiers to destroy.[1] Thomas, on July 7, 1774, began to print across the full width of the front page, under the title, a cartoon consisting of a dragon, to represent Great Britain, and Franklin's snake, then in nine segments, one for each colony, with Franklin's legend, "Join or Die." This cartoon he continued to use in every issue for nine months, until the paper ceased publication on April 6, 1775. Within a few weeks after its first appearance the following verses were published in *Rivington's New-York Gazetteer* ridiculing the device:[2]

> Ye sons of Sedition, how comes it to pass,
> That America's typ'd by a Snake — in the grass?
> Don't you think 'tis a scandalous, saucy reflection,
> That merits the soundest, severest Correction?
> New-England's the Head too; — New-England's abused;
> For the Head of the Serpent we know should be bruised.

Isaiah Thomas' Snake and Dragon Cartoon, Printed in the
Massachusetts Spy from July, 1774, to April, 1775

Having aroused the bitter enmity of the Government, and anticipating the imminent crisis, Thomas a few days before the battle of Lexington packed up his press and some of his type and left Boston. The last issue of the *Spy* in that city was dated April 6,

[1] *Boston Evening-Post*, September 19, 1774.
[2] *Rivington's New-York Gazetteer*, August 25, 1774.

1775. Thomas paused to aid in spreading the news of the approaching British troops, then joined the militia hastily collected to oppose the enemy, and finally went to Worcester, set up his press, and revived the *Spy*, on May 3, 1775.   Besides being a fearless Patriot publisher, Thomas, by his two-volume *History of Printing in America*, issued in 1810, supplied an invaluable account of the rise and development of the newspaper press in this country.

In most of the other colonies newspapers played rôles similar to those of the Massachusetts press, although in most instances they were less conspicuous.

The contribution to colonial journalism before the Revolution that attracted the most attention on both sides of the Atlantic, was John Dickinson's twelve *Letters from a Farmer in Pennsylvania to the Inhabitants of the British Colonies*, first printed serially in the *Pennsylvania Chronicle* between December 1, 1767, and the following February.   Both in substance and in style they constituted the most effective presentation of the position of the colonists in the controversy with the mother country.   Accordingly, they were reprinted in twenty-one of the twenty-five other colonial newspapers almost as fast as they came out in the *Chronicle*.   Shortly after the last letter appeared, they were republished in pamphlet form.   Eight different editions appeared in the several colonies, and within the same year two editions came out in London and one in Dublin.   The British editions contained a preface by Benjamin Franklin.   Dickinson, who has been termed the "penman of the American Revolution," was also the author of the popular "Liberty Song" of the Patriots, first published in the *Boston Gazette* in 1768, and given wide currency through republication in most of the other colonial newspapers.

When hostilities began in 1775, there were thirty-seven newspapers in the eleven colonies.   Of these, seven were published in Massachusetts; five in Boston, one in Salem, and one in Newburyport.   Rhode Island had two papers; one in Providence and one in Newport.   In Connecticut there were four; at Hartford, New Haven, Norwich, and New London.   New Hampshire had one, at Portsmouth.   Thus the four New England colonies contributed fourteen of the thirty-seven papers, or more than one third.   Pennsylvania could boast the second largest number, nine.   Of

these, six in English and one in German were published at Philadelphia, one in English and German at Lancaster, and one in
German at Germantown.   New York had four papers; three issued in New York City, and one in Albany.   In the five southern
colonies there were only ten papers; two in Maryland, at Annapolis and at Baltimore; two in Virginia, both at Williamsburg;
two in North Carolina, at Wilmington and at Newbern; three in
South Carolina, all at Charleston; and one in Georgia, at Savannah.[1]   Since the total population of all the colonies was about
three millions, of which half a million were negro slaves, there was
only one newspaper published for every 70,000 freemen.   About
one third of the principal men in the colonies, as John Adams estimated, were opposed to the Revolution, but only seven or eight of
the newspapers were avowed supporters of the Tory cause, while
twenty-three were loyal to the Patriots.[2]

The capture by the British of one after another of the seaports,
interfered with the publication of Patriot newspapers.   But the
failure of the enemy to hold any of these places throughout the
war, with the single exception of New York, made possible the reappearance of some of the papers as soon as the cities had been
evacuated.   Thus, while the British held Boston for a year —
from April, 1775, to March 17, 1776 — the *Massachusetts Gazette
and Boston News-Letter* was the only paper published there; but,
on the evacuation of the city, the *Boston Gazette*, which had been
taken to Watertown, Massachusetts, resumed publication in
Boston, and the *Massachusetts Gazette and Boston News-Letter* expired.   When Newport was captured by the British, the *Newport
Mercury* was moved to Rehoboth, Massachusetts, where it continued for three years, until the withdrawal of the enemy from
Newport made possible its return.   With the British occupation
of Philadelphia (September, 1777, to July, 1778) the *Pennsylvania
Gazette* and the *Pennsylvania Journal* ceased publication.   The
Pennsylvania Packet or General Advertiser removed to Lancaster
and remained there until the withdrawal of the British.   The
Philadelphia *Evening Post*, on the other hand, which had originally
advocated independence for the colonies, sought the favor of the

[1] Thomas, Isaiah. *History of Printing in America*, vol. II, pp. 294–95.
[2] Sabine, Lorenzo. *Biographical Sketches of Loyalists of the American Revolution*,
vol. I, p. 49.

enemy and continued publication. When Philadelphia was evacuated, it recanted and again supported the Patriot cause. While they held Philadelphia, the British revived the Tory *Pennsylvania Ledger*, which had been forced to suspend in November, 1776, and established a new paper, the *Royal Pennsylvania Gazette*, which continued until the British withdrew. Upon the capture of New York by the British, Hugh Gaine took his *New-York Gazette* to Newark, Samuel Loudon removed the *New-York Packet* to Fishkill, and John Holt transferred his *New-York Journal* to Kingston (then Esopus), and, when that town was burned by the enemy, to Poughkeepsie. When Gaine abandoned his attempt to publish a Patriot paper in Newark and returned to New York, Governor Livingston of New Jersey urged the colonial legislature to give aid in the establishment of a paper to uphold the Colonials. Accordingly, in December, 1777, the *New-Jersey Gazette* was issued at Burlington. Such were the vicissitudes of newspaper publication in the uncertain times of war.

The outbreak of hostilities also handicapped printers, by cutting off the importation of presses, type, and paper. An attempt had been made as early as 1750 to make wooden presses in Pennsylvania, but these were inferior to those imported from England. To secure presses and type, printers like Franklin and Rivington had to make trips to England. Although the first paper mill in the colonies had been built as early as 1690, paper-making developed slowly, and considerable difficulty was experienced, even before the Revolution, in getting enough paper at home or abroad to meet the needs of the few newspapers. When the war broke out, many skilled paper-makers left their work to join either the British or the colonial armies, and therefore the supply of paper became still more limited. Patriotic pleas to housewives to save rags for paper-making frequently appeared in the papers, and prizes were offered for the largest collections of rags. In some instances during the war, the shortage of paper limited the size of an edition and affected the regularity of publication.

The writer who undoubtedly did the most effective journalistic work during the Revolution was Thomas Paine. Having arrived in America from England late in 1774, with a letter of introduction from Franklin, he became editor of the *Pennsylvania Magazine, or American Museum*, and continued in that position until

August, 1776. His first newspaper contribution, published in the *Pennsylvania Journal* on January 4, 1775, was a brief imaginary "Dialogue between General Wolfe and General Gage in a Wood near Boston," in which Wolfe rebukes Gage for leading the British against the Americans. Later in 1775 he contributed another letter to the *Journal*, signed "Humanus," in which he came out not only for independence for the colonies but for the abolition of slavery: [1]

> ... I hesitate not for a moment to believe, that the Almighty will finally separate America from Britain — Call it Independency or what you will — if it is the cause of God and humanity, it will go on. — And when the Almighty shall have blest us, and made us a people, *dependent only upon him*, then may our first gratitude be shown, by an act of continental legislation, which shall put a stop to the importation of Negroes for sale, soften the hard fate of those already here, and in time procure their freedom.

Early in January, 1776, appeared his famous pamphlet, "Common Sense," which, according to a contemporary, Dr. Benjamin Rush, "burst from the press with an effect which has rarely been produced by types and paper in any age or country." Within three months over 120,000 copies had been sold. This pamphlet, more than any other single piece of writing, crystallized in the popular mind the idea of independence for the colonies. The president of the University of Philadelphia, the Reverend William Smith, under the name of "Cato," undertook to answer its arguments by a series of eight letters contributed to the *Pennsylvania Gazette* during March and April, 1776. To these Paine replied in four letters signed "Forester" in the *Pennsylvania Packet*. This "Cato-Forester" controversy was one of the significant pre-Revolutionary discussions, and the letters were widely reprinted.

Paine's journalistic ability was strikingly displayed also in the famous "Crisis," which was published in the *Pennsylvania Journal* on December 19, 1776, and was read to Washington's disheartened soldiers on the eve of his attack on Trenton. Its opening lines are familiar to all: [2]

> These are the times that try men's souls. The summer soldier and the sunshine patriot will, in this crisis, shrink from the service

---

[1] *Pennsylvania Journal and Weekly Advertiser*, October 18, 1775.
[2] Conway, Moncure D. *The Writings of Thomas Paine*, vol. I, p. 170.

of their country; but he that stands it *now*, deserves the love and thanks of man and woman. Tyranny, like hell, is not easily conquered; yet we have this consolation with us, that the harder the conflict the more glorious the triumph. What we obtain too cheap, we esteem too lightly: it is dearness that only gives every thing its value. Heaven knows how to put a proper price upon its goods; and it would be strange indeed if so celestial an article as FREEDOM should not be highly rated.

Paine wrote the "Crisis" while serving as a volunteer aide-decamp in Washington's army during the retreat through New Jersey. The half-clad, dispirited soldiers, heartened by Paine's ringing appeal, turned upon the enemy, took Trenton, and captured the hated Hessians. The second "Crisis," in pamphlet form, followed a month later. Addressing Lord Howe in this pamphlet, Paine declared that "'The United States of America,' will sound as pompously in the world or in history, as 'the kingdom of Great Britain.'" [1] Whenever occasion seemed to demand it during the seven years of war, he published another "Crisis." These pamphlets finally numbered sixteen. Samuel Adams, writing afterwards to Paine of the effect of "Common Sense" and of the "Crisis," declared that they "undoubtedly awakened the public mind, and led the people loudly to call for a declaration of independence." [2]

Paine, as Leslie Stephen has truly said, "possessed in the highest degree the gift of the born journalist," [3] the ability to write the timely argument and appeal that the occasion required, to interpret to the average man what he had thought and felt but had not formulated, and to do these things in a simple, direct, vigorous, and appealing style. "The secret of his strength," to quote Moses Coit Tyler, historian of the literature of the Revolution, "lay in his infallible instinct for interpreting to the public its own conscience and its own consciousness, and for doing this in language which, at times, was articulate thunder and lightning." [4]

His career as journalist again illustrates the fact that, in eighteenth-century English and American journalism, the most

---

[1] Conway, Moncure D. *The Writings of Thomas Paine*, vol. I, p. 181.

[2] Wells, W. V. *Life of Samuel Adams*, vol. II, p. 341.

[3] Stephen, Leslie. *English Thought in the Eighteenth Century*, vol. II, p. 260.

[4] Tyler, Moses Coit. *Literary History of the Revolution*, vol. II, p. 41.

significant figures were, not the men who edited and published the newspapers, but the contributors, many of whom, like Paine, sent their letters and essays now to one paper and now to another, and received no remuneration for them. Paine's extensive use of the pamphlet as a medium for discussing current issues at length, also shows that newspapers were still too small in size, and too limited in circulation, adequately to disseminate ideas among the largest possible reading public. In short, newspapers, even in great crises like the Revolution, were still primarily enterprises of printers, who gleaned news in comparatively small amounts from only a few of the possible sources, and who depended on public-spirited citizens to supply them gratis with editorial material.

Despite these limitations of the colonial press, its influence was unquestionably great. Loyalist testimony to this fact was given by Ambrose Serle when, temporarily in charge of the *New-York Gazette* under General Howe, he wrote to Lord Dartmouth, on November 26, 1776:[1]

> Among other Engines, which have raised the present Commotion next to the indecent Harangues of the Preachers, none has had a more extensive or stronger Influence than the Newspapers of the respective Colonies. One is astonished to see with what Avidity they are sought after, and how implicitly they are believed, by the great Bulk of the People.

How the Loyalists, just before and during the Revolution, sought to counteract the effects of the Patriot papers by establishing new papers and subsidizing existing ones, has already been pointed out. The extent of their financial aid to printers and writers, both in England and in America, was thus commented on in 1781 by the Patriot paper, the *New-Jersey Gazette:* [2]

> It is a fact well-established, that in the course of the last year the British government expended upwards of Fifty Thousand Guineas on hirelings employed to tell lies in pamphlets and in the news-papers in Europe and America. The present year will probably cost them double that sum, as their affairs are in a more critical state; and we may expect to see marks of redoubled industry in the trade of misrepresentation and falsehood. The news-papers begin to abound with this species of intelligence.

[1] Ford, Paul Leicester. *Journals of Hugh Gaine, Printer*, vol. I, p. 57.
[2] *New-Jersey Gazette*, July 4, 1781.

Partly because of the large number of Loyalists in New York City, and partly because the British held possession of the city to the end of the war, it became the center of their journalistic activities. Even as early as October, 1774, Lieutenant-Governor Colden of New York reported to the British Government that English inflammatory pamphlets and speeches which found their way to the colonies "are opposed in this Place by publishing more Papers [pamphlets and newspapers] in favour of administration, and against Measures which may be offensive to Parliament than in all the other Colonies put together."[1]

The most notable Loyalist editor and publisher in New York was James Rivington, an Englishman of education and ability. He began his career as journalist by issuing in 1773 a weekly paper with the comprehensive title of *Rivington's New-York Gazetteer: or Connecticut, Hudson's-River, New-Jersey, and Quebec Weekly Advertiser*. In 1777 he changed its name to the *New-York Loyal Gazette*, and later in the same year, to the *Royal Gazette*, with the royal arms between the two words. Apparently he did a thriving business, for in 1773 he claimed a circulation of 3600, and in 1775 declared that he employed sixteen workmen, paid out nearly £1000 annually in wages, and expended about the same amount for paper. These items doubtless included his book and job-printing business. At first Rivington undertook to give both sides a fair hearing in his paper, but, as in the case of the *Boston Evening-Post*, this policy was resented by the Patriots. When, in February, 1775, he was denounced by the Committee of Patriots in Newark, New Jersey, as a "ministerial hireling," he printed the condemnatory resolution, and defended his course thus:[2]

> His crime then is neither more or less, than the keeping a *free press* in a land of Liberty. . . .
>
> Every unprejudiced person, during the present unhappy dispute with the parent country, would no more wish to form his opinion, without hearing both sides of the question, than a jury would desire to give in their verdict, without examining the witnesses on both sides. While, therefore, he continues to lay before the public, all arguments *pro* and *con;* he is sure of the patronage, the protection and encouragement of the most respectable of his fellow subjects.

[1] *Colden Papers. New York Historical Society Collections for 1877*, p. 368.
[2] *New-York Gazetteer*, February 16, 1775.

Two months later, when he was hanged in effigy at New Brunswick, New Jersey, he printed a wood-cut of a man hanging from a tree, followed by another explanation of his policy, addressed "To the Public." [1]

> The Printer is bold to affirm, that his press has been open to publications from all parties; and he defies his enemies to produce an instance to the contrary. He has considered his press in the light of a public office, to which every man has a right to have recourse. But the moment he ventured to publish sentiments which were opposed to the dangerous views and designs of certain demagogues, he found himself held up as an enemy of his country, and the most unwearied pains were taken to ruin him. In the country wherein he was born, he always heard the liberty of the press represented as the great security of freedom, and in that sentiment he has been educated; nor has he reason to think differently now on account of his experience in this country. While his enemies make liberty the prostituted pretense of their illiberal persecution of him, their aim is to establish a most cruel tyranny, and the Printer thinks that some very recent transactions will convince the good people of this city of the difference between being governed by a few factious individuals, and the good old law and constitution, under which we have so long been a happy people.

Moreover, he published the British account of the battle of Lexington, with the Patriots' denial of its truthfulness and the affidavits of the minute-men to the effect that on that occasion they had been fired upon first by the British soldiers. As the denunciation of him and of his paper continued unabated, he again defended himself in the following address "To the Public": [2]

> As many Publications have appeared from my Press which have given great Offence to the Colonies, and particularly to many of my Fellow Citizens; I am therefore led, by a most sincere Regard for their favorable Opinion, to declare to the Public, that Nothing which I have ever done, has proceeded from any Sentiments in the least unfriendly to the Liberties of this Continent, but altogether from the Ideas I entertained of the Liberty of the Press, and of my duty as a Printer. I am led to make this free and public Declaration to my Fellow Citizens, which I hope they will consider as a sufficient Pledge of my Resolution, for the future, to conduct my

---

[1] *New-York Gazetteer*, April 20, 1775.   [2] *Ibid.*, May 18, 1775.

Press upon such Principles as shall not give Offence to the Inhabitants of the Colonies in general, and of this City in particular, to which I am connected by the tenderest of all human Ties, and in the Welfare of which I shall consider my own as inseparably involved.

In spite of these protestations, General Gage, commanding the British troops in Boston, was so well pleased with Rivington's paper that he is said to have distributed 400 copies each week among the army, the navy, and other Loyalists in Boston.[1] The Patriots finally showed their resentment by attacking Rivington's office, carrying away his type, and compelling him, on June 7, 1775, to take refuge on board a man-of-war in the harbor.[2] Later Rivington went to England to secure new equipment, and on his return, with the designation of king's printer, he made his *Royal Gazette* the mouthpiece of the Loyalists. He sought to hearten the Tories by publishing false news, such as the reported capture and death of Washington, the attempted assassination of Franklin, the supposed failures and cowardice of the "rebels," and the rumored acquisition of 36,000 Cossacks by the British forces. "There was a fool's paradise for the hopeful Tory" in every issue, it has been said.[3] So gross were these falsehoods that among the Patriots his paper came to be known as the "Lying Gazette." Such hopeful news was reinforced by plausible arguments in favor of the British and against the Patriots. After the war, Rivington sought to conciliate the Patriots with an admission of his errors, but was unsuccessful, and he discontinued his paper on December 31, 1783. In his apology he wrote:[4]

Sensible that his zeal for the success of his Majesty's Arms, his sanguine wishes for the good of his country, and his friendship for individuals, had at times led him to credit and circulate paragraphs without investigating the facts so closely as his duty to the public demanded. Hereafter he would err no more.

Philip Freneau, the journalist-poet, who satirized Rivington in half a dozen poems, characterized him as "The inventor as well as

[1] *New-York Journal*, March 30, 1775.
[2] *Colden Papers. New York Historical Society Collections for 1877*, p. 422.
[3] Van Tyne, C. H. *Loyalists in the American Revolution*, p. 251.
[4] *Ibid.*, p. 290.

the printer of lies," [1] and ascribed to him these words in his "Last Will and Testament": [2]

> I know there are some (that would fain be thought wise)
> Who say my Gazette is the record of lies;
> In answer to this, I shall only reply —
> All the choice that I had was to starve or to lie.

With his absurdly false news, published in the interests of the cause that he chose to serve, and with his specious defense of his policies, Rivington is a typical example of the war-time partisan journalist.

Another New York editor and publisher who served the British while they occupied that city, was Hugh Gaine of the *New-York Gazette and Weekly Mercury*, which he had established in 1752 as the *New-York Mercury*. For many years an ardent supporter of the Colonists' cause, he had in 1754 published Franklin's snake cartoon with the legend, "Join or Die." [3] At the time of the Stamp Act in 1765, he announced that he would discontinue the *Mercury* rather than print it on stamped paper, and, when the mob seized all the stamped paper, he continued to print the *Mercury* for three weeks without a title heading, and in place of it printed the announcement, "No Stamped Paper to be had." [4] When, early in 1768, he was made official printer for the colony and the city, he changed the name of his paper to the *New-York Gazette and Weekly Mercury*, to indicate the official status of the publication. As the Revolutionary War approached, he still showed his sympathy with the Patriots but sought to keep the columns of the *Gazette* open to both sides. He refused, however, to publish the British accounts of the battles of Lexington and Concord furnished him by the Lieutenant-Governor. [5]

After the British occupation of New York, Gaine took part of his printing equipment to Newark, and, for seven issues, beginning on September 21, 1776, published the *Gazette* there as the only newspaper in New Jersey. His difficulties in getting materials and in circulating his paper were so great that, when the British threatened to overrun New Jersey, he wavered in his

---

[1] *Freeman's Journal*, March 27, 1782.
[2] Pattee, F. L. *Poems of Philip Freneau*, vol. II, p. 121.
[3] *New-York Mercury*, May 13, 1754.   [4] Cf. p. 80, *supra*.
[5] *Colden Papers. New York Historical Society Collections for 1877*, p. 414.

allegiance, and was compelled by the New Jersey Patriots to return to New York.   During his absence, Ambrose Serle, a Loyalist, at the request of the Governor, supervised the publication of
the *New-York Gazette* as the only newspaper published in the city.
He had it printed in Gaine's shop and attached Gaine's name to
the first issue.   On returning to New York after his sojourn in
New Jersey, Gaine resumed control of the *Gazette.*

After his return, Gaine, like Rivington, deliberately published
false news designed to bolster up the British cause and to belittle
the successes of the Patriots.   This is evident from a comparison
of the entries made in his diary with the reports of the same
events printed in his paper.[1]   Nevertheless, he failed to win the
complete confidence of the British and hence was not always favored by them with the news, as was Rivington.   His course,
however, aroused the bitter hostility of the Patriots and led the
Pennsylvania Journal to characterize him as "the greatest liar
upon earth."[2]   Freneau satirized him in several poems in the
Freeman's Journal, putting him in the same class with Rivington.
When the British evacuated New York City, Gaine ceased to
publish the *Gazette* but continued as printer and bookseller.

In connection with their book and stationery business, both
Rivington and Gaine sold patent medicines, which they advertised freely in their papers.   These advertisements, some of which
were of an objectionable type, often included testimonials from
persons who had used the nostrums.   In attacking Rivington and
Gaine for their support of the Tories, some of the Patriot papers
took occasion to refer satirically to these patent medicine advertisements.

The protracted struggle between the colonies and the mother
country from 1765 to 1783, demonstrated the value of the press as
a means of influencing public opinion.   From the time of the
Stamp Act controversy, political leaders on both sides freely used
the newspapers to carry on discussion.   Until hostilities actually
began, each side sought to uphold its position by arguments set
forth not only in letters to newspapers but in pamphlets.   Although some of the papers opened their columns to contributions
from both sides, most of them were avowedly partisan.   After the

---

[1] Cf. Ford, Paul Leicester. *Journals of Hugh Gaine, Printer*, vol. II, p. vi.
[2] *Pennsylvania Journal*, February 19, 1777.

break came, arguments as weapons of journalistic warfare were generally superseded by satire, ridicule, and bitter attacks. The animosities inevitable to war were reflected and intensified in the press. Verse as well as prose served to satirize and ridicule the enemy, often in a coarse manner. News was colored and falsified, as invariably happens in time of war. The papers controlled by the British during their occupancy of the seaboard cities, were the worst offenders in the matter of publishing false and misleading reports and rumors. These methods of war-time journalism, carried out for eight years, affected the character of newspapers in the subsequent period, when the contest centered in partisan politics rather than in war.

CHAPTER IV

BEGINNINGS OF THE POLITICAL PRESS, 1783–1800

THE ending of the Revolutionary War made possible the resumption of newspaper publishing under normal conditions. At the beginning of 1784 the postmaster-general announced that mail would again be carried over the old post roads,[1] and by the end of that year the post was going from New York to Philadelphia three times a week. Even though stage coaches and post riders traveled but from thirty to fifty miles a day under favorable conditions, and carried newspapers merely by courtesy, since papers were not received by the post offices as regular mail, they brought to publishers the only news available from other parts of the country. With the reopening of the seaports, news from abroad entered more freely. Printing materials, likewise, were less difficult to obtain. The war had stimulated paper-making to such an extent that at its close there were between eighty and ninety mills in operation.

The general character of the newspapers, some forty of which survived the war, showed no immediate change. Essays, generally in the form of letters furnished by local contributors and frequently signed with Latin names, still occupied an important place as substitutes for editorials. The subjects debated were the funding of the debt, the status of the Loyalists who had remained in the country or who were refugees, the recently organized society of army and navy officers called the Order of the Cincinnati, the power of Congress to regulate trade, the desirability of the theater, and similar political, economic, and social problems of the day. The ridicule, coarse satire, and bitterness of war-time journalism were carried over into the post-war period. Historical and literary material, such as Robertson's *History of America*, *Capt. Cook's Voyages*, and poems by Gray, Cowper, and Goldsmith, was reprinted in some of the best papers of the period.[2]

News continued to be gleaned from other papers and from

[1] *Pennsylvania Packet*, January 6, 1784.
[2] Cf. Boston *Weekly Advertiser*, 1784; *Pennsylvania Packet*, 1784-85; and *Massachusetts Centinel*, 1784.

private letters solicited by publishers from merchants and others. Persons who received letters containing interesting information were asked to give them to the newspapers. "Reservoirs will be established in public houses for the reception of information, whether foreign, local, or poetical," announced the publisher of the *Massachusetts Centinel* in outlining his policy; and "Essays, Articles of Intelligence, Advertisements, &c, &c, are gratefully received" was the standing announcement in Loudon's *New-York Packet*. News from other parts of the country and from abroad took precedence over the very limited number of local items. With the revival of business after the war, the amount of advertising increased to such an extent that advertisements often occupied more than half the space in many papers.

The two marked advances in American journalism just after the war were the establishment of new papers and the change in the frequency of publication from weekly to semi-weekly, tri-weekly, and daily issues. The "Yankee curiosity" regarding current events that impressed all foreign travelers in America, the growth of the cities, and the increase in advertising were, no doubt, responsible for these forward steps. In response to the demand, some of the old weekly papers were issued twice, thrice, or six times a week, and new semi-weeklies and dailies were started.

The first daily newspaper in the United States came into existence in Philadelphia on September 21, 1784, when, without any previous announcement or any comment after the change took place, the tri-weekly *Pennsylvania Packet and General Advertiser* became the *Pennsylvania Packet and Daily Advertiser*. The price was reduced from sixpence to fourpence a copy, and David C. Claypoole became joint publisher with John Dunlop, who, since he founded it in 1771, had published the paper continuously. After a change of name in 1795 to *Claypoole's American Daily Advertiser*, and another, in 1800, to *Poulson's American General Advertiser*, it was finally absorbed, in 1839, by a new daily paper, the Philadelphia *North American*, which continued until 1925. Less than six months after the *Packet* became a daily, a new daily paper was set on foot by Francis Childs in New York City, the *New York Daily Advertiser*, the publication of which began on March 1, 1785.

With the political discussion centering in the new Constitution that was proposed to replace the ineffective Articles of Confederation, newspapers became increasingly important as a medium for presenting the arguments of the two factions that developed into the Federalist and Anti-Federalist parties. As in pre-Revolutionary days, political leaders sought to influence public opinion through anonymous letters in newspapers. Because newspaper pages were larger, because papers were more numerous, and because they were published at more frequent intervals, they served as a better medium for political discussion than they had been in colonial times, and thus largely replaced the pamphlet. Alexander Hamilton, James Madison, John Jay, DeWitt Clinton, and John Dickinson, author of the *Letters of a Farmer in Pennsylvania*, were among the distinguished men who contributed letters, singly or in series, discussing the proposed Constitution.

Unquestionably the greatest series of such letters was that known as *The Federalist*, written by Hamilton, Madison, and Jay, under the name of "Publius," and addressed "To the People of the State of New York." They were first published in the semi-weekly New York *Independent Journal: or General Advertiser*, beginning on October 27, 1787, and continuing into April, 1788. These letters explained in detail the various articles of the Constitution and urged its adoption. Jefferson wrote from Paris that they constituted "the best commentary on the principles of government which was ever written." [1]   As fast as they appeared in the *Independent Journal*, they were reprinted in other newspapers that favored the ratification of the Constitution. The publishers of the *Independent Journal* also reprinted the original letters with some additional ones — eighty-five in all — in two volumes, and then proceeded to print the additional letters in the *Independent Journal*, from June 14 to August 16, 1788. Hamilton, who had contributed essays and letters to newspapers from the beginning of the Revolutionary War, was the author of two thirds of these letters. As an exposition of the fundamental principles of constitutional government, *The Federalist* is the most important contribution to political science that has ever appeared in the American press.

In defending the omission from the Constitution of any guar-

[1] *Writings of Thomas Jefferson*, P. L. Ford, ed., vol. v, p. 52.

antee of freedom of the press, Hamilton had this to say in *The Federalist:* [1]

> What signifies a declaration, "that the liberty of the press shall be inviolably preserved"? What is the liberty of the press? Who can give it any definition which would not leave the utmost latitude for evasion? I hold it to be impracticable; and from this I infer, that its security, whatever fine declarations may be inserted in any Constitution respecting it, must altogether depend on public opinion, and on the general spirit of the People and of the Government.

Jefferson, on the other hand, favored a clause in the Constitution safeguarding the freedom of the press. Writing to Madison from Paris he said, "A declaration that the federal government will never restrain the presses from printing any thing they please, will not take away the liability of the printers for false facts printed." [2] Jefferson believed in a constitutional guarantee of the freedom of the press because he held that newspapers were essential to the success of the republic. He wrote in a letter early in 1787: [3]

> The people are the only censors of their governors; and even their errors will tend to keep these to the true principles of their institution. To punish these errors too severely would be to suppress the only safeguard of the public liberty. The way to prevent these irregular interpositions of the people is to give them full information of their affairs thro' the channel of the public papers, & to contrive that those papers should penetrate the whole mass of the people. The basis of our government being the opinion of the people, the very first object should be to keep that right; and were it left to me to decide whether we should have a government without newspapers or newspapers without a government, I should not hesitate a moment to prefer the latter. But I should mean that every man should receive those papers, & be capable of reading them.

The outstanding journalist of the period was a man who, unlike most of his colleagues, was, not merely a printer and publisher, but an editor as well — Benjamin Russell, founder in 1784 of the *Massachusetts Centinel and Republican Journal.* After learning

---

[1] *The Fœderalist,* H. B. Dawson, ed., pp. 599–600. (No. LXXXIV.)
[2] *Writings of Thomas Jefferson,* P. L. Ford, ed., vol. V, p. 47.
[3] *Ibid.,* vol. IV, pp. 359–60.

the printing trade under Isaiah Thomas, he had served in the Continental army and had risen to the rank of major. When the war was over, he established the *Massachusetts Centinel* in Boston, and for over forty years he made this paper a potent influence both locally and nationally. In 1790, in order to indicate the broader appeal that he desired his paper to make, he changed the title to the *Columbian Centinel*. A strong Federalist, Russell did valiant work in crystallizing public opinion in favor of ratification of the Constitution. A novel, cartoon-like device was one original and effective method that he employed. The illustration represented the "Federal Edifice," the "National Dome" of which was to be supported by thirteen pillars, one for each state. As the states ratified the Constitution, one pillar after another, each inscribed with the name of a state, was put in place in the picture. When in 1788 only North Carolina and Rhode Island still held back, the illustration showed the North Carolina pillar raised part way, with the caption, "Rise it will," and the Rhode Island pillar, broken off at the base, with the legend, "The foundation good — it may yet be saved."[1]

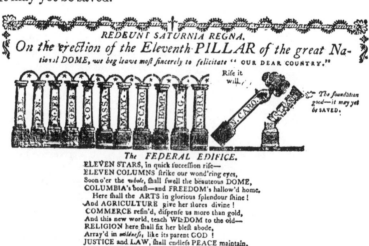

Benjamin Russell's Federal Edifice Cartoon, Printed at the Top of Two Columns on the Second Page of the *Massachusetts Centinel*, August 2, 1788.

Size of cartoon with verse, 5½ in. by 3½ in.

---

[1] *Massachusetts Centinel*, August 2, 1788.

Like Franklin's "Join or Die" device of the snake, and Thomas's dragon and snake, Russell's "Federal Edifice" cartoon deserves a high place in the history of patriotic pictorial journalism.

Russell remained a staunch Federalist throughout his career, supporting Washington and Adams, opposing the war against England in 1812, and fighting vigorously the French influence as represented by Jeffersonian Republicanism. He urged the wearing of a black cockade by the Federalists in opposition to the tricolored French cockade of the Republicans; he coined the term "Gerrymander" to describe the efforts of the Republicans under Governor Gerry to redistrict Massachusetts in the interests of their party; and he originated the phrase, the "era of good feelings," to characterize the period after the election of Monroe had ended the Federalist party. By his patriotism, originality, and strong personality, Russell placed his paper in the front rank of early American newspapers.

The cleavage that developed between the supporters and the opponents of ratification was accentuated after the Constitution had been accepted by the several states and the government had been organized under it. Hamilton, secretary of the treasury, continued in the leadership of the Federalist party. Jefferson, returning from France in 1790 to become secretary of state, was the leader of the Anti-Federalist, or Republican, party. Both men, as keen students of government and politics, recognized the importance of the press in a republic. Each sought to use newspapers to shape public opinion in support of the theories of government that he believed to be vital to the success of the first great experiment in democracy. Thus political party organs became inevitable. Newspapers, they realized, could no longer be mere enterprises of printers, entirely dependent on voluntary contributors for discussions of political and economic questions. Able editors were essential to a vigorous support of party policies. Out of this situation grew a new era in American journalism.

The first paper to be established as the avowed organ of the Government was the *Gazette of the United States*. It appeared at New York, the seat of the Federal government, on April 15, 1789, with John Fenno as editor. The fact that Fenno was not a printer but a Boston school teacher, recommended to Federalist leaders as a writer whose "literary achievements are very handsome," [1] is significant of the change that was taking place in the editing of newspapers. Fenno always referred to himself as the "editor" of his paper, not as the printer or publisher. That he had the assistance of prominent Federalists in editing the paper is shown by his statement, at the end of the second year of the *Gazette*, that "through the assistance of several distinguished literary characters, whose labors would give celebrity to works of a superior denomination, this Gazette has been continued for two years." [2] The two "literary characters" referred to were Hamilton and Vice-President Adams.

From Fenno's prospectus to the *Gazette* it is evident that he aimed to make it "a National, Impartial and Independent Conveyancer to all parts of the Union, of News, Politics, and Miscellanies." He promised to publish (1) the proceedings of Congress; (2) "impartial sketches of the debates of Congress"; (3) "essays upon great subjects of Government in general"; (4) "a series of paragraphs calculated to catch the 'living manners as they rise'"; (5) "the interests of the United States as connected with their literary institutions"; (6) "every species of intelligence, which may affect commercial, agricultural, manufacturing, or political interests of the American Republick"; (7) "a chain of domestic occurrences, collected through the Medium of an extensive Correspondence with the respective States"; (8) "a series of foreign articles of intelligence, so connected, as to form a general Idea of publick Affairs in the eastern Hemisphere"; and (9) "the state of national funds; also of the individual governments — courses of exchange — prices current, etc." With this comprehensive program he hoped to receive the support, not only of the "wealthy part of the community," but also of the mercantile classes, mechanics, and farmers. [3] The price of the paper was $3 a year, or sixpence a copy.

His firm determination to aid the newly established Federal government was best expressed in the following declaration published at the end of the second year: [4]

> To hold up the people's own government, in a favorable point of light — and to impress just ideas of its administration by ex-

[1] King, C. R. *Life and Correspondence of Rufus King*, vol. I, p. 357.
[2] *Gazette of the United States*, April 27, 1791.
[3] *Ibid.*, April 15, 1789.   [4] *Ibid.*, April 27, 1791.

hibiting FACTS, comprise the outlines of the plan of this paper —
and so long as the principles of the Constitution are held sacred,
and the rights and liberties of the people are preserved inviolate,
by *"the powers that be,"* it is the office of patriotism, by every
exertion, to endear the GENERAL GOVERNMENT to the people.

Because Hamilton, under various pen names, wrote letters on
current political topics for the *Gazette*, it came to be considered the
official organ of the Federal administration.

Fenno hoped that his paper would have value as a permanent
record, for he published an index to the first volume and offered
back numbers to subscribers who desired to bind their files. Advertisements were excluded for the greater part of the first year,
because "the object being an extensive circulation, the Editor
conceiving that their insertion would have counteracted that part
of his plan, has never admitted any." [1] Toward the close of 1789,
however, he explained that, since his paper circulated in every
state in the Union, as well as in Canada, the West Indies, and
Europe, he would accept some advertisements. He wrote: [2]

> This extensive circulation renders it a proper vehicle for Ad-
> vertisements of a general, commercial and governmental import:
> — By the particular desire and advice, therefore, of a number of
> its patrons, this paper will be open for the reception of advertise-
> ments of the above description; which as they will convey intel-
> ligence of an interesting nature, the Editor hopes their insertion
> will meet the approbation of his friends in general. Should the
> number at any time amount to more than a page in the Gazette,
> they will be given in a Supplement.

At the end of the first six months the circulation reached 650,
and at the end of two years 1400 copies were printed. [3] Later in
the year 1791, however, the editor admitted that the *Gazette* was
sent gratis to 120 postmasters and printers in the United States
and to only 1000 subscribers in different parts of the Union. [4]
When, in November, 1790, the seat of the Federal government
was moved from New York to Philadelphia, Fenno transferred
his paper to the latter place, beginning with the issue of November 3, 1790.

[1] *Gazette of the United States*, October 14, 1789.
[2] *Ibid.*, December 2, 1789.   [3] *Ibid.*, October 14, 1789, and May 4, 1791.
[4] *Ibid.*, December 7, 1791.

With a limited number of subscribers, many of whom apparently failed to pay, under the credit system then common among newspapers, Fenno had difficulty in maintaining the *Gazette*. "The receipts of the first year," he pointed out, "have fallen short one third of the actual expences of publication — so that it remains to be determined whether a newspaper can be supported in the United States, without deluging it with advertisements." [1]   A year later he wrote, "receipts for the year 1790, do not amount to more than one half of the actual expence of the publication during that period." [2]   That his losses increased rather than decreased is evident from a letter that he sent to Hamilton late in 1793, after the *Gazette* had been in existence for over four and a half years. In appealing for a loan of $2000 to keep the paper alive, he wrote: [3]

> After struggling for four and an half years with a complication of difficulties in supporting my publication, difficulties which no industrious person has perhaps been called to encounter since the organization of the general Government, I am reduced to a situation so embarrassing as incapacitates me from printing another paper without the aid of a considerable loan. . . . A loan of Two Thousand Dollars therefore would relieve me, and not only so but place me in a situation which would supercede probably the necessity of any further application of a similar kind. . . . Tho' I have incessantly importuned my distant subscribers & agents to make payment since the 18th of September, I have rec'd only 35¼ dollars; tho' accounts to the amount of 1500 Dollars have been forwarded during the period that has elapsed since.   I therefore conclude that tho' I have more than 4000 Dollars due, there is no dependence to be placed on a fund so wretchedly precarious. . . . Four years & an half of my life is gone for nothing; & worse (for I have a Debt of 2500 Dollars on my Shoulders), if at this crisis, the hand of benevolence & *patriotism* is not extended.

Hamilton wrote to Rufus King suggesting that King should raise $1000 in New York while he himself would raise a like amount in Philadelphia.   Apparently the loan was made, for the *Gazette* continued.

Although a vigorous supporter of the Administration, Fenno undertook at first to be fair and to avoid personalities.   He gave prominence in the *Gazette* to original letters on political topics and

---

[1] *Gazette of the United States*, May 8, 1790.   [2] *Ibid.*, January 8, 1791.
[3] King, C. R. *Life and Correspondence of Rufus King*, vol. I, pp. 501–02.

reprinted similar letters from other papers. Essays on social and general topics, like those in the *Spectator*, were also contributed by readers or were reprinted from other newspapers. While the contents of the *Gazette* were like those of its contemporaries, Fenno generally maintained a somewhat more dignified tone in controversy than did most of the other political organs. In 1798 he was succeeded in the editorship by his son, John Ward Fenno.

As a Republican organ opposed to the *Gazette of the United States*, the *National Gazette* was started by Philip Freneau, the poet of the Revolution. The first issue appeared in Philadelphia on October 31, 1791. Some months before this, Jefferson had declared that, since Fenno's *Gazette* was "a paper of pure Toryism, disseminating the doctrines of monarchy, aristocracy, & the exclusion of the influence of the people we have been trying to get another *weekly* or *half-weekly* paper set up excluding advertisements, so that it might go through the states, & furnish a whig vehicle of intelligence."[1] Jefferson, as secretary of state, offered Freneau the position of translating clerk in the Department of State at a salary of $250 a year, and promised him a better place when one was available; he also wrote to Madison that he planned to give Freneau "the perusal of all my letters of foreign intelligence & all foreign newspapers; the publication of all proclamations & other public notices within my department, & the printing of the laws, which added to his salary would have been a considerable aid."[2] Urged by Madison, Freneau finally decided to start the *National Gazette* and to accept the clerkship that Jefferson offered. He accordingly left New York, where he had been writing for the *Daily Advertiser*, and began his new duties in Philadelphia.

Fenno's *Gazette of the United States* and Freneau's *National Gazette* soon became rival political papers; the former representing Hamilton and the Federalists; the latter, Jefferson and the Republicans. Freneau vigorously attacked Hamilton's funding system, his national bank, his proposed perpetual public debt, and his advocacy of the extension of the powers of the Federal government under the "general welfare" clause of the Constitution. He also denounced the supposed monarchial tendencies of both

[1] *Writings of Thomas Jefferson*, P. L. Ford, ed., vol. v, p. 336.
[2] Pattee, F. L. *Poems of Philip Freneau*, vol. i, p. li.

Hamilton and Vice-President John Adams. Hamilton, as secretary of the treasury, resented these attacks on himself and on his policies, and believed that they were directly inspired by Jefferson. In anonymous letters published in the *Gazette of the United States*, he questioned the propriety of the paying out of public funds by the secretary of state to an office-holding editor who attacked the Administration. He also attacked Jefferson and his ideas of government in a number of letters contributed anonymously to the *Gazette*. In one of these letters Hamilton summed up his conception of the impropriety of Jefferson's relation to the policy of Freneau's *National Gazette* thus: [1]

> That he is the *instigator* and *patron* of a certain Gazette published in this city, the object and tendency of which are to vilify and depreciate the government of the United States, to misrepresent and traduce the administration of it, except in the single department of which that gentleman is the head; implicating in the most virulent censure the majorities of both houses of Congress, the heads both of the treasury and war departments, and sparing not even the Chief Magistrate himself; that in the support of this paper, thus hostile to the government, in the administration of which he holds so important a trust, he has not scrupled to apply the money of that very government; departing by this conduct from the rules of official propriety and obligation, and from the duty of a discreet and patriotic citizen.

This controversy between two members of his cabinet became so bitter that Washington was led to intervene. He had previously suggested, when angered by Freneau's attacks, that Jefferson should discharge Freneau as translating clerk, but this Jefferson refused to do. In reply to a letter from Washington calling attention to the charge that Jefferson was responsible for the attitude of the *National Gazette*, Jefferson denied absolutely any connection with Freneau's paper, except that he had furnished the editor with copies of the *Leyden Gazette* as a reliable source of foreign news. He wrote: [2]

> But as to any other direction or indication of my wish how his press should be conducted, what sort of intelligence he should give, what essays encourage, I can protest, in the presence of heaven,

---

[1] *Gazette of the United States*, September 15, 1792.
[2] *Writings of Thomas Jefferson*, P. L. Ford, ed., vol. VI, pp. 106 and 108.

that I never did myself, or by any other, directly or indirectly, say a syllable, nor attempt any kind of influence. I can further protest, in the same awful presence, that I never did by myself or any other, directly or indirectly, write, dictate or procure any one sentence or sentiment to be inserted *in his, or any other gazette,* to which my name was not affixed or that of my office.

In the same letter, Jefferson continued:

He [Freneau] & Fenno are rivals for the public favor. The one courts them by flattery, the other by censure, & I believe it will be admitted that one has been as servile, as the other severe. . . .

No government ought to be without censors: & where the press is free, no one ever will.

That Jefferson sincerely believed that Freneau's paper was performing a great patriotic service is evidenced by these comments on it written in May, 1793, after it had been in existence for a year and a half:[1]

His paper has saved our constitution which was galloping fast into monarchy, & has been checked by no one means so powerfully as by that paper. It is well & universally known that it has been that paper which has checked the career of the Monocrats, & the President, not sensible of the designs of the party, has not with his usual good sense, and sang froid, looked on the efforts and effects of this free press, & seen that tho' some bad things had passed thro' it to the public, yet the good have preponderated immensely.

In this belief Jefferson sought to secure new subscribers for the paper and to persuade old ones to pay up their subscriptions, and expressed his satisfaction when its circulation extended to New England and to other parts of the country.[2]

At the end of the second year, on October 26, 1793, the *National Gazette* ceased publication, doubtless, as Jefferson wrote, for "want of money."[3] When Jefferson resigned the secretaryship of state, Freneau gave up his clerkship. Notwithstanding its lack of financial success, the paper had claimed a circulation of 1500 copies, distributed in every state of the Union. The amount of its advertising, however, was very small, averaging scarcely more than a column out of the sixteen that each issue contained.

Another paper that exemplified the new tendency of having a

[1] *Writings of Thomas Jefferson*, P. L. Ford, ed., vol. I, p. 231.
[2] *Ibid.*, vol. VI, p. 134.   [3] *Ibid.*, vol. VI, pp. 438 and 443.

writing editor in charge rather than a practical printer, was the
daily *American Minerva*, edited by Noah Webster, who is now
best known as the compiler of a dictionary.   Published by George
Bunce & Co., New York, it began on December 9, 1793.   A
graduate of Yale, Webster taught school, was admitted to the bar
in his native city, Hartford, Connecticut, returned to school
teaching, and issued a textbook that was a speller, grammar, and
reader combined.   His journalistic activities included letters
written to the *Connecticut Courant*, one of the leading papers in the
country, and a pamphlet urging a strong central government to
take the place of the Articles of Confederation.   Webster always
claimed that this pamphlet, entitled *Sketch of American Policy*,
had helped to shape the form of government provided by the
Constitution.   To protect his textbook, he urged upon state
legislatures and upon Congress the adoption of copyright laws,
and was instrumental in securing such legislation by Congress in
1790.   Through these various activities he had become favorably
known to political leaders, and was encouraged by Hamilton,
Rufus King, and leading Federalists of New York to establish a
daily paper.   The plotting of Citizen Genêt made desirable the
publication of a strong Federalist daily in New York in order to
combat the French influence.   The Republicans had aroused considerable hostility against the Administration by their attacks on
Washington's declaration of neutrality and on his demand for
Genêt's recall.

In the first issue of the *Minerva*, Webster pointed out that "in
no Country on earth, not even in Great-Britain, are Newspapers
so generally circulated among the body of the people, as in
America"; that "from their cheapness, and the frequency and
rapidity of their circulation" they "may, in America, assume an
eminent rank in the catalogue of useful publications"; that "they,
in a great degree, supersede the use of Magazines and Pamphlets";
and that, in view of their importance in republican governments,
"like schools, they should be considered the auxiliaries of government, and placed on a respectable footing; they should be heralds
of truth; the protectors of peace and good order."   As his policy
for the *Minerva*, he announced that "the Editor will endeavor to
preserve this Paper *chaste* and *impartial*"; that "Personalities, if
possible, will be avoided"; that "Confidence, when secrecy is

The AMERICAN MINERVA,

Patroness of Peace, Commerce, and the Liberal Arts.

Published (Daily) by GEORGE BUNCE, & Co. No. 37, Wall-street, nearly opposite the Tontine Coffee-house, at Six Dollars per annum.

VOL. I.]　　　　NEW YORK, Monday, December 9, 1793.　　　　[NUMB. 1.

New-York, Dec. 2d. 1793.

PROPOSALS,

FOR PUBLISHING IN THIS CITY, A DAILY PAPER, UNDER THE TITLE OF

THE AMERICAN MINERVA,

Patroness of Peace, Commerce, and the Liberal Arts.

I. THIS Paper will be published every day, Sundays excepted, at 4 o'clock in the afternoon, or earlier if the arrival of the mails will permit, and delivered to Subscribers in the city at Six Dollars a year payable quarterly. This Paper will contain the earliest intelligence, collected from the most authentic Sources; and will be open to Advertisements and all valuable Essays. This Paper will be of a large size. The first number will appear on Monday the 9th instant.

II. One day in each week, the Paper will be calculated for country readers; containing a summary of the Intelligence of the preceding week, with such Advertisements as require a general circulation in the state; together with such valuable Essays on Civil Policy, Agriculture and the Arts, as shall be best calculated to diffuse useful knowledge. This paper for the country will be published on Wednesday evening, and sent to Subscribers by the most speedy conveyances, at Fourteen Shillings a year. Whenever the Advertisements in the Wednesdays Paper shall fill more than two pages, a supplement will be furnished without any additional expense to the subscribers.

III. The Editor will endeavor to preserve this Paper chaste and impartial. Confidence, when necessary or proper, will never be violated. Personalities, if possible, will be avoided; and should it ever be deemed proper to insert any remarks of a personal nature, it will be held an indispensable condition, that the name of the writer be previously left with the Editor.

IV. This Paper will be the Friend of Government, of Freedom, of Virtue, and every species of Improvement. In justice to their own views, the Publishers cannot say less; and they presume more will not be necessary to ensure the patronage of an enlightened and liberal Public.

N. WEBSTER, jun. Editor.
GEORGE BUNCE, & Co. Publishers.

☞ THIS PAPER will be enlarged and improved in proportion to the encouragement it receives.

THE EDITOR's ADDRESS TO THE PUBLIC.

IT is the singular felicity of the Americans, and a circumstance that distinguishes this Country from all others, that the means of information are accessible to all descriptions of people. Most of the Citizens of America are not only acquainted with letters and able to read their native language; but they have a strong inclination to acquire, and property to purchase, the means of knowledge.

Of all these means of knowledge, Newspapers are the most eagerly sought after, and the most generally diffused. In no Country on earth, not even in Great-Britain, are Newspapers so generally circulated among the body of the people, as in America. To this facility of spreading knowledge over our Country, may, in a great degree, be distributed, that civility of manners, that love of peace and good order, and that propriety of public conduct, which characterize the substantial body of Citizens in the United States.

Newspapers, from their cheapness, and the frequency and rapidity of their circulation, may, in America, assume an eminent rank in the catalogue of useful publications. They, in a great degree, supersede the use of Magazines and Pamphlets. The public mind in America, roused by the magnitude of political events, and impatient of delay, cannot wait for monthly intelligence. Daily or at farthest weekly communications are found necessary to gratify public curiosity. But Newspapers are not only the vehicles of what is called news; they are the common instruments of social intercourse, by which the Citizens of this vast Republic constantly discourse and debate with each other on subjects of public concern. It is by means of these, that in times of danger, either from open hostility or insidious intrigue, an alarm is instantly conveyed, and a unanimity of opinion is formed, from Maine to Georgia.

Montesquieu has declared virtue to be the principle of Republican governments. If by virtue he meant a disinterested love of one's Country, it may be doubted whether such a principle ever existed. If by virtue is meant an ardent public enthusiasm, this is a passion that has existed for a month, perhaps for a year or two; but it is a transient thing; the blaze of a meteor that flames for a moment and vanishes; it is not, and from the nature of man it cannot be, a steady permanent principle. But fixed permanent principles only will maintain government of any kind.

Besides, is it true that Republicans love their Country more than the subjects of arbitrary government? That they ought to do so is certain; but if Republicans fight pro focis, do not the subjects of power contend pro aris? If individuals under despotic governments have fewer rights and less property to attach them to their Country, do not their prejudices, their customs, their religion, create as strong attachments to their Country, as the liberty and the rights of free Citizens do to theirs. Will not a Turk, or a Spaniard fight arbravely for his Koran or his Crucifix, as any Republican for his property? Let History; let facts decide.

The foundation of all free governments, seems to be, a general diffusion of knowledge. People must know they have rights, before they will claim them; and they must have just ideas of their own rights, and learn to distinguish them from the rights of others, before they can form any rational system of government, or be capable of maintaining it. To know that we have rights, is very easy; to know how to preserve those rights, to adjust contending claims, and to prescribe the limits of each; here lies the difficulty. To form and to give duration to a system of government that shall ensure to every man his civil and political rights, and restrain every man from violating the rights of others, is a task of infinite magnitude. Indeed it is probably beyond the powers of man to devise a system for this purpose that can be perpetual; a system that will not in time crumble to pieces by its own imperfections, or be overthrown by the corruption and vices of men. The only anchor of hope left us by history and experience, is, that 'free governments may be rendered durable, perhaps perpetual, by the knowledge, the wisdom and the good sense of the mass of people who are to be governed.' It is the demonstration of ages that many provisions, checks and restraints in a constitution prove useful and necessary to control contending interests; but it is probably a serious truth, that if people are generally ignorant, the best constitution of government the wisdom of man can devise, will become corrupt. Charters of rights, constitutional articles, fundamental regulations may be essential to organize and direct the complex movements of a nation or state; but they are not the ultimate security of the rights of men. Power may assail or corruption may undermine with success the best parchment barriers of liberty; but when a constitution rests on the good sense of a well-informed people, the breach will always be repaired. Whole nations are never corrupt; let the body of people are often ignorant; every department of the best form of government may become vicious; but perhaps no nation as such was ever so corrupt and vicious, that an appeal to the citizens would not restore government to its purity. It is always the interest of a nation to be well governed; and men will never submit to a vicious government but thro ignorance or fear. A good portion of knowledge among the citizens of a free republic, is therefore the ultimate resort for a correction of the evils incident to the best systems of government. It is an important fact in the United States that the best informed people are the least subject to faction, intrigue and a corrupt administration. The utility of News-Papers is therefore most clearly asserted in Republican Governments; like schools, it should be a main point to encourage them; as the auxiliaries of government, and placed on a respectable footing; they should be the heralds of truth; the protectors of peace and good order.

But Newspapers may be rendered useful in other respects. In America, agriculture and the arts are yet in their infancy. Other nations have gone before us in a great variety of improvements. They have, by observations and experiments, discovered many useful truths of which the people of this country are yet ignorant; or which are not generally known and applied to practice. The compiler of a paper, who will take the trouble to select from authors, those facts and principles in the arts which are found in other countries to abridge labor and render industry more productive, will perform a most essential service to his country. A useful fact, a truth, which cost some ingenious inquirer the labor of ten year's experiment, may be contained in a single column of a Gazette, and diffused among millions of people. Some exertions to collect such useful truths for this paper will be made by the Editor, and he hopes, with success.

The First Page of the First Number of Noah Webster's *American Minerva*, New York, 1793

Size of page, 9 in. by 15 in.

necessary or proper, will never be violated"; and that "This Paper will be the Friend of Government, of Freedom, of Virtue, and every species of Improvement." [1]

Webster wrote for his paper letters under various names, and a series of essays entitled "The Times"; he also edited news matter from other newspapers, foreign and domestic. In defense of Jay's Treaty with England in 1795, which had called out bitter denunciation of the Administration from the Republicans, Webster prepared a series of twelve letters for the *Minerva* signed "Curtius"; and Hamilton and Rufus King, under the name of "Camillus," wrote a similar defense in thirty-eight letters, the last thirteen of which came out in the *Minerva*. Rufus King in a letter to Jay declared that "the essays of Curtius [Webster] had contributed more than any other papers of the same kind to allay the discontent and opposition to the treaty," because they were adapted to the average reader.[2] Jefferson also bore witness to the effectiveness of these letters in the *Minerva*, all of which he attributed to Hamilton, for he wrote to Madison on September 21, 1795: [3]

> I gave a copy or two, by way of experiment, to honest, sound-hearted men of common understanding, and they were not able to parry the sophistry of Curtius. I have ceased therefore, to give them. Hamilton is really a colossus of the anti-republican party. Without numbers, he is an host within himself. They have got themselves into a defile, where they might be finished; but too much security on the republican part will give time to his talents & indefatigableness to extricate them. We have had only middling performances to oppose him. In truth, when he comes forward, there is nobody but yourself who can meet him. His adversaries having begun the attack, he has the advantage of answering them, & remains unanswered himself. . . . For god's sake take up your pen, and give a fundamental reply to Curtius & Camillus.

The *Minerva* continued under Webster's editorship until October 2, 1797, when it was decided to change the name to the *Commercial Advertiser* and to enlarge the size of the pages. Under the latter name it went on for over a century, until in 1905 it was merged with the *New York Globe* as the *Globe and Commercial*

---

[1] *Minerva*, December 9, 1793.   [2] Scudder, H. E.   *Noah Webster*, p. 138.
[3] *Writings of Thomas Jefferson*, P. L. Ford, ed., vol. VII, p. 32.

Advertiser. The *Globe and Commercial Advertiser* continued until 1923, when it was purchased by Frank A. Munsey and combined with the New York *Sun.*

Webster introduced an important innovation in newspaper publishing when in 1794 he issued the *Herald*, a semi-weekly paper for country-wide circulation, made up from material already set in type and printed in the daily *Minerva.* This economical device was used during the greater part of the nineteenth century by practically all daily papers for their weekly editions.

The bitterness of political party journalism during the last decade of the eighteenth century reached its climax in Philadelphia, the seat of the Federal government, when Benjamin Franklin Bache's *Aurora* was pitted against William Cobbett's *Porcupine's Gazette.* After Freneau's *National Gazette* ceased publication, the *Aurora* became the leading exponent of Republicanism in Philadelphia. Bache, who had been educated in France while residing there with his grandfather, Benjamin Franklin, and who had later studied at the University of Pennsylvania, set up the *General Advertiser* in 1790, and in 1794 prefixed the word *"Aurora"* to the title. Although always sympathetic with France, he pursued a moderate policy toward the Federalists during the first years of the paper. Bache, according to a statement made by Temple Franklin in 1793, said that he had espoused the Republican cause because "he could not maintain his family," and that "he had determined to adopt a bold experiment and come out openly against the Administration," because "he thought the public temper would bear it." [1] As partisan bitterness increased after Washington's proclamation of neutrality, Citizen Genêt's activities and final recall, and Jay's Treaty with Great Britain, Bache published the most violent abuse of his Federalist opponents. Noah Webster, editor of the Federalist *Minerva* in New York, was called by Bache the "jackall of the British faction," and was characterized in the *Aurora* thus: [2]

> If ever there was a devoted tool to a faction, the editor of the New York Minerva, may be safely said to be one. If ever a man prostituted the little sense that he had, to serve the purposes of a monarchic and aristocratic junto, Noah Webster, Esq. must be the man.

[1] Beveridge, A. J. *Life of John Marshall*, vol. II, p. 165.
[2] *Aurora*, December 2, 1796.

Fenno's *Gazette* was described by a correspondent in *Aurora* as the "sink of prostitution, the British hireling Grub-Street gazette." [1]

The culmination of Bache's virulence is to be found in his two attacks on Washington when the latter was about to retire from the presidency. Three months after Washington's Farewell Address was published in *Claypoole's American Daily Advertiser*, Bache printed the following attack on Washington as "From a Correspondent": [2]

> It has been a serious misfortune of our country, that the President of the United States has been substituted for a Providence, and that the gifts of Heaven have been ascribed to his agency. The flattery, nay the adoration that has been heaped upon him, has made him forget that he is a mortal, and he has been persuaded to believe, and his actions squint that way, that like Alexander he is an immediate offspring of the Gods. . . . If ever a nation was debauched by a man, the American nation has been debauched by Washington. If ever a nation has suffered from the improper influence of a man, the American nation has suffered from the influence of Washington. If ever a nation was deceived by a man, the American nation has been deceived by Washington. Let his conduct then be an example to future ages. Let it serve to be a warning that no man may be an idol and that a people may confide in themselves rather than in an individual. — Let the history of the federal government instruct mankind, that the masque of patriotism may be worn to conceal the foulest designs against the liberties of the people.

Again, as Washington relinquished office when Adams was inaugurated on March 4, 1797, Bache's malignity found vent in another attack "From a Correspondent," as follows: [3]

> "Lord now lettest thou thy servant depart in peace, for mine eyes have seen my salvation," was the pious ejaculation of a man who beheld a flood of happiness rushing in upon mankind. — If ever there was a time that would license the reiteration of the exclamation, that time is now arrived; for the man, who is the source of all the misfortunes of our country, is this day reduced to a level with his fellow-citizens, and is no longer possessed of power to multiply evils upon the United States. — If ever there was a period of rejoicing this is the moment — every heart, in unison

[1] *Aurora*, January 16, 1795.   [2] *Ibid.*, December 23, 1796.
[3] *Ibid.*, March 6, 1797.

with the freedom and happiness of the people ought to beat high
with exultation, that the name of WASHINGTON from this day
ceases to give currency to political iniquity, and to legalize corruption. . . . When a retrospect is taken of the WASHINGTONIAN
administration for eight years, it is a subject of the greatest aston-
ishment that a single individual should have cankered the principles of republicanism in an enlightened people, just emerged from
the gulph of despotism, and should have carried his designs against
the public liberty so far, as to have put in jeopardy its very existence. — Such however are the facts, and with these staring us
in the face, this day ought to be a JUBILEE in the United States.

Bache also printed a series of letters purporting to be by Washington, which had been forged twenty years before in an effort to
prove that the latter had betrayed American soldiers to their
death at the hands of the British — an accusation that Washington felt called upon to deny, on the day that he left office, in a
letter which he requested should be deposited in the office of the
Department of State for the information of posterity.[1]   Undaunted by this denial, Bache published another accusation, to
the effect that Washington in 1754 had ordered soldiers to fire on
a party carrying a flag of truce and had thus been responsible for
the death of an officer.[2]

In his editorial work after 1797 Bache was assisted by William
Duane, who, following Bache's death in 1798, took charge of the
paper and continued to make it as rabidly partisan as it had been
under its founder.   Bache, according to Duane, "actually sunk
fourteen thousand seven hundred dollars of his private fortune in
supporting his paper" in the seven years that he published it.[3]

To uphold Federalism, and to champion the cause of Great
Britain against that of France, William Cobbett, an Englishman,
who came to America in 1792, entered the lists of partisan journalism.   Beginning as a pamphleteer, he later established *Porcupine's Gazette and United States Advertiser*, which first appeared in
Philadelphia on March 4, 1797.   Because of his fighting qualities,
displayed in pamphleteering, he had been likened to a porcupine,
and had thereupon adopted the pen name of "Peter Porcupine."
Other American newspapers, he declared, had done this country

---

[1] *Gazette of the United States*, March 10, 1797.
[2] *Aurora*, March 12, 1797.   [3] *Ibid.*, April 23, 1800.

"more real injury than all its open enemies ever did or can do" because "they misleed the people at home and misrepresent them abroad." Accordingly, he thus set forth his policy toward them in a prospectus published in other papers a month before he began his *Gazette*:[1]

> The only method of opposition then is to meet them on their own ground; to set foot to foot; dispute every hair's breadth; fight them at their own weapons, and return two blows for one.

With equal frankness, he disclaimed in his first issue any attempt at impartiality and thus announced his intention of supporting the Federal government:[2]

> Professions of *impartiality* I shall make none. They are always useless, and are besides perfect nonsense, when used by a news-monger: for, he that does not relate news as he finds it, is something worse than partial; and as to other articles that help to compose a paper, he that does not exercise his own judgment, either in admitting or rejecting what is sent him, is a poor passive tool, and not an editor. For my part, I feel the strongest partiality for the cause of order and good government, such as we live under, and against every thing that is opposed to it. To profess impartiality here, would be as absurd as to profess it in a war between Virtue and Vice, Good and Evil, Happiness and Misery. There may be editors who look on such a conflict with perfect indifference, and whose only anxiety is to discover which is the strongest side. I am not of these, nor shall a paper under my direction, ever be an instrument of destruction to the cause I espouse.
>
> I wish my paper to be a rallying point for the friends of government.

In his efforts to "return two blows for one," Cobbett was more than a match for Bache and Duane, whom he charged with being in the pay of France.[3] In his first issue he promptly characterized the *Aurora* as a "vehicle of lies and sedition," and he proceeded to fight it and the other Republican organs and pamphlets tooth and nail.[4] So violent was he in his vituperation and abuse of France that, even though he defended Washington against tra-

---

[1] *Aurora*, March 1, 1797.

[2] *Porcupine's Gazette and United States Advertiser*, March 4, 1797; reprinted in William Cobbett's *Porcupine's Works*, vol. v, pp. 3–7.

[3] *Porcupine's Gazette and United States Advertiser*, March 9, 1797.

[4] *Ibid.*, March 4, 1797.

ducers and supported the Federalists, Webster felt called upon to reprove him in the *Minerva*,[1] and President Adams considered deporting him under the Alien Act. Benjamin Russell, the ardent Federalist editor of the *Columbian Centinel*, took Cobbett to task for attacking President Adams and denounced him unsparingly. He wrote:[2]

> COBBETT was never encouraged and supported by the Federalists as a solid, judicious writer in their cause; but was kept merely to hunt Jacobinic *foxes, skunks,* and *serpents.* The Federalists found the Jacobins had the *Aurora, Argus* and *Chronicle*, through which they ejected their mud, filth and venom, and attacked and blackened the best characters the world ever boasted; — and they perceived that these vermin were not to be operated on by reason or decency. It was therefore tho't *necessary* that the opposite party should keep, and *feed a suitable beast* to hunt down these *skunks* and *foxes;* and "*the fretful Porcupine*" was selected for this business. . . .

Within six weeks after its appearance, *Porcupine's Gazette* claimed a circulation of 2000, and explained that "these subscribers have been obtained without any of those quack-like mendicant arts, that but too often disgrace undertakings of this kind."[3] His paper, nevertheless, was not financially profitable to Cobbett; he wrote in his farewell address to subscribers, "My Gazette, Gentlemen, instead of being a mine of gold to me, as it has generally been supposed, has never yielded me a farthing of clear profit, and, therefore, in laying it down, I lose nothing but a troublesome and weighty burthen."[4]

Cobbett abandoned his *Gazette* in its third year, after a judgment of $5000 had been secured against him for libel. He returned to England, and in 1802 began the publication in London of *Cobbett's Weekly Political Register*, which he continued to edit for over thirty years. Despite his brief career in this country, Cobbett's strong personality and vigorous controversial style were among the factors most potent in strengthening the bitterness of American partisan journalism.

[1] *Minerva*, March 21, 1797; reprinted with Cobbett's reply in William Cobbett's *Porcupine's Works*, vol. V, pp. 143–69.

[2] *Columbian Centinel*, April 10, 1799.

[3] *Porcupine's Gazette and United States Advertiser*, April 22, 1797.

[4] Cobbett, William. *Porcupine's Works*, vol. XI, p. 138.

In an effort to curb the abusive Republican organs and to rid the country of alien propagandists, the Federalist majority in Congress in 1798 passed the Alien and Sedition Acts. The Alien Act provided that the President might order the deportation of all such aliens "as he shall judge dangerous to the peace and safety of the United States, or shall have reasonable grounds to suspect are concerned in any treasonable or secret machinations against the government"; and that, if they failed to go, they were to be imprisoned. While the Alien Act could be used against Republican newspaper writers of foreign birth, the Sedition Act was aimed both at them and at the native American editors and writers who attacked the Government. Its second section read:

That if any person shall write, print, utter or publish, or shall cause or procure to be written, printed, uttered or published, or shall knowingly and willingly assist or aid in writing, printing, uttering or publishing any false, scandalous and malicious writing or writings against the government of the United States, of either house of Congress of the United States, or the President of the United States, with intent to defame the said government, or either house of the said Congress, or the said President, or to bring them, or either or any of them, into contempt or disrepute; or to excite against them, or either or any of them, the hatred of the good people of the United States, or to stir up sedition within the United States, or to excite any unlawful combinations therein, for opposing or resisting any law of the United States, or any act of the President of the United States, done in pursuance of any such law, or of the powers in him vested by the constitution of the United States, or to resist, oppose, or defeat any such law or act, or to aid, encourage or abet any hostile designs of any foreign nation against the United States, their people or government, then such person, being thereof convicted before any court of the United States having jurisdiction thereof, shall be punished by a fine not exceeding two thousand dollars, or by imprisonment not exceeding two years.

Two other significant clauses of this act provided that "the truth of the matter contained in the publication charged as libel" might be introduced as evidence in defense of it, and that "the jury who shall try the cause, shall have the right to determine the law and the fact, under direction of the court as in other cases." These were the two points that Zenger's lawyer had sought to maintain in 1735, and that had been established in England by the Fox Libel Act of 1792. Both laws were to continue in force for three years only, and, despite attempts to reënact them before their expiration, they went out of existence on March 3, 1801, the day before Jefferson became President.

Some of the leading Federalists, like John Marshall, saw the danger in these drastic measures, and even President Adams, who had been most bitterly attacked by the Republicans, did not take an active part in the advocacy of the bills or in their enforcement after he had signed them. With apparent impartiality, he suggested the application of the Alien Law alike to the virulent Republican editor, Duane, and to the equally vituperative Federalist editor, Cobbett.[1] Secretary of State Pickering desired to apply it to John D. Burk, an editor of the tri-weekly Republican *Time-Piece* of New York.[2] But there were no actual prosecutions of Republican editors under the Alien Act during the three years that it was in force.

In applying the Sedition Law, which was especially designed to curb attacks on the Administration by Republican editors, Secretary of State Pickering took an active part by reading newspapers carefully and by calling the attention of district attorneys in the several states to the alleged seditious material that he found in them. From incomplete records now available, it appears that about twenty-four or twenty-five persons, not all editors, were arrested; that at least fifteen of these were indicted; but that only ten or eleven of these cases ever came to trial.[3] Of the ten persons who were found guilty, three were not at the time newspaper editors. Three of the four leading Republican newspapers were attacked directly or indirectly through the Sedition Law: *Aurora; Argus, Greenleaf's New Daily Advertiser*, of New York; and the *Richmond Examiner*. Action against the fourth — the *Independent Chronicle*, of Boston — was brought under the English common law of seditious libel. At least four other less prominent Republican editors were indicted: Burk of the *Time-Piece;* Anthony Haswell of the *Vermont Gazette;* William Durrell of the

[1] Adams, Charles F. *Works of John Adams*, vol. IX, p. 5.

[2] Anderson, Frank M. "Enforcement of the Alien and Sedition Laws," in the *American Historical Association Annual Report for 1912*, p. 114.

[3] Anderson, Frank M. "The Enforcement of the Alien and Sedition Laws," in the *Annual Report of the American Historical Association for 1912*, p. 120.

Mount Pleasant, New York, *Register;* and Charles Holt of the New London, Connecticut, *Bee.* The two most prominent Republican leaders who were tried and convicted — Dr. Thomas Cooper and Matthew Lyon — were not primarily journalists, although Dr. Cooper was editor of the *Sunbury and Northumberland Gazette* in Pennsylvania. James Thompson Callender of the *Richmond Examiner* was the only outstanding Republican editor convicted, but the case against him was based on a pamphlet and not on anything that he had printed in his paper. Several cases were pending against Duane of the *Aurora* when Jefferson became President and put an end to the prosecutions.

In the case of the *Argus, Greenleaf's New Daily Advertiser*, Alexander Hamilton was responsible for the action, which was brought against David Frothingham, a printer employed by Mrs. Greenleaf, the proprietor. He was tried and convicted for the publication in that paper of an article that had appeared in several papers, charging Hamilton with trying to buy *Aurora* from Mrs. Bache in order "to suppress" it, and hinting that funds for the proposed purchase might be supplied by the British minister to this country from "British secret service money."[1] Hamilton, in a letter to the attorney-general of New York asking that action be taken against the paper, characterized the charge thus:[2]

> A bolder calumny; one more absolutely destitute of foundation was never propagated. And its dangerous tendency needs no comment; being calculated to inspire the belief, that the Independence and Liberty of the press are endangered by the intrigues of ambitious citizens, aided by Foreign Gold.
>
> In so flagrant a case, the force of the laws must be tried. I therefore request that you will take immediate measures towards the prosecution of the persons who conduct the enclosed paper.

Duane, commenting on the matter in the *Aurora*, asserted that unsuccessful efforts had been made to buy that paper, and that, although there was no "positive evidence" to connect Hamilton with these attempts, "yet there is the strongest reason to believe that he did take an active part in certain transactions calculated to destroy this paper."[3]

In at least three cases Republican editors were arrested at this

[1] *Argus, Greenleaf's New Daily Advertiser*, November 6, 1799.
[2] *Ibid.*, November 9, 1799.   [3] *Aurora*, November 11, 1799.

time, not under the Sedition Law, but under the English common law of seditious libel, which was then held to apply in this country and to be within the jurisdiction of the Federal courts. Bache of the *Aurora* was arrested under the common law, just before the Sedition Act went into effect, for "sundry publications and republications" of alleged libels upon the executive department of the United States, but his death put an end to the case. Abijah Adams, a bookkeeper in the employ of his brother, Thomas Adams, editor of the Boston *Independent Chronicle*, was convicted under the "common law of England" after the Sedition Law was in force. Both Thomas and Abijah Adams had been indicted, but, because of the serious illness of the former, only the latter was tried. The offense of the *Independent Chronicle* consisted in charging the majority of both Houses of the Massachusetts General Assembly with "wilful perjury, because that in their constitutional oath they had sworn that Massachusetts is a free, sovereign and independent state, and of right ought to be, &c, and yet that in their vote to reject" the resolutions of the Virginia legislature against the Alien and Sedition Laws, "they had disclaimed the right to decide the constitutionality of any law of Congress." [1] John D. Burk, of the New York *Time-Piece*, was arrested for seditious libel a few days before the Sedition Act went into effect. [2] Since he was an Irishman and might have been deported under the Alien Act, as Pickering had suggested to the federal district attorney in New York, he went into hiding until Jefferson became President.

None of the prosecutions served to silence the Republican editors in their attacks on the Federalists, or on President Adams, "His Rotundity, the Duke of Braintree," as they called him because his home was at Braintree, Massachusetts. On the other hand, the Alien and Sedition Laws helped to create the sentiment against the Federalists that led to their defeat and to the triumph of the Republicans in the election of Jefferson.

Early in 1800, the United States Senate sought to punish Duane of the *Aurora* for the publication of reports of "their proceedings, which are false, defamatory, scandalous, and malicious, tending to defame the Senate of the United States, and to bring them into

[1] *Independent Chronicle*, April 8–11, 1799.
[2] Cf. *Time-Piece*, July 9, 1798.

contempt and disrepute, and to excite against them the hatred of the good people of the United States," because "the said publication is a daring and high-handed breach of the privilege of this house." Duane was summoned before the bar of the Senate "to make a proper defense of his conduct." After he had appeared once and had asked permission to secure counsel, he refused to attend a second time and sent instead a letter written to him by Dr. Thomas Cooper, a prominent Republican, whom he had requested to serve as his counsel, denouncing the Senate for its action against Duane. The Senate thereupon voted to take Duane into custody for contempt, but he went into hiding to escape arrest, and announced in the *Aurora* that letters left at the office of that paper would reach him in forty-eight hours. This procedure by the Senate was similar to that of the two Houses of the British Parliament previous to 1772 in disciplining newspaper publishers for publishing their proceedings, and, after that date, even till late in the nineteenth century, for alleged misrepresentations or attacks on the honor of the Houses or of their members.

The advisability of undertaking to curb the excesses of partisan journalism by these various repressive measures may well be questioned, but it must be admitted that, during the last decade of the eighteenth century, the character of the American press that called them forth was deplorable. As early as 1782, Benjamin Franklin in France had been so impressed with the abusive tone of the American newspapers that he wrote to Francis Hopkinson, "You do well to avoid being concern'd in the Pieces of Personal Abuse, so scandalously common in our Newspapers, that I am afraid to lend any of them here, until I have examined and laid aside such as would disgrace us." [1] While to some extent newspapers only reflected the bitterness of partisan warfare, they also played an important rôle in increasing that bitterness. Vituperation and abuse were carried to unheard of lengths. The Republican papers, as opposition organs attacking the Administration, seem to have been the worst offenders, but some Federalist editors like Cobbett believed that they must return "two blows for one."

The leaders of both parties deplored the degradation of the press. "The publications in Freneau's and Bache's papers are

[1] *Writings of Benjamin Franklin*, A. H. Smyth, ed., vol. VIII, p. 647.

outrages on common decency," wrote Washington.[1] In 1796 Washington gave as one of his reasons for deciding to retire from public life "a disinclination to be longer buffeted in the public prints by a set of infamous scribblers."[2] Two weeks later he wrote to Jefferson, "nor did I believe until lately, that it was within the bounds of probability, hardly within those of possibility, that . . . the grossest and most insidious misrepresentations of them [the acts of his administration] [could] be made . . . and that too in such exaggerated and indecent terms as could scarcely be applied to a Nero, a notorious defaulter, or even to a common pickpocket."[3] "Is there any thing evil in the regions of actuality or possibility, that the Aurora has not suggested of me?" asked President Adams, writing to Pickering in 1799.[4] In 1801, just after Adams had retired from the presidency, he wrote of the defeat of the Federalists:[5]

> If we had been blessed with common sense, we should not have been overthrown by Philip Freneau, Duane, Callender, Cooper, and Lyon, or their great patron and protector [Jefferson]. A group of foreign liars, encouraged by a few ambitious native gentlemen, have discomfited the education, the talents, the virtues, and the property of the country.

Hamilton characterized Freneau's *National Gazette* as "an incendiary and pernicious publication."[6] Noah Webster wrote in 1800, "I . . . aver that . . . no government can be durable and quiet under the licentiousness of the press that now disgraces our country."[7] "The newspapers are venal, servile, base, and stupid," wrote Fisher Ames, a leading Massachusetts Federalist, in 1799.[8]

Jefferson strongly denounced the Federalist press, and after he had been President for two years, came to believe that prosecu-

[1] Letter to Henry Lee, July 21, 1793; *Writings of Washington*, Worthington C. Ford, ed., vol. XII, p. 310.

[2] Letter to Hamilton, June 26, 1796; *Writings of Washington*, Worthington C. Ford, ed., vol. XIII, p. 220.

[3] *Writings of Washington*, Worthington C. Ford, ed., vol. XIII, pp. 230–31.

[4] Adams, Charles F. *Works of John Adams*, vol. IX, p. 5.

[5] *Ibid.*, vol. IX, p. 582.

[6] Hamilton, Alexander. *Works*, vol. VII, p. 32.

[7] Gibbs, George. *Memoirs of the Administrations of Washington and Adams*, vol. II, p. 374.

[8] Ames, Fisher. *Works*, vol. I, p. 265.

tions of opposition editors were necessary, not under federal laws, but under those of the several states.   In 1803 he wrote to Governor McKean of Pennsylvania:[1]

> The federalists having failed in destroying the freedom of the press by their gag-laws, seem to have attacked it in an opposite form, that is by pushing it's licentiousness & it's lying to such a degree of prostitution as to deprive it of all credit.   And the fact is that so abandoned are the tory presses in this particular that even the least informed of the people have learnt that nothing in a newspaper is to be believed.   This is a dangerous state of things, and the press ought to be restored to it's creditability if possible. The restraints provided by the laws of the states are sufficient for this if applied.   And I have therefore long thought that a few prosecutions of the most prominent offenders would have a wholesome effect in restoring the integrity of the presses.   Not a general prosecution, for that would look like persecution; but a selected one.

Even some of the newspaper editors themselves were no less harsh in their criticism of the journalism of the period.   John Ward Fenno, who had succeeded his father as editor of the *Gazette of the United States*, wrote in 1799:[2]

> The American newspapers are the most base, false, servile and venal publications, that ever polluted the fountains of society — their editors the most ignorant, mercenary, and vulgar automatons that ever were moved by the continually rusting wires of sordid mercantile avarice. . . .
> The newspapers of America are admirably calculated to keep the country in a continued state of insurrection and revolution.

The remedy that he suggested is interesting.   He proposed the establishment of educational and professional standards for editors, "qualifications and pledges from men on whom the nation depends for all the information and much of the instruction that it received."[3]   "To well-regulated colleges we naturally look," he continued, "for a source whence such qualifications in proper form be derived."   But although he was a graduate of the University of Pennsylvania, he saw in colleges as they were then conducted little hope for the betterment of journalism.

Joseph Dennie, editor of the *Farmer's Weekly Museum* of Wal-

[1] *Writings of Thomas Jefferson*, P. L. Ford, ed., vol. VIII, p. 218.
[2] *Gazette of the United States*, March 4, 1799.   [3] *Ibid.*, March 4, 1799.

pole, New Hampshire, whom Duane in the *Aurora* described as "the only Federal editor in the United States worthy of the name of a man of talents," [1] agreed with Fenno in his characterization of American newspapers, and brought other charges against them, as follows: [2]

> Many of our American papers are not so valuable after being blackened and defiled by stupid printers and editors, as when immediately from the paper mill. Our domestic gazettes, when destitute of news, are not like European journals, replete with entertainment and sound instruction. They are generally destitute of wit and originality. Indeed, a gross and slovenly system of plagiarism prevails throughout. One wittol editor copies the nonsense of his simple brother; and false grammar, trivial remark, unimportant news, wire drawn poetry, and drowsy essays, pass from hand to hand, and dulness enjoys a kind of newspaper immortality. There are some respectable exceptions, but the majority of American newspapers fully deserve the severity of Mr. Fenno's reproof. He has described a large class of our Journals with truth, accuracy and acumen. From a most painful experience of four years, the writer of this article can abundantly testify to the plagiarisms, mawkishness, dreariness, and gross folly of many of those weekly things, which profess to convey novelty and amusement to gaping reader. The fact is, there are three or four good papers published, upon which all the rest live.

That this charge of papers' borrowing freely from one another was commonly made is indicated by Duane's statement in the *Aurora*, in 1800, to the effect that "hitherto the American newspapers have been complained of for their sameness, and plagiarism — their filtering folly out of one vapid medium into another." [3]

One significant influence on the journalism of the period was the character of the newspaper writers and editors. The leading Republican editors were English or Irish radicals who had fled from England and who were therefore only too ready to take up the anti-British side. "Very few of the abusive scribblers who slander his [Washington's] reputation have one drop of American blood in their veins," declared Fenno's *Gazette of the United States*.[4] President Adams referred to the Republican editors as

[1] *Aurora*, July 30, 1799.
[2] *Farmer's Museum, or Lay Preacher's Gazette*, April 15, 1799.
[3] *Aurora* (Tri-Weekly), April 7, 1800.
[4] Quoted in Edward Smith's *William Cobbett*, vol. I, p. 178.

"a group of foreign liars." Bache and Duane, though American born, had acquired abroad an anti-British point of view. Bache as a young man had studied in France. Duane had been driven out of India and had had his property confiscated by the English, "for advocating the cause of France and attempting to disseminate the democratic principles of Tom Paine in his paper," as a Calcutta correspondent wrote to a Philadelphia friend in a letter published in the *Aurora*.[1] James T. Callender of the *Richmond Examiner*, convicted under the Sedition Law, was a political refugee from England, whom Jefferson used as a hack-writer, but who turned upon his benefactor and attacked him in the *Richmond Recorder* when Jefferson refused to make him postmaster of Richmond. John D. Burk of the New York *Time-Piece*, who had gone into hiding to escape trial for seditious libel and to avoid possible deportation under the Alien Law, had fled from Ireland because of his activities with the rebellious United Irishmen. Of the Federalist editors, on the other hand, the only alien was William Cobbett, whose political activities in England had led him to come to America, but who took sides with, rather than against, his mother country. Benjamin Russell, Noah Webster, and John Fenno, the other leading Federalist editors, were all American-born of New England stock.

In contrast to these city newspapers, was a country weekly paper, best known as the *Farmer's Weekly Museum*, which attained a nation-wide circulation because of its literary features. It was published at Walpole, New Hampshire, with Joseph Dennie as editor. A graduate of Harvard, Dennie had practiced law for a short time but had abandoned the bar for journalism. After contributing some essays signed "The Lay Preacher" to the *New Hampshire and Vermont Journal, or Farmer's Weekly Museum*, as it was first called, he became its editor in 1795, and continued in that position until 1799. Dennie and a number of voluntary contributors from various parts of New England supplied a variety of general reading matter in prose and verse, under such names as "Peter Pencil," "Simon Spunkey," "Peter Pendulum," "Common Sense *in Dishabille*," and "The Pedlar." One popular department was entitled "From the Shop of Mess. Colon & Spondee," "Wholesale Dealers in Verse, Prose, and Music." These

[1] *Aurora*, June 22, 1795.

various features were later placed together on the fourth page under a page-wide cut of a basket, "emblematical of wine, fruit and flowers," with the heading, "The Dessert." The first page was devoted to "politics, biography, economicks, morals, and daily detail." Besides the wit and humor in prose and verse served up on the last page as "The Dessert," there were on the third page bright remarks on the news, under headings, "Incidents Abroad" and "Incidents at Home," as well as clever comments entitled "To Readers and Correspondents." Contrary to the practice of other newspapers, little was reprinted from American papers, but British publications were not infrequently drawn upon for poetry and prose. At the height of its popularity, late in 1797, the *Farmer's Weekly Museum* had a circulation of 2000 copies, which went to practically every state in the Union. Essays by "The Lay Preacher" on religious, moral, literary, and occasionally political topics, ninety of which appeared in the *Museum*, were widely reprinted in other newspapers. In 1796 forty essays were collected in a small volume, entitled *The Lay Preacher*. Some of these essays and various other selections from the paper, were also reprinted in book form in 1801 under the title, *The Spirit of the Farmer's Museum and Lay Preacher's Gazette*. The low subscription price of the *Museum*, at first a dollar a year and later a dollar and a half, together with the very limited amount of advertising available in so small a place as Walpole, made its financial condition so uncertain that Dennie was led to give up the editorship of the *Museum* and to accept a secretaryship in the Department of State at Philadelphia. There he wrote for Fenno's *Gazette of the United States*, and in 1807 started the *Port Folio*, a literary journal. Although an ardent Federalist, Dennie was offered the editorship of the Republican *Independent Chronicle* of Boston, just before he left Walpole, but he declared that, "if he had allowed me 12 million of dollars annually, I must have refused the offer. . . . It would have belied my feelings, my habits, my principles, my conscience." [1] With its variety of literary features and its wit and humor, the *Farmer's Weekly Museum* was unique as a popular, widely read, and widely quoted paper that did not descend to the prevailing bitterness of partisan journalism.

[1] Ellis, Harold M. *Joseph Dennie & His Circle*, p. 108.

CHAPTER V

THE POLITICAL PARTY PRESS, 1800–1833

THE latter part of the year 1800 was marked by two events of importance to journalism: the removal of the seat of government to Washington, and the defeat of the Federalists in the national election. Washington thus became the headquarters of the Administration organs. The ascendancy of the Republicans — or Democrats, as they came to be called — with Jefferson as President, involved a complete change in the political complexion of the Administration. The Federalist papers, which had been supporters of the Administration, became organs of the opposition, whereas the Democratic publications ceased to be opposition papers and became Administration organs.

For two years previous to 1800 Washington had been without a newspaper, two papers established in 1795 and in 1796 having failed to find sufficient support to continue. The announcement that Congress would meet in the new Capital on November 17, 1800, led to considerable journalistic activity. The publishers of the *Centinel of Liberty,* a Federalist paper that had been printed for two years at Georgetown, Virginia, near Washington, announced that they would start a daily paper "when Congress removes to the City of Washington." Accordingly, on November 18, the first issue appeared of the *Museum and Washington and Georgetown Advertiser.* Three other papers, however, got into the field ahead of the *Museum.* The *Washington Federalist,* with its offices in Georgetown, came out as a tri-weekly on September 25; the *Cabinet of the United States* began at Georgetown as a Democratic daily about October 1; and Samuel Harrison Smith brought out his tri-weekly *National Intelligencer* in Washington on October 31.[1] Thus, before Congress assembled, Washington had two Federalist and two Democratic papers.

It was on Jefferson's advice that Samuel Harrison Smith, then the twenty-eight-year-old editor of the weekly *Universal Gazette* in Philadelphia, moved his plant to Washington and began the *National Intelligencer* as a tri-weekly, with the *Universal Gazette,*

[1] Bryan, W. G. *History of the National Capital,* vol. 1, pp. 364–70.

transferred from Philadelphia, as its weekly edition.[1] Smith's ability had come to Jefferson's attention when the young editor's essay on a system of national education was awarded a prize by the American Philosophical Society of Philadelphia, of which Jefferson was president and Smith secretary. Jefferson soon established close social and business relations with Smith in Washington, and the *National Intelligencer* developed into the official organ of the Administration. This position it continued to occupy during the administrations of Jefferson, Madison, and Monroe, to the extent that "it was the medium through which the acts of the executive were authentically announced, and in which its advertisements were published." [2]

When Congress assembled, Smith, who wrote shorthand, presented a memorial to the House of Representatives "requesting permission to take the debates and proceedings of the house, from positions within the bar," because that liberty had been denied him by the Speaker.[3] As the House, however, was evenly divided between Federalists and Democrats, permission was refused by a tie vote, the Speaker voting in the negative. A month later the Speaker denied the Democratic editor access both to the lobby and to the gallery, as a result, Smith asserted, of his "fairly stating the unquestioned blunders of the Speaker." But, when the Democrats had a majority in the House at the second session held in Washington, the Speaker was directed to assign places on the floor to reporters and stenographers. Smith, as an expert shorthand reporter, was able to print in the *National Intelligencer* the best reports of the debates and proceedings. In fact, the congressional reports in this paper were for a number of years the only printed records of the proceedings of Congress. Other newspapers throughout the country depended on the *National Intelligencer* for their accounts of congressional speeches and proceedings. When Smith retired in 1810, this work of reporting was continued for nearly half a century by the new owners of the *National Intelligencer*, Joseph Gales, Jr., and William W. Seaton.

The bitterness of political controversy was in no way abated by

---

[1] Smith, Mrs. Samuel Harrison. *First Forty Years in Washington*, p. 9.
[2] *National Intelligencer*, January 1, 1840.
[3] Quoted from *National Intelligencer* by *American Citizen*, April 11, 1801.

the defeat of the Federalists and the triumph of the Democrats. The *Washington Federalist*, in announcing the result of the presidential election in 1800, turned a picture of the American eagle upside down and ran under it the caption, "Pluria e Uno."[1]   On the inauguration of Jefferson, Russell in the *Columbian Centinel* published a long "Monumental Inscription," which began thus:[2]

YESTERDAY EXPIRED

Deeply regretted by MILLIONS of grateful Americans,
And by *all* GOOD MEN

The FEDERAL ADMINISTRATION
Of the
GOVERNMENT of the *UNITED STATES;*

———

Its death was occasioned by the
Secret Arts, and Open Violence;
Of Foreign and Domestic Demagogues.

The Federalist press not only characterized Jefferson as an atheist, but claimed that the ultimate aim of the Democrats was an equal division of all private property among the people.   The Democratic papers, on the other hand, continued to assail Hamilton, Adams, Pickering, Oliver Wolcott, and other former members of the Federal Administration.   They opposed the appropriation of public funds for the erection of a monument to Washington in the new Capital, and pointed out the folly and danger of thus exalting unduly any citizen of a republic, however great had been his services to his country.   Editors also continued to denounce and ridicule their journalistic opponents in most unbridled fashion.   State political contests served to feed the flames of partisanship in the newspapers scarcely less than did national politics.

In New York City, journalistic controversy was stimulated by the accession to the ranks of Democratic editors of James Cheetham, an English radical, who had fled to this country after the Manchester riots in 1798, and who in 1800 became the editor of the *American Citizen*, the successor of the *Argus, Greenleaf's New Daily Advertiser*.   That Cheetham was not lacking in ability to

———

[1] *Washington Federalist*, February 17, 1801.
[2] *Columbian Centinel*, March 4, 1801.

uphold the tradition of journalistic vituperation is shown by his characterization of the Federalist *New-York Gazette and General Advertiser*, of which he wrote, "Destitute of claim to truth, to integrity, and to honour, it is a fit repository of the filth of the fallen faction, whose means are falsehood and misrepresentation, and whose end, the dissolution of our republican system of government, by endeavoring to bring the principle and its advocates into disrepute." [1] Cheetham was the first editor to print editorials in almost every issue of his paper. He continued to edit the *Citizen* for eight years until his death in 1809. Cheetham is another of those Englishmen who left their impress on American journalism by extreme political partisanship.

After the defeat of Federalism in both the national and the New York State elections, Hamilton, John Jay, and other leading New York Federalists felt the need of a strong Federalist daily in New York City to oppose Cheetham. Accordingly, they established the *New-York Evening Post*, the first issue of which appeared on November 16, 1801, nine months after Jefferson's inauguration. This was the fourth Federalist paper to which Hamilton had given financial aid, the others being Fenno's *Gazette of the United States*, Cobbett's *Porcupine's Gazette*, and Webster's *Minerva*. As editor of the new paper, William Coleman was secured. He was a Massachusetts lawyer, who had established and had written for the Greenfield *Impartial Intelligencer*. He had gone to New York in 1798, where two years later he was appointed clerk of the circuit court. With a knowledge of Latin and Greek and a taste for reading acquired at Phillips Andover Academy, and with political experience gained as a presidential campaign speaker and as a member of the Massachusetts legislature, he was better equipped for editorial work than were most of the editors of the period. So well did he accomplish the purpose for which the *Evening Post* was established, that in less than a year he was dubbed by Callender, "Field-Marshal of the Federalist editors." At the same time, opposing editors like Cheetham credited Hamilton with being the moving spirit of the new paper, and called Coleman a "mere hireling," a charge that Coleman vigorously and honestly denied. Nevertheless, in editing the *Post*, he had the advantage of Hamilton's keen mind and extensive knowledge of

[1] *American Citizen*, March 7, 1801.

political and economic affairs.   Describing how Hamilton aided him in his editorial work, he told a contemporary:[1]

> Whenever anything occurs on which I feel the want of information, I state the matter to him, sometimes in a note.   He appoints a time when I may see him, usually a late hour in the evening.   He always keeps himself minutely informed on all political matters.   As soon as I see him, he begins in a deliberate manner to dictate, and I note down in short-hand; when he stops, my article is completed.

That the policy of the *Evening Post* was to be somewhat broader and less partisan than that of most of its contemporaries, was indicated by these excerpts from its prospectus:[2]

> The design of this paper is to diffuse among the people correct information of all interesting subjects; to inculcate just principles in religion, morals, and politics; and to cultivate a taste for sound literature.

> Persuaded that the great body of people of this country only want correct information to enable them to judge of what is really best; and believing that nothing will so directly conduce to this desirable end, as candid and liberal discussion; this paper shall be equally free to all parties.

Although Coleman also aimed to avoid "personal virulence, low sarcasms, and verbal contentions with printers and editors," he soon found it difficult to fight Democratic editors with other than their own weapons.   He was driven to attacking his opponents, as is shown by the well-known lines against two of his strongest rivals:

> Lie on, Duane, lie on for pay,
>   And, Cheetham, lie thou too,
> More 'gainst truth you cannot say,
>   Than truth can say 'gainst you.

On another occasion he used Milton's description of Satan, who "Squat like a toad at the ear of Eve," with the comment, "I beg the devil's pardon for comparing him in any shape with Duane."[3]   In his use of such methods of political warfare,

[1] Clark, Gilbert J.   *Memoir, Autobiography and Correspondence of Jeremiah Mason*, pp. 31–32.
[2] *Evening Post*, November 16, 1801.
[3] Quoted in Allan Nevins's *The Evening Post*, p. 50.

however, he was merely living up to the prevailing traditions of journalism.

With the support of the strong Federalist mercantile interests of New York City, the *Post* was able to secure so large an amount of advertising as to fill four fifths of the paper. But its advertising rates, like those of the other papers of the period, were so low, and the proportion of delinquents among both advertisers and subscribers was so large, that for many years it had the usual financial difficulties.

To reach readers all over the country in the interests of Federalism, a weekly edition, under the name of the *Herald*, was made up from the type that had been used in the daily issues, after the manner of Noah Webster's innovation. Within a short time Coleman's *Herald*, with a subscription price of $3.50 a year, was circulating 1600 copies to the *Evening Post's* 1100.

In its almost complete subordination of news to political discussion in the form of editorials and letters to the editor, the *Evening Post* followed the journalistic practice of the day. The only news that papers could be depended upon to furnish regularly, was the arrival and departure of ships and similar commercial information, together with reports of congressional proceedings and speeches. No systematic scheme existed for gathering news, local, national, or foreign; nor were important events outside the limited field of politics covered with any show of journalistic enterprise. Political editors, like Coleman, were still satisfied to glean fragments of news from foreign papers and from those published in other American cities, as well as from private letters placed at their disposal by merchants and citizens. No attempt was made to appeal to the great bulk of the population by presenting news attractively. Business and professional men constituted a large part of the 1100 subscribers, who either paid $8 a year or received a subscription gratis if they inserted an advertisement for a year. When skilled workers like journeymen printers on newspapers received only from $6 to $8 a week in wages, the average workingman was obviously unable to subscribe for a paper that cost $8 a year. Editors were no doubt glad to have politically minded workingmen and clerks read newspapers in taverns, but they edited their journals for the classes and not for the masses.

Advertising was apparently the most important source of the income of newspapers as early as 1803. This is evident from the following comment made by the editor of the *Post* when, in the latter part of that year, it was proposed to have all the daily papers in New York raise their subscription price from $8 to $10 a year:[1]

> Subscribers alone, allowing them to be quadruple to what was ever known in this city would not support a Newspaper establishment; and, in fact, it is the advertiser who provides the paper for the subscriber. It is not to be disputed, that the publisher of a Newspaper in this country, without a very extensive advertising support, receives a less reward for his labour than the humblest mechanic.

Following the example of English newspapers, American papers did, however, give some reports of "shocking accidents," "horrid murders," suicides, and other crimes, when these stories could be obtained without much effort. This type of news called forth an interesting letter printed in the *New England Palladium* of Boston in 1801.[2] It was from the pen of Fisher Ames, a prominent Federalist, who had represented Massachusetts in the House of Representatives for two terms, who, in 1804, was offered the presidency of Harvard, and who wrote articles for the press not infrequently. Of the tendency of newspapers to print sensational news, he wrote, "Gazettes, it is seriously to be feared, will not long allow room to any thing that is not loathsome or shocking," and "A newspaper is pronounced to be very lean and destitute of matter, if it contains no accounts of murders, suicides, prodigies or monstrous births." His description of the effects of crime news on readers is also interesting. He pointed out that "some eccentric minds are turned to mischief" by it, since "the spirit of imitation is contagious and boys are found unaccountably bent to do as men do." The bad results, he showed, are caused "by dinning burnings and murders in every body's ears, to detain all rash and mischievous tempers on such subjects long enough to wear out the first impression of horror, and to prepare them to act what they so familiarly contemplate." Sensational news, he continued, creates a morbid taste in readers, for "Every horrid story

---

[1] *Evening Post*, December 1, 1803.
[2] *New England Palladium*, October 13, 1801.

in a newspaper produces a shock, but after some time the shock lessens," and "At length, such stories are so far from giving pain that they rather raise curiosity, and we desire nothing so much as the particulars of terrible tragedies." "Strange events are facts," he admitted, "and as such should be mentioned, but with brevity and in a cursory manner"; and "sensible printers and sensible readers will think that way of mentioning them the best that impresses them least on the public attention, and that hurries them on the most swiftly to be forgotten." This was as thoughtful and as accurate an analysis of the influence of sensational news as had hitherto been made.

Jefferson's advocacy of "a few prosecutions [under state laws] of the most prominent offenders" among the Federalist editors, for "a wholesome effect in restoring the integrity of the presses," bore fruit in 1804 in the arrest of Harry Croswell, editor of a Federalist paper at Hudson, New York, for reprinting from the New York *Evening Post* the following attack on Jefferson:[1]

> Holt says the burden of the Federalist Song is that Jefferson paid Callender for calling Washington a traitor, a robber, a perjurer; for calling Adams a hoary-headed incendiary and for most grossly slandering the private characters of men he knew well were virtuous. These charges not a democratic Editor has yet dared or ever will dare to meet in an open and manly discussion.

After Croswell had been tried and convicted, Hamilton argued for a new trial in a speech that is said to have been his greatest and that proved to be his last important one. Although his complete argument is not extant, the notes that he made in preparation for it have been preserved and are interesting as outlining his attitude on the freedom of the press and on the law of libel. Hamilton maintained that "the liberty of the press consists of the right to publish with impunity truth with good motives for justifiable ends though reflecting on government, magistracy and individuals," and that "the allowance of this right is essential to the preservation of free government, the disallowance of it is fatal." He also insisted that "the law and fact being blended, the jury . . . is entrusted with the power of deciding both law and fact," and that "truth, as an important defense, cannot be excluded."[2] Dis-

[1] Hamilton, A. McL. *Life of Alexander Hamilton*, p. 177.
[2] *Ibid.*, p. 181.

regarding Hamilton's plea, the higher court upheld the decision of the trial judge, who maintained the old English doctrine of seditious libel by ruling that the jury could decide only the fact, and that the truth of the alleged libel could not be admitted as a defense. Thus, so far as the State of New York was concerned, the truth was not considered an admissible defense, nor was the jury allowed to decide the law.

A remark in criticism of Burr, made by Hamilton while at Albany attending this trial, proved to be the culmination of the many unfavorable opinions that Hamilton had expressed concerning Burr, and was directly responsible for the duel between these two political rivals. Hamilton's death in the duel deprived his country of a great statesman and American journalism of one of its best writers and most generous patrons.

The great struggle in Europe between England and France, which vitally affected American shipping and finally involved the United States in the War of 1812, fanned the flames of American political partisanship and thus kept at white heat the journalistic controversy between the Democratic supporters of France and the Federalist advocates of Great Britain. Federalist papers representing the commercial and shipping interests of New England and New York were naturally aroused by Napoleon's restrictions on neutral commerce and by Jefferson's failure to protect American ships. Democratic papers attacked with equal force Great Britain's retaliatory restrictions and her disregard of this country's rights on the seas. The virulence of political journalism thus continued unabated.

The excesses of the partisan papers led Jefferson to declare in 1807:[1]

> It is a melancholy truth, that a suppression of the press could not more compleatly deprive the nation of it's benefits, than is done by it's abandoned prostitution to falsehood. Nothing can now be believed which is seen in a newspaper. Truth itself becomes suspicious by being put into that polluted vehicle. The real extent of this state of misinformation is known only to those who are in situations to confront facts within their knolege with the lies of the day.

Thomas Paine, writing in Cheetham's *American Citizen* in 1806,

[1] *Writings of Thomas Jefferson*, P. L. Ford, ed., vol. IX, p. 72.

said that the Federalist papers had lost their influence with the citizens of New York:[1]

> The number of Federalist papers in the city and state of New-York are more than five to one to the number of Republican papers, yet the majority of the elections go always against the Federalist papers; which is demonstrative evidence that the licentiousness of those papers is destitute of credit.

Duane explained in the *Aurora* that Federalist papers were maintained "by support in the form of commercial advertisements," and in a letter to Jefferson in 1809 he charged that they had "secret supplies" of British gold:[2]

> It cannot be supposed that six newspapers in this city [Philadelphia], four in New York, four in Boston, three in Baltimore, two in Norfolk, and two in Charleston could be supported as efficiently as they are without secret supplies. I find it impossible to get out of debt with the paper of greatest circulation in the country; and my personal expenses besides clothing and food would be discharged with fifty dollars a year.

But at the very time that these charges were being made, Coleman was seriously considering abandoning the *Evening Post* and returning to the practice of law, because the paper, despite good financial management, was not sufficiently remunerative. Coleman also undertook to disprove the charge that Federalist papers depended for their existence upon advertisements of Federalist commercial interests, by showing that the actual amount of this advertising in the Republican and in the independent papers in New York and Philadelphia was greater than in the Federalist papers.

From the time of the Embargo Act at the end of 1807 through the War of 1812, party animosities, intensified by the disastrous effects of the restrictions on American commerce, continued to find expression in the party press. "Madison's war," as the Federalist papers dubbed the War of 1812, was extremely unpopular with the mercantile and shipping interests of New England and

[1] *American Citizen*, October 20, 1806; reprinted in Moncure Conway's *Writings of Thomas Paine*, vol. IV, p. 475.

[2] Ford, Worthington C. "Jefferson and the Newspaper," in *Records of the Columbia Historical Society*, vol. VIII, p. 103.

New York.   The Federalist papers representing these interests not only opposed war measures but minimized American victories and dilated on American defeats.   Opposition to the war by the Baltimore *Federalist Republican* led to the destruction of its plant at the hands of a mob.   Later, when it was printed in George-town and distributed in Baltimore, another riot caused the death of several men who were defending its offices, including General James M. Lingan, a prominent veteran of the Revolutionary War. Against this violent attack on the liberty of the press, as the Federalists considered it, protest meetings were held in Boston and in other cities.   A funeral procession and memorial exercises in honor of General Lingan were held in Washington by his Fed-eralist admirers.   The hostility of the Federalists to the war and to the Administration culminated in 1814 in the Hartford Con-vention, which it was believed might result in the secession of New England from the Union.   In printing the news of Connecti-cut's decision to be represented at that convention, the ardent Federalist editor, Benjamin Russell, in the *Columbian Centinel* ran the headline, "Second Pillar of a New Federalist Edifice Reared," and, when Rhode Island made a similar decision, he headed the news, "Third Pillar Raised." [1]   These devices were reminiscent of his "Federal Edifice" cartoon used a generation earlier when he was urging the ratification of the Constitution.

In Washington during the war, the two editors of the *National Intelligencer*, William W. Seaton and Joseph Gales, Jr., managed to get out their paper, but only on a single sheet instead of a double one, because they were serving with the troops that were guarding the city and most of their printers were in the militia. When the British captured the city and burned the Capitol and the President's house, the office of the *Intelligencer* was sacked and its contents burned.   Fortunately some of the type was saved, and a week later the paper reappeared, but in a smaller form.

In 1810, Joseph Gales, Jr., who had been on the staff of the *Intelligencer* since 1807, purchased it from its founder, Samuel Harrison Smith, and in 1812 took into partnership his brother-in-law, William W. Seaton.   On January 1, 1813, it was changed from a tri-weekly to a daily.   Together Gales and Seaton edited and published the *National Intelligencer* for forty-eight years,

[1] *Columbian Centinel*, November 9, 1814.

until Gales's death in 1860. As both were stenographers, they were able to report the proceedings of Congress, one from a place beside the Vice-President in the Senate and the other beside the Speaker in the House. So well did they do their work that newspapers in all parts of the country depended on the *Intelligencer* for accounts of the doings of Congress.[1] Nevertheless, although for fifteen years from 1801 to 1816 the paper was the recognized Administration organ and did a large part of the public printing, it did not make enough money to enable the proprietors to buy the building it occupied or to free its plant from debt.

In the first year of the War of 1812, Boston was at last provided with a successful daily newspaper, the Boston *Daily Advertiser*, the first issue of which appeared on March 3, 1813. It is curious that Boston should have been unable to maintain a daily paper, when other large cities like New York and Philadelphia had supported dailies continuously for some thirty years.[2] The first editor of the Boston *Daily Advertiser* conducted the paper for a little over a year and then was succeeded by Nathan Hale, a nephew of the Revolutionary hero. Hale proved to be a journalist of unusual ability. In the "Editor's Salutatory" published in the first issue that Hale edited, he made these interesting observations in regard to newspapers, editors, and their readers:[3]

> ... it is only necessary to state that almost the total amount of the reading of at least one half of the people of this country, and of a great part of the reading of a large portion of the other half, is from the daily or weekly newspapers of the country. Many of these readers rely solely for information upon the amount afforded by a single paper. Thus the intellectual appetites of thousands of readers, through which nourishment or poison is to be afforded to their political, moral, and sometimes religious principles, by which arguments are to be supplied for their daily discussions, facts for their history, and an impetus to all their mental exercise, are dependent for their periodical supply upon the frail understanding of a single editor.

[1] Cf. *Federalist Republican*, November 27, 1821.

[2] The first daily paper in Boston, the *Polar Star and Boston Daily Advertiser*, edited by John D. Burk, afterwards one of the editors of the *Time-Piece*, continued for only six months, from October 2, 1796 to February 2, 1797. The second, the *Federal Gazette and Daily Advertiser*, established on January 1, 1798, became a semi-weekly three months later.

[3] *Daily Advertiser*, April 7, 1814.

From this single view of the subject, independent of any consideration of our political institutions, it is manifest that the office of an editor is one of great importance and responsibility; since through his agency a great portion of the people receive almost their whole stock of moral and intellectual furniture. It is not strictly his precepts which form their characters; but the impressions and excitements produced by the materials which he directly or indirectly furnishes, certainly give them a bias. — Accordingly we find, that if we have any striking traits of national character, their origin may be clearly discerned in our universal relish for newspaper reading, and in the general character of the papers which we read.

If we consider the influence which the opinions of every individual respecting public measures and men have upon the administration of the government and the laws, we find an additional importance belonging to the proper editing of the public papers. It is obvious, that under a government like ours, the public welfare is intimately connected with the correctness of public opinion. Newspapers ought to be illuminators of the public mind. But who is arrogant enough to maintain that his opinions are always correct, or if correct, that he is able to impress them in the most forcible manner on his readers? It is not sufficient to be on the right side, but that side must be supported in a right manner. Indiscreet zeal is often more injurious than open hostility, and a cautious and timid support, sometimes, by its disheartening example, more than counteracts the aid that it brings.

One of the peculiar traits of national character alluded to above, is the insatiable appetite which exists in all classes of the people in this country for *news*. It is a thirst so universal, that it has given rise to a general and habitual form of salutation on the meeting of friends and strangers: *What's the news?* This is an enquiry of such universal interest that he who can answer it, is always welcome; while he who brings the second report of an event, although it be much more full and correct in its details, is listened to with indifference. From this diseased state of the public taste, arises a very great obstacle to the suitable performance of the editorial duties. The most correct rumours are seldom the most rapid in their flight; and while the editor is waiting for the arrival of the true statement in any affair, his readers are satisfied with the distorted representations that have gone forward. If he would keep pace with the curiosity and anticipations of a great part of his readers, he must deal more in crude reports and loose conjectures, than in well authenticated facts and the materials of history. . . .

It must be an important object with every reader, who daily

peruses any one paper, to be able to rely upon it for a complete history of the times, and that it will present him all the important items of new intelligence which have been received on the day and hour of its date.

"Readers have become so unreasonable now-a-days," he pointed out in a later issue, that they expect the editor to condense news "into such short paragraphs, that it may be comprehended at a single glance."[1] "This is a luxury," he added, "with which we have strenuously refused to indulge the readers of this paper, both because we have thought the same labour much better bestowed in obtaining and publishing the most clear, full, and authentic accounts, and because the reading of select sentences, disconnected paragraphs, *items* and quotations, although calculated to give a momentary satisfaction, provided they be judiciously selected, makes but a transient impression on the memory, and never furnishes one with any thing like a fair history of the times." Although Hale has been credited with being the first editor to publish editorials regularly, there is no evidence that he did more in this respect than other editors, like Cheetham, had done a decade earlier.

"The era of good feelings," as Benjamin Russell in the *Columbian Centinel* called the post-war period following the inauguration of President Monroe and his tour through New England and New York in 1817, marked the end both of Federalism and of the influence of Great Britain and France on American political partisanship, and hence on party journalism.

American journalism received a notable recruit in the summer of 1826 when William Cullen Bryant joined the staff of the New York *Evening Post*. A struggling poet-lawyer, he had gone to New York from western Massachusetts the preceding year. He was trying to earn a living as co-editor of the *United States Review and Literary Gazette* when called upon to take the editorship of the *Evening Post* while William Coleman was incapacitated by a runaway accident. As Coleman's health failed steadily until his death in 1829, Bryant was virtually editor-in-chief of the paper from the time of his first connection with it, and continued at its head for half a century. Originally a New England Federalist, Bryant was converted to a belief in a low-tariff policy, and hence

[1] *Daily Advertiser*, December 6, 1814.

supported Jackson against John Quincy Adams for President in 1828. In the 1824 campaign, Coleman had deserted Adams because he regarded him as a traitor to Federalism. Thus, the paper that Hamilton had established with Coleman as "field-marshal of the Federalist editors," became an exponent of the democratic principles of Jackson. It fought the tariff of 1828, assisted Jackson when he sought to destroy the United States Bank, and opposed federal aid for internal improvements. Bryant denounced lotteries as early as 1827, and under his influence the *Evening Post* excluded lottery advertisements, as the *Journal of Commerce* did from the time of its establishment in 1827.

In the summer of 1834 Bryant went abroad, with the intention of abandoning journalism on his return and devoting himself to literary pursuits; he apparently expected that his one-third interest in the *Evening Post*, which had yielded him over $4500 that year, would be enough to maintain him. During his absence the paper was in charge of William Leggett, his associate and a part-owner for five years following Coleman's death. Leggett immediately launched a vigorous campaign against his journalistic opponents, a policy that Bryant had avoided. Leggett also took a more radical stand in his editorial utterances. Although he regarded the Abolitionist movement as impractical at that time, he defended the right of free speech for the unpopular Abolitionists and upheld the right, denied them by the Postmaster-General, to circulate their pamphlets in the South through the post offices. He advocated the abolition of property qualifications for voting in New York State, the organization of workers into trade unions, then just beginning, and other movements calculated to give the people a greater degree of political and economic equality. Such policies did not accord with the opinions of the readers of the *Evening Post*, who were substantial mercantile and professional men. Leggett's illness and the death of the business manager of the *Evening Post*, made necessary Bryant's return from Europe and his resumption of editorial work to restore the declining fortunes of the paper. As both Bryant and Leggett had published poems, they had been nicknamed the "chaunting cherubs of the *Evening Post*." [1]

The first keen competition in news-gathering in New York City

[1] Cf. *Evening Star*, February 28, 1824.

grew out of the founding, in the year 1827, of two new morning papers, the *Morning Courier* and the *Journal of Commerce*. Through uniting with the *New York Enquirer* in 1829, the *Morning Courier* came to be known as the *Courier and Enquirer*. Like most of their competitors, these two new dailies aimed to be primarily "mercantile papers," appealing to the business and professional classes. Previous to their advent, the New York morning papers had organized an association for the purpose of sharing the expense of $2500 a year incurred in maintaining boats to meet incoming ships which brought them foreign newspapers. When the *Journal of Commerce* was admitted to this Association of Morning Papers, the *Courier* withdrew and maintained a boat of its own for a year at a cost of $4300.[1] Thereupon the *Journal of Commerce* arranged to have a fast boat built. Expelled from the Association because of this independent enterprise, the *Journal of Commerce* began to collect its own foreign news from incoming ships. A sharp three-cornered rivalry in the matter of securing foreign news was thus precipitated in 1828 between the Association newspapers, the *Journal of Commerce*, and the *Courier*. By the summer of 1831 the competition had become so keen that six news schooners were being maintained, at a cost, it was said, of $25,000 a year.[2] Rival pony expresses were run from Washington to New York, at first to secure early publication of the President's messages, and later to obtain daily reports of the doings of Congress.

This rivalry led to the publication of "extras" at any time during the day when important foreign news arrived. Large, bold-face heads, such as "Twenty-Five Days Later from Europe," followed by brief headline summaries of the most important events, were employed to display this foreign news. These "extras" were often issued within two hours after the arrival of a ship, although, in order to select the news to be published, it was necessary to look over two or three dozen foreign papers.[3] In such "extras" this foreign news was displayed on the front page, displacing the usual advertisements and miscellaneous reprint, instead of being placed on the second page. Front-page display of news, however, was exceptional in this period. With flat-bed

[1] *Morning Courier and New York Enquirer*, September 24, 1831.   [2] *Ibid.*
[3] New York *Evening Post*, March 20, 1828.

presses it was still necessary to run each sheet through the press twice. In accordance with custom, the first and fourth pages were run off first, leaving the second and third to be printed last. Thus the inside pages normally contained news and editorials.

The amount of advertising in these papers, which filled from 20 to 24 columns of the total 28 columns, grew to such an extent that the number of the pages had to be increased at times from four to six and even to Eight. Following the combination of the *Morning Courier* with the *New York Enquirer* in 1829, the number of advertisements was so large that the *Courier and Enquirer* issued a two-page supplement on some days, and a four-page supplement on Saturdays, in which 35 of the 42 columns, and 50 of the 56 columns respectively, were filled with advertising. By 1828 there were in New York eight morning papers competing for advertising and circulation, of which five were devoted exclusively to commercial affairs. More newspapers were published in New York City in proportion to the population, as the *New York Enquirer* boasted, than were issued in the city of London.[1]

The circulation of these papers was comparatively small. At the end of its first year the *Morning Courier* claimed a circulation of 2150. It was probably the first paper to print its circulation figures daily under its "masthead," although it continued this innovation for only a week.[2] Early in its third year, as the *Courier and Enquirer*, it laid claim to the largest circulation in New York, with a daily issue of 4000.[3] The number of delinquent subscribers and advertisers was so large that in 1829 the New York newspapers agreed to furnish each other with lists of delinquents and to refuse credit to persons who failed to pay other papers for subscriptions and advertisements.[4]

The *Courier and Enquirer* was edited in its earliest years by Colonel James Watson Webb, with the aid of Mordecai M. Noah and James Gordon Bennett, both able and experienced journalists. In the forties he had the assistance of Henry J. Raymond, afterwards founder of the *New York Times*. Colonel Webb, who was a graduate of West Point and had had army experience, was an impulsive, belligerent editor, constantly engaged in journalistic

---

[1] *New York Enquirer*, July 3, 1828.   [2] *Morning Courier*, May 3, 1828.
[3] *Morning Courier and New York Enquirer*, May 25, 1829.
[4] *Ibid.*, September 29, 1829.

combat with his newspaper rivals. Quick to resent attacks on himself and on his paper, he twice came to blows in the street with his former associate, Bennett, when the latter was editing the *Herald*, was wounded in a duel with one congressman, and was indirectly concerned in a duel that led to the death of another congressman. Webb continued in charge of the *Courier and Enquirer* until his retirement in 1861, when it was merged with the *World* and lost its identity.

The *Journal of Commerce* was established in 1827 by Arthur Tappan, a prominent and public-spirited merchant, who desired to give New York City a daily paper of high moral tone and religious character. The purpose was, not to make it a distinctly religious paper, but, rather, "a commercial paper, true to its character and at the same time, decidedly and unequivocally friendly to the great and inseparable interests of religion and morality."[1] Advertisements of theaters, lotteries, and "business to be transacted on the Sabbath" were accordingly excluded, and no work connected with the publication was permitted between midnight on Saturday and midnight on Sunday. Because of this restriction, the paper appeared an hour later on Monday morning than on other days. The founder disclaimed any desire to reap "pecuniary advantage" from the paper.[2] The *Journal of Commerce* also expressed the intention to shut its "columns against all party and personal politics," as well as to "meddle as little as possible with our popular elections, and the angry altercations which they always excite."[3]

As the paper did not obtain much of a circulation, and within sixteen months cost its founder over $30,000, he decided to turn it over to his brother, Lewis Tappan. The latter entered into an arrangement with Gerard Hallock, former editor of the *Boston Telegraph*, and David Hale, business manager of the *Journal of Commerce* from its inception, by which in the course of two years they became its proprietors. Since they were able to pay $6000 to Arthur Tappan for the equipment of the plant, his loss on the experiment was only $25,000.[4] Under the name of Hale and

---

[1] *Journal of Commerce*, September 17, 1827.

[2] Advertisement of the *Journal of Commerce* in the *Morning Courier*, September 29, 1827.

[3] *Journal of Commerce*, September 6, 1827.

[4] [Tappan, Lewis], *Life of Arthur Tappan*, p. 94.

Hallock, the new owners conducted the paper in accordance with the principles of its founder, and were able to make it a financial success.   Hallock, because of a desire to be free from obligation to any interests, is said to have refused all the usual "deadhead" privileges, which were accorded even more freely to newspapers in those days than at present.[1]   After Hale's death in 1849, Hallock conducted the paper alone until he retired in 1861, the same year that Colonel Webb withdrew from the *Courier and Enquirer*.

Despite the stand taken by the *Journal of Commerce* and by the *New England Palladium*[2] against theater and lottery advertisements, most of the papers of this period accepted advertising of patent nostrums and of so-called medical specialists.   The *Journal of Commerce*, for example, two months after it published excerpts from an unfavorable report of the Medical Society of New York on several nostrums, including an analysis of one that was claimed to be a cure for intemperance, printed an advertisement of this same medicine.[3]   So, too, the New York *Evening Post*, after asserting that "we felt it our duty" to insert a contributed article giving extracts from a report of the Medical Society of Philadelphia on several nostrums, began the same day to run an advertisement of one of the patent medicines condemned in the report.   On the whole, however, there was very much less objectionable advertising, judged by present-day standards, in the six-penny papers at this time than appeared a little later in the first penny papers.   This, no doubt, was largely due to the class of readers to whom the papers appealed.   Before the advent of the penny papers, all the New York dailies aimed primarily at "commercial support," for, as the *Morning Courier* explained,[4]

> . . . commercial patronage is the best, safest, and most unchanging of any, and less affected by prejudice, whim, or petulance than any other.   Merchants are ever ready to bestow their confidence and their support on those who exhibit zeal, industry, and vigilance in their service and devotedness in their interests.

The *Journal of Commerce* also advertised that it was "devoted principally to commerce and manufactures, but including Politics, Literature, and whatever is interesting to intelligent men of busi-

---

[1] Hallock, William H.   *Life of Gerard Hallock*, p. 16.
[2] *Journal of Commerce*, September 15, 1829.   [3] *Ibid.*, October 16, 1827.
[4] *Morning Courier*, January 24, 1828.

ness." With a subscription price of $10 a year, these papers did not intend to reach the working-classes. Of newspaper readers in this period, Horace Greeley wrote, "No secular papers were generally read in our City save the large daily journals, which the great laboring mass were precluded by their cost from reading except at the grog-shop; and we believe that less than one-third of the adults of our City habitually read any paper whatever." [1]

In contrast with the large commercial papers in New York, three newspapers with much smaller pages, and with a subscription price of only $4 a year, were successfully established in Boston. These were the *Daily Evening Transcript*, which appeared in 1830; the *Boston Morning Post*, in 1831, and the *Mercantile Journal*, in 1833. The "hint that led to the establishment of the Transcript" as a paper of smaller size was obtained, according to the editor, Lynde M. Walter, from the *Daily Courier* of Portland, Maine, a publication that had been in existence for nine months when the *Evening Transcript* was first issued on July 24, 1830. [2] Of its small size the editor said in the first issue: [3]

> We are aware that it is not now the mode to appear in such stinted robes as we have adopted; but we have chosen to set fashion at defiance, and study our own convenience. We therefore beseech the Reader to judge us impartially; — not by the size of the casket, but by the value of the contents.

With four columns to the page, the paper was slightly larger than the first penny papers that began in New York in 1833. It was the only evening paper in Boston, the *Bulletin*, its predecessor in the evening field, having been discontinued.

Although smaller and cheaper, these three Boston papers did not undertake to make a popular appeal, as did the first penny papers, either by enterprise in local news-gathering or by the publication of reports of police courts and criminal trials. In fact, all three condemned objectionable news of crime and vice. Within the first month of its existence, the *Boston Morning Post* thus protested editorially against the publication of such matter: [4]

> The duties of an editor are not only to collect news, but to disseminate truth; to cater for the mind as well as the curiosity of the

[1] *New-Yorker*, March 13, 1841.
[2] *Daily Evening Transcript*, October 14, 1830.   [3] *Ibid.*, July 24, 1830.
[4] *Boston Morning Post*, December 8, 1831.

public. He should be an inspector, as well as surveyor, and see that no unwholesome article come to the public palate. . . .

We think there is generally too great a propensity among our editorial brethren to present some crimes, quite bad enough when only *alluded* to — to the public eye, in a garb as shameless as their own naked deformity. — We doubt the propriety of it — but have no doubt of the indecency of it. Let it be borne in mind that all newspapers fall into the hands of children — children of both sexes; and that it is desirable to have them contain nothing that we should blush to *hear* our children read — for that is not fit to be read, that is unfit to be heard.

The *Evening Transcript* took a similar stand when the first penny papers in New York were devoting disproportionate space to the sordid details of the Robinson-Jewett murder trial. The editor wrote in that connection, "we shall not . . . occupy our columns with a report of the testimony, as it is not only very voluminous, but is unmeet for every eye, and may be purchased by those who have an appetite for such garbage, of penny newsmen, for a cent."[1]

The Boston *Mercantile Journal*, like the New York *Journal of Commerce*, was established with a decided moral and religious purpose, and likewise was opposed to lotteries and theaters. This general policy, as outlined in the first number, on February 5, 1833, was stated thus:

We believe that both the wants and the voice of the community call for a paper, which, without partizan character in politics, shall aim only at the general good, and the communication of full and impartial information. . . .

We believe that both the wants and the voice of the public call for a daily paper of a high moral, or perhaps we ought to say, religious character, and avowedly such: — a paper which shall make the moral elevation of the community one of its chief objects; which shall keep up with, if not pioneer, public opinion on such subjects; which shall advocate openly the cause of temperance, and every other benevolent enterprise; which shall discourage all such public or private practices and amusements as are injurious to public or individual character even at the sacrifice of pecuniary profit and at the cost of opposition and reproach, and which shall, so far as a newspaper can, maintain the general diffusion of sound religious principles, — principles like those which have thus far been our support and our glory as a people, but which are in

[1] *Daily Evening Transcript*, June 6, 1836.

danger of falling a sacrifice to neglect occasioned by the universal and increasingly exclusive attention now paid to merely intellectual improvement.

The *Mercantile Journal* continued until 1845, when its name was changed to the *Evening Journal;* later it became a morning paper, and in 1917 was absorbed by the *Boston Herald*. The success of the Boston *Evening Transcript* and the *Boston Morning Post*, both of which have continued to the present time, demonstrated the possibility of maintaining smaller papers without resorting to sensationalism, at a subscription price of $4 a year, one half or less of that of the large papers.

In Washington, political changes resulted in newspaper changes. The *National Intelligencer* continued to be the organ of the Administration until the presidency of John Quincy Adams, and its proprietors, Gales and Seaton, not only were printers to both Houses of Congress after 1818, but did a large amount of the government printing. When Adams, as Secretary of State in Monroe's Cabinet, came out as a candidate for the presidency, the *National Journal* was established to advance his candidacy. It was changed to a daily in August, 1824, at the beginning of the presidential campaign. After Adams became President, the *National Journal* displaced the *National Intelligencer* as the official organ of the Administration. To aid General Jackson, who was preparing to become a candidate for the presidency again in 1828, his supporters established the *United States Telegraph* early in 1826, and later in that year Duff Green, of St. Louis, became its editor. The *Telegraph* waged a vigorous campaign for Jackson and against Adams, who characterized it as "a scurrilous and abusive print." When Jackson and his party came into power, Duff Green was chosen printer of both Houses of Congress to succeed Gales and Seaton, and the *Telegraph* became the Administration paper. The *National Intelligencer* and the *National Journal* were relegated to the place of opposition papers. Dissatisfied with the *Telegraph*, because Duff Green was believed to favor Vice-President Calhoun to succeed President Jackson, the latter secured Francis P. Blair of Kentucky to edit a new semi-weekly paper, the *Globe*, as the Administration organ. Begun in December, 1830, the *Globe* became a daily a few days after Jackson's second inauguration in 1833. With Blair in the editing of the

Globe were associated John C. Rives, who acted as business manager, and Amos Kendall, fourth auditor of the treasury.   The three constituted what was known as President Jackson's "Kitchen Cabinet" and exerted considerable political influence.   By reason of their close connection with the Jackson administration, Blair and Rives secured the public printing.   Late in 1832 they began issuing the proceedings of Congress in volumes entitled the *Congressional Globe*.   Thus they entered into rivalry with Gales and Seaton, who since 1828 had been publishing the debates and proceedings of Congress in book form under the name of *Register of Debates*.   The two publications continued until 1838, when the discontinuance of the *Register of Debates* left the field to Blair and Rives's *Congressional Globe*.   The financial success of Blair and Rives as printers and publishers is shown by the fact that, in less than six years after they began the publication of the *Globe*, they were able to purchase the property they occupied.   The *Globe* continued to be the government organ throughout the administration of President Van Buren.

A survey of American journalism for the first thirty years of the nineteenth century shows that newspapers continued to be primarily political party organs, the chief purpose of which was the discussion of political and economic issues, rather than the printing of news.   The bitterness of partisanship in politics was both reflected and intensified by the press.   The accession to the ranks of journalism of abler editors resulted in better editorial discussion.   Congressional proceedings, political speeches, messages of presidents and governors, and reports of various departments of government, filled columns and even whole pages, often to the exclusion of other reading matter and advertisements.   Routine shipping news, prices current, and similar information of interest to mercantile and commercial classes, together with reports of civil and criminal trials involving commercial or political matters, constituted the local news that was fully covered.   It was only in the printing of foreign news that the papers, particularly in the latter part of the period, showed any enterprise.   Thus foreign news still took precedence over domestic news, as it had done since the dawn of journalism in England and America.   The first special correspondence from Washington, begun about 1825, supplemented the reports of Congressional proceedings taken from

Gales and Seaton's *National Intelligencer*. With the subscription price of metropolitan papers at $8 or $10 a year, large circulations were out of the question, especially when papers could be obtained only by subscription and were not sold on the streets. The credit system entailed considerable loss through delinquent subscribers and advertisers, and in consequence few newspapers were very profitable. Many papers were started on small capital, only to die within a year or two for lack of support.

The influence of a few well-edited papers extended beyond local readers, partly because newspapers reprinted material freely from one another, and partly because they usually published weekly or semi-weekly editions "For the Country," that were made up from the daily editions. The subscription price of these semi-weekly and weekly issues was not more than half that of the daily, and the number of subscribers was often greater. The establishment and maintenance of administration and opposition organs at the National Capital, gave an importance to the newspapers of Washington almost equal to that of the strongest papers in New York, despite the fact that the Capital had a population of only 13,000 in 1820, and 23,000 in 1840. Government printing and advertising, given to its organ by the party in power, took the place of commercial advertising as a source of revenue for administration organs. The newspapers of the period were designed for the mercantile and professional classes, not for the masses. In Boston, three papers were successfully maintained that were smaller in size and lower in price than the prevailing type of metropolitan newspapers. Without telegraph lines, telephones, railroads, or trans-Atlantic steamships, means of communication were limited to stage coaches, pony expresses, sailing ships, and a few local steamboats. News in consequence came slowly.

CHAPTER VI

BEGINNINGS OF THE PENNY PAPERS, 1833–1840

THE successful publication of cheap, popular newspapers in the United States began with the appearance of the New York *Sun* on September 3, 1833. Three years previously a short-lived paper called the *Cent* had been established in Philadelphia, but little or nothing is known of its brief history. Eight months before the *Sun* appeared, the New York *Morning Post* began a three-weeks' career, first as a two-cent daily and then, during the last few days of its existence, as a one-cent paper. Its founder, Dr. Horatio D. Sheppard, a dentist, is said to have got his suggestion for a penny paper, to be sold on the streets by newsboys, from the "penny-apiece" articles offered for sale along the sidewalks of Chatham street.[1] But, after securing Greeley and Story as his printers, he was unable to convince Horace Greeley, senior member of the firm, of the feasibility of producing a paper to be sold for so small a price.[2] As Dr. Sheppard had only $50 in cash and a promise of $200 in credit, he reluctantly yielded to Greeley's proposal to make the price of the paper two cents instead of one. A severe snow storm on the day of the first issue, January 1, 1833, followed by several days of inclement weather, interfered with street sales and prevented the venture from having a fair trial. When, on the last two days of its third week, as a final resort, the price was reduced to a cent, it was too late to save the enterprise from failure.[3] Benjamin H. Day, founder of the *Sun*, is said to have obtained his idea for a penny paper from a fellow compositor who worked with him on one of the sixpenny dailies, some three years before he actually tried the experiment, and there is evidence that he prepared a headline for the proposed paper some time before he actually began its publication.[4] Whatever may have been his inspiration, he deserves the credit for demonstrating the possibility of a successful penny paper. Moreover, the success of the *Sun* led within the next four years to the establishment of similar small,

[1] Parton, James. *Life of Horace Greeley*, p. 105.
[2] *Ibid.*, p. 108.   [3] *Ibid.*, p. 110.
[4] O'Brien, Frank M. *Story of The Sun*, pp. 21 and 23.

cheap daily papers not only in New York City, but in Boston,
Philadelphia, and Baltimore.   Thus quickly did the idea take root
of the penny press for the people.

This apparently sudden rise of low-priced dailies for the masses
was due to several causes.   Chief among them was the growing
class consciousness of the workers, both in England and in
America.   This was manifested by the organization of the first
trade unions, with their demands for a ten-hour day, higher
wages, and better working conditions.   Even women workers,
"female operatives," as they were called, sought to improve their
condition.   Efforts to secure the right to vote for a larger proportion of citizens, resulted, in several of the states, in the removal of
property-holding as a qualification for voting, and in the extension
of the franchise.   Similar agitation in England led to the Reform
Bill of 1832.   To reach the masses in England, where newspapers
sold for fourteen cents a copy, because of the taxes on the papers
themselves, on their advertisements, and on print paper, Henry
Hetherington, who was interested in the formation of trade
unions, published in 1830 the *Penny Papers for the People*, and in
1831, the *Poor Man's Guardian*, both two-cent papers.   But his
efforts to evade the so-called "taxes on knowledge" were unsuccessful, for he was prosecuted and imprisoned for issuing these
unstamped periodicals.   The Society for the Diffusion of Useful
Knowledge, headed by Lord Brougham, Chancellor of the Ex-
chequer, began in London, in March, 1832, the weekly *Penny
Magazine*, which within a year attained the phenomenal circulation of over 200,000 copies at two cents each.[1]   An American edition of this magazine was brought out the following year.   The
immediate success of the *Penny Magazine* led in England to the
publication in 1832 of at least a dozen other popular publications
containing in their titles the word "penny" or "half-penny," and
one of them referred to this sudden outburst as "the mania for
cheap periodicals."[2]   Although the *Penny Magazine* and the
similar publications begun the same year in England, were not
newspapers but small, popular magazines of general information,
and hence escaped taxation, some of the first penny papers in this
country referred to them editorially as examples of the success of

[1] Preface to vol. 1 of the *Penny Magazine*, dated December 18, 1832.
[2] *True Half-Penny Magazine*, No. 1, May 4, 1832.

cheap, popular papers, and of the general demand for such publications.[1] The attention attracted by these new English periodicals, and the remarkable and immediate success of the *Penny Magazine*, undoubtedly suggested to American printers the possibility of publishing daily papers for a cent in this country, where newspapers were untaxed.

The two most popular features of the first American penny papers, the humorous treatment of police court news and the reports of more or less sensational criminal trials, were also borrowed from the English press. As early as 1820, the London *Morning Herald* had begun to attract attention by its humorous reports of the Bow Street police court, written by John Wight, one of its reporters, and largely because of this feature had increased its circulation within a year from 1200 to 3600 copies a day. The popularity of these reports was so great that, not only were they reprinted in provincial weekly papers, but individuals who could not afford to take the *Morning Herald* at the rate of fourteen cents a copy clubbed together to subscribe for it. To attract customers, "refreshment houses" posted signs in their windows, "The Morning Herald Taken in Here."[2] The great interest in these police court reports was shown by the fact that some of the "most humorous and entertaining" of them, written by Wight for the *Morning Herald*, were collected in book form in 1824 under the title, *Mornings at Bow Street*, and were illustrated by George Cruikshank, the well-known English artist. In 1827 a second volume was issued, *More Mornings at Bow Street*, also illustrated by Cruikshank. An American edition of the first volume was printed in New York in 1826. By 1828, largely as a result of its police court stories, the circulation of the *Morning Herald* had increased five-fold and approximated that of the London *Times*, the best daily paper in England. These police court reports with their humor and pathos may be regarded as the first examples of so-called "human interest stories."

In this country, not only were these stories imitated by the police court reporters on the first penny papers, most of whom were Englishmen, but in some instances the English original was

---

[1] *Boston Daily Times*, February 16, 1836; Philadelphia *Public Ledger*, March 27, 1837.
[2] Grant, James. *Newspaper Press*, vol. I, p. 318 ff.

printed in New York papers as a local story, with only slight changes to give it local color.[1] The fact that, "out of the ten or twelve reporters who attend our courts of justice, there are but two or three Americans," the others being Englishmen, was the explanation offered by the editor of the New York *Sun* in 1834 to a reader who asked why the court reports "in the daily papers savor so strongly of John Bull."[2] When in 1828 the first imitations of the English police court reports began to appear occasionally in the sixpenny *Morning Courier* and in one or two other New York papers, some of the metropolitan press, like the *National Advocate*,[3] the *Evening Post*, and the *Statesman*, condemned the practice and urged their fellow-editors to abandon it. The editor of the *Evening Post*, for example, wrote that "We fully concur in the sentiments contained in the following article from the Statesman" regarding "one of these indecent police reports, so justly reprobated by the editor of the Statesman":[4]

> The question is asked us by a correspondent, why we do not, like a few of our contemporaries of late, keep a regular chronicle of trials before the police, for the amusement and instruction of our readers? We have to reply, that it is a fashion which does not meet with our approbation, on the score of either propriety or taste. To say nothing of the absolute indecency of some of the cases which are allowed occasionally to creep into print, we deem it of little benefit to the cause of morals thus to familiarize the community, and especially the younger parts of it, to the details of misdemeanor and crime. . . . Besides, it suggests to the novice in vice all the means of becoming expert in its devices. The dexterity of one knave, arrested and sent to State Prison, is adopted from newspaper instruction by others yet at large. . . . There are now and then extraordinary cases, that require notice at our hands, and accordingly receive it; we also, at times, furnish from our foreign journals (for lack of other things) reports of a whimsical nature, in which there is considerable entertainment, totally unmixed with offence; but we are wholly averse to the task of dishing up the ingredients of which the majority of published trials are composed.

Although some of the New York papers occasionally imitated the London *Morning Herald's* police court reports, no American news-

---

[1] Cf. *Evening Star*, February 10, 1834. [2] *Sun*, June 30, 1834.
[3] Cf. *Morning Courier*, April 3, 1828.
[4] *Evening Post*, June 6, 1828, quoting the *Statesman* of June 5, 1828.

paper published police court stories regularly until they became the leading feature of the first penny papers.

Detailed reports of criminal trials with verbatim testimony, such as were featured in the first American penny papers, had been common in English newspapers from the middle of the eighteenth century, particularly in those published on Sunday only.

From England, therefore, it may fairly be said, came the suggestion for small, cheap, popular newspapers; and from England, unquestionably, came the "human interest" and sensational elements that characterized the first American penny papers. The importance of reports of police court and criminal trials, as the chief features used to attract the masses, will appear more clearly in the detailed analysis of the first American penny papers.

Benjamin H. Day, when he launched the New York *Sun* on September 3, 1833, was a twenty-three-year-old job printer with a small plant, who had learned his trade on the *Springfield Republican*, then a weekly, and who for three years had served as a compositor on New York daily papers. Thus, not only was he familiar with metropolitan journalism, but he saw life from the point of view of the workers, and knew what they were interested in. With the aid of one compositor and a boy, he ran off probably not more than one thousand copies of the first issue of his little four-page paper, on a hand press, at the rate of 250 sheets an hour, printing them first on one side and then on the other. It scarcely seemed an epoch-making event to get out such a paper, with only three columns to the page, and with each page hardly larger than a letter sheet of 8½ by 11 inches. The only introduction to prospective readers appeared on the front page at the top of the first column, as follows:

> The object of this paper is to lay before the public, at a price within the means of everyone, all the news of the day, and at the same time afford an advantageous medium for advertising. The sheet will be enlarged, as soon as the increase of advertisements require it — the price remaining the same.
>
> Yearly advertisers (without the paper) Thirty Dollars per annum — Casual advertising, at the usual prices charged by the city papers.
>
> Subscriptions will be received, if paid in advance, at the rate of Three Dollars per annum.

THE SUN.

NEW YORK:

MONDAY, JULY 21, 1834.

Fire.—Between one and two o'clock on Saturday morning, fire was discovered in the lower story of the building 208 Broadway, occupied by Mr. Branzon as a dry goods and fancy article store. The prompt arrival of the firemen prevented much damage to the building. Mr. B's goods were considerably injured. We understand the goods were insured.

Charge of False Pretences.—On Friday last, Lester West, of Maiden Lane, near William street, Merchant, lodged a complaint at the policce office, against Isaac Odell, late a merchant of 160 Chatham street. He stated that some time last winter, Odell, took the store, in question, which Franklin B. Case formerly occupied, and there commenced the mercantile business. That early in February, F. B. Case introduced Odell to complainant, as a merchant, stated that he, Odell, had a cash capital of $1500 to $2000 to begin business with, and recommended Odell to West, as a good and safe customer, to whom he might properly extend credit. That in consequence of this representation, West gave credit to Odell from that time to near the last of May, to the amount of upwards of $1000. He then determined to trust him no farther until this debt was paid. On the 31st of May, however, Odell went to the store of West, and told him that he was doing a very good business; selling $60 to $70 worth of goods a day; that he had plenty of cash, which he let out at a high rate of interest; that L. & S. Haight, merchants in Grand street, owed him a large sum of money, which he had loaned them; not mentioning the sum, but that it was as much or more than $275 dollars, and wanted West to loan him $275 for a few days, because the Messrs. Haights had failed to pay him, as he had expected. On the 7th June, Odell called again on West, reiterated his former story; said Haights had not yet paid him, and that he owed F. B. Case for his store of goods, only a very small sum, and could pay him any day. Odell then wanted credit for another bill of goods, which solely on account of his false representations in his own favor, he obtained tothe amount of $333 45. West stated that but for Odell's statements in relation to the prosperity of his affairs, he would not have trusted him at all. That Odell had since admitted that he had no capital of $1500 or $2000—that Haights did not owe him $275, nor any other sum on the 31st May, but that on that day Odell borrowed of Heights $200, that he was hard pressed for money, and had none to loan. On the 10th June, Odell assigned all his property to Franklin B. Case for the benefit of his creditors, making Case a preferred creditor, to the amount of more than $2400. At the time of this assignment, Odell owed West more than $1300.

It also appeared by the affidavit of Mr. L. Haight, merchant in Grand street, that Case had recommended Odell to him also as worthy of credit, that he had credited him to the amount of upwards of $1900; that he had never borrowed any money of Odell, except one or two hundred dollars for a few days, which he had returned, and that Odell was hard pressed and had no money to loan, and all his representations of his unembarrassed condition were false, and intended to deceive. In consequence of his thus obtaining the goods of West by false representations, process was issued and Odell brought up, and in his examination corroborated almost all that West and Haight had said, and confessed he had no capital to begin upon, had been a clerk of Case, and had given his notes for the goods he bought of him; that he had not paid him, and was now insolvent; had made an assignment to Case, and that he owed about $6000. From the facts of the case, as exhibited to the magistrates, Odell was ordered to find bail to answer, and in default was committed.

Infant Abandoned.—A woman named Ann Delamere, wife of William Delamere, of 12th street, between the 5th and 6th Avenues, came to the police office and stated that, on the 17th inst., Mary Ward, wife of John Ward, abandoned her infant, only two weeks old, without any provision for its support, and left it to the mercy of the world. She came with the infant in her arms, and made the complaint against the aforesaid John and Mary Ward, but when the oath was about to be administered refused to swear against them, and took the infant back, saying that if she swore, they might come and *murther* her.

Names.—The Directory, just published by Mr. Longworth, contains 1025 Macs, 619 Smiths, and 288 Browers.

COURT OF SESSIONS—[Saturday.]

The following sentences were passed.

Ephraim Parker, assault and battery on John L. Moses; placed under bonds to keep the peace for one year, himself in $500, and a surety in $250.

John L. Carter, a German Jew, receiving $900 worth of stolen goods, knowing them to be stolen; property of John Stevens. Penitentiary 6 months, and fined $250, to stand committed until the fine be paid.

Jacob Woolston, a Jew clother in Chatham street, a partner of Carter's in receiving the stolen goods. Same penalty.

Charles Rivers, commonly called Lord Rivers, grand larceny, stealing 12 yards of cloth. State Prison 2 years and 3 months.

Thomas Williams, alias Castro, alias John T. Longford, a black, stealing $1785 from Capt. Ghain of the schooner Hannah. State Prison 4 years and 6 months.

Walter Van Valen, grand larceny, stealing a horse from Arthur Quinn. State prison 2 years and 2 months.

Richard Lefroy, assault and battery with intent to commit manslaughter on Charles R. Havens, by stabbing him in the neck with a dirk. Penitentiary 4 months.

Joseph Thompson, alias Trim Sharp, a black man, and Thomas Jackson, alias Beau Jackson, a yellow man, grand larceny, stealing iron chest with $12,000; property of Charles Saxton. State Prison, Thompson, for 5 years, and Jackson for 4 years and 6 months. Before his sentence, Thompson made a most eloquent and pathetic address to the court and auditory. He had been twice in the Penitentiary, and once in the State Prison before, and possessed a good education and cultivated mind.

Joseph Shannon, grand larceny, in picking the pocket of Mr. Logan, of $250. State Prison 2 years.

Peter Bowerhan, petit larceny, 2d offence, being an old offender, State Prison 2 years 1 month.

Robert Thatcher and William Seymour, for a riot and assault and battery on James Moore, No. 6 James slip; Penitentiary, Thatcher 3 months, and Seymour 6 months.

John Mason, who had been guilty of embezzlement, in appropriating to his own use money with which he had been entrusted to take to the Chemical bank, was placed at the bar, when his counsel, Mr. Brady, who had filed exceptions to the opinions of the Court, and the verdict of the jury as founded on those opinions, argued at length, and read authorities to prove that the case did not properly constitute the crime of embezzlement under the statute; which was controverted by the District Attorney and left to the future decision of the Court.

The Rioters.—To-day is set apart by the Recorder of the city, for the special benefit of those who were recently engaged in the very laudable business of stoning churches, assaulting negroes, tearing down houses, &c. &c. We understand that from 50 to 100 young men are in durance vile awaiting the pleasure of the court.

Landlord's Warrants.—We had the honor to publish an article under this head a few days since, in which we stated the service of a landlord's warrant in favor of Col. Slam, by the officers to whom it was entrusted, on a man (named Moses Tarney, of 121 Delancy street) and the subsequent renconter between the officers and Tarney's Amazonian wife, in which a watch without wheels was the subject of contention. In this case the officers performed their duty to the *full* extent of their authority; both in relation to the furniture and also the wheel-less watch, which found its way into the mammoth lady's bosom.—Col. Slam every body knows is a *peaceable* and *enlightened* citizen, and one of the *best-natured* landlords of this or any other country. He requests us to state, that he had no disposition whatever to be oppressive, to his tenant, Mr. Tarney, or his *heroic wife*, who so courageously resisted the execution of the warrant. He simply, with the best feelings of his *generous nature*, wished to dispossess these tenants who had become disorderly; a course of conduct to which he had always been most *sensitively opposed*: that to effect this object he took out the process in question in order to eject them from his premises, in obedience to his *uniform determination to preserve the peace and prevent disorder*, and to support the *sanctity of the laws*. Of the *purity* of Col. Slam's intentions, no one who *knows him* will *dare* to doubt; and it is his fixed purpose, as it *always has been*, to unite himself to the cause of *uncontaminated virtue* and *good order*, regardless of the pecuniary consequences to himself. We highly commend his well-timed zeal, and hope he may *ever* pursue it and prosper.

POLICE OFFICE.—(Saturday morning.)

John Turner, of 111 Washington street, was charged with exposing himself naked in the street. Committed.

Charles Lynch, of 190 Washington street, was charged with committing an assault and battery on Mary Lynch. Mary forgave him, and he was discharged.

John Murphy, from York, U. C., had no home—no money—no clothes—and slept in the Park. Committed.

George McCarthy was charged with stealing a stove from 491 Pearl street. Committed.

William Riley, of 28 Norfolk street, was brought up for abusing his wife. Bound over to answer the charge at the Court of Sessions.

Michael McGuire, of 35 Spring street, was also charged with abusing his wife. Discharged.

Julia Brisco was found in the street in a state of gross intoxication. Committed.

Lawrence Leroy was charged with stealing a couple of oars from a boat in the North River. Committed.

Robert Canvon, of 8 Elizabeth street, was charged with choking his wife. Bound over to answer the charge at the Sessions.

Giving a Divorce.—Yesterday morning a little curly-pated fellow, by the name of John Lawler was called up on a charge of kicking over the mead stand of Mary Lawler, alias Miss Donohue, alias Mrs. Donohue.

Magistrate, [to the complainant.] Mrs. Donohue, what were the circumstances of this affair?

Complainant. You will be so good sir, if you please, as to call me Miss Donohue. It is my maiden name, and I wish no other.

Mag. Very good, MISS Donohue, how came he to kick over your stand, and break your bottles and glasses?

Comp. Aye yes, now, I like that better. Every vartuous woman should be called by her own right and proper name.

Mag. Well, let's hear your story. Do you know the boy?

Comp. The boy did you say. Indade, sir, divil a bit o' boy is there about the baste, nor man neither, barring he drinks brandy like a fish. [loud laughter.]

Mag. Did you ever see him before?

Comp. Indade I guess I did. Many years ago he was my husband; but your honor sees, I gave him a divorce. That is, ye see, I gave him a bit of paper, stating that I would'nt live with him no longer. [laughter.]

Pris. Its no sich thing, your honor. She used to go off with other men, and so I sold her for for a gill of rum.

Comp. [shaking her fist at the prisoner.] A *gill* was it, you baste? I'll take my bible oath that it was a whole blessed pint. [laughter.

Mag. Well, well, it matters not whether it was a gill or a pint.

Comp. Indade it matters a good deal—to say that a good vartuous woman like me is'nt worth no more nor a gill of rum. [turning to the prisoner.] You baste of the earth. I'll bung out your 'tother peeper. [The prisoner had but one eye.]

Mag. [getting out of patience.] Madam, if you want this man punished you must tell me what he has been doing.

Comp. Indade then, I'll tell you what he has been doing. You see, I was down to the market, selling some mead and spruce beer, to get a little money to support my children with. Last night the brute came down where I was, and, says he, Mary, says he, will you go and live with me again. And says I, go long you divil, for you know I gave you a divorce. And then says he, if you dont go and live with me, I'll break every damned bottle of made that you've got. Then says I, John Lawler, if you touch my made I'll break your head. And then your honor, he up with his foot—O, my poor children—he up with his foot, and he kicked the bottles, and the glasses, and the pea-nuts—all into the dirt!

The prisoner was committed.

☞ Timothy Donohue, who was committed to prison on Thursday morning for drunkenness and abusing his wife, is not the person who resides at 31 Vesey street of that name. On the contrary, Mr. D. of Vesey st. is a worthy citizen.

Charge of Libel.—On Friday afternoon a man named Thomas Fuller was brought before the police on complaint of Mr. Hutchings, in Chatham next door to Mott street, on a charge of having written and published a libel against Mr. Hutchings in the Democratic Chronicle, on the 2nd July, in relation to the riot that took place before his store door on the evening of July 1st. Fuller was held to bail in the sum of $500 to appear and answer.

A Typical Second Page of Benjamin Day's New York *Sun*, on which was Printed Most of the News, Including that of the Police Court

Size of page, 7⅝ in. by 10¼ in.

The contents of the little paper during the first years of its career were in marked contrast to those of its six-penny predecessors. The first and fourth pages, which, according to custom, were run off first, usually contained advertisements and miscellaneous non-news reprint consisting of brief fictitious narratives, anecdotes, and verse. The two inside pages included reports of police court cases, brief news stories of local crimes and accidents, short accounts clipped from other papers concerning murders, criminal trials, executions, fires, and similar events in this country and abroad. Day dismissed briefly, or entirely excluded, political news, the doings of Congress and of the state legislature, and political speeches, as well as editorials on political and economic questions, to all of which the sixpenny papers devoted most of their space. In the matter of politics, the *Sun*, like most of the penny papers that followed it, was not only neutral but quite unconcerned. This policy, and that of exposing evils wherever they might be found, were thus set forth by the editor of the *Sun* when the paper was a little more than six months old:[1]

> When we began the Sun, we were determined to conduct an independent paper — and we shall stick to our text. . . . We began an independent course, and nothing shall deter us therefrom. With TRUTH for our motto we alike disregard libel suits of the house-breaker, and the money of the office-seeker. And whenever the villainous conduct of a man, or a body of men — (no matter to what they belong) — may deserve exposure — so sure as we hold within our hands the whip, so sure will we
> "Lash the rascals naked through the world."

To write humorous stories of the police court, which began its sessions at three or four o'clock in the morning, Day employed George W. Wisner, a fellow printer, at a salary of $4 a week. So successfully did Wisner accomplish his task, to the extent of nearly two columns a day, that Day, when the paper was four months old, gave him a half interest in it, to be paid for out of the profits. The popularity of this feature, as well as the success of the idea of a small penny paper, was shown by the extraordinarily rapid increase in the *Sun's* circulation. Within four months it reached 5000, some 500 more than that of the *Courier and Enquirer*, the most successful of the New York six-penny papers. Within a

[1] *Sun*, March 31, 1834.

year of its establishment, the *Sun* was circulating 10,000 copies a day, and in less than two years it claimed 15,000, "a circulation far surpassing that of any other daily paper in the Union, and with one, perhaps two, exceptions, in London, in the whole world." [1]

Day's method of getting his paper into the hands of readers was also based on English practice.   He adopted what was known as the "London plan" of selling copies to newsboys and carriers. This was a radical change in the method of distributing papers in this country.   Hitherto newspapers had not been sold on the streets by newsboys, but had been delivered to regular subscribers by carriers employed by the paper.   Under the old system, publishers assumed the responsibility of delivering their papers to subscribers, and received payment for subscriptions either at the newspaper office or through their collectors.   Under the London plan adopted by Day, carriers bought as many copies as they needed at the office of the *Sun*, delivered the papers to the customers they had secured, and collected what was due them from these subscribers.   After Day had demonstrated the success of this method, it was adopted by all of the penny papers subsequently established.

Day also deserves credit for taking a stand against the ruinous credit system by which newspapers lost thousands of dollars in continuing to serve subscribers and advertisers who failed to pay their accounts.   Subscriptions, he announced in the first issue, would be received "if paid in advance."   By offering carriers a rate of 67 cents a hundred copies for cash, or 75 cents on credit, he encouraged them to pay when they took their papers.   He also refused to send his paper by mail unless it was paid for in advance. [2]   As to advertising, he explained that "we publish no advertisements (except yearlys) until we receive pay for the same in advance." [3]   Although James Gordon Bennett has been given credit for originating on the New York *Herald* the "cash system" for newspapers, it is evident that Day was the real innovator, although, in giving credit to yearly advertisers and to such carriers as were willing to pay a higher price for their papers, he did not entirely abandon the credit system.   But even Bennett, for a

---

[1] *Sun*, June 30, 1835.   [2] *Ibid.*, January 18, 1834.
[3] *Ibid.*, February 13, 1834.

year after the establishment of the *Herald*, did not demand payment in advance from yearly advertisers and from auctioneers that advertised in his columns.[1]

What was probably the greatest "fake" ever perpetrated by an American newspaper, the celebrated "Moon Hoax," appeared in the *Sun* during the last week of its second year. Richard Adams Locke, an Englishman who had been educated at Cambridge, who had engaged in newspaper work in England, and who, after coming to New York in 1832, had been a reporter on the *Courier and Enquirer*, was the author of this clever hoax while on the staff of the *Sun*. It consisted of a series of seven articles purporting to give the substance of "Great Astronomical Discoveries, lately made by Sir John Herschell at the Cape of Good Hope," concerning life on the moon, which, it was said, had just been published in the *Edinburgh Journal of Science*.[2] Beginning with a circumstantial account of the construction of a telescope with an immense lens, the articles proceeded to describe the flora and the fauna on the moon, and reached a climax with a detailed description of the inhabitants, bat-like men and women. By the skilful use of scientific terminology and of circumstantial detail, suggestive of Defoe, Locke was able to produce a 11,000-word story plausible enough, not only to convince the average reader, but to lead some of the other papers to reprint the articles with favorable comments on the magnitude of the discovery. Even after Locke explained to a reporter on the *Journal of Commerce* that he had written the "moon story" and declared that he had intended it as a satire, the *Sun* still pretended to believe in the story and to be awaiting confirmation of it from Edinburgh.

"From the epoch of the hoax the 'Sun' shone with unmitigated splendor," wrote Edgar Allan Poe, the first installment of whose story, "Hans Pfaall," dealing with lunar discoveries, had appeared in the *Southern Literary Messenger* only three weeks before the beginning of the "Moon Hoax" in the *Sun*. "Its success firmly established 'the penny system' throughout the country," he continued, "and (*through* the 'Sun') consequently, we are indebted to the genius of Mr. Locke for one of the most important steps ever yet taken in the pathway of human progress."[3]

[1] *Herald*, June 13, 1836.   [2] *Sun*, August 25, 1835.
[3] Stedman, E. C., and Woodberry, G. E. *Works of Edgar Allan Poe*, vol. VIII, p. 178.

Whether or not the end justified the means, there can be no doubt of the effect of the "Moon Hoax" on the circulation of the paper, for it passed the 19,000 mark and was "the greatest of any daily paper in the world (the daily edition of the London Times being only 17,000)."[1] Ten hours were required to run off so large an edition on a Napier press that printed from 2000 to 2200 copies an hour. Although the size of the page had been twice increased since the paper had started two years before, Day announced that he had been "compelled for a few weeks past to refuse yearly and in some instances monthly advertisers."[2] A month after, and again three months later, he increased the size of the pages, until, beginning on January 6, 1836, they were 14 × 20 inches, nearly twice as large as those of the first issue. The profits of the paper were between $20,000 and $25,000 a year.[3]

With the business depression of 1837, however, and the establishment of two rival penny papers, the *Transcript* and the *Herald*, the profits decreased, and, although the circulation had reached 30,000, Day sold the paper for $40,000, in June, 1838, to his brother-in-law, Moses Y. Beach, who had assisted in the business management. Thus, in less than five years, a young printer, beginning without capital, had built up a daily paper that had, not only the largest circulation in the world, but one which, he claimed, equalled the combined circulation of all the other New York papers; a paper that required two Napier double-cylinder presses to print it at the rate of 4000 an hour; that expended over $93,000 a year for wages and materials; and that was sold for $40,000.[4] Of the effect of the paper on the community, the *Sun* had the following to say editorially a year before Day sold it:[5]

> Since the Sun began to shine upon the citizens of New York there has been a very great and decided change in the condition of the laboring classes and the mechanics. Now every individual, from the rich aristocrat who lolls in his carriage to the humble laborer who wields a broom in the streets, read the Sun; nor can even a boy be found in New York City or the neighboring country who will not know in the course of the day what is promulgated in the Sun in the morning.

[1] *Sun*, August 28, 1835.   [2] *Ibid.*
[3] *Ibid.*, April 19, 1837; cited by Frank M. O'Brien, *Story of The Sun*, p. 127.
[4] *Ibid.*, June, 1838; cited by Frank M. O'Brien, *Story of The Sun*, p. 128.
[5] Quoted in Frank M. O'Brien's *Story of The Sun*, p. 129.

Already can we perceive a change in the mass of the people. They think, talk, and act in concert. They understand their own interest, and feel that they have numbers and strength to pursue it with success.

The Sun newspaper probably has done more to benefit the community by enlightening the minds of the common people than all the other papers together.

The basis of the *Sun's* success is unquestionably to be found in its giving the masses what they wanted — sensational, "human interest" news, the value of which as a circulation-builder had been demonstrated in England both by the London *Morning Herald* and by the London papers published on Sunday only. Police court news, treated humorously as a rule; reports of criminal trials, frequently with scandalous details; accounts of murders, suicides, and other crimes — these were the popular features. This sensational news was sought, not only in the local field, but also in newspapers from other cities in this country and from abroad. Other popular subjects of news stories were snakes, sea-serpents, and remarkable animals, unusually large families with triplets and quadruplets, infant prodigies, and monstrosities. Editorially the *Sun* was not concerned with government and politics; it discussed drunkenness, gambling, dueling, reckless driving, and such other "moral" topics as are always interesting to the class of readers to whom it appealed. In short, Day discovered that the secret of popular journalism lay in appealing to the emotions of the masses rather than to their intellects; in amusing, entertaining, and shocking them; in admonishing them against the moral evils of the day.

The small size of the *Sun* and of all the other penny papers, although at first a matter of necessity, was also, no doubt, a factor in their popularity. The large, unwieldy "blanket sheets" could not be conveniently carried about and read at leisure, as could the "tabloid" penny papers. James Gordon Bennett, in the first issue of the New York *Herald*, called attention to this fact when he wrote, "there is not a person in this city, male or female, that may not be able to say — 'well I have got a paper of my own which will tell me all about what's doing in the world — I'm busy now — but I'll put it in my pocket and read it at my leisure.'" [1] Thus the little penny papers foreshadowed the suc-

[1] *Morning Herald*, May 6, 1835.

cess attained many years later by the "tabloid" illustrated dailies that began in 1903 with the London *Daily Mirror*.

The popularity of the *Sun* led to the publication six months later of the second penny paper in New York, the *Evening Transcript*. It was brought out on March 10, 1834, by three compositors, with Dr. Asa Greene, a clever writer, as editor, and with William Atree, an Englishman, as police court reporter. The name was probably suggested by the Boston *Evening Transcript*, begun four years before as a small, cheap paper. In size, make-up, and contents, the New York *Evening Transcript* closely imitated the *Sun*. Doubtless the founders thought that what the *Sun* had done in the morning field, another penny paper could do in the evening field. At the end of the first month, however, it became a morning paper and changed its name to the *New York Transcript*.

The chief regular feature of the *Transcript*, police court reports written by Atree, were, like those in the *Sun*, broadly humorous, with dialogue, repartee between magistrate and prisoner, exaggeration, and salacious detail. The *Sun* declared that its rival "was chiefly distinguished by the humour of its fabulous police reports, which were concocted from an English publication called 'Mornings in Bow Street,' a reprint of police articles written for the London Morning Herald by a talented fellow named Wight; and the agent employed in new modeling these was the highly honorable individual known by the name of Attree." [1]   The *Transcript* had previously explained with pride that it employed two reporters, one of whom spent from three o'clock in the morning until eight at night in the police court, and it had given the *Sun* credit for equal enterprise. The editor of the *Transcript* had written: [2]

> There are eleven "large and regularly established daily papers" in this city; and with the exception of the Courier and Enquirer, and perhaps, the Times, not one of them employs a news reporter, or takes any other pains to obtain accurate and correct local information — on the other hand, there are two small daily NEWS papers, (ourselves and our cotemporary,) and those two employ four reporters, exclusively to obtain the earliest, fullest, and most correct intelligence of every local incident; and two of these

[1] *Sun*, May 26, 1835.   [2] *New York Transcript*, June 23, 1834.

latter arise at 3 in the morning, at which hour they attend the police courts, and are there employed, with short intermissions, till the close of the office at 8 in the evening, while others are obtaining correct information about the city.

The *Transcript* also claimed that its police court reports, by giving publicity to the names of offenders, were reducing the number of cases, and cited the magistrate to that effect:[1]

> There has recently been a striking decrease in the number of cases brought before the Police. Previous to the issuing of the *Transcript* there were fifty or sixty cases of a Sunday morning — the last two Sunday mornings there have been but six or seven. The presiding magistrate stated that he noticed the change with pleasure; and that he could attribute it to no other source than the publication of the names of the offenders in the Transcript, so soon after the cases were brought before the Bench.

Reports of cases of illicit sex relations, some of local origin and some clipped from other papers in this country and in England, as well as of criminal trials involving sex relations, were given prominence in the *Transcript*. News of horse races, prize fights, and foot races were printed whenever such events took place, the paper on one occasion devoting nearly two columns to an account of a forty-six round fight.[2] Thus the *Transcript* not only equalled the *Sun* in its sensational and human interest appeal but took advantage of the popular interest in sporting events.

The circulation of the *Transcript* rose in the first six months to almost 9000, a record slightly better than that of the *Sun* during its first half-year. Within a year and a half it had increased to 17,000,[3] at the time when the *Sun*, with 19,000, claimed the largest circulation in the world, and when Bennett claimed 8000 for the *Morning Herald*, which had come into the penny paper field in New York six weeks before. Thus, within slightly less than two years after the *Sun* appeared, the three penny papers in New York City made claims to a combined circulation of 44,000 copies daily. When the *Sun* was started in 1833, the combined circulation of the eleven daily papers in New York City was only 26,500, and the largest circulation of any one of these papers, that of the *Courier and Enquirer*, was only 4500. Moreover, the circulation

---

[1] *Evening Transcript*, April 7, 1834.
[2] *New York Transcript*, February 4, 1835.   [3] *Ibid.*, August 27, 1835.

of the *Transcript* was not confined to New York and Brooklyn. According to a table printed in its columns in April, 1836, when it was a little over two years old, its circulation of 21,575 was distributed as follows: New York and Brooklyn, 14,500; Albany, 1350; Newark, 950; Troy, 800; Providence, 800; Hartford, 700; New Haven, 700.[1]   In short, one third of its circulation was outside of the metropolitan district.

Editorially the *Transcript* followed the example of the *Sun* in eschewing politics.   In the first issue, referring to its "politics," the editor wrote, "we trust our readers will pardon us when we declare, that in common acceptation of the word, *we have none*," [2] and six months later he again asserted of the paper that "*it takes no part whatever in politics*." [3]

The *Transcript*, like the *Sun*, published much objectionable advertising of patent medicines and so-called medical specialists. When taken to task for this policy by the *Commercial*, it admitted the fact but pleaded that it was only following the practice of other papers.   It said: [4]

> In regard to advertisements — which come not at all under the supervision of the editor — the Transcript is doubtless as excusable for inserting those of quack medicines and quack cures, as the Commercial; the penny papers have generally the same privilege in relation to these things, as the "respectable sixpenny ones."

As a matter of fact, both the *Sun* and the *Transcript* printed more of this type of advertising than did the older papers.

The *Transcript* enlarged its size several times, as the *Sun* had done, to make room for the increased amount of advertising.   In 1839, after five years' existence, it ceased publication, doubtless because it was less profitable than it had been.

Following the success of these first two small, cheap papers, James Gordon Bennett began the publication of a third, the *Morning Herald*.   The first issue came out on May 6, 1835, twenty months after the *Sun* appeared and fourteen after the *Transcript*.   Modeled on its two predecessors, the *Herald* took on

[1] *New York Transcript*, April 29, 1836.
[2] *Evening Transcript*, March 10, 1834.
[3] *New York Transcript*, September 6, 1834.
[4] *Ibid.*, September 4, 1834.

so distinctive a character during the thirty-one years of Bennett's editorship that the contribution which he made to American journalism will be considered in a separate chapter.

The phenomenal success of the first penny papers — the *Sun*, the *Transcript*, and the *Herald* — resulted in a number of others in New York, all of which proved short-lived. Among them were the *Man*, the *Crisis*, the *Bee*, the *Irishman*, the *True Sun*, the *Citizen*, the *Serpent*, and the *Light*.[1] The most novel of these undertakings was a penny paper for women, the *Ladies' Morning Star*, established by William Newell on April 23, 1836. Two years earlier an attempt had been made to provide a penny paper for women, when in the fall of 1834 the *Woman* was established, under the editorship of some one who adopted the name of "Ann Oddbody." "There is a paper *Man* published," wrote the editor in the first issue; "why shall not a paper *Woman* be also seen daily in the city of Gotham?"[2] Apparently the paper was short-lived, for no copies of it seem to have survived.

The purpose and appeal of the *Ladies' Morning Star* were set forth in the prospectus and in the first editorial thus:[3]

> THE LADIES' MORNING STAR will sustain the character of a Literary Moral Newspaper, which it shall be the endeavor of the proprietor to enrich with every variety that may improve and adorn the female mind, enlarge and strengthen the understanding, purify the soul, and refine the senses. . . .
>
> THE LADIES' MORNING STAR will advocate the just claims and rights of that class of young women who live by their daily labor. . . .
>
> The manifest propriety of married ladies, in particular, practising great carefulness against admitting into their families publications deficient in decency, morals, and usefulness, few, if any, will deny. Papers have indeed been presented to their patronage, wanting some of these attributes, and more especially in that of delicacy, which ought not to be carelessly disregarded. Interest may have prompted some proprietors of papers, to publish what their better judgment would condemn. It is therefore a proper tribute of respect to themselves and families, that such should be excluded; and that mothers should practise a prudential caution

---

[1] *Sun*, March 27, 1834, and *Morning Herald*, July 22, 1835.
[2] Quoted in the *New York Transcript*, October 4, 1834.
[3] *Ladies' Morning Star*, April 23, 1836.

in the admission of papers to their daughters, without due examination of their character.

In an editorial on "Police Reports" in the initial number, the editor took exception to the way in which such news was presented in the other penny papers.   He wrote:[1]

> The *manner* in which many of the daily occurrences of the police department have been communicated to the public, is not in keeping with our opinions of propriety, or calculated to subserve any valuable moral purpose.   That some portions of the police reports, as given in the penny journals, are useful to citizens, we do not pretend to deny, as they contribute to guard the unsuspecting against the arts of the vicious, to promote vigilance in the unwary, and to expose to deserved opprobrium the incorrigibly wicked.   Thus far we commend them.   But to chronicle every story of the vices, associated with the names of those miserable and degraded beings, who are lost to all sense of femenine [*sic*] modesty and virtue, is apparently a work of supererogation, and ought better be witheld; as the disgusting details of infamy can never convert the wretched victims of vice into virtuous women, and is calculated to shock the delicacy of the virtuous, to plant the burning blush of shame on the cheek of the "pure in heart," and to prostrate the honourable feelings of the chaste of *one sex*, by an exposure of the frailties of its unworthy members, by means of the corrupt devices and unworthy arts of *the other*.

Police court news, accordingly, was not entirely excluded but occupied less space than in the other penny papers.   It was not treated in humorous fashion, and objectionable details were eliminated.   A similar policy was pursued with reference to the Robinson-Jewett trial, which took place shortly after the paper began publication.   The editor made it the subject of a series of editorials, in which he pointed out the lessons to be learned from the vicious lives of the two principals.   In an effort to interest his women readers, he published articles on "female operatives," as women workers were termed, on "female character," and on "female education."   These articles and editorials were written in a heavy style suggestive of the imitators of Dr. Samuel Johnson and were scarcely calculated to appeal to the average woman reader of the classes from which it might expect support.   The oppressively moral tone of these articles and editorials also de-

[1] *Ladies' Morning Star*, April 23, 1836.

tracted from the popular appeal that such a paper might have made.   At the end of three months, the *Ladies' Morning Star* could boast a circulation of only 2000 copies.

The character of its advertising was as unexceptionable as that of its news.   Although advertisements of patent medicines were not completely excluded, those that were printed were not objectionable.   Nevertheless, one of the readers felt it necessary to warn the editor to be "careful to exclude all '*pills*' — i.e. advertisements, which is the principal thing that destroys the reputation of the '*penny press*.'" [1]   The editor evidently construed this letter as a reflection on his patent medicine advertising, for in reply he wrote, "it must be remembered by our correspondent, that the pill speculation is a profitable one, for its agents as well as for the press; that by inserting such advertisements, or *some* advertisements, the paper alone can be supported, and without them no paper can live." [2]   In short, he regarded even advertising of nostrums as defensible, on the ground that, if other advertising was not available, a penny paper could not live without such support.

In attempting to publish a daily paper exclusively for women, the editor was obviously in advance of his time.   He could attract neither readers nor advertisers.   Although he pointed out the advantages of his paper as an advertising medium, New York merchants apparently objected to advertising in a paper intended exclusively for women.   To meet this objection, after a six months' struggle, the editor proposed a change in the name.   He wrote: [3]

> Many mercantile gentlemen of high and honorable standing, have objected to inserting their advertisements in our paper, on account of what they consider the singularity of its name, and express their conviction that if its title were altered, and if it were called simply "The Morning Star," without the prefixture of the word "Ladies'," it would not only obtain a much more extensive subscription, but also ten times the amount of advertising patronage, which they even promise to ensure us, if the change be made.

The change in title was made, but the character of the paper was not altered.   It still aimed to be "a moral daily paper," the purpose of which the editor set forth in his characteristic style thus: [4]

[1] *Ladies' Morning Star*, July 29, 1836.   [2] *Ibid.*, July 30, 1836.
[3] *Ibid.*, September 17, 1836.   [4] *Ibid.*, December 22, 1836.

The objects of the Morning Star are, to inculcate sound moral principles, to induce veneration of religion, and encourage the practice of vertue; to promote a taste for literature and mental culture; to excite attention to honest industry and economy; the improvement of the physical, moral, and pecuniary condition of the operative classes, male and female; a hatred of vice in all its forms; to ameliorate the social conditions of our fellow citizens; to disseminate sound sentiments, calculated to make mankind better and, consequently, happier; and withal to present to the public a paper containing all the most important news of the day, in a condensed form, always clothed in such language, and dictated by such a spirit, as will justify its introduction into every family, without alarming the most refined delicacy. In short, a paper that will exert a happy moral influence upon the community, free from the taint of opinions and sentiments calculated to corrupt the affections and to deprave the heart, and one that will improve and enlarge the mind in moral principles, in literature, and in mental and physical science. To this effect, private quarrels, notices and advertisements of immoral exhibitions, and improper medicines, will be excluded.

The change of name, however, failed to win sufficient circulation or advertising to warrant the paper's continuance.

Notwithstanding its lack of success, the editor of the Philadelphia *Public Ledger* declared that the *Sun, Transcript,* and *Ladies' Morning Star* "were the three penny papers in New York, which, for vigor and diversity of talent, are superior to any of the large papers in that city, and decidedly so to any in this"; and "that for correctness of general news, soundness of logic, and extent and variety of knowledge, these papers are not *equalled* by any large papers in Boston, New York, Philadelphia, or Baltimore." [1]

The popularity of the first three penny papers in New York soon led to similar publications in Boston, Philadelphia, and Baltimore. In Boston the first successful paper of this type was the *Boston Daily Times,* an evening paper, which appeared on February 16, 1836. It was modeled on the New York penny papers in size, contents, and method of distribution. Police court reports constituted the major part of the local news. News from other parts of the country and from abroad consisted largely of

[1] *Public Ledger,* September 2, 1836.

stories of crime, accidents, and criminal trials, clipped from other papers. No political news or political editorials were printed. In an editorial in the first issue, the editor professed a desire to exert a moral influence through his paper. "However little influence we may be able to exert," he wrote, "that little, we humbly trust, will be found on the side of morality and virtue, and will tend to aid the march of general improvement, refinement, good order, and good fellowship." [1] Desiring, also, to make his little paper "a welcome guest in every family," he urged that penny papers like his own "take in all cases a respectable stand" and "strive rather to be *good* than to be *popular*." [2] A few months later he again discussed editorially the responsibility of the press as an influence for good or for evil: [3]

> The newspapers of this country, at the present juncture, hold the " balance of power " between virtue and vice. On them rests the responsibility, if the morals of the community grow worse instead of better. The country is now ripe for reform, or for degradation, just as the current is turned. Let editors now come up to the work. Let them forget their political predilections, and strive for a time to give such a tone to public sentiment as shall make men wiser, better, happier. It is an object worthy of their highest ambition.

In spite of these excellent sentiments, the editor announced in the first issue of the *Times* that, "as soon as circumstances will permit, we shall employ a Police Reporter and a News Collector, who, in their respective departments, will add much to the value and interest of the Times, as far as regards local intelligence." [4] The publication of police court news in the *Times* called forth criticism from the other Boston papers. The editor of the *Spectator* wrote: [5]

> They [the penny papers] are doing infinitely more to promote licentiousness, and corrupt our youth, than they are doing good.
> No paper is more guilty in this respect, than the Daily Times, of this city. And it owes no little of its popularity to this very fault; and no one who regards good morals, should patronize it, (and we may say the same of other penny papers).
> In speaking of any crime, it appears to be the object of the

[1] *Boston Daily Times*, February 16, 1836.   [2] *Ibid.*
[3] *Ibid.*, May 4, 1836.   [4] *Ibid.*, February 16, 1836.
[5] Quoted in *Boston Daily Times*, October 18, 1836.

Times to turn away the thoughts from sin, and to create a laugh, and even sympathy for the criminal.

In a letter to the *Gazette*, "A Parent" complained that "the honest father, who truly cares for the present and future interests of his children, had rather see them in their graves while pure in innocence, than dwelling with pleasure upon these [police] reports, which have grown so bold, as to demand some check on their licentiousness." [1] Replying to these criticisms, the *Times* asked if "A Parent" would prefer to have children remain ignorant of crime and its consequences, and defended its position thus: [2]

> For our own part, we are confident that the publication of Police Reports is one great means of prevention of crime. There are very many, even of the more degraded of the recipients of the bounty of the Commonwealth, who dread more the appearance of their names in print, than the worst severities of their punishment. We have had many opportunities for observing this fact at Police Court, and we think we cannot be mistaken.

What the *Times* considered news was shown by the editor's complaint that "never was there a more plentiful scarcity of the article by which editors live. . . . there are not 'horrid murders,' 'awful catastrophes,' or 'melancholy accidents' enough, to make up a common string of newspaper pearls." [3] In the absence of such news, the *Times* published in turn the "Awful Disclosures" both of Maria Monk and of Rosamund Culbertson, who were then attracting widespread attention by their alleged sensational experiences while inmates of Roman Catholic convents.[4] It censured the New York papers because they were "all striving to outdo each other in horrible surmises relative to" the Robinson-Jewett murder "for the want of something more important to feed the morbid appetite of the public." [5] Nevertheless, it devoted much space to the trial of Robinson, practically the whole of one issue being given over to the first day's report of the testimony, to the exclusion of considerable advertising. Its reports of the trial, the *Times* explained, were obtained "conjointly with the New York Sun." [6] Clearly the paper followed the example of the

[1] Quoted in *Boston Daily Times*, October 10, 1837.
[2] *Boston Daily Times*, October 10, 1837. [3] *Ibid*., March 12, 1836.
[4] *Ibid*., February 22–26, 1836, and March 9–14, 1836.
[5] *Ibid*., April 16, 1836. [6] *Ibid*., June 4, 1836.

New York penny papers in serving its readers with sensational reading a plenty.

That its sensationalism bore immediate fruit is evident from the rapid increase in circulation. In its eleventh issue it claimed the largest circulation of any paper in Boston. Within a month after its appearance, it laid claim to 8000, and within four months, to 12,000. To print so large an edition, it secured a double-cylinder Napier press capable of running off 2500 copies an hour — the first press of its kind in New England, as the *Times* proudly announced.[1] A little later it published a two-column cut of its new press. "In Charlestown, Roxbury, Salem, Lynn, Lowell, Worcester, New Bedford, and many other towns," the *Times* reported, "we have regular carriers, who circulate great numbers, and we believe the paper is read by nearly the entire population of these places."[2] At the same time it claimed a larger circulation than any other three dailies in Boston and more than all the large daily papers combined. Like the other penny papers, it adopted the "London plan" of selling directly to carriers.[3] It resented, however, the charge made by a contemporary of Bangor, Maine, that it was "hawked about the streets." The papers, it explained in answering the charge, were "sold by regular carriers, mostly to regular customers," and it employed "no boys but . . . good, honest, substantial men to carry it, who make it a regular business, and who make their calling every way unobjectionable."[4]

Like the New York penny papers, the *Boston Daily Times* printed much advertising of patent medicine, some of which was of an objectionable type. It defended this practice thus:[5]

> Some of our readers complain of the great number of patent medicines advertised in this paper. To this complaint we can only reply that it is for our interest to insert such advertisements as are not indecent or improper in their language, without any inquiry whether the articles advertised are what they purport to be. That is an inquiry for the reader who feels interested in the matter, and not for us, to make. It is sufficient for our purpose that the advertisements are paid for, and that, while we reserve the right of excluding such as are improper to be read, to the advertising public we are impartial, and show no respect to persons,

[1] *Boston Daily Times*, May 21, 1836.   [2] *Ibid.*, July 12, 1836.
[3] *Ibid.*, March 4, 1836.   [4] *Ibid.*, February 23, 1836.
[5] *Ibid.*, October 11, 1837.

or to the various kinds of business that fill up this little world of ours. One man has as good a right as another to have his wares, his goods, his panaceas, his profession, published to the world in a newspaper, provided he pays for it.

Always "neutral in politics," the *Times* made the proposal, then considered novel, that, "if either or both parties wish to obtain the use of our advertising columns in order to disseminate their political doctrines or dogmas, they can have them by paying the customary fee";[1] and, when criticized for the suggestion, declared it could "see no impropriety in the offer," for "we advertise for individuals and associations of every kind, and why not for a political party?"[2]

The *Boston Daily Times* continued until April 23, 1857, when it was purchased by the proprietors of its chief rival in the Boston penny field, the *Herald*, which had been established on August 31, 1846.

The first successful penny paper in Philadelphia, the *Public Ledger*, was begun on March 25, 1836, a month later than the *Boston Times*, by three former compositors on the New York *Sun*, William Swain, A. S. Abell, and A. H. Simmons. Its editor, Russell Jarvis, who had received his training under Duff Green of the *United States Telegraph*, continued in his position for fifteen years, although during all that time he resided in New York City. In its first issue the *Public Ledger* announced that it had "secured the services of a police reporter and a collector of news, and it is hoped that their exertions will impart to its columns additional interest."[3] In its police reports and its stories of crime and criminal trials, the *Ledger* followed in the footsteps of its penny contemporaries. Criticized by the other Philadelphia papers for its police court stories, the *Ledger* defended itself by declaring that "the fear of exposure in such publications has saved more than one young man from the watch house at night, and a criminal examination in the morning, and thus arrested him in the road to ruin," and it spoke of these reports as "a terror, to deter such young men from violating the laws."[4] Furthermore, it insisted that "a very salutory influence has been produced by us, in publishing the names of individuals who cared little for exposure

[1] *Boston Daily Times*, October 22, 1838.   [2] *Ibid.*, October 23, 1838.
[3] *Public Ledger*, March 25, 1836.   [4] *Ibid.*, April 11, 1836.

before his honor, John Swift, Esq. [the Mayor, acting as magistrate] and some one or two dozen people who could forget every thing as soon as they left the office." [1]

The *Ledger* gave its readers a liberal amount of crime news, a single early issue containing two murder stories from the New York penny papers, two other murders from St. Louis, Missouri, and Norfolk, Virginia, papers, an account of a "stabbing match" from the New York *Herald*, and one of a "daring attempt to rob" from a Charleston, South Carolina, paper, together with a report of "more Indian Massacres." [2]   It printed full accounts of the Robinson-Jewett murder taken from the *New York Transcript*, followed by a detailed report of the trial of Robinson, and seven long editorials on the trial.[3]   In discussing the causes of "the impression that crime has multiplied," the editor attributed the apparent increase in the amount of crime to "the multiplication of newspapers, and the augmented facilities of intercourse between different parts of the country," and referred to the growing tendency of newspapers to "play up" crime news.   He wrote: [4]

> Formerly, crimes were not always known beyond their immediate vicinity.   Now, a crime in the remotest settlement of Arkansas is soon carried, by the press, through steam boats, and rail roads, to every dwelling in the Union.   This multiplication of newspapers creates competition among publishers, to provide for the gratification of readers; whence every crime is described in strong colors, and is made a theme of impassioned eloquence.

American newspapers in general were not held in high esteem by the editor of the *Public Ledger*.   He declared editorially that they were "contemptible" because partisan, "corrupt" in that "they must cater for the public taste," and lacking in independence for fear of losing advertising.   In a number of editorials on the American press printed during the first year of the *Public Ledger*, he wrote:

> Our own opinion, and an opinion founded on an extensive acquaintance with it in every one of the states, is that with some few exceptions, the character of the American press is VERY CONTEMPTIBLE.   With a very few exceptions, it is destitute of

---

[1] *Public Ledger*, July 26, 1836; cf. August 22, 1836.
[2] *Ibid.*, April 14, 1836.   [3] *Ibid.*, June 14–21, 1836.
[4] *Ibid.*, April 29, 1836.

talent, independence, liberality or honesty. With a few exceptions, it is a mere tool for the dissemination of particular views, or the support of local or personal interests.[1]

The press in our country is venal and corrupt beyond that of any other free country. It is immeasurably behind that of France in dignity, candor, truth, knowledge, deep investigation and bold averment; indeed inferior in every thing which a free press ought to be. It is far behind that of England in bold and fearless exposition of error, defence of right and denunciation of wrong. Why is this? Because in neither country does the press condescend to flatter prejudices; because in each, the editor dares to teach and scorns to follow. But in our own country, most editors are seekers of patronage, and governed by the corrupt and corrupting principle that *they must cater for the public taste;* and too large a portion of the public, unwilling to endure disagreeable truth, address corrupting appeals to the pecuniary interests of the editors.[2]

... if an editor attacks any abuse upon which any of these fragments [merchants, real estate men, ship owners, etc.] fatten, or proposes any thing for the general good, which any one of these fragments, with its vision circumscribed within its own small circle, blindly construes into opposition to itself, he is at once assailed with the cry of *stop my paper; I shall hereafter advertise in some other.*[3]

His own conception of the function of a newspaper editor, he set forth thus: [4]

The post of an editor is a post of high responsibility. His purpose ought to be to instruct, to improve the world; not *to take it as he finds it,* and as he finds it, to direct it to his own views or private interest. His duty is to assail prejudices, for the purpose of correcting them; not to flatter, for the purpose of profiting by them. His duty is to hold up folly and vice to ridicule and scorn; not to treat them tenderly if they have money in their pockets, for the purpose of buying their patronage. The editor who will be frightened from his duty by the cry of "*stop my paper,*" or who will withold one stroke of the lash from any back that deserves it, in hope of obtaining an advertisement or a subscriber, is a venal pandar. He is in the market; his services are for sale to any body or any cause, and the highest bidder may obtain him.

---

[1] *Public Ledger,* August 13, 1836.   [2] *Ibid.,* April 20, 1836.
[3] *Ibid.,* September 1, 1836.   [4] *Ibid.,* April 20, 1836.

Editorially, as the above quotations indicate, the *Public Ledger* was stronger than any of the other penny papers. It published regularly editorials of some length, and discussed a variety of subjects of general interest, such as intemperance, gambling, prize fighting, lynching, and dueling, as well as various local "nuisances." In its first issue it declared that it would give no place to "political discussions involving questions of merely partizan character," but "on all political principles and questions involving the common good," would "speak freely, yet temperately"; and added that, "in seeking this object, it will have especial regard to the moral and intellectual improvement of the laboring classes, the great sinew of all civilized communities." [1] Evidently the editor felt it incumbent upon him to defend the penny press and to attack the partisanship of the old established papers, for seldom did a week go by, during the first two years of the *Public Ledger's* existence, without editorial discussion of the new type of journalism and of the old. The *Public Ledger* believed that "the honor of the invention" of the penny press was "due to one of the most distinguished men in the British Empire, Lord Chancellor Brougham," head of the Society for the Diffusion of Useful Knowledge, because that organization had been responsible in 1832 for the publication of the *Penny Magazine*. [2]

In the rapidity with which the *Public Ledger* attained a very large circulation, it repeated the history of the other penny papers. At the end of its first eight months, the circulation was 10,000, which it claimed was from five to ten times that of any of the "Mammoth Dailies" of Philadelphia; [3] and, within eighteen months of its establishment, it printed a statement under its "masthead" to the effect that it circulated 20,000 copies a day. [4] For the first six months it was printed on a hand press; then a Napier press "propelled by steam" was secured; and, shortly after it entered upon its second year, a double-cylinder Napier press was installed capable of printing 3000 sheets an hour. [5] The *Public Ledger* was circulated on the "London plan," because, as it explained, "this is the only manner in which a publication of the kind, furnished at so low a price, can be sustained." [6]

[1] *Public Ledger*, March 25, 1836.   [2] *Ibid.*, March 27, 1837.
[3] *Ibid.*, November 26 and December 7, 1836.   [4] *Ibid.*, July 1, 1837.
[5] *Ibid.*, March 27 and April 10, 1837.   [6] *Ibid.*, May 27, 1836.

Like the other penny papers, also, the *Public Ledger* printed much patent medicine advertising, and in defense of this practice declared that "we do not indorse for the disease-dispelling potency of any of these drugs . . . such things are matters of opinion, about which the community are competent to decide."[1] It also laid down the rather unusual principle that, "if a patent medicine be deleterious whoever has a better can expose the imposition, and advertise his own."[2] Its general advertising policy it announced in these words:[3]

> Our advertising columns are open to the "public, the whole public, and nothing but the public." We admit any advertisements of any thing or any opinion, from any persons who will pay the price, excepting what is forbidden by the laws of the land, or what, in the opinion of all, is offensive to decency and morals. . . . We do not hold ourselves responsible for any thing which appears in them, with the limitations already mentioned. . . .
>
> Our advertising is our revenue, and in a paper involving so many expenses as a penny paper, and especially our own, the *only* source of revenue; and we get our living honestly by permitting our advertising columns to be a stage for the whole public to act upon, we excluding actors unlicensed by the law of morals or the law of the land.

The first successful penny paper in Baltimore, the *Sun*, established in 1837, was an offshoot of the Philadelphia *Public Ledger*, for it was published by A. S. Abell & Company, the head of which retained his interest in the firm of Swain, Abell, and Simmons, founders of the *Public Ledger*. In its initial number, issued on May 17, 1837, it expressed a desire to reach the young people of the city, since "very few of this numerous body of young men have access to the large daily papers in our cities. . . . the prices for which these papers are furnished" being "yet beyond the reach of a numerous portion of our population, and more especially of the young."[4] "While its cheapness shall place it within reach of the poorest artisan or laborer," continued the editor, "we shall endeavor to furnish the merchant and manufacturer with the earliest and most useful information relating to their respective interests." It also proposed to be neutral in politics.[5]

[1] *Public Ledger*, September 23, 1836. [2] *Ibid.* [3] *Ibid.*
[4] *Sun*, May 17, 1837. [5] *Ibid.*

We shall give no place to religious controversy nor to political discussions of merely partisan character. On political principles, and questions involving the interests or honor of the whole country, it will be free, firm and temperate. Our object will be the common good, without regard to that of sects, factions, or parties; and for this object we shall labor without fear or partiality.

Its contents, arranged in four columns on each of the four pages, were not unlike those of the other penny papers. Police court news was treated humorously, and such topics as drunkenness and gambling were discussed in editorials, which, as in the case of the *Public Ledger*, were a regular feature. Political topics were completely absent from its editorials. The *Sun*, in reviewing its first year, explained its success thus: [1]

We think the chief cause of our success, is the free and fearless manner in which we have proclaimed our sentiments, the candor with which we have at all times opened our Columns, without respect to politics, to such communications as in our humble opinion may with propriety appear in a newspaper, and the caution with which we have abstained from indulging in the vulgarity and bitterness of party rancour.

Within nine months of its establishment, the *Sun* claimed that "scarcely a mechanic in Baltimore does not read the *Sun*," and asserted that its circulation was nearly 11,000, "more than triple the circulation of any paper in Baltimore." [2] At the end of the first year, it had a circulation of 12,000, which, it said, was exceeded only by those of the Philadelphia *Public Ledger* and of the New York *Sun*.[3] Both its circulation and its advertising were on a strictly cash basis, and even its yearly advertisers were required to pay quarterly in advance. Like the other penny papers, the *Sun* placed no restrictions on advertisers, as it explained to a subscriber who stopped his paper because "too many pills" were advertised: [4]

... the advertising columns belong to the public, and any one has a right to use them for any purpose that is not illegal or immoral, provided they comply with our terms. We are not responsible for any thing contained therein. Our views and sentiments are to be found under the editorial head.

[1] *Sun*, May 16, 1838.   [2] *Ibid.*, February 16, 1838.
[3] *Ibid.*, May 16, 1838.   [4] *Ibid.*, March 7, 1838.

From the beginning it carried a considerable amount of patent medicine advertising, some of which was objectionable.

As a result of the sensationalism of these early penny papers, we have the first instance in American journalism of the creation by newspapers of widespread interest in a sordid murder case, and in the subsequent trial of the alleged murderer.   In New York City on April 10, 1836, Helen Jewett, an inmate of a house of ill-repute, was found murdered in her room, and a young clerk, Richard P. Robinson, who had been a resident of New York for only a few years, was charged with the crime.   Obviously neither of the persons concerned occupied a position in society that would warrant the press of the day in giving much space or prominence to the murder.   In fact, before the advent of the cheap popular papers, the crime and the trial would have been dismissed briefly by the New York papers, and would have remained practically unnoticed by the newspapers in other cities.   But to the *Sun*, the *Transcript*, and the *Herald*, competing sharply during their early years for popular favor, this murder afforded an opportunity to carry sensationalism to the greatest length that it had ever attained.

By giving detailed stories of the crime and of the persons involved, the three penny papers of New York, with a combined circulation of at least 50,000, were able to arouse popular interest, not only in the metropolis, which then had a population of about 250,000, but also in the neighboring cities in which the papers circulated.   James Gordon Bennett went to the scene of the crime, interviewed the woman who had discovered the murder, and wrote for his paper, the New York *Herald*, then less than a year old, a verbatim report of the interview in the first person.   To satisfy the curiosity of readers who had been unable to secure copies of the *Herald* on the first two days following the crime, he reprinted the stories that had appeared in these issues.   The circulation of the *Herald* in the next ten days increased from four or five thousand a day to from ten to fifteen thousand.[1]   Both the *Sun* and the *Transcript* did their best to equal the *Herald* in their reports of the crime.

By the time that the trial of young Robinson began, nearly two months later, the three penny papers had succeeded in arousing so

[1] *Herald*, April 21, 1836.

much popular interest that, according to the *Transcript*, "an immense multitude which had collected in the avenues, passages, and round the city hall (despite the extremely wet and boisterous weather) rushed in and literally jammed every nook and corner" of the large court room.[1] The three penny papers outdid themselves in reporting verbatim the sordid testimony, filling column after column of their small sheets, to the exclusion of other news. When Sunday intervened, after the first three days of the trial, the *Transcript* went to the length of issuing a Sunday "extra," in which fifteen of the twenty-four columns were devoted to the testimony of the preceding three days; the other nine columns were given up to advertising.[2] Again, on the following Wednesday, the *Transcript* announced that "An extra will be published at this office at an early hour this morning, containing a full report of the trial of Robinson from its commencement to its close, with a synopsis of the speeches of the counsel and the charge of Judge Edwards."[3] The *Herald* devoted practically its entire issues during the trial to detailed reports of the testimony.

In Boston, the *Times* had declared, just after the murder, that "the New York papers, for the want of something more important to feed the morbid appetite of the public, are all striving to outdo each other in horrible surmises relative to the late Thomas street murder"; nevertheless it devoted over twelve columns out of its sixteen to a report of the opening of the trial, which it had secured "conjointly with the New York *Sun*," and apologized to advertisers for omitting their advertisements to make room for this lengthy report.[4] The Boston *Daily Evening Transcript*, on the other hand, then one of the smaller and cheaper papers, refused to print the testimony, on the ground that it was "unmeet for every eye, and may be purchased by those who have an appetite for such garbage, of the penny newsmen, for a cent."[5] In Philadelphia, the *Public Ledger* gave its readers full reports of the trial, after having reprinted a column and a half of the murder story from the *New York Transcript*. It also published seven editorials on the trial, and later in several editorials defended its course in criticizing the judge and the verdict.

[1] *New York Transcript*, June 5, 1836.   [2] *Ibid.*
[3] *Ibid.*, June 8, 1836.   [4] *Boston Daily Times*, June 6, 1836.
[5] *Daily Evening Transcript*, June 6, 1836.

The exploitation of this crime and trial by the first penny papers, not only in New York but in Boston and Philadelphia, marked the culmination of their effort to attract readers by a degree of sensationalism hitherto unknown in American journalism. Having once discovered the possibility of increasing circulation by such means, they were not slow to continue such sensational methods whenever occasion offered. The inevitable influence on the public of the excessive publicity given to criminal cases like the Robinson-Jewett murder, was pointed out by the New York *Courier and Enquirer* in the following editorial, published immediately after the close of Robinson's trial: [1]

> In general, it may be said, that the moment a wretch commits, or is supposed to commit a murder, he becomes the hero of popular imagination. His likeness appears in the windows of print shops; his dress, features, actions and manners, are carefully described in the public prints, as if he were some great public benefactor. . . .
>
> That this growing sympathy in favor of all sorts of criminals, and this habit of making their crimes, as it were, illustrious, by conferring fictitious importance on the perpetrators, are calculated to diminish our abhorrence of crime and encourage its commission, will appear obvious to all those who look into their hearts.

In a word, the success of the earliest cheap, popular papers in increasing their circulation by "playing up" news of crime, created the problem of the treatment of such news in American journalism.

The success of the penny papers in four of the largest cities of the country, brought about a new condition in the economics of newspaper publishing. Since, under the system of cash sales to carriers at the rate of 67 cents a hundred copies, the management of a penny paper received only two thirds of a cent a copy, it is obvious that such a paper, in order to make any profit, would have to obtain a much larger proportion of its total income from advertising than was the case with papers that sold for six cents a copy, or $10 a year. Thus, the *New York Transcript* pointed out that it depended "mainly for support upon . . . advertising patronage," [2] and that, so far as its circulation was concerned, it made

---

[1] *Morning Courier and New York Enquirer*, June 10, 1836.
[2] *New York Transcript*, May 25, 1836.

"little or nothing on the paper."[1] As the penny papers enlarged their pages, the readers paid less and less toward the total cost of producing the paper, and the advertisers paid more and more. With the reduction of the price to one cent, therefore, began a situation in newspaper publishing wherein the financial success of a paper is almost entirely dependent on advertising.

Thus, by 1840 the penny papers, suggested by the success of cheap periodicals in England, and having as their principal features humorous police court stories and reports of criminal trials imitated from English newspapers, had become well established in the United States. By eliminating political news and political editorials, and by substituting for them entertaining and sensational news, with editorials on such "moral" topics as intemperance and gambling, they were able to secure almost immediately circulations greater than those of all the "respectable six-penny papers" combined. Distributed on the so-called "London plan," with both circulation and advertising on practically a cash basis, they demonstrated the possibility of sound financial management in newspaper publishing. Sold on the streets for one cent, or delivered by carriers for six cents a week, they were within the reach of everybody. For the first time in the world was demonstrated the possibility of appealing successfully to large masses of the population by cheap "tabloid" newspapers, edited so as to make the strongest possible appeal.

[1] *New York Transcript*, May 18, 1836.

CHAPTER VII

JAMES GORDON BENNETT AND THE NEW YORK HERALD

OF the founders of the first penny papers, James Gordon Bennett was the only one who was an experienced journalist. He had been a newspaper writer and editor almost continuously during the fifteen years since his arrival in America from his native Scotland, until, in 1835, he began the publication of the *Morning Herald*. After a short experience on the *Courier* of Charleston, South Carolina, he went to New York, wrote for several papers, and became associate editor successively of Major M. M. Noah's *New York Enquirer* and of Colonel James Watson Webb's *Courier and Enquirer*. As Washington correspondent for these papers, he came to know the leading figures of the National Capital, and wrote bright, gossipy letters in marked contrast to the first rather feeble correspondence from Washington. He also reported several criminal trials that, because of the prominence of the persons involved, were of more than usual interest. At various times previous to 1835, he had edited three papers of his own: one a Sunday paper, another a two-cent presidential campaign paper, and a third, the Philadelphia *Pennsylvanian*, a political organ of the prevailing type. Thus, before launching the *Herald*, he had come to be recognized as a reporter, correspondent, and editorial writer of ability, familiar with politics and political leaders in Washington, Philadelphia, and New York. As a result of his experiences, he apparently was disgusted both with political methods and with partisan journalism.

When, accordingly, he returned to New York in 1835, Bennett decided to cast in his lot with the new, cheap, politically independent press. He is said to have applied to Day for a position on the *Sun*, but, as Wisner, Day's partner, objected to the extra expense involved in employing Bennett, nothing came of the matter. He then approached Horace Greeley with a proposal to join him in starting a newspaper, but Greeley declined.[1] He decided, therefore, to start a penny paper of his own. With $500 and the aid of

[1] Parton, James. *Life of Horace Greeley*, p. 117.

a firm of printers who also printed the *Transcript*, he launched the *Morning Herald* on May 6, 1835.   The *Herald's* business and editorial office was one basement room, where its founder, seated at an improvised desk and counter consisting of a plank resting on two flour barrels, wrote news and editorials, received advertisements, and transacted all the business of the paper.[1]   At first glance, the paper he produced did not appear to differ in size or contents from its two penny predecessors, the *Sun* and the *Transcript*.   The first and last of the small four-column pages contained reprint, with some advertisements on the fourth page; the two inside pages were filled with editorials, local, domestic, and foreign news, more reprint, and advertising.   The style, however, of editorial and news writing was more sprightly than that of its rivals, and showed the hand of an experienced journalist.   In his salutatory, Bennett explained that, as there were about 150,000 persons in New York City who glanced at newspapers every day, with only 42,000 copies of daily papers to supply the demand, there must be room for at least 20,000 or 30,000 copies of the *Herald*.   His general policy he outlined thus in the initial issue:[2]

> We shall support no party — be the organ of no faction or *coterie*, and care nothing for any election, or any candidate from President down to Constable.   We shall endeavor to record facts, on every public and proper subject, stripped of verbiage and coloring, with comments when suitable, just, independent, fearless, and good tempered.

After this introductory bow to the public, the *Herald* did not begin regular publication until May 11.

Realizing at once that, in order to succeed in the face of competition from the other two penny papers, the *Sun* and the *Transcript*, he would have to appeal to a wider circle of readers, Bennett announced in his second issue that he would cover a larger field of local news than police and criminal courts, upon which these other papers relied for much of their news.   He wrote:[3]

> The broad relief which the lively Herald will afford to the dull business air of the large morning papers, will naturally induce

[1] Parton, James. *Famous Americans*, p. 277.
[2] *Morning Herald*, May 6, 1835.   [3] *Ibid.*, May 11, 1835.

JAMES GORDON BENNETT
1795–1872

every patron of the former to take in a copy of the latter, so as to diversify and exhilerate the breakfast table. . . .

But amusement and agreeableness are not our sole aim. We shall give a correct picture of the world — in Wall street — in the Exchange — in the Police Office — at the Theatres — in the Opera — in short, wherever human nature or real life best displays its freaks and vagaries.

In contrasting his own paper with his rivals, he again emphasized the wider appeal that he sought to make:[1]

The small daily papers around us were solely directed to mere police reports, melancholy accidents, or curious extracts. They indicated no mind, no intelligence, no knowledge of society at large. The larger [papers] were many of them without talent and without interest. There was plenty of room, therefore, for a cheap paper managed on our plan, calculated to circulate among all ranks and conditions; to interest the merchant and man of learning, as well as the mechanic and the man of labor.

The circulation of the *Herald*, he wrote shortly after, was "diffused among all classes — but principally among the business and commercial, private families, and men of leisure," and he added, "in this respect it differs from the other small daily papers."[2] In a word, Bennett sought to create a penny paper that would be read both by subscribers to the "sixpenny" dailies, the dull contents of which he sought to supplement in the livelier *Herald*, and by the masses, to whom he proposed to furnish sensational but more varied reading matter than did the other penny papers.

As his rivals had made police court reports their leading feature, Bennett promptly denounced their treatment of such news as "trash," and declared in his first issue that "we shall exclude all such folly from our columns; and only trouble our readers with that species of reading when there is something interesting or useful to relate."[3]   Nevertheless, within a few weeks, he advertised at the head of his editorial column for "a Police Reporter, of genius and education," adding that "none need apply unless he can report with far more taste and judgment than those of the Sun and Transcript."[4]   These police reporters he had character-

[1] *Morning Herald*, May 20, 1835.   [2] *Ibid.*, May 26, 1835.
[3] *Ibid.*, May 6, 1835.   [4] *Ibid.*, June 16, 1835.

ized as "dirty police scavengers, from the lanes and alleys of
London" that "ought to be put a stop to in this land of yet good
and uncontaminated taste in newspaper reading."[1]   Police court
reports began to appear in the *Herald* the day following the publication of the advertisement.   They were not, however, written in
the humorous vein of the other penny papers, for, as Bennett
later explained, "our reporters are some of the best in the city —
gentlemen of taste and refinement, not indulging in those low
scenes so vulgarly described, that too often disgrace the columns
of the small papers generally."[2]

As features to attract a larger clientele than police court reports
were likely to do, Bennett included in the *Herald* comments on
financial conditions in Wall Street, "theatrical chit chat," pointed
editorial paragraphs, a greater variety of local news, and the
latest foreign intelligence — all made readable by the personal
note given to them by the editor.   The Wall Street news and
comment, which appeared as a regular department after June 13,
1835, were written by Bennett himself and soon came to be recognized as a distinctive contribution to daily journalism.   As a result of these "elaborate reports of the operations in Wall street,
the state of the Money market, and the fluctuations in exchanges," Bennett claimed that there was "not a person in business in the lower part of the city that does not read the HERALD
every day"; that "every bank, every insurance company, every
broker, take it in"; that "some of the banks indeed, take half a
dozen copies every morning"; and that he even "had orders for
the Herald from several of the banks in the West."[3]

That there was room for the new paper is shown by the fact that
within six weeks after its appearance its circulation was nearly
7000 a day.   "At the end of the first three months of its existence," as Bennett wrote, "the receipts of the Herald pay its
expences, a fact which never happened before in any newspaper
enterprise," and the "advertising patronage is equal to that of the
Transcript, and close at the heels of the Sun."[4]   A few days after
the editor of the *Herald* had thus boasted of his prosperity, the
plant at which it was printed was completely destroyed by fire,
and the paper was compelled to suspend publication for nineteen

[1] *Morning Herald*, June 8, 1835.
[2] *Ibid.*, August 7, 1835.   [3] *Ibid.*   [4] *Ibid.*

days, just when its rival, the *Sun*, was increasing its popularity by printing the "Moon Hoax."

Undismayed by this disaster, Bennett secured a new office on Broadway, installed a Napier press, and as sole proprietor brought out his paper on August 31, with the title of the *Herald* instead of the *Morning Herald*. "We are again in the field," the editor proclaimed, "larger, livelier, prettier, saucier, and more independent than ever." "In every species of news," he continued, "the Herald will be one of the earliest of the early." [1] Bennett's description of his paper as lively, saucy, and spicy is evidence of the type of appeal that he was seeking to make. Coupled with this feature was the strong personal note in everything that he wrote. He preferred the pronoun "I" to the editorial "we." He wrote constantly of the remarkable success of the *Herald* and of his great mission as its editor. He printed letters from readers condemning and praising his policies, and announced that he received over a hundred of these letters in three days. [2] Typical of the personal element that he injected into his columns is the following account of his method of editing the paper: [3]

> The Herald alone knows how to dish up the foreign news — or indeed domestic events, in a readable style. Every reader — *numbering between thirty and forty thousand daily* — acknowledge [*sic*] this merit in the management of our paper. We do not, as the Wall-street lazy editors do, come down to our office about ten or twelve o'clock — pull out a Spanish segar — take up a scissors — puff and cut — cut and puff for a couple of hours — and then adjourn to Delmonico's to eat, drink, gormandize and blow up our cotemporaries. We rise in the morning at five o'clock — write our leading editorials, squibs, sketches &c., before breakfast. From nine till one we read all our papers, and the original communications, the latter being more numerous than those of any other office in New York. From these we pick out facts, thoughts, hints and incidents, sufficient to make up a column of original spicy articles. We also give audience to visitors — gentlemen on business — and some of the loveliest ladies in New York, who call to subscribe — God bless them. At one, we sally out among the gentlemen and loafers of Wall-street — find out the state of the money market — return, finish the next day's paper — close every piece of business requiring thought,

[1] *Herald*, August 31, 1835.   [2] *Ibid.*, July 27, 1836.
[3] *Ibid.*, August 16, 1836.

sentiment, feeling or philosophy, before four o'clock. We dine moderately and temperately — thank God for his mercies — read our proofs — take in cash and advertisements, which are increasing like smoke — and close the day by going to bed always at ten o'clock, seldom later.

That's the way to conduct a paper with spirit and success.

Bennett wrote grandiloquently of the great reform that he proposed to bring about through his paper, and compared himself as reformer and innovator with the greatest geniuses and prophets of all ages. Characteristic of his attitude are the following excerpts from editorials appearing during the summer of 1836: [1]

I go for a general reformation of morals — of manners. I mean to begin a new movement in the progress of civilization and human intellect. I know and feel I shall succeed. Nothing can prevent its success but God Almighty, and he happens to be entirely on my side. Get out of my way, ye drivelling editors and drivelling politicians — "I am the voice of ONE crying in the wilderness, prepare ye the way of the Lord, and make his path straight."

Every great reformer in the world has been objected to as I have been. . . . Zoroaster, Moses, Socrates, Seneca, Luther, were all considered madmen. Why should not I?

I speak on every occasion the words of truth and soberness — I have seen human depravity to the core — I proclaim each morning on fifteen thousand sheets of thought and intellect, the deep guilt that is encrusting over society. What is my reward? I am called a scoundrel — a villain — a depraved wretch — a base coward — a vile calumniator — a miserable poltroon. These anonymous assassins of character are leagued and stimulated by the worst men in society — by speculators — by pickpockets — by sixpenny editors — by miserable hypocrites — whose crimes and immoralities I have exposed, and shall continue to expose as long as the God of Heaven gives me a soul to think, and a hand to execute.

My great purpose is to upset — reform — knock up — and revolutionize the impudent, blustering, corrupt, immoral Wall street press.

In announcing his sudden decision to increase the price of the *Herald* to two cents, he wrote in a similar characteristic strain: [2]

[1] *Herald*, July 20, 22, and 27, and August 12, 1836.   [2] *Ibid.*, August 19, 1836.

After the usual quantity of reflection which I give any thing, I have come to the determination to advance the price of the Herald to TWO CENTS PER COPY to every subscriber and purchaser in the city or country. With my usual rapidity of thought and action, the new arrangement goes into effect TO DAY. There are Napoleons of the press, as well as of the camp.

... I mean to avail myself of the high value the public very properly put on my labors, and I shall do so. . . . I want to be rich — I shall be rich. . . .

I am determined to make the Herald the greatest paper that ever appeared in the world. The highest order of mind has never yet been found operating through the daily press. Let it be tried. What is to prevent a daily newspaper from being made the greatest organ of social life? Books have had their day — the theatres have had their day — the temple of religion has had its day. A newspaper can be made to take the lead of all these in the great movements of human thought, and of human civilization. A newspaper can send more souls to Heaven, and save more from Hell, than all the churches or chapels in New York — besides making money at the same time. Let it be tried.

When telling his readers, early in 1837, of the new quarters that were being prepared for the paper, he thus dilated on the success of the *Herald*, which he said was then worth $100,000, and on his great mission as its editor: [1]

This success [of the *Herald*] has undoubtedly arisen from the entire novelty which I have infused into the daily press. Until this epoch of the world, the daily newspaper press has been a mere organ of dry detail — uninteresting facts — political nonsense — personal squabbles — obsolete rows — tedious ship news — or meagre quotations of the market. I have changed all this. I have infused life, glowing eloquence, philosophy, taste, sentiment, wit and humor into the daily newspaper. . . . Shakespeare is the great genius of the drama — Scott of the novel — Milton and Byron of the poem — and I mean to be the genius of the daily newspaper press.

That Bennett fully appreciated the advertising value of keeping himself and his affairs before his readers, is indicated by the way in which he reported the assaults made upon him. In waging his journalistic war on the "respectable, sixpenny, Wall street papers" Bennett charged some of the editors with using their news

[1] *Herald*, February 28, 1837.

and editorial columns to advance their speculative stock operations in Wall Street.   As a result of such charges made in the
Herald, Colonel Webb, of the *Courier and Enquirer*, early in 1836,
knocked Bennett down in Wall Street and beat him with his cane.
In his account of the affair published in the *Herald*, Bennett described how Colonel Webb had "cut a slash" in his head, and
went on to say, "the fellow, no doubt, wanted to let out the never
failing supply of good humor and wit, which has created such a
reputation for the *Herald*, and appropriate the contents to supply
the emptiness of his own thick skull."[1]   Again, less than four
months later, when Webb attacked him a second time, he described the encounter fully and commented on it thus:[2]

> As to intimidating me, or changing my course, the thing cannot
> be done.   Neither Webb nor any other man shall, or can, intimi-
> date me.   I tell the honest truth in my paper, and leave the con-
> sequences to God.   Could I leave them in better hands?   I may
> be attacked, I may be assailed, I may be killed, I may be mur-
> dered, but I never will succumb.   I never will abandon the cause
> of truth, morals, and virtue.

The attitude of the *Courier and Enquirer* and of the *Journal of
Commerce* toward Bennett and the *Herald* is indicated by the following paragraphs from these papers, as reprinted by Bennett in
the *Herald:*[3]

(From the Courier and Enquirer)

> At the request of individuals, under circumstances which for-
> bid us listening to the promptings of our own feelings, we are
> compelled, for the first time, to soil our columns with an allusion
> to a beggarly outcast, who daily sends forth a dirty sheet in this
> city under the title of *The Herald*.

(From the Journal of Commerce)

> That little dirty penny paper the *Herald*, whose Editor, if he got
> his deserts, would be horsewhipped every day. . . .

Later in the same year Bennett was attacked in his office by the
manager of the Bowery Theater, because he had espoused the
cause of the manager's wife, from whom the latter had become

---

[1] *Herald*, January 21, 1836.   [2] *Ibid.*, May 10, 1836.
[3] *Ibid.*, May 13, 1836.

estranged, and because he had opposed in the *Herald* a benefit performance for the manager.

Despite his promises to work a great moral reform through his paper, Bennett's avowed purpose of making the *Herald* lively, saucy, and spicy led him to publish much material of a highly objectionable kind. Besides exploiting news of crime and criminal trials, like the Robinson-Jewett case, he published reports of private scandals, often without giving the names of those involved. In connection with these stories of scandal and vice, he sometimes promised to make astounding disclosures, but, as these revelations seldom appeared, his critics asserted that he used such threats to extort blackmail. Semi-fictitious stories of illicit sex relations were featured on the front page in place of reprint or of other general reading matter, commonly used in that position by other papers. This emphasis on salacious material extended even to the *Herald's* treatment of biblical and religious subjects, including church services and revival meetings, to a degree that was regarded by many persons as blasphemous. Thus the *Herald* was far more sensational than the other cheap, popular papers, and Bennett was vigorously denounced for its indecency.

Protests against the objectionable character of the *Herald* culminated in the so-called "Moral War" waged on Bennett and on his paper by most of the newspapers in New York and by some papers in other cities. The attack was begun late in May, 1840, by Park Benjamin in his *Signal*. Major Noah in his *Evening Star* and Colonel James Watson Webb in the *Courier and Enquirer*, under both of whom Bennett had served, joined in the denunciation and rallied to their support, not only other New York papers, such as, *Journal of Commerce*, the *Express*, the *Star*, the *Commercial*, and the *American*, but also the Philadelphia *North American* and the Boston *Advertiser*.[1] Bennett was charged with indecency, blasphemy, blackmail, lying, and libel. The *Herald* was declared unfit to be read by self-respecting men and women. Advertisers and subscribers were urged to withdraw their support. Hotels, clubs, and reading rooms were requested to exclude the paper. All respectable persons were encouraged to ostracize Bennett completely. These denunciations of Bennett and the *Herald* apparently met with considerable approval from the moral and

[1] *Courier and Enquirer*, June 3, 4, and 5, 1840.

religious elements in the community. Other persons attributed the attacks to jealousy of the success of the *Herald* on the part of competing papers. If Bennett's own statements as to the *Herald's* circulation were accurate, the "Moral War" affected in a marked degree the popularity of the paper. When the attacks began, the *Herald* claimed that it printed 17,000 copies daily and 19,000 of the weekly edition.[1] Two years later, the daily circulation was 14,460, and that of the weekly, 12,240.[2] Five years later, a sworn statement of circulation gave the daily as 12,000 and the weekly as 12,000.[3] In fact, the daily edition did not again reach 17,000 until 1844, a presidential campaign year; and the weekly did not begin to approach 19,000 until 1850.[4]

In spite of the large circulation and advertising patronage of the *Herald* and the recognized enterprise of its editor in securing news, neither Bennett nor his paper ever outlived the bad reputation resulting from the character of its contents and from these vigorous attacks, during the first half dozen years of its existence.

A much less serious fault of Bennett's, but one that disgusted persons of sensibility and tended to strengthen the unfavorable opinion of him and of his paper, was the lack of good taste he evinced in exploiting in the columns of the *Herald* the intimate details of his personal life. The announcement of his approaching marriage, just after the "Moral War" began, his description of the bride, and later the accounts that he wrote of his wife and their infant son, James Gordon Bennett, Jr., were unparalleled in American journalism. The signed announcement of his approaching marriage, which appeared in the editorial column on June 1, 1840, began thus:

TO READERS OF THE HERALD

Declaration of Love — Caught At Last — Going To Be Married
— New Movement in Civilization

I am going to be married in a few days. The weather is so beautiful — times are so good — the prospects of political and moral reform so auspicious, that I cannot resist the divine instinct of honest nature any longer — so I am going to be married to one of the most splendid women in intellect, in heart, in soul, in

[1] *Herald*, May 30, 1840. [2] *New York Herald*, December 16, 1851.
[3] *New York Herald*, July 2, 1845. [4] *Ibid.*, December 16, 1851.

property, in person, in manners, that I have yet seen in the course of my interesting pilgrimage through human life.

I cannot stop in my career. I must fulfil the awful destiny which the Almighty Father has written in broad letters of my life against the wall of Heaven. I must give the world a pattern of happy wedded life.

This lack of taste and reticence undoubtedly stimulated interest among the less critical of his readers and led many persons to read the *Herald* out of curiosity to see what the editor would do and say next.

Bennett was too shrewd a journalist, however, to depend entirely on sensational news and on his personal affairs to attract readers. Lacking inclination and character to assume editorial leadership, he turned to news as a means of outdoing his competitors. He was the first American editor to realize the widespread interest in society events, and from the earliest years of the *Herald* he printed accounts of important social affairs in New York and at Saratoga, then a fashionable watering place. His purpose in printing society news he set forth characteristically thus:[1]

No one ever attempted till now to bring out the graces, the polish, the elegancies, the bright and airy attributes of social life. ... Our purpose has been, and is, to give to the highest society of New York a life, a variety, a piquancy, a brilliancy, an originality that will entirely outstrip the worn out races of Europe. ...

Instead of giving names in full in society news, he printed only the first and last letters of the names, separated by dashes, a method that, no doubt, added to popular interest. However little New York society may have relished having their receptions and balls described in the tasteless manner in which the *Herald* treated such events, they feared to incur the displeasure of an editor who had it in his power to abuse and ridicule them if they refused him or his reporters admittance to these affairs. Philip Hone, prominent business man, philanthropist, and social leader, recorded in his diary in 1840 that, on the occasion of a fancy dress ball given by the Brevoorts, an old New York family, there appeared "a man in the habit of a knight in armour, — a Mr. Atree, reporter and

[1] *Herald*, March 17, 1837.

one of the editors of an infamous penny paper called the 'Herald,'" and continued the entry:[1]

> Bennett, the principal editor, called upon Mr. Brevoort to obtain permission for this person to be present to report in his paper an account of the ball. He consented, as I believe I should have done under the circumstances, as by doing so a sort of obligation was imposed upon him to refrain from abusing the house, the people of the house, and their guests, which would have been done in case of a denial. But this is a hard alternative; to submit to this kind of surveillance is getting to be intolerable, and nothing but the force of public opinion will correct the insolence. . . .

Nine years later, in 1849, Bennett devoted practically the whole first page of the *Herald* to an account of a fancy dress ball at Newport, Rhode Island, with a description of the costumes.[2]

In other fields Bennett showed a more commendable enterprise. His reports of financial affairs in Wall Street were the first attempt to cover adequately that important department of local news. In 1838 he went abroad on the return trip of one of the first two steamships to cross the Atlantic, and arranged for foreign correspondents in the leading European capitals. In 1841 he undertook to establish a corps of Washington correspondents, at a weekly cost of $200, who were to furnish the *Herald* with daily reports of the doings of Congress. His plans, however, miscarried for the time being, because the President *pro tem.* of the Senate refused to admit Bennett's correspondents to the reporters' desk in the Senate Chamber, thus perpetuating the monopoly enjoyed by representatives of the Washington papers in reporting the proceedings of the Senate. Commenting on what he called the "atrocious folly" of the presiding officer of the Senate, Bennett claimed that it was "caused by the selfish and malign influence of the Washington newspapers, in order to maintain a monopoly of Washington news, and to rob the public treasury, under the color of public printing."[3] He promised to give in the *Herald* "a daily report and circulation to these debates, better and more comprehensive, without asking a cent of the public treasury."

Another innovation in news-gathering was begun by Bennett in

---

[1] *Diary of Philip Hone*, vol. II, p. 13.
[2] *New York Herald*, September 3, 1849.
[3] Quoted in Pray's *Memoirs of James Gordon Bennett and His Times*, pp. 289–90.

1839 when he undertook to report fully the annual meetings in New York of the national religious societies, known as the "anniversary meetings." Although thousands of members of various denominations throughout the country contributed to the funds of these organizations, comparatively brief accounts of the meetings had been given in the secular press before the *Herald* began to report them. Largely because of the unsavory reputation of the editor and his paper, the clergy and the laity interested in these anniversary meetings resented the publication of their proceedings in the *Herald*. But, as usual in such cases of opposition, Bennett persisted in his course, and other newspapers followed the *Herald's* lead in reporting the meetings.

The enterprise of the *Herald* in covering important sporting events was illustrated in 1845 by the manner in which it handled the news of a race between horses representing the North and the South. The day before the event, the paper printed on the front page a two-column advance account with two-column "cuts" of the horses. Eight "competent reporters and writers," according to the *Herald*, were assigned to cover the race, and four extra editions were issued, one at eight o'clock in the morning and one after each of the three heats.[1]

In order to outdo his rivals, Bennett maintained news boats to meet incoming ships and chartered special trains to secure foreign news from ships that came to Boston. He also ran pony expresses from Washington when the importance of the news warranted them. By spending money freely on such enterprises, the *Herald* was frequently able to publish news ahead of its competitors.

The successful operation of the electric telegraph in 1844 was proclaimed by the *Herald* as marking a new epoch in journalism. Of the effect on newspapers of the new invention, he made this prediction:[2]

.... the mere newspapers — the circulators of intelligence merely — must submit to destiny, and go out of existence. That journalism, however, which possesses intellect, mind and originality, will not suffer. Its sphere of action will be widened. It will, in fact, be more influential than ever. The public mind will be stimulated to greater activity by the rapid circulation of news. The swift communication of tidings of great events, will awake in

[1] *New York Herald*, May 12 and 13, 1845.   [2] *Ibid.*, May 12, 1845.

the masses of the community a keener interest in public affairs.
Thus the intellectual, philosophic and original journalist, will have
a greater, a more excited, and more thoughtful audience than ever.

At the time this was written, the *Herald* was getting news from
Mexico a day or two ahead of the United States mail, by running
expresses from New Orleans in conjunction with the *Crescent* of
that city.[1]   Within five years of the successful demonstration of
the telegraph, Bennett pointed out in the *Herald* the effect that it
had had on the Washington newspapers, in lessening their importance as purveyors of congressional and governmental news.
In 1849, he wrote:[2]

> By means of the electric telegraph the local advantages of the
> Washington papers are transferred to this metropolis, and the su-
> perior enterprise and pecuniary means of the journals here will en-
> able them to turn these advantages to the best account.   Next
> session of Congress, we mean to show what can be done in this
> respect.   We will give telegraphic reports of congressional debates
> and proceedings which will defy competition, and fully satisfy the
> whole country.   As for official or semi-official information to be
> obtained at Washington, we will be able to give it here, and
> diffuse it throughout the country, before the indolent papers in
> that remote village have printed it in their columns.

> As matters stand there, no newspaper can exist in Washington
> without receiving the wages of corruption from Congress, in the
> shape of jobs and gratuities.

Bennett not only foresaw the value of the telegraph to newspapers but made liberal use of it in securing news.   A year before
these editorial comments appeared, the Boston *Evening Transcript*
had called attention to the fact that in one issue of the *Herald* ten
columns of telegraphic news had been published, including the
Governor's message, "markets from various quarters, legislative
proceedings, Mexican news, and Congressional proceedings . . .
including a long report of Mr. Calhoun's anti-war speech," and
added "who would have believed such a thing possible five years
ago?"[3]

In the matter of illustrations the *Herald* was also a leader.   As

---

[1] *New York Herald*, May 2, 1845.   [2] *Ibid.*, June 11 and 17, 1849.
[3] *Evening Transcript*, January 7, 1848.

THE WEEKLY HERALD

NEW YORK, SATURDAY, JUNE 28, 1845.

GRAND FUNERAL PROCESSION
IN MEMORY OF

First Full-Page Illustration in an American Newspaper, Printed in the
New York Herald, June 25, 1845, and in the *Weekly
Herald*, June 28, 1845

early as its first year, when a disastrous fire swept through the business section of New York, the *Herald* printed a two-column wood-cut of the ruins of the Merchants Exchange and a two-column map of the burned district.[1]   Three years later, when the Canadian Rebellion centered in the vicinity of Niagara Falls, the *Herald* printed a map of "The Seat of War."[2]   Bennett has been credited with being the first American newspaper editor to use a war map, but that distinction probably belongs to Zenger, who, in 1733, printed in his *New-York Weekly Journal* a map of the habor and fortifications of Louisburg.[3]   Besides illustrations of news events, the *Herald* in 1839 published a three-column cartoon of an election procession, in which the participants were humorously portrayed.[4]   The most ambitious of the *Herald's* attempts at pictorial journalism appeared in 1845, on the occasion of the "Grand Funeral Procession in Memory of Andrew Jackson."   This large wood-cut, the work of Thomas W. Strong, a New York wood engraver of note, filled the whole first page and part of the second.   When the editors of rival newspapers charged that this cut was "faked" from previously printed illustrations of Queen Victoria's coronation procession, the Croton Water Celebration, and President Harrison's funeral procession, Bennett published a letter from Strong to prove that the wood-cut had been made especially for the funeral of General Jackson.[5]   A year and a half later, the *Herald* eclipsed this achievement by issuing an eight-page pictorial annual containing a variety of wood-cuts, such as, scenes in the Mexican War, a cartoon, and pictures of an actor and an actress in the parts that they were then taking on the New York stage.[6]   In view of the fact that the making of wood-cuts was a slow, laborious, and expensive process, Bennett deserves great credit for his enterprise in pictorial journalism.

In organizing and managing the news-gathering of the *Herald*, Bennett had an unusually able assistant in Frederic Hudson. Hudson at the age of seventeen joined the staff of the paper early in its career, when Bennett had but one other assistant.   He soon showed marked proficiency in getting news, particularly that per-

---

[1] *Herald*, December 21, 1835.   [2] *Ibid.*, January 5, 1838.
[3] *New-York Weekly Journal*, December 24, 1733.
[4] *Herald*, November 5, 1839.
[5] *New York Herald*, June 25 and 30, 1845.   [6] *Ibid.*, December, 26, 1846.

taining to shipping. Bennett came to depend on him and eventually made him managing editor, a position that he held for many years. Not a little of the *Herald's* success in securing news more promptly and more fully than its rivals was due to Hudson's enterprise. After thirty years of service on the *Herald*, he retired in 1866 to his old home in Concord, Massachusetts. Although now best known as the author of the first comprehensive history of American journalism, which was published in 1873 under the title, *Journalism in the United States from 1690 to 1872*, Hudson was recognized by his contemporaries as the outstanding managing editor of his day.

When, in 1845, the *Herald* was ten years old, its circulation, according to a sworn statement of Bennett's, was about 12,000 on week days, approximately 7000 on Sundays, and 12,000 for the weekly edition — "the largest aggregate circulation," it boasted, "of any journal in the civilized world." [1] To print editions of this size, four double-cylinder presses were required, two for the daily and two for the weekly. The capacity of the presses used for the daily edition was 5000 an hour. Twenty compositors were employed to set type and sixteen hands to work the presses. The editorial staff consisted of thirteen editors and reporters, including Bennett himself. The weekly expenses of the paper ran from $1400 to $1600, and the receipts from circulation and advertising were said to average from $2000 to $3000 a week. [2] In 1849 the printing plant of the *Herald* was increased by the addition of a Hoe type-revolving cylinder press with a capacity of from 11,000 to 12,000 an hour. [3] This press was made necessary by the increase in circulation from about 12,000 daily in 1845 to over 33,000 in 1849.

From the beginning of its career, the *Herald* published objectionable advertising of patent medicines and of quack specialists, as did the other cheap papers. When, in the summer of 1836, one of the readers, a broker, complained about the advertisements of a maker of patent medicines, Bennett answered him thus: [4]

Send us more advertisements than Dr. Brandeth does — give us higher prices — we'll cut Dr. Brandeth dead — or at least curtail

[1] *New York Herald*, July 3, August 15 and 20, 1845.
[2] *Ibid.*, May 5 and August 27, 28, and 30, 1845.
[3] *Ibid.*, October 26, 1849.   [4] *Ibid.*, June 26, 1836.

his space.   Business is business — money is money — and Dr.
Brandeth is no more to us than Mr. "Money Broker." If he does
not like this proposition, he may cut and run.   We permit no
blockhead to interfere with our business.

A few weeks later another reader took exception, in these words,
to the advertising of quack doctors: "I say that people *have had*
a great passion for your paper, but they have lately begun to
grumble, because you are crowding your first page full of quack
doctors' advertisements, which are getting to be so indecent that
the ladies do not pretend to look on that side of the paper." [1]   To
this complaint Bennett made no reply, nor did he change his policy as a result of it.   Nine months later, however, he had some
business disagreement with Dr. Brandeth, of whom the broker
had complained, and thereupon threw out the doctor's patent
medicine advertisement and denounced him.   "Our purpose,"
Bennett wrote in the *Herald*, "is to warn the public throughout
the whole country, from being any longer deceived and cheated
by the quackeries of this most impudent charlatan BRANDETH," [2]
and later he said, "without a doubt Brandeth is the most super-
lative quack that ever appeared in the world." [3]

Bennett did not escape censure from other New York newspapers for the character of the advertising in the *Herald*.   "The
Herald," wrote Raymond in the *New-York Times* in 1852, "is
the recognized organ of quack doctors, . . . having a virtual monopoly of this business, it compels the doctors to pay double price
for their advertisements." [4]   Greeley, commenting in 1863 on Bennett's circulation claims, wrote in the *Tribune*, "Much the larger
portion of that circulation is in houses of infamy, in gambling-
hells, and in grog-shops and drinking saloons of the lowest character, to whose owners and frequentors no advertisements except
those which are admitted nowhere but into the columns of *The
Herald*, are of the slightest interest or importance," [5]   and again he
referred to some of the *Herald* advertisements, including "personals," as being such as "no decent paper publishes." [6]

Bennett in the '40s adopted three radical innovations with reference to advertising in the *Herald*.   First, he eliminated all illus-

---

[1] *Herald*, July 20, 1836.   [2] *Ibid.*, March 25, 1837.
[3] *Ibid.*, March 29, 1837.   [4] *New York Times*, July 17, 1852.
[5] *New-York Tribune*, February 16, 1863.   [6] *Ibid.*, February 18, 1863.

trations and large display type from the advertising columns. Besides improving the typographical appearance of the paper, this change was designed to put all advertisers on an equal footing, by preventing any of them from using striking display devices. Second, he decreed that no advertisement should be taken for insertion for a period of more than two weeks, and at the close of 1845 he went still further by announcing that "no advertisements will be taken for more than one day, or for one insertion, payment to be made at the delivery of it over the counter." Third, he decided that no editorial notices of advertisements would be published. Bennett had adopted the "cash in advance" plan for advertisements after Day had carried it out successfully in the *Sun*, although it was not until 1836, when the *Herald* had been running for over a year, that he gave notice that, "in consequence of the trouble, disputes, &c., growing out of the credit system, the advertisers in the Herald are informed that no advertisement will hereafter be inserted, unless paid for invariably in advance — yearly advertisers and auctioneers only excepted." [1]

The largest amount of space ever taken by one advertiser in a single issue of a daily newspaper was probably the seven pages used in the *Herald* on May 6, 1858, by Robert Bonner to advertise his popular weekly periodical, the *New York Ledger*. To make room for these seven pages of advertising, it was necessary to double the size of the paper, thereby increasing it from eight to sixteen pages.[2] Since no striking display was permitted in the *Herald*, most of this advertising of the *Ledger* consisted of announcements like the following, set in body type, and repeated over and over again in each column, with cut-off rules, like classified advertisements:

> At Daylight, This (Thursday) Morning, the New York Ledger will be on sale at all news offices in the United States, New Jersey and the Sandwich Islands.

Other forms used by Bonner in the *Herald* consisted of similar repetitions of single-line statements, such as, "Ledger — Out!" "Cobb and the Ledger," "Fanny Fern and the Ledger," "George D. Prentice and the Ledger." On another occasion Bonner took a whole page in the *Herald* to give the first chapters of a serial

[1] *Herald*, June 13, 1836.   [2] *Ibid.*, May 6, 1858.

then beginning in the *Ledger*.[1]   Although Bonner published no advertising in the *Ledger*, he was an extensive advertiser in newspapers.   He used more advertising space in the *Herald* than in any other paper.

Before the outbreak of the Civil War, the *Herald* opposed the anti-slavery movement and upheld the claims of the South. "When the Kansas-Nebraska bill was brought forward," Bennett wrote in the *Herald* in 1858, "about the only Northern newspaper that had the moral courage to come out boldly in its support was the NEW YORK HERALD."[2]   The same year Bennett declared that, "for twenty odd years, through good and evil report, the NEW YORK HERALD has been the only Northern journal that has unfailingly vindicated the constitutional rights of the South."[3] That Southerners, including members of Congress, found the *Herald* much to their liking is indicated by the account given by Samuel Bowles of the avidity with which it was received in the National Capital.   In one of his letters from Washington to the *Springfield Republican*, in 1859, he wrote:[4]

> It is amusing to see the greed with which the *Herald* is snatched up and devoured on its earliest arrival here in the evening; and what is worse, to see the simplicity of these Southern fellows who seem to pin their whole faith upon it.   Where Northern men look at it only for amusement, as they look at *Punch* or *Frank Leslie*, Southern men swallow it gravely with a sigh and a knowing shake of the head.

Its avowed sympathy with the South brought the *Herald* into open opposition to outstanding Republican papers of the metropolis, the *Tribune*, the *Times*, and the *Courier and Enquirer*, all of which bitterly attacked it and, in turn, were bitterly assailed by the *Herald*.

Because the *Herald* had a circulation of about 100,000, and was read and quoted abroad, its attitude caused considerable apprehension among leaders in the North.   The London *Times* had for years taken the utterances of the *Herald* as representative of the substantial commercial interests of this country.   It had

[1] *New York Herald*, May 13, 1858.
[2] *Ibid.*, February 28, 1858.
[3] *Ibid.*, January 23, 1858.
[4] *Springfield Republican*, December 9, 1859.

quoted its editorials with approval, because the *Times* represented the business interests of England which were disturbed over the possible effects on the cotton trade of the controversy between the North and the South. Recognizing the influence thus exerted by the *Herald*, President Lincoln brought to the attention of his cabinet the desirability of undertaking to secure Bennett's support. It was decided to make a personal appeal to him, and Thurlow Weed, editor of the *Albany Evening Journal*, was selected as the emissary of the Administration to approach Bennett. Although Weed had long been a journalistic opponent of his, he succeeded in impressing Bennett with the gravity of the situation, and the policy of the *Herald* was accordingly changed.[1] In appreciation of the altered attitude of the *Herald*, President Lincoln some years later offered to appoint Bennett minister to France, but the editor declined the post.

The enterprise in news-gathering previously shown by the *Herald* was even greater during the Civil War. Anticipating the tension that would result in the South from Lincoln's election in 1860, Bennett arranged to have correspondents at important points in the Southern States to report developments. The *Herald* published long news stories from these correspondents in regard to the feeling in the South. As the crisis approached, maps were printed of the places where hostilities were likely to break out, and, throughout the war, maps were freely used in the *Herald* to illustrate the accounts of battles. War correspondents, provided with tents and wagons, were assigned to every army corps. By using every material aid, the *Herald* was able to report the progress of the war more fully than any other newspaper. No expense was spared to secure and forward the latest news from the scene of action. During the four years of the war, Bennett is said to have maintained from thirty to forty correspondents in the field and to have spent nearly $500,000 to obtain news.[2]

Long one-column headlines summarizing the news to which they were attached, began to appear in the *Herald* during the 1860 presidential campaign, and in the course of the war grew longer and longer by the addition of many "decks." In these headlines developed during the Civil War, not only by the *Herald*,

[1] *Autobiography of Thurlow Weed*, Harriet A. Weed, ed., pp. 615–19.
[2] *New York Herald*, June 10, 1865.

but by other papers, are to be found the beginnings of the present-day newspaper "heads."[1]

The enterprise of the *Herald* in the matter of news, maps, and headlines was rewarded by a large increase in circulation, for every one sought the latest reports from the front. No American newspaper did more to supply that demand than did the *Herald*.

A year after the close of the war, the success of the trans-Atlantic cable was an epoch-making event for journalism. The failure of the first cable in 1857, after a few days of communication across the Atlantic, created doubts as to the ultimate success of the new cable, but these were soon dissipated. "We are now commencing a new era in journalism in this country," announced the *Herald* in commenting editorially on the significance of communication by cable with Europe.[2] The importance of the cable, in the opinion of the *Herald*, lay, not only in bringing Europe and America into closer relation, but in making for a more concise newspaper style. Of this new influence, the *Herald* said editorially:[3]

> There can be no doubt that the telegraphic communication with Europe will revolutionize the newspaper business on both continents. It will tend to produce a condensation of style in newspaper articles. Already we observe, since the telegraph has been established throughout Europe, a terseness in the writings of English journals which forms a strong contrast to the former long-winded style of the magazine school, which rendered the leading articles almost unendurable. The telegraph will bring us back to that succinct, simple and condensed method of expressing our ideas which prevailed in ancient times. . . . It is evident that the extension of the telegraph system will have a very marked effect upon the intellectual habits of the world at large. The telegraph teaches us that the days of the elaborate ten-column articles and three-volume books have gone by. Condensation of words to express thought will prevail.

George W. Smalley, for many years London correspondent of the *New-York Tribune*, brought out the same point in describing his experiences in sending one of the first cable messages across the ocean to his paper:[4]

---

[1] See reproduction of headlines in *New-York Times* on p. 249, *infra*.
[2] *New York Herald*, August 12, 1866.   [3] *Ibid.*, August 11, 1866.
[4] Smalley, George W. *Anglo-American Memories*, p. 164.

Nor, in truth, did news from abroad by mail ever present itself with the same suddenness and authority it derived from the cable. It came by mail in masses. It came by cable with the peremptory brevity which arrested attention. The home telegraph was diffuse. It was the cable which first taught us to condense. A dispatch from London was not, in the beginning, more than a flash of lightning; and went into print as it came, without being "written up"; and was ten times more effective.

Cable tolls at first were approximately five dollars a word, and correspondents, as Smalley went on to point out, "wasted no words at that price."[1]

In 1866, Bennett sought relief from the responsibility of editing the *Herald*, which he had borne for over thirty years, and turned over a large share of the burden to his son, James Gordon Bennett, Jr., then a young man of twenty-five. Although for the last five years of his life Bennett was no longer in active control of the paper, he took a keen interest in its success under his son's direction. The achievements of these years included the establishment of the *Evening Telegram* in 1867; the publication of the entire speech delivered by the King of Prussia at the end of the war with Austria, the cable tolls for which amounted to $7000; and the successful expedition of its correspondent, Henry M. Stanley, sent to find Dr. Livingstone, the traveler, who was lost in the heart of Africa. Bennett's health began to fail in 1871, and he died on June 1, 1872, at the age of seventy-seven years.

At the time of Bennett's death, the *New-York Tribune*, which had always been an opponent of the *Herald*, and which Bennett had constantly assailed with bitterness, contained a long sketch of his life with the following evaluation of his contribution to American journalism:[2]

It was as a collector of news that Bennett shone conspicuously. Editorially he was cynical, inconsistent, reckless, and easily influenced by others' opinions, and by his own prejudices. But he had an unerring judgment of the pecuniary value of news. He knew how to pick out of the events of the day the subject which engrossed the interest of the greatest number of people, and to give them about that subject all they could read. The quality might be bad, and generally was; but it suited the multitude, and the

[1] Smalley, George W. *Anglo-American Memories*, p. 165.
[2] *New-York Tribune*, June 3, 1872.

quantity at any rate was abundant. He had a method of impressing the importance of news upon others in his employ, which inspired many who served him to energetic action, some of them in
a remarkable degree, but he inculcated no principle of correctness.
The fact is, he was utterly indifferent to the correctness of details
or conclusions, provided the principal event of the narrative or
argument of the editorial was made clear and published ahead of
all competitors. He never tolerated defeat. . . .

He developed the capacities of journalism in a most wonderful
manner, but he did it by degrading its character. He made the
newspaper powerful, but he made it odious. Those who recognize
this, whether claiming it as his admirers or admitting it contemp-
tuously, know that his personal characteristics had everything to do
with forming his paper. He alone made it; it was personal journalism in all senses of the word. He associated with himself
a few remarkable men, but they were remarkable as much in consequence of his training as from a natural aptitude for the profession. . . . His hard early career, by embittering his nature,
isolated him from friends, unfitted him for friendly relations with
any one, for he suspected everybody. His conduct of *The Herald*
in its early existence isolated him from society, and all his subsequent great wealth brought no oblivion for what were called his
misdeeds. *The Herald*, without acquiring any principle, acquired
some decency as it grew great, and the discredit which once attached to any man seen reading it gradually passed away; but
it is rather a remarkable fact that Mr. Bennett personally never
was forgiven for the scandals of his early career.

The strength and the weakness of Bennett as a journalist were
accurately set forth as follows by Samuel Bowles in an editorial in
the *Springfield Republican* at the time of Bennett's death: [1]

He was a coarse and vigorous writer, but excelled more in organization and enterprise. He was never troubled with principles,
or accustomed to espouse and defend a cause from any far-sighted
conviction, or faith in the nobler springs of human action.

The character of the man has been reflected by his works.
Under him, the Herald was the first of American papers, indeed,
the first journal in the world, to apprehend the truth that the collection of news at any price was the first duty of journalism. This
was the conviction and the faith which served Mr. Bennett in
place of every other. The Herald, though fickle in politics and
worthless in editorial judgment, thus became the symbol of news-

[1] *Springfield Weekly Republican*, June 7, 1872.

paper enterprise all over the world. This was at times unfortunate for us as a nation, for the English in the days of the Herald's greatness used to think that its sentiments represented the American people. Even now they are not weaned from that delusion, and the vagaries in the tone of that journal, at which we smile, throw an Englishman into fits. But we must not deny to Mr. Bennett his place in journalism, as the great teacher and enforcer of the principle that in devotion to news-gathering lies at once the first duty and chief profit of a newspaper. Though other papers have in more recent years excelled the Herald in this respect, the first enunciation and demonstration of the principle will be yielded by history and popular tradition to Mr. Bennett.

Viewing Bennett and the *Herald* with the perspective of nearly half a century, Edwin Lawrence Godkin, in his "Random Recollections," published in 1899 in the New York *Evening Post*, had this to say concerning the influence on American journalism of both the editor and his paper: [1]

The secret discovered by the elder Bennett, from which he was already reaping a golden harvest when I arrived in New York [in 1856], was, that there was far more money to be made by catering to the tastes of the uninstructed, or the slenderly instructed, masses than to those of the educated few. . . . Bennett found there was more journalistic money to be made in recording gossip that interested bar-rooms, work-shops, race-courses, and tenement houses, than in consulting the tastes of drawing-rooms and libraries. He introduced, too, an absolutely new feature, which has had, perhaps, the greatest success of all. I mean the plan of treating everything and everybody as somewhat of a joke, and the knowledge of everything about him, including his family affairs, as something to which the public is entitled. This was immensely taking in the world in which he sought to make his way. It has since been adopted by other papers, and it always pays. It has, indeed, given an air of flippancy to American character, and a certain fondness for things that elsewhere are regarded as childish, which every foreign visitor now notices. Under its influence nearly all our public men are regarded as fair objects of ridicule by opponents. This is also true of most serious men, whether public men or not. Even crime and punishment have received a touch of the comic. I used to hear, at the time of which I write, that Bennett's editors all sat in stalls, in one large room, while he walked up and down in the morning distributing their parts for

[1] *Evening Post*, December 30, 1899.

the day.   To one he would say "Pitch into Greeley;" to another, "Give Raymond hell;" and so on.   The result probably was that the efforts of Greeley and Raymond for the elevation of mankind on that particular day were made futile.   By adding to his comic deportment wonderful enterprise in collecting news from all parts of the world, Bennett was able to realize a fortune in the first half century, besides making a deep impression on all ambitious publishers.

The steady growth of the Bennett type of journalism, which has ever since continued, and its effects on politics and morals are now at last patent. . . . It is ever substituting fleeting popular passion for sound policy and wise statesmanship.   Democratic philosophers and optimistic clergymen are naturally unwilling to admit that the modern press is what the modern democratic peoples call for, and try to make out that it is the work of a few wicked newspaper publishers.   But the solemn truth is that it is a display of the ordinary working of supply and demand.

CHAPTER VIII
HORACE GREELEY AND THE NEW YORK TRIBUNE

THE dissatisfaction of the respectable element in New York City with the character and tone of the cheap, popular newspapers, as shown particularly in the so-called "Moral War" against the *Herald* in 1840, together with the desire of the Whigs for a penny paper to represent their cause, led in 1841 to the establishment by Horace Greeley of the *New-York Tribune*. Much of the news and of the advertising matter that appeared constantly in both the *Sun* and the *Herald*, was felt by many persons to render these papers unfit for the family circle. Moreover, both papers, although avowedly neutral in politics, were more inclined to support the principles and representatives of the Democratic party than those of the Whigs. Since the *Herald* in 1836 had become a two-cent paper, and the *Transcript* had been discontinued in 1839, the *Sun* was the only successful penny paper in the field. Hence there was room for another cheap daily.

When he undertook the publication of the *Tribune*, Greeley, like Bennett, was an experienced journalist, and, like the founders of most of the other penny papers, he was also a practical printer. After an apprenticeship of more than four years as printer on a Vermont weekly newspaper, Greeley went to New York in 1831 and worked as a compositor on several metropolitan papers. In 1832 he and another compositor set up a job printing office, with a capital of about $250. Their first venture in the daily newspaper field, as printers of the unsuccessful *Morning Post*, resulted in a loss to the firm of $50 of their meager capital. In their next undertaking, the printing of a weekly paper devoted to news and advertisements of lotteries, as well as in job printing for lotteries, Greeley and his partner were more successful, so that by 1834 the firm considered itself worth $3000.

With the knowledge and experience gained from these ventures, and with a keen interest in political and economic questions, Greeley decided to edit and publish a weekly paper. The *New-Yorker*, accordingly, was launched on March 22, 1834. Its contents consisted of current literature, a digest of the week's news, and editorials — all selected or written by Greeley himself. The *Sun* characterized it as "most ably conducted, and — unlike most weekly newspapers of the day — well filled with instructive reading matter."[1]   In selecting current literature for the *New-Yorker*, Greeley declared that it was his aim "to blend the lessons of Science, History, Morality, and sound Criticism, as far as possible," and that he had "escaped the fashionable error of filling our columns from week to week with the buffoonery of Midshipman Easy and its compeers, the grovelling vulgarity of Snarley-yow, or the trashy though humorous absurdities of the Pickwick Papers."[2]   "The temptations to fall into this mistaken course," he continued, "are two-fold: a reduction of editorial labor, and a certainty of sailing in the popular current, and receiving large accessions of patronage."   Two years later he wrote of his policy, "we lack, or do not take kindly to, the arts which contribute to a newspaper sensation," and "we have a pride in believing that we might at any time render our journal more attractive to the millions by rendering it less deserving — and that, by merely considering what would be sought after and read with avidity, without regard to its moral or its merit, we might easily become popular at the mere expense of our own self-approval."[3]

While conducting the *New-Yorker*, he wrote editorials for the *Daily Whig*, had entire charge for a year of the *Jeffersonian*, a political paper issued at Albany in 1838 by the Whig State Central Committee, and for six months during the presidential campaign of 1840, edited and published a campaign paper, the *Log-Cabin*. Thus Greeley had had a variety of journalistic experience before he announced in an advertisement in the *Log-Cabin* that, beginning on April 10, 1841, he would publish a daily paper, the *New-York Tribune*.[4]

The purpose of the "new Morning Journal of Politics, Literature, and General Intelligence," he indicated thus in the same advertisement:[5]

THE TRIBUNE, as its name imports, will labor to advance the interests of the People, and to promote their Moral, Social, and

[1] *Sun*, May 5, 1834.
[2] *New-Yorker*, September 16, 1837.
[3] *New-Yorker*, March 21, 1839.
[4] *Log-Cabin*, April 10, 1841.
[5] *Log-Cabin*, April 10, 1841.

Political well-being. The immoral and degrading Police Reports, Advertisements and other matter which have been allowed to disgrace the columns of many of our leading Penny Papers will be carefully excluded from this, and no exertion spared to render it worthy of the hearty approval of the virtuous and refined, and a welcome visitant at the family fireside.

Of the political purpose and policy of the *Tribune*, Greeley wrote, in his autobiographical sketches, *Recollections of a Busy Life:* [1]

I had been incited to this enterprise by several Whig friends, who deemed a cheap daily, addressed more especially to the laboring class, eminently needed in our city, where the only two cheap journals then and still existing — The Sun and The Herald — were in decided, though unavowed, and therefore more effective, sympathy and affiliation with the Democratic party. . . .

My leading idea was the establishment of a journal removed alike from servile partisanship on the one hand and from gagged, mincing neutrality on the other. Party spirit is so fierce and intolerant in this country that the editor of a non-partisan sheet is restrained from saying what he thinks and feels on the most vital, imminent topics; while, on the other hand, a Democratic, Whig, or Republican journal is generally expected to praise or blame, like or dislike, eulogize or condemn, in precise accordance with the views and interest of its party. I believed there was a happy medium between these extremes, — a position from which a journalist might openly and heartily advocate the principles and commend the measures of that party to which his convictions allied him, yet frankly dissent from its course on a particular question, and even denounce its candidates if they were shown to be deficient in capacity or (far worse) in integrity.

In thus eschewing the three conspicuous features of all the cheap, popular dailies — police court news, objectionable medical advertising, and political neutrality — Greeley was undertaking to establish a new type of penny paper.

The *Tribune* began under almost as humble circumstances as did Bennett's *Herald*. Greeley entered upon the task of establishing a paper, as he afterwards said, "with no partner or business associate, with inconsiderable pecuniary resources, and only a promise from political friends to aid to the extent of two thousand

[1] Greeley, Horace. *Recollections of a Busy Life*, pp. 136–37.

dollars, of which but one half was ever realized." ¹   As editorial assistant he had Henry J. Raymond, a youth of twenty-one, just graduated from the University of Vermont, whom he employed at a salary of $8 a week, and who ten years later became one of the founders, and the first editor, of the *New-York Times*.   The price of the paper was one cent a copy, or sixpence a week.   Like the other penny dailies, it was circulated on the so-called London plan of selling its circulation to carrier boys.²   The *Tribune* started with less than 500 subscribers, and with an edition of 5000 copies, of which Greeley said he "nearly succeeded in giving away all . . . . that would not sell." ³   He had enough type to set up one issue, but no presses on which to print the paper.   His expenses for the first week amounted to $525, and his receipts were $92.⁴

Despite this inauspicious beginning, the *Tribune's* circulation rose even more rapidly than had those of the *Sun* and of the *Herald* on their inception.   Within three weeks of its first issue it claimed 5500, and at the end of seven weeks, 11,000.⁵   Owing to the fact that the pages of the *Tribune* were about four times the size of those of the first penny papers, it gave its readers "a greater amount of reading matter daily than has ever been given for One Cent in any paper ever published in the World." ⁶   When the *Tribune* was eight months old, Greeley explained that, although "our circulation is now exceeded by not more than three or four daily papers in the world; yet . . . its circulation at our low price is not directly profitable to us but the reverse." ⁷   In writing at this time to Thurlow Weed, editor of the *Albany Evening Journal*, Greeley said, "The 'Tribune' is just beginning to draw ahead in spite of the absence of all party and mercantile advertising from its columns." ⁸   From four columns of advertising in the first issue, the amount increased by the end of the second week to nine columns, and at the close of four months, to thirteen columns.

After trying for nearly four months to manage both the editorial and the business departments of the paper, Greeley formed a co-

¹ Parton, James. *Life of Horace Greeley*, p. 158.
² *New-York Tribune*, April 10, 1841.
³ Greeley, Horace. *Recollections of a Busy Life*, p. 139.   ⁴ *Ibid.*, p. 140.
⁵ *New-York Tribune*, May 31, 1841.
⁶ *Ibid.*, December 1, 1841.   ⁷ *Ibid.*
⁸ *Autobiography of Thurlow Weed*, Harriet A. Weed, ed., vol. 1, p. 468.

partnership with Thomas McElrath, a practical man of affairs. The latter thereupon became business manager of the *Tribune* and relieved Greeley of the financial management, for which he had no aptitude.[1]

Invading the metropolitan field as a large, well-edited penny daily, the *Tribune* immediately aroused the hostility of the *Sun* and of the *Herald*, the publishers of which adopted drastic measures to destroy it. *Tribune* carriers were bribed to give up their routes; they were attacked and beaten by *Sun* newsboys at the instigation of the proprietor of that paper; they were forbidden by the publishers of the *Sun* and of the *Herald* to handle these papers as long as they continued to sell or deliver the *Tribune*.[2] These unfair attempts on the part of his rivals to crush the new paper, led Greeley to attack them both for such tactics and for their news, editorial, and advertising policies.

Having denounced "the immoral and degrading Police Reports ... which have been allowed to disgrace the columns of many of our leading Penny Papers," Greeley proceeded to assail those papers for publishing detailed reports of crimes and of criminal trials. In an editorial on the manner in which a murder case had been handled by the sensational papers, he wrote:[3]

> The avidity with which all the particulars attending this horrid butchery, the murderer's trial, execution and the confessions, real or manufactured, said to have fallen from his lips, have been collected, published and read, evinces no less a depraved appetite in the community, than a most unprincipled and reckless disregard of consequences on the part of those who are willing — nay, eager, for the sake of private gain, to poison the fountains of public intelligence, and fan into destroying flames the hellish passions which now slumber in the bosom of Society. We weigh well our words when we say that the moral guilt incurred, and the violent hurt inflicted upon social order and individual happiness by those who have thus spread out the loathsome details of this most damning deed, are tenfold greater than those of the wretched miscreant himself. . . .
>
> The guilt of murder may not stain their hands; but the fouler and more damning guilt of *making murderers* — of raising and training to their tasks men who will dare to strike the blow the

[1] Greeley, Horace. *Recollections of a Busy Life*, p. 140.
[2] *New-York Tribune*, May 4, June 7, June 10, and August 30, 1841.
[3] *Ibid.*, April 19, 1841.

fear of the law perhaps restrains themselves from giving — rests upon their [the editors'] souls and will rest there for ever. The wretched plea of 'the duty of the Press to Society' — that it is bound to keep the public informed of all such acts — is urged: — but the same hypocrites who stab the public good under this pretence, turn a deaf ear to the higher duties which they owe to the best interests of society, to the good of their fellow-men and to the requirements of decent morality as well as of the highest justice.

A month later he characterized the *Sun* as "that depraved and filthy sheet, which has forced itself into a wide circulation by systematically pandering to the lowest appetites and most perverted tastes of the community." [1]

With equal moral earnestness he condemned the objectionable advertisements in the *Sun* and in the *Herald*. In two editorials he denounced both papers for permitting a notorious woman practitioner to use their advertising columns. Excerpts from these editorials read as follows: [2]

Two years ago, we (while temporarily conducting the New York Whig) called public attention repeatedly to the atrocious and abominable advertisements which then blazoned in *The Sun* and Bennett's *Herald*. . . . We remonstrated against the public toleration of such scandalous and depraving practices and the unblushing effrontery of the woman and her coadjutors of the Sun and the Herald in proclaiming their joint iniquity.

This was long after the conductors of that paper [the *Sun*] had been publicly and anxiously remonstrated with and shown the iniquity of publishing those advertisements. But what cared *they* for crime or misery, so long as either could fill their greedy coffers with gold? . . . And thus, by constant publication and puffing in *The Sun*, backed by puffing Editorials in the *Herald*, the dreadful trade of this wretch was made to thrive and gold flowed in streams into her den, and thence to the pockets of her newspaper accomplices.

In spite of his vigorous stand against such advertising and that of objectionable patent medicines, Greeley himself was not sufficiently in advance of the practices of the day to censor the advertisements of makers of nostrums. Later in the same year he wrote: [3]

---

[1] *New-York Tribune*, May 22, 1841.   [2] *Ibid.*, April 28 and 30, 1841.
[3] *Ibid.*, December 20, 1841.

A friend writes us to complain of the ingenuity of our advertisers in writing commendations of their medicines. He should complain to our advertisers themselves, who are not responsible to us for the style or language (if decent) of their advertisements, nor have we any control over them.

In the matter of theaters and theatrical advertising, however, he took a definite position, for he declared: [1]

> ...we have never refused to publish advertisements of Theatres, though we have not sought and do not desire them. We have not sought them mainly because we consider the Stage, *as it is*, rather an injury than a benefit to the community — vicious, licentious, degrading, demoralizing. Doubtless, the Stage might be — perhaps has been — a pure and powerful instrument of civilization and refinement; but it certainly is not so now. It never can be, so long as each Theatre contains within its walls a grog-shop and a place of assignation — a sort of exchange for lewdness and moral death. We say nothing of the notorious fact that a large proportion of those connected with the Stage are libertines or courtezans — a proportion much larger, we are confident, than can be found in any other tolerated profession.

In two other matters involving the ethics of journalism, Greeley early expressed himself unequivocally. When his assistance was sought in a campaign to curb vice by giving newspaper publicity to the names of owners and landlords of questionable resorts, he refused, evidently because he did not consider that such matters were suited to a family newspaper. "This is an undertaking," he wrote, "which we cannot aid through our columns; but we assure those who applied to us that they are right and that the public will justify them in the course they have resolved on." [2] Discussing a defense of "hoaxing" made by the *Boston Mail*, he deplored in no uncertain terms the evils of "faking." [3]

> The Mail here plainly declares that there is no difference in point of morality between deliberately forging a falsehood, which may cause infinite misery, and spreading it far and wide, and scribbling a fictitious tale which does not purport to be true, and to which no one can for a moment attach any importance....
>
> We are having by far too much of this of late. This same pleasant 'hoaxing' is sinking and degrading the character of the

[1] *New-York Tribune*, May 11, 1841.
[2] *Ibid.*, July 30, 1841.　　[3] *Ibid.*, December 11, 1841.

newspaper press as a faithful herald of a busy world.   These journals have already become almost the poorest authority that can be cited for the truth or falsehood of any statement; and, if the newspaper morals of the Mail are to prevail, they will soon deserve all the contempt and distrust the judicious are disposed to bestow upon them.

Ever ready in the columns of the *Tribune* to express his own convictions on all political, economic, industrial, and social questions, he believed that it was the duty of an editor to take a definite stand in his editorials.   In an early number of the *Tribune*, he discussed the so-called "neutrality" of the other cheap papers, and set forth his own ideas of an editor's attitude thus: [1]

> As regards the relative independence of avowed party and honestly neutral papers, we know from much experience that the advantage is decidedly with the former.   An openly party paper will, nine times out of ten, speak out its honest thought; a neutral paper seldom or never can.   If it does, it will lose subscribers at every turn.   Its only safe course is to avoid political discussion altogether, and thus leave the most important topics wholly untouched.   But the true, honest course for an individual would seem to be not to attempt Editorship until he has studied the great public questions of the day, and formed his opinions upon them; then, in coming before the public, he should frankly, candidly avow what these opinions are.   Having done this, he is prepared to act with freedom and independence, and to give to his arguments the weight of his known convictions.

Accordingly, he denounced the editorial policies of the "neutral" papers, declaring that "the professedly *neutral* journals of our city are the Journal of Commerce, Herald and Sun — each of them animated by the deadliest hostility to every distinctive principle and measure of the Whig party," and that "no opportunity is omitted by either to aim a deadly blow at any plan of creating a National Circulating Medium, the Protection of American Industry or the Land Distribution." [2]   Against the *Sun's* political policies Greeley wrote most vigorously: [3]

> That paper, steeped as it is in the gall of Loco-Focoism, circulates over thirty thousand copies daily — equal to more than the

[1] *New-York Tribune*, April 26, 1841.
[2] *Ibid.*, August 27, 1841.   [3] *Ibid.*, April 16, 1841.

circulation of all the Whig papers in the City. Ten thousand of these copies are taken by as many Whigs, and it is read by ten times the number. Professing entire neutrality and treating all political topics with catlike dexterity — fur outside, but sharp claws beneath — it exerts a most destructive and blasting influence throughout the whole extent of its circulation. There is no honesty in its management.

Again he wrote of the *Sun:* [1]

The iniquity of The Sun's course consists in its *suppression of the truth.* A neutral paper ought to present *both sides* of the party questions it discusses.

The *Herald* he also charged with unfairness in reporting political affairs with which the editor was not in sympathy.   He wrote: [2]

If any one really believes that the *Herald* gives any thing like fair reports of the Debates in Congress we ask him to read the substance of Mr. Botts's remarks in any other paper, and then look at the wretched travesty, the shameful suppression in the *Herald.* Mr. Botts spoke an hour, and the Herald report can be read in one minute! This is the way Marshall's and all the anti-cabal speeches have been treated by that print throughout.

In carrying out his determination, expressed early in the career of the *Tribune,* that his "readers shall have matter, not merely for a morning glance, but for an evening fireside hour if they can command the time," [3] Greeley published reviews of books and of magazines, as well as some of the best current literature. Carlyle's essay on Burns, Emerson's essay on "Man the Reformer," and Dickens' *Barnaby Rudge* were printed (the last named, serially) in early numbers of the paper, together with "the Spirit and Substance of all the best Lectures" delivered in New York.[4]   In order to provide as good a newspaper as they desired, Greeley and McElrath found it necessary, at the beginning of the second year, to increase the price to two cents a copy, as the *Herald* had done.

Always sympathetic with the working classes, and moved by the hardships imposed on them by the business depression of 1837–38, Greeley was led to consider ways and means of bringing

[1] *New-York Tribune,* April 29, 1841.   [2] *Ibid.,* September 14, 1841.
[3] *Ibid.,* November 24, 1841.   [4] *Ibid.,* December 1, 1841.

about better social and industrial conditions.   Thus he became interested in various idealistic proposals for a greater degree of economic equality for all classes.   One of these was the communistic plan advocated by Charles Fourier, a Frenchman, whose doctrines were being popularized in the United States by Albert Brisbane, a well-to-do young American, who had studied abroad, and who on his return to this country in 1840 had published a book expounding Fourierism.[1]   Greeley accepted this form of Socialism, known as "Association," the policy of which was to establish communistic agricultural settlements called "phalanxes."   He permitted Brisbane and a number of men associated with him to use, for a nominal amount, a column on the first page of the *Tribune* in which to set forth the principles of Association. These contributions, which took the form of letters, began in March, 1842, and continued, either daily or three times a week, for over two years.

At first Greeley did not advocate Fourierism editorially, but, as the plan created interest and gained adherents, he supported the principles of Association.   Naturally so radical a proposal for social reform aroused much opposition.   That Greeley realized the unpopularity of his editorial policy in this matter, is shown by a letter that he wrote in August, 1842, to Charles A. Dana, then a young man living at Brook Farm, an experimental communistic settlement near Boston.   He wrote: "I have encountered much opposition and ridicule on account of what I have published and the little that I have written in favor of association, and have shocked the prejudices of many worthy friends, some of whom have stopped my paper on account of this, and all been chilled in their friendship by my unyielding *fanaticism.*" [2]   Notwithstanding the unfortunate effects produced by this first of Greeley's "isms," he continued for many years to support the Association scheme, until the failure of one after another of the communities, or "phalanxes," in various parts of the country seemed to prove its futility.

In an effort to put his communistic ideals into practice, Greeley in 1849 arranged with his partner, Mr. McElrath, to organize the

---

[1] Albert Brisbane was the father of Arthur Brisbane, editor of Hearst newspapers.

[2] Wilson, J. H.   *Life of Charles A. Dana*, p. 42.

Tribune as a stock company, and to permit employees in all departments of the paper to become stock-holders.   The company was capitalized at $100,000, with one hundred shares of $1000 each.   Ten employees, including five assistant editors and five members of the business and mechanical departments, took sixteen shares, and the two original proprietors stood ready to sell some of their own stock whenever other employees wished to buy.[1] Two years later, Greeley wrote in the *Tribune* that the number of stock-holders had increased to twelve, "including all those responsibly connected with its conduct, editorial, financial, or mechanical," and he added that "thus the two chief proprietors purpose and hope in time to make still further application of the general principle that the workman should be his own employer and director, and should receive the full reward of his labor."   By 1854 the stock-holders numbered sixteen, including the publisher, seven editors, four clerks, the foreman of the composing room, the foreman of the press-room, one compositor, and one pressman.[2]

In connection with the capitalization of the *Tribune* at $100,000, which was a conservative valuation, it is interesting to recall that, eight years before, Greeley had started the paper with only $2000. Mr. McElrath, on becoming a partner, had furnished $2000 more in order to secure a half interest.   Thus, from a total investment of $4000, the *Tribune* during eight years had developed into a property worth $100,000.   It was not the daily *Tribune*, however, that was profitable, according to Dana, who was one of the stockholders.   In a letter of 1854, he wrote that it had "never made a cent, but . . . . existed solely that something might be made on the weekly and semi-weekly." [3]

In 1850 the staff of the *Tribune* consisted of twelve editors and reporters.   It had three regular correspondents in Washington, two in California, and one each in Philadelphia, Baltimore, and Boston.   Its foreign service included four permanent European correspondents, two in Canada, and one each in Mexico, Cuba, and Central America.   To produce the paper there were required thirty-seven compositors and thirteen pressmen, engineers, and

[1] *New-York Tribune*, August 30, 1850.
[2] Parton, James. *Life of Horace Greeley*, p. 362.
[3] Wilson, J. H. *Life of Charles A. Dana*, p. 128.

press-room workers.   When a four-cylinder, type-revolving press
was installed in 1850, at a cost of $12,000, the time necessary for
running off the daily edition was reduced by one half.[1]

Although Mr. McElrath was a co-partner before the stock company was organized, and afterwards held a majority of the stock,
he did not interfere with Greeley's conduct of the paper.   "During the ten years or over that The Tribune was issued by Greeley
& McElrath," wrote Greeley in his autobiography, "my partner
never once even indicated that my anti-Slavery, anti-Hanging,
Socialist, and other frequent aberrations from the straight and
narrow path of Whig partisanship, were injurious to our common
interest, though he must often have sorely felt that they were so;
and never . . . did he even *look* grieved at anything I did." [2]
This relation between the editorial and the business departments
of the *Tribune* was thus set forth in one of the articles of agreement entered into on January 1, 1849: [3]

> The Editor shall have entire and uncontrolled management of
> the Editorial Department of the said paper or papers, and also the
> right of determining the political character, views, or opinions of
> the said paper or papers; and the right, conjointly with the Pub-
> lisher, of determining upon the insertion or rejection of every
> communication, advertisement, or other matter, intended or of-
> fered for insertion therein.

Greeley's advocacy of Fourierism, and his attempt to put into
practice by the stock company ownership of the *Tribune* some of
the principles of Association, led Bennett to attack the *Tribune*
and its editor in editorials like the following: [4]

> We understand that the *Tribune* establishment, from top to
> bottom, has been recently converted into a socialistic phalanx,
> and that the editors, printers, publishers, reporters, all the way
> from the nigger to the lesser devils, are all interested, more or less,
> in that delectable sheet — a sheet that has produced on public
> affairs and on the public mind a more deleterious, anti-Christian,
> and infidel effect, during the last few years, than all the publica-
> tions that have hitherto appeared, from the time of Voltaire to
> the first issue of the *Tribune* sheet . . . the same phalanx of philos-

---

[1] *New-York Tribune,* August 30, 1850.
[2] Greeley, Horace.   *Recollections of a Busy Life,* p. 140.
[3] *Articles of Agreement of the New-York Tribune* (pamphlet).
[4] *New York Herald,* October 3, 1849.

ophers, Fourierites, socialists . . . have employed some of the most rabid infidels and socialists of France and England — steeped in the reddest of all red republicanism — to fulminate and disseminate in this community their atrocious and demoniac doctrines, which have nearly ruined, in its first inception and primary movements, the glorious republic of France.

Bennett not only charged the *Tribune* with being "steeped in abolition, folly, infidelity, demoralization of society, and various other iniquities," [1] but repeatedly maintained that Greeley, Dana, and Ripley advocated "the promiscuous intercourse of the sexes and free love." [2] The only basis for these charges was the *Tribune's* support of such idealistic communist experiments as Brook Farm.

Although Greeley's primary interest lay in the editorial columns, the *Tribune* did not lack enterprise in getting and publishing the news. It printed "extras," as did the other cheap papers, on the arrival of ships with foreign news. It also arranged with the Boston *Atlas* to have "extras" printed containing the foreign news obtained from trans-Atlantic ships that ran to Boston, and to have enough of these sent to New York to be distributed as a part of the *Tribune*.[3] The news published in "extras" on the arrival of ships was usually reprinted on the first page of the next morning's issue. The front page, however, was not supposed to contain news, as the two following apologies show: [4]

We are obliged to-day by a press of new advertisements to put most of our best matter and News on the First Page of our paper. We trust our readers will take the slight trouble of turning over the leaf for it.

We are constrained, by the necessity of making room in the evening for the Reports of Lectures, to place a great portion of our earlier News by the Mails on our First Page. As our paper can be opened without straining the arms, our readers will have no difficulty in finding it.

Greeley testified, in 1851, before an English parliamentary committee investigating the effects of the so-called "taxes on knowledge," that in the United States "more weight is laid upon in-

---

[1] *New York Herald*, August 15, 1845.   [2] *Ibid.*, April 30, 1858.
[3] *New-York Tribune*, August 21, 1841.   [4] *Ibid.*, November 19 and 25, 1841.

telligence [news] than on editorials; the paper which brings the quickest news is the thing looked to." Editorials, he declared, had less influence in America than in England, for in America "the telegraphic dispatch is the great point," while in England, he believed, the telegraph was employed by newspapers "not a hundredth part" as much as it was by the American press.[1]

On September 29, 1841, five months after the daily *Tribune* started, a weekly edition was launched. Later it absorbed Greeley's two weekly papers, the *Log-Cabin* and the *New-Yorker*. The scope of the *Weekly Tribune* was thus indicated by the prospectus:[2]

> The TRIBUNE — whether in its Daily or Weekly edition — will be what its name imports — an unflinching supporter of the People's Rights and interests, in stern hostility to the errors of superficial theorists, the influence of unjust or imperfect legislation, and the schemes and sophistries of self-seeking demagogues. . . .
>
> The proceedings of Congress will be carefully recorded; the Foreign and Domestic Intelligence early and lucidly presented; and whatever shall appear calculated to promote Morality, maintain Social Order, extend the blessings of Education, or in any way subserve the great cause of Human Progress to ultimate Virtue, Liberty and Happiness, will find a place in our columns.

The price of the *Weekly Tribune* was $2.00 a year. Of the first issue 18,000 copies were printed. The circulation of the weekly edition, which always exceeded that of the daily, extended throughout the northern states. In 1847, when the daily circulated 11,000 copies, the weekly had reached more than 15,000. By 1853 the weekly had risen to 51,000, and, in the following year, during the presidential campaign, it went up to over 100,000. Premiums and club rates were effectively used to increase the circulation of the weekly edition, which in 1860 exceeded 200,000. Of the influence of the *Weekly Tribune* in the '50s James Ford Rhodes, the historian, has said:[3]

[1] Parton, James. *Life of Horace Greeley*, p. 326; also *New York Herald*, October 7, 1851.

[2] *New-York Tribune*, September 14, 1841.

[3] Rhodes, J. F. "Newspapers as Historical Sources," in his *Historical Essays*, pp. 90–91.

The greatest single journalistic influence was the *New York Weekly Tribune* which had in 1854 a circulation of 112,000, and many times that number of readers. These readers were of the thorough kind, reading all the news, all the printed speeches and addresses, and all the editorials, and pondering as they read. The questions were discussed in their family circles and with their neighbors, and, as differences arose, the *Tribune*, always at hand, was consulted and re-read. There being few popular magazines during this decade, the weekly newspaper, in some degree, took their place; and, through this medium, Greeley and his able co-adjutors spoke to the people of New York and of the West, where New England ideas predominated, with a power never before or since known in this country.

Greeley gathered around him from the first an unusually capable staff of associates. Charles A. Dana, going to the *Tribune* when the Brook Farm community came to an untimely end, became city editor, and later, managing editor, a title that he is said to have been the first person to bear on any American newspaper. He not only had charge of the news but contributed editorials. During Greeley's trips abroad, he had entire direction of the editorial columns, and, whenever the editor was away from the office, he took over responsibility for the editorial policy. From the time that he rejoined the *Tribune* staff in 1849, after having been abroad for eight months, until he retired in 1862, he shared with Greeley the editing of the paper, and had no small part in determining its policy and character. Another former member of the Brook Farm group to join the *Tribune* was George Ripley. In 1849 he established the first regular department in any American daily paper devoted to the reviewing of current books and periodicals. He continued as literary editor for over thirty years, until his death in 1880. Margaret Fuller, who with Ralph Waldo Emerson and George Ripley had edited the *Dial*, a literary and philosophical quarterly published in Boston, was a member of the *Tribune* staff from 1844 to 1846, and was the first woman writer of distinction to engage in daily newspaper work. Solon Robinson was agricultural editor, but is best known for a series of "human interest" stories, the earliest of their kind published in any American newspaper, portraying the life of the less fortunate classes in New York City. The first of these sketches, entitled "Hot Corn," published in 1853, dealt with a little girl, a street waif, who sold boiled sweet corn on a street corner near the *Tribune* office until after midnight. In their exaggerated pathos and their sentimental treatment of the less fortunate classes, these stories were suggestive of the work of Charles Dickens. So popular were these stories, that in 1853 they were reprinted in book form under the title, *Hot Corn: Life Scenes in New York Illustrated,* and over 50,000 copies were sold in the first six months.[1] Another writer to join the staff in 1849 was Bayard Taylor, who became widely known, both through his travel sketches in the *Tribune,* which were later published in book form, and through lecturing on his travels. Dana, Ripley, and Taylor in due time became stock-holders in the *Tribune* company. With such writers the paper early took on a distinctly literary character, which differentiated it in a marked degree from other newspapers in this country.

Greeley encouraged the members of his staff to sign their articles. In a letter to Bayard Taylor early in 1849, he said, "I want everybody connected with the 'Tribune' to become known to the public (in some unobtrusive way) as doing what he does, so that in case of my death or incapacity it may not be fancied that the paper is to die or essentially suffer," and he suggested "initials or some distinctive mark at the bottom" as a means of identification.[2] Greeley himself occasionally signed his initials to his editorials.

During the first decade of the *Tribune* Greeley fearlessly advocated a variety of unpopular causes. In thanking his readers for their support, he wrote in 1844, at the beginning of the fourth year of the paper:[3]

Our gratitude is the deeper from our knowledge that many of the views expressed through our columns are unacceptable to a larger proportion of our readers. We know especially that our advocacy of measures intended to meliorate the Social condition of the Toiling Millions (not the purpose, but the means,) our ardent sympathy with the People of Ireland in their protracted, arduous, peaceful struggle to recover some portion of the common Rights of Man, and our opposition to the legal extinction of

[1] Derby, J. C. *Fifty Years Among Authors,* p. 130.
[2] Taylor, Marie H., and Scudder, H. E. *Life and Letters of Bayard Taylor,* vol. 1, p. 144.
[3] *New-York Tribune,* April 8, 1844.

Human Life, are severally or collectively regarded with extreme aversion by many of our steadfast patrons, whose liberality and confidence is gratefully appreciated.

Because of his violent hostility to the Mexican War, threats were made to mob the *Tribune* office. The woman's rights movement, as equal suffrage was then termed, called forth much ridicule, but Greeley himself reported the first national convention held at Seneca Falls, New York, in 1848, and wrote of the movement: [1]

> It is easy to be smart, to be droll, to be facetious, in opposition to the demands of these Female Reformers; and, in decrying assumptions so novel and opposed to established habits and usages, a little wit will go a great way. But when a sincere republican is asked to say in sober earnest what adequate reason he can give for refusing the demand of women to an equal participation with men in political rights, he must answer, None at all.

He also urged restrictions on the liquor traffic, the evils of which he constantly deplored. His attitude toward all movements calculated to improve society, he expressed thus: [2]

> It has been urged as an objection to The Tribune that it proposed to 'give hospitality to every *new* thought.' Our own expression here aimed at, contemplated not every new but every *generous thought*. To that profession we shall be constant at whatever sacrifice. Full of error and suffering as the world yet is, we cannot afford to reject unexamined any idea which proposes to improve the Moral, Intellectual or Social condition of mankind. Better incur the trouble of testing and exploding a thousand fallacies than by rejecting stifle a single beneficent truth.

The various constructive measures that received his endorsement included a protective tariff to safeguard American workers against unequal competition with foreign labor; distribution of public lands to *bona fide* settlers; the construction with government aid of railroad and telegraph lines to the Pacific; organizations of workers; the ten-hour day; an international copyright law; freedom of speech for radical abolitionists like William Lloyd Garrison; internal improvements such as those of rivers and harbors; and scientific agriculture.

[1] Quoted in Parton's *Life of Horace Greeley*, p. 289.
[2] *New-York Tribune*, May 29, 1845.

During the critical period from 1850 to 1860, when slavery became the one great issue, Greeley and the *Tribune* took journalistic leadership as exponents of the anti-slavery cause.   Never in
American journalism has a single editor or a single newspaper
wielded so great an influence throughout the country as did Greeley and the *Tribune* at this time.   In New York and Washington,
where the daily *Tribune* was read, and in other cities where the
daily edition was quoted and commented on by other newspapers,
the effect of Greeley's anti-slavery policy was unquestionably
great, but his influence was even greater in the towns and rural
districts west of the Alleghanies, where the *Weekly Tribune*
had the then phenomenal circulation of from 125,000 to 200,000
copies.   "The 'Tribune' comes next to the Bible all through
the West," wrote Bayard Taylor to his mother while he was
on a lecture tour.[1]   Throughout the North and West, the *Tribune*
was undoubtedly the most powerful of all forces in crystallizing
public opinion against slavery.

The *Tribune* from its inception had been a staunch supporter
of the Whig party, and through Greeley's vigorous editorial policy
it came to be recognized as that party's leading exponent.   But,
after the defeat of General Scott for the presidency in 1852,
Greeley declared that, "if an anti-slavery Whig must give up his
anti-slavery or his Whiggery, we choose to part with the latter."
Accordingly, when the new Republican party came into existence
in 1854 as the anti-slavery political organization, Greeley became
a Republican.

In national and state politics Greeley took an active part.
In New York state political activities he was a close associate
of the two Whig leaders, Thurlow Weed, editor of the *Albany
Evening Journal*, and William H. Seward, governor of New York
and later United States senator, the three constituting until 1854
what Greeley termed "the political firm of Seward, Weed, and
Greeley."   Disappointed by the failure of these political associates to secure for him the nomination for governor or for lieutenant-governor, especially as the latter position went to his journalistic rival, Henry J. Raymond, editor of the *New-York Times*,
he announced to Seward the dissolution of this political alliance.

[1] Taylor, Marie H., and Scudder, H. E. *Life and Letters of Bayard Taylor*, vol. 1,
p. 263.

For three months of the session of 1848–49, Greeley served as a member of Congress to fill a vacancy created by the death of a New York congressman, and wrote daily letters to the *Tribune* from Washington. In his brief congressional career, he attracted nation-wide attention by exposing the evils of the excessive mileage allowed by law to members of Congress. He also attacked the injustice of the postal rates and the abuse by congressmen of the franking privilege. He advocated cheap postage and retrenchment and reform in governmental expenditures. In the Republican National Convention at Chicago in 1860, Greeley exerted all his influence, both through the *Tribune* and as a substitute delegate from Oregon, to prevent the proposed nomination of Seward for the presidency. Seward's friends had their revenge the following year when they succeeded in blocking Greeley's nomination for the United States senatorship. Nevertheless, Greeley supported Seward for the secretaryship of state in Lincoln's cabinet.

The Civil War proved a sore trial for Greeley. All his humanitarian instincts made him hate war, but they also made him hate slavery. Thus he was constantly vacillating. When, after Lincoln's election, threats of secession became stronger and stronger, Greeley in the *Tribune* took the position that " the great principle embodied by Jefferson in the Declaration of American Independence, that governments derive their just power from the consent of the governed, is sound and just; and that if the Slave States, the Cotton States, or the Gulf States only, choose to form an independent nation, they have a clear moral right to do so." [1] After Fort Sumter had been fired on and Lincoln had issued the call for troops, Greeley changed his mind as to secession: [2]

> There has been a good deal of discussion, since the Southern rebellion began, of the propriety of allowing the Slave States south of the Potomac and the Ohio to separate themselves from the Union, and set up an independent Slave-holding Government for themselves. . . .
> It is now evident — and all men will do well to shape their calculations accordingly — that THE UNION CANNOT BE DISSOLVED. There cannot be two rival and competing Governments within the boundaries of the United States. The territorial integrity and

[1] *New-York Tribune*, February 23, 1861.   [2] *Ibid.*, April 25, 1861.

the political unity of the nation are to be preserved at whatever cost.

Urging vigorously that a decisive blow be struck at the Confederacy, the *Tribune* printed the following rallying cry at the head of its editorial column day after day, beginning in June, 1861:

THE NATION'S WAR-CRY

Forward to Richmond!   Forward to Richmond!   The Rebel Congress must not be allowed to meet there on the 20th July.   BY THAT DATE THE PLACE MUST BE HELD BY THE NATIONAL ARMY.

Dana, not Greeley, was responsible for the reiteration of this warcry, which was composed by a regular contributor, Fitz-Henry Warren.   The disaster to the Union army at Bull Run, which resulted from an attempt to carry out this military program of the *Tribune*, led Greeley to publish a signed statement explaining his position.   It read in part: [1]

> I wish to be distinctly understood as not seeking to be relieved from any responsibility for urging the advance of the Union Grand Army into Virginia, though the precise phrase "Forward to Richmond!" is not mine, and I would have preferred not to iterate it. I thought that that Army, One Hundred Thousand strong, might have been in the Rebel capital on or before the 20th inst., while I felt that there were urgent reasons why it *should* be there if possible.   And now, if any one imagines that I, or any one connected with THE TRIBUNE, ever commended or imagined any such strategy as the launching of barely Thirty Thousand of the One Hundred Thousand Union Volunteers within fifty miles of Washington against Ninety Thousand Rebels enveloped in a labyrinth of strong intrenchments and unreconnoitered masked batteries, then demonstration would be lost on his closed ear. But I will not dwell on this.   If I am needed as a scapegoat for all the military blunders of the last month, so be it!   Individuals must die that the Nation may live.   If I can serve her best in that capacity, I do not shrink from the ordeal. . . .
>
> Now let the wolves howl on!   I do not believe they can goad me into another personal notice of their ravings.

Greeley was so overwhelmed by the Union defeat at the battle of Bull Run that he was prostrated for six weeks with an attack of brain fever.

---

[1] *New-York Tribune*, July 25, 1861.

At the close of 1861, the *Tribune* insisted that Lincoln could end the war in three months if he would proclaim that "Slaveholding by rebels is not recognized and sustained by the Government and arms of the United States." [1] This proposal, which found repeated expression in the paper, finally took the form of a letter to the President entitled "The Prayer of Twenty Millions," which urged Lincoln to declare free all slaves who escaped into the Union lines, and to use negro labor in connection with military operations. [2] To this appeal Lincoln replied by a letter to Greeley, which included this famous paragraph: [3]

> My paramount object in this struggle *is* to save the Union, and is *not* either to save or destroy Slavery. If I could save the Union without freeing *any* slave, I would do it; and if I could save it by freeing *all* the slaves, I would do it; and if I could do it by freeing some and leaving others alone, I would also do that.

Greeley immediately wrote a reply to Lincoln, urging him to "instruct your Generals and Commodores, that no loyal person — certainly none willing to render service to the National cause — is henceforth to be regarded as the slave of any traitor." [4] When, less than a month later, Lincoln issued the Emancipation Proclamation, Greeley ceased to doubt the ultimate triumph of the Union cause. "It is the beginning of the end of the rebellion," he wrote; "the beginning of the new life of the nation." [5]

Bennett, always bitterly hostile to Greeley and the *Tribune*, made more vicious attacks on him during the first years of the war than ever before. He characterized Greeley in the *Herald* as a "crazy, contemptible wretch," a "monster, ogre, ghoul," who had "instigated this dreadful civil war for years past, and carefully nurtured and fostered the abolition sentiment, with which he hoped to poison and kill the Republic." Bennett declared that Greeley would "not cease to do evil until the government or the people shall lose all patience and suddenly annihilate him and his infamous Tribune," and predicted, "if we decide to hang the Abolitionists, poor Greeley shall swing on the post of high honor at the head or the tail of the lot." Such incendiary utterances in the *Herald* helped to incite a mob, during the draft riots in 1863,

---

[1] *New-York Tribune*, December 16, 1861. [2] *Ibid.*, August 20, 1862.
[3] *Ibid.*, August 25, 1862. [4] *Ibid.* [5] *Ibid.*, September 23, 1862.

to attack the *Tribune* office, and Greeley narrowly escaped with his life.

Desirous of bringing about peace at the earliest possible moment, Greeley in July, 1864, sought and obtained authorization from Lincoln to treat with commissioners of the Confederacy, but the attempt proved futile.

From the day of Lee's surrender, Greeley advocated a policy of magnanimity toward the South, in the face of widespread demands for drastic reprisals against the rebels. "Universal amnesty, — Impartial suffrage" became the *Tribune's* new watchword. The assassination of Lincoln strengthened popular opposition to a policy of clemency and brought down on Greeley the denunciation of extremists who had been urging vigorous measures against Jefferson Davis and the South. In describing the reaction against him and the *Tribune* that resulted from his conciliatory attitude, Greeley later asserted:[1]

> At once, a concerted howl of denunciation and rage was sent up from every side against me by the little creatures whom God, for some inscrutable purpose, permits to edit a majority of our minor journals, echoed by a yell of "Stop my paper!" from thousands of imperfectly instructed readers of THE TRIBUNE. One impudent puppy wrote me to answer categorically whether I was or was not in favor of hanging Jeff. Davis, adding that I must stop his paper if I were not! Scores volunteered assurances that I was defying public opinion — that most of my readers were against me — as if I could be induced to write what they wished said rather than what they needed to be told. I never before realized so vividly the baseness of the Editorial vocation according to the vulgar conception of it.

When, in May, 1867, Greeley went to Richmond to sign the bailbond of Jefferson Davis, who had been imprisoned in Fortress Monroe for two years, the storm that broke over his head was even more violent. So strongly did the tide of popular resentment run against Greeley because of this quixotic act, that the sale of his history of the Civil War, *The Great American Conflict,* which had been large and steady, "almost ceased for a season; thousands who had subscribed for it refusing to take their copies."[2]

[1] *New-York Tribune*, May 23, 1867.
[2] Greeley, Horace. *Recollections of a Busy Life*, p. 424.

Notwithstanding the criticism and abuse that were heaped upon him, Greeley remained unshaken in his belief that the greatest satisfaction of the journalist lay in his opportunities for leadership of public opinion. In an editorial in the *Tribune*, early in 1868, he declared: [1]

> An essential element in the truly literary or scholarly character is a love of the truth for the truth's sake. Nothing but this passion for the dissemination of sound and true views can compensate the editor for his intense and unremitting labor.
>
> He who is not conscious of having first interpreted events, suggested policies, corrected long-standing errors, or thrown forward a more searching light in the path of progress, has ever tasted the luxury of journalism. It is the province of journalism to lead and to lead.

From 1870 to 1872, Greeley, although still editor-in-chief of the *Tribune*, took a less active part in its conduct. A capable group of younger men, who supplemented the work of the veterans, Greeley, Ripley, and Taylor, continued to make it a paper of outstanding merit. Whitelaw Reid, a Civil War correspondent for the Cincinnati *Gazette*, joined the *Tribune* staff in 1869, and, after virtually editing the paper until Greeley's death, purchased a controlling interest in it. John Hay, who had been one of Lincoln's private secretaries, and later had been abroad in the diplomatic service, became an editorial writer. His first editorial elicited from Greeley the comment, "I have read millions of editorials, and this is the best of them all." [2] William Winter at this time was just beginning his long and notable career as dramatic critic. The staff also included such writers, well known in their day, as Isaac Bromley, Charles T. Congdon, Noah Brooks, J. R. G. Hassard, and George W. Smalley. "Greeley's young men," they were called, who carried on the *Tribune* traditions after their chief's death.

The climax of Greeley's career came in 1872, when he was nominated for the presidency by the Liberal Republicans and the Democrats. The Liberal Republican movement had begun early that year in Missouri under the leadership of Carl Schurz, editor of the St. Louis *Westliche Post*, with a platform of thorough

---

[1] *New-York Tribune*, February 27, 1868.

[2] Thayer, William Roscoe. *Life and Letters of John Hay*, vol. 1, p. 331.

reconciliation with the South, civil service reform, and reduction of the tariff.   It grew out of the dissatisfaction of many Republicans with the abuses that marked Grant's first term.   Journalists, rather than politicians, were the moving spirits in this proposed third party.   These editors were Samuel Bowles of the *Springfield Republican*, Horace White of the *Chicago Tribune*, William Cullen Bryant of the New York *Evening Post*, Edwin Lawrence Godkin of the *Nation*, Murat Halstead of the *Cincinnati Commercial*, and Henry Watterson of the Louisville *Courier-Journal*.   The nomination of Greeley by the Liberal Republicans came as a disappointment to these independent editors, but, with the exception of Bryant and Godkin, they gave him the support of their papers.   As the Democratic National Convention endorsed both the Liberal Republican platform and the nomination of Greeley, the contest lay between President Grant and the editor of the *Tribune*.   After one of the bitterest of all presidential campaigns, Greeley was able to carry only six states — all of them border or Southern states — and Grant was reëlected by a majority of nearly three quarters of a million votes.

Immediately after the election, Greeley published the following announcement of his new policy for the *Tribune:* [1]

The undersigned resumes the Editorship of THE TRIBUNE, which he relinquished on embarking in another line of business six months ago.   Henceforth, it shall be his endeavor to make this a thoroughly independent journal, treating all parties and political movements with judicial fairness and candor, but courting the favor and deprecating the wrath of no one.

If he can hereafter say anything that will tend to heartily unite the whole American People on the broad platform of Universal Amnesty and Impartial Suffrage, he will gladly do so.   For the present, however, he can best commend that consummation by silence and forbearance.   The victors in our late struggle can hardly fail to take the whole subject of Southern rights and wrongs into early and earnest consideration, and to them, for the present, he remits it.

Since he will never again be a candidate for any office, and is not in full accord with either of the great parties which have hitherto divided the country, he will be able and will endeavor to give wider and steadier regard to the progress of Science, Industry,

[1] *New-York Tribune*, November 7, 1872.

and the Useful Arts, than a partisan journal can do; and he will not be provoked to indulgence in those bitter personalities which are the recognized bane of journalism. Sustained by a generous public, he will do his best to make THE TRIBUNE a power in the broader field it now contemplates, as, when Human Freedom was imperiled, it was in the arena of political partisanship.

Greeley did not live to carry out this new policy. As a result of overwork during the campaign and of sleepless nights spent at the bedside of his dying wife, he suffered a nervous breakdown and died within three weeks after the election.

Greeley was the outstanding example of personal journalism in this country. For thirty years, through his editorial columns, he expressed opinions on a great variety of subjects. Because of the large circulation of the *Weekly Tribune* throughout the North and West, he had a wider circle of readers than did any other newspaper editor. His vigorous style, no less than his unquestioned sincerity, carried conviction to the minds of all who read the *Tribune*. He was "in all probability, the best known man in America," as a fellow journalist wrote.[1] This was due, not only to his writings, but also to his frequent appearances as a lecturer. From the earliest days of the *Tribune*, he spoke before popular lyceums and young men's associations all over the North and West. During the winter of 1853–54, he lectured, on an average, twice a week. Because of their desire to see and hear the man whose writings they had read from week to week, men and women from farms and small towns often drove miles over poor roads to the cities where he was to speak. Descriptions of his picturesque appearance added to the popular interest in his personality. His clothes usually appeared to be in a condition of neglect and disorder, as though he had been traveling in them in a stage coach, day and night, for six weeks.[2] He wore an old felt hat, an old white coat, shapeless trousers often tucked into the tops of his boots, and a large neckcloth that was generally awry. His oddity of dress and shambling gait made him a picturesque figure. So much interest had been aroused in Greeley, the man, that a fine steel engraving of him was offered as a premium to subscribers to the *Weekly Tribune*. All these things com-

---

[1] Browne, Junius Henri. *The Great Metropolis*, p. 214.
[2] Parton, James. *Life of Horace Greeley*, p. 297.

bined to make him more of a personage than any other editor in American journalism.

An interesting contemporary evaluation was made of Greeley in 1863, at the height of his editorial career, by Edwin Lawrence Godkin, who was then acting as American correspondent for the London *Daily News*, and who became the first editor of the *Nation* two years later. The impression produced by the editor of the *Tribune* upon this well-educated Anglo-Irish journalist, viewing American affairs with detachment, was recorded in these words:[1]

Mr. Horace Greeley is self-educated, and very imperfectly educated at that — has no great grasp of mind, no great political insight, and has a brain crammed with half truths and odds and ends of ideas which a man inevitably accumulates who scrapes knowledge together by fits and starts on his way through life. I cannot better describe his position in political life than by saying that he has about the same relation to a statesman that a leader of guerillas has to a general of the regular army. But he has an enthusiasm which never flags, and a faith in principles which nothing can shake, and an English style, which, for vigor, terseness, clearness, and simplicity, has never been surpassed except, perhaps, by Cobbett. Nothing can be more taking than the frank, forcible way in which he states his ideas; but I must also add that nothing can be coarser or more abusive than the language in which he defends them. He calls names and gives the lie, in his leading articles, with a heartiness and vehemence which in cities seem very shocking, but which out in the country, along the lakes, and in the forests and prairies of the Northwest, where most of his influence lies, are simply proofs of more than ordinary earnestness. I confess that, disagreeable as his ways are and must be to everybody who hates vulgarity in public life, and who would wish to see such power as Greeley undoubtedly wields lodged in hands of nicer touch and more careful training, when we remember that he founded the New York *Tribune*, sixteen years ago, as the organ of the then small and despised sect of anti-slavery men, and has never for one hour flagged or grown weary in the great struggle of which we are to-day witnessing the crisis, it is not fair to criticise too severely either his weapons or his manner of wielding them.

He has waged one of the most unequal battles in which any journalist ever engaged with a courage and tenacity worthy of the cause, and by dint of biting sarcasm, vigorous invective, powerful

---

[1] Ogden, Rollo. *Life and Letters of Edwin Lawrence Godkin*, vol. I, p. 254.

arguments, and a great deal of vituperation and personality, has done more than any other man to bring slaveholders to bay, and place the Northern fingers on the throat of the institution. His influence is now immense, for he has over 200,000 readers, and enjoys a confidence which his zeal and ability rather than his judgment or skill have won for him.

Greeley was the first American editor to demonstrate that it was possible to publish successfully a cheap daily paper without depending upon sensational news to secure and retain a large body of readers. Without featuring police court news, criminal trials, scandal, or vice, as the other cheap popular papers did, the *Tribune* was able to build up quickly a large circulation that compared favorably with those of its rivals. In 1847, six years after its establishment, it circulated as many copies of its daily and weekly editions as did the *New York Herald*, which had been in the field a dozen years. Unquestionably, if Greeley had not alienated many readers by his radical "isms," the *Tribune* would have had an even larger circulation. He also proved that a cheap popular paper need not be politically neutral, as were all of the first penny papers.

It was his vigorous editorial writing that won for the *Tribune* no small part of its success. Greeley was a great editorial propagandist, the greatest, possibly, that American journalism has ever possessed. He made the *Tribune* a medium for expressing his personal opinions on all the questions of the day. With an open mind he espoused new ideas in almost every field of human activity. Every movement for social, economic, and industrial betterment found in him an earnest advocate. Many of these so-called radical "isms" have long since been accepted as essential to social and political democracy; others, like communism, are still subjects of debate. It is very creditable to Greeley's sense of social justice that he was ever a strong advocate of the rights of labor to organize, to have its hours of work determined by law or by mutual agreement with employers, and to share in the profits of its toil. No less far-sighted was his advocacy of a sound currency on a gold basis, the building with government aid of railroad and telegraph lines across the continent, international copyright, scientific agriculture, freedom of speech for radical reformers like the abolitionists, and equal political rights for women.   His willingness to suffer the penalties of unpopularity for himself and for his paper, and thus to incur financial loss, shows a high degree of independence and a lofty conception of the duty of a journalist.

The influence he wielded through the editorial columns of his paper — an influence that has never been exceeded by that of any other American journalist — was the result, not of any willingness to yield to the popular clamor of the moment, but of his determination to proclaim the truth as he saw it, however much or little the truth might please his readers.   Believing in his sincerity, his more serious-minded readers accepted him as their recognized leader.

In his choice of a remarkably able staff of writers and editors for the *Tribune*, Greeley sought to realize his ideal of a daily newspaper that should be both interesting and significant.   No other American newspaper during Greeley's lifetime could boast of a better staff than that of the *Tribune*.   The *Tribune* not only was in truth a "great moral organ," as it was dubbed by its rivals, but maintained a literary character unusual in a daily newspaper.

CHAPTER IX

HENRY J. RAYMOND AND THE NEW YORK TIMES

THE success of the *New-York Tribune*, as a cheap newspaper of high moral character in avowed support of a political party, resulted in the establishment of the *New-York Times*, as a one-cent Whig daily. Henry J. Raymond's experience in journalism and politics led him to believe that there was room for a Whig paper which would maintain as high a standard as did the *Tribune* but which would avoid those of Greeley's "isms" that had alienated from the *Tribune* many high-minded though naturally conservative readers. A report that the profits of the *Tribune* for 1850 had been over $60,000 encouraged Raymond and George Jones, an Albany banker formerly on the business staff of the *Tribune*, to plan the establishment of such a paper. Jones, together with half a dozen "up-state" business men, organized a company with a capitalization of $100,000, and Raymond agreed to edit the paper. Accordingly, the new penny daily appeared in September, 1851.

Raymond had begun his journalistic work, while still an undergraduate at the University of Vermont, by contributing to Greeley's *New-Yorker*. After graduation he had assisted Greeley on this weekly paper. When the *Tribune* was started in 1841, Raymond, then just twenty-one, became Greeley's assistant at a salary of $8 a week. Of Raymond's work on the *Tribune* at that time, Greeley wrote, in his *Recollections of a Busy Life*, "I never found another person, barely of age and just from his studies, who evinced so signal and such versatile ability in journalism as he did. Abler and stronger men I may have met; a cleverer, readier, and more generally efficient journalist, I never saw." [1] Despite this appreciation of Raymond's talent, Greeley failed to retain him on the *Tribune* staff when, two years later, Colonel James Watson Webb offered this promising young journalist a

[1] Greeley, Horace. *Recollections of a Busy Life*, p. 138.

higher salary to become associate editor of the *Courier and Enquirer*. For four months during the winter of 1846–47, Greeley and Raymond carried on a spirited editorial debate on the merits of Fourierism, in which Raymond proved more than a match for his former chief. Raymond entered politics in 1849, when he was elected to the New York State Assembly. The following year he was chosen speaker of that body. It was while acting in that capacity at Albany that he arranged with George Jones to establish the *Times*.

The first issue of the *New-York Daily Times* appeared on September 18, 1851, just ten years after Raymond had begun work on the *Tribune*. In his salutatory editorial Raymond justified the establishment of the *Times* on the ground that the reading public had doubled in New York in five years, while the number of newspapers was no greater. He pointed out that many of the newspapers "now published are really *class* journals, made up for particular classes of readers; — that others are objectionable upon grounds of morality; and that no newspaper, which was really *fit* to live, ever expired for lack of readers." Of his policy for the *Times*, he wrote, "as a *Newspaper*, presenting all the news of the day from all parts of the world, we intend to make THE TIMES as good as the best of those now issued in the City of New York .... its influence shall always be upon the side of Morality, of Industry, of Education and Religion." Raymond's temper of mind and attitude toward life were also expressed in this first editorial, when he wrote, "we do not believe that *everything* in Society is either exactly right, or exactly wrong; — what is good we desire to preserve and improve; — what is evil, to exterminate, or reform." He continued with this equally characteristic statement: [1]

> We do not mean to write as if we were in a passion, unless that shall really be the case; and we shall make it a point to get in a passion as rarely as possible. There are very few things in this world which it is worth while to get angry about; and they are just the things that anger will not improve. In controversies with other journals, with individuals, or with parties we shall engage only when, in our opinion, some important public interest can be promoted thereby; — and even then, we shall endeavor to rely

[1] *New-York Daily Times*, September 18, 1851.

HENRY J. RAYMOND
1820–1869

more upon fair arguments than upon misrepresentation or abusive language.

In this proposal to produce "a *Newspaper*, presenting all the news of the day from all parts of the world," and to discuss questions of the hour in a fair-minded, good-tempered manner, without anger or abuse, the *Times* approached more nearly to the news and editorial policies of well-edited newspapers of to-day than did most of the papers of Raymond's own generation. As Charles A. Dana wrote in the New York *Sun* many years later, Raymond "aimed at a middle line between the mental eccentricity of the *Tribune* and the moral eccentricity of the *Herald*, at the time of those great newspapers' greatest greatness, marking out for the *Times* a mean between the two extremes." [1]

During the first year of the paper, Raymond continued from time to time to discuss his ideals of journalism and the policies of the *Times*. "The majority of thinkers are indolent," he declared in an editorial on the mission of the newspaper. "One man in ten thousand does his own cogitation," while "the rest have a belief in 'the paper' for a sole confession of faith." "The press, the country more than the city — the weekly more than the daily," he wrote in the same editorial, "does create and rule the prevailing sentiment." He continued: [2]

> Such *being* the fact, greatly is the need of a more elevated editorial character. Make the press answerable for its emanations, as the sources of immense issues for good or ill, and we shall benefit it infinitely more than by depreciating its power. Its propositions would then be more maturely considered; its language more cautiously measured; and its influence more benignly felt. The editorial of an American paper is usually the first warm impression of a fact, set down at first white heat. The editorial of the German or English redacteur is generally a sober, elaborate essay, embracing none but mature results of reflection. When we have borrowed a few of these foreign traits, the press may be equal to its mission. They are needed, and are easily had.

Again, a year later, in an editorial on "The Model Newspaper," he held up the London *Times* as an exemplar, but called attention to the fact that probably no American paper would ever imi-

[1] *Sun*, March 13, 1875.
[2] *New-York Daily Times*, October 11, 1851.

tate that publication, because, as he was doubtless the first to point out, American women exert a potent influence on the character of our newspapers. He wrote: [1]

> The London *Times* is emphatically a paper for men; a paper for coffee-house and club-room reading. Its topics do not commend it to the "merry homes of England." English women seldom read the *Times*. . . . This absence of domestic qualities is a defect in the great paper; a defect scarcely appreciated in England, but which would prove a serious objection to it here. American women read newspapers as much as their liege lords. The paper must accommodate itself to this fact; and hence the American sheet involves a variety of topics and diversity of contents, of which the *Times* has nothing. Our dailies have domestic habits. They possess the requirements of the family journal. They speak to the parlor and sitting room, as well as to the office and shop.

His own paper he aimed to make a family newspaper. In an early issue he wrote, "special pains are taken to exclude from its columns everything objectionable, and to make it, in all respects, *a good Daily Family Newspaper*." [2]

In reviewing the first year of the *Times*, he referred thus to the purpose of the paper: [3]

> Its readers are among the best portion of our citizens, — those who read it because they like it, and not because it panders to any special taste, and least of all to any low or degrading appetite. It is made up for all classes, and it is designed to cover all departments. Whatever has interest or importance for any considerable portion of the community has found a place, according to its limits, within its columns.

"Whatever has interest or importance for any considerable portion of the community," constitutes as accurate a definition of news as has ever been framed.

Replying to the charge made by Greeley in the *Tribune*, that the *Times* had not lived up to its promise to advocate reforms regardless of political parties, Raymond wrote editorially in 1853: [4]

> If the TIMES has avoided *all* that was unpopular, because unsafe or unsound, in the *Tribune's* character, we submit it has been none the worse on that account. It certainly has not specially devoted

[1] *New-York Daily Times*, October 14, 1852.   [2] *Ibid.*, October 11, 1851.
[3] *Ibid.*, September 12, 1852.   [4] *Ibid.*, April 1, 1853.

its columns to such "reforms" as should meet the views of that very clamorous class of professional reformers who continually boast of being some ages or generations "in advance of public sentiment;" nor did its "original prospectus" contain any "promise," or give any reason to expect from it anything of the kind. The TIMES professed then, as it professes now, to be "*Conservative* so as best to promote needful and practical *Reform*." It has endeavored steadily and earnestly to fulfil that promise and to carry out that purpose: — and in so doing it certainly has not trespassed upon the *Tribune's* province nor "appropriated" anything of its peculiar character. . . . it has pursued its own course, and acted upon its own convictions of justice and expediency.

After six years of editorship of the *Times*, Raymond wrote an editorial on his "Theory of Journalism," in which he thus contrasted the party organ with the independent paper:[1]

But such papers [party organs] ought not to be mistaken for the PUBLIC PRESS. They are not legitimate members of the profession of JOURNALISM. They are not held to its responsibilities — they are not entitled to its honors — they should not be allowed to burden it with accountability for its offences. . . . But the Public Press should not be judged by Editors who sink their regard for journalism in their zeal for party. Its functions are higher, and if properly performed its duties are much more elevated. A Newspaper to command public confidence must be independent of parties. It must be felt that what it says is said — not because the interest of a party requires it, or loyalty to a party exacts it, — but because it is deemed true and essential to the public good.

This is the theory of Journalism, — and we trust it is gradually becoming the basis of its practice. We believe that the public at large demand *independence of judgment and expression* in the journals to which they give their confidence. They do not want independence of all principle, — recklessness of truth, of sound policy, or the public welfare; — nor yet the ascendancy of passion and prejudice, either personal or political. But they want to feel, when they take up a newspaper, that the views they find expressed in it are not the dictates of a caucus or a Committee, — not put forth to serve the private ends of some politician ambitious of place, or of some party greedy for power, — but the honest convictions of an unbiased judgment, dictated by a desire to promote the welfare of the whole community. We believe this to be the tendency of public sentiment, from experience as well

[1] *New-York Times*, January 13, 1857.

as observation. We know that the DAILY TIMES has been most prosperous and most popular, when it has been most free from partisan entanglements, when it has been least exposed to the suspicion of seeking political, rather than public ends; and when it advocated measures, and interpreted passing events, with reference to the general good of the whole country, rather than any section or any party in it. We believe the same thing holds true of the Press at large — and that those journals prosper most everywhere, which combine the best ability and the soundest common sense with decorum of language and independence of party aims. The London *Times* is the most influential journal in the world, because it is at once the ablest, the most enterprising, and the most independent.

That Raymond had gauged accurately the opportunity for another penny paper in New York City, is clearly shown by the circulation that the *Times* achieved immediately. When, within ten days after its first issue, the paper circulated over 10,000 copies, it complacently said, "If any other newspaper ever started in this City or in any other part of the world, ever reached so large a circulation in so short a time, we should be very glad to be informed of the fact." [1] Before the first two months had elapsed, it was issuing over 15,000 copies, and during the third month, 20,000. "There are but two daily papers in the United States which have a larger circulation than this," proclaimed the *Times*.[2] That it was "taken by business men at their stores, and by the most respectable families in town," and that it gave "all the news of the day" were the explanations offered for its immediate success.[3] The *Times* quoted with approval the explanation given by the editor of another new paper, the *Day Book*, to the effect that "Those who have experience in the newspaper business, do not hesitate to say, that the money which pays for the news it contains, alone has done the work; and that without it, the circulation of *The Times* would hardly have reached one thousand." [4]

The *Times* during the first year consisted of four six-column pages. News, both foreign and local, was placed on the first page, under such headlines as, "The News from Europe," "New York," and "Brooklyn." From three fourths of a column to two columns of "Latest Intelligence, By Telegraph to the New-York

[1] *New-York Daily Times*, September 27, 1851.   [2] *Ibid.*, January 1, 1852.
[3] *Ibid.*, September 27, 1851.   [4] *Ibid.*, October 15, 1851.

Times" appeared from day to day. Other "heads" for news were "Foreign Intelligence from our European Files," and "News by Mails." Although these news headlines were of the conventional "label" type, the *Times* showed some appreciation of the value of the bulletin type of "head" when, within the first few months of its existence, it placed the following headline over a story of a panic in a New York schoolhouse:[1]

TERRIBLE ACCIDENT

AT PUBLIC SCHOOL No. 26

FORTY-FOUR CHILDREN KILLED

Twenty-one Children Injured

SEVERAL TEACHERS INJURED

and

Two not expected to Live

In this story it also tabulated the list of killed and injured. Excerpts from editorials and articles taken from other New York newspapers were grouped under the headline, "Topics of the Day," and miscellaneous items bore the head, "Snap Shots at Books, Talk and Town." From two and a half to three columns were daily occupied by editorials.

Like the other penny papers, the *Times* was circulated on the London plan of selling copies directly to carriers to be distributed on their own responsibility, at one cent a copy or six and one quarter cents a week delivered daily. "Carriers, of course, make their profit upon this," the paper explained in its first issue, so that "the amount which we receive barely covers the cost of the paper upon which it is printed, the deficiency being made up by advertisements."[2] "We have chosen this price, however, deliberately and for the sake of obtaining for the paper a large circulation and corresponding influence." "All payments for subscriptions and advertising," it was announced, "must be made in advance." When the paper was a year old, it increased its price to two cents, and at the same time doubled its size from four to eight pages. Although this higher price resulted in a drop in circulation from 26,000 to 18,000 copies, the paper eventually regained its former numbers. The *New-York Evening Times,*

<hr>

[1] *New-York Daily Times*, November 21, 1851.

[2] *Ibid.*, September 18, 1851.

a reprint of the morning paper, with the addition of such later news as came in before noon, and the *New-York Weekly Times*, were both issued soon after the morning paper began. The evening paper, however, was later abandoned.

The *Times* started "without a subscriber or a dollar's worth of advertising pledged in advance." [1] No advertising solicitors were employed, it announced in its fourth number, because "we design to make it the *interest* of advertisers to come to us; and until they feel it to be so, we shall not annoy them by solicitations." [2] This unusual but thoroughly sound advertising policy was again stated a few days later in these words: [3]

> We understand very distinctly that no paper can be sustained by advertising given as a *favor*. Bu iness men must feel that their *interest* is promoted by it, before they will give any great amount of advertising to any paper.

Against objectionable advertising, the *Times* took an unequivocal stand, which it stated thus: [4]

> It may save others, as well as ourselves, some trouble to state that Advertisements of certain classes of Medicines, Doctors, Books &c, &c, will not be inserted in the DAILY TIMES at any price. . . .
> This class of advertisers has a special organ in this city with whose monopoly of the business we have no wish to interfere: — nor shall we allow the TIMES, by the insertion of any such notices or any other of an objectionable character, to be rendered unfit or unsafe for family perusal.

With its large circulation in both the offices and the homes of the substantial business and professional classes of New York City, the *Times* commanded a good advertising patronage.

The amount of capital required to establish and maintain the *Times*, in competition with the other successful New York papers, the *Sun*, the *Herald*, and the *Tribune*, is significant as indicating the extent to which the business of newspaper publishing had developed in the decade since Greeley had been able to launch the *Tribune* with only $2000. Of the $100,000 subscribed by eight stock-holders, $20,000 was required for the purchase of a Hoe

[1] *New-York Daily Times*, May 3, 1852.
[2] *Ibid.*, September 22, 1851.
[3] *Ibid.*, September 27, 1851.
[4] *Ibid.*, May 28, 1852.

Mammoth type-revolving press, and $30,000 more for other mechanical and office equipment. Thus, half of the capital, or $50,000, was invested in the plant before the paper was issued. The first year's expenses included $40,000 for paper; $25,000 for wages in the mechanical and business departments; and $13,000 for the salaries of editors, reporters, and correspondents. The salary scale in the editorial department was not high, however, for Raymond himself received only $2500 a year. Despite its circulation of about 25,000 daily throughout the first year, the *Times* did not pay expenses at one cent a copy. By doubling its price at the beginning of the second year, and also by doubling the number of its pages, it sought to increase its income from both circulation and advertising. The larger paper made room for more advertisements, but the loss of a third of its circulation cut down part of the expected gain. Before the paper was on a paying basis, the remaining half of the original capital had to be spent for operation. "Capital, and large capital too, is essential now-a-days to the establishment of a daily newspaper, upon any scale sufficient to make it successful," commented the editor of the *Times* after a few months' experience. [1] The experience of the *Times* bore out Dana's statement in the *Tribune*, made the year before the *Times* was established: [2]

> It is no exaggeration to say that the same talent which in 1840 could, with a capital of $5000, or $10,000, establish a daily journal in this city, could not now do it with less than $100,000, most of which would have to be expended without any tangible result before the establishment would begin to pay.

During the fourth year the circulation went up to 35,000, and within five years of its establishment the *Times* was able to pay $20,000 a year in dividends. Shares of its stock of $1000 par value accordingly sold for $1666. To establish their paper on so profitable a basis within five years in the face of strong competition, was an achievement for both Raymond, as editor, and George Jones, as business manager.

In spite of his onerous duties as head of the new paper, Ray-

---

[1] *New-York Daily Times*, January 5, 1852.
[2] *New-York Tribune*, August 30, 1850.

mond continued to take an active part in politics, both state and national.   In the Whig National Convention of 1852 at Baltimore, he played a conspicuous part by challenging the right of the Southern delegates to control the presidential nomination.   Two years later, he was a delegate to the anti-Nebraska convention in New York State, and shortly after was nominated lieutenant-governor by the New York Whigs.   After a two-year term as lieutenant-governor, he was offered the nomination for the governorship by the newly organized Republican Party, but he declined.   At the first Republican National Convention, held at Philadelphia in June, 1856, he wrote the long declaration of principles that constituted the first platform of the new party. During the Civil War and the Reconstruction period, Raymond continued active in politics.   He was a delegate to the New York State Republican Convention of 1864, and in the same year was chairman of the state delegation to the Republican National Convention that renominated Lincoln.   As chairman of the Republican National Committee in that year, he directed the campaign that resulted in Lincoln's reëlection.   In the same election, he was chosen congressman from the sixth New York district, and he served in the Thirty-Ninth Congress, from 1865 to 1867.   He supported President Johnson, and, in an effort to assist in the adoption of a sane reconstruction policy, attended the National Union Convention at Philadelphia in August, 1866, a meeting that unfortunately was dominated by Northern Democrats, the so-called "Copperheads."   His attendance at this convention, he afterwards admitted, cost the *Times* $100,000, because his attitude was misunderstood by many loyal Republican readers who felt that, by taking part in such a convention, he had deserted those who had fought and won the war.   After this, Raymond withdrew from politics completely, and during the last three years of his life he gave his undivided attention to his paper.   In spite of his active participation in politics, he never used the *Times* to advance his own political fortunes or those of the factions with which he was identified, although he gave editorial support to the political policies in which he believed.

During the years from 1866 to 1869, the *Times* regained the prestige and support that had been lost by Raymond's political activities in the National Union Convention.   Its flourishing

VOL. XIV......NO. 4220.

GRANT.

RICHMOND

AND

VICTORY!

The Union Army in the Rebel Capital.

Rout and Flight of the Great Rebel Army from Richmond.

Jeff. Davis and His Crew Driven Out.

Grant in Close Pursuit of Lee's Routed Forces.

Richmond and Petersburgh in Full Possession of Our Forces.

ENTHUSIASM IN THE REBEL CAPITAL.

The Citizens Welcome Our Army with Demonstrations of Joy.

RICHMOND FIRED BY THE ENEMY

Our Troops Save the City from Destruction.

THE EVACUATION OF PETERSBURGH.

FIRST DISPATCH.
[OFFICIAL.]
WAR DEPARTMENT,
WASHINGTON, April 3—10 A. M.

To Major-Gen. Dix:

The following telegram from the President, announcing the EVACUATION OF PETERSBURGH and probably of Richmond, has just been received by this department:

EDWIN M. STANTON, Secretary of War

CITY POINT, Va., April 3—8.30 A. M.

To Hon. Edwin M. Stanton, Secretary of War:

This morning Lieut.-Gen. GRANT reports Petersburgh evacuated, and he is confident that Richmond also is.

He is pushing forward to cut off, if possible, the retreating rebel army. A. LINCOLN.

THE CAPTURE OF RICHMOND.
SECOND DISPATCH.
WAR DEPARTMENT, WASHINGTON, D. C.,
April 3—10 A. M.

VOL. XIV......NO. 4225.

HANG OUT YOUR BANNERS

UNION

VICTORY!

PEACE!

Surrender of General Lee and His Whole Army.

THE WORK OF PALM SUNDAY.

Final Triumph of the Army of the Potomac.

The Strategy and Diplomacy of Lieut.-Gen. Grant.

Terms and Conditions of the Surrender.

The Rebel Arms, Artillery, and Public Property Surrendered.

Rebel Officers Retain Their Side Arms and Private Property.

Officers and Men Paroled and Allowed to Return to Their Homes.

The Correspondence Between Grant and Lee.

VOL. XIV......NO. 4230.

AWFUL EVENT.

President Lincoln Shot by an Assassin.

The Deed Done at Ford's Theatre Last Night.

THE ACT OF A DESPERATE REBEL

The President Still Alive at Last Accounts.

No Hopes Entertained of His Recovery.

Attempted Assassination of Secretary Seward.

DETAILS OF THE DREADFUL TRAGEDY.

[OFFICIAL.]
WAR DEPARTMENT,
WASHINGTON, April 15—1.30 A. M.

Maj.-Gen. Dix:

This evening at about 9:30 P. M., at Ford's Theatre, the President, while sitting in his private box with Mrs. LINCOLN, Mrs. HARRIS, and Major RATHBURN, was shot by an assassin, who suddenly entered the box and approached behind the President.

The assassin then leaped upon the stage, brandishing a large dagger or knife, and made his escape in the rear of the theatre.

The pistol ball entered the back of the President's head and penetrated nearly through the head. The wound is mortal. The President has been insensible ever since it was inflicted, and is now dying.

About the same hour an assassin, whether the same or not, entered Mr. SEWARD's apartments, and under the pretence of having a prescription, was shown to the Secretary's sick chamber. The assassin immediately rushed to the bed, and inflicted two or three stabs on the throat and two on the face. It is hoped the wounds may not be mortal. My apprehension is that they will prove fatal.

The nurse alarmed Mr. FREDERICK SEWARD, who was in an adjoining room, and hastened to the door of his father's room, when he met the assassin, who inflicted upon him one or more dangerous wounds. The recovery of FREDERICK SEWARD is doubtful.

It is not probable that the President will live throughout the night.

Three Headlines Printed in the First Columns on the Front Pages of the
New-York Times, April 4, 10, and 15, 1865

financial condition in 1869 was shown by the facts that it paid a dividend of eighty per cent and that its owners refused an offer of a million dollars for the paper.   Thus, within eighteen years, the *Times* had increased in value from $100,000 to $1,000,000. Raymond's own fortunes, notwithstanding his political activities, rose with those of the *Times*, for in 1869 he owned one third of the stock, and his salary was advanced to $10,000 a year.

Just at the height of his career as a journalist and of the financial success of the *Times*, Raymond died suddenly, on June 19, 1869. Only forty-nine years old, he was in the prime of life, and might reasonably have been expected to attain even greater distinction as a journalist.   During all but the last three of his eighteen years as editor of the *Times*, he had devoted so much of his time and energy to politics that journalism could scarcely be said ever to have had his undivided attention.   That the *Times*, under his editorship and Jones's management, was able within three years to recover completely from the set-back of 1866, indicates that, had Raymond lived, the paper might easily have become even more successful and influential than it was at the time of his death.

Although the *Tribune* and the *Times* had long been rivals, Greeley, in an editorial on the occasion of Raymond's death, paid this tribute to him as journalist: [1]

> Mr. Raymond's official career, though evincing ability, did less than justice to his comprehensive knowledge and rare intellectual powers.   Never so positive and downright in his convictions as his countrymen are apt to be, he was often misjudged as a trimmer and a time-server, when in fact he spoke and wrote exactly as he felt and thought. . . . He saw both sides of a controverted issue, and, if one of them seemed juster to-day, the other might nevertheless command his preference to-morrow.   This mental constitution or mental habitude is rare with us, and he would have been more favorably judged as a journalist or politician in Great Britain than in this country. . . .

Raymond's contribution to the development of the American newspaper was accurately summarized at the time of his death in the following editorial, written for the *Nation* by its editor,

[1] *New-York Tribune*, June 19, 1869.

Edwin Lawrence Godkin, who for a time had been an editorial writer on the staff of the *Times:* [1]

> In this art of making a good newspaper, we need hardly say, he was a master. The *Times* under his management probably came nearer the newspaper of the good time coming than any other in existence; in this, that it encouraged truthfulness — the reproduction of facts uncolored by the necessities of "a cause" or by the editor's personal feelings — among reporters; that it carried decency, temperance, and moderation into discussion, and banished personality from it; and thus not only supplied the only means by which rational beings can get at the truth, but helped to abate the greatest nuisance of the age, the coarseness, violence, calumny, which does so much to drive sensible and high-minded and competent men out of public life or to keep them from entering it. Moreover, it rendered journalism and the community the essential service of abstaining from the puffery of worthless people, which does so much for the corruption of our politics.

Because Raymond was able to see both sides of a question, and consequently did not always support the causes that he espoused with as much fervor as did an editor like Greeley, he was sometimes accused of inconsistency. "If those of my friends who call me a waverer," he once remarked to a friend, "could only know how impossible it is for me to see but one side of a cause, they would pity me rather than condemn me; and, however much I may wish myself differently constituted, yet I cannot unmake the original structure of my mind." [2]

Raymond demonstrated that there was a place in New York for a newspaper that presented "all the news of the day from all parts of the world" without personal or party bias, that furnished "whatever has interest or importance for any considerable portion of the community" without "being objectionable on the grounds of morality," and that discussed current issues without "misrepresentation or abusive language," that "interpreted passing events, with reference to the general good of the whole country, rather than any section or party of it." In accomplishing these ideals of Raymond's, the *Times*, as Godkin wrote, "probably came nearer the newspaper of the good time coming than any other in existence."

[1] *Nation*, vol. VIII, p. 490 (June 24, 1869).
[2] Maverick, Augustus. *Henry J. Raymond*, p. 225.

CHAPTER X

SAMUEL BOWLES AND THE SPRINGFIELD REPUBLICAN

THE outstanding newspapers the influence of which shaped the course of American journalism during the first half of the nineteenth century, were naturally to be found at the National Capital or in the metropolis of the country. Until the extension of telegraph lines, following the success of Morse's experiment, on May 24, 1844, in transmitting messages by electricity between Baltimore and Washington, the Washington newspapers enjoyed practically a monopoly in the publication of the proceedings of Congress and other official news of the Federal Government. Since there was little commercial advertising available in the National Capital, these papers were dependent for their success on government printing and government advertising. The New York newspapers, on the other hand, had the first opportunity to publish foreign news, since most of the trans-Atlantic ships entered at that port. They also had the advantage of the large amount of advertising available in the largest city of the country. Other newspapers, accordingly, were compelled to await the arrival of the Washington papers to secure congressional and governmental news, and of the New York papers to obtain news from abroad. The rapid extension of telegraph lines, however, made it possible for newspapers in other cities to print both foreign and domestic news simultaneously with the papers at the points where it became available. The result was a decentralizing tendency in American journalism and the rise to importance of daily newspapers in inland cities.

Just two months before the first message was sent by telegraph, a small four-page evening paper appeared in Springfield, Massachusetts, the first daily to be published in that state outside of Boston. In charge of it was eighteen-year-old Samuel Bowles, Jr. Twenty years before, his father had journeyed up the Connecticut River from Hartford on a flat boat, bringing with him a hand printing press, and had established the *Springfield Republican* as a weekly paper. Beginning with a circulation of 250

SAMUEL BOWLES
1826–1877

among the citizens of the town and the farmers of the surrounding country, the little weekly had grown into a moderately successful newspaper. Springfield became a place of some importance in western Massachusetts, as a result of the location there of the United States Armory and of the building of railroad lines to Boston and Albany, and to Hartford and New York.

After leaving school at the age of seventeen, Samuel Bowles, Jr., assisted his father in getting out the weekly *Republican*. With youthful ambition and enthusiasm, young Bowles urged his father to publish a daily edition of the *Republican*. Although reluctant to try so uncertain an experiment, the father finally yielded, on the condition, it is said, that his eighteen-year-old son should take the "main responsibility of working and pushing it." [1] On March 27, 1844, accordingly, appeared the first issue of the Springfield *Daily Evening Republican*. The second number did not come out until April 1. The new daily was a small four-page paper with four columns to the page. The price was two cents a copy, or $4 a year.

In the introductory editorial, the publisher explained that he had considered the possibility of a daily edition two years before but had been dissuaded from it by friends and business men as "an unprofitable undertaking." [2] He also announced that "we commence now, without a single subscriber or advertising customer promised." He was still uncertain of the success of the project, and wrote that, "after continuing the publication six months, or a year, if we find in it too much of a loss, we shall stop." "If our little daily could have one half of what is paid in Springfield, for New York and Boston papers," he continued, "it would ensure its support." Publication in the evening was adopted, he explained, "not from choice, but because it is most economical and convenient at first; but if the experiment succeeds, and a morning paper be found preferable, we shall adopt it."

Of the policies of the paper, the editor wrote in this first editorial:

We need hardly say that the politics of the Daily Republican will be WHIG — FANEUIL HALL WHIG. . . . In this [presidential]

---

[1] Merriam, G. S. *Life and Times of Samuel Bowles*, vol. I, p. 21.
[2] *Daily Evening Republican*, March 27, 1844.

campaign we intend the Daily Republican shall be a vigilant and active auxiliary of the Whig cause.

The paper, the editor went on to say, "will not be particularly devoted to politics, but we mean to make it also a *news paper*, and especially a *local* one — as well as a medium for the discussion of matters of local interest."

During the first month the editor explained to his readers that "what we most need at first, to ensure its support, is a stable subscription of three hundred,"[1] but that number of subscribers was not secured until the paper had been in existence for two years. At the end of the first six months the paper was still losing money. "If we were to consult our interest," the editor wrote at that time, "we should now discontinue it, having lost enough, as we think, on its publication."[2] "But as its circulation and income slowly increase," he added, "we are induced to continue it, as a permanent publication." Again, at the end of the first year, the editor pointed out that the paper, small though it was, had not paid its way, and that its continuance was made possible only because the type set for the daily could be used in the weekly.[3] At the close of 1845, it was changed from an evening to a morning paper. Although, when the journal was six years old, it claimed the largest circulation of any New England daily outside of Boston, the editor admitted that, "up to the present time, the Republican has been no direct source of profit to its proprietors," and added, "as fast as money had been made it had been invested in improvements, and even to a greater extent, by several thousands, but we have now reached a point where we hope to see the scale descending on the other side."[4]

During the early years of the *Republican*, young Bowles seems to have devoted himself to gathering and writing news and to assisting his father in the management of the paper, rather than to writing editorials. The determination expressed in the first issue to make the *Republican* "a *news paper* and especially a *local* one," continued to be foremost in the mind of Bowles. He aimed particularly to meet the needs of the people of western

Daily Evening Republican, April 23, 1844.   [2] *Ibid.*, October 2, 1844.
[3] *Ibid.*, March 31, 1845.   [4] *Springfield Republican*, May 8, 1850.

Daily Evening Republican.

Vol 1.   SPRINGFIELD, MARCH 27, 1844.   No: 1.

The Daily Evening Republican,
IS PUBLISHED BY
SAMUEL BOWLES.

TERMS—Four dollars a year, or one dollar per quarter, payable in advance. Subscriptions received for a shorter time, at ten cents a week. Single copies, two cents each.

ADVERTISING—Yearly advertisers, with privilege of one square daily, (changed when wished) and a card in Business Directory, are charged $20 a year.

CASUAL ADVERTISEMENTS.

One square, one day, $0.75c.
   "   "   3 days,   1.00
   "   "   1 week,   1.50
   "   "   2 weeks,   2.50
   "   "   1 month,   3.50
   "   "   3 months,   5.50
Business Directory, (1 year) 6.00

For one half a square, two thirds of the above rates will be charged. Twenty lines make a square.

Longer advertisements will be inserted on favorable terms.

Advertisers are requested to hand in their favors before noon of the day of publication. And they are particularly requested to note on the copy, the number of insertions desired.

The office of the Republican, is in the 2d story of Byers' building, Main street;—entrance between the Chicopee Bank and Exchange Hotel.

The Springfield Republican, weekly, is published at the same office every Saturday morning, on a large sheet, for $2 per year.—A liberal discount to agents and companies. Advertisements inserted for $1 per square for 3 weeks, and 20 cents for each week thereafter.

C. E. WHITE, Printer.

FACTS IN RELATION TO THE COMMON SCHOOLS OF SPRINGFIELD.

We are able to communicate to our readers, the following facts and statistics in relation to the Schools of this town, for the past year;—but we cannot say that we do it with pride or even with a feeling of satisfaction.— The fact herein stated, that the average attendance has been only 1700, while the number of children in town of the proper ages, is about 3000, should bring a blush upon the cheek of every parent and guardian, and incite them to redoubled efforts in order to change the melancholy picture. Will it not do it? The farewell advice of Washington, should never be absent from the minds of every one of us;—Promote its objects of primary importance, institutions for the general diffusion of knowledge.

The whole number of scholars in all the schools in the Summer was 2645; in the Winter, 2916. The average attendance in the Summer was 1604; in the Winter, 1771.—The entire number of children between the ages of four and sixteen in the town on the first of May last, was 2981. About 50 have attended school who were under four, and 231 who were over sixteen. The whole amount of time occupied by all the schools has not been less than 326 months, which is an average of about 10 months to a school;—there having been at the commencement of the school year 31 schools, and there now being 35. In the Summer, 5 male teachers were employed, and 40 female; and in the Winter, 19 male teachers and 27 female, including assistants. The amount of money, from all sources, applicable to the schools during the year was $10,162.89, which is not quite $3.50 for each scholar. It will be seen from this statement that a large amount of time and money is lost by absence from the schools.—While we have in the town about 3000 children between the ages of four and sixteen, the average attendance upon the schools for the year has been only about 1700.

More than 100 scholars have attended private schools within the town, at an expense of between $2000 and $3000.

From the N. Y. Com. Adv.

LATE AND INTERESTING FROM OREGON.

At the meeting of the Board of Managers of the Missionary Society of the Methodist Episcopal church—held last evening—late and interesting communications were received from the Rev. Jason Lee, the superintendent of the Oregon mission. The dates are to the 28th of October, and came via Pensacola. These detachments of emigrants from the Western section of the United States had arrived at the Columbia river, some of whom had suffered severely by sickness, and want of provisions. One man in the last detachment had died on the way, and his widow and four children had arrived at the mission station on the Williamette.

The emigrants, on their arrival at the Willamette Valley, expressed their surprise at finding the religious state of the inhabitants so much better than they expected to find it. Many of them, after their arrival, had attended the ministry of the missionaries and had given evidence of a desire to change their mode of life. Some had joined the Church on probation, and it was evident that their example had its effect on many others.

The Rev. Dr. Whitman, belonging to the American Board of Missions, who recently visited the United States, had returned to his charge on the Columbia, in good health.

An excellent state of christian fellowship pervaded the entire family of the Methodist mission, and the prospects of its success were never before so flattering. They have suffered both by sickness and death, but when these letters were despatched, Mr. Lee says, those who had been sick were recovering.— Mr. Brewer is spoken of as having been dangerously ill.

The Rev. Mr. Perkins had been assaulted by one of the Indians from the interior. The chiefs had assembled in council, assisted by Dr. White, the United States agent, and determined that the Indian should be publicly whipped, and he received twenty-five lashes. Mr. Perkins interceded for the prisoner, and was anxious that he should be pardoned, but it was thought that prudence required an example.

ANECDOTE OF MR. CLAY.

The following anecdote of Henry Clay, so eminently characteristic of the man, and so honorable to the statesman, we have upon the authority of a distinguished Senator of the United States. We give it as nearly as we are able in the language in which we had it from the lips of the Honorable Senator himself.

It was during the last Session of Mr. Clay's service in the Senate—that session during which the nomination of Edward Everett, as minister to England, was confirmed. It will be remembered that, for a number of weeks after the nomination of Mr. Everett, great suspense and anxiety were felt throughout the country, as to the course which the Senate... for might take upon the question of his confirmation. The Southern members, or, at least, a portion of them, demanded his rejection, on the ground of his having expressed sentiments upon the subject of abolition, highly offensive to the South, and such as the South was called upon, both directly and indirectly, to rebuke and condemn. Matters stood thus, when, at the close, or near the close, of one of the Executive sessions of the Senate, on a long Summer's day, Mr. Clay had left his seat and taken up his broad brimmed straw hat which he was accustomed to wear in the warm season, began walking slowly backward and forward near the door of the Senate, expecting every moment when an adjournment would take place. Just then a Senator from the South, whose name the gentleman to whom we are indebted for these facts did not feel himself at liberty to mention, rose in his place, and called the attention of the Senate to a published correspondence which he held in his hand, between Mr. Everett and certain abolitionists who had addressed to him a series of questions touching the subject of slavery. The correspondence had taken place at a time when, if we recollect rightly, Mr. Everett was candidate for Governor of Massachusetts. The language used by Mr. Everett, said the narrator, was strong, stronger than we of ... should consider to have been justifiable. The Senator having read the correspondence, made it the text of a strong, denunciatory speech against Mr. Everett, earnestly and vehemently appealing to the representatives of the Southern interests and institutions of that body, to record their sentence of condemnation against such dangerous sentiments, by rejecting the nomination of the man by whom they were put forth. The correspondence, together with the speech of the Senator who brought it forward, arrested the attention of the whole Senate and awakened new and strong apprehensions among the friends of Mr. Everett, as to the fate of his nomination. Soon after the Senator in question had arisen from his seat and commenced speaking, Mr. Clay was observed to pause in his walk to and fro, and as the Senator from the South proceeded in his speech, he [Mr. C.] became, evidently, more and more interested till, at length, he gradually returned to his accustomed seat, and was standing by it when the gentleman who was occupying the floor, finished his speech with the following emphatic language:—"If, under these circumstances, the Senate shall confirm the nomination of Mr. Everett, I consider the Union virtually dissolved!"

"And I say, sir," said Mr. Clay, instantly taking up the words of the Honorable Senator"—that if this Senate, acting on the nomination of Mr. Everett, or any other man, as Minister to a foreign Court shall take upon itself to reject that nomination, on the ground that the person nominated, has expressed to his neighbors and fellow citizens of the State to which he belongs, sentiments not in accordance with our own, yet in no way impeaching his character, or affecting his qualifications for the post to which he is nominated, then, Sir," said Mr. Clay, elevating himself to his full height and raising his voice to that clarion-like tone of impassioned eloquence for which he, above all living men, is so justly distinguished, "then, Sir, I tell the Honorable gentleman and the Senate THAT WE HAVE NO LONGER ANY UNION TO DISSOLVE!" Proceeding from that point, Mr. C. poured forth, for the space of about ten minutes, the most eloquent speech I ever heard from him in all my life. And that speech," said the gentleman from whom these facts were derived, "settled the question of Mr. Everett's nomination."

Norwich Courier.

The First Page of the First Number of the Daily *Springfield Republican,* 1844

Massachusetts, and thus to supplant the New York and Boston dailies in this field.   This policy the editor outlined in an editorial at the end of 1851, as follows: [1]

> What we aim to make, is a Daily and a Weekly newspaper, not only better suited to the wants of the citizens of the four Western counties of Massachusetts than any Boston or New York journal can be, but beyond that, one *cheaper* in price than a journal of any pretensions can be obtained from either of the great cities.   We think we have already done both, and that the future will only make both advantages more apparent.   We do not wish to interfere with the local county journals.   Their interests and ours are the same.   But we do seek to supplant in Western Massachusetts, city journals, both daily and weekly, by papers which give the live news to those who take them, from six to twenty-four hours sooner, than it can be got from Boston or New York papers. . . .
>
> We aim first of all to make a live newspaper — to give everything in this region that people want, briefly, intelligently, succinctly stated — to weed out the verbiage and present the kernel. . . .
>
> After the news, which is the great distinctive object of the Republican, and to which all other things must bend, we aim to discuss politics, morals, religion, physics, — anything in fact which editors may discuss now a days — as honestly, frankly, fairly and intelligently as our abilities, knowledge and time will admit.

The extension of the telegraph to Springfield made it possible for the paper to print promptly the news of the outside world, beginning in the latter half of 1846.   For five years afterwards, the telegraph news was confined to only a few short items which filled scarcely half a column.   Late in 1851, however, the *Republican* was able to announce that "new telegraphic arrangements have recently been made which place us on an equality with the most advanced of the metropolitan press. . . . now our reports swell to columns, and embrace the fullest particulars of every occurrence received at New York up to a late hour of the previous night." [2]

Bowles not only held that the printing of the news was the prime function of the *Republican*, but early recognized the importance of giving his readers the significant aspects of events

---

[1] *Springfield Republican*, December 31, 1851.   [2] *Ibid.*

taking place everywhere in the world.   In an editorial on "The Newspaper," early in 1851, he wrote this prophetic vision of the future of the press: [1]

The increase of facilities for the transmission of news brought in a new era.   The railroad car, the steamboat, and the magnetic telegraph, have made neighborhood among widely dissevered States, and the Eastern Continent is but a few days' journey away. — These active and almost miraculous agencies have brought the whole civilized world in contact. . . .

The appetite for news is one of those appetites that grows by what it feeds on. . . . The mind accustomed to the gossip of nations, cannot content itself with the gossip of families.

The tendency of this new state of things has, as yet, hardly claimed a moment's consideration from the moralist and the philosopher.   Nations and individuals now stand immediately responsible to the world's opinion, and the world, interesting itself in the grand events transpiring in its various parts, and among its various parties, has become, and is still becoming, liberalized in feeling; and, being called away from its exclusive home-field, has forgotten, in its universal interests, the petty interests, feuds, gossips and strifes of families and neighborhoods.   The wonderful extension of the field of vision; this compression of the human race into one great family, must tend to identify its interests, sympathies and motives.

The brilliant mission of the newspaper is not yet, and perhaps may never be, perfectly understood.   It is, and is to be, the high priest of History, the vitalizer of Society, the world's great informer, the earth's high censor, the medium of public thought and opinion, and the circulating life blood of the whole human mind. It is the great enemy of tyrants, and the right arm of liberty, and is destined, more than any other agency, to melt and mould the jarring and contending nations of the world into that one great brotherhood which, through long centuries, has been the ideal of the Christian and the philanthropist.   Its mission has just commenced.   A few years more, and a great thought uttered within sight of the Atlantic, will rise with the morrow's sun and shine upon millions of minds by the side of the Pacific.   The murmur of Asia's multitudes will be heard at our doors; and laden with the fruit of all human thought and action, the newspaper will be in every abode, the daily nourishment of every mind.

For the first ten years of its existence, the *Republican* supported

[1] *Springfield Republican*, January 4, 1851.

the Whig Party.   When the annexation of Texas in 1844, and the Mexican War in 1846, brought the question of slavery into the foreground, the *Republican* opposed the annexation and took its stand against slavery and the war.   Although these policies doubtless were dictated by the elder and the younger Bowles, the *Republican's* editorials at this time were not written by them but by men outside the office.   When the Whig Party wavered on the question of the extension of slavery, the *Republican* ceased to give the Whigs its support.   After the passage of the Kansas-Nebraska Bill in 1854, Samuel Bowles, Jr., declared in an editorial that "the national whig party is surely a defunct institution . . . it has been tottering for some years, resorting to various expedients to maintain itself, but has finally gone by the board." [1]   At the same time he came out strongly for the non-extension of slavery, and, in the following editorial, promised his support for that principle, regardless of party: [2]

> For ourselves, — whatever others may do, — we shall advocate the doctrines we have enunciated, party or no party.   In the great internal struggle between slavery extension and non-extension, we plant ourselves with the non-extensionists; and we shall join that organization, whatever its name, whoever its leaders, that promises most successfully, most surely and most safely for the common weal, to carry out and establish the non-extension principle.   In this, we shall be only fulfilling the convictions and advocating the principles that we have ever cherished.

This determination to make the *Republican* independent of party ties, found more complete expression in an editorial written by Bowles the following year, when he declared: [3]

> Whatever it [the *Republican*] has been in the past, no more shall its distinction be that of a partizan organ, blindly following the will of party, and stupidly obeying its behests.   It has its principles and purposes.   But these are above mere party success.   To these it will devote itself.   Wherever and whenever the success of men or of parties can advance those principles and purposes, the Republican will boldly advocate such success; whenever men and parties are stumbling blocks to the triumph of those principles, they will be boldly opposed and denounced.

[1] *Springfield Republican*, May 31, 1854.
[2] *Ibid.*   [3] *Ibid.*, February 3, 1855.

In taking this stand for political independence, Bowles felt that he was following the tendency of the best journalism of the period; he continued in the same editorial:

> The independent press of the country is fast supplanting the merely partizan press. Parties are taking their form and substance from the press and the pulpit, rather than the press and pulpit echoing merely the voice of the party. A merely party organ is now a thing despised and contemned, and can never take rank as a first class public journal. The London Times, the great journal of the world, is the creator, not the creature, of parties. There is not in New York city, where journalism, in this country, has reached its highest material and intellectual perfection, a single party organ in existence. All are emancipated. None conceal facts lest they injure their party. None fear to speak the truth, lest they utter treason against merely partizan power. The true purpose of the press is understood and practised upon. They are the mirrors of the world of fact and of thought. Upon that fact do they comment with freedom, and to that thought do they add its freshest and most earnest cumulations.

Although, in the heat of controversy during the slavery agitation, the Civil War, and the Reconstruction period, partisan journalism again became the rule rather than the exception, Bowles maintained an unusual degree of political independence in the editorial policy of the *Republican*. After the Republican Party, at its first national convention in 1856, took a stand against the extension of slavery, Bowles gave it his support in the *Republican*. On the eve of the election of that year, he wrote: [1]

> If the principle upon which this party is established do not prevail, then the days of this confederacy are numbered; for slavery is not right, slave rule is not right, the whole policy growing out of wrong is wrong, and a government which recognizes wrong as the controlling force within it, fosters the seeds of its own absolute and inevitable dissolution.

While Bowles was successfully developing the news and editorial departments of the *Republican*, another member of the staff, Dr. J. G. Holland, was adding to its popularity by his editorials and articles on the conduct of life. Dr. Holland, who had been both preacher and teacher, wrote editorials which might

[1] *Springfield Republican*, November 1, 1856.

be characterized as lay sermons, in that they stressed the practical application of the fundamental principles of Christianity to the affairs of everyday life.   He also wrote three series of articles entitled "Timothy Titcomb's Letters to Young People," one addressed to young men, another to young women, and a third to young married couples.   These articles undertook to give advice on matters of conduct in a familiar, almost homely style, well adapted to the average newspaper reader.   When published in book form they enjoyed great popularity.   His "History of Western Massachusetts," which ran serially once a week throughout the year 1854, was another contribution particularly well suited to the readers of the *Republican*.   This was followed by "The Bay Path," an historical novel of colonial times in and about Springfield.   The popularity of his books and lectures diverted him from newspaper work after 1857, although his contributions to the *Republican* did not entirely cease until 1864. Later he found a more congenial field as editor of *Scribner's Monthly*, out of which developed the *Century Magazine*.

By 1857, after a dozen years of hard work, Bowles felt that he had developed the *Republican* as fully as was possible in its limited field, and, as he was but thirty, he looked about for a wider sphere.   Greeley had offered him a place on the *New York Tribune* as editorial writer and head of its Washington bureau.   Dana in 1857 negotiated with a group of Philadelphians for the establishment of a new paper, with a capital of $100,000, of which Bowles was to be the editor, but nothing came of the proposal.

The same year Bowles was attracted by a project to unite three Boston papers under the name of one of them, the *Traveller*. Despite the fact that the *Republican* had the year before netted him between $4000 and $5000, Bowles decided to accept the editorship of the new *Traveller* at a salary of $3000 a year, with a bonus of about one tenth of the capital stock, and he invested $10,000 in the enterprise.   He retained his financial interest in the *Republican*, which he left in the hands of Dr. Holland and other members of his staff.   With a staff of some fifteen, "such as no Boston journal ever yet dreamed of,"[1] he hoped to make the new Boston paper a "popular, progressive journal."

[1] Letter by Bowles, dated April 9, 1857, quoted in Merriam's *Life and Times of Samuel Bowles*, vol. I, p. 292.

Although within a month the *Traveller* circulated 21,000 copies daily, 16,000 weekly, and between 4000 and 5000 semi-weekly,[1] Bowles soon found that his policies for the paper did not agree with those of his associates in charge of the financial management.   After six months of unsatisfactory relations with the new enterprise, Bowles withdrew from the *Traveller* and returned to Springfield to resume the editorship of the *Republican*.   After this ill-starred venture, he remained at the head of the paper until his death.

By 1860 the circulation of the daily *Republican* had reached 5700, of which 1850 was in Springfield, then a city of 15,000, and the remainder largely in western Massachusetts.   The demand for news during the Civil War, and the growth of Springfield as a result of the enlargement of the United States Armory, more than doubled the circulation of the daily.

The weekly *Republican* had a circulation in 1860 approximately twice that of the daily, or 11,280, of which 7271 was in Massachusetts, and the other 4000 distributed over almost every state and territory in the Union.   To the weekly *Republican*, which was made up from the best material published in the daily, Bowles always gave his personal supervision, for he realized that, with its nation-wide circulation, the weekly *Republican* influenced a much larger circle of readers than he could reach through the daily. Although the *Weekly* never attained to a circulation approximating that of the weekly edition of the *New-York Tribune*, Bowles, like Greeley, had a large following of faithful readers throughout the North and West.

Bowles supported Lincoln after his nomination in 1860, and, like most of the leaders in the North, did not believe that Southern politicians and editors were serious when they declared that the election of a "Black Republican" would result in the secession of the Southern states.   During the campaign, Bowles prophesied, concerning the effect on slavery of Lincoln's election, that "What changes may occur within the next half century to hasten the work of negro emancipation on this continent, no one can foresee, but present appearances indicate its gradual retreat southward, and an 'irrepressible conflict' in the slave states protracted long

[1] Letter by Bowles, dated May 14, 1857, quoted in Merriam's *Life and Times of Samuel Bowles*, vol. I, p. 293.

after the question has been completely removed from national politics." [1]   After the results of the election of 1860 were known, the *Republican* again predicted that its effect would be "to completely remove the question of slavery from national politics." So little were the results of Lincoln's accession to the presidency anticipated among representative men in the North, in spite of the South's repeated threats of secession.

When war broke out, the *Republican* could not afford any special correspondents in the field, as could the New York papers, but it supplied from day to day the demand for news of the campaigns.   The eagerness with which persons of all classes sought for the latest news from the front greatly increased the circulation of the *Republican*, as it did that of all other papers.   The size of the staff also increased between 1860, when Bowles and Holland had but three assistants, and 1864, when they had seven.

Editorially the *Republican* gave Lincoln whole-hearted support.   Its attitude is summed up in the following quotation from a letter written by Bowles in 1863: [2]

> The present duty is clear — to push on the war, conquer all we can, as fast as we can, and stir up the "social institution" of the South as deeply as possible.   We may have to stop, or be stopped, any time.   The future is not clear.   But what we want is to make sure that slavery shall be destroyed, whether there be peace or war.   The white man seems to have failed us, and so the black man, as yet; but God is on our side, and it must come right.

During the Reconstruction period, Bowles urged a sane, just policy towards the South.   At first he advocated universal suffrage for all men, black or white, who could read and write.   He opposed the disfranchisement of the men of the South who had fought against the Union.   "There can be no real, no true, no lasting reconstruction in the South," he wrote, "that does not include all classes of its people. . . . Disenfranchisement is as great folly, as applied to the whites, as omission to enfranchise is wickedness toward the negroes." [3]   Throughout the struggle between President Johnson and Congress, the *Republican's* policy was fair, temperate, and broad-minded.   Bowles was not swept away by

---

[1] *Springfield Republican*, October 20, 1860.
[2] Quoted in Merriam's *Life and Times of Samuel Bowles*, vol. I, pp. 392-93.
[3] *Springfield Republican*, March 18, 1867.

the passions of the moment, but pursued a course which, viewed in the perspective of half a century, seems particularly well-balanced.

After the first problems of reconstruction were disposed of, Bowles turned to other issues. In State politics, the *Republican* strongly opposed the reëlection of General Benjamin F. Butler to Congress, on the ground of his "notorious and conceded uncertainty and infidelity in public life," a fight in which it had Godkin's *Nation* as an ally. It then attacked two New York financiers, Jay Gould and "Jim" Fisk, Jr., for their stock-jobbing deals in connection with the Erie Railroad. Through the political influence of Fisk, Bowles was arrested, while in New York City, on a charge of criminal libel, and was held in jail for a night. The press and leading citizens resented this high-handed action. Early in 1871 Bowles engaged in a lively controversy with David Dudley Field and his son, David Field, prominent New York attorneys, over the ethics of their defense of Gould and Fisk in legal matters involving the management of the Erie Railroad.[1] He also attacked the railroad lobbyists in the Massachusetts Legislature, as well as the efforts of the railroads to secure large grants of money from the State without giving adequate return. In the "Crédit Mobilier" scandal, growing out of the construction of the Pacific Railroad, the *Republican* took an equally unequivocal stand against corruption.

In thus undertaking to reform abuses in politics and business that had grown up during and after the Civil War, Bowles realized the difficulties of maintaining the ground that was won, because of the general apathy that follows every fight against corruption. After the exposure of the Tweed Ring, Bowles showed how short-lived was the popular interest in preventing the recurrence of a similar situation. He wrote:[2]

> We have a spasm of public spirit, and while it lasts we perform wonders. But it does not last long. The unaccustomed exertion brings on the inevitable reaction. We say to our souls: "We have done this or that; we have ousted these rogues and put honest men in their places; we have discharged our duties; now let us rest and take our ease." And we rest and take our ease accordingly. We

[1] Cf. *Springfield Republican*, January and February, 1871.
[2] *Springfield Weekly Republican*, November 17, 1871.

go off to our farms and our merchandise. We again find it too much trouble to go to the caucus and the polls. In a word, we drop off again into political sleep. And meanwhile the ship drifts, — and drifts. . . .

We ought to know by this time, — we have had a sufficiently costly experience to teach us, — that what good men will not do for love of their country, bad men will do for love of themselves, whether it be to run caucuses, or manage elections, or hold office. This whole caucus system, from the ward meeting up to the national convention, has been converted into a machine to relieve the people of the task of governing themselves. What is the result? That the whole framework of our government, from top to bottom, is being eaten out and worn away by a dry rot; that we have almost come to look upon self-seeking and place-hunting and thieving the public money as matters of course, disagreeable to be sure, but inevitable; that in this free democratic country, politician has become a term of reproach.

The only solution lay, he believed, in the creation by the press and the pulpit of a sound public opinion, to keep up the fight to maintain clean, efficient government. Continuing in the same editorial, he wrote:

Press and pulpit and platform must take on a higher usefulness than they have hitherto. Party must be shoved for some time to come into the background. Every honest, God-fearing man must make the performance of even trivial public duties a question of conscience. A higher, more searching test must be applied to public acts and public men. Public opinion must be straightened out and put in shape to discharge rightly and effectively its tremendous function. An incessant war must be kept up upon abuses, wherever found. All hands must fall to work to clean out and disinfect the national premises. It will be a long and a tedious job. In fact, there will be literally no end to it, — since after we have once got the establishment into a good and wholesome working condition, we shall have the task of keeping it so. But unless we can bring ourselves to undertake the drudgery — if we choose to think and speak of it by this name — of taking care of our institutions, we cannot hope to keep them. More than that, we shall not deserve to keep them.

"The first step in the protection of society from any evil," Bowles believed, is publicity, and he declared that, since "the first demand of the public in these modern days is knowledge, . . .

the first duty of the journalist is to furnish it." [1] Bowles, therefore, defended the press against those critics who objected to the
type of searchlight journalism that seeks to expose evils in society
and government. [2]

> The topics of daily journalism are by no means matters of its
> own choice, nor, to a great extent even, is the manner of their
> treatment. Its first duty is to report life, not the ideal, but the
> actual. Even if it could suppress discreditable things by ignoring
> them, it has no right to do it. The newspaper exists mainly to
> describe what is. The event of the hour, the topic of the day,
> must be its event, its topic, whether it be cholera, murder, abor-
> tion, tornado, revival, Jim Fisk, Tweed, Ben Butler — any
> anomaly of nature, or vice of man, or visitation of Providence.
> This is its theme, and every theme decides its own treatment.
> Faithful reporting, faithful comment; there is no other law of
> journalism. Little is left to the journalist but the intelligence and
> fidelity with which he shall perform the duty of reporting, the
> motive, and the independence, and the intelligence with which he
> shall comment.

Although Bowles did not believe in suppressing unpleasant facts
in the news if they were significant, he did not advocate sensational journalism. He declared that "that was the most successful journal which lays before its readers the highest class of news,
most intelligently discriminated and wisely set forth, and which
cultivates a taste for such among its readers." [3]

Bowles's independence of party was shown by the critical attitude that he, like other independent editors, took toward President Grant's mistakes during the second half of his first term. In
the latter part of 1870, Bowles took part in a meeting of the Free
Trade League, together with Carl Schurz of the St. Louis *Westliche Post*, E. L. Godkin of the *Nation*, Horace White of the *Chicago Tribune*, and William Cullen Bryant of the New York *Evening
Post* — all independent, forward-looking journalists interested in
a reduction of the high war tariffs. This group of editors, with
the addition of Murat Halstead of the Cincinnati *Commercial* and
Henry Watterson of the Louisville *Courier-Journal*, exerted the
dominant influence in the demand for reform in federal adminis-

---

[1] *Springfield Weekly Republican*, September 22, 1871.
[2] *Ibid.*   [3] *Ibid.*, September 13, 1872.

tration that culminated in 1872 in the Liberal Republican movement.   Although Bowles was disappointed, as were these other
editors, in the nomination of Greeley for the presidency, he supported him and deprecated the attacks on Greeley made by Bryant in the *Evening Post* and by Godkin in the *Nation*.   By opposing the reëlection of Grant and by supporting Greeley, Bowles in-
curred the hostility of many of his Republican readers, but he was
willing to risk unpopularity for the sake of bringing about the
reforms that he felt were necessary.

Reviewing his editorial policy in the presidential campaign
of 1872, Bowles outlined in the following editorial the reforms
that he had hoped might be accomplished by the success of the
Liberal Republicans: [1]

> It [the *Springfield Republican*] wanted to see an end to the old
> controversy over the rights of man, and the old bitterness which
> that controversy had engendered.   It wanted to see the evil spirits
> of sectional rancor and distrust exorcised by a genuine reconcilia-
> tion.   It wanted to see the newly enfranchised voters merged and
> blended in the great mass of American citizenship.   It wanted to
> see the color line at last disappear from American politics.   It
> wanted to see the carpet-bag highwaymen, who were rifling the
> pockets of prostrate and bleeding American commonwealths, at
> last driven from their prey.   It wanted to see an arrogant partisan-
> ship taught that the country was still above political organizations
> in the thoughts and affections of the American people.   It wanted
> to see the national book-keeping pass into new hands, — the na-
> tional accounts brought to light and examined.   It wanted a check
> put to that subtle but powerful materialistic tendency which
> produces Simon Camerons and Credit Mobiliers.   It wanted to
> see the "spirit and intelligence of reform" installed in the White
> House.   It wanted a higher tone in the administration of the
> government, cleaner legislation, a business-like, efficient civil
> service, politics unencumbered with carcasses of dead issues and
> dealing with the new and pressing questions of the new day.

Throughout Grant's second term, Bowles continued a fearless
critic of the Administration and a strong advocate of reform.
In the 1876 campaign he supported Hayes, believing that the
much-needed improvement in government would be accomplished
by his election.

[1] *Springfield Weekly Republican*, December 27, 1872.

Thus, during the last ten years of his life, from 1867 to 1877, Bowles made the *Republican* one of the outstanding examples of that independent journalism which placed public welfare above party success, which was ready to risk unpopularity to support just causes. Bowles acquired a nation-wide reputation as a fearless, independent journalist, and his editorial opinions were constantly quoted in other newspapers throughout the country. To merit such recognition, his editorial utterances had to measure up with those of the other great independent editors of the period, such as Godkin, Bryant, Schurz, Halstead, Watterson, and Horace White.

The political independence of these prominent journalists, in Bowles's opinion, marked a distinct forward step in journalism, and he justly claimed credit for the *Springfield Republican* as a pioneer in the movement. Writing at the close of 1872, he said: [1]

> Along with this political revolution and new birth, though only partly allied to it, has come a grand growth in Journalism. The Independence, which has been held and despised as Indifference, and the Impersonality, which was denounced as Irresponsibility, are now seen in their higher and broader character, and their reforming and elevating influences are fast possessing the government of the press, and growing in public appreciation. Party Journalism began to fall with the death and retirement of its great representatives — Isaac Hill, Francis P. Blair, Edwin Croswell and Thurlow Weed; but it has held on with great pretense, though with weakening power, and now in 1872 has fought its last campaign. The growth of Journalism as a business, and the extinction of the old party lines and divisions have united to make a date, as it were, of its emancipation. With the deaths of James Gordon Bennett and Horace Greeley, Personal Journalism also comes practically to an end. They did much to create modern American journalism in its two different characters: both sought news as the first and chief element, — the one went farther and added criticism, opinion, reform; the one gathered and organized fact and recorded opinions; the other sought to control and make those opinions. Their personality was the necessity of their creative work; it could not be suppressed by types and ink; but they have no successors, because there is no call for them, — the creators have given place to the conductors; and henceforth, American Journalism, in its best illustrations, will exhibit its outgrowth both of Partyism and Per-

[1] *Springfield Weekly Republican*, December 20, 1872.

sonalism.   It will become a profession, not a stepping-stone; and
a great journal will not longer be the victim of caprice and passion,
or the instrument of the merely personal ambition, of its chance
writer or conductor.   Its traditions, its conscience, its responsibilities and its constituency will assume their appropriate powers
over itself; and instead of a man, called to direct and contribute
to its columns, importing himself into it, the paper will import
itself into him.

In the Political Revolution, — that insures the burial of the
dead past, and carries like assurance of a new and larger national
life, and a better type of political administration, — as in the
growth of this Higher Journalism, — that promises so much for
itself in elevation and enlargement of power, and so much for the
public in a nobler leadership and a wider instruction, — THE
SPRINGFIELD REPUBLICAN may honorably claim to have been both
a pioneer and a prophet.   Through the imperfections of its materials, with the limitations of its provincial field, it has sought
long and earnestly for the results so happily promised in our
politics, — the extinction of sectionalism, the protection of all
men in equal rights, and the reform of the administrative service;
and it has given token that, in seeking these results, it was independent both of parties and of men, — that it cared more for the
ends than for maintaining in power any party organization or in
office any set of men.

The significance of Bowles in the development of American
journalism was accurately described by his fellow editors in the
tributes paid to him at the time of his death in 1877.   Horace
White of the *Chicago Tribune* declared: [1]

... Mr. Bowles was the pioneer and leader of independent
journalism in the United States.   He made the experiment in an
interior town, in the midst of a population overwhelmingly Republican in politics.   He made it under the most adverse circumstances, against the most inveterate prejudices, and yet with
the most triumphant success. . . . As Mr. Bowles was a model of
what I conceive to be the highest aims of journalism, so was he a
prince of the journalistic art.   No American journal during the
last ten or twenty years has been more diligently studied by editors
than the Springfield *Republican*.   This is the crucial test of a public journal. . . . Mr. Bowles had an instinctive perception of what
was important to a newspaper, and the finest sense of the degrees
of importance among various sorts and classes of news, and he

[1] Quoted in Merriam's *Life and Times of Samuel Bowles*, vol. II, p. 442-43.

possessed an analytical faculty which enabled him at all times to
spy out the grains and kernels of important fact in the midst of
endless chaff. . . . In all that constitutes taste in journalism, —
good taste, condensation, dress, perspicuity, and elevation of tone,
— Mr. Bowles was *facile princeps* among his contemporaries.

Henry Watterson, in the Louisville *Courier-Journal*, summed up
Bowles's contribution to American journalism thus: [1]

To say of a man that he edited the model provincial newspaper
in the most newspaper-reading country on the globe, that he gave
this provincial newspaper national influence and importance, and
that he was a statesman rather than a politician, is to say all that
could be claimed for a journalist.   Yet it is no more than of right
belongs to Samuel Bowles.

[1] Quoted in Merriam's *Life and Times of Samuel Bowles*, vol. II, p. 449.

CHAPTER XI

EDWIN LAWRENCE GODKIN, THE NATION, AND THE NEW YORK EVENING POST

FOR over a generation, from 1865 until 1899, Edwin Lawrence Godkin exerted a nation-wide influence both on American public opinion and on American journalism through the medium of a weekly paper, the *Nation*, the circulation of which never greatly exceeded 10,000 copies. So wide-spread an influence was possible only because his readers were newspaper editors, college professors, students, and "intellectuals" generally, through whom his ideas filtered down to thousands of others who never saw the *Nation* or even knew of its existence. His editorship of the New York *Evening Post* for eighteen years, from 1881 to 1899, gave him an opportunity to reach a larger number of readers, especially in New York City, but it was through the *Nation*, as a weekly edition of the *Evening Post*, that he made his influence felt the country over.

When Godkin undertook the editorship of the *Nation* in 1865, he had had a dozen years' experience in journalism, partly as newspaper correspondent and partly as editorial writer. Born in Ireland in 1831 of English stock, he was educated in an English preparatory school and at Queen's College, Belfast. After receiving his degree in 1851, he went to London to study law, but soon entered a publishing house. At the age of twenty-two he wrote a *History of Hungary*, because of his interest in Kossuth and in Hungary's struggle for independence. During the Crimean War, from 1853 to 1855, he was war correspondent for the London *Daily News*. On returning to Belfast, he wrote editorials for the *Northern Whig* of that city. Late in 1856, he went to New York and made a tour of the South and West, contributing letters to the London *Daily News* on his impressions of the United States and especially on the conditions growing out of slavery. Early in 1857, he took up residence in New York City, and, after completing his study of law, was admitted to the bar in 1858. Meanwhile he continued to contribute to the columns of the London *Daily News*. Impaired health led to his sojourn abroad during

EDWIN LAWRENCE GODKIN
1831–1902

1860–61, but he returned to the United States and became an editorial writer on the *New-York Times* under Raymond. Impressed by his ability, Raymond offered him a permanent position on the *Times* with the opportunity to become a part owner, but Godkin declined the offer.

As early as 1863, Godkin had in mind the establishment of a high-grade weekly journal devoted to politics and literary criticism, like the *Spectator* and the *Saturday Review* in England, and he discussed the project with his friends at Harvard and Yale, and in Boston and New York. Finally, in 1865, through the efforts of friends, the sum of $100,000 was subscribed to form a stock company with some forty stock-holders. Thus the *Nation* was launched. Godkin was made editor, and Wendell Phillips Garrison, then recently graduated from Harvard, was literary editor.

In the publisher's prospectus announcing the first issue for July 6, 1865, the purposes of the new weekly were set forth as (1) "The discussion of the topics of the day, and, above all, of legal, economical, and constitutional questions, with greater accuracy and moderation than are now to be found in the daily press"; (2) "the maintenance and diffusion of true democratic principles in society and government, and the advocacy and illustration of whatever in legislation or in manners seems likely to promote a more equal distribution of the fruits of progress and civilization"; (3) "the earnest and persistent consideration of the condition of the laboring class at the South," since "there can be no real stability for the Republic so long as they are left in ignorance and degradation"; (4) "the fixing of public attention upon the political importance of popular education, and the dangers which a system like ours runs from the neglect of it in any portion of our territory"; (5) "sound and impartial criticism of books and works of art." [1] The *Nation*, the prospectus continued, "will not be the organ of any party, sect, or body," but "will, on the contrary, make an earnest effort to bring to the discussion of political and social questions a really critical spirit, and to wage war upon the vices of violence, exaggeration and misrepresentation by which so much of the political writing of the day is marred." As to the criticism of books and works of art, which was to be "one of its most prominent features," it was announced that "pains will be taken to

[1] Ogden, Rollo. *Life and Letters of Edwin Lawrence Godkin*, vol. I, pp. 237–38.

have this task performed in every case by writers possessing special qualifications for it." [1]   The list of regular and occasional contributors, as given in the prospectus, included such men as Henry Wadsworth Longfellow, James Russell Lowell, John G. Whittier, Charles Eliot Norton, Richard Grant White, William Lloyd Garrison, Professor Francis J. Child of Harvard, Professor William Dwight Whitney of Yale, Daniel Coit Gilman, then professor at Yale, Frederick Law Olmsted, the Reverend Phillips Brooks, and Bayard Taylor.[2]

Although with the third issue the circulation reached 5000, the task of putting the paper on a paying basis, with the subscription price at $3 a year, was a difficult one.   Within the first year the experiment was tried of increasing the price to $6 a year, and later the paper was issued semi-weekly, but this plan was abandoned at the end of the second volume in favor of weekly publication.[3] By the end of the first year practically all of the capital had been used, and Godkin, with the aid of a few of his friends, took over the business under the name of E. L. Godkin & Co. [4] He had been engaged to edit the paper for two years, under an agreement that he was to have complete control over the editorial department. In the course of the first year, however, differences had arisen between some of the stock-holders and the editor over the policy of the *Nation*, and these disagreements were partly responsible for the change of ownership.   In writing to Charles Eliot Norton of the situation that had thus developed, Godkin said: [5]

> When the editorship was offered me, I took it on the understanding, which was afterwards reduced to writing, that I was to be completely independent to any extent that an honorable man could be. . . .
>
> I, on my part, undertook not to produce a paper that would be certain to sell well, but to produce a good paper, one that good and intelligent men would say *ought* to sell, and whose influence on those who read it, and on the country papers, would be enlightening, elevating, and refining.   Commercial success I never guaranteed.   The whole thing was well understood to be an experi-

---

[1] *The Nation*, vol. I, p. 63 (July 13, 1865).
[2] *Ibid.*, vol. I, p. 127 (July 27, 1865).
[3] *Ibid.*, vol. II, p. 822 (June 29, 1866).
[4] *Ibid.*, vol. III, No. 60 (August 23, 1866).
[5] Ogden, Rollo. *Life and Letters of Edwin Lawrence Godkin*, vol. I, p. 247.

The Nation.

VOL. L—NO. 9.   THURSDAY, AUGUST 31, 1865. $3 PER ANNUM.

Three Dollars per annum, in advance; Six months, Two Dollars. When delivered by Carrier in New York or Brooklyn, Fifty Cents additional.

JOSEPH H. RICHARDS, PUBLISHER, 130 NASSAU STREET, N. Y.

The Week.

The chief sensation of the week has been disaster by land and flood. On Monday, the 21st, a train on the Chicago and North-western Railway ran at night into a culvert washed away by a storm. On Tuesday, a train was thrown from the track of the Shore Line Railroad, Connecticut, by running over a cow. On Wednesday, there was an accident on the Oil Creek Road, Pennsylvania, and another on the Old Colony Road, Massachusetts—the results of culpable carelessness and misconduct. On Friday, a train on the Alabama and Tennessee Railroad ran off the trestle-work of a bridge. All these involved the destruction of at least twenty persons, and the maiming of more than a hundred others. A collision on the Chesapeake drowns one person and injures two, while an explosion on the Ohio causes the death of twelve and the scalding of eight. Lastly, we hear of the total loss of the steamer *Brother Jonathan*, on the Pacific coast, on the 30th of last month, in which but seventeen lives were saved out of two or three hundred. Among those who went down were Brig.-Gen. Wright and his family. He was on his way to Fort Vancouver, to take command of the Department of the Columbia.

An important organization was effected in this city on Friday. Representatives of the principal Freedmen's Associations, East and West, met together and formed the "American Freedmen's Commission," with the following list of officers: Bishop Simpson, President; Wm. Lloyd Garrison and John V. Farwell, Vice-Presidents; Fred. Law Olmsted, General Secretary; Jacob R. Shipherd, Associate Secretary; and George C. Ward, Treasurer; which officers, with J. Miller McKim and J. M. Walden, Corresponding Secretaries of the Eastern and Western Departments, will constitute the Board of Managers. Other prominent and representative names embraced in this new Association are Francis George Shaw and Rev. Henry Ward Beecher, of this city; Stephen Colwell and Francis R. Cope, of Philadelphia; Judge Bond and Archibald Stirling, Jr., of Baltimore; C. G. Hussey and Dr. Howard, of Pittsburg; Adam Poe and Abraham M. Taylor, of Cincinnati; Dr. Newberry, of Cleveland; Dr. Patterson, of Chicago; Dr. Duffield, of Detroit; Calvert Fletcher and Robert Morrison, of Indiana; James E. Yeatman and Dr. Elliott, of St. Louis; Judge Russell and Rev. John Parkman, of Boston; John G. Whittier, of Amesbury; Postmaster Bowen, of Washington, etc., etc. This Commission completes the unity, so long desired, of the various philanthropic combinations which,

under whatever name, have the welfare of the freedmen at heart. It will work in harmonious co-operation with the Bureau at Washington, to which it will bring no small measure of strength and public support. It is another guaranty that the revolution of to-day shall go forward and not backward, nor cease till the rights of man are acknowledged in every citizen of this Republic.

The Mississippi Convention finished its business and adjourned on Thursday the 24th. It declared the ordinance of secession null and void. It prohibited, by a constitutional amendment, the revival of slavery, by a vote of 86 to 11. It ratified the proceedings of the courts, the sales of administrators, and all marriages since January, 1861. It fixed upon the first Monday in October as the day for the State and Congressional elections. Judge E. S. Fisher was nominated for Governor. The delegates, in their unofficial capacity, drew up a memorial to the President asking for the pardon of the two State offenders, Jefferson Davis and Governor Clark. The convention received a telegraphic dispatch from the President through Governor Sharkey, congratulating them upon their action, and the prospects of Mississippi's readmission into the Union, and promising the restoration of the *habeas corpus* and the removal of the troops as soon as practicable.

A correspondent calls our attention to the fact that a petition was presented to the Senate in February of this year, by Senator Morgan of this State, praying for the passage by Congress of a "General Election Law" regulating the suffrage in all the States, in the manner indicated by "T. F." in the last number of The Nation, and in virtue of the power claimed by him under the Constitution for the national legislature.

The Kentucky Court of Appeals have reversed a decision of the Louisville Chancery Court, by which the appellant was required to accept Treasury notes in discharge of his contract for money. Judge Williams dissented, but the majority held the act of Congress of Feb. 25, 1862, to be unconstitutional in so far as it made these notes "lawful money and a legal tender in payment of all debts, public and private, in the United States." Judge Robertson summed up his conclusions in two propositions: that the people, on adopting the national Constitution, emphatically and aforethought "established gold and silver coin as the money, and the only legal money, of the United States;" and that, to secure this deliberate object, "they determined that no legislation, State or national, should ever make anything else a legal tender for money, demandable on any contract made between citizens under the sanction of State laws." He added, as a necessary corollary, "that all power not expressly delegated over money is constructively *forbidden*," and that, therefore, "there can be no implied power to make Treasury notes a legal tender in private contracts."

The trial of Wirtz, which was commenced on Monday the 21st, then suddenly interrupted, and resumed on Wednesday, promises to drag its slow length along like the Assassination trial, which it will probably resemble, in evoking a great deal of testimony more pertinent to the general character of the rebellion than to the charges against the prisoner. Wirtz is beyond question a villain, but then a regard for decency ought to restrain people from pelting him with rotten eggs as he sits in the pillory. The following delectable morsel is from a correspondent of the Boston *Advertiser* :—

" Yet the central figure in the room is, after all, this Swiss-American, Henry Wirtz, whom God probably made, and yet whom no man thinks

ment, and it was this very fact that rendered a large capital so
necessary.

Again, a few months after the *Nation* was started, he wrote to
Norton of its prospects: [1]

> If the thing fails, or I fail, I shall try to fall with honor, but in
> the meantime I shall, owing to the rotten condition of the press
> and the fixed belief of the public that no paper can be conducted
> with purity or independence, have a great deal to endure.

Those who did not agree with the policies advocated by the
Nation were not slow to point out that the editor was an Englishman, and a Richmond, Virginia, paper insinuated that "British
gold" was invested in the new undertaking in an attempt to overthrow the Government. Such were some of the obstacles encountered in the effort to give the United States an independent
weekly paper.

That the *Nation* was appreciated by thoughtful men is indicated by the enthusiastic encouragement given Godkin by James
Russell Lowell and Charles Eliot Norton, during the early years
of the paper, when it was struggling to establish itself. Lowell,
writing to Godkin in 1866, praised the *Nation* for "its good taste,
good temper, and good sense." [2] Two years later, he said that the
paper was his "weekly refreshment," and that in his judgment it
was "really *excellent* — so full of good manners, good sense and
good writing," while "our journals are commonly crammed with
crudeness, commonplace, and cussedness!" [3] Again, in 1870,
Lowell contrasted the *Nation* with other papers, thus: [4]

> When I see, as every one daily sees, the influence of bad or
> foolish newspapers, I cannot doubt that a good and strong one like
> the *Nation* is insensibly making public opinion more wholesome
> with its lessons of sound sense. There is no journal that seems to
> me on the whole so good as yours — so full of digested knowledge,
> so little apt to *yaw*, and so impersonal. And yet, take away *your*
> personality, and it would sink to the ordinary level.

Lowell had little patience with those who found fault with the
Nation because its editor was a foreigner. The fact that Godkin

[1] Ogden, Roilo. *Life and Letters of Edwin Lawrence Godkin*, vol. 1, p. 245.
[2] *Ibid.*, vol. 11, p. 74.   [3] *Ibid.*, vol. 11, p. 76.   [4] *Ibid.*, vol. 11, p. 67.

had been born and educated abroad was felt by Lowell to be a distinct advantage, as it enabled him to take "an impartial view." "The cause you advocate in the *Nation*," Lowell wrote, "is not specially American — it is that of honest men everywhere and acknowledges no limits of nationality." [1] "You can hold American opinions without American prejudices," said Lowell in another letter, "and I know very few of my countrymen who have a large enough intellectual and moral past behind them to deal with politics in their true sense." [2] Charles Eliot Norton wrote to Godkin in 1867, "It is no delusion of friendship to regard you as the soundest and best-trained writer on social and economical questions — the topics of political economy — that we have." [3] Of the influence that Godkin exerted on college men, Professor M. Stuart Phelps of Andover wrote in 1870, "You are giving weekly lessons in history to hundreds of college graduates, as well as undergraduates, and we cannot spare you." [4]

A Utilitarian of the school of Bentham, and an economist of the school of John Stuart Mill, Godkin accepted the creed of mid-Victorian English Liberalism, which was "peace, retrenchment, and reform." In applying these ideas to American political and economic conditions, he urged a complete reconciliation with the South, reduction of the tariff, civil service reform, a sound currency, and a progressive improvement in government. He also fought strenuously against corruption and maladministration in municipal, state, and federal departments. During the Reconstruction period, he stood for the withdrawal of Federal troops from the South and for the control of the State governments by the Southerners themselves rather than by "carpet-baggers" from the North. In espousing the merit system in civil service, as opposed to the prevailing idea that to the victors belong the spoils of political office, he was among the pioneers in this country. His dissatisfaction with Grant's first administration led him to join in the movement for the nomination of a liberal candidate to oppose Grant's candidacy for a second term. But, because of distrust of Greeley and of his protectionist doctrines, he opposed his election to the presidency on the Liberal Republican ticket in 1872, and sharply criticized Greeley. His idea of the necessity of progres-

---

[1] Ogden, Rollo. *Life and Letters of Edwin Lawrence Godkin*, vol. II, p. 78.
[2] *Ibid.*, vol. II, p. 67.   [3] *Ibid.*, vol. II, p. 60.   [4] *Ibid.*, vol. II, p. 67.

sive improvement in government, and his conception of the function of a democracy, he set forth thus in an editorial on the hundredth anniversary of the signing of the Declaration of Independence celebrated at the Centennial Exhibition in 1876:[1]

> And a progressive and improving government is not one which every year covers a wider area with its laws and makes large additions to its population.   Nor is it even a government under which each generation clings to its nationality with a more passionate and proud affection.   These things have all been seen under governments whose subjects paid for the glory of their flag and the spread of their sway by the sacrifice of their highest ideals, the blunting of their moral perceptions, and the increase of public misery.   Government is not an emblem, or a name, or an army with banners.   It is a bundle of mutual services; and its goodness or badness, and the value of its contribution to the moral growth of the world, depend on the efficiency with which they are rendered. Unless we are supplying the poor and the rich with better justice; unless we are striving to make taxation lighter and its collection simpler and easier; unless we are discovering modes of making the execution of the laws more efficient and more certain — of taking better care of the poor and the insane — of giving the young a better education — of bringing the highest intelligence of the community to bear on its legislation and administration — of enabling the weak and unlearned to feel surer about the future — of making firmer the hold of the frugal on their savings — of making marriage a more honorable and sacred relation and children a more solemn responsibility, — all that we heard . . . of the novelty or the success of our political system was reproach and not glory. . . . . The truth is that no nation is under such weighty obligations as ours to make constant and steady improvement in every branch of political machinery.

Godkin's freedom from partisanship on all current issues made the *Nation* for over a generation an outstanding example of independent journalism.   The presentation of the truth as he saw it, Godkin conceived to be his duty as editor.   Sound reason and common sense were the bases of his judgments, not the passions of the moment or the popular clamor.   On these points he made his position clear, both in the prospectus of the *Nation* already quoted, and again in the following editorial, published two years later:[2]

[1] *The Nation*, vol. 23, pp. 20–21 (July 13, 1876).
[2] *Ibid.*, vol. v, p. 326 (October 24, 1867).

We profess to supply opinions exactly as we have formed them, and not in the shape in which they will be likely to please or encourage or console. If we damage the Republican party or any other good party, we are sorry for it; but we cannot, for the benefit of that party, either say what we do not believe or suppress what we do believe while professing to supply our readers with honest comments on public affairs. . . . We treat our readers as grown-up men and women who can bear to hear the truth, and know how to reason from it with regard to their own duty, and not as children who have to have pretty stories told to them and fine promises made to them to keep their courage up.

Godkin took issue with critics of the press who held that the influence of the editorial was waning. "A good editorial" he defined, as "the earnest address of an exceptionally able and an exceptionally well informed man to some fifty thousand, more or less, of his fellow citizens." Of the need of such editorials, he wrote: [1]

When the world gets to be so intelligent that no man shall be more intelligent than any other man, and no man shall be swayed by his passions and interests, then there will be no need of editorial expressions of opinions, and editorial arguments and appeals will lose their power.

Because he insisted that men in public life should measure up to the high standards that he believed in, Godkin often criticized honest, public-spirited leaders who, realizing the exigencies of practical politics, sought to accomplish their ends by compromise or by other methods of political expediency. Hence he was often characterized as a carping critic. But his critical comments were only the result of a rigorous application to all men and measures of his high ideals of conduct and morality. Even to the progressive, independent journalist Samuel Bowles, who appreciated the *Nation's* fearless independence, Godkin's attitude seemed "often conceited and priggish; coldly critical to a degree sometimes amusing, and often provoking; and singularly lacking, not only in a fine enthusiasm of its own, but in any sympathy for that great American quality." [2] Undaunted, however, by such criticism from friends and foes, Godkin continued in the *Nation* to

[1] *The Nation*, vol. II, p. 584 (May 8, 1866).
[2] *Springfield Republican*, November 30, 1868.

present the truth as he saw it, regardless of its unpopularity. "The weekly day of judgment" was Charles Dudley Warner's apt characterization of the paper.

Godkin's clear and logical reasoning found expression in an equally clear and effective style. His editorial paragraphs had, as Lowell said, both "a lightness of touch and a weightiness of good judgment." [1]   In characterizing his style, James Bryce, a life-long friend and admirer, wrote: [2]

> Even when he was writing most swiftly, it [his style] never sank below a high level of form and finish.   Every word had its use and every sentence told.   There was no doubt about his meaning, and just as little about the strength of his convictions.   He had a gift for terse vivacious paragraphs commenting on some event of the day or summing up the effect of a speech or a debate.   The touch was equally light and firm.   But if the manner was brisk, the matter was solid; you admired the keenness of the insight and the weight of the judgment just as much as the brightness of the style. Much of the brightness lay in the humour.

Humor was used to advantage by Godkin, especially in puncturing the bubbles of popular and party pretense.   To be made light of infuriated those against whom he directed his humorous shafts, while it furnished abundant amusement to most of his readers. Irony was an equally effective weapon used by him in disposing of adversaries.   Since the *Nation* was widely read by other editorial writers, Godkin's clean-cut, trenchant style, as well as his effective use of humor and irony, tended to influence editorial style the country over.

In its criticism of current literature, the *Nation* exerted a no less potent force.   Godkin and Wendell Phillips Garrison, literary editor of the *Nation*, assigned the reviewing of books to "writers possessing special qualifications" for the task.   Thus they gave the book reviews an authoritative character hitherto lacking in most journalistic criticism in this country.   In replying to the charge that the *Nation* "devoted too large a portion of its space and attention, in its literary department, to the consideration of foreign literature and literary news, neglecting American books, and American authors, and the current subjects of American

[1] Ogden, Rollo.   *Life and Letters of Edwin Lawrence Godkin*, vol. II, p. 74.
[2] Bryce, James.   *Studies in Contemporary Biography*, pp. 367–68.

thought," the editors pointed out that one half of the books reviewed during the first six months of the publication were American and one half foreign. After analyzing the publishers' statistics for the same period, the *Nation* showed that "the reading matter of this country is almost entirely foreign." The editors outlined their conception of the relation of criticism to literature as follows: [1]

> It is certainly no part of our purpose, any more than that of any newspaper, to build up a literature. It would be silly and presumptuous for us to entertain or proclaim any such intention. The *rôle* of a weekly critic is, after all, a very humble one. It is to examine the fields from which it finds the community drawing its mental food, and to point out, to the best of its ability, what those fields produce — what is bad and what is good; what had better be tasted, what digested, and what thrown away; to keep before the public the best standard in every department, and point out departures from it, according to the critic's understanding of it. If people go to England for political economy and history, to Germany for philology and metaphysics, to France for everything by turns, it is our business to go with them and find out what the English, French, and Germans are getting ready for their entertainment; and we are no more responsible for the extent to which those markets are ransacked for our literary wares, than we are for the condition of our dry goods trade. We protest against the shallow notion that a peculiar standard of art or literary criticism has been evolved by our political and social system. This is one of those bits of Anglo-Saxon conceit which gives Frenchmen and Germans so much amusement. Truth and beauty are eternal and immutable, and of no country.

This cosmopolitan point of view was in sharp contrast with that of many other American newspapers and periodicals, which undertook to stimulate American literature by praising the work of native authors rather than by passing critical judgment upon them, a method of dealing with American books followed generally by the pioneer journalistic book-reviewer, George Ripley, of the *New-York Tribune*. The higher standard of criticism set by the *Nation* influenced the reviewing of books by other American journals.

Because he believed that the practice followed by theatrical

[1] *The Nation*, vol. II, pp. 266–67 (March 1, 1866).

managers of giving newspapers free tickets tended to hamper freedom in dramatic criticism, Godkin opposed these "deadhead" privileges, and maintained that "all the best journals would be willing to waive their courtesies and pay for the ticket of their critic on the usual terms." [1]

In 1881 Godkin sold the *Nation* to Henry Villard, Wendell Phillips Garrison's brother-in-law, who had just purchased the New York *Evening Post*. Through the change Godkin became editor of the *Post* jointly with Horace White, formerly of the *Chicago Tribune*, and with Carl Schurz, formerly editor of the St. Louis *Westliche Post* and a leader in the Liberal Republican movement of 1872. Villard, a native of Germany, who had engaged in newspaper work after coming to this country in the '50s, had reported the Lincoln-Douglas debates and had served as correspondent during the Civil War. Later he became president of several railroads, including the Northern Pacific, for the completion of which he was directly responsible. Of Villard's part in the purchase and control of the *Post*, Horace White said: [2]

> He wished to do something useful to his adopted country by taking a daily journal of established reputation and putting it in charge of men who would give it increased influence and authority. He informed them that they were absolutely independent of himself, independent of the counting room, and independent of party. To make good this declaration, he placed all of his shares in a trust, with David A. Wells, Benjamin H. Bristow, and Horace White, trustees, with all the powers that he could have exercised. This trust remained in force for several years, and at its expiration Mr. Villard turned the property over wholly to other members of his family.

By this change, the *Nation* became virtually a weekly edition of the *Evening Post*. The relation between the two publications was thus explained by Godkin in a letter to Charles Eliot Norton: [3]

> I sold the *Nation* yesterday, after much deliberation and perplexity, to the *Evening Post*, as the weekly edition of which it will appear after July 1st. It will not be changed in appearance, and I hope not in quality, but most of the articles will have previously

---

[1] *The Nation*, vol. II, p. 634 (May 18, 1866).
[2] *Evening Post*, April 13, 1907.
[3] Ogden, Rollo. *Life and Letters of Edwin Lawrence Godkin*, vol. II, p. 121.

appeared in the *Post*. Garrison goes over with me, and will continue in special charge of the *Nation*, and our publisher becomes publisher of the *Post*. . . .

The *Post* will be somewhat harder work for me in some ways, but I shall have the great relief of being able to leave it, without anxiety, for vacations, and of knowing that I can withdraw from it altogether without loss whenever I feel any signs that the night is coming.

"The change might not have come about," as Garrison wrote, "had the *Nation* prospered so as to warrant an enlargement of its staff," but, as it was, "the strain of writing from three to five pages for it weekly was felt at last to be too severe as well as too unremunerative, in view of the scrutiny to which Mr. Godkin was subjected while all but single-handed." [1]

As Carl Schurz became editor-in-chief of the *Evening Post*, Godkin was relieved of much responsibility. Within the first two years, however, differences arose between the two men over some points of editorial policy, and Schurz resigned. Godkin thereupon took over editorial control, with Horace White as his assistant. On the *Evening Post* he continued to be an editorial writer, as he had been on the *Nation* for eighteen years. It was to such work that he was best adapted, for "he had, strictly speaking," as Garrison wrote, "no business instinct, no faculty for details, nor any liking for the task of coördinating the departments of a daily newspaper." [2]

Of his policy for the *Post*, Godkin wrote to Garrison in 1883, "My notion is, you know, that the *Evening Post* ought to make a specialty of being the paper to which sober-minded people would look at crises of this kind, instead of hollering and bellering and shouting platitudes like the *Herald* and *Times*." [3]

When Godkin took over the editorial direction of the *Post* in 1883, it seemed probable that James G. Blaine would be the Republican nominee for the presidency the following year. Because he believed that Blaine, as a member of Congress, had used his official position for private gain, Godkin opposed his nomination, and, after he was nominated, fought his election. Other influential journals like the *Springfield Republican*, the *New-York*

[1] *The Nation*, vol. 74, p. 403 (May 22, 1902).   [2] *Ibid*.
[3] Ogden, Rollo. *Life and Letters of Edwin Lawrence Godkin*, vol. II, p. 127.

Times, the *Boston Herald*, and *Harper's Weekly* also bolted after the nomination, and, together with the *Nation* and the *Evening Post*, led the independent, or "Mugwump," movement, as it was dubbed by Dana in the New York *Sun*.

By means of the "deadly parallel" column, the *Evening Post* undertook to demonstrate that Blaine, while serving in Congress, had been guilty of deliberate misrepresentation in regard to his relations with corporations. Grover Cleveland, the Democratic nominee, on the other hand, was defended by Godkin against the charge that, because of a moral delinquency in his youth, he was unfitted for the presidency. Never had Godkin fought harder than in this 1884 campaign. He realized that New York was the pivotal state in the election. The *Evening Post*, accordingly, did its utmost to convince the voters of that state, not only of the unfitness of the Republican nominee, but of the promising character of the Democratic candidate. After an unusually bitter campaign, marked by unsparing attacks on the personal character of both candidates, the contest was so close that both sides claimed victory for several days after the election, while the vote of New York State, upon which the final outcome depended, was being tabulated.

The fact that the "Mugwump" element defeated Blaine and elected Cleveland, the first Democratic President since the Civil War, showed the growing strength of the independent voters, whom papers like the *Nation* and the *Springfield Republican* had been training up to put public welfare ahead of party loyalty. Thus the victory was in part the result, not only of Godkin's strenuous fight in the *Evening Post*, but of his strong advocacy of reform, week by week, for nearly twenty years. The *Nation* undoubtedly influenced the rising generation of young men. Eight years later, when Cleveland was again elected President, Godkin attributed the victory to these young independent voters. He wrote: [1]

> Mr. Cleveland's triumph today has been largely due to the young voters who have come on the stage since the reign of passion and prejudice came to an end and the era of discussion has opened. ... Nothing is more important, in these days of "boodle," of indifference, of cheap bellicose patriotism, than that this con-

[1] *The Nation*, vol. 55, p. 346 (November 10, 1892).

fidence in the might of common sense and sound doctrine and free speech should be kept alive.

Although Godkin approved of Cleveland's attempts, during his first administration, to carry out the Civil Service law, to curb congressional extravagance, and to reduce the tariff, and commended his opposition to the free coinage of silver while out of office in 1891, he denounced with the greatest vigor Cleveland's belligerent Venezuelan message late in 1895, which threatened to lead to war between the United States and Great Britain. Godkin and Pulitzer of the *World* helped to stem the wave of "jingoism" before it swept the country into war, but this experience shook Godkin's confidence in democracy and in the press. In a letter written to Charles Eliot Norton ten days after Cleveland's Venezuelan message, Godkin reviewed the whole situation and discussed its causes and its significance thus: [1]

> I was thunderstruck by Cleveland's message, and have seen so much Jingoism even among intelligent people, and so much cowardice in the face of Jingoism, that the prospect which seemed to open itself before me was a long fight against a half-crazed public, under a load of abuse, and the discredit of foreign birth, &c, &c. It was in this state of mind we opened our batteries on that Friday morning, and I am bound to say relief came promptly. We were literally overwhelmed with laudatory and congratulatory letters, as well as oral applause of every description, and our circulation rose 1,000 a day. In fact our course has proved the greatest success I have ever had and ever known in journalism. . . .
>
> . . . But the situation to me seems this: An immense democracy, mostly ignorant, and completely secluded from foreign influences, and without any knowledge of other states of society, with great contempt for history and experience, finds itself in possession of enormous power and is eager to use it in brutal fashion against any one who comes along, *without knowing how to do it*, and is therefore constantly on the brink of some frightful catastrophe like that which overtook France in 1870. The spectacle of our financial condition and legislation during the last twenty years, the general silliness and credulity begotten by the newspapers, the ferocious optimism exacted of all teachers and preachers, and the general belief that we are a peculiar or chosen people to whom the experience of other people is of no use, make a pretty dismal picture,

[1] Ogden, Rollo. *Life and Letters of Edwin Lawrence Godkin*, vol. II, pp. 202–03.

and, I confess, rather reconcile me to the fact that my career is drawing to a close. I know how many things may be pointed out as signs of genuine progress, but they are not in the field of government. Our two leading powers, the legislature and the press, have to my knowledge been running down for thirty years. The present crisis is really a fight between the rational business men, and the politicians and the newspapers, and the rational business men are not getting the best of it.

The press is the worst feature in the situation, and yet the press would not be what it is without a public demand for it as it is. I have been having cuttings about the present situation sent in to me from all quarters, and anything more silly, ignorant, and irrational you could not imagine. I am just now the great object of abuse, and the abuse is just what you would hear in a barroom row.

Godkin again fought "jingoism" before the outbreak of the Spanish-American War in 1898, and assailed the "yellow journals" for their part in inflaming popular passions. Sensational journalism, intended to appeal to the masses, had come to the front in New York City with the purchase of the *World* by Joseph Pulitzer in 1883, and with that of the *Journal* by William Randolph Hearst in 1895. By 1898 these two rivals in the penny paper field had built up very large circulations. The *Journal* had also begun to attract attention by its use of large headlines and a bizarre make-up. To Godkin, who hated sensationalism and exaggeration, the efforts of the "yellow press" to attract readers by catering to the "jingo" spirit seemed a heinous offense against good journalism. Two months before war was declared, he denounced unsparingly the policies of the "yellow journals" with reference to news from Cuba and Spain. He wrote: [1]

Nothing so disgraceful as the behavior of two of these newspapers in the past week has ever been known in the history of American journalism. Gross misrepresentation of the facts, deliberate invention of tales calculated to excite the public, and wanton recklessness in the construction of headlines which outdid even these inventions, have combined to make the issues of the most widely circulated newspapers firebrands scattered broadcast through the community. . . . It is a crying shame that men should work such mischief simply in order to sell more papers. . . .

[1] *The Nation*, vol. 66, p. 139 (February 24, 1898).

The reason why such journals lie is that it pays to lie; or, in other words, this is the very reason for which they are silly and scandalous and indecent. They supply a want of a demoralized public. Moreover, such journals are almost always in favor of war, because war affords unusual opportunities for lying and sensation.

Shortly after the war began, in an editorial on these papers as "The New Political Force," Godkin presented this scathing arraignment of the evils of yellow journalism: [1]

> The fomenting of war and the publication of mendacious accounts of war have, in fact, become almost a special function of that portion of the press which is known as "yellow journals." The war increases ·their circulation immensely. They profit enormously by what inflicts sorrow and loss on the rest of the community. They talk incessantly of war, not in the way of instruction, but simply to incite by false news, and stimulate savage passions by atrocious suggestions. . . .
>
> . . . His [the yellow journalist's] one object is to circulate widely and make money. And he does circulate widely. He treats war as a prize-fight, and begets in hundreds of thousands of the class which enjoys prize-fights, an eager desire to hear about it and read about it. These hundreds of thousands write to their Congressmen clamoring for war, as the Romans used to clamor for *panem et circenses;* and as the timid and quiet are generally attending only too closely to their business, the Congressman concludes that if he, too, does not shout for war, he will lose his seat. . . .
>
> This is an absolutely new state of things. . . .
>
> They [the multitude] have already established a régime in which a blackguard boy [Hearst] with several millions of dollars at his disposal has more influence on the use a great nation may make of its credit, of its army and navy, of its name and traditions, than all the statesmen and philosophers and professors in the country. If this does not supply food for reflection about the future of the nation to thoughtful men, it must be because the practice of reflection has ceased.

Godkin also deplored the spirit of imperialism which the acquisition of the Philippines and Hawaii seemed to have developed in the United States.

With equal force and fearlessness, both in the *Nation* and in the *Evening Post*, Godkin kept up a continuous warfare on Tammany

[1] *The Nation*, vol. 66, p. 336 (May 5, 1898).

rule in New York City.   His editorial control of the *Post*, beginning in 1883, gave him the opportunity to fight at close range such municipal maladministration and corruption.   The defeat of the Tammany candidate for mayor in 1884 by a reform Democrat, and the resulting downfall of Kelly, Tweed's successor, of whom Godkin wrote, "he stole nothing himself, but he enabled others to steal with great freedom," filled Godkin with hope for better things in city government.   That hope again seemed to be realized when, two years later, another good Democratic candidate was chosen mayor.   Both in these and in subsequent elections, the *Evening Post* made effective use of a "Voters' Directory," a device, invented by Joseph Bucklin Bishop of the *Post* staff, for presenting concisely the record and character of every candidate.   The election in 1888 of another typical Tammany candidate, served to arouse the *Post* to even greater aggressiveness against Tammany when, in 1890, he came up for reëlection.   In this campaign the *Post* developed the "Voters' Directory" into a detailed exposure of the record and character of every man connected with the Tammany organization.   Beginning with biographical sketches of twenty-seven members of the executive committee, it printed a similar exposure of the 1970 members of the committee on organization, and, finally, of the 4564 members of the general committee.   Suits for criminal libel were immediately begun, and Godkin was arrested three times in one day, but, as the facts published by the *Post* could not be controverted, nothing came of these actions except annoyance to the editor.   In spite of the *Post's* fight, the Tammany candidates won in this election and again in 1892.

But the ceaseless exposure by the *Post*, supplemented by the opposition to Tammany of the *World* and the *Times*, eventually bore fruit.   Investigation by the City Club, charges made by the Reverend Charles H. Parkhurst, and finally the inquiry conducted by the Lexow Committee of the State Legislature, revealed so wide-spread a corruption, notably in the police department, that the reform elements in the Republican and Democratic parties were able in 1894 to elect a Republican mayor, a man of high character and integrity.   That Godkin deserved most of the credit for the overthrow of Tammany was recognized by all who had watched the course of the *Post*.   Colonel George E. Waring, a prominent figure in the reform administration, wrote to Godkin just after this election, "I am glad to see that Parkhurst gives you such cordial recognition; but Parkhurst don't know, as do those who have watched your course during all the years of your work here, to what extent you alone are to be credited with the maintaining, among the leaders of the community, of the spirit which at last made Parkhurst and his work possible." [1]   That the fight for clean government in New York won by Godkin would have its effects in other cities was the opinion of President Daniel Coit Gilman of Johns Hopkins University, who wrote to Godkin just after the election, "You — next perhaps to Dr. Parkhurst — seem to me deserving the personal and unqualified thanks of all who are fighting for good government in cities.   The moral effect of this victory in strengthening the independent voters and in showing how reforms can be accomplished will be felt throughout the land for decades to come." [2]

In recognition of this work, Godkin was presented with a loving cup by a number of his friends on December 31, 1894.   He wrote to Charles Eliot Norton, "nearly every one here whose good opinion I care for came forward to cover me with praise and felicitation. . . . there is a fair prospect of good government in the city for a few years at all events."   But he was "not sanguine about the future of democracy."   His lack of confidence he explained thus: [3]

But with a villanous press — venal and silly, — and a somewhat frivolous and distinctly *childish* public, it is difficult to be sure of more than a few years [of good government].   I know of no good influence now which is acting on the masses, and the practice of reading trivial newspapers begets, even among men of some education, a puerile habit of mind.

Of this puerility of the American press, Godkin wrote two years later as follows: [4]

The note of the press to-day which most needs changing is childishness.   Even if the papers are clean and decent, they are fit only for the nursery.   The pictures are childish; the intelli-

[1] Ogden, Rollo. *Life and Letters of Edwin Lawrence Godkin*, vol. II, pp. 174-75.
[2] *Ibid.*, vol. II, pp. 175-76.   [3] *Ibid.*, vol. II, p. 199.
[4] *The Nation*, vol. 62, p. 356 (May 7, 1896).

gence is mainly for boys and girls. The "good stories" are trivial, and are intended chiefly for junior clerks and laborers. The observations on public as distinguished from purely party affairs, are quite juvenile. The abuse is mostly boyish or street abuse, with neither rhyme or reason to it. What is wanted in the way of reform is mainly maturity, the preparation of the paper for grown people engaged in serious occupations. Gravity either in discussing or in managing our affairs is fast vanishing under the journalistic influence. We laugh over everything; make fun of everybody, and think it will "all come out right in the end," just like ill-bred children who hate to have their games interrupted.

Declining health forced Godkin's retirement from active editorial work at the end of 1899, but he wrote occasional signed articles for the *Post* almost to the time of his death in May, 1902.

No other American journalist during his lifetime received such marked recognition as Godkin won from leaders of thought in England and in America, for his influence both on them personally and on public opinion. James Russell Lowell's tributes to Godkin in the early years of the *Nation* have already been quoted. When James Bryce learned of the loving cup that had been given to Godkin for his services in advancing the cause of good government, he wrote, "no person in this generation has done as much to stem the current of evil and preach a high ideal of public duty and of political honesty as you have." [1]   Again, when Godkin retired, Bryce wrote, "I do regret it terribly, for there is no one in the U.S.A. that one has heard of who can do the tithe of what you have done for principles of good government and purity and for sound reason as against demagogism." [2]   President Charles W. Eliot of Harvard University, on hearing of Godkin's resignation, wrote to him: [3]

> Now I am conscious that the *Nation* has had a decided effect on my opinions and my actions for nearly forty years; and I believe it has had like effects on thousands of educated Americans. This does not mean that your readers have always adopted your opinions; but if you have not convinced them, you have forced them to find some good reasons for holding opinions different from yours; and that is a great intellectual service. Then you have pricked any number of bubbles and windbags, and have given us keen en-

[1] Ogden, Rollo. *Life and Letters of Edwin Lawrence Godkin*, vol. II, p. 179.
[2] *Ibid.*, vol. II, p. 232.   [3] *Ibid.*, vol. II, p. 231.

joyment in the process. And how often you have exposed humbug and cant to the great refreshment of sincere people!

President Daniel Coit Gilman of Johns Hopkins University wrote to Godkin in 1895, "Few numbers of the *Nation* have appeared in all that time [thirty years] which I have not read, and if I have kept a steady head during this long period it is due in no small degree to the intellectual and political inspiration that I have received from its pages." [1] Likewise, in expressing regret at Godkin's retirement, President Gilman paid this tribute to the editor's influence on himself and on others: [2]

> But you have fought a good fight for law and order, for honesty, learning and unselfishness in politics; and you have influenced by your precept, and by your example, multitudes of good citizens in every part of this country. Personally I am very grateful to you for guidance in many of the political perplexities of our times. I can make these expressions all the more heartily because I have not always been able to agree with the *Evening Post*, and can add that when I have been obliged to differ, an extra amount of consideration has been necessary before forming an opinion.

That the *Nation* was the one significant contribution to American journalism in the decade from 1860 to 1870, was the opinion of Samuel Bowles, editor of the *Springfield Republican*. In an editorial in 1868, commenting on the invaluable service which Godkin was rendering, he wrote: [3]

> [The *Nation*] has become a permanent and proud addition to American journalism . . . the paper . . . shows such vigor and integrity of thought, such moral independence of party, such elevation of tone, and such wide culture as to demand our great respect and secure our hearty praise. It is the one contribution to American journalism of the last ten years; and happy may the profession call itself if every decade shall offer another gift so positive and so progressive. The Nation may not ever be popular in the common American sense; popular as the New York Ledger, or the Boston Journal, or even the New York Tribune is; as a sort of moral policeman of our society, our politics, and our art, it can hardly expect to be, — but it assuredly has been and will be most useful. In the great necessity and duty of the time, the reformation of the ad-

---

[1] Ogden, Rollo. *Life and Letters of Edwin Lawrence Godkin*, vol. II, p. 179.
[2] *Ibid.*, vol. II, p. 227.   [3] *Springfield Republican*, November 30, 1868.

ministration of our government, the substitution of competence for incompetence, of integrity for corruption, it is laboring with noble zeal and telling influence, and is worthy of every patriot's praise.

Of the influence of the *Nation* on other newspapers, and through these on hundreds of thousands of newspaper readers, Wendell Phillips Garrison, for thirty-five years Godkin's associate on the paper, declared, "The *Nation* was eagerly read in every newspaper office of importance, and its ideas filtered down without acknowledgment through a thousand channels."[1]   How this influence operated was well shown by Rollo Ogden of the *Evening Post*, who wrote in the fiftieth anniversary number of the *Nation:*[2]

> The *Nation's* influence in shaping the American press was out of all proportion to the mere number of its readers.   It did not strive or cry.   The effects it wrought were subtle and insinuated, never clamorous.   A virtue went out from it which was unconsciously absorbed by many newspaper writers.   They could scarcely have said where they got their new impulse to exercise a judgment independent of party.   All can raise flowers now, for all have got the seed.   To-day the most powerful newspapers in the United States are those which have the reputation of being always ready, on a question of real principle, to snap the green withes with which politicians would bind them.   But until twenty years after the *Nation* was founded, how few they were, how sneered at, how disliked!   The steady light which Mr. Godkin burned in the *Nation*, and later in the *Evening Post*, had its slow but cumulative radiations.   Not merely did it become impossible to employ, with a grave face, the partisan shibboleths which he was continually holding up to ridicule, but it was made easier for editors to refuse to give up to party what was meant for country.   In this way, the *Nation* was as leaven in the lump of American journalism. . . . And in the whole matter of unbiassed and informed comment upon great affairs, it gradually became a sort of external conscience to other publications.   They waited to see what it would say before finally committing themselves.   Coming down to a later period, that of Mr. Godkin's larger identification with the *Evening Post*, we have the remark of a veteran Western journalist, in reply to some one who was lamenting the fact that such a paper had not a larger circulation.   "You idiot," he exclaimed, with profane emphasis, "don't you know that there isn't a decent editor in the

[1] *The Nation*, vol. 55, p. 403 (May 22, 1902).
[2] *Ibid.*, vol. 101, p. 33 (July 8, 1915).

United States who does not want to find out what it has to say on any subject worth writing about, before getting himself on record in cold type?"

When the retirement of Godkin from the editorship of the *Evening Post* and the *Nation* was announced, Dr. Fabian Franklin, editor of the *Baltimore News*, wrote editorially in that paper: [1]

> From the moment of its [the *Nation's*] establishment, it became a powerful agency in the formation not only of public opinion but of something that lies far deeper than mere opinion. It stirred the thoughts of the most serious and the most high-minded men and women in the country, and it stamped indelibly upon the minds of thousands of earnest young men standards of political thinking and of political conduct which would otherwise have existed for them but as vague ideals. While its immediate circle of readers was never very large — its subscription list seldom exceeding 10,000 — it was read with care in every respectable newspaper office, and the strong doctrine so mightily poured out at the fountain-head filtered through, we may be sure, in a thousand ways, and slowly but steadily made itself felt by the multitude. Improbable as it may seem to many readers, we have no hesitation in saying that, taking the entire period of thirty-five years, the influence of the Nation and the Evening Post upon the history of the time has been incomparably greater than that of any other American publication.

Godkin aimed to make both the *Nation* and the *Evening Post* journals that would appeal to the thinking classes rather than to the unthinking masses. He never expected that either publication would be "popular" in the ordinary sense of the term. Intellectually an aristocrat, he nevertheless believed in democratic government. No doubt he would have accepted for the *Nation* and the *Post* Thackeray's description in *Pendennis* of the fictitious *Pall Mall Gazette*, a newspaper "written by gentlemen for gentlemen." Size of circulation meant little to him, either when his livelihood depended on the success of the *Nation* or when he was part owner of the *Post*. Neither was he concerned about advertising patronage. Because of his attacks on New York retail merchants for their opposition to a proposed increase in the exemption from customs of purchases made by Americans return-

[1] Franklin, Fabian. *People and Problems,* p. 184.

ing from abroad, a large number of them withdrew their advertisements from the *Post*, at a loss to the paper of thousands of dollars. Nor was he interested in the news published in the *Post*, except to the extent that nothing undignified or in any way sensational was ever permitted in its columns. In short, his conception of the function of a newspaper editor was that of nineteenth century English journalism, namely, that he should be primarily a leader-writer. To present the truth as he saw it on every matter of public concern, and to demonstrate the truth by sound logic, were his constant aim. That the truth might be unpalatable to many of his readers was to him all the stronger reason why he should present it to them. For editors who constantly had their ears to the ground to catch the popular feeling of the moment, and who catered to readers by giving them only what they wanted, he had the greatest contempt. Fearlessly independent, he felt free to attack whatever seemed to him wrong. But he was not merely a destructive critic, for he presented constructive policies to remedy the evils he denounced. His mastery of a lucid, trenchant style, shot through with humor and irony, gave a keenness to his attacks, and a cogency to his argument, that have never been equaled in American editorial writing. Alike to his journalistic and non-journalistic readers, he always furnished food for thought, whether they agreed or disagreed with him. Finally, his cosmopolitan point of view, the product of his European background and liberal education, gave him a detachment in viewing American affairs that was lacking in the work of other American journalists.

CHAPTER XII

CHARLES A. DANA AND THE NEW YORK SUN

FROM 1838, when Benjamin H. Day, founder of the New York *Sun*, sold the paper to his brother-in-law, Moses Y. Beach, it continued in the hands of the Beach family for thirty years, until it was purchased by Charles A. Dana and his associates in 1868. For the first ten of these thirty years, Moses Y. Beach managed the paper. In 1848 he retired in favor of his two sons, and, when one of them withdrew in 1852, the other, Moses S. Beach, became sole owner. During twenty-five of the thirty years under the Beaches, the *Sun* continued to be a penny paper, the only successful newspaper at that price in New York City. The *Herald*, the *Tribune*, and the *Times*, after having begun on a one-cent basis, had increased their price to two cents within a year or so of their establishment. The circulation of the *Sun*, approximately 50,000, was chiefly among the working classes. Its advertising patronage was large, but, because of the character of the circulation, its columns were used for much objectionable advertising. The size of the pages was increased from time to time to meet the demands of advertisers for more space, until the paper consisted of four seven-column pages. When the Civil War increased the price of print paper and other costs of production, the *Sun* was cut down to a five-column page set in agate type. But even this economy proved insufficient, and, accordingly, in 1864 the price was increased to two cents. At this price it remained for over half a century, until it was purchased by Frank A. Munsey in 1916. The general character of the paper continued much the same under the Beaches as it had been under Day, except that a new feature was added in the serial publication of fiction by such popular authors of the day as Mary J. Holmes, Ann S. Stephens, and Horatio Alger, Jr. For seventeen months — from August, 1860, to January 1, 1862 — the *Sun* was published as a moral and religious paper by a rich young man who paid Beach $100,000 for the rental of its plant and for its good will. When this experiment failed, the *Sun* reverted to Beach and resumed its former character. As a cheap paper catering to the masses, it was so successful financially that, before the Civil War, it netted over $20,000 a year in profits.   Begun by Day in 1833 practically without capital, it was sold by him to the elder Beach in 1838 for $40,000; fourteen years later, when Moses S. Beach became sole owner, it was said to be worth $250,000; but in 1868 the latter sold it to Dana and his backers for $175,000.

Charles A. Dana was at this time in his forty-ninth year, with an established reputation as journalist, author, and federal government official.   As a youth he had spent two years at Harvard, and had then entered the Brook Farm community, in the affairs of which he took an active part for five years until its dissolution. During this time he contributed to the *Harbinger*, the Brook Farm publication, and to the *Dial*, a transcendental quarterly with which Emerson and Margaret Fuller were associated.   Then, after a brief connection with a religious weekly in Boston, Dana early in 1847 joined the staff of the *New-York Tribune* as city editor, at a salary of $10 a week.   The following year he went abroad, paying his expenses by writing weekly letters for the *Tribune* and for papers in Boston and Philadelphia.   The revolutionary movement that swept through Europe in 1848 gave him an opportunity to study at first hand the new spirit of democracy abroad, particularly in France and in Germany.   His early connection with the communistic Brook Farm experiment led him to regard with interest the various movements for association, cooperation, and social reform that were being tried in France and in the United States, and, after he rejoined the *Tribune* staff in March, 1849, he wrote much on these topics.   The sympathies of Greeley, Dana, and Ripley with the association of labor in cooperative enterprises by which workers became their own employers, resulted, in the year of Dana's return, in the reorganization of the *Tribune* as a stock company with partial ownership by the employees of the several departments.

From the time that Dana, as managing editor of the *Tribune*, became Greeley's right-hand man, until his retirement from the paper in 1862, he shared with the editor the shaping of its news and editorial policies.   During Greeley's many absences, Dana was in charge.   He also engaged in various forms of literary work, including the editing of a successful anthology, *The Household Book of Poetry* (1857), and *The American Encyclopedia* (1858–63).

CHARLES A. DANA
1819–1897

Differences between the two editors over matters of policy for the *Tribune*, led Greeley, with characteristic impulsiveness, to ask the board of directors to demand Dana's resignation. Although Greeley apparently regretted his hasty action, Dana withdrew from the paper in March, 1862, never to return.

During the remaining years of the Civil War, Dana served the Government in various capacities, in 1864 becoming Assistant Secretary of War under Stanton. On terminating his connection with the War Department in July, 1865, he undertook the editorship of the *Daily Republican*, a new journal just started in Chicago. The paper was capitalized at $500,000, but not enough of this sum was paid in to maintain the new enterprise in competition with the well-established Chicago papers, and, after a year's struggle, Dana withdrew.

While considering the advisability of establishing a new daily in New York City, Dana and his associates learned of the possibility of buying the *Sun* for $175,000, and decided to take it. Although Dana, as he wrote to a friend, considered this a large sum, he pointed out that the purchasers of the paper acquired at once "a large and profitable business" and "a circulation of from fifty to sixty thousand a day, and all among the mechanics and small merchants of this city." [1] Associated with Dana in the new company were such well-known business and professional men as William M. Evarts, Roscoe Conkling, Alonzo B. Cornell, Cyrus W. Field, Edwin D. Morgan, and William H. Webb. The company, which was capitalized at $350,000, purchased a building known as Tammany Hall, at the corner of Nassau and Frankfort streets, which was destined to become famous as the home of the *Sun* for nearly half a century.

In the first issue under the new management, Dana, in a signed statement as "manager and editor," set forth his policies thus: [2]

In changing its proprietorship, THE SUN will not in any respect change its principles or general line of conduct. It will continue to be an independent Newspaper, wearing the livery of no party, and discussing public questions and the acts of public men on their merits alone. It will be guided, as it has been hitherto, by uncompromising loyalty to the Union, and will resist every attempt

[1] Wilson, J. H. *Life of Charles A. Dana*, p. 378.
[2] *Sun*, January 25, 1868.

to weaken the bonds that unite the American people into one Nation.

THE SUN will support Gen. GRANT as its candidate for the Presidency. It will advocate retrenchment and economy in the public expenditures, and the reduction of the present crushing burdens of taxation. It will advocate the speedy restoration of the South, as needful to revive business and secure fair wages for labor.

THE SUN will always have All the News, foreign, domestic, political, social, literary, scientific, and commercial. It will use enterprise and money freely to make the best possible newspaper, *as well as the cheapest.*

It will study condensation, clearness, point, and will endeavor to present its daily photograph of the whole world's doings in the most luminous and lively manner.

It will not take as long to read THE SUN as to read the *London Times* or *Webster's Dictionary;* but when you have read it, you will know about all that has happened in both hemispheres. . . .

We shall endeavor to make THE SUN worthy the confidence of the people in every part of the country. Its circulation is now more than fifty thousand copies daily. We mean that it shall soon be doubled; and in this, the aid of all persons who want such a newspaper as we propose to make, will be cordially welcomed.

This announcement that the writing in the *Sun* was to be marked by "condensation, clearness, point" in presenting "the whole world's doings in the most luminous and lively manner," forecast the qualities of the *Sun's* style that were to give the paper its distinctive character among American journals. These qualities made it "the newspaper man's newspaper."

The time was ripe for an innovation in the style of newspaper writing. From the days of the first colonial newspapers, American writers and editors had had before them constantly the current English newspapers. This was partly due to the fact that, until the trans-Atlantic cable proved successful in 1866, by far the greater part of all foreign news printed in American papers was taken directly from English journals. All the ships that crossed the Atlantic from England brought bundles of English papers for all the important New York newspapers. The London *Times,* with its unrivaled foreign news service, was an invaluable aid to New York editors in their efforts to give American readers the news of the whole world. It was not surprising, therefore, that the English style of news-writing should have influenced that of American journals.   So, too, the style of editorial writing in English papers was not without its effect on that of American editors.   Because of the importance attached to the "leaders," or editorials, of the London *Times*, not only in England but on the Continent as well, they could not be overlooked by American editorial writers seeking enlightenment as to English public opinion.   In the decade before the Civil War, American editors like Raymond and Bowles paid editorial tribute to the London *Times* as an exemplar of independent journalism and as "the greatest newspaper in the world."   Even during the war, the denunciation of the *Times* by Republican editors of the North for its sympathy with the South, was an implied recognition of its influence abroad.   Whatever effect, direct or indirect, the style of English leader-writers may have had on the American editorial, was reinforced by the high repute in which the work of British men of letters was held in this country.   The result was a more or less conscious imitation of English literary style by American writers. It is not without significance, accordingly, that Dana should have declared in his first editorial that "it will not take as long to read THE SUN as to read the *London Times*," or that he should have written later:[1]

> The American newspaper reader demands of an editor that he shall not give him news and discussions in heavy chunks, but so condensed and clarified that he shall be relieved of the necessity of wading through a treatise to get at a fact, or spending time on a dilated essay to get a bite at an argument.
> Six or seven dreary columns [in New York newspapers] are filled with leading articles, no matter whether there are subjects to discuss of public interest, or brains at hand to treat them. . . .
> Another thing has been bad.   Men with actual capacity of certain sorts for acceptable writing, have been frightened off from doing natural and vigorous work by certain newspaper critics and doctrinaires, who are in distress if the literary proprieties are seemingly violated, and if the temper and blood of the writer actually show in his work.   They measure our journalistic production by an English standard, which lays it down as its first and most imperative rule that editorial writing shall be free from the characteristics of the writer.   This is ruinous to good writing, and damaging to the sincerity of writers.

[1] *Sun*, July 24, 1875.

The English journals have admirable qualities, but they are deficient often in directness and earnestness, intellectual courage, and incisive vigor and pungency. . . .

Besides, the American is a curious person — hot and heavy in his work, desperate in his desire to get rich, not quite so fearfully over industrious as he imagines himself to be, but engrossed in his affairs; yet he is also a creature of quick sentiments and dearly loves fun. He is bored by ponderous leading articles, didactic and doctrinal, and cries out for sharp, incisive writing, wit and laughter; and he requires now and again, a tender touch of genuine heartiness.

In short, Dana sought to encourage originality in American newspaper writing and to discourage imitation of English journalistic style, long considered a model. His utterances on this point may be regarded as a journalistic declaration of independence.

In making up his staff, Dana secured a number of men who had been associated with him on the *Tribune*. Among his editorial writers were James S. Pike, from 1855 to 1860 a Washington correspondent and an associate editor of the *Tribune*, and Fitz-Henry Warren, originator of the *Tribune's* disastrous war-cry, "Forward to Richmond," and head of its Washington bureau previous to the war. Isaac W. England, managing editor of the *Sun* during Dana's first year, and then for many years its business manager, had been city editor of the *Tribune* until after the war, and later had gone to Chicago with Dana on the *Daily Republican*. Amos J. Cummings, who succeeded England as managing editor, had been editor of the *Weekly Tribune* and a political reporter on the daily *Tribune*. Cummings was regarded as one of the best judges of news in his day. He also developed the "human interest" methods of news-writing among the reporters on the *Sun*. Another former writer for the *Tribune*, whom Dana secured as an editorial contributor and reviewer of books, was Henry Brewster Stanton, husband of Elizabeth Cady Stanton, pioneer leader of the woman's rights movement. One of the mos brilliant of the new *Sun's* editorial writers, William O. Bartlett, not a *Tribune* man, was responsible for two famous phrases generally attributed to Dana himself. The first was this couplet, reiterated with great effect in fighting against the Tammany boss and his candidates for mayor:

No king, no clown
To rule this town!

The other phrase was the *Sun's* description of General Hancock, the Democratic presidential candidate in 1880, as "a good man, weighing two hundred and forty pounds."

With this able staff under Dana's direction, the *Sun* took on a new character, and appealed to a much wider circle of readers than the "mechanics and small merchants" who had constituted the old *Sun's* circulation. The expectation expressed in the prospectus that its circulation of 50,000 would soon be doubled, was realized, for, within three years, the *Sun* was printing 100,000 copies daily, and by 1875, 120,000. Thus, in a short time Dana was able to place the *Sun* in the front rank of New York newspapers, beside the *Herald*, the *Tribune*, and the *Times*. In the matter of price, the *Sun* had an advantage over these rivals, for it gave readers a four-page paper for two cents, while they charged four cents for their eight pages.

Dana was a firm believer in the possibility of keeping editorials, news, and advertisements within four pages, and of maintaining the price at two cents. In fact, he went so far as to suggest the desirability of discouraging advertising and depending on circulation for profits. After pointing out, in an editorial in 1875, that the other successful New York papers, the *Tribune*, the *Times*, and the *Herald*, had "ceased to expect a profit from their circulation" and sought large circulation "to attract advertisers," he set forth his own theory of newspaper economics thus:[1]

> It was then that THE SUN conceived of the idea of a daily newspaper that should yield more satisfactory dividends from large circulation than had ever been declared by the journals that had looked to the organism of political parties and to enterprising advertisers for the bulk of their income. It saw in New York a city of sufficient population to warrant the experiment of a two-cent newspaper whose cost should equal that of the four-cent dailies in every respect, the cost of white paper alone excepted. Accordingly, we produced THE SUN on a sheet that leaves a small margin for profit, and by restricting the space allotted to advertisers and eliminating the verbiage in which the eight-page dailies hide the news, we made room in THE SUN for not only all the real news of the day, but for interesting literature and current political dis-

[1] *Sun*, March 13, 1875.

cussion as well. It was an enterprise that the public encouraged with avidity. The edition rapidly rose to one hundred and twenty thousand copies daily, and it is now rising; while the small margin of profit on that enormous circulation makes THE SUN able to exist without paying any special attention to advertising — approaching very closely in fact to the condition of a daily newspaper able to support itself on the profits of its circulation alone.

Only a single further step remains to be taken. That step was recently foreshadowed in a leader in which THE SUN intimated that the time was not far distant in which it might reject more advertising than it would accept. With a daily circulation of fifty or a hundred thousand more, there is little doubt that THE SUN would find it necessary to limit the advertisers as the reporters and other writers for its columns are limited, each to a space to be determined solely by the public interest in his subject. It will be a long stride in the progress of intellectual as distinguished from commercial journalism, and THE SUN will probably be the first to make it, thus distancing the successors of RAYMOND, BENNETT, and GREELEY in the great sweepstakes for recognition as the Journal of the Future.

Following the policy announced in the prospectus, Dana made the *Sun* "an independent newspaper, wearing the livery of no party, and discussing public questions and the acts of public men on their merits alone." He not only supported Grant for the presidency in 1868 but, in collaboration with General James H. Wilson, wrote a campaign biography of Grant, which was based partly on his personal knowledge, gained during the Civil War, when he was an observer for Lincoln and Stanton at Grant's headquarters. Notwithstanding his admiration of Grant's military ability, Dana did not hesitate to attack his administration when it became evident that men appointed to positions of trust were unfit for office through incompetence or dishonesty. Dana maintained a firm belief in Grant's personal integrity, but this did not prevent him from denouncing the President for lack of good judgment or from attacking those office-holders who were involved in the scandals that marked Grant's two terms. This policy of the *Sun* alienated many good Republicans, including some of the stock-holders of the paper. The hostility to Dana thus engendered on the part of his old friends and supporters was intensified when, in 1872, the *Sun* supported Greeley for the presidency in opposition to Grant. During Grant's second term, the *Sun* was an unsparing critic of every questionable act and policy, and with telling effect reiterated its watchword, "Turn the rascals out."

Dana's independence was again manifest when, in the presidential campaign of 1876, he supported Tilden, the Democratic nominee, against Hayes. The *Sun* never recognized, either the authority of the Electoral Commission to decide the contested election, or its decision against Tilden and in favor of Hayes. It printed Hayes's picture with the word "Fraud" across the forehead, and referred to him, not as President, but only as "the Fraudulent President." Throughout the Hayes Administration, Dana continued a bitter opponent of the President. How strongly Dana felt in this matter was shown by a letter in which, as a former Harvard student, he declined to contribute toward a fund that was being raised at the close of the President's term to place a portrait of Hayes, a graduate of Harvard, in the University's Memorial Hall. He wrote that he was "not willing to do anything that may be designed or construed as a compliment to Mr. Hayes or that may recognize his tenure of the executive office at Wash ngton as anything other than an event of dishonor." [1]

In the presidential campaign of 1880 Dana opposed General Garfield, the Republican nominee, whose record in Congress, as the *Sun* had demonstrated two years before, had involved him in various governmental scandals and irregularities that marked the Republican administrations following the Civil War. The *Sun* was not enthusiastic over the Democratic nominee, General Hancock, whom it described as "a good man, weighing two hundred and forty pounds," and whose letter of acceptance it characterized as being "as broad and comprehensive as the continent, as elastic as india-rubber, and as sweet as honey." Four years later the *Sun* refused to support Cleveland because it thought him lacking in experience in national affairs, or Blaine, because as congressman he had been concerned in questionable transactions. Instead, Dana came out for General Benjamin F. Butler, the independent nominee, who had been successively a pro-slavery Democrat, a radical Republican, and a Greenbacker, and whose "notorious and conceded uncertainty and infidelity in public life" had been denounced by Bowles in the *Springfield Republican*. In view of Butler's record of instability and insincerity and his reputed lack

[1] Wilson, J. H. *Life of Charles A. Dana*, p. 457.

of honesty, Dana's support of his candidacy, even as a protest against the other two nominees, scarcely showed good political judgment.   Moreover, it cost the *Sun* heavily in circulation and prestige.   This defection of the *Sun* from the Democratic Party coincided with the rise of the New York *World*.   Following its purchase by Pulitzer in 1883, the *World* had become a rival of Dana's paper and now came out strongly for Cleveland.[1]   Between May, 1883, when Pulitzer took over the *World*, and January, 1885, its circulation increased from approximately 16,000 to 116,000, while that of the *Sun* fell off from about 150,000 to 98,000.[2]

Throughout the period of nearly thirty years during which the *Sun* was under Dana's editorship, it maintained its policy of independence in national politics.   It criticized those policies of Cleveland's two terms with which it did not agree, but praised other acts of the President and of Congress.   In the campaign of 1888, it supported Cleveland for reëlection, in spite of its opposition to the free trade policy of the Democratic Party.   Four years later, it opposed Cleveland's candidacy, because he had been the Democratic nominee twice before.   When free silver became an issue with the nomination of Bryan by the Democrats in 1896, the *Sun* advocated the election of McKinley.   Thus, although the paper was credited with leaning toward the Democratic Party, it could not be counted on to support either Democratic candidates or Democratic measures when Dana considered them inimical to the best interests of the country.

In New York City politics, the *Sun* fought Tammany and its misrule.   It just missed being the means of exposing the Tweed Ring, for the proofs of the Ring's operations were brought to the *Sun* office by a disgruntled member of Tammany during Dana's absence, and, as the editor in charge was unwilling to assume responsibility for publishing them, they were taken to the *New-York Times* and were printed in that paper.[3]   A year before this exposure by the *Times*, the *Sun* had sought to ridicule "Boss" Tweed by proposing the erection of a monument to him, a movement that was taken seriously by some of his followers, who

---

[1] See the *World's* cartoon depicting Dana and Butler, p. 331, *infra*.
[2] *World*, January 19, 1885.
[3] Mitchell, Edward P.   *Memoirs of an Editor*, p. 220.

undertook to raise the necessary funds. Not until Tweed wrote from Albany, where he was a state senator, discountenancing the proposal of the *Sun* as "one of those jocose sensations for which that journal is famous," were his followers convinced that the proposed monument was only another of the *Sun's* bits of ridicule. After Tweed's downfall, the *Sun* fought the Tammany boss who succeeded him, reiterating constantly the watchword, "No king, no clown, To rule this town!"

Dana believed firmly in the value of iteration as the best means of impressing his ideas upon his readers. On the *New-York Tribune* he had employed the battle cry, "Forward to Richmond"; on the *Sun* he used with telling effect such phrases as, "the Fraudulent President" and "Turn the rascals out." In explanation of the reason for this method, Dana is quoted as saying:[1]

> If you say a true and important thing once, in the most striking way, people read it, and say to themselves, "That is very likely so," and forget it. If you keep on saying it, over and over again, even with less felicity of expression, you'll hammer it into their heads so firmly that they'll say, "It *is* so"; and they'll remember forever it is so.

From the beginning of Dana's control of the paper, it was known for its sprightly style in presenting news. The headlines were no less original than the news stories. It accomplished brilliantly the aim set forth in Dana's prospectus, of presenting "the whole world's doings in the most luminous and lively manner." Among the characteristics that made the paper distinctive, according to Edward P. Mitchell, its editor-in-chief, were "no waste of words," "the abolishment of the conventional measures of news importance, the substitution of the absolute standard of real interest to human beings," and "bright and enjoyable writing." The test that the reporter was asked to make to determine the length of his "story" was, not what is a piece of news worth when judged by conventional standards of news value, but rather, "How much can you make interesting?"[2] Good writing and "human interest" characterized its news stories. To the *Sun*

[1] Mitchell, Edward P. "Mr. Dana of 'The Sun,'" *McClure's Magazine*, vol. III, p. 391 (October, 1894).

[2] Irwin, Will. "The New York Sun," *American Magazine*, vol. 67, p. 303 (January, 1909).

belongs the credit for coining the term, "human interest stories," to designate the little comedies and tragedies in the day's news that made its pages readable.

The *Sun* attracted to its staff of reporters an unusually large number of young men who afterwards became prominent as newspaper and magazine writers and editors. In the twenty years from 1880 to 1900, it numbered among its reporters Arthur Brisbane, Julian Ralph, John R. Spears, David Graham Phillips, Will Irwin, Samuel Hopkins Adams, E. W. Townsend, Rudolph E. Block, and Charles M. Fairbanks; while the *Evening Sun*, begun in 1887, had such reporters as Richard Harding Davis and Jacob Riis. The *Sun* probably employed more college-trained men than most newspapers. In 1878 Dana wrote that in the *Sun* office were "many college-bred men who are very skilful reporters," and pointed out that "the theory that a university education unfits a young man to become a successful newspaper writer is not sound, of course; for whatever trains him intellectually and broadens the scope of his knowledge, makes him better fitted to write for the public, provided he learns to understand what they want, and gets the knack of putting things attractively." [1]

The *Sun's* bright young men had the advantage of direction by two very able executives, Chester S. Lord, managing editor from 1880 to 1913, and Selah M. ("Boss") Clarke, night city editor from 1881 to 1912. The entire staff, except the editorial writers, occupied places in one large room, an arrangement that not only made for a greater degree of democracy than existed in other large newspaper offices but also brought reporters into closer contact with the news executives than was generally the case. Mr. Lord, it has been said, picked his staff "as much for personality as for brains." "Boss" Clarke was called the "greatest living school master of newspapermen" of his day. The paper came to be regarded as a kind of school of journalism for young college graduates before such professional schools were organized in American universities. The "*Sun* spirit" thus developed led, not only to the recognition that "once a *Sun* man, always a *Sun* man, wherever you go," but to the organization, by former members of the staff, of the *Sun* Alumni Association, which for many years has held regular meetings. Through long continued service, un-

[1] *Sun*, January 6, 1878.

broken by the changes and "shake-ups" that were not infrequent in many newspaper offices, Lord and Clarke were able to establish and maintain standards of newspaper writing and editing that made the *Sun* "the newspaper man's newspaper."

In summing up Dana's contribution to the development of the American newspaper, Edward P. Mitchell, for many years editor-in-chief of the *Sun*, wrote thus, three years before Dana's death:[1]

> The revolution which his genius and invention have wrought in the methods of practical journalism in America during the past twenty-five years can be estimated only by newspaper makers. His mind, always original, and unblunted and unwearied at seventy-five, has been a prolific source of new ideas in the art of gathering, presenting, and discussing attractively the news of the world. . . . To Mr. Dana's personal invention are due many, if not most, of the broad changes which within a quarter of a century have transformed journalism in this country. From his individual perception of the true philosophy of human interest, more than from any other single source, have come the now general repudiation of the old conventional standards of news importance; the modern newspaper's appreciation of the news value of the sentiment and humor of the daily life around us; the recognition of the principle that a small incident, interesting in itself and well told, may be worth a column's space, when a large dull fact is hardly worth a stickful's; the surprising extension of the daily newspaper's province so as to cover every department of general literature, and to take in the world's fancies and imaginings, as well as its actual events. The word "news" has an entirely different significance from what it possessed twenty-five or thirty years ago under the ancient common law of journalism as derived from England; and in the production of this immense change, greatly in the interest of mankind and of the cheerfulness of daily life, it would be difficult to exaggerate the direct and indirect influence of Mr. Dana's alert, scholarly, and widely sympathetic perceptions.

By encouraging originality and good writing on the part of his reporters and editorial writers, Dana exerted a powerful influence on journalistic style throughout the country. The *Sun* had a nation-wide reputation for the cleverness and originality of its news stories and editorials. The emphasis placed by Dana upon

[1] Mitchell, Edward P. "Mr. Dana of 'The Sun,'" *McClure's Magazine*, vol. III, pp. 392–93 (October, 1894).

the "human interest" elements in the news, also tended to modify the conventional standards of news values followed by other papers.   The so-called "human interest stories" of the *Sun* were imitated by reporters on many other newspapers.   The result was that humorous and pathetic incidents in the day's news that, before the vogue of the *Sun's* "human interest stories," would have received but a few lines, or would have been omitted entirely, were often given as much space and prominence as reports of significant news.   This revised standard of news values undoubtedly made newspapers more readable, but it also tended to place news that was merely entertaining on almost the same plane as informative news.   Thus, the tendency of American newspapers to seek constantly for incidents in the news that will afford entertainment rather than food for thought, can be traced back to Dana and the *Sun*.

CHAPTER XIII

WILLIAM ROCKHILL NELSON AND THE KANSAS CITY STAR

WHEN William Rockhill Nelson established the *Kansas City Evening Star* in 1880, he was in his fortieth year and was without journalistic experience save such little as he had gained as manager of the Fort Wayne, Indiana, *Sentinel*, during a short time just previous to his going to Kansas City. A restless boy, difficult to manage, he had been sent to the College of Notre Dame, now the university of that name, in his native State of Indiana, but he did not prove amenable to the strict discipline of that institution and at the end of two years was compelled by the college authorities to withdraw. Then he read law, was admitted to the bar before he was twenty-one, and for a time practiced in his native city, Fort Wayne. After an unsuccessful venture in growing cotton in Georgia just after the close of the Civil War, he returned to Indiana and engaged in the contracting business, constructing roads, bridges, and buildings. He was responsible for Indiana's first good roads legislation and for the use in that state of the Nicholson wooden block pavement for city streets. So successful did this business become that, at the age of thirty-five, he had amassed a fortune of some $200,000, but, through the failure of his partner in the Georgia enterprise, whose notes he had endorsed, this entire capital was wiped out. All that remained was an interest in the Fort Wayne *Sentinel*. After managing this paper for over a year, he decided to cast in his lot with journalism. Looking about for a larger field than his native city afforded, he considered Brooklyn, St. Louis, and Kansas City, as the three most promising cities, and finally chose the last.

Kansas City in 1880 was the gateway through which settlers passed on their way to the western country, over the trails to Pike's Peak, Santa Fé, California, and Oregon. It was then an overgrown frontier town, sprawling over the clay hills along the Missouri River, with unpaved, muddy streets, wooden sidewalks, street cars drawn by mules, and all the evils common to a raw

western community.   Between 1860 and 1880 it had increased
in population from slightly over 4000 to more than 55,000.
Unattractive though the city appeared, Nelson realized that in
its strategic position lay great possibilities for future development.

With four daily papers already in the field, however, the need of
another did not seem great.   Nevertheless, with the small amount
of capital derived from the sale of his share of the *Sentinel*, and
with the editorial aid of his former partner on that paper, Samuel
E. Morss, he established the *Kansas City Evening Star*.   The first
issue appeared on September 18, 1880, as a six-column, four-page
paper.   It was printed on an old flat-bed press.   Lacking an
Associated Press franchise, the new paper contained little telegraphic news.   The price was two cents a copy, whereas that of
the other dailies was five.   As pennies were scarce in Kansas City
in those days, Nelson secured a keg of them to distribute among
his newsboys so that they might make change.   In a display advertisement in the first issue, the *Star* announced that at its office
"Pennies and Two Cent Pieces" would be "Furnished in Quantities to Suit."

In an introductory editorial over a column in length, the proprietors explained, both the growing popularity of cheap evening papers, and the advantages of Kansas City as a field for such
a journal.   It read: [1]

> Among the most successful products of recent journalism in the
> United States is the cheap afternoon paper.   Experience has
> demonstrated that the great morning journals printed in our large
> cities, admirable and enterprising as they are, do not meet the
> wants of the great masses of the people.   Their broad pages filled
> with elaborate details of all news matters, with lengthy, ponder-
> ous editorials, with long, prosy sermons and other matter of the
> same class, which occupy a large amount of space, and demand
> much time for their perusal, while they make them journals in-
> valuable to many, at the same time render them unattractive to
> the great majority of dwellers in cities.   The hour at which they
> are published and the price at which they are furnished, combine
> to deter thousands from taking them, who, however, feel the need
> of a daily newspaper of some kind.   They have neither the time
> nor the inclination to read these large papers, nor do they feel that

[1] *Kansas City Evening Star*, September 18, 1880.

WILLIAM ROCKHILL NELSON
1840–1915

they can afford to pay for them. But some kind of a daily newspaper has become, in our modern civilization, a necessity to every intelligent person, who desires to keep posted as to the current events of the day with the minimum expenditure of time and money. To meet this want the cheap afternoon journal was devised, and the unqualified success which all well managed enterprises of this class have achieved whenever they have had a proper field, proves beyond cavil a demand for them. In almost every city and large town in the country cheap afternoon newspapers are printed which enjoy very large circulations and prosperous advertising patronage. . . . The newspapers of this type are small in size, but present in a condensed form all the news of the day. . . . The reader is not compelled to wade through columns of surplusage in order to get a kernel of news, and the writers are not obliged to cover reams of white paper with words, in conveying a few ideas which might better be stated in one-quarter of the space. Everything is told in terse, concise, direct language. There is no occasion for or temptation to verboseness, exaggeration or surplusage of any kind. The price at which such a newspaper can be supplied places it within the reach of everyone, and the hour of publication makes it especially desirable to that very large number who must postpone their newspaper reading until they have completed their day's labor.

The publishers of The Evening Star, after a careful survey of the country, came to the conclusion that Kansas City offers as inviting a field for an enterprise of this character as any city in the United States. At the present time Kansas City is large enough and partakes sufficiently of a metropolitan character to render a first-class cheap afternoon newspaper an absolute necessity. In addition, however, it is the commercial center of the great Missouri valley, and no city in the country contains within itself greater possibilities or offers brighter prospects for the future. No city in the land is growing more rapidly, or attracting more attention in all quarters. It is universally conceded that Kansas City, in a very few years, will be one of the largest and most important cities in America. Having entire confidence in the future of this city The Evening Star enters the field without a doubt in the minds of the proprietors that it will achieve unqualified success and in a very short time become one of the recognized institutions of Kansas City.

In another column on the editorial page, headed "The Evening Star, A Paper for the People, Independent, Enterprising, Spicy,

Readable, Truthful, Entertaining," the news and editorial policies were set forth thus: [1]

> The Kansas City Evening Star is offered to the people of the
> Missouri Valley, in order to meet a demand, which evidently
> exists, for a cheap afternoon newspaper, of the highest class,
> absolutely independent in politics, entirely disconnected from rings
> and cliques of all description, and wholly free to labor for the inter-
> ests of the people and to wage warfare upon corrupt and extrava-
> gant tax eaters of all parties.
>
> ... It will contain, in a condensed form, all the news of the day,
> presented to its readers in an impartial and truthful manner, with-
> out exaggeration or partisan coloring.   Arrangements have been
> made for first-class telegraphic reports, including the leading
> markets, and thus all the important events of the day will be
> recorded in the columns of The Evening Star on the day of their
> occurrence or development. . . .
>
> As a family journal The Evening Star will be strictly first-class,
> every issue containing one or more short stories, together with
> poetry, selected miscellany, etc.
>
> In its editorial department, as well as in its news columns, The
> Evening Star will seek to deal impartially and fairly by all. While
> it will be entirely independent, politically, it will by no means be
> neutral, but will express itself fully and freely concerning all
> matters of public interest, and will support such men and measures
> as are, in its judgment, best calculated to advance the popular
> welfare. . . .
>
> The Evening Star will devote its best energies to aiding the work
> of building up the material and moral interests of Kansas City,
> and developing the great Missouri Valley, of which this is the
> metropolis.

In still another editorial it called attention to its typographical
appearance and pointed out that the type, which had been especially cast for the paper, had as "its chief merit, aside from
its beauty . . . a clear and distinct face . . . perfectly legible to
all." [2]

Practically all of the characteristics of the paper outlined in its
first issue were maintained by Nelson throughout his lifetime, including its political independence, its efforts to advance the material and moral interests of the city and to develop the advantages
of the whole Missouri Valley, its high character as a family news-

[1] *Kansas City Evening Star*, September 18, 1880.   [2] *Ibid.*

paper, its attractive and legible typography, and its price of ten cents a week.

Of the initial number, 3000 copies were issued, and at the end of the first month the *Star* announced that it had "a great many more readers in Kansas City than any other newspaper published here."[1]   As Morss's health failed during the first year, Nelson, as sole proprietor, took over both the business and editorial management.   During the second year he was able, with the aid of borrowed funds, to secure an Associated Press franchise through the purchase of a small paper.

The *Star's* policy of political independence was shown by an editorial published in connection with the local election of the spring of 1881, within six months after its establishment.   It declared:[2]

> The Star has no axe to grind, no candidate to elect, no party to serve.   Its only interest is in the growth and prosperity of Kansas City and the proper administration of city government. It is for the best men, entirely regardless of party.   It is, however, forced to admit that most of the men who are seeking nominations from both parties are utterly unfit for the positions to which they aspire.   Briefless barristers, to whom no sane man would intrust a lawsuit involving five dollars, want to be city attorney.   Irresponsible and incapable men whom no one would think of selecting for cashier or bookkeeper, ask for the city treasurership. Ignorant peddlers of whiskey aspire to the city council.   Such of these men who seek nominations may expect that The Star will tell the truth about them.   The voters of the city have a right to know all the facts as to the character and capacity of those who ask their suffrage.   These they cannot find in their party organs.

Against fraud in city and county elections, and corruption in municipal government, the *Star* from the beginning took a firm stand.   It exposed and denounced those responsible for dishonesty in elections; it offered rewards for the conviction of election crooks; it employed detectives to watch for fraud on election days.   It waged unrelenting warfare against gang rule and against the protection of gambling and vice.   When many years later the commission form of municipal government seemed to

[1] *William Rockhill Nelson*, p. 18.
[2] *Kansas City Evening Star*, March 10, 1881.

offer a remedy for some of these evils, Nelson sent reporters to investigate this form of government in cities where it was being tried.   To make the information thus secured available for municipalities interested in better government, the *Star* published a pamphlet on the commission plan, for free distribution anywhere in the country.   It also encouraged members of its staff to speak on the subject wherever municipalities in its territory were considering the commission plan.   With the aid of the *Star*, Kansas City, Kansas, adopted this type of government.

Early in its career, the *Star* began a long fight against monopoly in street railway transportation, and against the granting of long-term franchises without adequate return to the city.   In 1882 it succeeded in securing a franchise for a new company that later constructed the cable system as a rival to the old mule-drawn street cars.   Two years later, it prevented a thirty-year extension of the franchise of the old company, by arousing sufficient public sentiment against it to induce the mayor to veto the proposed grant after it had been passed by the city council.   To the end of Nelson's life, the *Star* kept up the struggle to protect the city against the traction interests.

Within its first year the *Star* began a campaign for city parks. Eventually a remarkable system of parks and boulevards was secured, which may be said to be Nelson's greatest achievement. In the face of apathy on the part of the average citizen, and of opposition from men of wealth who objected to increased taxation, the *Star* carried on a fifteen-year campaign before the first public park was secured.   Organized opposition not only denounced the proposed park system as needless extravagance, "confiscation," and "robbery," but carried the fight against it into the courts. These enemies of parks were dubbed by the *Star* the "Hammer and Padlock Club," because they sought to destroy the project and to protect their own pockets.   "Of all the measures for which The Star labored," wrote Nelson after the struggle was over, "the one most despairingly blocked by this spirit of benighted non-comprehension was the project of parks."[1]   Not satisfied with urging a park system for Kansas City, Nelson published and distributed pamphlets showing the advantages of public parks for smaller communities in the territory served by the *Star*.

[1] *William Rockhill Nelson*, p. 36.

While carrying on the campaign for a park system, Nelson also advocated the development of boulevards bordered by shade trees. He experimented with various kinds of trees to determine which were best suited to the soil and climate. He had trees grown in his own nurseries and then transplanted to permanent locations along the boulevards. Similar tests were made under his direction to find out the grasses, shrubs, and flowers most suitable for beautifying streets, parks, and lawns.

The interest in building that he had acquired as a contractor in Indiana continued throughout his life. Through the columns of the *Star* he encouraged the erection of substantial, attractive, moderate-priced homes, particularly in the residential sections that were being opened up along the new boulevards in outlying parts of the city. By building his own home on a site some two miles from the city limits, in what was then an undeveloped section, he set an example for others and showed his faith in the future growth of the city. In the construction of his home he demonstrated the possibility of using effectively the then neglected native limestone. That Kansas City came to be known as a "city of beautiful homes," was a source of great pride to Nelson.

For five years, beginning in 1893, he urged through the *Star* the desirability of a municipal auditorium for Kansas City, and one was finally erected. When, within a year after the completion of the auditorium, it was destroyed by fire, he launched another campaign to have it rebuilt in time for the Democratic National Convention of 1900, the first convention of its kind to be held in Kansas City. The *Star* was likewise instrumental in bringing about the construction of viaducts to connect the city with Kansas City, Kansas. All these campaigns were carried out in accordance with Nelson's belief that it is the function of a newspaper to bring about all forms of civic improvement. "Anybody can print the news," he declared, "but the *Star* tries to build things up. That is what a newspaper is for." [1]

Nelson always tried to maintain the highest journalistic standards. Despite the success of sensational journalism in New York and other cities during the period in which Nelson was building up the *Star*, he never permitted in his paper any of the striking devices of that type of journalism. During his lifetime the *Star* had

[1] Street, Julian. *Abroad at Home*, p. 304.

no large headlines, colored "comics," sensational Sunday features, or even half-tone illustrations. In fact, the paper was conspicuous among American newspapers for its conservatism in typography and "make-up." Nelson believed that "the people will support the best that can be furnished them" in the way of a newspaper.[1] That other newspapers gained large circulations by methods of which he could not approve, did not influence his policy for the *Star*. "Don't let the other fellow make your newspaper," he said. "Make your own newspaper just as good as you can every day, and if it shows progress you are on the right trail."[2] Developing the same idea on another occasion, he said:[3]

> What the other fellow does doesn't interest me. Newspapers that are edited with a view to attracting attention from other newspapers are failures. We are running The Star for our readers, not for other newspapers.

Nelson demonstrated that a newspaper could be cheap in price without being cheap in quality. When, in 1894, he decided to issue a Sunday edition of the *Star*, he did not increase the subscription price, but gave his readers seven issues for ten cents a week, the same price that he had charged for six issues. Seven years later, in 1901, when he bought the *Kansas City Times*, he continued it as a morning edition of the *Star*, and supplied his readers with a morning, evening, and Sunday paper, all for the original price of the *Evening Star* alone — ten cents a week. By this unique arrangement, subscribers received thirteen issues a week for less than a cent a copy, the lowest price at which any American newspaper has ever been offered. Thus he was able to meet the competition of other papers without resorting to the use of "comics," which he regarded as inartistic and vulgar, or to sensational news and large headlines, which he considered objectionable.

Although the *Star* eschewed many of the so-called popular features that appeared in other papers, it published much informative and entertaining reading matter other than news and editorials. From its earliest days, it reprinted all kinds of in-

---

[1] *William Rockhill Nelson*, p. 117.
[2] Rogers, Jason. *Newspaper Building*, p. 23.
[3] *William Rockhill Nelson*, p. 122.

teresting material taken from American and English periodicals. In this respect it followed the practice of earlier American newspapers rather than that of its contemporaries. In his choice of non-news features, Nelson always sought to maintain the standard set for the *Star* in its prospectus, that of "a family journal . . . strictly first-class." Moreover, he aimed to make his paper one that would appeal to the average reader. "Always keep in mind the family that is paying us ten cents a week — and particularly its women members," was one of his favorite bits of advice to his staff.[1]

The *Star's* circulation attested the success of his policies. Beginning with 3000 for the first issue, it doubled in the first year, and passed the 10,000 mark by the end of 1883. At that time it claimed "the largest circulation of any daily newspaper published between St. Louis and San Francisco."[2] By 1886 the average daily circulation had reached 25,000, and by 1892 had exceeded 50,000. When, at the beginning of 1896, its circulation reached 60,000, the *Star* announced that this figure was "more than double the combined circulation of all other daily newspapers" in Kansas City.[3] In 1900, at the end of its first twenty years, the circulation had gone up to over 87,000,[4] and eleven years later it was practically double that figure, or 171,134.[5]

The influence of the *Star* was not measured solely by the daily edition, for, in 1890, ten years after the daily had begun publication, Nelson decided to issue a weekly edition. Of the origin of the *Weekly Kansas City Star*, Nelson said:[6]

> I took pencil and paper and figured that we could afford to print a four-page farm weekly for twenty-five cents a year. Nobody else had ever done it. But I felt that it was possible, that we were in a position to do it, and that we ought to do it. For we had a lot to say to the farmers and we weren't reaching them through the daily.

At this remarkably low price the *Weekly Star* attained a circulation of 45,000 during the first year, and within three years ex-

[1] *William Rockhill Nelson*, p. 118.
[2] *American Newspaper Directory* for 1884, p. 874. [3] *Ibid.*, 1896, p. 555.
[4] *American Newspaper Annual* for 1901, p. 473. [5] *Ibid.*, 1912, p. 502.
[6] *William Rockhill Nelson*, p. 117.

ceeded 100,000. Ten years after its first appearance, the circulation reached 150,000.[1]

The most important single factor in newspaper-making, in Nelson's estimation, was the work of the reporter. He said:[2]

> ... the reporter is the essential man on the newspaper. ...
> We could get on pretty well without our various sorts of editors.
> But we should go to smash if we had no reporters. They are the
> fellows whose work determines whether the paper shall be dull or
> interesting; whether it shall attract readers or repel them.

"The reporter who can get facts straight and put them into plain, concise language," he once declared, "is the real man in the newspaper office."[3] Reporting, however, should not consist merely in recording what had happened. From his point of view, its most important function was to investigate subjects affecting the home and business affairs of readers and their relations to the community as citizens. In accordance with his idea that "you can always trust the people to do what is best when they know what is best," he would assign his reporters to make an intensive study of whatever seemed of most vital concern to the community at a given moment. He was accustomed to say to his staff:[4]

> You must remember that a reporter has something to do be-
> sides sitting at a desk and writing. He must have an idea and
> develop that idea in every possible way. It is his business to get
> results; to bring things about, whether it is writing an article or
> making a speech.
>
> Remember this: The Star has a greater purpose in life than
> merely to print the news. It believes in doing things. I can em-
> ploy plenty of men merely to write for the paper. The suc-
> cessful reporter is the one who knows how to get results by working
> to bring about the thing he is trying to do.

"Make it your ambition to be great reporters," was his advice to students in the University of Missouri School of Journalism; "And everything else shall be added unto you."[5]

To get things done, and to serve the community, he regarded as much more important for a newspaper than to win elections or to

---

[1] *American Newspaper Annual* for 1901, p. 473.
[2] *William Rockhill Nelson*, p. 126.
[3] Grasty, Charles H. "The Best Newspaper in America," *World's Work*, vol. 18, p. 11729.
[4] *Ibid.*, pp. 46 and 73.   [5] *Ibid.*, p. 129.

maintain a rigidly consistent editorial policy. In a letter to his staff, some years before the close of his life, he wrote:[1]

> The loss of a local election has never been a matter of very serious concern to The Star, which constantly is occupied with greater things than filling offices and is concerned in election results only as they accelerate or retard those important purposes.

On one occasion when a reporter, after investigating the problem of an adequate water supply for Kansas City, Kansas, came to the conclusion that municipal ownership was the best solution, Nelson, although doubting the success of such ownership under existing political conditions, said to the young man:[2]

> I want you to know this. The Star is the only paper in the world, I suppose, without a "fixed policy." It is always for the thing that is most efficient and most feasible. What it advocated yesterday, it feels at perfect liberty to "kick over" today if it finds that what it advocated yesterday stands in the way of what it finds is a good thing today.

To achieve what the *Star* stood for, as Nelson believed, required the coöperation of every member of the staff. In a letter addressed to them he said:[3]

> In the permanent things, both great and small, with which The Star is engaged, every one having a part in its production should have a hand. Every one should clearly understand those purposes and have them constantly in mind, so that no news or information or influence bearing upon any of them shall be overlooked or disregarded. Every reporter, every writer, every deskman should regard each of these subjects as a continuous assignment in which the best interest of the paper is concerned. And, in general, every one should strive to furnish ideas and suggestions; to find new opportunities for the paper's active service; new features of interest; new ways of doing things.

This ideal of close coöperation among all members of the staff in carrying out the policies of the *Star*, found expression in the arrangement of the news and editorial room. Every one, from Nelson himself to the youngest reporter, had a desk in this one large room. Thus Nelson was able to keep in touch with all the members of his staff, and they felt free to consult him at any time.

[1] *William Rockhill Nelson*, p. 50.   [2] *Ibid.*, p. 74.   [3] *Ibid.*, p. 50.

Nelson himself seldom wrote anything for publication.   He was in the habit of talking over with his writers whatever he desired to say, and then they put his ideas into form for publication.   In this way the *Star* to a remarkable degree expressed the personality of its editor without containing anything that he himself had written.   No other American editor of a paper as large as the *Star* ever directed more completely all the workings of his organization than did Nelson.   He was not unwilling, however, to consider and accept ideas and policies other than his own when they were supported by facts and arguments that seemed to him cogent.

Although the *Star* was always an intensely local paper, it did not neglect national political issues.   Originally a great admirer of Samuel J. Tilden, Nelson had in 1876 been his Indiana manager for the presidential nomination, but in 1880, when the Democratic Party failed to nominate Tilden for the presidency, Nelson broke with the Democrats, and during the rest of his life he was an independent.   He gave the support of the *Star* to Cleveland in the 1884 campaign and again in the 1892 election.   Although he distrusted the Republican Party in national politics, believing that it was dominated by special interests, he favored McKinley rather than Bryan on the free silver issue in the presidential campaign of 1896, and again, in the 1900 campaign, on the issue of imperialism.   Nelson had been attracted by the fighting qualities displayed by Roosevelt both as civil service commissioner in New York and as governor of that state.   After making the acquaintance of Roosevelt in the 1900 presidential campaign, Nelson was henceforth a warm supporter of him and of his policies.   He supported Taft for the presidency, but the failure of the Republicans to revise the tariff downward, and Taft's acquiescence in the Payne-Aldrich high tariff measure, alienated Nelson and the *Star*.   Despairing of any reform within the Republican ranks, Nelson in 1912 urged the establishment of the new Progressive Party, with Roosevelt at its head, and, contrary to his principle of refusing to participate personally in political organizations, he signed the call for the new party.   After the third party was established, however, he promptly withdrew as temporary national committeeman from Missouri, but continued his support of Roosevelt and of the Progressive program of social and political reform.   At the same time he urged the Democrats to nominate Woodrow Wilson for the presidency, as a liberal candidate, and, after Roosevelt and the Progressives were defeated, he gave President Wilson his whole-hearted support. In state politics the *Star* showed a similar independence by supporting, sometimes a Republican, and sometimes a Democrat.

The *Kansas City Star*, during its thirty-five years under Nelson's personal direction, demonstrated what a newspaper can do toward building up and improving a community. No other American newspaper ever rendered so continuous and efficient a service to its community as did the *Star*. It did not confine its efforts to Kansas City, but extended them to cover the whole section in which it circulated. That in most of its campaigns for civic betterment it was compelled to fight against determined and well-organized opposition, makes its achievement all the greater.

No American newspaper has expressed more completely the personality of its editor than has the *Star*. Nelson was a fighting editor, determined to accomplish what he believed to be for the best interests of the city, the state, and the nation. When he and his paper were violently attacked and maligned, they both fought all the harder. "I've tried to be gentle and diplomatic," he once remarked, "but I've never done well in my stocking feet."[1] That he was called "Colonel" by his admirers and "Baron" by his enemies, shows that he was an outstanding personage in the community. His strong personality found expression only through the columns of the *Star*, for, unlike other exemplars of personal journalism such as Greeley, he never aspired to public office and did not take part personally in public affairs. He rarely attended public meetings or served on committees, even when they were concerned with matters in which he was keenly interested. When, during Taft's administration, it was rumored that he was to be offered the ambassadorship to France, he promptly declared that he "regarded himself as holding a place of greater responsibility and usefulness than any within the gift of the President or the electorate."[2] Of all the great American journalists, he alone was not a writing editor. His ideas found expression only in the writing of members of his staff. His terse, picturesque phrases were not infrequently embodied in what they wrote, but the actual composition of the editorials and articles was theirs, not his.

[1] *National Floodmarks*, p. 44.   [2] *William Rockhill Nelson*, p. 113.

The success of the *Star* showed that it was possible to build up a large circulation at a very low subscription rate without cheapening the quality of the reading matter or resorting to sensational typography.   To furnish for ten cents, a morning, evening, and Sunday paper, thirteen issues a week, was in itself a unique achievement.   To retain modest headlines and a conservative "make-up" throughout a period that was marked by a widespread adoption of large display "heads" and striking effects in "make-up," was scarcely less remarkable.   The *Star* during Nelson's lifetime was probably the only important American daily paper that never published half-tone illustrations.   Because the first attempts to print half-tones on newspaper perfecting presses did not produce very clear or attractive illustrations, Nelson preferred to use zinc etchings reproducing line drawings.   Although the printing of newspaper half-tones was in time perfected, he never used them in the *Star*.   The Sunday issue included no colored comic section.   The *Star* was a clean, well-printed, readable family newspaper, which contained, in addition to news and editorials, a variety of wholesome, entertaining, and informative matter.

What William Rockhill Nelson and the *Star* had stood for was briefly set forth, after his death, in the following editorial signed by his widow and his only daughter:[1]

> The Star was dedicated by Mr. Nelson to the great purposes and high ideals in the service of humanity — to honest elections, to democratic government, to the abolition of special privilege, to fair dealing on the part of public service corporations, to larger opportunities for boys and girls, to progress toward social and industrial justice, to all things that make for the richer, fuller life that he coveted passionately for every man, woman and child.
>
> Particularly was it dedicated to the advancement of Kansas City.   Whatever helped the city The Star was for.   Whatever hurt the city The Star was against.   For thirty-five years this newspaper has warred with all the resources at its command against election thievery, against boss rule, against grasping corporations that came to town only to make money out of it, against the whole brood of enemies of Kansas City.   For thirty-five years it has given its zealous support to every movement for the upbuilding of the city.   There has been no citizen, no matter

[1] *William Rockhill Nelson*, p. 182.

what his station, but has known that if he came forward with a practical, effective plan for the city's benefit, he could count on the heartiest help and coöperation from The Star.

Mr. Nelson never regarded his newspaper as a commercial proposition. To him it was always a sacred trust.

CHAPTER XIV
JOSEPH PULITZER AND THE NEW YORK WORLD

THE development of the New York *World* into an aggressive, crusading, sensational newspaper by Joseph Pulitzer, following his purchase of it in 1883, marks the beginning of a new epoch in American journalism. In the fifteen years following the close of the Civil War, all of the pre-war leaders in journalism ended their careers. Raymond died in 1869, Greeley and Bennett in 1872, Bowles in 1877, and Bryant in 1878. Within the same period, New York City journalism received two notable accessions: Godkin, who became editor of the *Nation* in 1865, and of the New York *Evening Post* in 1883; and Dana, editor of the *Sun* after 1868. The sensationalism that had marked the first cheap papers of the thirties, such as the New York *Herald*, the New York *Sun*, the Philadelphia *Public Ledger*, and the Baltimore *Sun*, had been considerably tempered by their success. None of the outstanding papers in the decade following the Civil War could be characterized as sensational. Although earnest efforts to reform abuses in municipal and federal government were made by papers like the *Springfield Republican*, the *New-York Times*, the New York *Sun*, the New York *Evening Post*, and the *Chicago Tribune*, these activities scarcely placed them in the category of crusading newspapers. Pulitzer in the *World* revived, not only the aggressive editorial leadership shown by Greeley in the *Tribune*, but also the sensational treatment of news common to the first penny papers, and to these policies he added a crusading spirit, in both the news and the editorial columns, that was new in American journalism.

When Pulitzer purchased the *World* in 1883, he was thirty-six years old and had been engaged in journalism for the greater part of fifteen years. Born in Hungary in 1847 of a good family, he had run away from home at seventeen, in hope of pursuing a military career. Weak eyesight and an unmilitary physique led to his rejection for service successively in the Austrian army, the French Foreign Legion, and the British army; but an American agent in Hamburg, seeking recruits for the Union army, shipped him as an emigrant to the United States. On his arrival in

JOSEPH PULITZER

1847–1911

Boston harbor in the fall of 1864, he and a companion decided to collect their own enlistment bounties by jumping overboard and swimming ashore. Making straight for New York City, he enlisted in a company of the Lincoln Cavalry. His military career, however, was short and comparatively uneventful, for, following Lee's surrender, six months after his enlistment, he was mustered out of the army without having engaged in any fighting. Lacking money or prospect of employment in New York City, then overrun with former soldiers out of work, he made his way to St. Louis. He cared for army mules at the barracks near St. Louis, acted as fireman on Mississippi packets, and did other manual labor. Finally a chance acquaintance, made over the chess board, with Dr. Emil Preetorius and Carl Schurz, editors and publishers of the *Westliche Post*, resulted in his beginning his journalistic work as a reporter on that influential German daily newspaper of St. Louis. His aggressiveness and persistence in newsgathering, coupled with his broken English and ungainly appearance, made him the laughing stock of his rivals on the English daily papers. Nevertheless, he outdid them in securing news. Then, partly as the result of a joke, he was nominated for the Missouri legislature on the Republican ticket in a strong Democratic district of St. Louis. To the surprise of every one, he not only made a vigorous personal canvass of the voters, but won the election.

Pulitzer's efforts to reform abuses, while he was acting both as a member of the legislature and as legislative correspondent for the *Westliche Post*, led to an encounter between him and a well-known St. Louis politician whose lobbying he had attacked. He shot and slightly wounded his detractor, but, when he was convicted of the offense, his fine was paid by prominent Missourians who admired his reform efforts. As one of three police commissioners of St. Louis, he fought gambling and other local evils. In 1870 with Carl Schurz he participated in the revolt against the Republicans that began in Missouri. During the presidential campaign of 1872, he took the stump for Greeley and made sixty speeches in German throughout Missouri and Indiana. After Greeley's defeat and the failure of the Liberal Republican movement, Pulitzer became a Democrat. As a result of the election he acquired a part ownership in the *Westliche Post*, for some of the proprietors were willing to dispose of their stock because, as he wrote, they "thought the paper was ruined by the Greeley campaign." [1]   But he proved too aggressive for his associates, Preetorius and Schurz, and accordingly they purchased his interest in the paper, paying him $30,000.   Schurz long afterwards half humorously remarked that Dr. Preetorius and he were rather glad when Pulitzer sold his interest, for they were afraid that, if he continued with them much longer, he would own the whole paper.[2]

Following his retirement from the *Westliche Post*, Pulitzer went abroad, but he returned to St. Louis early in 1874.   He straightway made $20,000 almost overnight by purchasing a struggling German daily and selling its Associated Press franchise to J. B. McCullagh, who made use of it in 1875 to bring about the consolidation of the *Globe* and the *Democrat* into the successful *St. Louis Globe-Democrat*.   On returning from another trip abroad, Pulitzer took the stump for Tilden, the Democratic nominee in the 1876 presidential campaign.   Then he reported for the New York *Sun* the deliberations of the Electoral Commission at Washington.   Dana published these news stories and contributions to the editorial page over Pulitzer's signature.   Following two more trips to Europe and his admission to the bar of the District of Columbia, Pulitzer returned to St. Louis and again took up journalism.

He purchased the St. Louis *Dispatch* for $2500 at a sheriff's sale on December 9, 1878, and three days later combined it with the *Post*, owned by John A. Dillon.   Known first as the *Post and Dispatch* and then as the *Post-Dispatch*, the new paper was controlled jointly by Pulitzer and Dillon.   Its prospectus, written by Pulitzer, explained the policies of the publication thus: [3]

> The *Post and Dispatch* will serve no party but the people; will be no organ of Republicanism, but the organ of truth; will follow no causes but its conclusions; will not support the 'Administration,' but criticise it; will oppose all frauds and shams wherever and whatever they are; will advocate principles and ideas rather than prejudices and partisanship.   These ideas and principles are

---

[1] Seitz, Don C.   *Joseph Pulitzer*, p. 75.

[2] Meloney, W. B.   "Joseph Pulitzer," *American Magazine*, vol. 69, p. 120, footnote (November, 1909).

[3] Seitz, Don C.   *Joseph Pulitzer*, pp. 101–02.

precisely the same as those upon which our Government was originally founded, and to which we owe our country's marvellous growth and development. They are the same that made a Republic possible, and without which a real Republic is impossible. They are the ideas of a true, genuine, real Democracy. They are the principles of true local self-government. They are the doctrines of hard money, home-rule and revenue reform.

The *Post-Dispatch* carried on campaigns to remedy various abuses, such as tax-dodging by the well-to-do, gambling, the sale of lottery tickets, and the failure of the city to keep the streets clean and in good repair. At the end of the first year, Pulitzer bought out his partner and became the sole owner. As editorial assistant he secured John A. Cockerill, an experienced newspaper man. The paper proved a financial success from the beginning and became the leading evening paper in St. Louis.

Pulitzer's four and a half years' experience with the *Post-Dispatch* was valuable, not only in furnishing him with money with which to buy the *New York World*, but also in giving him the opportunity to try out in a smaller field the ideas and ideals that he afterwards developed on a larger scale in the metropolis. In a history of the *World* issued in 1890, it was said that "the foundation of the New York World was laid in St. Louis. . . . The battle of new ideas and new theories of journalism was fought there under the banner of the Post-Dispatch. The spirit and character which have distinguished The World were imparted to the Post-Dispatch by Mr. Pulitzer on the day that he became the sole director." [1]

Ill-health, due to overwork and to anxiety over the killing of a prominent St. Louis attorney by Cockerill, following the *Post-Dispatch's* attacks on the former, led Pulitzer to go to New York in 1883 with the intention of traveling abroad for six months. In the metropolis he learned of Jay Gould's desire to dispose of the *World*, then a well-edited but financially unsuccessful Democratic morning paper. Acting on the impulse of the moment, Pulitzer decided to buy it at Gould's price, $346,000, the amount that Gould had paid for it plus the losses that he had sustained during the four years of his ownership.

The *World* had begun in 1860, as a one-cent religious daily, but

[1] *The World, Its History and Its New Home* (pamphlet), p. 94.

had not proved a success even after it was combined in 1861 with the old, well-established *Courier and Enquirer*.   During the Civil War it was ably edited by Manton Marble as a Democratic paper. In 1864, with the *Journal of Commerce*, it was suppressed by the Federal Government for three days for publishing a proclamation, supposedly issued by President Lincoln, but in fact "faked" to influence the stock market.   After the 1876 presidential campaign, it became the property of the head of the Pennsylvania Railroad, and three years later passed into the hands of Jay Gould, who had amassed a fortune by his exploits in Wall Street.   At the time Pulitzer bought it, the *World* was a two-cent, eight-page paper, with a circulation of about 15,000.   Its rivals in the metropolitan field were the *Herald*, with from twelve to sixteen pages, at three cents a copy, directed by James Gordon Bennett, Jr.; the *Times*, with eight pages at four cents, managed by George Jones; the *Tribune*, with eight pages at four cents, edited by Whitelaw Reid, and the *Sun*, with four pages at two cents, edited by Dana.

In a signed statement in the first issue of the *World* under his control, Pulitzer announced his policy thus:[1]

> There is room in this great and growing city for a journal that is not only cheap but bright, not only bright but large, not only large but truly Democratic — dedicated to the cause of the people rather than that of purse-potentates — devoted more to the news of the New than the Old World — that will expose all fraud and sham, fight all public evils and abuses — that will serve and battle for the people with earnest sincerity.

A week later he published his platform in ten lines and recommended it "to the politicians in place of long-winded resolutions." It read:[2]

1. Tax luxuries
2. Tax inheritances
3. Tax large incomes
4. Tax monopolies
5. Tax the privileged corporations
6. A tariff for revenue
7. Reform the civil service
8. Punish corrupt office-holders
9. Punish vote-buying
10. Punish employers who coerce their employees in elections

[1] *World*, May 11, 1883.   [2] *Ibid.*, May 17, 1883.

Although the first five planks in this platform seemed to be aimed at capitalists and big corporations, the *World* had made plain, in its first issue under Pulitzer, that it recognized the rights of capital. In an editorial headed "True Democracy," the paper had said:[1]

> Democracy, sometimes from ignorance, more frequently from malice, has been represented as radicalism and destructiveness. It is nothing of the kind. True Democracy, based on equal rights, recognizes the millionaire and the railroad magnate as just as good as any other man, and as fully entitled to protection for his property under the law. But true Democracy will not sanction the swallowing up of liberty by property any more than the swallowing up of property by communism.

The typographical changes introduced by Pulitzer made the *World* less striking in appearance than it had been. A smaller and lighter face of type was adopted for the headlines at the top of the columns on the front page. Four single-column display headlines, with a cross-line for the first "deck," appeared on the first page. Except for its use of news illustrations in the form of line drawings, the *World* did not differ materially in appearance from the other New York morning papers.

The only typographical innovation was the printing of "ears" in the blank spaces created on both sides of the shorter name, *The World*, which Pulitzer substituted for the former title, the *New York World*. These "ears," which began to appear at the end of the first month, were originally in circular form and advertised the *Post-Dispatch* as having "a larger circulation in St. Louis than any other paper," and the *World* as the "only 8-page newspaper in the United States sold for 2 cents." A little later the "ears" became rectangular in form and announced that "The Daily World prints every day more news for 2 cents than any 8-page paper in the United States," and that the Sunday *World* with twelve pages for three cents was the "Brightest and Best Sunday Paper." This innovation in journalism, credit for which belongs to the *World*, has been widely adopted by newspapers throughout the country.

That the *World* under Pulitzer's control sought to attract readers by striking headlines, was evident from the first issues.

[1] *World*, May 11, 1883.

Local and telegraph news on the front page within the first month bore such sensational display "heads" as, "Screaming for Mercy," "All for a Woman's Love," "A Mother's Awful Crime," "Love and Cold Poison," "A Bride but Not a Wife," "Withered Bridal Roses," "A Mystery of the River," "Victims of His Passion," "Death Rides the Blast," "The Wall Street Terror." Alliterative headlines like the following were frequent: "Baptized in Blood," "Bachelor Bang's Bridal," "Terrible Times in Troy," "Little Lotta's Lovers," "A Preacher's Perfidy," "Jim-Jams in the Jury," "Duke Meets his Doom," "A Riddle of the River." To arouse curiosity, the question form of headline was occasionally used, such as, "Was It Peppermint Mary?" "A Heroine or a Criminal?" "What has Become of Him?"

Sensational news, to which these headlines were attached, was gleaned from the local field and surrounding states, as well as from all over the country and even from abroad. The "human interest" elements in the day's news were "played up" in the news stories. Colonel John A. Cockerill, who had been Pulitzer's right-hand man on the St. Louis *Post-Dispatch*, was brought to New York and placed in charge of the *World's* news department, as managing editor. That the paper strove to make a popular appeal, is evident from the editorial statement to the effect that "the tone and sentiment of THE WORLD we believe to be in accord with the mass of the American people."[1] Its success was attributed to the fact that it was "a bit breezy." In an editorial apropos of its Sunday circulation's having reached 100,000, it said:[2]

> It is certainly demonstrated that the Eastern public appreciates a style of journalism that is just a bit breezy while at all times honest, earnest and sincere, and a journalism that represents every day a laborious effort to meet the popular demand for news seasoned with just convictions.

The use of illustrations, both in the daily edition and in the Sunday paper, also contributed to the immediate success of the *World*. Within six months of its appearance under Pulitzer's ownership, diagrammatic illustrations of murders were published on the front page.[3] Pictures were likewise used in connection

[1] *World*, August 25, 1884.   [2] *Ibid.*, September 29, 1884.
[3] Cf. *World*, October 17 and November 19, 1883.

with feature articles in the Sunday *World*. The unprecedented circulation attained by the *World* during its first two years was attributed to its illustrations by the *Journalist*, a weekly magazine published in New York in the interests of the profession of journalism. The editor of the *Journalist* wrote in 1885: [1]

> It is the woodcuts that give the World its unparalleled circulation. When Joseph Pulitzer went to Europe he was a little undecided about the woodcuts. He left orders to gradually get rid of them, as he thought it tended to lower the dignity of his paper, and he was not satisfied that the cuts helped in its circulation. After Pulitzer was on the Atlantic Col. Cockerill began to carry out the expressed wishes of its editor and proprietor. He found, however, that the circulation of the paper went with the cuts, and like the good newspaper general that he is, he instantly changed his tactics. He put in more cuts than ever, and the circulation rose like a thermometer on a hot day, until it reached over 230,000 on the day of Grant's funeral.

The success of Pulitzer's efforts to attract readers to the *World* was reflected in the circulation. The average daily circulation for the first three months of his ownership, 30,326, was twice what it had been previous to his purchase of it. At the end of the first year its circulation had reached 61,152, four times what it had been when he bought the paper. The circulation of the Sunday *World*, which outstripped that of the daily, had, by the end of the first sixteen months of Pulitzer's control, reached 100,000. This achievement was celebrated by the firing of a hundred rounds from a cannon in City Hall Park. By the close of the second year, in 1885, the circulation of the daily had gone up to over 100,000, and that of the Sunday edition to over 135,000. When, in September, 1886, the circulation passed the 250,000 mark, a silver medal was struck off to commemorate "the largest circulation ever attained by any American newspaper." Thus, within less than three and a half years, the *World*, a cheap, popular, sensational newspaper, had broken all circulation records in America.

The immediate success of the new *World* led its rivals to reduce their prices. On September 18, 1883, four months after Pulitzer bought the *World*, the *Times* cut the price of its daily edition

[1] *Journalist*, August 22, 1885.

from four to two cents, and that of its Sunday issue from five to three cents; the next day the *Tribune* came down from four to three cents for its daily, and from five to three cents for its Sunday edition; and the following week the *Herald* reduced its price for the daily from three to two cents, but continued to charge five cents for the Sunday paper. To announce the price reduction of the *Herald*, James Gordon Bennett, Jr., took a full-page advertisement in the *World* for a week, with the single sentence in the center of the page, "Herald at Two Cents, Cheapest Paper in America." [1] Unfortunately the *Herald*, in cutting its price, antagonized the news dealers by reducing their profits on each copy, and was compelled to establish news-stands of its own to insure sales. This struggle proved costly to the *Herald*, both in added expense and in reduced circulation. Pulitzer often said that Bennett and Dana had made him a present of the city, the former by his injudicious contest with the news dealers, the latter by deserting the Democratic Party upon Cleveland's nomination in 1884. [2]

With the rapid gains in circulation came equally rapid increases in the *World's* advertising. When Pulitzer took over the paper, it had less advertising than the *Times*, the *Tribune*, or the *Herald*. After the first year, it boasted of "nearly four times as many [advertisements] as either the *Times* or *Tribune*," [3] and by November, 1884, it had passed the *Herald* in the number of columns of advertising.

Having gone over to the Democratic Party in 1876, Pulitzer did not find it necessary to change the politics of the *World*, which had always been a staunch Democratic paper. Impressed by Grover Cleveland's majority of 193,000 for governor in the 1882 election in New York State, and by his "clean record for honesty, capacity, and economy in his administration of the State government," the *World* strongly urged his nomination for the presidency on the Democratic ticket and later supported him vigorously in the campaign. Large four- and five-column cartoons by "Walt" McDougall and Valerian Gribayédoff were printed on the first page of the *World* belittling Blaine, the Republican nominee, and ridiculing Dana together with his candi-

[1] *World*, September 27–October 3, 1883.
[2] Seitz, Don C. *Joseph Pulitzer*, p. 145. [3] *World*, July 28, 1884.

ONLY A "BLIND" FOR BLAINE.

**Travelling in an Expensive Car to Beg Votes for His
Republican Master.**

One of a series of political cartoons drawn by Walt McDougall for the
New York *World*, during the Presidential Campaign of 1884.   It shows
Gen. Benjamin F. Butler, the Independent candidate, holding the hand of
Charles A. Dana, who supported him in the New York *Sun*, while James G.
Blaine, the Republican candidate, is catching the votes

Size of cartoon, 9¼ in. by 9¼ in.   New York *World*, October 20, 1884

date, General Benjamin F. Butler.[1]   This was the first series of
political cartoons published in an American newspaper.   That
the *World* was a potent force in the election of Cleveland, the
first Democratic President since the Civil War, was recognized by
Cleveland himself.   On the occasion of the twenty-fifth anniversary of the paper, he wrote:[2]

And I recall . . . how brilliantly and sturdily the World then
fought for Democracy; and in this, the first of its great party

[1] Cf. *World*, August 30 and 31, September 7, 13, and 15, 1884.
[2] Seitz, Don C. *Joseph Pulitzer*, p. 149.

fights under the present proprietorship, it was here, there and everywhere in the field, showering deadly blows upon the enemy. It was steadfast in zeal and untiring of effort until the battle was won; and it was won against such odds and by so slight a margin as to reasonably lead to the belief that no contributing aid could have been safely spared. At any rate, the contest was so close it may be said without reservation that if it had lacked the forceful and potent advocacy of Democratic principles at that time by the New York World the result might have been reversed.

In the same election Pulitzer was elected to Congress. When the first session got under way, however, over a year after the election, he found that his duties as congressman interfered with his journalistic work, and he therefore resigned his seat the following April, after serving only four months. This was the only political office that Pulitzer ever held during his ownership of the *World*.

By the powerful editorial aid that the *World* rendered Cleveland in this campaign, it not only won recognition as one of the outstanding Democratic papers in the country, but realized Pulitzer's ideal of a newspaper as a force in creating sound public opinion. His interest always centered in the editorial page. To the details of newspaper publishing he was indifferent. He said on one occasion that in all his newspaper career he had "never spent an hour at any one time in the business office." [1] Sensational news, presented in an interesting way, he apparently regarded largely as a means of securing readers for the editorials. A large circulation meant to him the opportunity to influence through editorials a large number of citizens. He is said to have confessed that his favorite New York newspaper was Godkin's *Evening Post*, and, when asked why he did not make the *World* a paper like the *Post*, replied, "Because I want to talk to a nation, not to a select committee." [2] In commenting on the success of the paper in attaining, by the fall of 1884, a Sunday circulation of over 100,000, the *World* declared editorially, "We can conscientiously say that we believe the success of THE WORLD is largely due to the sound principles of the paper rather than to

---

[1] *World*, October 31, 1911.

[2] Creelman, James. "Joseph Pulitzer — Master Journalist," *Pearson's Magazine*, vol. XXI, p. 246 (March, 1909).

its news features or its price." [1] Whether or not this explanation was correct, it undoubtedly expressed Pulitzer's hope and desire for the *World*.

During the years 1885 and 1886, the *World* engaged in a series of crusades of a sensational type. It uncovered the bribery of New York aldermen in connection with the Broadway street car franchise, and reported brilliantly the trial of the accused "boodlers." It sought the prosecution and conviction of a contractor for erecting flimsy tenement houses. It assailed a police sergeant charged with criminally assaulting a little girl, and a janitor for murdering a young woman. In the latter case it raised funds by popular subscription to erect a statue of the victim. It exposed the white slave traffic carried on by a pseudo-astrologer, and thereby won the commendation of the judge before whom he was arraigned. "Every mother of foolish girls and every father of flighty daughters," the judge declared, "is indebted to the *World* for a Christmas gift beyond all price." [2]

Its campaign for funds to erect in New York Harbor a pedestal for Bartholdi's statue of "Liberty Enlightening the World" was its first great public service to win nation-wide recognition. This gigantic statue, funds for which had been secured by popular subscription among the French people, was to have been presented to the United States in connection with the Centennial celebration in 1876, but the task of making it had proved greater than was anticipated and it was not completed until eight years later. After Congress had failed to appropriate money for a pedestal, and a citizens' committee had been unable to secure the necessary amount from private sources, the *World* in the spring of 1885 took up the cause, declaring that "THE WORLD is the people's paper, and it now appeals to the people to come forward and raise this money." [3] After a five months' campaign in its news and editorial columns, the *World* succeeded in raising the $100,000 needed for the pedestal. This amount was collected chiefly in small contributions, many of which were of five and ten cents. [4] There were over 120,000 contributors to the *World* fund. Pulitzer was perhaps the first to realize the significance of the Statue of Liberty as a symbol to the millions who, like himself, had come to America seeking freedom and opportunity.

[1] *World*, September 30, 1884.   [2] *Ibid.*, December 25, 1886.
[3] *Ibid.*, March 16, 1885.   [4] *Ibid.*, August 11, 1885.

With the profits of the *World* for 1886 exceeding half a million dollars, Pulitzer suddenly decided in 1887 to enter the evening field in New York with the *Evening World*. The immediate success of the *Evening Sun*, following its appearance as a four-page penny paper in March, 1887, no doubt influenced him to launch a similar venture. On October 10th of that year, the twentieth anniversary of his arrival in St. Louis, appeared the first issue of the *Evening World*, which, like the *Evening Sun*, consisted of four pages and sold for one cent. The new enterprise entailed a loss of $100,000 the first year, but, by the end of the second year, it was on a paying basis and had passed its rival, the *Evening Sun*. The success of both papers demonstrated the hitherto unrealized possibilities of the evening newspaper field in New York City.

The growth of the daily, Sunday, and evening editions of the *World* necessitated larger quarters. Accordingly, in April, 1888, Pulitzer purchased French's Hotel at Park Row and Frankfort Street. A penniless soldier just mustered out of the army, he had been ordered out of this same hotel by the porter twenty-three years before. On this site he determined to erect a home for the *World* that should tower above all the buildings in the vicinity, including that of the *Sun* next door. But shattered nerves and impaired eyesight made it necessary for him to go abroad to seek relief from work and worry and to consult leading European specialists, in the hope of preventing a complete breakdown. When the corner-stone of the new *World* building was laid on October 10, 1889, he could not be present, but from his sick bed in Germany he dispatched the following message, which embodied all his hopes and aspirations for the institution in which his life centered:[1]

God grant that this structure be the enduring home of a newspaper forever unsatisfied with merely printing news — forever fighting every form of wrong — forever Independent — forever advancing in enlightenment and progress — forever wedded to truly Democratic ideas — forever aspiring to be a moral force — forever rising to a higher plane of perfection as a Public Institution.

God grant that THE WORLD may forever strive toward the highest ideals — be both a daily school-house and a daily forum —

[1] *World*, October 11, 1889.

both a daily teacher and a daily tribune — an instrument of Justice, a terror to crime, an aid to education, an exponent of true Americanism.

Let it ever be remembered that this edifice owes its existence to the public; that its architect is popular favor; that its moral corner-stone is love of Liberty and Justice; that its every stone comes from the people and represents public approval for public services rendered.

God forbid that the vast army following the standard of THE WORLD should in this or future generations ever find it faithless to those ideas and moral principles to which alone it owes its life and without which I would rather have it perish.

Before the building was completed he was stricken with blindness, and, two months before the paper was settled in its new home, he announced his retirement from its active editorship.[1]

Commenting on Pulitzer's withdrawal from the *World*, the *New York Herald* appraised his contribution to American journalism during the seven and a half years of his editorship. It said:[2]

What the Greeleys and the Raymonds and the Bennetts did for journalism thirty years ago, Pulitzer has done to-day. It is true his methods have been queer and peculiar; but, after all, they have suited the present American public.

As for us of the HERALD, we droop our colors to him. He has made success upon success against our prejudices; has succeeded all along the line; has roused a spirit of enterprise and personality which, up to this time, has not been known. This man, however, who has given us a new line of thought and action, now becomes a part of the past.

We have not always agreed with the spirit which has made his ideas a journalistic success, and we cannot refrain from regretting that he did not encourage us in the new departure which he made, instead of merely astonishing us, frightening us, and, we may add — now that it is past — perhaps a little bit disgusting us.

But, *le Roi est mort, vive le Roi!* The New York *World* is dead. Long live the *World! Pace!*

But, if the *Herald* and the *World's* other rivals thought that the blind "king" and his paper were no longer to be reckoned with, they were mistaken. They were destined to see both make greater innovations, break more journalistic traditions, and secure a much larger circle of readers.

[1] *World*, October 16, 1890.   [2] *New York Herald*, October 17, 1890.

Pulitzer's retirement from active control of the *World* did not affect vitally its policies or general character. Although, during the last eighteen years of his life, he visited the *World* office only three times, he always kept in close touch with the men in charge of the paper. His summers he spent at Bar Harbor or in cruising along the Atlantic coast in his steam yacht. His winters were passed at his villa at Cap Martin on the Riviera or on his yacht in the Mediterranean. Wherever he was, he constantly had the *World* in mind. Copies of every issue were read to him by his secretaries. He frequently sent instructions and suggestions by cable or by mail to various members of the staff regarding its news and editorial policies. Editors responsible for the conduct of the paper were often summoned for conference with him wherever he happened to be, at home or abroad. Thus he continued to direct the affairs of the *World* to the time of his death.

After supporting Cleveland in the 1888 campaign, in which he was defeated, and in the 1892 campaign, in which he was victorious, the *World* did not hesitate to take issue with him when it could not approve his policies. In 1895 an old dispute between Great Britain and Venezuela over the boundary line of British Guiana came to a head, and Venezuela, appealing to the Monroe Doctrine, succeeded in arousing considerable interest in the matter in the United States. Goaded by American "jingoes" in and out of Congress, President Cleveland finally sent a belligerent message to England demanding that Great Britain arbitrate, and in a message to Congress urged that, if this demand were refused, the United States should intervene and, if necessary, fight to uphold the Venezuelan claims.[1] Despite the disastrous effect of this threat of war on Stock Exchange prices, other leading New York papers like the *Sun*, the *Times*, and the *Tribune* supported the President. Only the *Evening Post* and the *World* took a strong stand against him. Four years before, when a difference had arisen between Great Britain and the United States over fur-seal rights in Alaskan waters, the *World* had come out strongly for arbitration, in these words:[2]

Arbitration is civilization's substitute for the brutality of war.

[1] Cf. *World*, December 18, 1895. [2] *Ibid.*, November 12, 1891.

Arguments cost less than ammunition. Reasoning comes cheaper than throat-cutting.

Justice is all that any civilized nation really wants in any dispute, and justice is much more likely to be the outcome of arbitration than of armed conflict.

In agreeing to submit the Behring Sea question to arbitration the governments of Great Britain and the United States have made their bow to the enlightened sentiment of the people of both countries.

This is civilization. This is progress.

Again, in the Venezuelan dispute, the *World* was no less outspoken. In an editorial headed "No Cause of War," it showed that the Monroe Doctrine was not involved in the question at issue, and ended with this unmistakable declaration: [1]

The reasons urged for the forcible application of a false Monroe doctrine in the Venezuela case therefore fall to pieces at a touch. There is no substance to them. There is no menace to the boundary line. It is not our frontier. It is none of our business. To make it such without cause, and to raise the spectre of war over a false sentiment and a false conception, is something more than "a grave blunder." If persisted in it will be a colossal crime.

Not satisfied merely to state his own views as to the "colossal crime" of a war between the two great English-speaking nations, Pulitzer sent cable messages to many prominent leaders in England and Ireland asking for their opinions. This list of notables included the Prince of Wales, the Duke of York, Lord Salisbury of the Foreign Office, former Prime Minister Gladstone, John Redmond, the Irish leader, and the English and Irish bishops and archbishops. All responded in unanimous opposition to war. In publishing facsimiles of the cablegrams from these prominent men, the *World* used for the first time a banner headline; it read, "Messages of Peace, Common Sense and Humanity to the People of the United States." [2] In an effort to prove that Pulitzer's actions in this matter were a violation of the law, Secretary of State Olney, who had written the bellicose message to England, cited a statute of 1799 that provided a heavy fine and imprisonment for "any citizen of the United States, who, without permission of the Government," carried on "any verbal correspondence or intercourse with any foreign govern-

[1] *World*, December 21, 1895.   [2] *Ibid.*, December 24, 1895.

ment . . . in relation to any controversy with the United States."
In the Senate, Henry Cabot Lodge quoted the same statute
against Pulitzer. But, as the " jingo " spirit subsided, the country
realized the truth of the famous phrase in Gladstone's reply to
Pulitzer's cable message, "Only common sense is required," and
war was averted.[1]

Again, in December, 1895, the *World* took issue with the Cleveland Administration when, for the second time within a year, the
Secretary of the Treasury proposed to sell privately to a syndicate
headed by J. P. Morgan and Company a large issue of United
States bonds at what was regarded by Pulitzer as less than their
market value.[2] Pulitzer ordered 10,000 telegrams sent to all the
national banks and to other financial institutions of the country,
asking whether or not they would subscribe for these bonds if they
were offered at public sale.[3] The mass of evidence thus secured
proved that the bonds could be sold directly to the public at
higher prices than the Morgan syndicate had paid for the first
issue or had offered for the second one. The *World* called on
President Cleveland to "trust the people," "reject the steal,"
and "smash the ring" of big financiers.[4] The *World's* striking
crusade again proved successful, and, when the bonds were offered
to the public, not only was the issue largely over-subscribed, but
the price secured by this method was much higher than that at
which the bond syndicate was to have bought them. Pulitzer
himself subscribed for $1,000,000 of the bonds at the highest price
bid, and in a short time was able to realize a profit of $50,000 on
them. The *World* heralded its success thus:[5] "the victory of
publicity and patriotism is complete. The World's greatest
triumph is secure."

The entry into New York journalism of William Randolph
Hearst, with his purchase of the *Morning Journal* in the fall of
1895, brought Pulitzer face to face with the most formidable
antagonist he had ever encountered. Mr. Hearst, with millions at
his command, began to lure away men from the *World* by offers of
larger salaries. Thus commenced "the most extraordinary dollar-

---

[1] *World*, December 22, 1895.
[2] Cf. *World*, December 17–31, 1895, and January 1–14, 1896.
[3] *World*, January 6, 1896.   [4] *Ibid*., January 3, 4, and 5, 1896.
[5] *World*, January 14, 1896.

matching contest in the history of American journalism." [1]
First the editor and entire staff of the Sunday *World* were won
over by financial inducements; next the managing editor of the
Evening World was captured; then the publisher of the *World*
succumbed; and finally Arthur Brisbane, who had developed
the Sunday *World* into a most strikingly original paper, went
over to the enemy. When, early in 1896, the *Journal* as a one-
cent paper had reached 150,000 in circulation, Pulitzer decided
to reduce his price to one cent, hoping thus to stop the progress
of the *Journal*.[2] The *World*, in announcing the reduction, declared that its aim was "One Million Per Day." Although the
World gained 88,000 a day by the move, the *Journal* did not suffer
but continued to increase in circulation.[3]

The journalistic battle royal had just begun. Before Arthur
Brisbane went over to the *Journal* in 1897, he had built up a circulation of over 600,000 for the Sunday *World*, of which he was
editor. Striking feature articles in the Sunday Supplement were
in 1893 illustrated by the first colored pictures ever attempted on
a fast newspaper press. Then some comic cuts by R. F. Outcault,
picturing child life in "Hogan's Alley," were tried in colors —
the first attempt in any newspaper to produce colored "comics."
In experimenting with color effects, it was decided to print in
bright yellow the dress of the leading figure, "The Kid of
Hogan's Alley." The success of using solid colors in these
Sunday "comics" was instantaneous. Outcault, the creator
of the "Yellow Kid," was soon taken over by Mr. Hearst for his
Sunday *Journal*, but the *World* secured George B. Luks, afterwards a painter of merit, to continue the "Yellow Kid" in its
Sunday edition. Advertisements of the rival "Yellow Kids"
in the two papers adorned the billboards of New York. This
war of "comics," coupled with the sensationalism that marked
both papers in their daily and Sunday editions, led an editor of one
of the other New York newspapers to coin the term, "yellow
journalism."

The *World* was the first American newspaper to add a colored
supplement to its Sunday edition. In 1893 a Walter Scott Company color press was installed, and on Sunday, November 19,

[1] Seitz, Don C. *Joseph Pulitzer*, p. 212.   [2] *World*, February 10, 1896.
[3] Seitz, Don C. *Joseph Pulitzer*, p. 212.

NEW YORK JOURNAL, SATURDAY, NOVEMBER 14, 1896.

THE YELLOW KID AT THE HORSE SHOW!

"The Yellow Kid," originally a colored "comic," drawn by R. F.
Outcault for the New York *World*, and then taken over by the
New York Journal. It gave rise to the term "Yellow Journalism"

New York Journal, November 11, 1896

appeared a four-page section called the "Colored Supplement."
The two outside pages were printed in five colors and the two
inside pages in black. The front-page illustration, which filled
most of the page, reproduced a wash drawing in colors depicting
"The Cathedral at Eleven O'Clock Mass," and the fourth page
contained a similar illustration in colors, entitled "Scene in the
Atlantic Garden Saturday Night."[1] The following year a Hoe
color press was secured, which printed an eight-page supplement,
with four pages in colors and four in a single color. These colored
sections of the Sunday paper included the forerunners of the
"colored comics" in the form of illustrated jokes consisting of
three or four separate sketches. Humorous drawings by "Walt"
McDougall, the *World's* cartoonist, were also printed in colors in
these supplements.

Early in 1898, the *World* installed a new Hoe multi-color and
half-tone press, which was described by its makers as "the largest Color Perfecting Machine we have ever placed in operation,
printing either four, six, eight or sixteen page papers in nine
separate colors simultaneously."[2] This press marked an advance on the Hoe color machine which the *New York Journal*
had installed a year and a half before.[3] The new press enabled
the Sunday *World* to print more attractive magazine and comic
sections.

The sensationalism of the *World* and of the *Journal* was vigor-

---

[1] *World*, November 19, 1894.   [2] *Ibid.*, March 12, 1898.
[3] Cf. *New York Journal*, September 28, 1896.

ously condemned, not only by the more conservative press, but by well-known civic leaders. Clubs banished both papers from their reading rooms. The reaction against "yellow journalism" was not unlike the "Moral War" waged on Bennett's *Herald* in 1840. Although this outcry did not reduce circulation, it did result eventually in Pulitzer's toning down the more sensational features of the *World*, just as Bennett had done after the attacks on the *Herald*. The *New York Journal*, on the other hand, did not materially change its policies.

The "jingo" spirit, which had been smouldering since the threat of war with Great Britain over the Venezuelan boundary in 1895, broke out again in 1898 as a result of the inhuman methods employed by Spain to put down a Cuban revolution. Spanish oppression of the Cubans had been a source of irritation to this country for many years, but war would probably have been averted had not the battleship "Maine" been mysteriously blown up in the harbor of Havana. Both the *World* and the *Journal* seized the opportunity to "play up" the news by the most striking typographical devices ever before employed by any newspaper. Page-wide "streamer heads" and full-page line-drawing illustrations were employed for the first time. A few days after the disaster, the *World* gave over its entire front page to a large illustration of the "Maine," with a banner headline and a caption. The *Journal*, not to be outdone, spread a similar illustration over two inside pages.[1] For the second week following the explosion, the *World's* circulation exceeded 5,000,000, and was heralded as the "largest circulation of any newspaper printed in any language in any country."[2] Editorially the *World* counseled patience and moderation until an investigation should reveal the cause of the disaster, but the manner in which every phase of the news was displayed no doubt tended to arouse readers to demand drastic action.

When a two months' investigation as to the cause of the blowing up of the "Maine" proved inconclusive, the *World* urged a "short and sharp" war to free the oppressed Cubans. In a signed editorial on April 10, 1898, Pulitzer summed up his position in these words:

[1] *New York Journal*, February 18 and 21, 1898.
[2] *World*, February 28, 1898.

No lover of peace, no lover of justice, no lover of his country
ought to hesitate in urging the Government to strike one swift and
decisive blow, now that a conflict is made inevitable by the mad
folly of Spain, and thus end the suspense, the uncertainty and the
expenditure of $1,000,000 a day in mere preparation. To be
"short and sharp" in war is to be merciful as well as economical.
Further dilly-dallying . . . will be criminal.

In view of Pulitzer's vigorous fight for arbitration on two previous
occasions, when differences had arisen between Great Britain
and the United States, this demand for war with Spain seemed a
complete reversal of policy. There were two reasons for this
change. One was the fact that human liberty was at stake.
The other was to be found in the sharp rivalry between the
World and the *Journal*. Pulitzer, as he afterwards confessed,
thought that war would arouse wide-spread interest and would
give him an opportunity to test its effect on the *World's* circulation.[1] In the two months between the "Maine" disaster and the
declaration of war, the daily circulation of the *World* rose from
about 800,000 to more than 1,000,000, and by April 26 it had
reached the phenomenal record of 1,300,000 copies a day. To
the sober-minded Godkin, "nothing so disgraceful" as the course
of the *World* and the *Journal* had "ever been known in the history
of American journalism." He considered it a "crying shame
that such men [Pulitzer and Hearst] should work such mischief
simply in order to sell more papers."[2]

During the month before hostilities began, the *World* appeared
with striking front-page headlines and "make-up." The usual
"make-up" of the paper at this time consisted of two four-column
drop-line "heads" on the first page. Banner "heads," however,
were not uncommon. On April 1, the first page banner read,
"Spain Must Choose Peace or War in a Few Hours," and was
followed by two eight-column "banks"; on April 7, "The President and Congress Now United for War," also with two eight-
column "banks"; and on April 11, "President M'Kinley Will Not
Wait. Message to Congress Due To-Day." The two largest

---

[1] Seitz, Don C. *Joseph Pulitzer*, p. 238.
[2] *Evening Post*, February 19, 1898, and *Nation*, February 14, 1898, vol. 66, p. 139.
For further criticisms of the *World* and the *Journal* by Godkin, see Chapter XI,
pp. 284–85 and Chapter XV, pp. 377–78.

banner "heads" were a two-line drop-head in type an inch high, on April 14, "House Adopts War Resolution by a Vote of 322 to 19. Flying Squadron Sails South, Perhaps for St. Thomas"; and the single-line " streamer " in type an inch and a half high, on April 17, "Declaration of War!" Streamer headlines were not used on the inside pages as they were in the *Journal*, and, on the whole, the typographical display was less sensational in the *World* than in the *Journal*.

Although the Spanish-American War lasted less than four months, it gave the *World* ample opportunity for striking displays of news in big headlines, large illustrations, and hitherto unknown forms of "make-up." Through the enterprise of one of its correspondents, the *World* was able to print the first news of Dewey's victory at Manila, but only in an "extra," too late for wide circulation.[1] The cost to the paper of cable messages and of the special fleet of tugs maintained in the vicinity of Cuba, proved so great that, despite large gains in circulation, the *World* did not make its usual profits during the war. Except in so far as the war freed Cuba from Spanish oppression and increased circulation temporarily, its results were unsatisfactory to Pulitzer. To compete with the large banner "heads" and bizarre "make-up" of the evening edition of the *Journal*, the *Evening World* had to adopt similar typographical devices, and Pulitzer disliked big display headlines. In an attempt to eliminate them after the war, he ordered the melting-up of all the large headline type, but the use by rival evening papers of big display "heads" prevented their permanent elimination from the *Evening World*.[2]

The so-called "imperialism" which victory threatened to impose on this country was also distasteful to Pulitzer. While the treaty of peace was being negotiated, he came out strongly in the *World* against the proposal to retain the Philippines. In an editorial protest against such a policy, the *World* declared that "the Great Republic has won a position as a world power, a world influence, by means of a war not for 'criminal aggression' but for humanity and liberty alone." [3] The paper accordingly attacked the Treaty of Paris, both while its ratification was under discussion in the Senate, and after it had been ratified. Although

[1] *World*, May 7, 1898.   [2] Seitz, Don C. *Joseph Pulitzer*, p. 242.
[3] *World*, November 3, 1898.

the *World* had in 1896 opposed Bryan as the Democratic presidential nominee, because of his stand for "free silver," it supported him in 1900, because of his stand against "imperialism." With Bryan's defeat, "anti-imperialism," for which the *World* had fought valiantly, ceased to be a vital issue.

That Pulitzer later came to realize the part that "jingoism" had played in bringing on the Spanish-American War, is shown by his directions to his editorial writers in 1907, when President Roosevelt proposed to send battleships to the Pacific coast to impress Japan. "Show that Spain had granted to Cuba all that we demanded," he wrote, "but passion in Spain and here forced the hands of government. . . . Give further details of jingoism causing Cuban War after Spain had virtually granted everything." [1]

Desiring to be relieved to a greater extent of the responsibility for the editorial page of the *World*, in which his chief interest centered, Pulitzer sought some new editorial writers. Through the efforts of a personal representative, who visited a number of cities and studied the editorial pages of their papers, Frank I. Cobb, editorial writer on the *Detroit Free Press*, was secured for the editorial staff of the *World*. In due time Cobb was able to adapt himself to the needs of Pulitzer and of the *World*, and, after becoming chief editorial writer, continued to direct the editorial policies of the paper for many years until his death in 1923. In 1904 Ralph Pulitzer, the oldest son of the editor, also joined the editorial staff, and, upon the death of his father in 1911, became head of the *World*.

The greatest crusade carried on by the *World* was that begun in 1905 against abuses in the management of the great life insurance companies in New York City. A struggle for the control of the Equitable Life Assurance Society, one of the three largest life insurance companies in this country, led to the exposure of certain questionable uses to which the funds were being put that were accumulating from premiums paid by policy-holders. The *World* took advantage of these revelations to demand a thorough investigation by a committee of the state legislature into the manner in which the great life insurance companies were conducted. In the face of strong opposition, the *World* was

[1] Seitz, Don C. *Joseph Pulitzer*, pp. 312–13.

finally able to enforce its demand for an investigation. Through its efforts, Charles E. Hughes, who had been assisting in a campaign of the *World's* against the so-called "Gas Trust," was appointed as legal counsel for the committee of investigation. Hughes's careful conduct of the investigation revealed that the insurance companies were exerting great financial and political influence by means of the millions of dollars of premiums paid by the hundreds of thousands of policy-holders all over the country. The investment of the vast assets of these companies was being used as a means of financial profit to those in control of the companies. Large amounts of the funds that should eventually have been returned to policy-holders were being paid out for a variety of purposes, including contributions to political campaign funds. This crusade initiated by the *World* aroused public opinion throughout the country and led, the following year, to the enactment of legislation in New York State designed to prevent the recurrence of such abuses. The prominence achieved by Hughes in this investigation led to his election in 1906 to the governorship of New York.

Although Hughes was nominated for governor on the Republican ticket, the *World* supported him vigorously against his Democratic opponent, William Randolph Hearst. Pulitzer, however, was unwilling that the previous struggle between the *World* and the *Journal* should color the attitude of the *World* toward Mr. Hearst as a candidate for the governorship. He telegraphed to John L. Heaton, then in charge of the editorial page, as follows:[1]

Treat Hearst without a particle of feeling of prejudice, if this is possible. Concentrate on the one point previously telegraphed, that while as a matter of conviction sincerely detest most of his professions, principles, purposes and party, the same conviction compels an expression of respect for his courage in accepting a candidacy which cannot lead to his election and must appear as devotion to his principles. If he will give vigorous articulation and organization to the deep conviction among all intelligent Democrats that the name, spirit, spell and fame of the ancient Democratic party is used by unscrupulous bosses and politicians purely for moneymaking for their own pocket all the time, . . . he will render a public service whatever his motives. If he will de-

[1] Seitz, Don C. *Joseph Pulitzer*, pp. 287–88.

tach from the blind followers of the Murphy machine a large body, and if he will teach the voter that his first duty is to vote in accordance with his own conscience and as a free man, he will render a service to the cause of independence and intelligence. . . .

Late in 1908, the *World* became involved in a controversy with President Roosevelt over the conditions under which the United States had acquired its rights to build the Panama Canal. This issue, when finally settled by the United States Supreme Court in 1911, had important bearings on the right of the Federal Government to interfere with the freedom of the press. The controversy began with an editorial by Frank I. Cobb in the *World* of December 8, 1908, demanding a congressional investigation of "the entire Panama Canal scandal." In this editorial President Roosevelt was charged with "deliberate misstatements of fact in his scandalous personal attack upon Mr. Delavan Smith, editor of the Indianapolis *News*," who had published an editorial raising pertinent questions in regard to the so-called Panama Canal scandal.[1] Incensed by these charges, the President, on December 15, 1908, sent a special message to Congress in which he excoriated Pulitzer as editor and proprietor of the *World*. Some of the statements in the President's message follow: [2]

It is idle to say that the known character of Mr. Pulitzer and his newspaper are such that the statements in that paper will be believed by nobody; unfortunately, thousands of persons are ill informed in this respect and believe the statements they see in print; even though they appear in a newspaper published by Mr. Pulitzer. . . .

While the criminal offense of which Mr. Pulitzer has been guilty is in form a libel upon individuals, the great injury done is in blackening the good name of the American people. It should not be left to a private citizen to sue Mr. Pulitzer for libel. He should be prosecuted for libel by the Governmental authorities. . . .

It is therefore a high national duty to bring to justice this vilifier of American people, this man who wantonly and wickedly and without one shadow of justification seeks to blacken the character of reputable private citizens and to convict the Government of his

[1] This editorial and others dealing with the same subject are reprinted in J. L. Heaton's *Cobb of " The World,"* pp. 1-25.

[2] *World*, December 16, 1908.

own country in the eyes of the civilized world of wrong-doing, of the basest and foulest kind, when he has not one shadow of justification of any sort or description for the charge he has made. The Attorney-General has under consideration the form in which the proceedings against Mr. Pulitzer shall be brought.

These charges were based on the fact that, in seeking to prove President Roosevelt's "deliberate misstatements of fact," the *World* had reviewed the whole history of the United States Government's relation to the Panama Canal. It had shown by documentary evidence how the Republic of Panama had been set up by means of a "manufactured" revolution with the aid of the United States Government; how Congress had then voted $10,000,000 to this Republic in return for the grant of the Canal Zone; how Congress had appropriated $40,000,000 to reimburse an American company for what it claimed it had spent in purchasing the rights of the old French Panama Canal company, although the *World* declared that the control of the bankrupt company could have been bought in the open market for $4,000,000.[1]

Indictments were secured in the District of Columbia charging Pulitzer and two of his editors with criminal libel. Indictments were also secured against Delavan Smith and another editor of the *Indianapolis News*. As the indicted editors could not be arrested and brought to trial unless they volunteered to go to Washington, indictments were sought against the editors and publishers of the *World* in the United States District Court in New York, the charge being that copies of the paper containing the matter alleged to be libelous had been circulated on the Government reservation at West Point and in the New York Federal Building. Before either of the cases against the *World* came to trial, the Federal judge in the United States District Court at Indianapolis ruled against the Government's attempt to make the editor of the *Indianapolis News* answerable to the indictments brought in the District of Columbia. His decision against the Government was based on the Sixth Amendment to the Constitution, which guarantees an accused person the right to a trial in the state or district where the crime was committed. When the *World's* case came up in the Federal District Court in New York, the Federal judge held that there was no national

[1] *World*, December 8, 1908.

statute in force covering the crime of libel against the Government of the United States, and that, since the libelous matter complained of had been published in the State of New York, it came within the jurisdiction of state courts. The Government carried the case to the United States Supreme Court, which, in a unanimous decision handed down on January 3, 1911, upheld the *World*. The two essential points in this decision, which was written by Chief Justice White, were:[1]

> First, That adequate means were afforded for punishing the circulation of a libel on a United States reservation by the state law and in the state courts, without the necessity of resorting to the courts of the United States for redress;
> Second, That resort could not be had to the courts of the United States to punish the act of publishing a newspaper libel by circulating a copy of the newspaper on the reservation upon the theory that such publication was an independent offense, separate and distinct from the primary printing and publication of the libellous article within the State of New York, without disregarding the laws of that State and frustrating the plain purpose of such law, which was that there should be but a single prosecution and conviction.

This decision was heralded by the *World* as "the most sweeping victory won for freedom of speech and of the press in this country since the American people destroyed the Federalist party more than a century ago for enacting the infamous Sedition law," and the paper declared that "no other President will be tempted to follow the footsteps of Theodore Roosevelt, no matter how greedy he may be for power, no matter how resentful of opposition."[2]

In the New York mayoralty campaign of 1909, the *Evening World* adopted a new feature by giving the supporters of each of the three candidates an opportunity to present their arguments day by day. Arthur Brisbane offered to contribute daily to the *Evening World* a signed article in support of his chief, William Randolph Hearst, who was running as an independent candidate against the regular Democratic and Republican nominees. Mr. Brisbane's offer was accepted by Pulitzer, and a twenty-four sheet poster containing a six-foot portrait of Mr. Brisbane appeared on the bill-boards of New York announcing his signed

---

[1] *World*, January 4, 1911.   [2] *Ibid.*

contributions to the *Evening World*. So violently did Mr. Brisbane assail Judge Gaynor, the Democratic nominee, that the latter brought a libel suit against the *World*, in spite of the fact that it was giving him strong editorial support. Although the suit caused some anxiety in the *World* office, Frank I. Cobb used it as an argument for electing Gaynor. He wrote in the *World:*[1]

> Judge Gaynor's libel suit against The World for the publication in its evening edition of one of Mr. Brisbane's entertaining articles in behalf of Mr. Hearst is to be accepted as further proof of the Democratic candidate's militant independence.
>
> If Judge Gaynor, in the midst of the campaign, brings suit against The World, which is his chief newspaper supporter, we have high hope that as Mayor he would be equally courageous in starting litigation in the public interest. That kind of a man could bring all the tax-dodgers to time, collect the franchise taxes that the corporations have evaded for years and compel the traction companies to fulfil their contract obligations. That is what we want a Mayor to do.
>
> New York needs a Mayor who is not afraid to start lawsuits against anything or anybody, and who will not be swerved by personal considerations of any sort.

Gaynor won the election but was with difficulty persuaded to withdraw his suit against the *World*.

In the fall of 1911, while cruising southward from New York on his yacht, Pulitzer was taken ill, and, in the harbor of Charleston on October 29, he lapsed into unconsciousness and died.

A little over a year before his death, in a letter to Charles M. Lincoln, managing editor of the *World*, Pulitzer summarized his ideals for the *World* in these words:[2]

> Concentrate your brain upon these objectives:
> 1st. What is original, distinctive, dramatic, romantic, thrilling, unique, curious, quaint, humorous, odd, apt to be talked about, without shocking good taste or lowering the general tone, good tone, and above all without impairing the confidence of the people in the truth of the stories or the character of the paper for reliability and scrupulous cleanness.
> 2nd. What is the one distinctive feature, fight, crusade, public service or big exclusive? No paper can be great, in my opinion,

[1] *World*, October 26, 1909; reprinted in John L. Heaton's *Cobb of "The World,"* p. 136.
[2] Seitz, Don C. *Joseph Pulitzer*, pp. 416–17.

if it depends simply upon the hand-to-mouth idea, news coming in anyhow.   One big distinctive feature every day at least.   One striking feature each issue should contain, prepared before, not left to chance.

3rd. Generally speaking, always remember the difference between a paper made for the million, for the masses, and a paper made for the classes.   In using the word masses I do not exclude anybody.   I should make a paper that the judges of the Supreme Court of the United States would read with enjoyment, everybody, but I would not make a paper that only the judges of the Supreme Court and their class would read.   I would make this paper without lowering the tone in the slightest degree.

4th. Accuracy, accuracy, accuracy. Also terseness, intelligent, not stupid condensation.   No picture or illustration unless it is first class both in idea and execution.

Some years before, he had given the following advice to his editors: [1]

Always tell the truth, always take the humane and moral side, always remember that right feeling is the vital spark of strong writing, and that publicity, *publicity*, PUBLICITY is the greatest moral factor and force in our public life.

Because he believed in the importance of establishing and maintaining high standards for the profession of journalism, Pulitzer became interested, some eight years before his death, in the idea of founding a school of journalism. The project seemed to have taken shape in his mind during the winter of 1903, and was presented to the authorities of Columbia University in the spring of that year.   As some questions arose concerning the personnel of the advisory board of the proposed school, Pulitzer decided to postpone further action during his lifetime.   After his death, the school was established, with an initial endowment of a million dollars and a provision for a second million after the school had been in successful operation for three years.   The School of Journalism at Columbia University opened in the fall of 1912.   The proposal to found a school of journalism called forth considerable criticism from newspaper men and from educators.   In reply to these strictures, Pulitzer wrote an article, which appeared in the *North American Review*, setting forth at

[1] *World*, December 29, 1895.

length his conception of the purposes and methods of a school of journalism.[1]

Among numerous bequests provided for by Pulitzer were several designed to stimulate interest in better journalism. A $500 gold medal was to be awarded annually "for the most distinguished and meritorious public service rendered by any American newspaper during the year." A prize of $1000 was to be given "for the best example of a reporter's work during the year; the test being strict accuracy, terseness, the accomplishment of some public good, commanding public attention and respect." The third prize was one of $500 for the best cartoon published during the year. Three traveling scholarships of $1500 each were provided to enable graduates of the Columbia School of Journalism to spend a year abroad studying social, political, and journalistic conditions in Europe. Annual awards were also provided for the best American novel, the best history of the United States, the best American biography, and the best book of verse.

During a little less than half a century, since the time when Pulitzer reached Boston, a penniless immigrant, he had amassed a fortune which, according to the final appraisal, amounted to more than $18,650,000. This was unquestionably the largest fortune ever made in America through the editing and publishing of newspapers.

Pulitzer's contribution to the development of the American newspaper was four-fold. To the editorial page of the *World*, in which his interest was centered, he gave a vigor of style and an aggressiveness of policy that had been lacking in American newspapers since the days of Greeley, Bowles, and other editors of the era of personal journalism before and during the Civil War. His only editorial rival in the New York field was Godkin of the *Evening Post*. The fact that the *Post* was his favorite newspaper is not without significance. Pulitzer undoubtedly sought through the editorial columns of the *World* to create sound public opinion. His aim was always to make the *World* a paper that would "expose all fraud and sham, fight all public evils and abuses, . . . serve and battle for the people with earnest sincerity,"[2] "a newspaper

[1] *North American Review*, vol. 178, pp. 641–80 (May, 1904).
[2] *World*, May 11, 1883.

forever unsatisfied with merely printing news — forever fighting
every form of wrong — forever Independent — forever advancing
in enlightenment and progress — forever wedded to truly Democratic ideas — forever aspiring to be a moral force — forever
rising to a higher plane of perfection as a Public Institution." [1]
That he was able to realize this ideal to a marked degree is evidenced by the success of the various laudable crusades that were
carried on through the editorial and news columns of the *World*.
The paper was an independent, fearless advocate of many good
causes.

By its news policies, the *World* revived the sensationalism
begun by the first penny papers.   In giving prominence to sensational news, Pulitzer aimed to secure as large a circle of readers
as possible.   Believing as he did that the *World* should be "both
a daily school-house and a daily forum — both a daily teacher
and a daily tribune," [2] he sought to obtain readers for his editorials by offering them sensational news.   To reach the masses,
he felt that he must give the masses what they wanted in the way
of news.   Whether the end justified the means may well be questioned.   The success of this sensationalism in building up rapidly
the largest circulation in this country, led a host of newspapers
to imitate the *World's* sensational methods.   Thus it exerted an
unwholesome influence on the American press.   In so far as it
secured readers among the masses who had not hitherto read
newspapers, it marked another step toward the democratization
of the press.

Once firmly established with a large circulation, the morning
World, like most of the first penny papers half a century earlier,
abandoned much of its sensationalism.   The *Evening World*,
on the other hand, continued to display conspicuously the more
sensational aspects of the day's news, as well as to use striking
headlines and "make-up."

By his advocacy of professional education for journalism, and
by his liberal endowment for the establishment of a school of
journalism, Pulitzer gave a powerful impetus to what has since
become the most important movement for the advancement of
the profession.   In his proposal to endow a school of journalism
he was a pioneer, but, by delaying its establishment until after

[1] *World*, October 11, 1891.   [2] *Ibid*.

his death, he lost for that institution the claim of being the first of its kind in the world.

By the innovations that he introduced into the Sunday *World*, Pulitzer was instrumental in extending the scope of the American Sunday newspaper. In the Sunday *World* were printed the first colored illustrations and the first colored "comics." Sensational feature articles, with striking illustrations, also appeared for the first time in the Sunday *World*. As a result of the keen rivalry between the *World* and the *New York Journal*, all these features of the Sunday editions of both papers were developed until they became so popular that they were adopted by many other newspapers.

The duality of the man is suggested by John S. Sargent's well-known portrait of Pulitzer. The right side of the face is depicted with the saturnine expression of the sensationalist, the left side with the benevolent aspect of the idealist.

CHAPTER XV

WILLIAM RANDOLPH HEARST AND THE NEW YORK JOURNAL

THE success of the New York *World* during its first two years under Pulitzer's direction, furnished the inspiration and the ideas that William Randolph Hearst, then a student at Harvard University, later developed in the newspapers under his control. "I was watching all the while I was at Cambridge the rise of Mr. Pulitzer's *World*," Mr. Hearst has said, "and I thought I saw the principles underlying his methods." [1]   During his two years at Harvard, from 1883 to 1885, he became so interested in journalism that he not only visited Boston newspaper offices, to learn their methods of editing and publishing, but analyzed representative papers from various parts of the country.   On leaving college at the end of his sophomore year, he returned to his native city, San Francisco.   His father, George Hearst, one of the successful California pioneeers, had amassed a large fortune in mines and ranch lands.   Aspiring to be governor and later United States senator, he had acquired the *San Francisco Examiner* in order to advance his political interests, but it had not proved a financial success.   When the son returned from college, his father is said to have tried to interest him in the management of his mines and ranches, but William Randolph Hearst preferred journalism.   Finally he secured his father's reluctant consent to his taking over the direction of the *Examiner*.   When, early in 1887, George Hearst was elected to the United States Senate, his son assumed complete charge of the paper, and thus became a publisher at the age of twenty-four.

By applying the principles that had proved successful for the New York *World* under Pulitzer, Mr. Hearst undertook to transform the *Examiner* from an unprofitable business into a profitable one.   "I wanted to make the *Examiner* pay," he said afterwards.   "A newspaper should be self-supporting.   It can't last if

[1] Steffens, Lincoln. "Hearst, the Man of Mystery," *American Magazine*, vol. 63, p. 11 (November, 1906).

it isn't, no matter how much money is behind it." [1]   He secured
as editor Samuel S. Chamberlain, who had been on the *New
York Herald* and on the *Evening Telegram* under the younger
Bennett, and who in 1884 had established *Le Matin* in Paris.
Other outstanding members of the *Examiner* staff under Hearst
were Arthur McEwen, an effective writer, who later became
prominent on other Hearst papers; Edward H. Hamilton, a star
reporter and special writer; Andrew M. Lawrence, who, during
fourteen years' connection with the paper, was successively city
editor, Washington correspondent, and managing editor, and who
afterwards took charge of the *Chicago American* and of the
Chicago *Examiner;* "Annie Laurie" (Mrs. Winifred Black), a
pioneer among women reporters of the new type developed by the
Hearst journalism; Ambrose Bierce, who for years contributed
the "Prattle" column to the paper, and whose short stories later
won for him a national reputation; James Swinnerton, who drew
"comics"; and Homer Davenport, political cartoonist, who later
achieved national fame. Thus Mr. Hearst began the policy, which
he has since continued, of securing the best men obtainable.

The *Examiner* gave Mr. Hearst the opportunity to experiment
with various methods of attracting readers for nearly a decade
before he entered the New York newspaper field, quite as Pulitzer had "tried out" different appeals on the St. Louis *Post-
Dispatch* before he bought the *New York World*.   Mr. Hearst
initiated crusades and campaigns, presented news in a striking
manner, and carried out a variety of promotion "stunts" to advertise the paper.   That his efforts proved successful was shown
by the fact that, within two years after taking charge of the
Examiner, he was able to make the paper not only pay its way
but net a good profit.

In 1895, Mr. Hearst entered the New York field by buying the
Morning Journal.   In the purchase was included the *Morgen
Journal*, a German daily.   The *Morning Journal* had been es-
tablished in 1882 by Albert Pulitzer, a younger brother of Joseph
Pulitzer, with a capital of $25,000.   As a one-cent paper it proved
successful, and, early in 1895, Albert Pulitzer sold it to John R.
McLean of the Cincinnati *Enquirer* for $1,000,000.   McLean

---

[1] Steffens, Lincoln.   "Hearst, the Man of Mystery," *American Magazine*, vol.
63, p. 11 (November, 1906).

raised the price to two cents and undertook to change it from a rather irresponsible paper to a more substantial one. Brought thus into competition with the other two-cent papers, the *Morning Journal* was unable to hold its circulation, and McLean was willing to dispose of it. On September 25, 1895, the *Morning Journal* passed into the hands of Mr. Hearst, but formal announcement of the change was not made until November 6. The price was restored to one cent, and the circulation increased.

Mr. Hearst immediately began building up a strong staff for the *Journal*. He brought from the *San Francisco Examiner* Arthur McEwen, Winifred Black, and Homer Davenport. He secured Julian Hawthorne, son of Nathaniel Hawthorne; Edward W. Townsend, creator of the popular "Chimmie Fadden" sketches in the New York *Sun;* Julian Ralph, a brilliant writer, who had been a member of the *Sun* staff for over twenty years; Rudolph Block ("Bruno Lessing"), formerly a writer on the *Sun* and on the *World;* Stephen Crane, a promising young novelist; Alfred Henry Lewis, a writer of fiction; A. C. Wheeler ("Nym Crinkle") and Alan Dale, dramatic critics; and James L. Ford, a well-known newspaper man and critic. From the New York office of the *San Francisco Examiner*, on the eleventh floor of the World Building, Mr. Hearst succeeded in luring away from the *World* Morrill Goddard, Sunday editor, and the staff of writers and artists of the Sunday *World*. Among the latter was R. F. Outcault, the creator of the "Yellow Kid of Hogan's Alley," a popular colored "comic" in the Sunday *World*, which thenceforth appeared in the Sunday *Journal*.

This defection to the *Journal* of the members of the Sunday *World's* staff aroused Pulitzer to action. He demanded that Mr. Hearst should give up the *Examiner* offices in the World Building. Then he sought to stifle the *Journal* by reducing the price of the *World* to one cent. The reduction in price cut deeply into the *World's* profits, and, not only failed to stop the advance of the *Journal*, but served to stir Mr. Hearst to greater activity. Pulitzer many years afterwards said: "When I came to New York Mr. Bennett reduced the price of his paper and raised his advertising rates — all to my advantage. When Mr. Hearst came to New York I did the same. I wonder why, in view of my experience?" [1]

[1] Seitz, Don C. *Joseph Pulitzer*, p. 214.

Despite the competition the *Journal* gained steadily in circulation, until by the end of the first year it approached 400,000.

To outdo the Sunday *World*, Mr. Hearst ordered a special Hoe color press capable of printing from four to sixteen pages, all in colors, "something," as the makers declared, "that had never before been attempted." [1] When this press was installed, there was added to the Sunday *Journal* an eight-page colored comic section, called the *American Humorist*. This section was described by the *Journal* as "eight pages of iridescent polychromous effulgence that makes the rainbow look like a lead pipe." [2] The *World's* colored comic supplement was characterized by the *Journal* as "black and tan," with four pages of "weak, wishwashy color" and four pages of a "desolate waste of black." Shortly after this, a sixteen-page section was added to the Sunday edition, under the name of the *Sunday American Magazine, Popular Periodical of the New York Journal*, and, a little later, an eight-page supplement, the *Woman's Home Journal*, parts of both of which were printed in colors. Thus, by the end of the year 1896, the Sunday *Journal* included three colored supplements.

The feature sections of the Sunday editions presented a much more striking appearance than did the daily. This was especially true after Morrill Goddard and the staff of the Sunday *World* were taken over by Mr. Hearst. Although the features of the Sunday *Journal* themselves did not differ greatly from those that Goddard had developed in the *World*, they were presented in a more sensational manner. Streamer headlines were regularly used on Sunday feature articles before they were so employed in the daily edition. These headlines, combined with large, striking illustrations, often arranged to produce a bizarre effect, made the feature pages of the *Journal* unique. Except for the fact that only zinc etchings reproducing pen-and-ink drawings were used, these pages were not unlike those of the Hearst Sunday papers in recent years.

Outstanding feature articles dealt with alleged scientific discoveries, with crime and vice, and with all kinds of material that could be treated in a sensational or suggestive manner. The finding of some fossil remains, for example, furnished the basis for a

[1] *New York Journal*, September 28, 1896.　　[2] *Ibid.*, October 17, 1896.

story entitled "Real American Monsters and Dragons," which was illustrated by a half-page sketch of prehistoric creatures labeled "The Jumping Laelaps of 5000 Years Ago." [1] Supposed discoveries in the field of medicine and surgery were presented with such headlines as, "A Marvellous New Way of Giving Medicine; Wonderful Results from Merely Holding Tubes of Drugs Near Entranced Patients." [2]   Strikingly illustrated stories of crime bore banner "heads" such as, "The Mysterious Murder of Bessie Little," [3] "Startling Confession of a Wholesale Murderer Who Begs to be Hanged," [4] "What Made Him a Burglar?   A Story of Real Life in New York by Edgar Saltus." [5]   Stephen Crane, the novelist, wrote a series of sketches for the Sunday *Journal* describing his experiences in the "Tenderloin" district, and these articles were illustrated with drawings of scenes in that notorious section.   When the *Journal's* dramatic critic interviewed the French comédienne, Anna Held, on her first visit to this country, the article appeared with the "streamer head," "Mlle. Anna Held Receives Alan Dale, Attired in a 'Nightie,'" and the actress thus attired was presented in a pen-and-ink sketch a page in length.   Winifred Black's contributions to the Sunday paper bore such titles as, "Why Young Girls Kill Themselves," and "Strange Things Women Do for Love." [6]

Even well-known authors and their works were exploited to furnish sensational articles for the Sunday *Journal*.   Henry James's story, *The Other House*, was reviewed under the headline, "Henry James' New Novel of Immorality and Crime; The Surprising Plunge of the Great Novelist into the Field of Sensational Fiction." [7]   A review of F. Marion Crawford's new novel, *Taquisara*, was given the headline, "A Story of a Woman's Passions; Marion Crawford's New Italian Society Novel of Love, Revenge, Suicide, and Poison." [8]

The popularity of this type of journalism was shown by the gains in circulation of the Sunday *Journal*.   During the last month of the first year under Mr. Hearst, the number of copies printed increased from 321,946 to 437,636, a gain of over 125,000. [9]

[1] *New York Journal*, October 4, 1896.   [2] *Ibid.*, October 18, 1896.
[3] *Ibid.*, September 29, 1896.   [4] *Ibid.*, November 1, 1896.
[5] *Ibid.*, October 27, 1896.   [6] *Ibid.*, September 13 and 27, 1896.
[7] *Ibid.*, October 18, 1896.   [8] *Ibid.*, October 25, 1896.
[9] *Ibid.*, November 8, 1896.

The increase in circulation of the Sunday edition for the whole of the first year amounted to over 380,000.

During its first year, the daily *Journal* did not depart in any marked degree, either in its news-writing or in its headlines, from the practices of the *World*. Both papers gave prominence to news of crimes, criminal trials, accidents, and disasters. Both papers illustrated such stories with large pen-and-ink sketches reproduced in zinc etchings. Criminal acts, suicides, and accidents were vividly and sensationally portrayed in these illustrations. Single-column headlines in type of moderate size were the rule. The wording of the heads, however, was as striking and as sensational in the *Journal* as in the *World*. Two-line drop-heads at the top of the column in the *Journal* consisted of such statements as, "One Mad Blow Kills Child," "Used Little Girls to Cloak Her Crime," "Death Came Over Telephone Wire." [1]

In the fall of 1896, Mr. Hearst began the publication of the *Evening Journal*, which also sold for one cent, and thus was a rival of the *Evening World*.[2] He sought to make it a more striking paper than the morning edition. Among the well-known writers whose work appeared in the *Evening Journal* were Julian Hawthorne, Edward W. Townsend, R. K. Munkittrick, James L. Ford, A. C. Wheeler, Alfred Henry Lewis, Arthur McEwen, Paul West, and Rudolph Block. These men were described in the *Journal* as writing for the evening edition "true stories of the new romances, mystery, pathos and humor, caught from the whirl of every-day life,"[3] and as furnishing "news novelettes from real life; stories gathered from the live wires of the day and written in dramatic form."[4] The aim obviously was to have these writers present the news of the day in the fictionized, melodramatized, "human interest" form that has become identified with yellow journalism.

Editorials in the *Journal* during its first year did not differ in form from those in other papers. It was not until the beginning of the second year that editorials were printed in a wider measure, a result secured by dividing the first three columns on the editorial page into two columns.[5] The editorial page appeared in the middle of the paper, in accordance with the general practice that

---

[1] *New York Journal*, September 16, 17, and 21, 1896.
[2] *Ibid.*, September 28, 1896.   [3] *Ibid.*, November 25, 1896.
[4] *Ibid.*, November 26, 1896.   [5] *Ibid.*, November 13, 1896.

had been followed by the English and American press ever since editorials were first published. It was not until 1900 that the last page became the editorial page.

Both the *World* and the *Journal* were taken over by new owners a year before a presidential election. Just as the *World* in 1884 became the leading Democratic newspaper by supporting Cleveland when the *Sun* had abandoned him, so in 1896 the *Journal* was the only important New York paper to rally to Bryan, the Democratic nominee, when the *World* deserted him on the free silver issue. In its effort to elect Bryan, the *Journal* devised a new plan to raise a campaign fund. It started a popular subscription "for the education of the voters of the United States," and offered "to duplicate every dollar so subscribed with a dollar of its own."[1] Over $40,000 was subscribed by its readers. Just as the *World* in the campaign of 1884 had printed large cartoons to defeat Blaine, so the *Journal* published big cartoons by Homer Davenport in an effort to defeat McKinley. These cartoons depicted Mark Hanna, the backer of McKinley, as a gross figure in a checked suit of clothes covered with dollar signs, generally carrying or protecting his money bags, and often holding McKinley, portrayed as a puny figure, in the hollow of his hand. That Bryan appreciated the *Journal's* efforts in this campaign was shown by a telegram from him that was displayed on the front page of the paper just before election day. It read in part, "The Journal deserves great credit for its splendid fight in behalf of bimetallism and popular government. Its influence has been felt in the West as well as in the East."[2]

On the day following the election, the *Journal* printed 1,506,634 copies, of which 956,921 were of the morning edition, 437,401 of the evening edition, and 112,312 of the German *Morgen Journal*. This, it declared, was "an achievement not only unparalleled in the history of the world, but hitherto undreamed of in the realm of modern journalism."[3] "To distribute this enormous output within a radius of 500 miles of New York the ordinary facilities of the railroads were insufficient," it continued, and so "the Journal chartered three special trains; one to Buffalo, one to Boston and one to Washington."[4] As a matter of fact, the circulation of the

[1] *New York Journal*, September 28, 1896.   [2] *Ibid.*, November 3, 1896.
[3] *Ibid.*, November 5, 1896.   [4] *Ibid.*

One of a series of political cartoons drawn by Homer Davenport for the *New York Journal* during the Presidential Campaign of 1896. It shows Mark Hanna in a checked suit covered with dollar signs, reading a statement by William J. Bryan, the Democratic candidate, in the *New York Journal*, while William McKinley, the Republican candidate is looking over his shoulder

Size of cartoon, 11 in. by 10½ in. *New York Journal*, Oct. 6, 1896

morning and evening editions of the *World* on the same day exceeded by a few thousands that of the morning and evening *Journal*, and hence it was only the German edition with its 112,312 copies that gave the *Journal* the advantage.[1] That these two papers printed only a little short of 3,000,000 copies in a single day, was undoubtedly a remarkable achievement in American journalism.

In celebrating its first anniversary under Mr. Hearst's ownership, the *Journal* published an editorial entitled "One Year's Progress," in which it explained its success thus:[2]

[1] *World*, November 5, 1896.   [2] *New York Journal*, November 8, 1896.

What is the explanation of the Journal's amazing and wholly unmatched progress? It lies on the surface. When the paper was purchased by its present proprietor, a year ago to-day, the work contemplated was at once begun, and has been carried forward without a moment's abatement of energy. In the first place, it was determined to get all the news, and the Journal realized what is frequently forgotten in journalism, that if news is wanted it often has to be sent for. The Journal had made it its business to reach out for news wherever it is to be had, considering neither precedent, difficulty nor cost. When the ordinary news channels are blocked or inadequate, the Journal dispatches its own correspondents to the points, however distant, where the news is to be obtained, and even presses monarchs and statesmen into its service. And these dignitaries are often gracefully obliging. His Highness the Pope and the Queen of Spain and her Prime Minister are among those who have been kind enough to respond to the Journal's cabled requests for news.

No other journal in the United States includes in its staff a tenth of the number of writers of reputation and talent. It is the Journal's policy to engage brains as well as to get the news, for the public is even more fond of entertainment than it is of information. In short, during the past year we have been publishing a first-rate, all-around newspaper that has given a history of the world's most important events each day; that has been outspoken in its opinions, taking the side of public interests as against special interests, such as those of the trusts; that has been as brisk, good humored and amusing as the pens of bright writers and the pencils of clever artists could make it.

In its second year under Mr. Hearst, the *Journal* proclaimed itself the great exemplar of the "New Journalism," and as such began a more spectacular career. [1] Early in December, 1896, it managed to secure in London the full text of the treaty of arbitration in regard to the boundary between Venezuela and British Guiana, which had just been negotiated by Secretary of State Olney and the British ambassador to this country. The exclusive publication of the whole treaty in the *Journal* before its ratification created a profound sensation, not only in the United States, but in England and in Venezuela. [2] This was the boundary dispute that had in the preceding year threatened war between this country and England. The news stories in the *Journal* regarding this treaty of arbitration were decidedly anti-British in tone.

[1] Cf. *New York Journal*, February, 1897.   [2] *Ibid.*, December 6 and 7, 1896.

Editorially the *Journal* characterized its exclusive publication of the treaty as "one of the most notable achievements of journalism in recent years." [1]

At the same time the *Journal* began its agitation to free Cuba, apparently with a view to influencing Congress, then convening. It sent out to the governors of all the states these two questions: [2]

First — Do you favor on the part of the United States such interference in the Cuban revolution, by recognition or the giving of material aid, as would promote the war of independence?

Second — How many volunteers would your State probably furnish for the sea and land forces respectively, in case of war with a foreign power?

The results of this canvass were published conspicuously on the front page of its Sunday edition. The following day the whole first page was devoted to a message to the people of the United States from the Spanish prime minister, relative to Spain's attitude toward Cuba. This statement had been secured through the efforts of James Creelman, "the Journal's special commissioner in Spain." From this time on, the *Journal* featured news pertaining to the Cuban insurrection, and it secured a fast yacht to carry its news from Cuba to this country. Richard Harding Davis was dispatched as special correspondent with the insurgent army, and Frederick Remington was sent to furnish sketches of the Cuban struggle for independence. [3]

In the local field, the *Journal* also sought to attract attention to itself. It provided a theatrical benefit for the poor of New York that netted over $5000. [4] When, two days later, a family prominent in New York society gave an elaborate fancy dress ball, the *Journal* devoted most of its first five pages to the event. [5] The entire front page was given over to a large sketch of the ball drawn by Archie Gunn, then a popular illustrator. The second page contained a large four-column illustration and was surrounded by a border of silhouettes of some of the guests. Nearly the whole of the third page was covered with a drawing by Granville Smith, another well-known magazine artist. On the fourth page were two seven-column sketches drawn by E. W. Kemble portraying

[1] *New York Journal*, December 7, 1896.   [2] *Ibid.*, December 18, 1896.
[3] *Ibid.*, January 17, 1897.   [4] *Ibid.*, February 10, 1897.
[5] *Ibid.*, February 11, 1897.

"Some of the Four Thousand Who Were Not in the Cotillion," in contrast with the so-called "Four Hundred" who were present. On the fifth page the *Journal* printed statistics to show that the total cost of the ball was estimated at $369,200. Thus did it seek to satisfy the interest of the masses in the doings of New York society.

It also emulated the *World* by starting crusades to remedy local abuses. "While Others Talk the Journal Acts" read the first page banner "head" on the story of an injunction that the *Journal* had just secured to prevent the aldermen from granting to a gas company a franchise which the *Journal* claimed was worth $10,000,000.[1] Two days later it declared that the franchise had been found to be illegal, and the following day it announced that the proposed measure had been withdrawn — all as a result of the paper's efforts. In the course of the year it took up other alleged abuses. In order to show that its efforts in invoking the aid of the courts to prevent abuses in city government were meeting with nation-wide approval, the *Journal* sent out requests for opinions on its action to mayors of American cities and to other prominent citizens. The favorable replies received were spread over two pages of the Sunday *Journal*. Across these two pages ran the heading, "The Development of a New Idea in Journalism," followed by two "banks" that read, "The Value and the Propriety of the Action of a Newspaper in Invoking the Courts When Public Interests are in Jeopardy" and "First Employed by the Journal, the Novel Conceit Seems Likely to Become an Accepted Part of the Function of the Newspapers of This Country."[2] In December, 1897, it printed another two-page "spread" with the heading, "Journalism that Acts; Men of Action in All Walks of Life Heartily Endorse the Journal's Fight in Behalf of the People."[3] The pages were filled with letters from mayors of cities in all parts of the country approving the paper's crusades in municipal affairs. The *Journal* declared that it had stopped "the gas franchise grab in Brooklyn, the trolley franchise grab in Brooklyn, the death terminal of the [Brooklyn] Bridge, the dilatory work on Fifth Avenue, the $10,000,000 light monopoly in New York."[4] Discussing these accomplishments editorially, the *Journal* said:[5]

[1] *New York Journal*, December 13, 1896.   [2] *Ibid.*, October 3, 1897.
[3] *Ibid.*, December 2, 1897.   [4] *Ibid.*, December 3, 1897.
[5] *Ibid.*, December 3, 1897.

Within the past year a new force has appeared on the side of good government in New York. It has been a simple matter hitherto for unfaithful servants to squander the resources and trample on the rights of the public. Complaints and denunciations in the press have been as idle as the breeze from a lady's fan. There seemed to be no remedy. But suddenly the jobbers have discovered that the control of a corrupt or careless or stupid board is not enough to carry through a scheme of plunder or of oppression. Above the boards and councils and commissions stand the courts, and by the side of the courts stands the New Journalism, ready to touch the button that sets the ponderous machinery in motion.

When the Journal, by means of an injunction blocked the scheme of the New York Aldermen to give away a gas franchise worth millions, its action was the result of no sudden whim. When it saved the people from the trolley slaughter pen on the Bridge, when it stopped the theft of miles of Brooklyn's streets for a perpetual trolley system, when it prevented the gift of $5,000,000 worth of franchises to gas and electric light companies, it was pursuing a systematic policy. And that policy it intends to continue to the end. No doubt venal officials will find its proceedings monotonous. They will protest that a newspaper ought to stick to its sphere, and refrain from annoying the courts. They will cheerfully agree to endure any number of columns of solemn reprobations, after the fashion of the old journalism, if only the Journal will be satisfied to talk and not act.

But the Journal has adopted the policy of action deliberately, and it means to stick to it. It thinks that it has discovered exactly the engine of which the dwellers in American cities stand in need. When it adopted the two mottoes, " While others talk the Journal acts" and " What is everybody's business is the Journal's business," it showed how the multitudes that are individually helpless against the rapacity of the few could be armed against the despoilers. With an Advocate of the People to keep a vigilant eye on the proceedings of public servants and bring them into court when they prove unfaithful, our judges will have a chance to show that they are ready to render justice in all cases, and the dying popular confidence in the bench will revive.

The Journal intends to be that advocate.

Early in the year 1897, the *Journal* began its streamer headlines — the first ever used regularly in any paper. The occasion for them was furnished by the possibility of war between the United States and Spain. On February 22, 1897, the first three pages bore banner "heads." On the first was a two-line drop-headline reading "Sherman for War with Spain for Murdering Americans." Senator John Sherman was to be Secretary of State in McKinley's cabinet. The banner on the second page proclaimed, "Fleets of the Great Powers Bombard the Cuban Insurgents." On the third page a banner was also used, over a story on the approaching prize fight between Robert Fitzsimmons and James J. Corbett; it read, "Exclusive News of the Fight by the Fighters for the Journal." The next day's front-page streamer, "King George Sends a Message to the Journal," concerned a cable dispatch sent to the paper by King George of Greece regarding the threatened war between Greece and Turkey. On the following day, the banner on the first page, "President Faure of France to the Journal," referred to an interview with the French President secured by James Creelman in Paris concerning the Anglo-American Arbitration Treaty. On February 26, banners appeared on the first three pages: that on the front page, "First Statement of McKinley's Cuban Policy," was attached to a news story from Cleveland, Ohio, dealing with the supposed attitude toward Cuba of the president-elect; that on the second page read, "Coal Barons Wanted Forty Million More" and concerned the disclosures made before a committee investigating the so-called trusts; that on the third page was "Senators Declare for War with Spain." The type in these headlines was not so large or so heavy as that employed later, just before and during the Spanish-American War. The use of banner "heads" day after day was an important innovation in American newspapers.

In reporting the inauguration of President McKinley on March 4, 1897, the *Journal* quite outdid any previous journalistic exploits. It ran a special train from Washington to New York that covered the distance of 228 miles in 249 minutes, and thus broke the speed record between these cities.[1] Its artists drew their sketches while the train traveled a mile in 34 seconds. Typewriters were provided so that its special writers might prepare their stories while the train sped on to New York. Vitascope moving pictures were taken of the inauguration, and the *Journal* promised that "in a few weeks these pictures will be on exhibition in almost every city in the country." [2]

[1] *New York Journal*, March 5, 1897.   [2] *Ibid.*, March 7, 1897.

To secure an Associated Press membership for the *Journal*, Mr. Hearst purchased the *Morning Advertiser* on April 2, 1897, and called the combination the *New York Journal and Advertiser*. In announcing the change, the *Journal* explained that the New York *World* had been plotting to bring about the collapse of the United Press, from which the *Journal* was securing its news, and then, by excluding the *Journal* from the Associated Press, to put the paper "at an enormous disadvantage."[1] The hostility of Mr. Hearst toward Pulitzer had cropped out a week before this, when the *Journal* attacked Pulitzer editorially, denouncing him as "a journalist who made his money by pandering to the worst tastes of the prurient and horror-loving, by dealing in bogus news, such as forged cablegrams from eminent personages, and by affecting a devotion to the interests of the people while never really hurting those of their enemies, and sedulously looking out for his own."[2]

The Greco-Turkish War in the spring of 1897 gave the *Journal* another opportunity to outdo all of its competitors in enterprise. James Creelman, "the Journal's commissioner at Athens," not only interviewed King George of Greece, but succeeded in getting him to send a cable message to the *Journal*.[3] It also had seven war correspondents in the field, among whom were Stephen Crane, Julian Ralph, two women, one of whom was described as the only woman correspondent at the front, George W. Steevens of the London *Daily Mail*, and Herbert White of the London *Daily News*, the last two serving these papers and the *Journal* jointly. It sold its war news to other American papers, including the *Chicago Tribune* and the *Buffalo Evening News*, the proprietors of which praised the service highly in letters published in the *Journal*.[4]

The enterprise of the *Journal* in giving the news of important sporting events was shown in the case of the Corbett-Fitzsimmons prize fight in Nevada in the spring of 1897. Mr. Hearst arranged with the managers to secure for the *San Francisco Examiner* and for the *Journal* the exclusive rights to all photographs, interviews, and signed statements given out by the principals.[5] For a month before the event, these statements appeared from time to time

---

[1] *New York Journal*, April 4, 1897.
[3] *Ibid.*, March 5 and 6, 1897.
[5] *Ibid.*, February 28, 1897.

[2] *Ibid.*, March 29, 1897.
[4] *Ibid.*, May 7, 1897.

conspicuously displayed in the *Journal*.   Its story of the fight
covered three and a half pages.   The front-page story was written
by ex-Senator John J. Ingalls, who had been sent out for the
purpose.   The illustrations were furnished by Homer Davenport,
the cartoonist, who also was dispatched to Nevada.[1]   At this
time the *Journal* attracted attention by devoting two pages to
sporting news, and on one occasion ran a banner "head" across
these two pages, "All the Sporting News of the Day Told by the
Most Competent and Accurate Writers." [2]

The *Journal* also sought to excel in running down criminals.   In
the summer of 1897, the finding of parts of the dismembered body
of a man created a "murder mystery" that the *Journal* undertook
to solve.   "The Journal," the paper explained, "threw the entire
force of its news-gathering machinery into the work, under the
personal direction of the best editorial brains in the world." [3]
After printing in colors a reproduction of the pattern on a piece of
oil cloth in which a part of the body of the murdered man had been
wrapped, the paper assigned thirty reporters to find the purchaser
of the oil cloth.   This quest led to the arrest of the wife of the
murdered man and her lover, an accomplishment for which the
Journal claimed sole credit.   In discussing this murder editorially,
the paper thus explained what it conceived to be the function of
the so-called "New Journalism" with reference to crime: [4]

> Time has been when the utmost art of the literary man or the
> journalist has been employed in making a criminal a heroic figure
> in an engrossing romance.   That was in the era of the old jour-
> nalism.   The new journalism strives to apprehend the criminal,
> to bring him to the bar of justice and thereafter not to convict him
> but to show him as he is.

Two years later, in connection with another mysterious murder,
when the *Journal* offered a $5000 reward for the arrest and con-
viction of the murderer, it explained its activities thus: [5]

> Some hold that a newspaper has no business to do anything but
> to print the news, and not that until after the news has become
> public property.

[1] *New York Journal*, March 18, 1897.   [2] *Ibid.*, May 11, 1897.
[3] *Ibid.*, July 4, 1897.   [4] *Ibid.*, September 11, 1897.
[5] *Ibid.*, January 28, 1899.

The Journal acts upon a different theory. It believes that it is the right and duty of a newspaper to do anything whatever that will promote the public interests, and that can be better done by the newspaper than by any other agency. . . .

The Journal has made itself the most efficient ally of justice in this city. By the terror it has inspired among criminals it has added materially to the safety of human life. Not only has its staff of reporters constituted a detective force at least as efficient as that maintained at public expense by this or any other city, but by enlisting its millions of readers in the work it has created a new instrument of detection of incomparable power.

In an editorial comment on its efforts in this murder case, the *Journal* quoted the *New York Times* on "the immense usefulness of the public press as an agent of detection," and went on to say: [1]

"This immense usefulness" has been repeatedly demonstrated by the Journal. . . . Without waiting for the slow developments of the case under the cautious handling of professional detectives, the Journal has investigated along its own lines, examining every clew, tracing every rumor and unravelling every theory.

So thorough has been its work, and so accurate its deductions, that the detectives of New York City and Newark, and the entire metropolitan press, have been compelled to accept its views of the subject.

In covering the news of all special occasions the *Journal* showed marked enterprise. Mark Twain, for example, was secured to write the leading account of the celebration of the sixtieth anniversary of Queen Victoria's coronation.[2] When General Grant's Tomb on Riverside Drive was dedicated, the *Evening Journal* published five editions with the first page printed in colors.[3] When the first rush of gold seekers to the Klondike began in the summer of 1897, the *Journal*, in conjunction with the *San Francisco Examiner*, sent two expeditions to the gold fields. An entire twelve-page section of the Sunday *Journal* of August 22 was devoted to news, articles, and pictures of the Klondike.

Besides such outstanding events, the *Journal* featured the romantic, melodramatic, and sensational news of the day. Across the second and third pages of one issue, for example, ran the banner headlines, "Woman — She Grieves, Loves, Deceives. She

[1] *New York Journal*, January 7, 1899.   [2] *Ibid.*, June 23, 1897.
[3] *Ibid.*, April 27, 1897.

Hates, Fears, Sympathizes, Dies." ¹   Under these "heads" were
a series of news stories and illustrations dealing with events in
which women were the chief actors.   On another occasion, the
third-page banner was "Stories of Love and Romance Gathered
from the News of the Day," and heart-shaped illustrations appeared at the beginning of each of the seven columns.²

Another feat of the *Journal*, for which it laid claim to great
credit, was the rescue of "the Cuban girl martyr," Evangelina
Cisneros, who had been tried for treason by a Spanish court
martial in Havana.   It was feared that she would be banished to
a penal settlement.   Following a graphic story of the young
woman's plight sent from Havana by a woman correspondent, the
Journal started a vigorous campaign to effect her release.   So
much interest was aroused that Mrs. Julia Ward Howe was led to
address an appeal to the Pope, and Mrs. Jefferson Davis sent a
similar one to the Queen Regent of Spain.³   A few days later, the
banner headline on the front page read, "The Whole Country
Rising to the Rescue," and the "bank" below it continued, "More
than Ten Thousand Women in all Parts of the United States
Petition for the Release of Miss Cisneros." ⁴   Nearly three pages
were devoted to the subject, one of which was filled with a list of
names of women signers of the petition to the Queen Regent of
Spain.   Two months later, in a front-page banner "head" with a
seven-column pyramid "bank" below it, the *Journal* suddenly
announced, "Evangelina Cisneros Rescued by the Journal; An
American Newspaper Accomplishes at a Single Stroke What the
Red Tape of Diplomacy Failed Utterly to Bring about in Many
Months." ⁵   Men employed by the *Journal* had, by a carefully
worked out plan, aided her to escape from the Havana prison in
which she was confined.

For the ensuing two weeks the *Journal* made the most of this
exploit.   A half-page sketch was printed showing President Mc-
Kinley and his cabinet discussing the rescue, while the President
held a copy of the *Journal* from which he was reading Secretary
of State Sherman's statement to the effect that "every one will
sympathize with the Journal's enterprise in releasing Miss Cis-

¹ *New York Journal*, May 4, 1897.   ² *Ibid.*, May 27, 1898.
³ *Ibid.*, August 19, 1897.   ⁴ *Ibid.*, August 23, 1897.
⁵ *Ibid.*, October 10, 1897.

neros." President McKinley was reported to have said, "Well, Mr. Secretary, I think that you have correctly voiced the unofficial sentiment of the administration. It was a most heroic deed." [1] When Miss Cisneros arrived in New York, the *Journal* gave a reception for her in Madison Square. It printed a full-page sketch of the scene, and in the magazine section gave three pages to the story of her experiences.[2] When she was taken to Washington to meet President McKinley, the *Journal* had another front-page "spread," with a half-page cut.

To celebrate its enterprise in the Cisneros rescue, the *Journal* printed in the "ears" on each side of the title, "The Journal's Motto: While Others Talk, the Journal Acts." [3] Discussing the subject in an editorial entitled "Journalism that Does Things," it declared: [4]

> Action — that is the distinguishing mark of the new journalism. It represents the final stage in the evolution of the modern newspaper of a century ago — the " new journals" of their day told the news and some of them made great efforts to get it first. The new journalism of to-day prints the news too, but it does more. It does not wait for things to turn up. It turns them up.

During the year 1897, the Sunday *Journal* was increased in size and attractiveness. In the spring of that year, it contained eighty pages, including a section of thirty-six pages, called the *American Magazine*, which was "devoted to science in popular form, news of the week and human interest"; another section, of twenty-four pages, of which four were in colors, entitled the *American Woman's Home Journal;* and a third, of eight pages, all in colors, called the *American Humorist.* The Easter Sunday edition consisted of 116 pages, including an extra supplement of four pages printed on calendered paper, with half-tone reproductions of Frederick Remington's Cuban sketches.[5] The special Christmas edition of the Sunday paper contained 112 pages. The first half-tone illustrations printed on news-print paper appeared in the Sunday magazine sections in March, 1897.[6] The editorials in the Sunday *Journal* during this period dealt with religious and ethical topics and were written and signed by New York clergy-

---

[1] *New York Journal*, October 13, 1897.
[2] *Ibid*., October 17, 1897.
[3] *Ibid*., October 13, 1897.
[4] *Ibid*., October 13, 1897
[5] *Ibid*.. April 11, 1897.
[6] *Ibid*., March 21, 1897.

men.   The circulation of the Sunday paper at the end of its second year was 340,870.[1]

Since one of the most serious charges brought against the so-called "yellow journals" was, not merely that they exploited news of crime and vice, but that, in order to sell more papers, they deliberately aroused the spirit of "jingoism" that led the United States into war with Spain, it may be well to examine the course of the *New York Journal* in this matter.

As early as December, 1896, when Congress was about to meet, the *Journal*, as we have seen, began to agitate the question of war between this country and Spain.   During 1897, special articles from Cuba written by Richard Harding Davis, sketches of Spanish cruelty in Cuba drawn by Frederick Remington, the rescue and exploitation of Miss Cisneros, and news of the oppression of Cuban patriots and their families under the Spanish commander, "Butcher" Weyler, as the *Journal* called him, all served to keep the possibility of war before its readers.   In February, 1898, the paper devoted its first two pages to a facsimile of a private letter written by the Spanish minister in Washington to the editor of a Madrid newspaper, in which President McKinley was described as "a low politician, catering to the rabble." [2]   The front-page banner on this story read, "The Worst Insult to the United States in Its History."   The letter was discussed in an editorial three columns wide, in which quotations from the letter were printed in bold-face type.   The next day the banner " head " on the first page declared, "Journal's Letter Gets DeLome His Walking Papers," with the first "bank," "Spanish Minister Couldn't Deny the Journal's Exclusive Fac-Simile Reproduction of His Infamous Letter, so He Makes a Confession by Silence." [3]   Two days later the *Journal* printed a two-line drop-head across both the first and second pages which read, "Threatening Moves by Both Spain and the United States; We Send Another War Vessel to Join the Maine in Havana." [4]   This repetition of the front-page streamer at the top of the second page was an innovation.   The Sunday *Journal* the following day contained a two-page "spread" in which the "horrors of starving Cuba" were described by Julian Hawthorne and were illustrated by ghastly pictures of emaciated

---

[1] *New York Journal*, February 28, 1898.   [2] *Ibid.*, February 9, 1898.
[3] *Ibid.*, February 10, 1898.   [4] *Ibid.*, February 12, 1898.

Cuban children.[1]   Again, two days later, on the front page, appeared a four-column, three-line drop-head in bold-face type an inch high reading, "Spain Refuses to Apologize; Arms Six Merchant Ships; We Order Shot and Shell." Below it were three four-column pyramid "banks." Obviously, the *Journal* treated the tension between the two countries in a manner calculated to arouse its readers.

The destruction of the United States warship "Maine" by an explosion in the harbor of Havana gave the *Journal* an opportunity to outdo any previous display of important news. Above the title, *New York Journal and Advertiser*, was printed, "$50,000 Reward — Who Destroyed the Maine? — $50,000 Reward," and, in the "ears," "The Journal will give $50,000 for information, furnished to it exclusively, that will convict the person or persons who sank the Maine."[2]   In the regular edition the banner head in three-quarter inch, bold-face type read, "Destruction of the War Ship Maine Was the Work of an Enemy." Below this, in the middle of the page, were two three-column pyramid "banks," the first of which declared, "Assistant Secretary Roosevelt Convinced the Explosion of the War Ship was Not an Accident." These "banks" were flanked on both sides by other two-column announcements of the $50,000 reward, while across the bottom of the page was a seven-column drawing of the "Maine" anchored above explosive mines connected with the Spanish fortress on shore. In an "extra" issued at 6 A.M. the same day, the banner was changed to a two-line drop-head in large bold-face type, "The War Ship Maine Was Split in Two by an Enemy's Secret Infernal Machine!"[3]   The first eight pages of the paper were given over to large pictures and details of the event. The next day the banner head in three-quarter inch, bold-face type proclaimed, "The Whole Country Thrills With the War Fever." Beneath this was a seven-column cut of a conference of President McKinley with the Naval and Finance Committees of Congress. A two-page illustration of the wreck of the "Maine," drawn from cabled descriptions, filled the whole of the fourth and fifth pages, with a two-page banner in large type, "Divers Searching For the Dead and the Evidence That They were Murdered under the

[1] *New York Journal*, February 13, 1898.   [2] *Ibid.*, February 17, 1898.
[3] *Ibid.*, February 17, 1898.

Murky Waters of Havana Bay." A streamer headline on the eighth page announced that "The Journal's Reward Excites the Admiration of Europe." On Sunday, February 20, the first-page banner "head" read, "Journal Here Presents, Formally, Proof of a Submarine Mine." It was followed by three large illustrations of the wreck, labeled "First Photographs of the Wreck of the Maine that Has [sic] Reached New York." Streamer heads appeared on seven pages, all of which were filled with material about the "Maine."[1] An "extra" of the *Evening Journal* was published on Sunday, February 20, the first instance of a Sunday edition of an evening paper. It contained a two-page illustration of "How the Maine Actually Looks as it Lies, Wrecked by Spanish Treachery, in Havana Bay."

The circulation of the *Journal* on the three days following the destruction of the "Maine," bore witness to the effectiveness of its striking treatment of the event. On the first day, 1,025,644 copies were printed; on the second, 1,063,140; and on the third, a rainy day, 1,011,041.[2] The total of 3,098,825 copies in three days broke all circulation records.

For the next week the *Journal* kept before its readers the idea that war was inevitable. Banner headlines on various pages read, "'No War' — But Night and Sunday Work on Big Guns Goes on, Sabbath Toil and Rush of Soldiers to All Seaside Forts"; "Recruiting Already Begun; Troops Impatient to March"; "Official Washington Now Regards War as Inevitable"; "Desperate Work to Hold the United States Senate in Check." On February 25, the fourth and fifth pages consisted of a double-page "spread" printed in colors, with the headline, "One United Country." A picture of "Uncle Sam" in the middle of the pages was flanked with the headings, "No North, No South," and with "banks" that read, "Sections Widely Apart Welded by a Common Impulse to Avenge Heroes of the Maine" and "The Union Ablaze with Patriotism — Every State Ready to Spring to Arms at a Moment's Notice." An eight-page "Maine Memorial Album," consisting largely of illustrations, appeared as a part of the issue of February 23. The next day the first eight pages appeared as the "Maine News Section," the front page of which consisted entirely of pictures of "The Journal's War Fleet, Correspondents and

[1] *New York Journal*, February 20, 1898.   [2] *Ibid.*

Artists." In the "Maine News Section" of the following days were to be found such heads as, "Citizens Demand that Congress Shall Take Action," "Citizen Soldiers Everywhere are Roused by the War Spirit," "Two More Big Cruisers are Ordered Made Ready for Service."

By February 27 the circulation of the Sunday *Journal* had mounted to 632,227, an increase of nearly 200,000 since the first of the year. The *Evening Journal* at this time reached 519,032, "a record," the *Journal* declared, "never equalled by any afternoon paper published in the English language or in any other language."[1]

The two largest front-page typographical displays made previous to the war, appeared in the *Journal* on March 7 and 8. The first-page banner on March 7 consisted of a three-line drop-head in type an inch high, with four seven-column "banks." The remainder of the page was divided into two columns, the reading matter of which was printed in large type. The banner read, "Nearer Than Ever to War With Spain. Flat Denials to Both Her Protests. Lee Shall Stay — War Ships Shall Go to Cuba." On March 8 the banner, in type one and three fourths inches high, proclaimed, "For War! $50,000,000." The news concerned the appropriation by Congress of that sum for national defense.

President McKinley's policy of delay, apparently in the hope that war might be averted, called forth from the *Journal* abuse of him, of his cabinet, and of his adviser, Mark Hanna. In its news stories, editorials, and cartoons, the *Journal* charged that the purpose of the delay was to enable speculators to make huge profits in the stock market. Hanna was depicted in a cartoon by Davenport as the Goddess of Liberty in a robe covered with dollar signs, holding the tape of market quotations as it came from the ticker.[2] In a news story on the first page was printed, in large boldface type, the statement that "McKinley and the Wall Street Cabinet are ready to surrender every particle of national honor and dignity."[3] In support of its attitude, the *Journal* displayed conspicuously on the front page what purported to be a verbatim report of an interview secured by its Washington correspondent with Theodore Roosevelt, then Assistant Secretary of the Navy, in which he was quoted as saying:

[1] *New York Journal*, February 28, 1898.   [2] *Ibid.*, March 16, 1898.
[3] *Ibid.*, April 7, 1898.

The Journal's attitude as reflected in its Washington dispatches during the past few days, is most commendable and accurate. All who know the situation will concede that.

It is cheering to find a newspaper of the great influence and circulation of the Journal tell the facts as they exist and ignore the suggestions of various kinds that emanate from sources that cannot be described as patriotic or loyal to the flag of this country.

Roosevelt, however, indignantly denied that he had been interviewed by a *Journal* reporter, and in a letter to the Associated Press declared:[1]

The alleged interview with me in to-day's New York *Journal* is an invention from beginning to end. It is difficult to understand the kind of infamy that resorts to such methods. I never in public or private commended the New York *Journal*.

When the Washington correspondent of the *Journal* wrote to Roosevelt asking him not to deny the interview, Roosevelt replied in part:[2]

The statement in to-day's *Journal* was an absolute falsehood. I told your reporter, not once, but again and again, as he was persistent, that I would not give him an interview of any kind. His conduct was infamous, and you yourselves should have known that no such interview as that could possibly have come from me, if for no other reason than that I never have given a certificate of character to the *Journal*.

The *World* took advantage of the occasion to print on the front page Roosevelt's denunciations of its rival, and, in a headline attached to the story, it characterized the *Journal's* war news as "Written by Fools for Fools."

The *Journal* suffered another rebuff when, a week later, publicity was given to the reply written by ex-President Grover Cleveland to an invitation from Mr. Hearst to become a member of the *Journal's* committee that was raising funds for a memorial to the American sailors who had lost their lives in the "Maine" disaster. Cleveland wrote:[3]

I decline to allow my sorrow for those who died on the Maine to be perverted to an advertising scheme for the New York Journal.

[1] New York *Evening Post*, March 21, 1898.   [2] *Ibid.*   [3] *Ibid.*, March 28, 1898.

While the *Journal* was seeking to arouse the war spirit with banner headlines, sensational news stories, huge illustrations, and triple-column editorials, Godkin, in the New York *Evening Post*, was constantly inveighing against both the *Journal* and the *World* for their sensationalism and "jingoism." The following excerpts from his editorials show how a serious-minded journalist regarded these "yellow journals": [1]

The admirable conduct of the government officials at Washington renders the course of the sensational press in this city the more shameful by contrast. Nothing so disgraceful as the behavior of two of these newspapers this week has been known in the history of American journalism. Gross misrepresentation of the facts, deliberate invention of tales calculated to excite the public, and wanton recklessness in the construction of headlines which even outdid these inventions have combined to make of the issues of the most widely circulated newspapers firebrands scattered broadcast throughout the country. . . . It is a crying shame that men should work such mischief simply in order to sell more papers.

The reason why such journals lie is that it pays to lie, or, in other words, this is the very reason for which they are silly and scandalous and indecent. They supply a want of a demoralized public. Moreover, such journals are almost always in favor of war, because war affords unusual opportunities for lying and sensation. That war involves much suffering and losses, does not matter. Their business is not to promote public happiness or morality, but to "sell the papers."

The resources of type have been about exhausted. Nothing in the way of larger letters can be used, unless only a single headline is to be given on the first page. Red ink has been resorted to as an additional element of attraction or terror, and if we had a war, the whole paper might be printed in red, white, and blue. In that case, real lunatics instead of imitation lunatics should be employed as editors and contributors.

As we see to-day, in spite of all the ridicule that has been lavished on the "yellow journals," in spite of the general acknowledgment of the mischief they do, in spite of the general belief in the baseness and corruption and satanism of their proprietors, their circulation is apparently as large as ever. The government and decent people are still obliged, as much as ever, to keep contradicting their "fake" stories and to keep reassuring the public against

[1] New York *Evening Post*, February 19, 21, and 26; March 14, 17, and 21, 1898.

their alarms. . . . None of these things seems to produce much of any effect.

A yellow journal office is probably the nearest approach, in atmosphere, to hell, existing in any Christian state.

A better place in which to prepare a young man for eternal damnation than a yellow-journal office does not exist.

During the war, both the morning and evening editions of the *Journal* reached the climax of typographical display. Arthur Brisbane had introduced large block-letter headlines into the evening edition shortly after he became managing editor in 1897, and the evening *Journal* outdid the morning paper in big "heads." In announcing Dewey's success at Manila, the evening paper on May 2, 1898, used type three and three quarters inches high for the banner "head," "Manila Ours!" Below this was a headline in two and seven-eighths inch type that read, "Dewey's Guns Shell the City." In the night edition of May 7, practically the whole first page was covered with headlines.

The circulation of the *Journal* reached over 1,600,000 on May 2, the day that Dewey's victory was announced. During the war it continued at about 1,500,000, and at the close of the year was still over 1,250,000. To print such large editions daily, the number of presses was increased, until, at the close of the year 1898, the press-room equipment consisted of eight octuple color presses, three quadruple presses, and two multi-color presses.[1] The capacity of these presses was 912,000 four-, six-, or eight-page papers an hour; 456,000 ten-, twelve-, fourteen-, or sixteen-page papers an hour; or 228,000 twenty-, twenty-four-, or twenty-eight-page papers an hour. All of these pages could be printed in two, three, or four colors, or in half-tone.

Among the national policies in the interests of which the *Journal* carried on editorial campaigns during and immediately after the Spanish-American War, were the annexation of Hawaii, the development of "a mighty navy," the construction of a Nicaragua Canal to connect the Atlantic and Pacific oceans, the establishment of strategic bases in the West Indies, and the development of "great national universities at West Point and Annapolis" to train officers for the army and navy.[2] When, early

[1] *New York Journal*, December 11, 1898. [2] *Ibid.*, November 15, 1898.

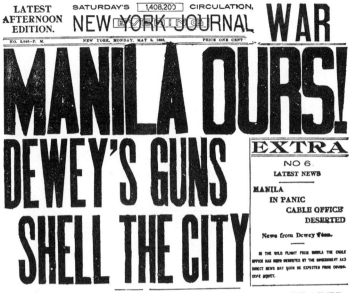

The Whole Front Page of the *New York Evening Journal*, May 2, 1898. The reading matter "boxed" under the heading "Extra" was printed in red ink

in 1899, most of these projects had been or seemed likely to be accomplished, the *Journal* came out for "an American internal policy" that should include the public ownership of public franchises, the "destruction of criminal trusts," a graduated income tax, the election of senators by popular vote, and a "national, state and municipal improvement of the public school system." [1] In a signed statement setting forth this program. Mr.

[1] *New York Journal*, February 5, 1899.

Hearst pledged himself to devote the columns of the *Journal* and of the *San Francisco Examiner* to its realization.[1]   The *Journal* also conducted a vigorous fight against polygamy among the Mormons in Utah, in connection with the question of permitting Brigham H. Roberts, representative-elect from that state, to take his seat in Congress.[2]   Winifred Black was sent to Utah to interview Mormon women on polygamy.   One of the headlines in this crusade read, "Crush the Harem; Protect the Home." [3]

An achievement in the field of news was the exclusive publication by the *Journal* of the proceedings of the Spanish-American Peace Commission, with the full text of the peace treaty and the bulk of the secret protocols of the negotiations from which the treaty emerged.[4]   The paper heralded this as "a journalistic achievement believed to be entirely without precedent." [5]   Such "journalistic enterprise," it declared, "had made Senatorial secrecy an absurdity." [6]   A few days later, the Senate made public both the treaty and the protocols.

Striking and sensational treatment of the day's news was continued by the *Journal*.   Typical headlines read, "She Fell in Love with a Man's Face in a Soap 'Ad'" and "Fight for Fair One; Both Lads in Limbo." [7]   A diagrammatic illustration of a robbery and murder was given the caption, "Burglar, Hard Pressed, Slays to Win Freedom." [8]   At this time the *Journal* gave much space and prominence to a "murder mystery" that was attracting some attention, and offered a reward of $5000 for the arrest and conviction of the murderer.[9]   It also continued to "feature" important events in New York society.   On one occasion, for example, it devoted its first two pages to a ball given by a member of the Vanderbilt family, and, a few days later, "featured" a ball given by Mrs. Astor.   Both stories were copiously illustrated.[10]

In the presidential campaign of 1900, the *New York Journal* supported Bryan, the Democratic nominee, and bitterly assailed his Republican opponent, President McKinley, as the representative of big business, the trusts, and plutocracy.   Editorial de-

[1] *New York Journal*, February 5, 1899.

[2] Cf. *New York Journal*, beginning December 22, 1898.

[3] *Ibid.*, January 27, 1899.   [4] *Ibid.*, January 1, 1899.

[5] *Ibid.*, January 1, 1899.   [6] *Ibid.*, January 5, 1899.

[7] *Ibid.*, January 24, 1899.   [8] *Ibid.*, January 25, 1899.

[9] *Ibid.*, January 28, 1899.   [10] *Ibid.*, January 7, 9, and 10, 1899.

nunciations were supplemented by large cartoons drawn by Homer Davenport. After President McKinley's reëlection, the attacks were continued. In an editorial published in April, 1901, the *Journal* declared that, "if bad institutions and bad men can be got rid of only by killing, then the killing must be done." [1] When President McKinley was assassinated by an anarchist at Buffalo, on September 6, 1901, Mr. Hearst and his papers were vigorously denounced for their incendiary utterances and cartoons. President Roosevelt, in his first message to Congress after the death of McKinley, spoke of the assassin as: [2]

> ... a professed anarchist, inflamed by the teachings of professed anarchists, and probably also by the reckless utterances of those who, on the stump and in the public press, appeal to the dark and evil spirits of malice and greed, envy and sullen hatred. The wind is sowed by men who preach such doctrines, and they cannot escape their share of the responsibility for the whirlwind that is reaped. This applies alike to the deliberate demagogue, to the exploiter of sensationalism, and the crude and foolish visionary who, for whatever reason, apologizes for crime or excites aimless discontent.

In the New York gubernatorial campaign of 1906, when Mr. Hearst was a candidate, President Roosevelt authorized Secretary of State Elihu Root to declare in a public address that Roosevelt "in penning these words of the above quoted message, with the horror of President McKinley's murder fresh before him, ... had Mr. Hearst specifically in his mind." [3] The Hearst papers praised McKinley highly after his death, and the *New York Journal,* in answering the attacks made upon it, declared editorially: [4]

> The sum of the Journal's offenses is that it has fought for the people, and against privilege and class pride and class greed and class heartlessness, with more and varied weapons, with more force and talent and enthusiasm, than any other newspaper in the country.

Following the success of the *New York Journal,* Mr. Hearst established or purchased a number of other newspapers in various parts of the country. In these journals he carried out the same

[1] *New York Journal,* April 10, 1901. [2] *New York Tribune,* December 4, 1901.
[3] New York *Evening Post,* November 2, 1906.
[4] Quoted in the *Outlook,* vol. 84, p. 403 (October 20, 1906).

general policies with reference to news, editorials, and features that he had developed in the *New York Journal*. In 1900 he started the *Chicago American* as an evening paper, and two years later, the *Chicago Examiner* as a morning paper. In 1904 he established the *American* in Boston as an evening paper. During the year 1912, he added two papers to his list by acquiring the *Atlanta Georgian* and by starting the *Los Angeles Examiner*. By the purchase in 1917 of the century-old *Boston Advertiser*, he secured a morning paper in Boston to supplement his evening *American*. He bought the *Chicago Herald* in 1918 and combined it with the *Examiner* under the name of the *Chicago Herald-Examiner*. The following year he took over two evening papers that had been acquired by Arthur Brisbane, the *Wisconsin News*, formerly the *Evening Wisconsin*, of Milwaukee, and the *Washington Times*. In 1920 he bought the *Boston Record* and combined it with his *Boston Advertiser*, which he later transformed into a "tabloid" illustrated paper. The *Detroit Times* was acquired by Mr. Hearst in 1921. During 1922 he increased his list of papers by seven — the *Syracuse Evening Telegram*, with a Sunday edition called the *American*, the *Rochester Evening Journal* and the Sunday *American*, the *Washington Herald*, the Oakland, California, *Post-Enquirer*, the *San Francisco Call*, the *Los Angeles Herald*, and the *Seattle Post-Intelligencer*. In 1923 he purchased three papers, the *Baltimore American*, the *Baltimore News*, and the Fort Worth, Texas, *Record*. The next year he bought two more papers, the *Albany Times-Union* and the San Antonio, Texas, *Light*, and started his second morning paper in New York, the *Daily Mirror*, an illustrated "tabloid." Thus, at the beginning of 1925, Mr. Hearst owned twenty-five papers in seventeen cities.

Mr. Hearst outlined his policies for his newspapers in reply to a series of questions submitted to him in the summer of 1924. Excerpts from these replies follow: [1]

> I have no intention to possess any given number of newspapers nor any plan to possess any more newspapers or to take on any more work or trouble.
>
> But occasionally somebody wants to get rid of a paper and tries to sell it to me, and if I think I can see a way to make it a success, I am very likely to take over the job and try out my program.

[1] *Editor and Publisher*, vol. 57, p. 3 (June 14, 1924).

I organize our newspapers with the best men available in a community and they consult me in general matters, but endeavor to carry out the desires of the community in all community matters.

In addition I generally have a local advisory board of leading citizens to help the local publisher to obtain accurate information in regard to local requirements and sentiments.

The whole purpose of our papers is to serve loyally the communities in which they are respectively published; and the papers are united into one large organization only to make that service more effective.

The power of a newspaper depends not merely upon the number of its readers, but upon the confidence which they repose in it. That confidence is earned by intelligent and unselfish service — by a long record of effort for the public good as the editor sees it.

The power of a newspaper which has deserved and won the confidence of its readers is considerable; but the American people do not follow blindly the lead of any newspaper, even though they may entirely respect its motives.

The American people are an independently thinking people.

Newspapers do not form the opinion of the public; but if they are to be successful they must express the opinion of the public.

To a degree circulation is a test of merit. If any manufactured article sold more and at a higher price than another similar article, you would naturally infer that the one which sold the greater amount at the higher price was better — or at least that it pleased the public better; and that is the main standard of comparison.

I expect a newspaper to make as much profit as is compatible with giving the public a good newspaper, and making subscribers and advertisers feel that they are getting full return for their money in excellence and service.

I spend a lot of money in making my newspapers. As a matter of fact I put back into the making of my newspapers over ninety percent of the money these newspapers take in from subscribers and advertisers. This I think I ought to do in order to give adequate service.

When in 1906 Mr. Hearst had six newspapers in New York, Boston, Chicago, and San Francisco, he organized the International News Service, in order to provide news and features for them and for such other papers as might desire to obtain this material. The International News Service, like the Associated Press, served both morning and evening papers, while the United Press, begun in 1907, confined its service to evening and Sunday papers.   In 1914 the King Features Syndicate was organized, both as a producing syndicate and as a selling agency for the International News Service, the International Feature Service, and the Newspaper Feature Service, the last named of which had been established in 1912.   Later the Universal Service and the Premier Syndicate were started, and the King Features Syndicate became their selling agent.   At the close of the year 1925, the King Features Syndicate was supplying to papers in about a thousand cities a great variety of features, which were translated into sixteen different languages, and which were read daily by approximately 32,000,000 persons.

In 1905 Mr. Hearst entered the magazine field by buying the *Cosmopolitan*.   Started in 1886, this magazine had been the pioneer among the cheap, popular illustrated monthlies.   He purchased another magazine in 1911, the *World Today*, and changed its name to *Hearst's International* magazine.   These two publications were consolidated in 1925 as the *Cosmopolitan*.   In 1913 he acquired *Harper's Bazaar*, and later, *Good Housekeeping*, *Motor*, and *Motor Boating*.   In London he has published *Nash's Magazine* and an English edition of *Good Housekeeping*.   Later he entered the motion picture field by producing news and feature films, under the names of the International News Reel and the Cosmopolitan Productions.

Mr. Hearst for many years took an active part in politics. From 1903 to 1907 he served as member of Congress from one of the New York City districts.   At the Democratic National Convention in St. Louis in 1904, he received over two hundred votes as a candidate for the presidency of the United States.   In the New York mayoralty campaign of 1905, he was a candidate on the municipal ownership ticket, but was defeated by the regular Democratic nominee.   In 1906 he was nominated for the governorship of New York by the Democratic Party, but was beaten by Charles E. Hughes.   He was defeated for a second time as a candidate for mayor of New York City in 1909, when he ran on the ticket of the Independence League, a political organization that he had helped to establish.   Since then he has been considered at various times as a possible candidate for the New York mayoralty and for the governorship of New York State, but he has not been nominated again for either position.   He has, however, been regarded as a power to be reckoned with in New York municipal elections, because of the large circulations of his three papers in New York City.

During the World War the Hearst newspapers were subjected to bitter attacks, both before and after the United States entered the conflict. Of the nature of these attacks the editor wrote in the *New York American* of August 8, 1918: "Some have said that we were pro-German; some have said that we preached treason; some have accused us of printing falsehoods in order to frighten our people and to give aid and comfort to the enemy." On October 11, 1916, by official action of the British Secretary of State, the International News Service was deprived of the use of the mails and of the cables controlled by Great Britain. The reasons given by the British Government for its course were the "continued garbling of messages and breach of faith on the part of the International News Service." The manager of the International News Service, in a signed statement published in the *New York American*, explained the position of his organization in these words: "The English censors have been threatening for many months to deny the International News Service the privilege of the mails and cables because the International News Service did not print the kind of news that the English desired to have printed in this country." [1] When the London representative of the International News Service cabled to Mr. Hearst suggesting that the latter give his "personal guarantee of non-garbling by any one under pain of dismissal and of the publication of all dispatches exactly as received," [2] Mr. Hearst replied that he was convinced that "the exclusion of the International News Service is not due to any delinquency on its part or on the part of the Hearst papers, but is due to the independent and wholly truthful attitude of the Hearst papers in their news and editorial columns." [3]

The French Government took similar action against the International News Service a month after the British Government's decree. Within the same month the Canadian Government issued an order barring the Hearst newspapers from Canada. At various places in the United States attempts were made to prevent

[1] *New York American*, October 11, 1916.
[2] *Los Angeles Examiner*, October 13, 1916.　　　[3] *Ibid.*, October 13, 1916.

the sale of Hearst papers, but in most instances the courts forbade such interference.

The Hearst newspapers, as the outstanding examples of so-called "yellow journalism," have often been given credit for originating the distinctive characteristics that became associated with them. As a matter of fact, however, the Hearst papers were not pioneers in developing new features. It was the New York *World*, not the *New York Journal*, that first gave prominence to sensational news; that first made extensive use of news illustrations, particularly those of a sensational kind; and that first launched local and national crusades in the interest of the common people. The *World*, also, was the first paper to include in its Sunday edition colored "comics," colored magazine sections, and sensational special articles. Banner headlines were first used in the morning edition of the *World*, and large display type in banner "heads" was first employed in the *Evening World*. The Hearst papers were not the first to demonstrate that a very large circulation could be secured by appealing to the emotions of the masses. That fact was discovered by the first penny papers in the thirties, and was rediscovered half a century later by Pulitzer.

The idea of a chain of newspapers originated, not with Mr. Hearst, but with the Scripps brothers in the Middle West, fifteen years before he bought the *New York Journal*. The credit for organizing a press association and a feature syndicate in connection with a chain of newspapers, also belongs to Edward W. Scripps and his associates in the Scripps-McRae League. The first press association established for a chain of papers was the Scripps-McRae Press Association, which was organized in 1897, nine years before the International News Service came into existence. The Newspaper Enterprise Association, founded in 1901 by E. W. Scripps to furnish the Scripps-McRae papers and others with news features, pictures, and cartoons, was the first newspaper syndicate established in connection with a chain of papers, and antedated the syndicates for the Hearst papers.

By spending money freely, the Hearst newspapers, together with the news and feature services connected with them, were able to adapt to their own needs innovations that had been made by other papers, press associations, and syndicates. By paying higher salaries, the Hearst papers secured writers and editors who had created successful innovations for other newspapers, and encouraged them to develop these ideas in ways that would appeal to the type of reader that the Hearst papers sought to reach. Sensational news and features were given more space and prominence by the Hearst newspapers than by other papers, and were generally presented in a more melodramatic form, with a stronger emotional appeal. Similar methods were pursued with reference to the subject-matter and the treatment of material published in the Sunday editions. Everything that money could buy in the way of talent and equipment was secured.

Because these methods were generally successful in obtaining circulation among the masses, they were not infrequently imitated by other newspapers. The advent of a Hearst newspaper in a city often resulted in the adoption of Hearst methods by rival papers, in the belief that they could thus meet the competition. These attempts at imitation, however, scarcely ever proved successful, because individual papers lacked the resources in the way of special news and feature services that a Hearst newspaper could command. Nevertheless, the ensuing competition often modified the character of the rival papers.

The influence of the Hearst papers was, no doubt, greatest in the field of newspaper typography. The constant use by the Hearst newspapers of large display type in headlines, led to its adoption by many papers that were not sensational in character. This was true both of banner "heads" and of "heads" of several columns in width. The typographical form of the editorial page in the Hearst papers was also imitated to a greater or less extent by other papers. Thus, the editorials in many newspapers were printed in wider columns and in larger type than was the other reading matter. So, too, some newspapers have followed the Hearst method of placing the editorials on the last page. Even the *Christian Science Monitor*, which represents the antithesis of the Hearst type of journalism, not only adopted the wider column and larger type for its editorial page, but placed its editorials on the last page.

The use by many papers of features syndicated by the various services connected with the Hearst newspapers, also changed the character of their non-news content. The brief editorial comments by Arthur Brisbane in the first column of the front page of the Hearst papers, under the heading "Today," were syndicated to other papers all over the country and were printed by them in the same position.   Other non-news features syndicated by the Hearst services were often used in the same manner as they were in the Hearst papers.

On the whole, the influence of the Hearst type of journalism on the form and contents of American newspapers has been as great as that of any other single force.

CHAPTER XVI

THE DEVELOPMENT OF THE PRESENT–DAY NEWSPAPER

THE present-day newspaper has been profoundly influenced in its development by the changes that took place in American life during the last generation. The period from 1890 to 1925 was marked by tremendous mechanical progress, by mass production and standardization of products, by greater rapidity in communication and transportation, by a steady increase in the population of cities, by a speeding up of life and consequent high nervous tension, by the growth of huge business organizations, and by the development of higher standards of business and professional ethics. All these factors have affected the character of the press.

The age was one of machinery. Ingenious machines were devised to do practically everything that had previously been done by hand. Mechanical inventions and improvements were as important in newspaper production as they were in other fields. The modern newspaper would have been impossible without huge perfecting presses, the linotype, the autoplate, color printing, and the half-tone and rotogravure processes. Other inventions that were of great value to newspapers were the telephone, the typewriter, radio communication, the telegraph printing machine, and the automobile. From one point of view, the present-day newspaper is a machine-made product to a greater extent than ever before.

Perfection of machinery led to mass production and standardization in manufacturing. This was also true of newspaper publishing. By means of the linotype, the autoplate, and high-speed presses, newspapers were produced rapidly in large quantities. Without these mechanical aids large circulations would have been out of the question. Rapid transmission of news was greatly facilitated by the telephone, by wireless, and by printing telegraph machines. Speedier distribution of papers was made possible by motor trucks. Newspapers very naturally took advantage of every improvement in communication and transportation.

A large part of the contents of the modern newspaper also

became standardized. This change was due in part to the press associations and in part to the newspaper syndicates. Press associations, covering the whole world, supplied the same news in identical or similar form to newspapers all over the country. In New York and Chicago, the city and suburban news was gathered and distributed to the papers of these cities by local press bureaus, in the same way that the press associations handled national and foreign news. Syndicates furnished a large number of papers with the same or with similar features and illustrations. Thus the press both reflected and contributed to the standardization of American life.

The steady growth of cities, which resulted from the increase in manufacturing and business, afforded newspapers the opportunity to secure larger circulations and a greater volume of advertising. The influx of immigrants, most of whom settled in cities, was an important factor in the rise of sensational journalism. As soon as these immigrants acquired a little knowledge of the English language, they were naturally attracted by the primer-like sensational papers with their large type and numerous illustrations. Yellow journalism, accordingly, flourished in large cities where the number of half-assimilated foreigners was greatest.

The rapid pace and high nervous tension everywhere manifested in American urban life affected the character of newspapers. The average person spent only from twenty minutes to half an hour in reading a newspaper. Hundreds of thousands of men and women in large cities read papers in the midst of the distracting conditions of subway and surface cars and suburban trains. Newspapers, therefore, found it advantageous to present news so that it could be read at a glance. Display headlines, condensed news reports, illustrations, and other devices to aid the rapid reader were accordingly adopted. Evening papers became more numerous and more popular than morning papers. In the evening, after the day's work is over, the powers of concentrated mental effort are largely exhausted. Under such conditions most persons seek relaxation and entertainment rather than information and instruction. The three most easily available sources of entertainment were newspapers, motion pictures, and radio receiving sets. In rivalry with attractions like the "movies" and radio programs, evening papers had to present their contents in a bright, interesting, and entertaining manner. The dramatic and melodramatic phases of life to be found in accidents, crime, and scandal afforded the readiest means of appealing to the largest number of persons in search of interesting and entertaining reading matter.

The development of big business enterprises that resulted partly from natural growth and partly from the consolidation of smaller business units, also influenced the press. With the rise of department stores and other large retail establishments, newspapers secured a greater volume of local advertising. When the nation-wide distribution of products became more common, manufacturers found the newspaper a valuable medium, and national, or "foreign," advertising in newspapers increased accordingly. The tendency both in manufacturing and in wholesale and retail business toward consolidation as a means of reducing competition and effecting economies, had its counterpart in the merging and elimination of newspapers. Chains of retail stores were paralleled by chains of newspapers.

Newspaper publishing, following the tendencies of the times, became a big business enterprise. The rapid growth in the volume of advertising not only necessitated an increase in the number of pages in newspapers, but also added greatly to the newspaper's revenues. The larger number of pages and bigger circulation made necessary more elaborate and more costly mechanical equipment. To preserve the proper proportion between advertising and reading matter, newspapers required more news from press associations and more features from syndicates. As revenues and costs increased, the business of newspaper publishing grew larger and larger. Thus the business department tended to overshadow the news and editorial departments.

Various movements for higher ethical standards in business and the professions affected newspaper editing and publishing. Agitation against dishonest and objectionable advertising, which led to the adoption by the Associated Advertising Clubs of the principle of "Truth in Advertising," resulted in marked improvement in the character of newspaper advertisements. By combining with advertisers, advertising agencies, and magazine publishers in the establishment of the Audit Bureau of Circulations, newspaper publishers were able to furnish accurate information about their circulation, in place of the exaggerated claims that had frequently been made.   The adoption of codes of professional ethics by state press associations and by the American Society of Newspaper Editors, a new organization of leaders in daily journalism, was in line with similar movements in the business and professional world.   Finally, the establishment by colleges and universities of schools, departments, and courses of journalism tended to give greater emphasis to the professional status of newspaper writing and editing.

The year 1890 marked a turning-point in the evolution of the American newspaper.   The decade from 1880 to 1890 witnessed a revolution in newspaper editing and publishing.   In that period the most important developments were the reappearance of sensationalism, the rise to prominence of evening papers, and great improvements in the mechanics of newspaper production.   The changes were followed by much larger circulations, a greater volume of advertising, and an increase in the number of pages in newspapers.

The phenomenal success of the morning edition of the New York *World* during the first six years of Pulitzer's ownership, demonstrated anew the possibility of building up a very large circulation by means of sensationalism.   The methods by which he transformed an old, run-down paper into a popular daily, with the largest circulation in the country, were not lost on editors and publishers the country over.

In New York the *Evening Sun* and the *Evening World*, both of which began publication in 1887 as one-cent papers, aimed to make the same wide appeal in the evening that the *World* made in the morning.   Low-priced popular evening papers were not confined to the metropolis.   The Detroit *Evening News*, launched by James E. Scripps in 1873, as a two-cent, four-page sheet, proved so popular that, between 1878 and 1881, his brother, E. W. Scripps, was led to publish similar evening journals in Cleveland, St. Louis, and Cincinnati.   In Chicago, the *Daily News*, established late in December, 1875, as a four-page, one-cent paper, had by 1890 reached an average daily circulation of over 130,000.   In Kansas City, during the eighties, William Rockhill Nelson proved that a successful evening paper could be maintained at the price of two cents a copy, or ten cents a week.   By 1890, therefore, it was recognized that the evening field offered at least as great possibilities as did the morning field.

In response to the demand of these and other newspapers with rapidly increasing circulations, important advances were made in the mechanics of newspaper production. Between 1885 and 1890 an invention was perfected that was to revolutionize newspaper composition. The linotype, as the new machine was called, because it cast solid lines of type, was devised by Ottmar Mergenthaler, a German-American of Baltimore. In 1885 a company was organized by several well-known newspaper publishers to develop the invention, and in 1886 the first twelve linotype machines were installed in the *New York Tribune* plant by Whitelaw Reid, owner of that paper and one of the organizers of the linotype company. The second large installation of twelve machines was in the office of the *Chicago Daily News*, of which Melville E. Stone, another member of the linotype company, was part owner. By 1890 the linotype had been so greatly improved that it found a ready sale to newspapers throughout the country, and in the next few years hundreds of machines were built. Soon all the reading matter in newspapers, except headlines and display advertisements, was set on linotype machines instead of by hand. The greater speed in composition thus attained made it possible for newspapers to increase the number of their pages and to reduce the time required to get news into type form.

Great improvements were made from time to time in machines for printing newspapers. From the middle of the fifteenth century, when printing was invented, until 1812, all printing, including that of newspapers, was done on hand presses. In 1812, Friedrich König, a German mechanic, perfected in England the first cylinder press, and two years later designed a two-cylinder model. Two of these double-cylinder presses were set up in the plant of the London *Times*, and on November 29, 1814, that paper was printed on these presses. Not only was this the first occasion on which a newspaper was printed on a cylinder press, but it marked the first use of a steam engine as the motive power in newspaper printing. In 1828 the Napier double-cylinder press superseded the König machine for printing papers, both in England, where it was invented, and in the United States, where it was developed by R. Hoe and Company. Some of these presses were operated by hand and some by steam.

The large circulations of the first penny papers led in 1846 to the next great advance in printing, the invention of the Hoe type-revolving press. For this machine, the pages were made up in curved forms with wedge-shaped column rules to hold the type in place. When these curved forms were placed on the large revolving cylinder of the press, their surfaces constituted a true circle. As the huge cylinder revolved, sheets of paper, fed into the press from several platforms, were printed rapidly on one side only. The first of these type-revolving presses was installed by the Philadelphia *Public Ledger* in 1846. When improved, these machines had a capacity of 20,000 sheets an hour printed on one side. In 1860, stereotype plates, cast in papier-mâché matrices, were substituted for the curved forms of type. This stereotyping process had the advantage, not only of saving wear on the type, but of making possible the casting of duplicate plates for simultaneous printing on two or more presses.

After several years of experimentation, the first successful web perfecting newspaper press was installed in 1868 in the plant of the London *Times*. Named the Walter press, after John Walter, proprietor of the *Times*, who was responsible for its development, it embodied all the principles of present-day newspaper presses except that of the folder. Paper was fed from a roll into the Walter press, passed between cylinders on which were clamped semi-cylindrical stereotype plates, was printed on both sides, was then cut, and was finally delivered in flat sheets. The *New York Times* used one of these Walter machines, but most of the large American newspapers installed similar perfecting presses built in this country by R. Hoe and Company. A folding device and other improvements were later incorporated in these presses both in England and in America. By 1890 large perfecting presses were being constructed by several American companies for newspapers in all parts of the country.

When the New York *World* went into its new building in 1890, its plant contained presses that could print 312,000 eight-page papers an hour. From two single presses arranged in tandem, two sheets of paper ran to one folder, so that sixteen-page papers could be produced. Before the introduction of the linotype into its plant, the *World* employed 210 compositors. The composing room was equipped with forty make-up tables. For one Sunday edition of the *World* in April, 1899, 732 stereotype plates were cast. The photo-engraving department of the paper could produce 150 zinc etchings for one Sunday paper.[1] Never before had newspaper production been possible on so large a scale.

Color printing on newspaper presses began in the early nineties. The New York *World* in 1893 installed a color press made by the Walter Scott Company, which could print a four-page supplement with the two outside pages in five colors and the two inside pages in one color. The following year that paper added a Hoe color press, which produced an eight-page section, with four pages in several colors and four in a single color. Improvements in these color presses were made so rapidly that in 1896 the *New York Journal* was able to secure a press that could print supplements of twenty-four pages all in colors. The *World* and the *Journal* used these presses for printing the first colored "comics" and the first colored magazine sections of the Sunday edition, and occasionally for printing in colors some pages of the daily editions.

Not a little of the success of the *World* was due to its illustrations. These "cuts" were made possible by important inventions in engraving processes. Previous to the early seventies, woodcuts were the only kind of illustrations available for newspapers. The long-practiced method of cutting type-high blocks of wood by hand was, however, a slow one. In 1873 a new process came into use by which illustrations drawn on zinc plates were etched with acid to produce printing surfaces like those of wood-cuts. This "paniconography," as it was called, was described as "a cheap substitute for wood engraving." [2] The same year appeared the first illustrated daily paper, the New York *Daily Graphic*, which sold for five cents a copy. Its illustrations were made by a newly devised photo-lithographic process. In December, 1873, this paper printed the first illustrations made directly from photographs, by a process known as "granulating photography." [3] The next step in photo-engraving was the photographing of pen and ink drawings and the transferring of these photographs to zinc plates, which were etched with acid to produce what have come to be known as zinc etchings. These zinc etchings, which were

[1] *The World, Its History and Its New Home* (pamphlet).
[2] *American Journalist*, December, 1873, p. 378.
[3] *Daily Graphic*, December 2, 1873.

first used by newspapers in 1884, continued for the next ten years to be the most common form of newspaper illustration.

The first half-tone process for making illustrations was patented abroad in 1882. A little later, this method was greatly improved in the United States by the invention of the half-tone screen, which served to break up the masses in reproducing photographs and wash drawings. Although these "half-tones" were soon used to illustrate American magazines that were printed on slow-running presses, it was not until 1894 that they were successfully stereotyped and printed on fast newspaper perfecting presses. In May of that year, a Sunday edition of the *Boston Journal* contained half-tone pictures printed from stereotype plates on presses that ran off from 30,000 to 50,000 copies an hour.[1] Thus half-tones became possible for newspapers, but they did not immediately displace zinc etchings in the daily and Sunday papers.

Illustrations were not confined to the metropolitan press. By 1892 the American Press Association, which through its branch offices all over the country was supplying over 500 newspapers with column-wide stereotype plates, furnished these papers with some 250 pictures a week.[2] As nine tenths of all the daily papers in this country used this plate matter, which included even telegraph news, the stereotyped zinc etchings that were sent out in connection with it appeared in a large number of papers.

The value of newspaper pictures as a means of attracting readers was pointed out in 1892 by John A. Cockerill, who had been managing editor of the New York *World* for some years after its purchase by Pulitzer. In a magazine article on the contemporary press, he wrote:[3]

> News stand illustration is, indeed, a part of the newspaper business, just as big headlines are. The most attractive picture must be put on the upper fold of the first page, in order to serve its purpose as an advertisement to purchasers at the news stand.

To increase the speed with which stereotype plates could be produced from papier-mâché matrices, Henry A. Wise Wood in 1900 devised an ingenious machine known as the autoplate.

---

[1] *Fourth Estate*, May 24, 1894.   [2] *Journalist*, vol. 16, December 17, 1892.
[3] Cockerill, John A. "Some Phases of Contemporary Journalism," *Cosmopolitan*, vol. XIII, p. 701 (October, 1892).

From the beginning of stereotyping for newspaper printing, in the sixties, until the autoplate was invented, the casting, shaving, and trimming of stereotype plates had been done entirely by hand. With the autoplate all of these processes were performed automatically after the matrix had been placed in the machine. A simplified form of this machine, known as the junior autoplate, was later placed on the market, which cast stereotype plates at the rate of three or four a minute, but did not shave or trim them. The autoplate was soon installed in a large number of newspaper offices.

Two inventions that were of great importance to newspapers were the telephone and the typewriter. Between 1876, when the first telephone messages were transmitted by an overhead wire, and 1892, when New York and Chicago were successfully connected by telephone, the development of telephonic communication was very rapid. By 1890 there were over 200,000 Bell telephone stations in this country. Ten years later the number had tripled. The development of the typewriter was scarcely less phenomenal. Following the perfecting of the first machine in 1878, a number of typewriter companies put various models on the market. By 1890 typewriters had begun to find their way into newspaper offices, but it was not until some years later that they were generally used by members of the news staff.

These mechanical devices in due time changed the whole character of the American newspaper. By telephoning the bare facts of the news to rewrite men in the newspaper office, reporters and correspondents tended to become news gatherers rather than news writers. Although this method saved time, it increased the danger of inaccuracy. Linotype machines and fast presses made it possible for papers to be sold on the streets within a very short time after the latest news reached the newspaper office. Keen rivalry between competing papers in the same field supplied a strong motive for increasing the speed with which the latest news was rushed into print. Again there was constant danger of sacrificing accuracy for speed. In large cities, rapid production and keen competition tended to increase the importance of street sales. With the advent of illustrations, and the introduction of large headlines in the Spanish-American War period, the "make-up" of the front page became increasingly important as a means of catching the eye of the purchaser when papers were displayed on

news-stands or in the hands of news boys.   Extensive mechanical
equipment also encouraged the publication of different editions at
frequent intervals throughout the day.   In New York, the *World*,
the *Sun*, and the *Journal*, all of which had originally been morning
papers, established semi-independent evening editions, which in
time exceeded the morning editions in circulation.   The circulation of the *World* and that of the *Journal*, each of which exceeded
a million and a quarter copies a day during the Spanish-American
War, broke all records.   Striking front-page displays of news, a
reduction in the price of papers, and a variety of original promotion schemes were employed to stimulate sales.   The greatest
possible circulation seemed to be the only goal of many papers.

The rise of department stores and the growth of other retail
establishments, by providing new sources of advertising, also
affected in a marked degree the character of the American press.
The increased circulation secured by the illustrated Sunday editions made them an attractive advertising medium.   So, too, the
success of low-priced evening papers attracted advertisers and resulted in the use by merchants of larger display advertisements
than had been customary in daily papers.   The greater use of advertisements by retail stores necessitated the addition of more
pages to accommodate them.   In order that space given to advertising might not be disproportionate to the total contents of a
paper, the amount of reading matter was increased as advertising
increased.   Thus papers that originally had consisted of four or
eight pages were enlarged to twelve and sixteen pages.   As more
display advertising was obtained for Sunday editions, these issues
were enlarged from sixteen and twenty-four pages to thirty-two,
forty-eight, and, on special occasions, even one hundred pages.
Cheap papers with large circulations, such as the *World*, also
secured a large amount of classified advertising.   Since the value
of a newspaper as an advertising medium is largely determined by
the size of the circulation, there was a strong incentive to promote
large circulations.   When the price of many papers was reduced
to one or two cents a copy, a large volume of advertising became
essential to their financial success.   Thus less and less of a paper's
revenue came from circulation, and more and more from advertising.   The result was a profound change in the economics of newspaper publishing.

With the rise of evening and Sunday papers and the increase in the amount of display advertising, the importance of making special appeals to women readers was more fully appreciated by newspaper editors and publishers. In the early nineties, three New York papers, the *World*, the *Sun*, and the *Recorder*, were all devoting considerable attention to their departments for women. Articles on fashions, cooking recipes, and similar material were grouped together, often with society news, in women's departments or women's pages. In 1892, the *New York Recorder*, a well-edited general newspaper, was characterized by the *New York Herald* as "pre-eminently a women's paper" that was read by a hundred thousand women.[1] The large Sunday editions of the New York papers gave considerable space and prominence to departments primarily of interest to women. In the latter part of the year 1896, the *New York Journal* added to its Sunday edition a supplement, the *Woman's Home Journal*, part of which was printed in colors. With the aid of the first newspaper syndicates, newspapers the country over were able to follow the example of the New York papers in appealing to women readers.

Newspaper syndicates, which began in this country in 1884, became an important factor in modifying the character of the present-day press. The first attempt to syndicate material to newspapers was made in England as early as 1870, when Tillotson and Son, publishers of a paper in Bolton, England, began to sell serials to other English newspapers. The head of that syndicate came to this country in the summer of 1884 to arrange for the syndication of novels and short stories to American newspapers. At the same time, Charles A. Dana of the New York *Sun* syndicated some short stories by Bret Harte and Henry James that he had bought for his own paper. These first attempts to syndicate fiction suggested to S. S. McClure, then on the staff of the *Century Magazine*, the possibility of an American newspaper syndicate. Accordingly, in the fall of 1884, he began the weekly syndication of 5000 words consisting of short stories. Within a year he had enlarged the scope of his service to include general articles and was offering newspapers 30,000 words a week.[2] Included in this material were cooking recipes written by Mr. McClure himself

---

[1] *New York Recorder*, December 12, 1892.

[2] Letter by S. S. McClure in the *Critic*, vol. VIII, p. 43 (July 16, 1887).

under the name of "Patience Winthrop." [1] By 1892 the "S. S. McClure Newspaper Features" consisted of new novels by Mark Twain, Robert Louis Stevenson, William Dean Howells, and Bret Harte; new short stories by Rudyard Kipling, Conan Doyle, and Mary E. Wilkins; special articles by Henry Cabot Lodge and Theodore Roosevelt; a woman's page; and a youth's department. In the same year that Mr. McClure began his service, Irving Bacheller started to syndicate a novel by a popular English author, and later added a London weekly letter, short stories, and special articles.[2]

The third American syndicate was established in 1886 by Edward W. Bok, who later became prominent as editor of the *Ladies' Home Journal*. Mr. Bok began with the syndication of a weekly article on current events written by Henry Ward Beecher, the distinguished pastor of Plymouth Church, Brooklyn. The success of this weekly article led Mr. Bok to organize the Bok Syndicate Press, with his brother as partner. He observed that "the American woman was not a newspaper reader," and decided, after looking over representative newspapers, "that the absence of any distinctive material for women was a factor." [3] He accordingly secured the right to syndicate "a bright letter of New York gossip published in the *New York Star*, called 'Bab's Babble.'" [4] This feature proved an immediate success, and helped him to secure a clientèle of some ninety newspapers in various parts of the country. He then engaged Ella Wheeler Wilcox, whose *Poems of Passion* had attracted much attention, to furnish a weekly letter on topics of interest to women. He also secured contributions from famous women writers and from men who were able to write on subjects of interest to women. By furnishing much syndicate material that appealed primarily to women readers, Mr. Bok encouraged newspaper editors all over the country to make a feature of the woman's department or the woman's page. Newspaper publishers soon realized that these syndicate features attracted more women readers and increased circulation, thus enhancing the value of their papers as advertising mediums.

---

[1] McClure, S. S. *My Autobiography*, p. 79.
[2] Bacheller, Irving. "The Rungs in My Literary Ladder," *American Magazine*, vol. 85, p. 19 (April, 1918).
[3] *The Americanization of Edward Bok*, p. 104.   [4] *Ibid.*, p. 105.

In 1891 the United Press added to its service a "literary department" that offered newspapers 10,000 words weekly of "the highest class of Sunday miscellany," consisting of short stories, serials, fashion articles for men and women, and special articles.[1]   Tillotson and Son, the pioneer English syndicate, established a New York office in 1889, and served American newspapers with short stories, serials, a London letter, a women's letter, and a children's letter.[2]   Thus, during the last decade of the nineteenth century, the newspaper syndicate came to be a recognized part of American journalism.

After the success of the first newspaper syndicates, their number grew steadily, and the amount of syndicated material published by newspapers increased correspondingly.   At first the fiction, special articles, matter of interest to women, and illustrations supplied by syndicates were published only in the Sunday editions, but in due time they were used to enliven the pages of the daily issues.   The popularity of syndicated material was due partly to the need of newspapers for more reading matter and illustrations to balance the great volume of advertising, and partly to the character of the new reading public created by the cheap popular newspapers.   By building up a sufficiently large clientèle among newspapers, syndicates could afford to furnish a great variety of features at comparatively low prices.   Many newspapers were thus enabled to publish reading matter and illustrations which they could not otherwise have afforded to buy.   The larger public that was attracted by low-priced popular papers was one which confined its reading largely to newspapers and hence welcomed the entertainment that syndicated reading matter and illustrations supplied.   Material furnished by syndicates, therefore, served to increase newspaper circulation.   Because successful features originated by one syndicate were often imitated by other syndicates, the material that they furnished newspapers tended to become standardized.   The use of the same or similar syndicated features by a large number of newspapers, accordingly, resulted in a considerable degree of sameness in these papers.

The extent of the business of syndicating reading matter and

---

[1] Advertisements in the *Journalist*, vols. XII and XIII, January 10, February 8, and August 8, 1891.

[2] Advertisement in the *Journalist*, vol. XIV, October 3, 1891.

pictures is indicated by the fact that in 1926 more than 100 syndicates were offering some 2000 features, prepared by 750 writers and artists.[1]   In this number were included those newspapers in New York, Chicago, Philadelphia, and other cities which syndicated various features published in their own columns.

One of the outstanding developments in American journalism during the decade from 1890 to 1900 was the rise of the Associated Press to a position as the dominant news-distributing agency. Coöperation in news gathering began in New York in the late eighteen-twenties when the Association of Morning Newspapers was organized for the purpose of maintaining boats to meet incoming ships bringing European news.   In 1849 the Harbor News Association was established in New York, and later the Telegraphic and General News Association was founded.   These two organizations were consolidated in 1856 into the General News Association of the City of New York, with a membership consisting of the *Journal of Commerce*, the *Express*, the *Herald*, the *Tribune*, the *Courier and Enquirer*, and the *Times*.   Out of this association grew the New York Associated Press, a coöperative news-gathering organization of New York papers, which sold to papers outside of New York City the news collected for its members.   In time sectional news-gathering agencies sprang up, such as the New England Associated Press, the Southern Associated Press, and the Western Associated Press.   A rival national association, the United Press, was established by newspapers that were not affiliated with the New York Associated Press.   In 1892 the United Press combined with the New York Associated Press. Late in the same year the Associated Press was incorporated in Illinois, to succeed the Western Associated Press, and Melville E. Stone, founder of the Chicago *Daily News*, was elected its general manager.   One of his first moves was to obtain European news for the Associated Press.   He went to London and secured a contract with the Reuter Telegram Company, and through it with the Agence Havas of Paris and with the Continental Telegraphen Compagnie (the so-called Wolff Agency) of Berlin.   This new arrangement was possible because the contract which had been in existence since 1865 between these European news agencies and

[1] *Editor and Publisher*, vol. 59, p. 3 (June 5, 1926).

the New York Associated Press expired on January 1, 1893. The loss of its valuable European connections was a hard blow to the United Press, and in 1897 it went into the hands of a receiver.

Although, after the failure of the United Press, the Associated Press had no rival except the Scripps-McRae Press Association, its success was seriously menaced in 1900 by a decision of the Illinois Supreme Court. Threatened with expulsion from the Associated Press for violating one of its by-laws, the Chicago *Inter-Ocean* had brought suit against the organization to retain its membership, and the Supreme Court of Illinois, to which the case was appealed, held that the Associated Press partook of the nature of a common carrier and, as such, must furnish its news to any paper that was willing to pay for it. As this decision deprived the Associated Press of the right to restrict its membership and made the service available to non-members who were competing in the same field with Associated Press members, it was necessary to find some way out of the difficulty. The management of the Associated Press discovered that, by incorporating under the Membership Corporation Law of New York State, a law intended to apply to social clubs, the organization could limit its membership. Therefore, in May, 1900, the Associated Press was incorporated in New York State as a purely coöperative association that could declare no dividends and that shared the cost of operation among its members. Under the direction of Melville E. Stone, the Associated Press became the leading American news agency, with a membership that included many important newspapers in all parts of the country.

The Scripps-McRae Press Association was organized in January, 1897, primarily to serve the newspapers in the Scripps-McRae League, although later it sold its news to other papers. After the United Press went into receivership in 1897, the Publishers' Press Association was organized in New York City. Through an arrangement entered into between the Scripps-McRae Association and the Publishers' Press, the former covered the territory west of Pittsburgh and the latter that east of Pittsburgh. In 1904 the Scripps-McRae interests bought out the Publishers' Press, and in 1907 these two associations were reorganized as the United Press Associations, or the United Press, as it came to be called despite the fact that it had no connection with the former United Press.

The United Press maintained a news service only for evening and Sunday papers.   Later the United News was established in connection with the United Press, to serve morning papers.   Both of these organizations furnished news to any newspaper that was willing to buy it, whether or not competing papers in the same field were already using it or were members of the Associated Press.   Roy W. Howard, who had been New York manager of the Publishers' Press Association and then of the United Press Associations, was president and general manager of the United Press from 1912 until 1920, and was largely responsible for its rapid growth and success.

In 1906 the International News Service was organized to serve the Hearst papers and such other newspapers as might desire it. Because its service was available for morning and evening papers, it became a competitor of both the Associated Press and the United Press.   Some of the Hearst papers that were members of the Associated Press were able to use news furnished by that organization and by the International News Service.

Early in 1917 the Associated Press sought by an injunction to prevent the International News Service from furnishing its clients with news that was sent exclusively to Associated Press members. Copyright laws afforded inadequate protection in the matter of news, because they covered only the form in which news was written and not the facts of the news.   Thus an Associated Press news dispatch might be rewritten and used by the International News Service without violating the law of copyright.   When the action brought by the Associated Press against the International News Service was finally decided by the United States Supreme Court in 1918, this decision, by giving to a newspaper or press association the exclusive right to news obtained through its own effort, established the principle of a property right in news.   The court, however, did not indicate for how long a period of time this exclusive right might be maintained.   English courts have ruled that it extends over twenty-four hours.

One of the remarkable achievements in American journalism during the first quarter of the twentieth century was the rise of the *New York Times* from bankruptcy to a position as the leading newspaper in this country.   From the time of Raymond's death in 1869 until 1891, the *Times* was successfully carried on by

George Jones, who had been Raymond's associate from the inception of the paper in 1851. Through its exposure, in 1871, of the Tweed Ring in New York City, the paper attracted nation-wide attention. In 1875 it paid a hundred per cent dividend on its original capital stock of $100,000. The following year Jones acquired a majority of the stock by purchasing ten shares, for which he paid $15,000 each, although their par value was only $1000. Thus, in twenty-five years the value of the paper had increased from $100,000 to $1,500,000.

After George Jones's death in 1891, his children were unable to make the paper pay and within two years sold it for $1,000,000 to a company headed by Charles R. Miller, its editor. Lack of capital to rehabilitate the plant and carry on the paper in successful competition with the other New York morning papers so seriously handicapped the new company that, in hope of a reorganization, Miller applied for the appointment of a receiver. Adolph S. Ochs, publisher of the *Chattanooga Times*, who had become interested in the possibility of entering the New York field, was asked to undertake the task of reëstablishing the *Times* on a sound financial basis. In accordance with the plan that he submitted, he invested $75,000 in the bonds of the company, with an agreement that, as soon as the paper had paid its expenses for three consecutive years, he was to be given a controlling amount of stock in the new company. Under this arrangement he acquired a majority of the stock of the *Times* within less than four years.

In the first issue after the reorganization, Mr. Ochs expressed his intention to conduct "a high-standard newspaper, clean, dignified and trustworthy," giving "the news, all the news, in concise attractive form, in language that is parliamentary in good society." [1] Its editorial policy, he declared, would be non-partisan.

When Mr. Ochs became publisher of the *Times*, he was a self-made man of thirty-eight. Beginning as a carrier boy at the age of eleven, he had worked up through every position on a newspaper, until, at the age of twenty, he purchased the *Chattanooga Times* for $250. During his eighteen years as owner of that paper, he built it up into a successful journal.

On assuming control of the *New York Times*, he found that its net circulation had fallen to 9000 a day, for, of the 19,000 copies

[1] *New York Times*, August 19, 1896.

printed daily, some 10,000 on an average were returned by news dealers.   At that time the *New York Journal* claimed a circulation of 385,000, the morning *World* 370,000, the *Herald* 80,000, and the *Tribune* 60,000.   The *Times* sold for three cents a copy; the *World* and the *Journal*, for one cent.

Within the first few months of his management, Mr. Ochs introduced several new features into the *Times*.   One of these was the motto, "All the News that's Fit to Print," which on October 25, 1896, appeared on the editorial page, and in the following February was transferred to an "ear" on the front page. To the Sunday edition he added a sixteen-page magazine section, printed on a good grade of paper and illustrated with half-tones.   The appearance and contents of this supplement were in keeping with the substantial character of the paper and were in striking contrast with the colored magazine and "comic" supplements of the Sunday editions of the *World* and the *Journal*. An eight-page section devoted to book reviews and art became a part of the Saturday edition in October, 1896, but later was transferred to the Sunday issue.   A weekly financial review was introduced as a supplement to the Monday issue.

In order that its editorial independence might be unquestioned, the *Times* in its early years under Mr. Ochs refused several opportunities to make what would ordinarily be regarded as legitimate profit.   When it was selected by the New York Board of Aldermen as one of the six newspapers in which the complete canvass of the vote in the election of 1896 was to be published, at a cost to the city of $200,000, the management refused to become a party to what it denounced as a waste of public money.   Again, when a Tammany administration offered it all of the city advertising, amounting approximately to $150,000 a year, the *Times* rejected the offer in the belief that, if the paper with the smallest circulation in the city accepted the municipal advertising, its motives might be impugned.   In the presidential campaign of 1900, when for the first time in eighteen years the *Times* supported the Republican Party, it refused an order from the Republican National Committee for a million copies of one issue containing an editorial favorable to the Republican cause.   Although these opportunities for profit came at a time when the paper needed money, Mr. Ochs decided that he could not afford to accept them.

Lack of funds prevented the *Times* from competing with the other New York papers during the Spanish-American War in the matter of special correspondents, dispatch boats, and special cable service, and so it had to rely on the war news furnished by the Associated Press. When, at the close of the war, the paper had been under Mr. Ochs's management for two years, it had more than doubled its circulation, but the 25,000 copies that it printed daily seemed very few compared to the million and a quarter of the morning and evening editions of the *World* and of the *Journal*. As some radical action seemed necessary, Mr. Ochs decided to reduce the price from three cents to one. In an editorial announcing the reduction, the paper declared that its character would remain unchanged. "In appealing to a larger audience," it said, "THE TIMES by no means proposes to offend the taste or forfeit the confidence of the audience it now has." The editorial continued:[1]

> The proposition that many thousands of persons in this city of three and one-half million souls buy and read one-cent newspapers chiefly on account of their price and not on account of their character and quality seemed sound. We believe these thousands would like to read a newspaper of the character and quality of THE TIMES in preference to, or let us generously suppose in conjunction with the papers they have been reading. THE TIMES has determined to extend its appeal beyond those readers with whom quality is indispensable and price a matter of no consequence to the presumably much larger number to whom both price and quality are of consequence.

The soundness of Mr. Ochs's contention was shown by the tripling of the circulation within a year after the reduction in price.

On the occasion of its golden jubilee, in September, 1901, the *Times* announced that it had secured from the London *Times* exclusive American rights to the world-wide news service of that paper. In return the London *Times* received the sole right to publish in England the news gathered by the *New York Times*.[2] This mutually advantageous contract, entered into when the London *Times* was still owned by the Walter family, was continued for some years after Lord Northcliffe secured control of the paper. Because of a disagreement between Mr. Ochs and

[1] *New York Times*, October 10, 1898.   [2] *Ibid.*, September 25, 1901.

Lord Northcliffe, this exchange of news ceased at the beginning of the World War.

The *New York Times* was the first American newspaper to recognize the importance of wireless telegraphy across the Atlantic. When the first regular Marconi trans-Atlantic service was established on October 17, 1907, the initial westward message was one from the London office of the *New York Times*. From 1907 to 1912, the paper published every Sunday considerable foreign news sent by wireless, and from early in 1912, when the speed of transmission was increased, until the beginning of the World War, practically all of its news from London was sent daily by wireless instead of by cable.[1]

The success of the *Times* was shown by its gains in circulation. From 9000 in 1896, when Mr. Ochs took over the paper, the circulation rose in a little over two years to 25,000. Within a year after the reduction in price it had reached 75,000. At the time of its jubilee in 1901 it had passed the 100,000 mark, and two years later exceeded 200,000. At the outbreak of the World War in 1914, it was close to a quarter of a million.

It was during the World War that the *New York Times* won its preëminence. The publication in its columns of the complete text of official documents, speeches, reports and other utterances of the various governments and of their leaders, made it an invaluable source of information. Within the first month of the war, it secured and published advance copies of the English and German White Books, in which these two governments set forth their versions of the events leading up to the declaration of war. It then reprinted these documents in pamphlet form and sold them at cost. As fast as the French, Belgian, Austrian, and Russian governments issued similar books, the *Times* reprinted them in full, both in its columns and in pamphlets. Thus, within a few months, American readers were furnished with all the information given out officially by the various countries involved in the struggle. As a further aid to an understanding of the issues raised by these documents, the *Times* printed on Sunday, October 25, 1914, a detailed analysis of them considered as briefs presented to "the supreme court of civilization." This study, with conclusions drawn from it, was made for the paper by James M. Beck, former

[1] Davis, Elmer. *History of the New York Times*, p. 281.

assistant attorney general of the United States, and was published in a pamphlet entitled, "The Evidence in the Case." Because Mr. Beck's conclusions, based on the documents then available, placed the responsibility for the war on Germany, the pamphlet was extensively used by the Allied Powers in support of their cause and was translated into other languages. The *Times* also published a large number of contributions from writers both foreign and American, advancing arguments in support of the cause of the Central Powers and of that of the Allied Powers. Ex-President Roosevelt wrote for the paper early in the war a series of articles on "What America Should Learn from the War." In these various ways, the *Times* sought to furnish a basis for sound opinion as to the cause of the war. In recognition of its "publishing in full so many official reports, documents, and speeches by European statesmen relating to the progress and conduct of the war," the *Times* won in 1918 the first award of the Pulitzer gold medal thereafter offered annually to the American newspaper that is judged to have rendered the most disinterested and meritorious service of the year.

Because the completeness of the *Times's* war news made the paper invaluable to readers who desired as accurate information as was available, it secured a nation-wide circulation, which at the close of the struggle averaged 370,000 a day. The paper had the distinction of being the only newspaper in the world that printed the whole draft of the treaty of peace. Twenty-four telegraph and telephone wires were used to transmit the document from Washington, and it filled sixty-two columns of the paper.[1]

The success of the *New York Times* demonstrated the possibility of building up a large circulation, with subscribers all over the country, for a newspaper that confined itself entirely to news and editorials. Unlike practically all other American newspapers, its daily issues contained no non-news features and only occasional illustrations. Its primary purpose was to furnish timely information rather than entertainment. A similar policy was pursued with reference to its Sunday edition. Besides news, editorials, special articles, and musical, art, and dramatic criticism, the Sunday paper included two illustrated "tabloid" supplements — a magazine section and a book-review section — together with

[1] *New York Times*, June 10, 1919.

two or three pictorial supplements, all printed by the rotogravure process. Editorially the paper has been independent and conservative.

The idea of a chain of newspapers under one control, which was later developed by Frank A. Munsey and William Randolph Hearst, originated in the late seventies and early eighties when the Scripps brothers established and acquired several evening papers in the Middle West. After the success of the *Detroit News*, started by James E. Scripps in 1873, two of his brothers, Edward and George H. Scripps, and his cousin, John Scripps Sweeney, obtained his assistance in founding the *Penny Press*, afterwards known as the Cleveland *Press*. It began publication as an evening paper on November 3, 1878, with a capital of $10,000. Two years later Edward W. Scripps started the St. Louis *Chronicle*, as a two-cent evening paper, in competition with Pulitzer's *Post-Dispatch*, then in its second year. In 1881 the Scripps interests secured control of a small sheet in Cincinnati, the *Penny Press*, which had begun publication the year before. The name of the paper was changed in 1883 to the *Penny Post*, then to the *Evening Post*, and finally to the *Cincinnati Post*. In 1882 Milton A. McRae, who had been in the business office of the *Detroit News*, became advertising manager of the *Cincinnati Post* and thus was brought into close contact with Edward W. Scripps. As a result of this association, they entered into a partnership in 1889, which six years later developed into the Scripps-McRae League of Newspapers. When this League was established in 1895, Edward W. Scripps was chosen president, George H. Scripps, treasurer, and Milton A. McRae, secretary and general manager. The four papers in the League were the Cleveland *Press*, the St. Louis *Chronicle*, the Cincinnati *Post*, and the *Kentucky Post* of Covington, Kentucky, which had been founded by Mr. McRae in 1885. This was the first chain of newspapers in the United States.

For the purpose of gathering and distributing telegraph news for the Scripps-McRae papers, the Scripps-McRae Press Association was organized in 1897, and thus was the first news agency established in connection with a chain of newspapers. In 1901 Edward W. Scripps started the Newspaper Enterprise Association in Cleveland, a newspaper syndicate formed to supply the Scripps-McRae and other papers with news features, pictures, and cartoons. This was the first syndicate connected with a chain of papers.

Meanwhile Edward W. Scripps, who had taken up his residence in California, entered the Pacific coast field in 1892 by purchasing the San Diego *Sun*. After adding to his holdings the Seattle *Star*, the Tacoma *Times*, the Spokane *Press*, the San Francisco *Daily News*, and the Los Angeles *Record*, he organized the Scripps Coast League, as well as the Scripps Coast Press Association to serve these League papers with telegraph news. By 1906 four other papers had been included in the Coast League — the Sacramento *Star*, the Fresno, California, *Tribune*, the Portland *News*, and the Denver *Express* — making nine papers in all.

The Scripps-McRae League extended its activities by purchasing the *Citizen* of Columbus, Ohio, in 1904, and by launching six new papers in 1906 — the *Press* at Evansville, Ohio; the *Post* at Terre Haute, Indiana; the *Dispatch* at Dallas, Texas; the *Oklahoma News* at Oklahoma City; the *Press* at Memphis, Tennessee; and the *Times* at Nashville. In 1908 both Edward W. Scripps and Milton A. McRae decided to retire from active control of their papers, and James G. Scripps, eldest son of Edward W. Scripps, took over the management.

Roy W. Howard, who since 1912 had been president and general manager of the United Press, was in 1920 made general business manager of the twelve Scripps-McRae League papers, and Robert P. Scripps, another son of Edward W. Scripps, became editorial director. Under this new management a policy of expansion was begun, with the result that during 1921 five new papers were launched — the *Post* at Birmingham, Alabama; the *Post* at Norfolk, Virginia; the *News* at Knoxville, Tennessee; the *Press* at Fort Worth, Texas; and the *Daily News*, a " tabloid " picture paper, at Washington, D.C. During the next year four more papers were added to the chain. Two of these were new papers — the *Post* of El Paso, Texas; and the *Post* of Baltimore, a " tabloid " — and two were acquired by purchase, the *Indianapolis Times* and the *Telegram* of Youngstown, Ohio. In November, 1922, the name of the Scripps-McRae League was changed to the Scripps-Howard Newspapers. During the year 1923, two papers were purchased — the *New Mexico State Tribune* of Albuquerque, and the *Pittsburgh Press*. In connection with the price of $5,000,000 paid for the *Pittsburgh Press*, it is interesting to note that thirty years before, in 1892, Milton A. McRae had taken an option to buy that paper for $51,000.   At the close of the year 1925, the Scripps-Howard chain consisted of twenty-three papers in eleven states and the District of Columbia.   After the death of James G. Scripps in January, 1921, the *Dispatch* of Dallas, Texas, and some of the Pacific coast papers — the Seattle *Star*, the Spokane *Press*, the Tacoma *Times*, the Portland *News*, and the Los Angeles *Record* — passed into the hands of his widow and her associates. The other papers that had been included in the Scripps Coast League — the Denver *Express*, the San Diego *Sun*, and the San Francisco *News* — became Scripps-Howard newspapers.   Edward W. Scripps died on March 12, 1926, at the age of seventy-one.

The Scripps papers, from the beginning, were low-priced, popular evening papers designed to appeal to what Edward W. Scripps called the "95 per cent," the plain people.   By reducing its price in 1887 to one cent a copy, the St. Louis *Chronicle* became the first penny paper west of the Mississippi River.   Editorially, the papers have been independent and liberal.   In the 1912 presidential election they supported Colonel Roosevelt, and in the 1924 campaign, Senator LaFollette.   They also championed the cause of union labor.   In the financial organization of the Scripps companies, provision was made for stock ownership by their editors and business managers.   Holding companies were also organized in which employees were permitted to become stock-holders.   Approximately forty per cent of all the stock of the Scripps-Howard Newspapers in 1925 was in the hands of present or former executives and managers, and several hundred employees were stock-holders in the holding companies that held diversified blocks of stock in the various Scripps enterprises.

The tendency to buy, reorganize, and consolidate old, well-established companies, that developed in the business world during the first quarter of the twentieth century, had its effect on newspapers.   Large increases in circulation and in the volume of advertising, heavy investments in mechanical equipment, and the great cost of newspaper production, made the business side of the newspaper the dominant one.   The magnitude of the business of newspaper publishing placed newspapers on a par with other large business enterprises. The result was that old, well-established papers were bought, sold, and consolidated in the same manner as were other companies.

The career of Frank A. Munsey, as a newspaper publisher, exemplifies this new tendency in journalism. After achieving success as a publisher of popular magazines, he entered the newspaper field in 1901 by purchasing for $500,000 the New York *Daily News*, which for over thirty years had been a cheap evening sheet closely identified with Tammany Hall. He changed it to a Republican morning paper, but, as it lost money steadily, he abandoned it at the end of three years. The same year he bought the *Washington Times* for $200,000, and in 1902 he acquired the seventy-year-old *Boston Journal* for $625,000. With the intention of securing papers in a number of the largest Eastern cities, he purchased in 1908 the *Philadelphia Times* and the *Baltimore News*.

That Munsey considered the consolidation of newspapers inevitable was shown by the following statement made by him in connection with the purchase of the *Baltimore News:* [1]

> There is no business that cries so loud for organization and combination as that of newspaper publishing. The waste under existing conditions is frightful and the results miserably less than they could be made. For one thing, the number of newspapers is at least 60 per cent greater than we need.

A chain of newspapers under one management seemed to him the best solution for the problem. In the same connection he said:

> Think of the possibilities involved in a chain of 500 newspapers under a single control! Such a faculty could be so maintained as no college could support; the greatest authors, artists, engineers, essayists, and statesmen could write with authority on every question of importance, each of the 500 papers getting the benefit of these great minds, while maintaining their individuality on purely local matters.
>
> There could be a $100,000 or $200,000 a year man at the head of the editorial force and another God-made genius in charge of the business end. Such economies would be effected that the highest salaries would be mere details of the business, and the product of the combined genius of the men in control would be the most uplifting force the world has ever known.

[1] Quoted in *Editor and Publisher*, vol. 58, p. 8 (December 26, 1925).

In 1912 Munsey again entered the New York field by purchasing the *New York Press* for $2,500,000.   Thus he owned papers in New York, Boston, Philadelphia, Baltimore, and Washington. Not all of his papers, however, proved successful.   After spending a million dollars on the *Boston Journal* in ten years, he disposed of it in 1913 for about $400,000, and four years later it was combined with the *Boston Herald*.   He sank another million in the *Philadelphia Times* before he abandoned it in 1914.   Undaunted by these failures, he bought the New York *Sun* and the *Evening Sun* in 1916, paying over $3,000,000 for them.   He combined the *Press* with the *Sun*, thus securing an Associated Press membership for the latter.   In 1920, following the death of James Gordon Bennett, Jr., he purchased for $4,000,000 the *New York Herald*, the *Evening Telegram*, and the Paris edition of the *Herald*.   He consolidated the *New York Herald* and the *Sun* into one morning paper in January, 1920, and continued this arrangement until October of that year, when he decided to use the name of the *Herald* for the morning paper, and that of the *Sun*, in place of the *Evening Sun*, for the evening paper.   In May, 1923, he purchased the New York *Globe and Commercial Advertiser*, then the oldest daily newspaper in the United States, and combined it with the *Sun*.   Early in 1924, he bought the New York *Evening Mail* and consolidated it with the *Evening Telegram*.   He is said to have paid $2,000,000 each for the *Globe* and the *Evening Mail*.   Two months after buying the *Mail*, he sold to the *New York Tribune* the *New York Herald* and its Paris edition, and these two old rivals appeared as one paper under the ownership of Ogden Mills Reid, proprietor of the *Tribune*.   Thus, in the New York field, Munsey practically wiped out six well-known papers — the *Daily News* (1867), the *Press* (1887), the *Evening Sun* (1887), the *Globe* (1797), the *Evening Mail* (1867), and the *Herald* (1835).

By 1917 Munsey had apparently given up his idea of a chain of papers, since in that year he sold the *Washington Times* to Arthur Brisbane, who in turn sold it to Mr. Hearst.   After buying the *Baltimore American* and the *Star* in 1921, Munsey combined the latter with his *Baltimore News*, and then sold to Mr. Hearst, first the *News*, in 1922, and then the *American*, in 1923.   At the time of his death in December, 1925, he owned only two newspapers, both in the New York evening field, the *Sun* and the *Evening Telegram*.

The movement to reduce the number of newspapers, largely through consolidations, was nation-wide. This was particularly true in the morning field. After the rise of the evening papers and their more extensive use by retail advertisers to reach women readers, it became increasingly difficult for morning papers to obtain enough advertising to maintain themselves. How the change took place is illustrated by the Chicago morning papers. In 1892, when that city had a population of 1,100,000, there were six morning papers printed in English. These papers, with the date of their establishment, were the *Tribune* (1847), the *Times* (1854), the *Inter-Ocean* (1872), the *Herald* (1881), the *News Record* (1892), and the *Globe* (1888). In 1895 the *Times* was consolidated with the *Herald*, under the name of the *Times-Herald*. Six years later, the *Record* was combined with the *Times-Herald* as the *Record-Herald*. In 1914, the *Inter-Ocean*, then in the hands of a receiver, was consolidated with the *Record-Herald*, which had failed to pay the interest on its bonds, and the name of the paper was changed to the *Chicago Herald*. Five years later, the *Herald* was merged with Mr. Hearst's *Examiner*, which had begun publication in 1902, under the name of the *Herald and Examiner*. Thus by 1918 the number of morning papers in Chicago was reduced to two — the *Chicago Tribune* and the *Herald and Examiner*. With the exception of the *Chicago Journal of Commerce*, which was established in 1920, primarily as a financial and business paper, no other morning papers continued in the field up to the end of 1925, although the population of the city had increased to nearly 3,000,000. Throughout the quarter of a century ending in 1925, four newspapers continued to occupy the evening field in Chicago — the *Journal* (1844), the *Daily News* (1875), the *Evening Post* (1889), and the *American* (1900).

As a result of consolidation and elimination, a number of large cities were left with only a single morning paper. Through the merger in Cleveland of the *Leader* (1848) and the *Plain Dealer* (1843) in 1917, the *Plain Dealer* remained alone in the morning field. Detroit, with a population in 1925 of over 1,000,000 had had for ten years but one morning paper, the *Free Press*. In

1919, the elimination of the Milwaukee *Free Press* (1901) left the metropolis of Wisconsin with only one morning paper, the *Milwaukee Sentinel*. By the purchase of the St. Louis *Republic* (1808), the *Globe-Democrat* in 1919 became the sole morning paper in St. Louis. In Minneapolis the *Tribune*, and in St. Paul the *Pioneer-Press*, were the only morning papers. Indianapolis had long had but one morning paper, the *Star*. In New Orleans, through the consolidation in 1914 of the *Times-Democrat* (1863) and the *Picayune* (1837), the *Times-Picayune* became the only paper in the morning field. Atlanta had but one morning paper, the *Constitution*. In 1926 the *Buffalo Courier* (1831), the *Buffalo Express* (1846), both morning newspapers, were consolidated as the *Buffalo Courier and Express*, which thus became the only morning paper in Buffalo. In each of these cities there were at least two evening papers.

A number of other well-known newspapers changed hands. In some instances they passed out of existence through consolidation; in others their character was greatly changed. The New York *Evening Post*, which had been owned by the Villard family since its purchase by Henry Villard in 1881, was sold in 1917 by his son, Oswald Garrison Villard, to Thomas W. Lamont of the firm of J. P. Morgan and Company. It was placed in charge of Edwin F. Gay, dean of the Harvard Graduate School of Business Administration, who in 1922 became head of a company which bought the paper from Mr. Lamont. The following year it was sold for over $1,500,000 to Cyrus K. Curtis, who, after his success as a magazine publisher, had in 1913 purchased the Philadelphia *Public Ledger*. The appearance and contents of the *Evening Post* were completely changed to resemble those of the *Public Ledger*, some of the features of which appeared thereafter in the *Evening Post*. In 1925, Mr. Curtis bought another one of the oldest American newspapers, the Philadelphia *North American*, established in 1839, and combined it with his *Public Ledger*. He is said to have paid $1,700,000 for the *North American*. By purchasing the *Detroit Tribune* for over a million dollars, the *Detroit News* in 1922 reduced the number of evening papers in Detroit to two. Thus Detroit, a city of over a million population, had but three papers in the morning and evening fields. In order to reduce competition, the Pittsburgh Newspaper Publishers Association, consisting of the *Chronicle Telegraph*, the *Press*, and the *Sun* in the afternoon field, and the *Gazette Times* and the *Post* in the morning field, bought and eliminated in 1924 the *Dispatch* and the *Leader*. The purchase by Mr. Hearst of several long-established newspapers resulted in changing their character completely.

The high valuation placed upon newspapers by 1926 was shown by the reorganization of the *Chicago Daily News* and by the sale of the *Kansas City Star*. The assets of the company organized to take over the *Daily News* after the death of Victor Lawson, its publisher and owner, were over $19,000,000, of which $12,000,000 consisted of its circulation, good-will, Associated Press membership, and reference library. Its annual net profits for the preceding five years had averaged $1,325,000. When the *Kansas City Star* was sold, in accordance with the terms of the will of William Rockhill Nelson, it brought the sum of $11,000,000.

Marked improvement in the character of newspaper advertising was made during the first quarter of the twentieth century. One of the first important steps in the direction of excluding undesirable advertising was taken by the Scripps-McRae League of Newspapers in 1903, when Robert E. Paine was appointed as advertising censor of all the newspapers in this chain. Every advertisement submitted to any of the Scripps-McRae papers had to have his approval before it could be published. Approximately $500,000 worth of advertising in one year was barred from papers in the chain because it was considered to be objectionable.[1]   In a series of ten articles published in *Collier's Weekly* during 1905 and 1906, Samuel Hopkins Adams, a former star reporter on the New York *Sun*, exposed the fraudulent claims of makers of patent medicines, of quack doctors, and of proprietors of so-called medical institutes, many of whom were advertising extensively in newspapers. He also showed how manufacturers of patent medicines sought to throttle the press by inserting in their advertising contracts a "red-line" clause that provided for the cancellation of the contract if any law were enacted, either by the state in which the newspaper was published or by Congress, restricting or prohibiting the manufacture or sale of proprietary

[1] McRae, Milton A. *Forty Years in Newspaperdom*, p. 213.

medicines.[1] The passage by Congress of the Federal Food and
Drug Act in 1906, as well as the enactment of similar legislation
by various states, tended to discredit fraudulent advertising by
quacks and makers of nostrums.   A number of newspapers,
accordingly, proceeded to bar such advertising from their columns.

A growing sentiment in favor of honesty in newspaper advertising found definite expression in the Standards of Newspaper Practice adopted by the Newspaper Division of the Associated Advertising Clubs of the World at their annual convention in June, 1914.   These Standards, which were endorsed by
representatives of the leading newspapers throughout the country, declared that "it is the duty of the newspaper (1) to protect
the honest advertiser and the general newspaper reader, as far as
possible, from deceptive or offensive advertising; (2) to sell advertising as a commodity on the basis of proven circulation and
the service the paper will render the manufacturer or the merchant; and to provide the fullest information as to the character
of such circulation and how it was secured; (3) to maintain uniform rates, according to classifications, and to present these rates,
as far as possible, in a uniform card; (4) to accept no advertising
which is antagonistic to public welfare; (5) to effect the largest
possible co-operation with other newspapers in the same field
for the establishment and maintenance of these standards." [2]

The *New York Tribune* four months later announced the adoption of a new advertising policy by which it guaranteed its readers
"absolutely against loss or dissatisfaction through the purchase
of any wares advertised in its columns." [3]   At the same time it
adopted as its motto, "First to Last the Truth; News, Editorials,
Advertisements."   It also established a department to investigate advertisements, and readers were encouraged to report any
unsatisfactory experiences they had had in purchasing advertised
commodities. On investigating the advertising in its own columns,
the *Tribune* found that one of the largest department stores in
New York was guilty of misrepresentation, and accordingly

---

[1] Adams, Samuel H. "The Patent Medicine Conspiracy Against the Freedom of
the Press," *Collier's Weekly*, vol. 36, p. 13 (November 4, 1905).
[2] *Editor and Publisher*, vol. 14, pp. 54-72 (July 8, 1914).
[3] *New York Tribune*, November 17, 1914.

barred the advertisements of this store from its columns. Although this policy of guaranteeing advertising was not followed by other papers, the *Tribune's* pioneer effort attracted much attention and tended to raise the standards of newspaper advertising.

Various agencies for improving the character of advertising in general were of assistance to those newspapers that undertook to maintain higher standards. In 1913 the Associated Advertising Clubs of America adopted a declaration of principles based on the idea of "Truth in Advertising," and provided for a National Vigilance Committee to expose fraudulent advertising. *Printers' Ink*, a periodical devoted to advertising, prepared in 1911 a statute that made dishonest advertising a misdemeanor, and in the following ten years thirty-seven states adopted laws substantially in accord with this statute. Through the efforts of the National Vigilance Committee, later known as the National Better Business Commission, local Better Business Commissions were organized in some forty cities. Local advertising clubs, affiliated with the Associated Advertising Clubs of the World, were instrumental in securing for their cities ordinances against dishonest advertising.

Outstanding newspapers like the *New York Times* and the *Chicago Tribune* published in pamphlet form detailed rules covering every kind of display and classified advertising, with the purpose of protecting their readers against misleading, dishonest, and objectionable advertisements. Many newspapers sacrificed hundreds of thousands of dollars of possible revenue by excluding from their columns undesirable advertising. Although advertisements of patent nostrums, quacks, and fake investment schemes continued to appear in newspapers, the amount of dishonest and objectionable advertising decreased greatly.

The Bourne Newspaper Publicity law, passed by Congress in 1912, was designed to protect both readers and advertisers by requiring newspapers to make public their circulation and the names of their owners. It required daily newspapers to publish sworn statements semi-annually, giving the average daily circulation during the preceding six months, as well as the names of the publisher, the editor, the managing editor, the business manager, the stock-holders, and the holders of the bonds and mortgages of the paper. Another clause provided that "all editorial and other reading matter . . . for the publication of which money or other valuable consideration is paid, accepted, or promised, shall be plainly marked 'advertisement.'"

In 1913 the Audit Bureau of Circulations was established by advertisers, advertising agents, and publishers, to furnish reliable information in regard to the size and character of the circulation of such newspapers and periodicals as belonged to the Bureau. The Bureau, commonly known as the "A.B.C.," makes an annual audit of the circulation of newspapers and magazines, and then issues an official report of the audit. A similar semi-annual report is required by the Bureau from each publisher. These reports show the total net paid circulation — city, suburban, and country — and the total number of free copies furnished to advertisers, employees, exchanges, and others. They also indicate what part of the circulation was secured by means of premiums, contests, and similar promotion methods, because many advertisers do not regard circulation secured by such means as of equal value with that obtained by the merits of the paper. As a result of these A.B.C. reports, the exaggerated claims as to circulation that were formerly made by some newspapers have been largely eliminated.

The growth in the business of newspaper publishing resulting from the increase in circulation and advertising, led to the formation of a number of organizations of business executives of newspapers. The first of these was the American Newspaper Publishers Association, founded in 1887. The International Circulation Managers Association was organized in 1898, the Association of Newspaper Advertising Executives in 1918, and the Newspaper Classified Advertising Managers in 1920. All these associations have aided in standardizing the business methods of newspapers.

A great increase in the amount of publicity and propaganda material furnished to newspapers marked the period beginning about 1890. Even before that date, press agents employed by circuses and theatrical companies had supplied the press with publicity matter designed to advertise these forms of entertainment. Theatrical press agents had often shown great ingenuity in devising novel events and situations that seemed to afford material for good news stories, and had arranged either to write the stories of these events themselves or to have them written by regular newspaper reporters. When, during the nineties and early nineteen-hundreds, attacks were being made upon the so-called trusts, these and other big business enterprises discovered that it was to their advantage to employ press agents to present their side of the controversies to the public through the medium of the press. This system of supplying newspapers with publicity and propaganda in the guise of news became so popular that a census of the regular, accredited press agents taken by the New York newspapers shortly before the outbreak of the World War showed that they numbered about 1200.[1]

Almost as soon as war was declared in 1914, both sides sought to influence American public opinion by furnishing newspapers in this country with propaganda favorable to their cause. Diplomatic agents of each of the nations involved in the struggle supplied the press with a steady stream of propaganda. Before the United States entered the conflict, the value of propaganda as a means of influencing public opinion at home and abroad, and of maintaining morale within a nation, as well as of breaking down the morale in enemy countries, had come to be well recognized. Of the work of the Committee on Public Information, which was organized by the American Government immediately after this country entered the war, George Creel, its director, wrote, "In all things, from first to last, without halt or change, it was a plain publicity proposition, a vast enterprise in salesmanship, the world's greatest adventure in advertising."[2] Newton D. Baker, Secretary of War, declared that "the whole business of mobilizing the mind of the world so far as American participation in the war was concerned was in a sense the work of the Committee on Public Information."[3] Newspaper publicity was also effectively used in "drives" for the Red Cross and the Liberty Loans, as well as in campaigns conducted for the conservation of food and fuel. Every organization, public and private, interested in its own particular efforts to win the war sought to secure newspaper publicity for its cause.

After the Armistice was signed, various nations undertook to

[1] Heaton, J. L. Cobb of "The World," p. 331.
[2] Creel, George. How We Advertised America, p. 4.   [3] Ibid., p. xiii.

influence American public opinion through propaganda furnished to newspapers, in order to attain their nationalistic ambitions through the treaty of peace.   Newspaper offices also continued to be flooded with great quantities of publicity material sent out by all kinds of organizations to advance their own interests. In some instances a newspaper received enough of such matter in a single day to fill an entire issue.   Finally, newspapers rebelled against these excesses and began to wage a determined fight against all forms of free publicity.

The World War affected newspapers in various other ways. A rapid rise in the cost of producing papers necessitated increases in price during the years 1917 and 1918, so that papers that had sold for one cent a copy went up to two cents, and two-cent papers advanced to three cents; at the same time, the price of Sunday papers increased from five to seven and then to ten cents a copy.   Although popular interest in war news led to larger circulations, the volume of advertising and hence the advertising revenues decreased.   The cost of maintaining special war correspondents by leading papers and heavy cable tolls also added to the financial burden.   The Associated Press spent four times as much for its foreign news in 1918 as it had done in 1913.

The importance of war news led many papers to use much larger headlines than had been customary.   Banner heads in big display type, which had previously been confined to sensational papers, became common in many newspapers.   Headlines extending across two, three, and four columns were also used more frequently than hitherto.   After the war, many newspapers continued to use large banners and other kinds of display heads.

A great advance in pictorial journalism was made when, in April, 1914, the *New York Times* added a rotogravure section to its Sunday edition.   The success of the new process, which had originated in Germany, was instantaneous.   Within four years after the *New York Times* made the innovation, forty-seven American papers included a rotogravure section in their Sunday issues, and by 1925 this number had been increased to seventy-two.   In 1921 the *Chicago Tribune* experimented with rotogravure printing in four colors, and shortly after was able to use this process for printing part of its Sunday magazine.   The *Tribune* named this color rotogravure process "coloroto."

The appearance of the *Illustrated Daily News* in New York City on June 26, 1919, as a daily "tabloid picture paper," was the beginning in this country of a new type of daily paper. The *News* was started by Robert R. McCormick and Joseph Medill Patterson, publishers of the *Chicago Tribune*. It contained sixteen four-column pages, which were half the size of those of a seven-column newspaper. Half-tone pictures appeared on almost every page. On the front page was a picture of the Prince of Wales in military uniform on horseback, with the overline, "Newport to Entertain Prince of Wales in August." The last page consisted of pictures of young women who had entered the paper's contest for "the most beautiful girl in Greater New York," the first prize in which was $10,000, the second, $2500, and the third, $1000. The paper contained some of the most popular features of the *Chicago Tribune*, such as "The Gumps"; Dr. Evans's department, "How to Keep Well"; Bert Leston Taylor's column, "A Line o' Type or Two"; "Bright Sayings of Children"; and a McCutcheon cartoon. There was also the first installment of a serial by E. Phillips Oppenheim. The price of the paper was two cents a copy.

In the first editorial, entitled "Who We Are," the paper set forth its aims thus:[1]

THE ILLUSTRATED DAILY NEWS is going to be your newspaper. Its interests will be your interests. Its policy will be your policy. It is not an experiment, for the appeal of news pictures, and brief, well-told stories will be as apparent to you as it has been to millions of readers in European cities. It will not be a competitor of other New York morning newspapers, for it will cover a field that they do not attempt to cover.

We shall give you every day the best and newest pictures of the interesting things that are happening in the world. Nothing that is not interesting is news. The story that is told by a picture can be grasped instantly. Ten thousand words of description could not convey to you the impression you receive when you look at Millet's painting, "The Angelus." You could read all that has ever been written about the Clock Room in Paris, where the peace conference is being held and get no clear idea of it. Look at a single picture of the same room, and you know exactly what it is like.

[1] *Illustrated Daily News*, June 26, 1919.

With the pictures we shall give you short, concise news stories, covering every happening recorded by the news gatherers. Pictures and stories together will supply a complete understanding of the events of the day, and that is liberal education.

No story will be continued to another page — that is to save you trouble. The print will be large and clear. You can read it without eye strain. The paper is, as you see, of convenient size. You can turn the pages in the subway without having it whisked from your hands by the draft. You can hang to a strap and read it without the skill of a juggler to keep its pages together.

The policy of THE ILLUSTRATED DAILY NEWS, as we said in the beginning, will be your policy. It will be aggressively for America and for the people of New York. . . . This newspaper always will be fearless and independent. It will have no entangling alliance with any class whatever — for class feeling is always antagonistic to the interests of the whole people.

Because the doings of the very fortunate are always of interest we shall print them as interestingly as possible in our society column. Because good fiction will always be appealing we shall print the best and newest that is to be had. . . . We shall print the best features that are to be found. The United Press dispatches, covering the whole world, will augment our own news service.

In form, make-up, and contents the *Illustrated Daily News* was plainly modeled on the London *Daily Mirror*, which had been started in November, 1903, by Viscount Northcliffe (then Alfred Harmsworth) as a daily paper for women. Because it did not succeed as a woman's paper, it was changed, within three months, to a "tabloid picture paper." In its first issue the *Daily Mirror* claimed to be the "first illustrated halfpenny paper in the history of journalism," and to occupy "a unique place among the journals of the world." [1] It had been preceded in the field of illustrated daily journalism by the *Daily Graphic*, a penny tabloid. The success of the *Daily Mirror* led in 1909 to the establishment of another small-size picture paper, the *Daily Sketch*. Thus, before the New York *Illustrated Daily News* was begun in 1919, three similar papers had been successfully maintained in London for ten years, and the most successful of them, the *Daily Mirror*, had reached a circulation of a million copies a day.

The success of the *Daily News* in New York brought it into keen rivalry with Mr. Hearst's *American*, as both of these morning

[1] *Illustrated Daily Mirror*, January 26, 1904.

papers appealed to the same class of readers. To meet the competition, the *American* added a tabloid illustrated supplement to its regular issue. In the ensuing fight for circulation, each paper tried to outdo the other by means of lottery schemes, the daily prizes of which were forced up by competition from $1000 to $25,000. In June, 1924, Mr. Hearst finally launched a tabloid in New York City, the *Daily Mirror*, borrowing the name from the long successful London picture paper, and imitating closely the New York *Daily News*. In September, 1924, a few months after the *Daily Mirror* began publication, Bernarr Macfadden, successful publisher of physical culture and popular fiction magazines, entered the New York evening field with a tabloid, the *Evening Graphic*. "To dramatize the news and features" and "to appeal to the masses in their own language," were his avowed purpose. At the end of the year 1925, the approximate circulation of these three New York picture papers was 1,350,000, of which the *Daily News* had 1,000,000, the *Daily Mirror*, 350,000, and the *Evening Graphic*, 100,000. Thus, within six years of its establishment, the *Daily News* had secured the largest circulation of any daily paper in the United States.

Following the remarkable rise of the *Daily News*, illustrated daily papers in tabloid form appeared in other cities. In Boston in 1921, Mr. Hearst changed the century-old *Advertiser* into that form. The same year the *Daily News* was started in Washington, as an evening tabloid, by the Scripps-McRae League. In Baltimore the *Post* was established in 1922, as a Scripps-Howard newspaper. In 1923 Cornelius Vanderbilt, Jr., started two tabloids in California — the Los Angeles *Illustrated News* and the San Francisco *Illustrated Herald*. Mr. Vanderbilt's policy for these papers was to make them clean newspapers, avoiding sensational and objectionable treatment of news. He also announced his intention to establish "a chain of nonsalacious journals throughout the United States," with "a clean newspaper in every town in which vileness and sensationalism now play so great a part in the local press." [1] The third tabloid in this chain was begun by Mr. Vanderbilt in 1925 at Miami, Florida, as the *Illustrated Daily Tab*. Two of these tabloids —

---

[1] Selden, Charles A. "Young Vanderbilt's Crusade Against Filth," *Ladies' Home Journal*, vol. 41, p. 20 (May, 1924).

those published in San Francisco and in Miami — ceased publication in the spring of 1926 because of financial difficulties. In Buffalo, the *Enquirer* became a tabloid in 1924, under the name of the *Star-Enquirer*. The only city besides New York that at the end of 1925 had more than one tabloid was Philadelphia. Late in 1925, Bernarr Macfadden took over the *Philadelphia Daily News*, which had been started as a tabloid in March of that year. Another tabloid, the *Sun*, was established in Philadelphia by Cyrus K. Curtis in 1925.

The success of these tabloid illustrated dailies was due to four factors: their convenient size, the large number of pictures, the condensed form in which the news was presented, and the emphasis upon human interest. Daily papers, particularly in large cities, had become so bulky that they could not be easily handled in crowded subway and surface cars. The tabloids, with pages only half the size of those of other papers, proved much more convenient not only to read but to slip into the pocket. Attractive news pictures and condensed news stories enabled busy readers to skim the day's news at a glance. In England, when Alfred Harmsworth (Viscount Northcliffe), after making a success of the *Daily Mail*, began the *Daily Mirror* as a tabloid illustrated paper, Lord Salisbury remarked that, "having invented a daily newspaper for those who cannot think, Mr. Harmsworth has now invented one for those who cannot read." The drama of the day's news as found in accidents, crimes, and scandal was given a prominent place in these tabloids, and the human interest phase of all types of news was emphasized.

The two morning tabloids in New York City apparently created a new group of readers. Between 1919, when the *Daily News* was launched, and 1925, when the *News* and the *Mirror* had reached a combined circulation of approximately 1,140,000, the other New York morning papers decreased in circulation only 26,000. The two tabloids, therefore, seemed to have attracted over a million persons who had not previously read a morning paper.

A significant movement for the improvement of the profession of journalism was the establishment of schools, departments, and courses in journalism by a number of American universities and colleges. Although various attempts were made during the thirty-five years following the Civil War to provide academic instruction in journalism, it was not until after 1900 that the movement took tangible form. The first courses in journalistic writing and the technique of journalism were given in Middle Western state universities, usually in the departments of English composition. In some instances the first instruction was in the form of lectures by newspaper men in active service. Impetus was given to this movement by the proposal made by Joseph Pulitzer in 1903 to endow a school of journalism, and by his detailed exposition of the possibilities of such a school made the following year in an article in the *North American Review*.[1] Despite the avowed scepticism of leading newspaper editors as to the feasibility of teaching the elements of journalism in the college class room, the pioneers in the movement were not discouraged. In 1908 the first school of journalism was established at the University of Missouri. Departments of journalism and four-year courses in journalism leading to a bachelor's degree were also organized in other state universities. The first school of journalism in an Eastern university was that established at Columbia University in 1912 with the Pulitzer bequest of $2,000,000. In the same year, the American Association of Teachers of Journalism was organized. In 1917 representatives of ten universities in which instruction in journalism was fully developed founded the Association of American Schools and Departments of Journalism. These two organizations in 1923 provided for a Council on Education for Journalism, and the next year adopted the Principles and Standards of Education for Journalism formulated by this Council. By 1925 over two hundred American colleges and universities were offering instruction in journalism, and some twenty universities had fully organized schools, courses, or departments of journalism.

Although state and national organizations of daily and weekly newspaper publishers had been successfully maintained for many years, it was not until 1922 that a national association was formed of editors of large city newspapers. This organization, known as the American Society of Newspaper Editors, consisted of "editors-in-chief, editorial writers, and managing editors having immediate charge of editorial and news policies of daily news-

[1] *North American Review*, vol. 178, p. 641-80 (May, 1904).

papers in cities of not less than 100,000 population." The Society began with a membership of 107. In 1924 the scope of the Society was enlarged by opening membership to editors of newspapers in cities of 50,000 or more, and the number of members increased to 174. One of the most important steps taken at the first meeting was the appointment of a committee to draw up a code of ethics, and, accordingly, at the second meeting, in 1923, seven "Canons of Journalism" were adopted by the Society. These canons dealt with the responsibility of the newspaper, with freedom of the press, and with journalistic independence, sincerity, truthfulness, accuracy, impartiality, fair play, and decency. Although the membership of the Society was too restricted to be as representative of the profession of journalism as the American Medical Association is of the medical profession and the American Bar Association is of the legal profession, the organization marked an important advance toward the recognition of the professional status of journalism.

Since 1910 various attempts have been made to improve the profession of journalism. The first National Newspaper Conference was held in 1912, under the auspices of the University of Wisconsin, to discuss the problems of journalism, and two years later the second Conference was held, at the University of Kansas. A number of state press associations adopted codes of ethics designed to improve news, editorial, and advertising policies of daily and weekly newspapers. Bills were introduced in several state legislatures providing for the licensing of journalists, but none of them was passed. In a few cities, unions of news writers were formed, which were affiliated with the American Federation of Labor through charters granted by the International Typographical Union, but this movement never gained much headway. Several efforts to organize local, state, and national professional societies of newspaper reporters and editors were not permanently successful, partly through the lack of interest of the members, and partly because of the hostility of newspaper publishers toward such associations. In an era when organizations of all sorts flourished as never before, it seemed remarkable that the rank and file of the news and editorial staffs of daily papers remained unorganized.

While thus keeping pace with the rapidly changing conditions of American life, the press underwent a great transformation. The merits and the defects of the newspapers of the period were largely a reflection of the strength and the weakness of the society of which they were a part. To the extent that newspapers became superficial and standardized, they showed the effect of the superficiality and standardization everywhere manifested in American life. In their efforts to secure the largest possible circulation, they succeeded in reaching a greater proportion of the whole population than had ever before been reached by the press of any other country. To accomplish this result, many papers found it necessary to present such news and features as would make the widest appeal. Since newspaper publishing became a highly competitive business, editors and publishers generally sought to meet the demand by giving the public what it wanted to read. The democratization of the press thus ran parallel with the democratization of other American institutions that attempted to furnish all classes of people with information, instruction, and entertainment. On the whole, however, a greater advance was made during the first quarter of the twentieth century, both by the press and by the profession of journalism, than during the same length of time in any previous period.

READINGS IN THE HISTORY OF JOURNALISM

CHAPTER I

EARLY ENGLISH JOURNALISM

Addison, Joseph, and Steele, Richard. *The Tatler;* G. A. Aitken, ed. 4 vols. London, 1899.

Addison, Joseph, and Steele, Richard. *The Spectator;* G. A. Aitken, ed. 8 vols. London, 1898.

Ames, John Griffith, Jr. *The English Literary Periodical of Morals and Manners.* Mt. Vernon, Ohio, 1904.

Andrews, Alexander. *History of British Journalism.* 2 vols. London, 1859.

Bleackley, Horace. *Life of John Wilkes.* London, 1917.

Bourne, H. R. Fox. *English Newspapers.* 2 vols. London, 1887.

Cambridge History of English Literature. Vol. VII, pp. 389–415; J. B. Williams, "Beginnings of English Journalism." Vol. IX, pp. 1–28; W. P. Trent, "Defoe — The Newspaper and the Novel." New York, 1908–13.

Collet, C. D. *History of the Taxes on Knowledge.* 2 vols. London, 1899.

Escott, Thomas H. S. *Masters of English Journalism.* London, 1911.

Hunt, Frederick K. *The Fourth Estate.* 2 vols. London, 1850.

Kitchin, George. *Sir Roger L'Estrange.* London, 1913.

Lee, William. *Life and Times of Defoe.* 3 vols. London, 1869.

Letters of Junius; John Wade, ed. 2 vols. London, 1868.

Lewis, Lawrence. *Advertisements of The Spectator.* Boston, 1909.

Lounsbury, Thomas R. *The Text of Shakespeare;* chap. XIX, "The Grub-Street Journal." New York, 1906.

Macdonagh, Michael. *The Reporters' Gallery;* pp. 81–298. London, n.d.

Marr, George S. *The Periodical Essayists of the Eighteenth Century.* London, 1924.

Minto, William. *Daniel Defoe.* New York, 1879.

Muddiman, J. G. *The King's Journalist.* [Henry Muddiman.] London, 1923.

Paterson, James. *The Liberty of the Press, Speech, and Public Worship.* London, 1880.

Printing Number of the London Times; pp. 18–42, and 68–72. London, 1912.

Sampson, Henry. *History of Advertising.* London, 1875.

Stevens, David H. *Party Politics and English Journalism, 1702–1742.* Chicago, 1916.

Stockum, van, Wilhelmus P., Jr. *The First Newspapers of England Printed in Holland, 1620–21.* The Hague, 1914.

Tercentenary Handlist of English and Welsh Newspapers, Magazines, and Reviews. [Compiled by J. B. Williams, *pseud.* J. G. Muddiman.] London, 1920.

Trent, William P. *Daniel Defoe; How to Know Him.* Indianapolis, 1916.

Underhill, John, ed. *The Athenian Oracle.* [Selections from Dunton's *Athenian Mercury.*] London, 1892.

Williams, J. B. *A History of English Journalism to the Foundation of the Gazette.* London, 1908.

CHAPTER II

EARLY COLONIAL NEWSPAPERS, 1690–1750

Buckingham, Joseph T. *Specimens of Newspaper Literature.* 2 vols. Boston, 1850.

Cambridge History of American Literature. Vol. 1, pp. 111–23; Elizabeth C. Cook, "Colonial Newspapers and Magazines, 1704–1775." New York, 1917.

Cook, Elizabeth C. *Literary Influences in Colonial Journalism, 1704–1750.* New York, 1912.

Duniway, Clyde A. *The Development of Freedom of the Press in Massachusetts.* New York, 1906.

Ford, Paul Leicester. *The Many-Sided Franklin.* New York, 1899.

Ford, Worthington C. *The Boston Book Market, 1679–1700;* [Benjamin Harris], pp. 35–41; also plate opp. p. 88. Boston, 1917.

Hudson, Frederic. *Journalism in the United States;* pp. 43–101. New York, 1873.

McMaster, John Bach. *Benjamin Franklin as a Man of Letters.* Boston, 1900.

Oswald, J. Clyde. *Benjamin Franklin, Printer.* New York, 1917.

Rutherfurd, Livingston. *John Peter Zenger.* New York, 1904.

Schuyler, Livingston R. *The Liberty of the Press in the American Colonies before the Revolutionary War.* New York, 1905.

Smyth, Albert H. *Writings of Benjamin Franklin.* 10 vols. New York, 1905–07.

Thomas, Isaiah. *History of Printing in America.* 2 vols. Albany, N. Y., 1874.

Weeks, Lyman H., and Bacon, Edwin M. *An Historical Digest of the Provincial Press* [1689–1707]. Boston, 1911.

Chapter III

The Press During the Struggle Between the
Colonies and England, 1750–1783

Buckingham, Joseph T. *Specimens of Newspaper Literature.* 2 vols.
Boston, 1850.
Cambridge History of American Literature. Vol. I, pp. 111–23; Elizabeth C. Cook, "Colonial Newspapers and Magazines, 1704–1775."
Vol. II, pp. 176–95; Frank W. Scott, "Newspapers, 1775–1860."
New York, 1917–18.
Conway, Moncure D. *Life of Thomas Paine.* 2 vols. New York,
1899.
Conway, Moncure D. *Writings of Thomas Paine.* 4 vols. New
York, 1894–96.
Ford, Paul Leicester. *The Journals of Hugh Gaine, Printer.* 2 vols.
New York, 1902.
Ford, Paul Leicester. *Writings of John Dickinson. Memoirs of the
Historical Society of Pennsylvania.* Philadelphia, 1895.
Ford, Paul Leicester. *The Many-Sided Franklin.* New York, 1899.
Hudson, Frederic. *Journalism in the United States;* pp. 102–40. New
York, 1873.
Lee, James Melvin. *History of American Journalism;* pp. 17–99.
Boston, 1917.
McMaster, John Bach. *Benjamin Franklin as a Man of Letters.*
Boston, 1900.
Payne, George H. *History of Journalism in the United States;* pp. 58–
134. New York, 1920.
Stille, Charles J. *Life and Times of John Dickinson. Memoirs of the
Historical Society of Pennsylvania,* vol. XIII. Philadelphia, 1891.
Thomas, Isaiah. *History of Printing in America.* 2 vols. Albany,
N.Y., 1874.
Tyler, Moses Coit. *Literary History of the American Revolution.*
2 vols. New York, 1897.
Wells, William V. *Life and Public Services of Samuel Adams.* 3 vols.
Boston, 1866.

Chapter IV

Beginnings of the Political Press, 1783–18

Anderson, Frank M. "Enforcement of the Alien and Sedition Laws.'
American Historical Association Annual Report for 1912, pp. 115–26.
Bowers, Claude G. *Jefferson and Hamilton; the Struggle for Democracy
in America.* Boston, 1925.

Cambridge History of American Literature. Vol. II, pp. 176–95; Frank W. Scott, "Newspapers, 1775–1860."

Cobbett, William. *Porcupine's Works.* 12 vols. London, 1801.

Dawson, Henry B. *The Fœderalist.* 2 vols. New York, 1863.

Ellis, Harold M. *Joseph Dennie and His Circle. Bulletin of the University of Texas,* No. 40. Austin, Texas, 1915.

Forman, Samuel E. *The Political Activities of Philip Freneau. Johns Hopkins University Studies in Historical and Political Science,* Series 20, Nos. 9–10. Baltimore, 1902.

Hudson, Frederic. *Journalism in the United States;* pp. 141–94, and 210–81. New York, 1873.

Lee, James Melvin. *History of American Journalism;* pp. 101–39. Boston, 1917.

Lodge, Henry Cabot. *Alexander Hamilton.* Boston, 1882.

Lodge, Henry Cabot. *Works of Alexander Hamilton.* 9 vols. Boston, 1878.

Paltsits, Victor H. *Bibliography of the Separate and Collected Works of Philip Freneau;* pp. 1–16, "Freneau and Journalism." New York, 1903.

Pattee, Fred L. *Poems of Philip Freneau;* vol. I, pp. vi–cxii. [Life of Philip Freneau.] 3 vols. Princeton, N.J., 1902–07.

Payne, George H. *History of Journalism in the United States;* pp. 135–89. New York, 1920.

Scudder, Horace E. *Noah Webster.* Boston, 1889.

Smith, Edward. *William Cobbett.* 2 vols. London, 1878.

Wharton, Francis. *State Trials of the United States during the Administrations of Washington and Adams.* [Alien and Sedition Law Trials.] Philadelphia, 1849.

CHAPTER V

THE POLITICAL PARTY PRESS, 1800–1833

Benton, Thomas H. *Thirty Years' View;* vol. I, pp. 128–30. [Duff Green and the *United States Telegraph,* and F. P. Blair and the *Globe.*] New York, 1858.

Bigelow, John. *William Cullen Bryant.* Boston, 1897.

Bryan, Wilhelmus B. *A History of the National Capital.* Vol. I, pp. 364–70, and 586–96. Vol. II, pp. 168–79, and 225–29. [Newspapers in Washington, D.C.] 2 vols. New York, 1916.

Cambridge History of American Literature. Vol. II, pp. 176–95; Frank W. Scott, "Newspapers, 1775–1860."

Godwin, Parke. *Life of William Cullen Bryant.* 2 vols. New York, 1883.

[Hallock, William H.] *Life of Gerard Hallock.* New York, 1869.

Hudson, Frederic. *Journalism in the United States;* pp. 344–407. New York, 1873.

Kendall, Amos. *Autobiography;* William Stickney, ed. pp. 370–74. [Duff Green and the *United States Telegraph,* and F. P. Blair and the *Globe.*] Boston, 1872.

Lee, James Melvin. *History of American Journalism;* pp. 140–63. Boston, 1917.

Nevins, Allan. *The Evening Post; a Century of Journalism;* pp. 9–227. New York, 1922.

Parton, James. *Men of Progress;* pp. 349–404. [James Watson Webb.] New York, 1870–71.

Payne, George H. *History of Journalism in the United States;* pp. 190–239. New York, 1920.

Seaton, Josephine. *William Winston Seaton of the "National Intelligencer."* Boston, 1871.

[Tappan, Lewis.] *Life of Arthur Tappan.* New York, 1871.

Thompson, Joseph P. *Memoir of David Hale.* Hartford, Conn., 1871.

Chapter VI

Beginnings of the Penny Papers, 1833–1840

Cambridge History of American Journalism. Vol. II, pp. 176–95; Frank W. Scott, "Newspapers, 1775–1860."

Hudson, Frederic. *Journalism in the United States;* pp. 416–27. New York, 1873.

Lee, James Melvin. *History of American Journalism;* pp. 185–205. Boston, 1917.

O'Brien, Frank M. *The Story of The Sun;* pp. 21–198. New York, 1918.

Parton, James. *Life of Horace Greeley;* pp. 103–12. Boston, 1872.

Payne, George H. *History of Journalism in the United States;* pp. 240–54. New York, 1920.

[Pray, Isaac C.] *Memoirs of James Gordon Bennett and His Times;* pp. 178–91. New York, 1855.

Wight, John. *Mornings at Bow Street.* London, 1824.

Wight, John. *More Mornings at Bow Street.* London, 1827.

Chapter VII

James Gordon Bennett and the New York Herald

Coleman, Albert E. "New and Authentic History of the Herald of the Bennetts." *Editor and Publisher;* vol. 56 (March 29, 1924) to vol. 58 (June 13, 1925).

Hudson, Frederic. *Journalism in the United States;* pp. 408–15, and 428–90. New York, 1873.

Parton, James. *Captains of Industry;* pp. 264–74. Boston, 1869.

Parton, James. *Famous Americans of Recent Times;* pp. 259–305. Boston, 1867.

Payne, George H. *History of Journalism in the United States;* pp. 255–68. New York, 1920.

[Pray, Isaac C.] *Memoirs of James Gordon Bennett and His Times.* New York, 1855.

Villard, Oswald Garrison. *Some Newspapers and Newspaper-Men;* pp. 273–81. New York, 1923.

Chapter VIII

Horace Greeley and the New York Tribune

Congdon, Charles T. *Reminiscences of a Journalist;* pp. 215–28. Boston, 1880.

Cornell, William M. *Life and Public Career of Hon. Horace Greeley.* Boston, 1872.

Frothingham, Octavius B. *George Ripley.* Boston, 1883.

Greeley, Horace. *Recollections of a Busy Life.* New York, 1868.

Hudson, Frederic. *Journalism in the United States;* pp. 522–73. New York, 1873.

Ingersoll, Lurton D. *Life of Horace Greeley.* Philadelphia, 1874.

Linn, William A. *Horace Greeley.* New York, 1903.

Parton, James. *Life of Horace Greeley.* Boston, 1872.

Payne, George H. *History of Journalism in the United States;* pp. 269–94. New York, 1920.

Reaves, L. U. *A Representative Life of Horace Greeley.* New York, 1872.

Robinson, Solon. *Hot Corn; Life Scenes in New York Illustrated.* New York, 1854.

Chapter IX

Henry J. Raymond and the New York Times

Davis, Elmer. *History of the New York Times, 1851–1921;* pp. 3–80. New York, 1921.

Hudson, Frederic. *Journalism in the United States;* pp. 618–45. New York, 1873.

Maverick, Augustus. *Henry J. Raymond and the New York Press for Thirty Years.* Hartford, Conn., 1870.

Payne, George H. *History of Journalism in the United States;* pp. 282–94. New York, 1920.

CHAPTER X

SAMUEL BOWLES AND THE SPRINGFIELD REPUBLICAN

Bradford, Gamaliel. *Union Portraits;* pp. 263–94. Boston, 1916.

Hooker, Richard. *The Story of an Independent Newspaper.* New York, 1924.

Merriam, George S. *Life and Times of Samuel Bowles.* 2 vols. New York, 1885.

Payne, George H. *History of Journalism in the United States;* pp. 323–46. New York, 1920.

CHAPTER XI

EDWIN LAWRENCE GODKIN, THE NATION, AND THE NEW YORK EVENING POST

Bryce, James. *Studies in Contemporary Biography;* pp. 363–81. New York, 1903.

Franklin, Fabian. *People and Problems;* pp. 183–88. New York, 1908.

Godkin, Edwin Lawrence. *Problems of Modern Democracy.* New York, 1896.

Godkin, Edwin Lawrence. *Reflections and Comments.* New York, 1895.

Godkin, Edwin Lawrence. *Unforeseen Tendencies in Democracy.* Boston, 1898.

Nevins, Allan. *The Evening Post; a Century of Journalism;* pp. 519–45. New York, 1922.

Ogden, Rollo. *Life and Letters of Edwin Lawrence Godkin.* 2 vols. New York, 1907.

Pollak, Gustav. *Fifty Years of American Idealism; the New York Nation, 1865–1915.* Boston, 1915.

Rhodes, James Ford. *Historical Essays;* pp. 265–97. N.Y., 1909.

Villard, Henry. *Memoirs of Henry Villard, Journalist and Financier.* 2 vols. Boston, 1904.

Villard, Oswald Garrison. *Some Newspapers and Newspaper-Men;* pp. 282–313. New York, 1923.

CHAPTER XII

CHARLES A. DANA AND THE NEW YORK SUN

Casual Essays of The Sun. New York, 1905.

Dana, Charles A. *The Art of Newspaper Making.* New York, 1895.

Hudson, Frederic. *Journalism in the United States;* pp. 677–87. New York, 1873.

Mitchell, Edward P.   *Memoirs of an Editor;* pp. 98–157; and 198–227. New York, 1924.
O'Brien, Frank M.   *The Story of The Sun;* pp. 198–433.   New York, 1918.
Wilson, James H.   *Life of Charles A. Dana.*   New York, 1907.

CHAPTER XIII

WILLIAM ROCKHILL NELSON AND THE KANSAS CITY STAR

Rogers, Jason.   *Newspaper Building;* pp. 20–37.   New York, 1918.
Street, Julian.   *Abroad at Home;* pp. 302–12.   "Colonel Nelson's 'Star.'"   New York.
Villard, Oswald Garrison.   *Some Newspapers and Newspaper-Men;* pp. 210–16.   New York, 1923.
William Rockhill Nelson; the Story of a Man, a Newspaper, and a City. Cambridge, Mass., 1915.

CHAPTER XIV

JOSEPH PULITZER AND THE NEW YORK WORLD

Heaton, John L.   *Cobb of "The World."*   New York, 1924.
Heaton, John L.   *The Story of a Page.*   New York, 1913.
Ireland, Alleyne.   *Joseph Pulitzer; Reminiscences of a Secretary.* New York, 1914.
Payne, George H.   *History of Journalism in the United States;* pp. 360–69.   New York, 1920.
Seitz, Don C.   *Joseph Pulitzer; His Life and Letters.*   New York, 1924.
Villard, Oswald Garrison.   *Some Newspapers and Newspaper-Men;* pp. 42–62.   New York, 1923.

CHAPTER XV

WILLIAM RANDOLPH HEARST AND THE NEW YORK JOURNAL

Brisbane, Arthur.   "William Randolph Hearst."   *Cosmopolitan,* vol. 33, pp. 48–51 (May, 1902).
Brisbane, Arthur.   "William Randolph Hearst."   *North American Review,* vol. 183, pp. 519–25 (September 21, 1906).
Brooks, Sydney.   "The Significance of Mr. Hearst."   *Fortnightly Review,* vol. 88, pp. 919–31 (December, 1907).
Commander, Lydia K.   "The Significance of Yellow Journalism." *Arena,* vol. 34, pp. 150–55 (August, 1905).
Croly, Herbert D.   *The Promise of American Life,* pp. 163–67, "William R. Hearst as a Reformer."   New York, 1909.

Editorials from the Hearst Newspapers. New York, 1906.

Irwin, Will. "The Fourth Current." *Collier's Weekly*, vol. 46, pp. 14–17 (February 18, 1911).

Irwin, Will. "The Spread and Decline of Yellow Journalism." *Collier's Weekly*, vol. 46, pp. 18–20 (March 4, 1911).

Irwin, Will. "The Unhealthy Alliance." *Collier's Weekly*, vol. 47, pp. 17–18 (June 3, 1911).

Russell, Charles E. "William Randolph Hearst." *Harper's Weekly*, vol. 48, pp. 790–92 (May 21, 1904).

Russell, Isaac. "Hearst-Made War News." *Harper's Weekly*, vol. 59, pp. 76–78 (July 25, 1914).

Steffens, Lincoln. "Hearst, the Man of Mystery." *American Magazine*, vol. 63, pp. 3–22 (November, 1906).

Wheeler, H. D. "At the Front with Willie Hearst." *Harper's Weekly*, vol. 61, pp. 340–42 (October 15, 1915).

CHAPTER XVI

The Development of the Present-Day Newspaper, 1890–1925

Bok, Edward W. *The Americanization of Edward Bok.* New York, 1920.

Davis, Elmer. *History of the New York Times, 1851–1921.* New York, 1921.

Hoe, Robert. *A Short History of the Printing Press.* New York, 1902.

Irwin, Will. "The American Newspaper." *Collier's Weekly*, vols. 46 and 47 (January 21 to July 29, 1911).

McClure, S. S. *My Autobiography.* New York, 1914.

McRae, Milton A. *Forty Years in Newspaperdom.* New York, 1924.

Mahin, Helen O. *The Development and Significance of the Newspaper Headline.* Ann Arbor, Mich., 1924.

"*M. E. S.*" *His Book.* [Melville E. Stone and the Associated Press.] New York, 1918.

Mitchell, Edward P. *Memoirs of an Editor.* New York, 1924.

Nevins, Allan. *The Evening Post; a Century of Journalism.* New York, 1922.

O'Brien, Frank M. *The Story of The Sun.* New York, 1918.

Stone, Melville E. *Fifty Years a Journalist.* New York, 1921.

Swerling, Jo. "The Picture Papers Win." *The Nation*, vol. 121, pp. 455–58 (October 21, 1925).

English Journalism, 1800–1925

Angell, Norman. *The Press and the Organization of Society.* London, 1922.

Atkins, John B. *The Life of Sir William Howard Russell, the First Special Correspondent.* 2 vols. London, 1911.

Bourne, H. R. Fox. *English Newspapers.* 2 vols. London, 1887.

Cambridge History of English Literature. Vol. xiv, pp. 184–225; J. S. R. Phillips, "The Growth of Journalism." New York, 1917.

Carson, William E. *Northcliffe, Britain's Man of Power.* New York, 1918.

Collet, C. D. *History of the Taxes on Knowledge.* 2 vols. London, 1899.

Cook, Edward T. *Delane of The Times.* London, 1916.

Dark, Sidney. *The Life of Sir Arthur Pearson.* London, 1922.

Dasent, Arthur I. *John Thadeus Delane, Editor of The Times.* 2 vols. London, 1908.

Dibblee, George H. *The Newspaper.* New York, 1913.

Escott, T. H. S. *Masters of English Journalism.* London, 1911.

Friedrichs, Hulda. *The Life of Sir George Newnes.* London, 1911.

Gardiner, A. G. *Life of George Cadbury.* London, 1922.

Gibbs, Philip H. *Adventures in Journalism.* New York, 1923.

Jones, Kennedy. *Fleet Street and Downing Street.* London, 1920.

Kitchin, Frederick H. *The London "Times" under the Management of Moberly Bell.* New York, 1925.

Lucas, Reginald J. *Lord Glenesk and the "Morning Post."* New York, 1910.

McKenzie, F. A. *The Mystery of the Daily Mail, 1896–1921.* London, 1921.

Mills, J. Saxon. *Sir Edward Cook.* New York, 1921.

Mills, W. Haslam. *The Manchester Guardian; a Century of History.* New York, 1922.

Pemberton, Max. *Lord Northcliffe; a Memoir.* London, 1922.

Pendleton, John. *Newspaper Reporting in Olden Time and To-Day.* London, 1890.

Scott-James, R. A. *The Influence of the Press.* London, 1913.

Simonis, H. *The Street of Ink.* London, 1917.

Steed, H. Wickham. *Through Thirty Years, 1892–1922.* 2 vols. New York, 1924.

Symon, James D. *The Press and Its Story.* London, 1914.

Whyte, Frederic. *Life of W. T. Stead.* 2 vols. Boston, 1925.

BIBLIOGRAPHIES ON JOURNALISM

Bleyer, Willard G. *The Profession of Journalism;* pp. 279–89. Boston, 1918.

Cambridge History of American Literature. Vol. i, pp. 452–57; vol. ii, pp. 518–24; vol. iv, pp. 779–82. New York, 1917–21.

Cambridge History of English Literature. Vol. xiv, pp. 589–94 [British journalism]. New York, 1917.

Cannon, Carl L. *Journalism; a Bibliography.* New York, 1924.

Ely, Margaret. *Some Great American Newspaper Editors.* New York, 1916.

Payne, George H. *History of Journalism in the United States;* pp. 399–427. New York, 1920.

Pendleton, John. *Newspaper Reporting in Olden Time and To-Day;* pp. 205–29. London, 1890.

Stockett, Julia C. *Masters of American Journalism.* New York, 1916.

Wieder, Callie. *Daily Newspapers in the United States.* New York, 1916.

INDEX